More Praise for *The Clinton Wars*

"Highly readable . . . compelling."
—Janet Maslin, *The New York Times*

"Witty and smart."
—Jonathan Yardley, *The Washington Post*

"More than a personal memoir or an intimate, up-close portrait of a marvelously complex president during an extraordinary time, *The Clinton Wars* is a sweeping account of the forces arrayed to derail the Clinton presidency . . . wildly colorful."
—*The Baltimore Sun*

"An important document . . . Blumenthal's riveting account [of the impeachment] is sharp, spare, and focused. It pulses with the energy of clashing ideologies and strategies and is propelled by the force of the legal, political, and reputational stakes involved."
—Bill Bell, *New York Daily News*

"A vigorous bravura performance that brings home again what a tragedy and travesty Clinton's impeachment really was . . . The central problems with our political culture that Blumenthal identifies and smartly analyzes remain with us."
—David Greenberg, *The Washington Monthly*

Sidney Blumenthal wrote for *The Washington Post, The New Yorker,* and *The New Republic* before serving as assistant and senior adviser to President Clinton from 1997 to 2001. He is the author of several other books, including *Pledging Allegiance: The Last Campaign of the Cold War.* He lives in Washington, D.C., with his wife.

ALSO BY SIDNEY BLUMENTHAL

The Permanent Campaign: Inside the World of Elite Political Operatives

*The Rise of the Counter-Establishment: From Conservative
Ideology to Political Power*

The Reagan Legacy (coeditor with Thomas Byrne Edsall)

Our Long National Daydream: A Political Pageant of the Reagan Era

Pledging Allegiance: The Last Campaign of the Cold War

SIDNEY BLUMENTHAL

The Clinton Wars

A PLUME BOOK

PLUME
Published by the Penguin Group
Penguin Group (USA) Inc., 375 Hudson Street, New York, New York 10014, U.S.A.
Penguin Books Ltd, 80 Strand, London WC2R 0RL, England
Penguin Books Australia Ltd, 250 Camberwell Road, Camberwell, Victoria 3124, Australia
Penguin Books Canada Ltd, 10 Alcorn Avenue, Toronto, Ontario, Canada M4V 3B2
Penguin Books (N.Z.) Ltd, Cnr Rosedale and Airborne Roads,
Albany, Auckland 1310, New Zealand
Penguin Books (South Africa) (Pty) Ltd, 24 Sturdee Avenue,
Rosebank, Johannesburg 2196, South Africa

Penguin Books Ltd, Registered Offices: 80 Strand, London WC2R 0RL, England

Published by Plume, a member of Penguin Group (USA) Inc. This is an authorized reprint of
a hardcover edition published by Farrar, Straus and Giroux. For information address Farrar,
Straus and Giroux, 19 Union Square West, New York, New York 10003.

First Plume Printing, May 2004
1 3 5 7 9 10 8 6 4 2

Unless otherwise credited, all photographs in this book are Official White House Photographs.

 REGISTERED TRADEMARK—MARCA REGISTRADA

The Library of Congress has catalogued the Farrar, Straus and Giroux edition as follows:
Blumenthal, Sidney, 1948–
    The Clinton wars / Sidney Blumenthal.— 1st ed.
      p.   cm.
    Includes bibliographical references and index.
    ISBN 0-374-12502-3 (hc.)
    ISBN 0-452-28527-5 (pbk.)
    1. Clinton, Bill, 1946–   2. United States—Politics and government—1993–2001.
3. Presidents—United States—Biography.   4. Political culture—United States—History—
20th century.   5. Political culture—Washington (D.C.)—History—20th century.   I. Title.

E885.B58 2003
973.929—dc21

                                                                                    2003044066

Printed in the United States of America

For Jackie

CONTENTS

THE CLINTON WARS

ONE

The Challenge to the Old Order

I

Bill Clinton had been president for only a few weeks, less than half of the fabled First Hundred Days by which all presidents have been early judged since Franklin D. Roosevelt's first burst of the New Deal. "Action, action, and more action," FDR had demanded. Now it was March 1993, sixty years later, and President Clinton was coming to Hyde Park.

I arrived early because I wanted to wander around Roosevelt's presidential library to soak up the atmosphere before the clamorous entourage wheeled in. Usually, the press corps traveling with the president misses any sense of place. The media are everywhere and nowhere at once. Acrobats in the circus get to see more of where they are while the tent is pitched. The press corps lives with the motorcade. My White House pass, showing that I represented *The New Yorker* magazine, got me quickly past the checkpoints of the local police and the sentries of the Secret Service. Their cordon for the new president made this plot of land something of a sanctuary, untrammeled by tourists or even stray scholars burrowing in the yellowing archives.

The cold gray sky cast no shadows down the long lawn stretching from the road to the single-story library. I walked undisturbed and alone past the exhibits. The whole Roosevelt life was encapsulated there. A bronzed statue of the lanky, carefree boy Franklin lounged on his back. Campaign buttons and banners traced the journey from the New York state senate to his last race for the presidency in 1944. Around the corner was the matter-of-fact typewritten letter from Albert Einstein in 1939 urging Roosevelt to develop an atomic bomb before the Nazis did. The artifacts displayed in the old oak cases were like pieces of bone in a natural history museum. The fragments could just hint at the passions, hatreds, and turmoil aroused by the squire who often conducted the swirling business of the nation from his serene Hudson Valley estate. Neatly contained, row after row, from beginning to end, from bucolic boyhood to world statesman, here it was: the past under glass. The story has been drummed into us as though foretold. Every chapter makes complete sense because we know every twist and turn, including the death of the President near Easter in 1945 on the eve of a redemptive victory in war, as Lincoln's death had been. The story, told in retrospect through our parents' lives in the Depression and the Second World War, remains vibrant in almost every family.

But to those who bore its responsibilities, much of this story of an American president appeared as an unlit passage, and the ghosts were not speaking. Their silence was a false signal that what had occurred before was, if not simpler, then always clearer to those working their way through the events. Roosevelt and those around him, even those in his "brain trust" who had been ascribed omniscient understanding, could not predict the storms that would envelop them. No matter how bold their devices, they were constantly disrupted and recast. The president and his advisers could not see around every turn or know when dangerous obstacles might suddenly appear. Often, they could not predict the consequences of their own plans. Exactly what destiny they would arrive at and by what rendezvous they could not say. It is easy to imagine the past as an epic, like a movie seamlessly edited and comfortably paced; it is hard to imagine it as it was experienced. No matter how vivid a vision of the future one may have, the real future is always wrapped in obscurity.

I could hear my own footsteps as I walked past black-and-white photographs of FDR grandly gesturing to roaring crowds. Then, suddenly, came whirling lights, sirens, and black vans soon catching up with their alarms. Out tumbled aides and reporters, hitting the ground running, like an army landing on a beachhead. The present was invading the preserve of the past.

I mingled inside the library with the expectant trustees and dignitaries. The chairman of the library, William vanden Heuvel, a former aide to Robert F. Kennedy and former ambassador, keeper of the perpetual Roosevelt flame, lovingly opened a book as large as a Gutenberg Bible with vellum pages. It was an unusual guest book: he turned to the signatures of Winston Churchill and then Lyndon Johnson.

The friendship between the American president and the British prime minister was at the heart of the Grand Alliance that won the Second World War. It cemented the Anglo-American "special relationship" as the enduring basis of the Western Alliance that weathered the Cold War. Every president since has had to act out a presidential role that Roosevelt established. Would Clinton ever have such a "special relationship," and what would it mean now that the Cold War was over?

If the relationship between Roosevelt and Churchill was that of cousins, the one between Roosevelt and Johnson was between a "daddy," as LBJ called Roosevelt, and his boy. The gangly congressman from Texas, an ardent New Dealer, saw his own presidency as fulfilling his political daddy's mission, realized at last as the Great Society. But Johnson's shattered presidency had left an unfinished legacy for another generation. What would Clinton make of it? The book was readied for Bill Clinton to sign his name.

President Clinton brought in with him a stream of cool, brisk air from outside. At six feet, two inches, with a jutting jaw, gray-green eyes, a ruddy complexion, and loose long limbs, Clinton was the most physically imposing person in the room, as he almost always was. He was immediately accessible, never at a loss for words, yet the strangeness of having a brand-new Democratic president roaming around FDR's home created what seemed a startle reflex among the older legatees. Suddenly, the Hyde Park library didn't feel like Harvard's Peabody Museum. The dust started to be shaken; the pinned exhibits almost seemed to want to move; the past was no longer at rest. It would in time be seen in a new shadow and a new light. But nobody knew what those would be.

Just before New Year's Eve in 1987, I had gone to Hilton Head, South Carolina, for what was then a little-known gathering called Renaissance Weekend, attended by a few hundred mostly Southern participants. Almost everyone there appeared on one or another panel, on any number of political, cultural, and religious subjects. Friends of mine had suggested to me that if I should go to this weekend, I should try to meet a contemporary, the forty-one-year-old governor of Arkansas. I was then a writer on the national staff of *The Washington Post*.

Clinton and I sat squinting in the winter sun and talked for an hour about his ambitions to be a national figure. He just didn't know how that was going to happen. He was little known beyond Arkansas and had little hope of getting recognized. Governors knew him, of course, but to the general public he was a cipher. I thought he was being perhaps too blunt about his ambition with someone he had just met. He fitted into the enduring category of rising stars to whom nothing might ever happen. Energy in politicians does not necessarily equal mass or the speed of light. Governors and senators from larger states, touted by newspaper columnists as future presidents, regularly melt away. With the Democratic primaries about six weeks away, Clinton wasn't even a candidate. The political talk was focused on the chances of Governor Michael Dukakis of Massachusetts. Clinton was on the sidelines, yet he was feeling his way to a starting gate in the distant future. In his conversation with me, however, he grasped that he was venturing forth during a moment when politics was changing, in particular because of the evolving role of the media, which were disturbingly erasing the distinction between public and private life. Already, two prospective Democratic candidates, Gary Hart and Joseph Biden, had been forced out of the race by the increasingly antagonistic media. Reporters had staked out Hart, who they believed rightly was having an affair, and at a crowded news conference one asked him if he had ever committed adultery. The invisible barrier protecting politicians from probes into their private behavior that had no public impact or appearance was removed. With the heat shield gone, Hart was incinerated. Biden's sin was that he had engaged in a rhetorical flight of fancy about his family's grit, from time immemorial as common a technique for a candidate as extolling his own patriotism, and had done so in words borrowed from a British politician. The intense media glare wilted his financial backers and campaign staff overnight. For his old-fashioned stem-winding eloquence, Biden was shamed into quitting as an exaggerator and a plagiarist.

Though different in detail, the Hart and Biden incidents together showed that power had shifted. Long before the voters entered into the presidential selection process, the media had changed their unwritten rules. A story sparked by one newspaper or television outlet rapidly spread into what was hailed in newsrooms as a "firestorm." Prestigious news organizations that had once disdained stories about sex inevitably wound up justifying covering them as part of a reality they just couldn't ignore. It was not simply that the press was rightfully being more independent in its scrutiny of politicians' claims. In the new game, the politicians' effort at self-presentation would be met as a challenge to the media's self-proclaimed prerogatives.

That winter evening in 1987, Clinton stepped onto the stage at Renaissance Weekend and spoke extemporaneously for about a half hour about his decision not to run for the presidency in the coming campaign. He admitted that he wanted to run, but wasn't ready. Clinton explained himself at the same time as a member of his generation and as a completely engaged politician. Politics was clearly his calling—how he thought, felt, and spoke. At forty-one, he vibrated with the idea of running for national office but was unprepared to enter a terra incognita, and he worried aloud about what the erasure of the distinction between public and private life would mean. Even in voicing his uncertainty, he was involving his listeners in his drama, enlisting their hopes and anxieties; they were caught up in concern about his fate. Later he drew on a number of them for posts in his administration.

A heated discussion ensued about the fate of the leaderless Democratic Party, still entrapped in the age of Reagan. In the middle of the free-for-all, a woman with shoulder-length brown hair and thick glasses stood up. It was the thirty-nine-year-old Hillary Rodham Clinton. She spoke deliberately and pointedly. Her thoughts were framed with great logic. She was emphatic but composed. She referred to what her husband had said and provided steel bracing for his expansive talk. Hillary had the effect of settling in Bill's favor whatever matter was at issue. The issue here, of course, was Bill himself. When the formal session concluded, Bill and Hillary stood a few yards apart, continuing the discussion with separate knots of people, but they were a team.

The next day I noticed that Clinton was carrying a book filled with papers under his arm as he made his way from table to table at the buffet lunch: it was *The Truly Disadvantaged: The Inner City, the Underclass, and Public Policy*, by William Julius Wilson. This was a rethinking of the reasons for job loss and welfare, and it focused on how the deindustrialization of America's cities had left blacks there structurally removed from employment. Clinton and I chatted about Wilson's policy approach compared to others. After a few days' exposure to him, my initial impression of a young man in a hurry was evolving and deepening. To be sure, he had ambition, but he possessed more than that essential quality. He was a charismatic if loquacious speaker who had an easy facility with the arcana of public policy. His formidable wife was a force in her own right. He was ambivalent about his future in a swirling political world and hinted at personal difficulties. Underlying it all was a determination to bring the Republican era to a close and alter the coordinates of politics.

Now, at Hyde Park in 1993, President Clinton spotted me and waved me over. He wanted me to accompany him as he toured FDR's library. In his wake trailed a group that personified various aspects of the Democratic tradition—James Roosevelt, FDR's grandson; Robert F. Kennedy, Jr., an environmental lawyer in the Hudson River Valley; and Senator Daniel Patrick Moynihan of New York, who, in his inimitable staccato rhythm,

held forth about writing his doctoral dissertation right here at the FDR
library, about FDR's vacations at Campobello Island off the Maine coast,
and about Roosevelt's tenure as assistant secretary of the navy during the
First World War.

Clinton headed directly for Roosevelt's desk that had been in the Oval
Office, now stationed in the middle of the exhibits, and slowly circled it.
It is smaller than the massive nineteenth-century desk made from the
timbers of the HMS *Resolute* that President Kennedy used and that Clinton chose to use, too, in his Oval Office. From behind this smaller desk,
Roosevelt, cigarette holder firmly fixed at an angle, had held bantering
press conferences with the press corps. None of the reporters wrote
about or photographed his wheelchair.

Clinton and his entourage trooped up the hill behind the library to
the looming mansion. The rooms in the house have been maintained as
they were in the 1940s, when Roosevelt conferred with Harry Hopkins
and Henry Morgenthau, or when Eleanor would point him to a social
problem that needed his special attention. Clinton took his time in every
room, absorbing every phase of Roosevelt's life. He stood before the portrait of James Roosevelt, FDR's father, who was in his fifties when he and
his young wife, Sara Delano, had their only adored child. On the walls of
the room FDR occupied as a youth still hung his copy of the Declaration
of Independence and a Harvard Crimson banner. Clinton jumped into
the little elevator, hand-operated by a rope, that had been installed
for FDR after he was stricken with polio. It still worked efficiently. At the
far end of the second floor, overlooking the rolling Hudson, was the
spartan room he always stayed in. The wooden wheelchair remained.
Outside, Clinton laid a red rose atop the white marble tomb on which
was engraved: FRANKLIN D. ROOSEVELT, and, underneath, ELEANOR
ROOSEVELT. Clinton stood awhile in the cold.

An aide gently but insistently reminded him that his time was limited.
The turbulent world was tugging at him, starting with a boisterous
crowd waiting at the local high school. "It's so peaceful," Clinton whispered as he stared at the tomb. His mind was filled with great plans: universal health care, reducing the federal deficit, investments in education
and the environment, cutting crime, remaking the welfare system, ending
discrimination, to begin with. "I believe that government must do much
more," Clinton had told a joint session of Congress on February 17,
quoting repeatedly Roosevelt's call for "bold, persistent experimentation." With those words, the old familiar politics since 1980 and even
since 1968 dissolved, for these phrases refuted the central tenet of Rea-

ganism: "Government is the problem." But more than principle was at stake. So was every vestige of power, from federal contracts to White House invitations.

In his pilgrimage to Hyde Park, Clinton sought to identify his innovations with the Rooseveltian spirit. Clinton had seen for himself the reliquaries, and now he could fix his sights on the road ahead. "I belong here," he remarked to me as he left Hyde Park.

II

When the Clintons first moved into the White House in January 1993 they ordered that portraits of Franklin D. Roosevelt and Harry S. Truman be hung prominently. But the pictures were not put in place. The instructions to the staff were relayed again. Only after a month, and further prodding, was the order carried out. Some of the White House staff held, it seemed, a class deference to the previous Republican residents. From their upstairs-downstairs angle, patricians were being replaced by outlanders who didn't know their place. Their recoil from the Clintons was almost as great as if that ruffian Andrew Jackson were moving in. It felt to them like an invasion and occupation. Putting Roosevelt and Truman where the Clintons wanted would mark symbolically that the presidency was not what it had been.

The resistance of the old household retainers to the Clintons' intrusion was a reactive impulse. Hanging pictures of long-ago presidents might seem a small gesture of little note, but the entrenched conservative members of the staff understood that it was not. It wasn't merely an issue of party, though it was that, nor was it only about class, though there was some of that, too. FDR, after all, was more of a patrician than George H. W. Bush, let alone Ronald Reagan. It was that the presidency was being changed.

Ten days after the inauguration, the President and First Lady flew for the first time in the presidential helicopter, *Marine One*, to Camp David, the presidential retreat in the Catoctin Mountains of Maryland. Their guests were the newly appointed cabinet members and senior White House staff. After dinner in the lodge everyone gathered for a discussion. Talk about immediate issues facing the new administration, including the overriding ones of the budget and the economy, soon gave way to talk about how to explain them to the public. That turned into a discussion of how Clinton's presidency should be presented. What were its themes?

What was its narrative line? In his inaugural address, Clinton had spoken of the need to "force the spring"—a metaphor about reform that implied that it would be difficult, if not unnatural. He had also quoted the prophet Isaiah: "Where there is no vision the people perish." Now Hillary briefly reviewed Clinton's career as governor of Arkansas, when he had tried to do too much in his first term and lost his second election. But he had learned and gone on in the next election to win it all back, making change after change. It was almost as though she were prophesying a cycle of return. But she was making a point beyond that about Clinton's perseverance. She and Bill knew how to struggle through turmoil. Laying out the nuts and bolts of policy was like showing off the bins in a hardware store. A story also had to be told; even more, the place in history needed to be located.

Men and women of the generation born after the Second World War who grew up in the 1960s may have thought that the high tide of American Century liberalism was permanent. In their formative years, they had been imbued with the optimistic notion that improvement was inevitable, and their rising expectations went far to explain the sharpness of their later disillusion. FDR's four electoral wins had established the realignment. Dwight Eisenhower's Republican interregnum between two Democratic presidents was felt to be merely a holding pattern. He had been classically conservative, and what he had conserved was the New Deal—"a dime-store New Deal," Barry Goldwater later called it. Eisenhower's aides' effort to fashion what they called "modern Republicanism" never amounted to more than a phrase. It was, as John F. Kennedy put it, time to get the country moving again. When the young Bill Clinton shook President Kennedy's hand in the Rose Garden in 1963, liberalism was in flower again, and with Lyndon Johnson's landslide in 1964, liberalism as conventional wisdom seemed ratified; it was felt to be a constantly rolling wave of the future.

Moving into the White House is not the same thing as walking onto a stage set. Protocol may inform the president about how to greet visiting heads of state in the Diplomatic Reception Room, but little else. There is no script. The constitutional functions of the office lay out only the minimal design. Whether and how it will be filled and expanded is left to the occupant, but not exactly as he wishes.

At Hyde Park, Clinton noticed FDR's clothes still hanging on hooks in his room, his shoes neatly lined up and polished. "Those are still his clothes?" he wondered. Roosevelt's political clothes had been tailored to fit each new generation of Democrats that followed him. Even Republicans stood in his shadow, none more so than Ronald Reagan.

Reagan had once been a left-wing Democrat, "a near-hemophilic liberal," he labeled himself in his autobiography, who regaled parties of Hollywood stars with his imitations of FDR's speeches. Though he turned FDR's politics on their head, he kept his attachment to Roosevelt. His background—as the son of a small-town, hard-drinking Irish Democrat, saved from the Depression by a job with the Works Progress Administration—was elemental in his appeal to Northern ethnic voters, the Reagan Democrats. In his acceptance speech to the Republican convention in 1980, he quoted Roosevelt liberally and claimed a "rendezvous with destiny." On the centennial of FDR's birth, in 1982, Reagan mounted a tribute with a lavish lunch at the White House to which he invited presidential aides from Roosevelt through Jimmy Carter. Reagan's optimism was still trying to echo Roosevelt's. "Happy days, now, again, and always," he said in his toast. President Carter had refused to approve the funding for an FDR memorial, but Reagan eagerly signed the bill, even as he tried to inter Roosevelt's actual political legacy.

In 1980, the very year of Reagan's presidential victory, which shattered the New Deal electoral coalition once and for all, the young governor of Arkansas addressed the Democratic convention. "It seems," said Clinton, "that everyone in this convention and half the people at the Republican convention quoted Franklin Roosevelt. Everyone can quote him, but his words out of context mean little."

Under President Clinton, the progressive tradition of the Democratic Party had to be re-created on a new basis, he believed. This required more than reinventing government rules and regulations. No one could claim that liberalism was a logical choice and blithely proceed as though the majority of the American people agreed. Clinton realized there had to be a remaking of the presidency, renovating the authority of government itself, discredited not only by the nightmares of assassinations, racial violence, and the Vietnam War but also by the concerted antigovernment campaign of the conservative movement. With Barry Goldwater as their standard bearer in 1964, the Republicans had lost in a landslide, but with Ronald Reagan in 1980, they had swamped the Democrats. By 1992, the consensus of the 1960s had been long smashed.

Massive fissures had widened between the realities of social and economic life and the routines of governance. Solutions to the new problems were not resting on a shelf, readily available. At the beginning of 1993, the United States was at the end of a half century of settled politics, but uncertain what would follow. The long twilight struggle of the Cold War was over. And the Democrats, still reeling from the Vietnam War that had so divided the party, had no coherent foreign policy and were widely considered pacifist. Old-style mass production of the industrial age was becoming obsolete. And the Democrats were pulled toward protection-ism. A new economy based on microchips and the Internet—a postindus-trial revolution—was in the making. And hardly any politician except for the new vice president, Albert Gore, Jr., had given it much thought. Im-migration, especially from Latin America and Asia, was creating large new minorities; California soon would have no single racial group in the majority. And the Democrats were perceived as a centrifugal party of identity politics. Republicans had tainted them as soft on racial quotas, crime, and the abuses of welfare. In sum, voters did not believe the Democrats could be the party to define the American nation.

The presidency is the chief engine of progress in American history; its leadership and power are central. No social movement, however broad or righteous, from abolition to labor rights, has seen its aims made into law without presidential power. How a president leads depends upon why he's leading. And in truth, despite what the post–Second World War gen-eration may have thought, progressive Democratic presidents are a rela-tive exception. Opportunities for them to gain power have been irregular. Excluding the Virginians of the early republic, only three Democrats be-fore Clinton had been elected to two consecutive terms: Andrew Jackson, Woodrow Wilson, and FDR. (Jackson, in fact, was elected three times, but his first win was stolen from him in what became known notoriously as "the corrupt bargain" of his rivals in the Congress.) Wilson first gained office when Theodore Roosevelt split the Republican Party by running on his Progressive Party platform.

Of the progressive Republicans, Abraham Lincoln won with a plural-ity of the votes over a divided field of two Democrats and a Constitu-tional Unionist candidate. Theodore Roosevelt—called a "madman" by Mark Hanna, the Republican Party boss—acceded to power by accident: he was put into the vice presidency by conservative Republicans who thought of the position as a locked safe, only to have the anarchist's bul-let that killed McKinley put TR in the White House.

By its dynamic nature, the tradition of the progressive presidency is not static, and any president who belongs in it must alter it. Progressive presidents are elected because they stand for the idea that the old ways will not work—and should not work. They object to the status quo on the grounds of both pragmatism and principle. They challenge existing political and social arrangements. They seek to expand democracy by re-defining the social contract, transforming the connection between the people and their government. They do not believe that the business of government is mere business. They try to reconcile democracy and new technologies, power, and property. Progressive presidents see themselves as the sole legitimate agent of the majority—"the direct representative of the people," in Jackson's words. In their mission to extend opportunity and rights, they constantly improvise their relationship with the people. They believe it is their unique responsibility and prerogative to reshape the country. As they see it, the United States would drift and divide without their intervention. They use the authority of the presidency to advance the idea that the United States is one nation. For them, liberty and union are "one and inseparable."

The case for a strong president was early made by Alexander Hamilton, in *Federalist Paper* Number 70. In his article on behalf of passage of the Constitution, he refuted arguments of the Anti-Federalists, who favored states' rights and a weak central government. "Energy in the executive is a leading character in the definition of good government," wrote Hamilton. "A feeble executive implies a feeble execution of government." Hamilton meant to forge a strong state but not necessarily a strong democracy. Thomas Jefferson, who was elected in 1800 in opposition to Hamiltonian political goals and pledged to reduce the power of the federal government, used the presidency for ends contrary to his own doctrine. Jefferson was a sinuous and elusive politician who pulled the strings of the Congress without being exposed as a puppeteer and who radically expanded the powers of the presidency without being denounced as a new Caesar. His robust use of the office succeeded gloriously with the Louisiana Purchase but failed miserably when he imposed an embargo on European imports. In the one case, the country's territory was augmented by one-third; in the other, a quixotic effort at peaceable coercion, American government and industry were bankrupted. Whatever the case, Jefferson never explained that his actions contradicted his theory.

Andrew Jackson created the sinews of the progressive presidency as we know it. In his battles against the forces of entrenched privilege (the Bank of the United States) and disunion (the Nullifiers, who were defenders of states' rights), he boldly asserted the executive branch as the surest defender of the people's will and the federal union. In his proclamation to the people of South Carolina, hotbed of secession, Jackson said, "I consider, then, the power to annul a law of the United States, as-

sumed by one state, incompatible with the existence of the Union, contradicted expressly by the letter of the Constitution, unauthorized by its
spirit, inconsistent with every principle on which it was founded, and destructive of the great object for which it was formed."

Lincoln kept a copy of Jackson's proclamation at hand when he was
drafting his early speeches during the Civil War. Without Jackson, there
could have been no Lincoln. Lincoln's notion of the presidency was
predicated on Jackson's, on a tradition that the Democratic Party had repudiated in the debates over slavery. After Lincoln, in the Gilded Age,
the presidency shriveled, despite a few shafts of energy. For decades, the
Congress, devoted mostly to the dispensing of special-interest favors,
ruled together with a deeply conservative Supreme Court and a compliant presidency.

Only with the advent of Theodore Roosevelt and the progressive era
did the presidency revive. "I did greatly broaden the use of executive
power," TR wrote triumphantly in his *Autobiography*. His "New Nationalism" was inspired by a book, *The Promise of American Life*, by Herbert
Croly, the editor of *The New Republic* magazine, who proposed Hamiltonian means for Jeffersonian ends. But TR's intertwined vision of the
office and the nation was abandoned in the 1920s, and the Republicans
reverted to their late-nineteenth-century conservatism as though TR had
been a passing delirium. Herbert Hoover, whom some voters presumed
to be some kind of progressive, "the great engineer," retreated into
clichés about voluntarism in the face of the Depression.

In the New Deal, the domestic equivalent of a war mobilization,
Franklin Roosevelt blended the approaches of his cousin, TR, and
Woodrow Wilson, whom he had served as assistant secretary of the navy.
A generation later, John F. Kennedy and Lyndon Johnson directly built
upon Roosevelt's and Truman's policies. Most important, they wielded
the presidency so as to make the greatest advance in civil rights since Reconstruction.

Progressive presidents follow conservative ones, but their election is
not foreordained. The alternation in power of the two principal political
parties, of liberalism and conservatism, of public purpose and private interest, mark what Arthur M. Schlesinger, Jr., has termed "the cycles of
American history." But the cycles encompass tragedy and accidents.
What if Lincoln had not been assassinated? Would Reconstruction have
been more effective? What if McKinley had not been shot? Would there
have been a progressive era? What if Kennedy had lived and had man-

aged to end American involvement in the Vietnam War before it became a quagmire? Would Nixon or any Republican have come to power?

Often, external crises blast apart a seemingly placid order. For Lincoln, his election itself precipitated the crisis; the Depression created one that brought FDR to power. Without external shocks of that magnitude, progressive presidents like Kennedy and Clinton, arriving with thin mandates, have had to maneuver their way into office through superior political skill. And yet, there *are* cycles. American government does move cyclically, in fits and starts. And however presidents arrive in the office, their energy in great part determines whether their eras become progressive or whether inertia overwhelms them.

Conservative presidents preserve their power through inertia, which has powerful momentum and interests. The allies of conservative presidents are indifference, passivity, and complacency. Nostalgia is the emotion that underlies many conservative sentiments—a magical belief that if little is done, a simpler, happier time can be restored and a world of change kept at bay. The desire to roll back a previous progressive tide usually gives the impetus to conservative presidential agendas, to the extent that there are any. And they typically fall back on retrograde elements in the other two branches of government, the Congress and the judiciary, often becoming their willing prisoner.

In the twentieth century, every progressive president inherited the unfinished programs and disappointments of the previous progressive era. The progressive era itself ended in ashes, with Teddy Roosevelt dead and President Wilson paralyzed, the leaders' conditions symbolic of the fate of their politics. TR left behind him an unrealized platform for workmen's compensation, laws governing workers' hours and wages, an inheritance tax, and more. A ruined Wilson saw his hopes for U.S. participation in the League of Nations defeated, the American commitment to collective security in the world unfulfilled. At FDR's death the New Deal was truncated by war, and a coalition of conservative Republicans and Southern Democrats dominated the Congress. Harry Truman, desperately unpopular during the unresolved Korean War, left national health insurance and a civil rights agenda unattended. Johnson left the Great Society wrecked by his own continued policies in Vietnam. It was because of these failures that conservative presidents were able to promise, as President Harding memorably put it, a "return to normalcy."

Just as FDR could not re-create the progressive era and Kennedy could not conjure up another New Deal, Clinton could not summon the

Great Society. If anything, he had to appear as a contrast to the politics of the preceding generation. He had to overcome an inheritance of voter disillusionment with his own party and of failure in the other. And the disruption in the Democratic tradition was greater between Clinton and the Kennedy and Johnson years than it had been between them and Roosevelt-Truman. Only a dozen years separated the administrations of Wilson and FDR, and only eight separated Truman and Kennedy, but there were three decades between Clinton and a usable Democratic past. The idea of a Democratic executive leading an activist government and an effective party had been discredited. The discontinuities in the progressive tradition were very great in the twentieth century. The landmark legislation of the Kennedy-Johnson period—the laws establishing Medicare, Medicaid, and civil rights—had been readied for years before they were passed. Even on long-standing policies such as health insurance, Clinton now had to remake legislative plans from scratch. Despite the handshake with Kennedy, the torch was not easily passed.

Clinton could not turn to the immediate past for help, because the last Democratic president and the last Republican president had left not only contrasts but burdens. The Democrats had lost five out of the previous six presidential elections. Jimmy Carter, the only Democratic president to punctuate the Republican period from Nixon through Bush, seemed to recapitulate the Democratic errors of the 1960s in trying to overcome them, adding new disabling handicaps—and cautionary lessons—for any Democratic successor.

III

Jimmy Carter was elected in 1976 as the anti-Nixon. He was a Baptist Sunday-school teacher who promised he would never lie and who campaigned against the evils of Washington. His understanding of the basic decency of Americans and their longing for leaders who respected them set him apart from Nixon. A youthful governor from the South, he had a strong appeal to blacks for his civil rights record and an empathy with blacks that went beyond politics and that was rare in his generation of white Southerners. His moderation and his desire to move beyond the slogans of past liberalism set him apart from his rivals in the battle for the Democratic nomination. He made being an outsider a point of principle, linking his professions of morality to denunciations of politics. Once in the White House he sold off FDR's yacht *Sequoia*, intending to separate himself from Nixon's grandiosity, but he was also symbolically downsizing the presidency.

The Democrats had become an entrenched congressional party, a kaleidoscope of competing constituencies, regions, and interests. Undisciplined and unwilling to take a president's lead, they were ready to punish Carter for any deviation from any constituency's demand. His program became a series of unfocused priorities, each deemed vitally important, multiplying confusion and diffusing his power. He failed to observe the niceties with Democratic congressional leaders, who grew to hold him in contempt. The party turned into a cacophony of discontent, feeding a Washington press corps that was becoming imbued with the idea that its business was to unmake presidents.

Carter was overwhelmed by economic and foreign crises, many inherited from the Nixon and Ford administrations. Inflation ran above 10 percent and interest rates soared above 20 percent. A seemingly intractable energy crisis caused frustrated motorists to wait for hours in long lines to fill their tanks. In July 1979, Carter retreated to Camp David, where he invited a procession of Washington wise men, thinkers, and religious figures to counsel him. He chose to listen to those pessimistic voices counseling him that mass alienation was the problem. The crisis atmosphere incited further anxiety that he didn't know how or where to lead.

Carter came down from his mountaintop to deliver a singularly self-undermining speech. "It is a crisis of confidence," he said. "It is a crisis that strikes at the very heart and soul and spirit of our national will. We can see this crisis in the growing doubt about the meaning of our own lives and in the loss of a unity of purpose for our nation. The erosion of our confidence in the future is threatening to destroy the social and the political fabric of America. . . . The symptoms of this crisis of the American spirit are all around us." This "malaise" speech, as it became commonly known, seemed to concede to overpowering events and to sentence confidence to exile. Rather than identifying specific forces that could be brought under control by presidential power, he was blaming the American people for their existential crisis. Through self-diminishing nobility, Carter had turned himself into an anti-Roosevelt.

In Washington, congressional Democrats, constituency groups, and political columnists implored Senator Edward M. Kennedy to run against the Democratic incumbent. Carter was, they believed, an accident, an interloper, whose candidacy had happened only because Ted had not run. Polls showed him beating Carter among Democrats by a two-to-one margin. On November 7, 1979, Kennedy announced his candidacy, evoking past glories: "We can light those beacon fires again." The theme song from *Camelot* blared through the loudspeakers into the hall. But on that very day, Iranian student militants seized American hostages at the U.S. Embassy in Teheran, and overnight, Carter assumed a presidential stature that he had not had before. Kennedy's challenge was easily defeated. Yet it is too simple to see his loss as the loss of liberalism. Carter's primary victories also demonstrated stirrings of a chastened Democratic Party. One of Carter's favorite quotations was from Bob Dylan: "He not busy being born is busy dying."

Yet the vise tightened around him, a good man caught in bad times. A hostage rescue mission crashed. Then, when the Soviet Union invaded Afghanistan, Carter expressed surprise. With the USSR appearing as an expansive, growing threat, the conservative worst-case scenario was seemingly confirmed. National pride demanded more than a diagnosis of "malaise." Many voters perceived Carter as combining the cold but ineffectual technician's sensibility of a Hoover with the moralistic but ineffectual sensibility of Democratic losers through the ages. Carter's campaign autobiography in 1976 was entitled *Why Not the Best?* By 1980, his purity of heart was regarded as naïve softness in a dangerous world, his unblemished character taken as proof of his innocence.

Just as Carter had been elected as the anti-Nixon, Reagan was elected in 1980 as the anti-Carter. Reagan borrowed Ted Kennedy's nationalist rhetoric from the Democratic primary campaign, echoed Carter's incessant talk against Washington, and festooned his speeches with quotations from FDR. His confidence, optimism, and age rubbed the harsh edge off his conservatism. He wiped away Nixon's scowl and never mentioned him. FDR's conservative pretender mimicked Roosevelt's style against his substance. Paying his peculiar homage, Reagan was the last Rooseveltian.

Reagan was astonishingly successful in his plan to paralyze the federal government. After a rush in his first year to pass an enormous regressive tax cut, accompanied by a large increase in the military budget to meet what he claimed was an ever-larger Soviet threat, Reagan was a president at leisure. He delegated his authority and paid little attention to detail. Congress enacted the fewest number of administration-proposed bills since Eisenhower. His achievement of presiding over a government that permitted the federal deficit to grow to astronomical proportions made a federal social policy virtually impossible to realize. Once he learned that the supply-side economic theory his advisers had advocated was backfiring, producing deficits instead of the promised Niagara of revenues, he was pleased with the deadening effect. He revived the grandeur of the presidency for his stage set but put the executive branch to sleep. At the end of 1986, his senescent presidency was jolted by the Iran-Contra scandal, in which his aides were discovered to have arranged illegally to sell weapons to Iran to raise money for the anticommunist "Contra" insurgency against the leftist government in Nicaragua. Reagan claimed ignorance. Yet with Mikhail Gorbachev leading the Soviet Union toward new freedoms and openness, perestroika and glasnost, Reagan, after missing several years of cues about these developments, rose to the occasion to sign an arms-control treaty with the USSR and proclaim the close of the Cold War. He claimed the happy ending as his.

Reagan's successor was a classic heir in every respect. George Herbert Walker Bush had not made his own way in the world or in politics but had been elevated by appointment in the government hierarchy largely because of his pedigree. He was a remnant of a waning part of the Republican Party, straining to belong to the waxing part. A Connecticut Yankee, the son of a Wall Street banker who had become a moderate Republican senator, Bush had been prepared for the duties and customs of his class. He was sent to Phillips Andover Academy and Yale, where he belonged to his father's club, Skull and Bones. After Yale, he struck out for Texas to prove himself in the oil business, staked with funds from his family and his father's friends. All his enterprises failed. Slated for a safe Republican congressional seat from a wealthy Houston district, he promptly began adjusting his politics. Bush's political career thereafter was a long effort to overcome his moderate Republican heritage. His father had been a close ally of the two-time GOP presidential nominee Thomas Dewey; Bush backed Barry Goldwater. His father had been head of the United Negro College Fund; Bush voted against civil rights. Presidents Nixon, Ford, and Reagan ratcheted him up the chain of command, his patrician background being his strongest apparent qualification, until he was chosen to be the vice presidential candidate in 1980. He had once been an active member of Planned Parenthood, but now opposed abortion. In the 1980 GOP primaries, he had criticized Reagan's supply-side tax cuts as "voodoo economics," but as a presidential candidate in 1988 he promised, "Read my lips—no new taxes!"

When his 1988 campaign began to falter, Bush put his fate in the hands of his political centurions, who ran a relentlessly negative campaign against the Democratic candidate, Governor Michael Dukakis of Massachusetts, arousing the voters' racial fears by using the image of Willie Horton, a black convict who had abused a prison furlough under a program initiated by a previous Republican governor. Bush also challenged Dukakis's patriotism and raised nativist prejudice by urging mandatory school recitation of the Pledge of Allegiance (a requirement that had been declared unconstitutional by the Supreme Court); and he demonized the "liberal governor" and the "L word" (for "liberalism"). Yet Bush hinted that he would practice a "kinder, gentler" conservatism than Reagan had. He proposed that America be illuminated by "a thousand points of light" through voluntary charity. He promised to be "the education president." His wife took up the cause of literacy. Priding himself on his realism, Bush considered Reagan a dreamer about the end of the Cold War. He would be a class above Reagan—"kinder, gentler," and tougher. After he won, Bush said about the vicious campaign, "That's history."

In the spring of 1991, Bush appeared invincible, standing at the foot of Pennsylvania Avenue, saluting thousands of troops marching by him in review. The commander in chief was the victor in the one-hundred-hour Gulf War that had freed Kuwait from its occupation by forces under the command of Iraqi dictator Saddam Hussein. It was a splendid little war. Bush took to comparing himself to Theodore Roosevelt, the patrician Rough Rider. He spoke of his "defining hour" (evoking Churchill's phrase "their finest hour" about the Battle of Britain). The war, Bush proclaimed, had been fought on behalf of "a new world order," a phrase first used by Woodrow Wilson to define the hoped-for structure of peace after the First World War. Bush's approval rating as president stood at 91 percent, the highest ever recorded for a president, even higher than that given President Truman on V-J Day. Bush's reelection, generally conceded to be a foregone conclusion, would certify conclusively that the Republican Party had a "lock" on the White House. According to the "lock" theory, Republican presidential dominance reflected a profound shift that had taken place in the American electorate—geographically to the south and west, and ideologically to the right—against the very idea of affirmative government.

But Bush presided over the Republicans' fall. The party's manifest destiny proved less predictable than events foreseen by Nancy Reagan's astrologer. Issues that Republicans deployed to divide and conquer the Democrats perversely turned against them. The crisis was not located in the evaporation of an ineffable Reagan magic. It was that the walls of the Republican presidency were closing in on its current occupant. Reagan's policies had set a trap for his successor. After the spending as if there were no tomorrow, tomorrow had arrived—on Bush's watch. Paralyzing government through deficits, manipulating "wedge" issues on race and women to tear apart the Democratic coalition, and accusing the Democrats of appeasement in the face of the Red Menace were all policies that now had a reverse effect.

On domestic policy, Bush was indifferent and distant. Deficits ranged as far as the eye could see. Unemployment rose above 10 percent. At a supermarket checkout line, Bush had no idea what anything cost; he confessed his wonder at electronic scanners, which had been in use for years. Especially because Bush had dispelled his image as a wimp through the Gulf War, people were embittered. He had demonstrated that he could be strong and decisive, so his incapacity on the domestic front seemed cruel. Where was the Rough Rider? There was no charge up this San Juan Hill, just a thousand points of light. In the New Hampshire primary in 1992, Bush proposed a new theme: "Message: I care."

The Republican Party began to crack up. Pat Buchanan, an extremely conservative isolationist and pundit, who had been an aide to both Nixon and Reagan, gave the incumbent president a scare in New Hampshire. And an eccentric Texas billionaire, Ross Perot, formerly a big contributor to the Republican Party, entered as an independent candidate to rescue the country from Bush and his deficits.

The end of the Cold War left Bush and the conservatives at sea. Even after the fall of the Berlin Wall in 1989, Bush persisted in his belief that the Cold War would continue. The ruins of the former Soviet empire left him virtually speechless about the shape of things to come. He had no idea how to fill in the blank.

Vertigo was a commonly felt social sensation. Donald Bartlett and James Steele, two journalists on *The Philadelphia Inquirer*, reported on a deindustrialized and demoralized country, turning their articles into a book called *America: What Went Wrong?*, which became a best-seller. In April 1992, when the ghetto of south central Los Angeles was consumed by the flames of racial violence, Bush had little to say and less to offer. The racial conflagration, he said, was not "a message of protest." His press secretary, Marlin Fitzwater, blamed the Great Society. Vice President Dan Quayle put the onus on a "poverty of values," symbolized by Murphy Brown, a character on a popular television situation comedy who was an unwed mother.

No prominent senator or governor in the Democratic Party chose to run for president against Bush. They had become convinced in the aftermath of the Gulf War that he was impregnable. They wanted the presidency conferred upon them without struggle. Most of them were a generation older than the governor of Arkansas. Snug in the Senate cloakroom and their statehouses, they left the field to someone they thought foolhardy enough to undertake the race.

IV

"One as yet unremarked dimension of the cyclical process deserves particular attention," wrote Arthur Schlesinger, Jr. "For in basic respects it is the generational experience that serves as the mainspring of the political cycle."

Perhaps only two other presidents came from backgrounds as modest as Clinton's, the poorest president elected in the twentieth century. His early childhood was spent in a hermetic Southern gothic world, little changed over the decades since the nineteenth century. Segregation was the law. There had not been a lynching in Hope, Arkansas, since the 1920s, but blacks lived in "Colored Town," literally on the other side of the railroad tracks. Hope's claim to fame was as the nation's watermelon capital. Clinton was born there to a single mother, was partly raised by his grandparents, and grew up with an abusive, alcoholic stepfather. The characters surrounding young Clinton combined the endurance described by Faulkner with the emotional turbulence dramatized by Tennessee Williams.

Yet on the eve of the Democratic convention that was to nominate him, his private polling showed that the public thought he was a son of privilege who came from a family similar to the Bushes. After all, he was a graduate of Georgetown University and the Yale Law School and a Rhodes scholar. His wife, who had attended Wellesley College and Yale Law, was a noted attorney. He was unusually articulate. He had none of the telltale upper-lip sweat of a resentful and insecure lower-middle-class person like Nixon. His tone was buoyant and optimistic, reminiscent of patrician Democrats. It was not until the convention that most people learned about "the man from Hope."

Clinton was neither a Southern boy posing as a cosmopolitan nor an intellectual pretending to be Bubba (his young brother's name for him, by the way). He was not one thing or the other; he was many things at once and all of a piece. He was the first president of his generation, and he had not been a passive bystander to its experiences. He had witnessed the civil rights revolution, protested the Vietnam War, and promoted women's rights. He was inspired by President Kennedy, hoped for Robert Kennedy, and campaigned for George McGovern. He stood in concentric circles: the New South, post–Cold War America, and the generation of 1968 that was coming to power throughout the Western world. In each area, he was something new.

His protean nature was revealed through his eclectic relationship with music. He had played the saxophone in his high-school band and in a sunglass-wearing combo called Three Blind Mice. He entertained his friends with imitations of Elvis. When he was president, he collected books about Elvis. Late in his presidency he kept a large framed picture of the young Elvis on display, propped up against the small Christmas tree in the Oval Office, a present from someone who knew what he liked. Clinton's affinity with Elvis was striking. Elvis, too, was a poor Southern boy, close to his mother, ingratiating and magnetic, who drew on black music and gestures to create a crossover appeal that the traditionally minded warned was the devil's sign. In Clinton's famous (or infamous) appearance on *The Arsenio Hall Show*, in June 1992, he put on black shades and belted out Elvis's standard on his sax, "Heartbreak Hotel." (His performance offended a number of Washington pundits, who felt he had violated norms of propriety.) During the 1992 campaign, the advance staff produced baggage tags with Elvis's picture. Clinton wore a baseball cap with the image of the U.S. postage stamp of the youthful Elvis. Asked on the NBC *Today Show* who he would pick as the greatest entertainer of the century, he replied in a snap, "The early Elvis."*

Clinton sang in Southern Baptist church choirs from his boyhood. In college he was so exhilarated after a Ray Charles concert that he ran for miles into the night. When he was governor, he attended an annual Pentecostal evangelical music festival held outside Little Rock. He joined a church with black members and sang in the choir every Sunday. At his invitation, Bob Dylan—and Ray Charles—played at his presidential inaugural on the steps of the Lincoln Memorial. As part of the White House Millennium Program, he presided over an evening of gospel choirs, framed by a lecture on the subject. When Václav Havel took him in 1994 to the smoky Reduta Jazz Club in Prague, Clinton jumped onstage to join a jazz sextet in "Summertime." He gave a National Medal of the Arts to the bluegrass icon Bill Monroe—and another to Quincy Jones. Sheryl Crow—and Itzhak Perlman—played the East Room. One evening, without advance notice, Clinton conducted the National Symphony at the Kennedy Center. A member of the orchestra told me he was the only guest conductor they'd ever had who knew what he was doing.

*See Greil Marcus, *Double Trouble*, Picador, 2000, p. xiii.

Born in something like a log cabin, Clinton emerged as the leading meritocrat of America's first mass generation of college-educated meritocrats. This was both more and less than part of his identity. And he was a member of a loose network that had grown up together politically since the 1960s. This network of people kept in touch through the Vietnam protests, the McGovern campaign, and outward into activism on hundreds of fronts, all the while pursuing professional careers. Many had been involved in Jimmy Carter's campaign and administration, though they never shared Carter's antigovernment rhetoric and ultimately were disappointed in his failure. Hillary, for example, had directed the Indiana campaign for Carter and was active as a board member of the Children's Defense Fund. The lingua franca of this network was the language of policy, the specifics of governmental activism. To be part of the network meant to be connected to its ongoing conversation. It was a large moveable feast, meeting at foundations, nonprofit issue-based organizations, universities, think tanks, journals, and the Democratic Party in all its manifestations. The conversation was amorphous, diffuse, and completely open. The first principle, after all, was merit. Almost all of those engaged came from middle-class backgrounds. They were self-made—not through having made great fortunes, but by reaching high professional standing. Education was more than an issue to them; it was how they had risen. And they had a will to govern because they believed in governing—and not out of a sense of class entitlement or noblesse oblige. They did not see public service as a kind of charitable contribution or themselves as Lady Bountiful; they hoped to be emblems of merit using public policy to extend merit.

Their rethinking of liberalism moved erratically, from issue to issue, with no fixed label (early on, neoliberalism, Atari Democrats, New Age Democrats, and others). Orthodoxy and dogmatism were antithetical to them; practicality and modernism were paramount. Their conversation was the opposite of a fixed ideological one, asserting all answers from unwavering preconceptions. Ideology, masquerading as policy, dresses as either pseudoscience, for which any jerry-rigged justification will serve, or as an act of faith. By contrast, this conversation was in the tradition of progressive pragmatism—a restless search for possible workable solutions to empirically defined problems. But it could not acquire clarity until it became a politics, and it was politically headless.

Clinton, in 1992, at the age of forty-five, was the longest-serving governor in the country. He was also one of the few elected officials of his generation who was organically part of this rising meritocracy. He was the meritocrat's meritocrat, but that hardly confined him. He reveled in long seminars on policy, but there was none of the metallic grind about him. After a while you almost got the sensation that his endless discussions were like jazz riffs. He played with them until he felt he had improvised the right composition. And then he would start again. Everything was ongoing and in motion. He read extensively in social science and demanded all the arguments from his policy advisers. He was intrigued by technology and its transformations, from the Internet to the human genome project. But he never confused social science with science or technology with a doctrine. He did not believe social problems were reducible to technical means. He disdained the idea that society should be governed by administrators or engineers. Clinton insisted on facts and valued expertise, but he never made claims of omniscience. Just as he was suspicious of political ideology, he was suspicious of the absence of political ideas.

Above all, Clinton believed in the difficult, frustrating, and often humiliating work of politics. Time and again, he said that he thought of the presidency as his "job," not as an exalted title. In private, he spoke frequently about how he wished to demystify the office so that people would always see the president as someone who was working. He saw himself operationally as the opposite of Reagan. He did not intend to strip the presidency of its accoutrements of grandeur, as Carter had done, but he wanted everyone to understand that it was what the president *did* that mattered, not how he posed near the presidential seal. He went out of his way to emphasize that the labor-intensive parts of the presidency were what moved the agenda.

Politics was Clinton's calling and vocation—and more. It provided the means for social change by which the majority benefited more equitably from prosperity and more justly from order and by which a sense of society in a vast, polyglot country was fostered. Politics, to him, was the work of democracy.

Clinton never left a roomful of people until he had spoken to and physically touched as many as he could. He liked to shake hands, always looking the person in the eyes, never darting a glance at who might be behind him or her, continuing to hold on to the hand and arm. Partly this was old-fashioned courtesy, but it also reflected his desire to meet everyone he could. Politics to him was tactile. He wanted to hear opinions and stories firsthand. He learned from these hundreds of thousands of encounters, receiving countless bits of information. In political strategy meetings, he would often make a point by telling an anecdote he had picked up from a random person he had just happened to meet recently. He remarked to me once that the best part of being president was being able to see so many more varieties of human nature than he might otherwise have encountered. He felt he gained the most from the interactions. Some on the staff joked that the Secret Service was there to protect the people from the president.

Franklin Roosevelt's empathy came from the great distance he had traveled from the heights overlooking the Hudson River to the swimming pool in Warm Springs. At Hyde Park, he was raised as a patroon. At Warm Springs, he dog-paddled with children who were afflicted with polio like himself. His kindness to them was accepted as sympathy by ordinary people, not simply because his programs helped them. His suffering brought him to their level. His immobility made him use his charm to draw people to him. FDR's enemies and a number of political columnists resented or dismissed the human element that bound millions to him. They believed that they saw through his ruses to the naked politician beneath. To them, he was an opportunist, a chameleon, a habitual liar, and an untrustworthy trimmer. They considered him shifty and unprincipled, someone who would do anything for political gain, even maneuver the country into war and kill our boys. No sacrifice was too great for his political viability.

Clinton's empathy did not require his being stricken with a dreadful disease. He never had to cross much social distance to be in direct contact with whomever he met. Clinton's critics, however, saw him as a meretricious operator. His compassion was disdained as sheer manipulation. If he was liked, it was because he was seductive. If he was believed, it was because he was false. If he was conciliatory, it was because he was compromised. If he was smooth, it was because he was inauthentic. Whether lodged in the aristocrat or the scholarship boy, these political figures were considered less as genuine personalities than as bundles of pathologies. At the bottom of the distaste was the unpleasant truth that progressive presidents were politically skillful and therefore had prevailed.

Roosevelt was born to rule, if he could manage it. Clinton was born to be something, but not likely president. Yet his energy was in perpetual motion, unstoppable by any outside force. Where did it come from? "Did you know his mother?" Hillary asked me once. As a matter of fact, I did.

Virginia Kelley lived in her dream house, on a small lake in Hot Springs, with her fourth husband and a German shepherd. When I went out to spend a day with her in the summer of 1992 she had already been diagnosed with the cancer that would kill her. She knew it, though she didn't show it. Her black hair had a shock of white in the front. She wore long eyelashes and painted-on arching eyebrows. She had a large ring in the shape of a horseshoe on her finger. On her walls were pictures of horses with black velvet motifs. She liked to go to the track and make two-dollar bets. Hanging up on a rafter was an old sepia photograph of a working man in a lumber mill. "That's my daddy," Virginia said.

Eldridge Cassidy said that when he died he would "go to Roosevelt." He worked in a lumber mill and an icehouse and, at the urging of his wife, Edith, bought a general store in Hope. "My mother said when I was born, 'I won't bring up this child in the country,' so we moved." The store was on the wrong side of the tracks, in Colored Town. Eldridge extended credit to his customers and accepted barter. Edith took a correspondence school course to become a practical nurse. The Cassidys were unusual in their racial liberalism, and Virginia recalled her mother admonishing her, as a child, for using a racial epithet.

Virginia married William Blythe III, a mechanic from Sherman, Texas, in a flash, and then he was off to the war. When he returned she got pregnant and he got a job in Chicago as a heavy equipment salesman. He bought a house there and was driving back to get his wife when, after a rainstorm, at night, near Sikeston, Missouri, his tire blew and he was thrown from the car. He was found in the morning in a shallow ditch. "There was only one little blue mark on his forehead," Virginia said. "So it wasn't the wreck that killed him. He was just stunned enough. He had really drowned. Oh, mercy." She cried all over again and then regained her composure. "It was just terrible, just terrible. So I was five months pregnant."

She decided to train as a nurse to support herself and her baby. "I guess that I had the same drive that my mother had in deciding she wasn't going to bring me up in the country." But Virginia had to enroll in a program in New Orleans and leave her son with her parents. "I didn't think that he would remember how emotional I was when my mother brought him to see me on a visit and they had to leave. It's not even easy now. But he remembered how I knelt at the train station and wept." (Indeed, Clinton described the scene in his acceptance speech to the 1992 Democratic convention.) Eldridge and Edith cared for the boy, while teaching him to read. When Virginia returned she married a local Buick car salesman, Roger Clinton, who had dreams of living large. They moved to Hot Springs, a resort town.

Virginia was surprised when teachers called her to school to tell her that her son was unusually bright. "I thought he was just special to me," she said. He was an avid newspaper reader and asked questions that other children did not. He wondered aloud why he attended a segregated school: "I'll never forget he asked me the question one day and he was so little, seven, eight, nine, something like that. He said, 'Can anybody tell me why the color of a man's skin makes so much difference?' " She also remembered him raising his head from a newspaper after reading about Arkansas's poor national ranking in education and saying, "Mom, aren't the kids in Arkansas born with the same brain as other people?"

Virginia had another boy, Roger, Jr., who turned to his older half-brother as to a father figure. Bill changed his name from Bill Blythe to Bill Clinton to make his family seem more harmonious. But Roger Clinton was an abusive drunk who ignored his children, beat his wife, and fired guns in the house. "Most of the time he just wouldn't be able to do what you do for your children," she said. "Roger just could hardly stand the way his father was treating me, and Bill couldn't either. He tried so hard in his own way as a child to make peace." Bill grew to be more than six feet tall by the time he was fifteen, bigger than his stepfather, and once he confronted him when Roger, in a drunken fit, was hitting his mother. "And Bill told him to stand up, and I thought, my goodness, he can't stand up. Then Bill said to him, 'Daddy, you must stand up to hear what I have to say. And if you can't, then I'll help you.' He helped him get to his feet. And Bill, he just said, 'Don't you ever lay a hand on my mother again.' I believe those were his exact words. Roger had some sort of fear of Bill. He never raised a hand at me again." She filed for divorce.

Virginia worked at the local hospital. She was a fount of stories about injustices she had seen. "It ain't right, but it's so" was her constant refrain. When Bill was eight he handed out palm cards to help elect his stepuncle to the state legislature. He was fascinated by politics and ran for offices at school. In the summer of 1963, he was chosen as one of Arkansas's two representatives to the American Legion Boys Nation. When the boys were brought to the White House, Bill fast-walked his way to the front and managed to shake the hand of President Kennedy. He brought the picture to his mother: "It was just the expression of his face. He was just so happy. It was the experience of a lifetime for him, it really was. That's when I knew he was going into politics."

During his Washington visit, Bill had lunch in the Senate Dining Room with his idol, Senator J. William Fulbright, the former president of the University of Arkansas, a Rhodes scholar, and chairman of the

Senate Foreign Relations Committee. When Bill applied to college, he applied to only one place: Georgetown University's School of Foreign Service. He was launched.

While he was at Georgetown, Bill worked as an intern in Fulbright's office. His job was to clip newspapers about the Vietnam War, which Fulbright opposed. In the 1960s, Georgetown was not a hotbed of student protest and not swept up in the counterculture, and Clinton's education on Vietnam took place in Fulbright's office. In his senior year, after the assassination of Martin Luther King, Jr., Clinton could see the burning of Washington's ghetto from the top of his dormitory. He tried to deliver food and clothing to a shelter there but was chased away by a mob. His hopes for the New Frontier and civil rights were now dashed. He applied to be a Rhodes scholar, like Fulbright. He grew his hair and a beard, traveled extensively throughout Europe, and helped organize the Vietnam moratorium protests in London. He returned from Oxford to attend the Yale Law School, where he soon met Hillary Rodham.

Clinton always intended to go home again. He wanted to bring back to Arkansas what he had learned in the broader world. He got a job as a law professor at the University of Arkansas at Fayetteville, where the black students called him Wonder Boy for his utter absence of racial distinction. Clinton then started running for office. In 1974, he ran for the Congress and barely lost. Two years later, he won for state attorney general. Two years after that he won for governor, becoming the youngest, at thirty-two, in the country. He tried to do as much as he could as fast as he could. He offended some local conservative sensibilities with his team of young, smart aides in a hurry and by his wife's insistence on keeping her maiden name. Raising the tax on car tags alienated more. When the Mariel boat people from Cuba, many of them criminals released by Castro in 1980, burst out of a military camp in Fort Smith, where they were detained, and rioted in the west Arkansan town, Clinton was caught up in the chaotic events that marked the last year of the Carter presidency. He lost his reelection campaign for the governorship by a narrow margin.

His first incarnation as the Comeback Kid came two years later. He was more tempered, more attentive to the Arkansas legislators, and more careful about building coalitions. And he won and won and won. In 1987, Thomas Caplan, Clinton's college friend, accompanied Clinton's mother, Virginia, to yet another gubernatorial inauguration. As he did so often, Clinton abandoned his text and spoke extemporaneously to the crowd. Caplan recalled to me that Clinton remarked that the day before he had been to a funeral, where the widow had vividly remembered his grandfather, Eldridge Cassidy. Clinton said, in Caplan's recollection: "It occurred to me, driving back, that when you get older you don't remember everything in your life. You just remember when you were most alive. I don't want to leave this moment, when I am here and most alive, and fail to do what I could to give every child an opportunity." "Virginia was crying," Caplan said. "And she hit me on the thigh and said, 'I'm so proud of that boy.' "

Clinton's empathy and sense of fairness, his impulse to conciliate and persevere, and his reliance on strong women can be traced to his relationship with his mother. Virginia herself believed that his ambition had to do with her, too. "I always kind of thought in the back of my mind," she told me, "that Bill at an early age had thought that life hadn't dealt me the best hand in the world. And I think in the beginning he was determined that I would have something to be proud of. Accomplishments make Bill happy."

But there was another factor. The only political memento that Clinton had in his private office, upstairs in the White House residence, was a framed letter from Speaker of the House Sam Rayburn to a Clinton cousin, one of Rayburn's constituents, expressing condolences on the death of William Blythe. The parental tragedy inescapably entered into Clinton's ambition and appetite for living.

When I told him, sometime later, about the day I had spent with his mother and what she had said, he reflected for a moment. Then he spoke about how he had always had an impinging feeling of mortality: "I knew that my mother really loved my father and it struck me, even as a child, as so profoundly sad that he would die at twenty-nine in a freak accident. I sort of immersed myself in my friends and my work. But I think some of that was trying to compensate for my mother and some of it was trying to do it for my father. I always felt like that, too. I always felt like maybe I could live the life that he never was able to live. It was like living for two people. And it got harder as I got older."

V

In his first year in office, in September 1989, George H. W. Bush, seeking to create a reputation as "the education president," held a summit on the subject in Charlottesville, Virginia. Governor Clinton emerged as the key figure shaping the goals set at the conference. During one of the luncheons, Bush sat next to the governor's wife. "You know, Mr. President, depending upon what statistic you look at, we're at seventeenth or nineteenth in the whole world in infant mortality," said Hillary. Bush dismissed her claim, informing her that the American health care system was "the envy of the world." She told him she would have Governor Clinton give him the statistics, which he did. Bush conceded that Hillary was right.

This was the first contest between Clinton and Bush. When Bush found himself vulnerable in 1992, he replaced his courtesies with vicious attacks, which had worked for him in 1988, when he was seventeen points behind and his political advisers hastily cobbled together a negative campaign. The feebleness of the kinder and gentler part of Bush's agenda inevitably opened onto the meaner and more malicious part of his politics. Bush thought of public service as a higher, clean calling and politics as a lower, dirty business.

There had been a number of chairmen of the Democratic Leadership Council before Clinton. He was the least prominent when he took the position in 1990. Richard Gephardt, Sam Nunn, and Charles Robb were all bigger names. The DLC was founded after the disastrous Democratic defeat in 1984 to try to develop a more "centrist" politics. None of the previous chairmen had figured out how the DLC could be an effective vehicle to promote their own ambitions and engage in recombinant Democratic politics at the same time. Al From, the DLC president, urged Clinton to use the DLC organization and network to run for president.

On May 6, 1991, Clinton delivered a keynote address to the DLC convention in Cleveland that was the de facto beginning of his campaign. But it was also the start of his redefinition of the Democratic Party. The DLC proposed a program, long in the making, that included a number of key policies that Clinton later championed, including market mechanisms and incentives for poverty-stricken areas, welfare reform, and tradable permits to lower greenhouse gases. Clinton understood that market devices could be integrated into new government solutions; he was eager to develop them. This hardly made him a Reaganite, but it did separate him from Democrats who had not imagined such new methods. Clinton saw his presidential candidacy as a way to use innovative policy to reanimate the Democratic Party.

In his speech in Cleveland, he began by describing how the United States was lagging in the new global economy, suffering from a fall in real income, declining productivity, and paltry investment in education. Clinton had been an education reformer for years in Arkansas, but the idea that education is central to the standing of nations in the global economy because human capital is the most important factor in productivity came in part from Clinton's fellow Rhodes scholar Robert Reich, then teaching at the Kennedy School of Government at Harvard. Reich laid out his analysis in a series of books, most notably *The Work of Nations*. Clinton was to appoint him secretary of labor.

Clinton lambasted the "greed and self-interest" of the Reaganite 1980s, pointing to the "explosion of poor women and their little children." But rather than continuing to hammer Republicans, he swiveled to address his own party:

> You may say, "Well, if all these things are out there, why in the wide world haven't the Democrats been able to take advantage of these conditions?" I'll tell you why. Because too many of the people who used to vote for us, the very burdened middle class we're talking about, have not trusted us in national elections to defend our national interests abroad, to put their values into our social policy at home, or to take their tax money and spend it with discipline. We've got to turn these perceptions around, or we can't continue as a national party. . . . We've got to have a message that touches everybody, that makes sense to everybody, that goes beyond the stale orthodoxies of "left" and "right."

He invoked the themes of opportunity, responsibility, and community—words that he would use throughout his presidency and in his farewell address.

Some liberals criticized Clinton's speech, partly because the DLC did not invite Jesse Jackson to its convention. But if Clinton had not begun speaking to the perceived failures of the party and of government, his appeal to voters on the issue of revitalizing the economy would not have been as wide. The DLC without Clinton would have remained on the fringe of the party, and Clinton without the DLC would have lacked a national organization to project his politics and the notion that he was transcending the Democrats' old shibboleths. In addition to the DLC, Clinton embraced, or had inroads into, or personal ties with, nearly every other constituency in the party. In his campaign were Harold Ickes, son of FDR's secretary of the interior, a master of New York politics, ally of Jesse Jackson; Ron Brown, the Democratic National Committee chairman, a patrician of Harlem if ever there was one; the Daleys of Chicago; the liberals of Hollywood; his fellow Southern governors; and just about every black clergyman in the country. Clinton's unique ability to fuse the myriad parts of the Democratic Party, using policy as a salient means of building a new coalition, buoyed his candidacy. Alone among the candidates, he was able to begin putting the fractured factions together in a new way. But his self-defined task also opened him to suspicions whenever he faltered. The constant improvisations required for him to craft a new message and coalition made it easy to criticize him as an unprincipled, shambling huckster, and to see in his stumbles profound personal flaws.

Politics in Arkansas had been Clinton's school, preparing him for national politics. When he returned to Arkansas after graduating from Yale Law School the state was among the poorest in the nation, its per capita income only 43 percent of the rest of the United States. The cartoon image of Arkansas as Dogpatch was an old joke even in the nineteenth century, when Mark Twain, in *Huckleberry Finn*, depicted "Arkansaw lunkheads" who wanted "low comedy—and maybe something ruther worse than low comedy." Little Rock was the only big city, with a metropolitan area containing about 300,000 people. Economic centers were principally located there and in the northwest corner of the state, where Wal-Mart and Tyson Foods had headquarters. Southeastern Arkansas, along the Mississippi River, was poverty-stricken. Among the old Confederate states, Arkansas had the lowest percentage of blacks, about 15 percent—it had not had a cotton-growing plantation culture—but race remained pivotal to its politics, and since the battle over the desegregation of Little Rock's Central High School in 1957 it had been an open wound. About a third of the voters were embittered segregationists. Clinton was in the line of liberal governors who had built black-white coalitions to win office, and none of his elections were certain. As late as 1990, politics was circumscribed almost completely by the Democratic Party, but there was no political machine or party boss. All the players—political and economic—knew each other well. And politics was intensely personal, ambition against ambition, given to blood feuds.*

Perhaps the best description of Clinton's political survival and legislative record was offered by his two predecessors as governor, Dale Bumpers and David Pryor, both subsequently U.S. senators, who jointly wrote a succinct letter in 1994 to *The New York Times* to correct a long, caricaturing article in the *Times Magazine*:

---

*See Gene Lyons, "Anything Goes," *The New York Review of Books*, August 8, 1996.

We have become increasingly exasperated with those who write that Mr. Clinton's years in the governor's office were a kind of wasteland, during which a hollow man played it slick and safe to insure a certain path to the Presidency. Governor Clinton demonstrated the courage, tenacity and other leadership qualities that caused the people of Arkansas to elect him time and again. "The President's Past" by Michael Kelly (*Magazine*, July 31), styled as political biography, devoted but one paragraph, amid much dubious psychological speculation, to Mr. Clinton's 12 years of gubernatorial service in Arkansas, dismissing that record as simply "a number of moderate reforms."

Is it "moderate reform" for a Governor to produce thousands of new jobs paying higher wages, make the state's tax system fairer, increase access to public health programs, establish the state's first ethics law to regulate the relations between lobbyists and lawmakers, appoint record numbers of women and African-Americans to high office, dramatically reduce infant mortality rates, stiffen environmental regulation of polluters and, with the help of his amazing wife, significantly improve state-supported education at all levels?

It takes energy, determination and perseverance to effect change as an Arkansas governor. The Legislature needs only a simple majority to override a governor's veto, while a raise in income tax requires a 75 percent vote. Until 1986, a governor was limited to debilitating two-year terms. All this for the lowest gubernatorial salary in America.

There is no party machine in predominantly Democratic Arkansas. The political scientist V. O. Key long ago observed that a one-party state is a no-party state. The governor of Arkansas must form a new coalition on each issue. The resulting bartering and negotiating may look slick to the unpracticed eye, but the novice should try it before judging.*

In the fall of 1989, Lee Atwater, chairman of the Republican National Committee, whose negative campaign had rescued the feckless Bush the year before, had had a plan to destroy Bill Clinton. Atwater, then a thirty-eight-year-old South Carolinian, strutted as a Southern bad boy, masking his insecurities. In my extensive dealings with him, beginning in the 1984 Reagan campaign, he was eager to demonstrate to me that he was intellectually serious. He drew diagrams showing politics divided between the poles of "populism" and "the establishment." And he made

---

*Dale Bumpers and David Pryor, "On Governing Arkansas: Mr. Clinton Moved the State Forward," *The New York Times*, September 5, 1994.

references to history, especially the Civil War. He prided himself on his mastery of "populism." His pose as an electric-guitar-playing bluesman added to his image as a rebel. But Atwater's political skill was in updating an old-fashioned Southern antipopulism, using coded racial issues to prevent the white working class from allying with blacks on common economic interests, and to peel off enough white votes on that basis to defeat the New South Democrats. He had interned with Senator Strom Thurmond, father of the Dixiecrats and the Southern Strategy that had realigned the GOP (he eventually ran Thurmond's reelection efforts). Atwater used all the modern tools of campaigning, fine-tuning polls whose results he drew on to shape television commercials. He was relentless and shrewd and knew no limits. As a consultant to other politicians, he had exploited an opponent's psychiatric record, done a poll against a Jewish opponent for not accepting Christ as his personal savior and leaked the result, and was the one who devised the Willie Horton campaign for George Bush. Bush, the candidate who saw politics as unclean, hired Atwater to do the dirty political work for him.

Atwater shrewdly saw Clinton as a potential threat to Bush, and he wanted to eliminate him before the 1992 campaign. He flew two local Republican operatives to Washington for a secret meeting at the Republican National Committee headquarters. His strategy was to use the first, Tommy Robinson, an Arkansas congressman and former sheriff who had switched to the Republican Party, as a weapon. "We're going to take Tommy Robinson," Atwater said, "and use him to throw everything we can think of at Clinton—drugs, women, whatever works. We may or may not win, but we'll bust him up so bad he won't be able to run again for years." Their plan was to make Robinson the Republican candidate against Clinton for governor in 1990—and Clinton would never recover. Atwater was descending into the dark byways of Arkansas politics to strike him down.

The second operative, J. J. Vigneault, whom Atwater had made the RNC regional chairman in Little Rock, told me in detail how this initial plan was upset by the embittered ambition of another figure they had not counted on. Sheffield Nelson was a poor boy who had been virtually adopted as a surrogate son by Witt Stephens, patriarch of the Stephens holding company, the most influential business in Little Rock, which included the largest bond-trading firm west of Wall Street. But Stephens had expelled Nelson from paradise when Nelson refused to make a deal he wanted, and by 1990 they were at war. Clinton had always got along

with Nelson and in 1984 had given him an important state post in economic development. The Stephens family had never supported Clinton,
who was too liberal for them. Indeed, Jackson Stephens, Witt's brother,
was close to the Bushes and a major Republican contributor. And as
Robinson's bankroller, he became an indispensable element in Atwater's
scheme against Clinton.

However, Sheffield Nelson, once a Democrat, enraged at the Stephenses, decided to run against Tommy Robinson in the Republican
primary. Vigneault described to me how Nelson spent his own money to
smash Robinson—resorting to dirty tricks, Vigneault claimed, including
break-ins at campaign headquarters to steal files. Thus the Republican
primary, pitting two former Democrats against each other, was a contest
of ulterior motives. Nelson's vengeance was aimed at the forces looming
behind Robinson, Atwater's pawn against Clinton.

When Nelson defeated Robinson, the Stephenses for the first time
backed Clinton in the general election. At their orders boxes of damaging information about Nelson's financial dealings were delivered to Clinton's campaign headquarters. But Clinton didn't need them. Nelson—a
neophyte now running against the most popular, entrenched politician in
the state as well as the most powerful economic empire, and having split
his newfound Republican Party, confounding the well-laid plans of its
national chairman—had no chance.

Nelson's rage against the Stephenses stoked his new dislike of Clinton. Nelson, the rejected son, was determined to mangle the Stephenses'
newly favored one. His useful idiot was a former state employee, Larry
Nichols, whose life was a shipwreck. Nichols had been forced to resign
from his job after getting caught making thousands of dollars of telephone calls to Contra leaders in Nicaragua and to a disreputable business
partner, Darrell Glascock, a low-level Republican operative known for
dirty tricks. Nichols's marriage had disintegrated into an acrimonious divorce. When his wife fled the state with their daughter, Hillary Clinton
was one of the lawyers representing her, giving him a personal motive for
his animosity toward the governor.

Three weeks before the election, Nichols distributed a statement
claiming he had been fired as Clinton's "scapegoat" in order to conceal
the governor's misuse of state funds to pay off five alleged mistresses,
and he filed a lawsuit against the governor. Sheffield Nelson distributed Nichols's statement from his campaign headquarters and faxed it
to reporters. It received little attention. But Nelson insisted that the
race turned on "character." Meanwhile, all five women, including Gen-

nifer Flowers, denied Nichols's charges; three of them threatened to sue.

"Two days before Election Day, Nichols tipped his hand," Joe Conason and Gene Lyons wrote in *The Hunting of the President*. "At a meeting in a diner with Clinton press secretary Mike Gauldin, he offered to settle his lawsuit if the governor arranged to pay off the mortgage on his house and give him an additional $150,000."* Clinton won by eighteen points. But it was in this dank political atmosphere that the anti-Clinton campaign began.

In July 1991, Clinton decided to brush off the rumors about his personal life by directly confronting them at a Washington press breakfast hosted by Godfrey Sperling of *The Christian Science Monitor*. Hillary accompanied him. "Like nearly anybody who has been together for twenty years, our relationship has not been perfect or free from difficulties, but we feel good about where we are and we believe in our obligation to each other, and we intend to be together thirty or forty years from now, whether I run for president or not." He believed the matter settled.

The right-wing *Washington Times* published a front-page article about Clinton's breakfast appearance, signaling that personal lives would be subject to search-and-destroy missions in the upcoming campaign. In *The New Republic*, where I was then a senior editor, I followed with an editorial entitled "Predators," which I quote here because it summarizes virtually all the themes that were to dominate press and politics during the Clinton years:

> The press treatment of Gary Hart was the exception that has proved to be the rule. Mr. Hart's case, we were solemnly informed by his media prosecutors at the time, was unique. But in the four years since, the peculiarities of his particular fate have become routinized. Now, however, there is no sharp gasp at questions about adultery and the like. The artifice of justification that surrounded the Hart episode—the self-destructive hypocrisy ascribed to the subject—is hardly deemed essential. No explanation is given for each new humiliating exposure. Private lives are fair game. The stakeout, the dragnet, and the inquisition have become quintessential methods of contemporary political coverage. Any self-protective gesture is considered an ipso facto confession of guilt and thus an incitement.

*Joe Conason and Gene Lyons, *The Hunting of the President: The Ten-Year Campaign to Destroy Bill and Hillary Clinton*, St. Martin's Press, 2000, p. 17.

The unspoken claim that private acts, especially sexual ones, have a direct bearing on public acts is, at best, extremely confused. When it comes down to such slippery terms as "character," rather than specific claims about the professional qualifications for public office, it is close to being a blanket justification for all manner of media excess. . . .

But the press has also devised an elaborate system for privacy raiding. Rumors are circulated; off-the-record quotes are pursued. Once a certain level of controversy has been stirred up, the controversy itself becomes the story, in which all the details of a private life are "incidentally" revealed. There are variations on this Hart-model, of course. In the last resort, the prestige press and the tabloids enter into a parasitic relationship, where the former reports the reporting of the latter. Increasingly, the media does not even go through the motions of civility. . . .

In the endless snipe hunts for bedroom hypocrisy, the media may boost circulation or ratings. But, so far, there has been no discernible rise in political virtue. . . . Instead, in the name of honesty, integrity, and candor, the trend toward supplanting serious political discourse with dubious distractions has been accelerated. The press, naturally, has no program of its own. But in its slow slide toward undiscriminating prurience, it has contributed to the trend of illiberalism.*

In January 1992, a month before the New Hampshire primary, Clinton emerged as the front-runner, poised to win. New York governor Mario Cuomo, thought by many observers to be the strongest candidate, had dithered Hamlet-like for months before deciding not to make the race. The field included Paul Tsongas, retired U.S. senator from Massachusetts; Edmund G. "Jerry" Brown, former governor of California; Tom Harkin, U.S. senator from Iowa; and Robert Kerrey, U.S. senator from Nebraska. With polls showing Clinton pulling ahead of the rest of the field, Larry Nichols and Gennifer Flowers sold stories to the *Star* tabloid about Flowers's supposed "twelve-year affair" with Clinton, for which Nichols received $50,000, Flowers $150,000. The Clintons went on CBS's *60 Minutes*, appearing immediately following the Super Bowl. Bill called the allegation "false," though he acknowledged causing "pain in my marriage," and Hillary said that if people didn't like it they didn't have to vote for him. Sheffield Nelson stepped forward to say that Clinton was lying. Tommy Robinson claimed that Nelson had "orchestrated"

*Sidney Blumenthal, Editorial, "Predators," *The New Republic*, August 19–26, 1991.

Flowers's accusations and that *she* was lying. She had, in fact, become close to Republican officials, even contributing to one Republican campaign. Nichols dropped his lawsuit and apologized to Clinton. "In trying to destroy Clinton, I was only hurting myself," he said. Quietly, he demanded $200,000 from Clinton. His bid for a payoff was rejected.

The sluice gates of scandal were opening. On February 18, a tabloid called the *Globe* headlined, "New Scandal Hits Dems' Front-Runner; Bill Clinton's Four-in-a-Bed Sex Orgies with Street Hookers—and he's the father of my child, claims ghetto gal he had sex with 13 times!" It was, of course, completely false. The story was exhumed from Arkansas's racial past: it was a canard that had first been used years before to tar Governor Winthrop Rockefeller, the liberal Republican.

The Flowers incident lofted the "character" issue into the presidential campaign. Clinton's carefully devised platform was being overshadowed by scandalmongering on the part of a press pack that was developing a uniform and instant line. Lars-Erik Nelson, one journalist who stood independently apart from the herd, wrote in his column in the New York *Daily News,* not widely read in Washington, in the aftermath of the Flowers incident:

> Not a vote has been cast this election year, and yet it is clear that strong and bipartisan opinion feels Clinton must be destroyed, and the sooner the better. Who are these people? And why do they want to kill him? The media campaign against Clinton is the most fascinating. The attacks on Clinton have been peddled first and foremost by the *Star* tabloid, the *Boston Herald,* the *New York Post,* the TV show "A Current Affair," and the Fox television network. Clinton would appear to be under a generalized media barrage. Yet what do the above named outlets have in common? They are all either owned or formerly owned—and all are currently staffed by long-time associates of—Rupert Murdoch, the one-time Australian who delights in his ability to destroy political candidates on three continents. . . . And then the TV networks, based in New York, find they cannot ignore the story that blares at them from every newsstand and from Murdoch's Fox network. . . . The onslaught becomes self-fulfilling. Truth doesn't matter. Clinton is whispered to be "damaged" by allegations. His campaign is "rocked" by charges. He is "mortally wounded." Except he is still standing.*

*Lars-Erik Nelson, "Despite Mauling, Clinton Still on Feet," New York *Daily News,* February 10, 1992.

Then came a new barrage. A letter Clinton had written in 1969 to a Colonel Eugene Holmes, who had been on Clinton's draft board, thanking him for helping him get out of the draft, was mysteriously released to the media. His letter made plain that the Vietnam War was "a war I opposed and despised with a depth of feeling I had reserved solely for racism in America before Vietnam." The young Clinton also explained that he planned for a political life: "The decision not to be a resister and related subsequent decisions were the most difficult of my life. I decided to accept the draft in spite of my beliefs for one reason: to maintain my political viability within the system. For years I have worked to prepare myself for a political life characterized by both practical political ability and concern for rapid social progress. It is a life I still feel compelled to try to lead."

The story about the draft turned on memories of events that had occurred decades earlier. There had been no law broken, no wrongdoing. But Clinton did not remember everything about his getting out of the draft in the correct sequence, and he said he had forgotten about a mistaken draft notice that had been instantly rescinded. The press treated this as a question of "character." Many in the mainstream press corps who had once been uncomfortable with the Flowers story but who were losing their discomfort with such tales now basically accepted and amplified the draft story, which they thought they could report legitimately. Reporters a generation older than Clinton held him in special disdain as two-faced, a would-be practical politician but in fact a countercultural, antiwar protester out only for himself. To them, the episode revealed deception, opportunism, and a lack of patriotism. Other reporters took his explanations as falsehoods. Among those who professed to be personally offended were some who had once defended Nixon's Vietnam policy.

In the deep freeze of New Hampshire, in February, Clinton's poll numbers fell to a single digit. The Clintons decided to throw themselves at the voters. Bill would fight "until the last dog died," he told a rally. Finishing second to Paul Tsongas, he proclaimed himself the Comeback Kid.

On the campaign trail, he continued trying to overcome the burdens borne by the Democratic Party because of its racial inclusiveness, which the Republicans used against it in a coded way. He told separate audiences of blacks and whites in Michigan that they each had to change. He criticized Sister Souljah, a rap artist, for her racial invective against whites. And finally, at the Democratic National Convention in New York City, in July, in his effort to redefine the party he chose Senator Al Gore of Tennessee as his running mate—not someone older, not someone from another region, not someone more or less liberal. Clinton decided to double himself. He put all his chips on one square.

By mid-October, President Bush was desperate. His campaign was frantically searching for a "silver bullet," a story like a magic projectile that, once it hit Clinton, would make him crumple to the ground. Republican operatives trolled for sex tales in Arkansas, calling every potential source of dirt. Plane tickets to Washington were offered to unidentified women telephone callers who plied them with lurid stories and then hung up. Aides were even dispatched to the phone booths used by these callers in futile efforts to track them down. Resources were poured into an operation to prove an apocryphal story that Clinton during his years in Oxford had tried to renounce his American citizenship to protest the Vietnam War. The British Home Office was asked to search its files, which it did. State Department officials looked to see if Clinton or his mother had even withdrawn their passports. Tory strategists were imported to advise on the negative themes that John Major had used to win as prime minister earlier in the year. The press corps was like a burned-over district, scorched by rumors and swept with fervent belief that the end was near: soon the *Los Angeles Times* will publish a story about Clinton's cocaine use!

Bush had trained to be a Cold War president and arrived in office in time for the fall of the Berlin Wall. The Gulf War had been swift, hardly the same as a decades-long confrontation that had divided the globe. Clinton's repositionings baffled and upset him. This was not the kind of Democrat that Republicans were used to deconstructing. Clinton did not act like a convenient and familiar sitting target. His rapid responses to the Bush campaign's attacks disoriented Bush, who took to calling him "the new man," half in bafflement and half in sarcasm. He was genuinely perplexed that he seemed to be losing. He lashed out at Gore for his environmentalism as "Ozone Man." On CNN's *Larry King Live*, he lunged at Clinton's patriotism: "But to go to Moscow one year after Russia crushed Czechoslovakia, not remember who you saw, I think, I really think the answer is, level with the American people." Bush's plight as yesterday's man might have appeared poignant if he had not indulged in these smears.

His administration then reached for a last straw, a failed real-estate investment called Whitewater. On March 8, 1992, seven months earlier, *The New York Times* had published a front-page article by Jeff Gerth: "Clintons Joined S&L Operator in an Ozark Real Estate Venture." Much of the article had been in error, beginning with the headline. When the Clintons had made their investment in 1978 in a property called White-water, their partner was not yet a savings-and-loan operator; he started the bank in 1983. Nor was Clinton yet governor. Gerth implied that the Arkansas securities commissioner, Beverly Bassett Schaffer, appointed by Clinton, had granted favors to the S&L operator at the prodding of the Clintons in 1985 and then, when questioned by Gerth about this, had had a convenient memory lapse. In fact, before his article appeared she had given him a twenty-page memo spelling out in detail what had actu-ally happened—she had requested federal regulators to close the S&L—an account Gerth ignored. (After the article appeared she considered filing a libel suit; later, her version was vindicated.)

The S&L operator in question was a flamboyant figure from Ar-kansas's political past, now fallen on hard times. Jim McDougal had been an aide to Senator Fulbright (convincing Fulbright to invest in his deals, too), a former state Democratic Party chairman, who lived large. His bank, the Madison Guaranty Savings and Loan Association, had col-lapsed and he had been acquitted in 1990 of federal bank fraud. He had tried an insanity defense during the trial but then withdrew it. Every-thing was gone: he was manic-depressive, drug-addicted, alcoholic, di-vorced, bankrupt, subsisting on Social Security. He was embittered that he was not getting something from a rising Bill Clinton. Who had put him in contact with Gerth? The helpful Sheffield Nelson. McDougal and Nelson had been business partners in a deal to buy Campobello Island, FDR's famous summer place, and turn it into resort lots. More than any other scheme, that failed one had helped pull the Madison bank under. But the Campobello deal went unmentioned in Gerth's account.

I interviewed Nelson shortly after the *New York Times* article was pub-lished. He sat behind a big desk in a spotless, generic office atop a build-ing overlooking Little Rock. But his initial appearance as a corporate manager soon altered as he adopted a low voice, arched his eyebrows, and let loose a stream of innuendoes about Clinton. By the end, he was leering. He made it clear to me that he had spoken to many reporters.

After Gerth's article was published in the *Times*, McDougal retracted his charges, saying Clinton had done nothing illegal or unethical. A forensic accountant scratched through the confused records and issued a report showing no wrongdoing by the Clintons, while they lost about $65,000. But in Tulsa, Oklahoma, an investigator for the regional office of the Resolution Trust Corporation—the temporary federal agency that had been created to sort out the assets of failed savings-and-loan banks and to assist their depositors—L. Jean Lewis, an ardent Republican, read the now forgotten *Times* piece and, working overtime for the next few months, produced a criminal referral drawing a picture of a large conspiracy. Bill and Hillary Clinton, according to the papers Lewis filed, were to be called as witnesses. The head of investigations for her RTC office had dismissed the idea that the Clintons had anything to do with Madison Guaranty, but this did not inhibit the aroused Lewis.

In October President Bush's White House counsel, C. Boyden Gray, called the chief executive of RTC to inquire about the existence of the referral. And Attorney General William Barr demanded information from the U.S. attorney in Arkansas, Charles Banks (who had once run unsuccessfully for the Congress as a Republican and served as the state party chairman). On October 7, the FBI office in Little Rock sent a telex to superiors in Washington:

> It is the opinion of Little Rock FBI and the United States Attorney . . . that there is indeed insufficient evidence to suggest the Clintons had knowledge of the check-kiting activity conducted by McDougal . . . and does not suggest the Clintons had access to checking account statements that would have reflected the questionable transactions. . . . It was also the opinion of [Banks that] the alleged involvement of the Clintons in wrong-doing was implausible, and he was not inclined to authorize an investigation or render a positive prosecutive opinion.*

Bush's attorney general did not accept Banks's opinion as final. He sent an assistant to demand a review of Lewis's referral. Banks sent a stern rebuke to his boss in Washington in the form of a letter to the head of the FBI office in Little Rock:

> While I do not intend to denigrate the work of the RTC, I must opine that after such a lapse of time the insistence of urgency in this case appears to suggest an intentional or unintentional attempt to intervene into the political process of the upcoming presidential election. You and I know in investigations of this type, the first steps, such as issuance of grand jury subpoenas for records, will lead to media and public inquiries [about] matters that are subject to absolute privacy. Even media questions about such an investigation in today's modern political climate all too often publicly purport to "legitimize what can't be proven." For me person-

*Conason and Lyons, *Hunting of the President*, p. 43.

ally to participate in an investigation that I know will or could easily lead to the above scenario . . . amounts to prosecutorial misconduct and violates the most basic fundamental rule of Department of Justice policy. I cannot be a party to such actions.*

On October 16, the Little Rock FBI office sent another telex to Washington stating categorically that there was "absolutely no factual basis to suggest criminal activity on the part of any of the individuals listed as witnesses in the referral."

With that, the Whitewater scandal withered. Despite Nelson's having planted the story at *The New York Times*, despite Lewis's referral, and despite prodding by the Attorney General, it never developed into Bush's hoped-for October surprise. Unlike previous Democratic candidates, Clinton triumphed over the personal assaults. And once he won in November, he held an illusion that the scandalmongering would fade and that the focus would turn toward the serious problems facing the country. Yet, in time, the least effective negative tactic used in the campaign against him, the bogus Whitewater scandal, had the most profound effect on his presidency.

Conservatives were enraged that Bush had lost. They had believed that Republicans had a perpetual "lock" on the White House. A Democrat was never supposed to occupy it. For some the loss was akin to all the Cold War betrayals by liberals: Who lost Eastern Europe? Who lost China? Who lost Vietnam? Now the issue was: Who lost Reagan? At first, they blamed Bush himself. At the Heritage Foundation in Washington, a group of young conservatives called the Third Generation held a frenzied postelection anthropological rite. They filled an auditorium with partisans and then entered with a plastic mask of Bush on a platter with red crepe paper to represent his blood; by this symbolic beheading, they tried to exorcise the defeat.

Clinton had won partly by default. Bush's ratings had declined an unprecedented fifty-seven points between the end of the Gulf War and the Republican National Convention. Ross Perot's third-party candidacy represented an inchoate and unstable revolt against the Republican Party on the part of rank-and-file members and Republican-leaning independents. Bush's rejection was decisive. But the rage instantly turned against the one who had beaten him. The new Democratic president aroused the furies simply by existing. From the RNC to the *Wall Street Journal* edito-

*Conason and Lyons, *Hunting of the President*, p. 44.

rial board, from the special-interest associations of K Street to Rupert
Murdoch, Clinton was seen as a usurper who must be driven from the
White House.

To the Republicans, Clinton's defeat of Bush undid the natural order.
He was unimaginable in the White House. He was a cracker who would
never have been admitted to Bush's Yale, certainly not tapped for Skull
and Bones. In any case, Clinton had been not at Yale College but at the
Yale Law School, a different kettle of fish entirely, especially by the late
1960s. Conservatives *knew* he was a liberal, only worse than a liberal because he kept eluding their campaigns to destroy him as such. He was
unpatriotic, a libertine who had not only opposed the war but said so in a
letter to his draft board (unlike Bush's sons, who used their father's connections to get out of serving in Vietnam and never uttered a word about
the war, either for or against it). Something had to explain the rise of this
figure to them, but they didn't know what. Clinton couldn't have gotten
to where he was naturally. His victory had to be illegitimate.

Like Roosevelt, Clinton came to power after long years of Republican
rule. But FDR had faced an immediate crisis with the Great Depression,
and his political room for maneuver was greater, since the Democrats had
large majorities in the Congress. Clinton, on the other hand, confronted a
vacuum and resistance whichever way he turned. The old politics had
been played out, and the country was pinioned between a liberalism fashioned during an age of scarcity and war and the reaction to it.

When I left Hyde Park after Clinton's visit, I went back to a capital
that was not an open city. Washington had not been ready for Clinton,
and his every move there had shaken things up and created uncertainty.
The Democrats were divided and confused, the Republicans were determined to bring him down, and the media were already lurching from
scandal to scandal. Whether Clinton would be able to pass his programs
or not, whether the Democrats would achieve political momentum, and
where the Republican assault and the media gyrations would lead were
all unknown. It was as though gravity had suddenly been suspended. At
the beginning, Clinton seemed to be all possibility. But in Washington
almost everything old felt threatened by everything new; the possible im-
periled the settled. And not everyone wanted to start the world over
again. Clinton referred me to a passage from Machiavelli's *The Prince*:
"There is nothing more difficult to plan, more doubtful of success, nor
more dangerous to manage, than a creation of a new order of things."

TWO

The Forces Are Arrayed

I

"It's the economy, stupid!" The campaign slogan, once pinned to the wall of the "war room" in Little Rock, was now foremost in the mind of the president-elect.

A month after the election, Bill Clinton convened a conference about economics. Dozens of pilgrims made the journey to Little Rock, where he was preparing himself for the presidency—chief executive officers of major corporations, Nobel Prize–winning economists, labor leaders, the president of the Navajo nation, and people whom he had just chosen for positions in his new administration. At the conference, the main lines of a new policy for prosperity were hammered out. The federal deficit, the new economy, globalization, education—all were examined at length.

Clinton sat rapt through the entire two days. It was the sort of detailed yet far-ranging discussion that he liked, and the participants competed with one another for his attention through sharp analysis and bold charts, while Clinton synthesized arguments that might have seemed at odds. Working on how to square the circle, he saw no contradiction between the need to "increase investment" in education and infrastructure and the need to "stop the cycle of borrow-and-spend economics." To be sure, he said, "Let's not kid ourselves; these are hard questions."*

The next eight years were to be consumed in making these difficult

*See *President Clinton's New Beginning: The Complete Text, with Illustrations, of the Historic Economic Conference Conducted by President Bill Clinton and Vice President Al Gore in Little Rock, Arkansas, December 14–15, 1992*, Donald I. Fine, 1993.

choices. Clinton had to remedy and reconstruct at the same time. He had to try to reduce the deficit *and* provide for new social investments, a juggler's trick that seemed an impossible stunt. Clinton's initial suggestion that he could accomplish both did little but arouse skepticism. It was a commonplace that the deficits stretched as far as the eye could see. Despite the Republicans' supposed doctrinal aversion to spending more than they had, the towering deficits erected during their years in power were a lasting monument in Washington to Reaganism.

Some economists argued to the president-elect that he must go back to renewed deficit spending, as a classic Keynesian stimulus to the economy to lift it out of the doldrums of lingering recession. Some argued for a drastic reduction in the deficit without any social spending, since the costs of social programs were depicted as a source of the problem. Some argued for simply doing nothing, saying that government activism could only create unintended consequences, all bad; if things were left alone, the economy would naturally improve on its own, according to its invisible but iron laws. But Robert Rubin, a partner at Goldman Sachs and soon to be appointed director of the National Economic Council, would propose the novel and heterodox theory by which a radical reduction in the deficit would free room for social investment in a new, virtuous cycle of prosperity. It had not happened before.

A week after the Little Rock conference, Clinton's transition team presented him with an "economic overview": "You have inherited a two-part challenge of historic proportions. Either challenge by itself would be daunting but manageable. Both challenges together, with their contradictory elements (cutting the deficit, while increasing the deficit) amount to a formidable task." Two weeks later, the departing Republican budget director sent his yet-unveiled new numbers to the next president. They showed a previously unforeseen increase of $60 billion in the deficit. Clinton's expansive plans were being squeezed even before he assumed office. He was incredulous.

Clinton was experienced in dealing with unpredictable difficulties. He was not jolted into a state of shock when things didn't work out just as he had planned. If anything, he had survived because he dealt with setbacks better than others. But the presidency was on a qualitatively different scale from being a governor or campaigning to be president. Clinton was entering territory that he may have thought he had mapped out but was filled with unmarked traps. He believed he could begin to implement his program, "Putting People First," by doing politics in the ways he understood. There would be ups and downs, maneuverings, deals, and, finally, the passing of bills, not in pristine condition, but more than good enough. He was convinced that gradually but surely he would forge a new consensus. Early in the campaign, he told me that he thought about three-quarters of the people agreed with his positions. He just needed to reach them and secure their support.

At every point when he found the atmosphere becalmed during his early presidency, he deluded himself into believing that the eye of the hurricane was firm ground. At least in the beginning, he didn't think the sudden stillness was eerie; he thought he was in a normal place. He knew from the campaign that the Democratic Party was in disarray, but he didn't expect it to be so ramshackle. He knew the Republicans were against him, but he didn't expect an opposition that wasn't an opposition but an enemy. He knew the media indulged in sensationalism, but he didn't expect the press corps to lose its moorings and standards. He thought he knew Washington, having been in and out of the city since he was a student at Georgetown, but he didn't expect a capital seething with resentment, envy, and hostility directed at him and his wife, much of it of unfathomable origin.

Clinton believed he could move his agenda reasonably, making his case, fighting his battles, and pushing extremists to the fringes, where they belonged. But the irrational element in politics isn't a virus isolated in extremism. Uncontrollable emotional passion in politics has roots in a thousand sources deep in the social soil. It can be located in the loss of power, in frustration at trying to grasp it, or just in the slightest proximity to power; in status anxiety, a moment of unsteady attention, or economic insecurity; in the desire for fame, influence, wealth, or ratings. These combustible feelings can never be quite gratified—because there is an insistent pressure for more, an ever-nagging sensation that whatever has been gained is never enough, and a dread that a speck of reflected glory can be capriciously lost in a twinkling.

The intensity of reaction, defying logic and reason, acquires its own logic. Rage and hatred swiftly develop images that masquerade as ideas, and the heightened imagination can make the figures on the cave wall appear to be a higher truth. The stronger the feeling, the more ingenuous it feels. Once in its grip, a person can make any remark or incident fit the mesmerizing pattern and confirm its reality. And the more a figure of hate tries to alter that reality to escape from the picture, the more he or she (Bill or Hillary) is thrust back into the stereotype. Doubt, uncertainty, and skepticism are banished. Credulous and impulsive hatreds then become contagious. Political gatherings and even dinner parties can suddenly be transformed into occasions when crowds become atavistic. As the pioneer sociologist Gustave Le Bon wrote in his nineteenth-century study *The Crowd*, "social illusions" of a "hypnotic order" can take on the power of a crowd in many forms, from rabble to noble castes, from groups of thousands to those of a half dozen. American history from the Salem witch trials to the present was not immune: it had its own peculiar vulnerability to these frenzies, given its heritage of moralistic absolutism, anti-intellectualism, populist demagogy, and instability in its elite and governing classes.

Clinton had all sorts of natural opponents, whose differences with him were based on their interests, partisan attachments, and professional work. But his clashes with them summoned up irrational forces almost from the start. Clinton's triumph over the personal assaults made on him during the campaign—the ones centered on sex, class, and patriotism—hardly quelled the animosities; in fact, his electoral victory aroused them further. Each of his enemies had an individual interest in damaging him; unreason found many constituencies. Almost any incident in his presidency set off a cascade of vituperation. Endless apocryphal stories, tall tales, and legends were generated that supposedly revealed the true Clinton—or the true Mrs. Clinton.

If there is a law about progressive presidencies it is not that they run in recurring cycles like a regular alignment of the planets, but that in their efforts to create a new consensus they become the object of intense opposition. The opposition fails to distinguish between hatred of the man and hatred of his politics. And an attack on morals has always gone hand in hand with an attack on politics. Members of what became Thomas Jefferson's party were hounded, fined, and imprisoned under the Alien and Sedition Acts signed by President John Adams—"the reign of witches," Jefferson called it. Jefferson himself was assailed as a godless anarchist, a sexual mauler, an adulterer, a betrayer of friends, a chronic liar, and, lastly, a keeper of a black concubine. Andrew Jackson had an election stolen from him; in the next contest, he was painted as the son of a prostitute and a mulatto, a bigamist, crook, and murderer; in the next, as "King Andrew," trampling the Constitution. In office, in payment for his fiercely fought positions, he became the first president ever censured by the Senate, for having, it charged, "assumed upon himself authority and power not conferred by the Constitution and laws, but in derogation of both." Had his enemies had a majority in the House, he would undoubtedly have been the first president to be impeached. Lincoln was caricatured as a baboon, a primate from the frontier Midwest, a "black

Republican," perhaps black himself, a trickster storyteller, Dishonest Abe. Franklin Roosevelt was despised as a traitor to his class, a dictator, habitually dishonest, a feebleminded playboy, and a warmonger. John F. Kennedy was loathed as a betrayer of national security, a communist sympathizer, a traitor, a Catholic Negro-lover, a libertine liberal, an illegitimate pretender, a fraud, and a calculating dissembler.

The pattern of these attacks cannot be dismissed as the usual cut and thrust of political combat, as mere name-calling or the customary jockeying for office. These presidents were castigated as they were because they represented new and broader forms of democracy. And there were essentially no built-in limits to the attacks on them. If the presidents could have been destroyed or removed from office, their enemies would have gladly done so. They were perceived as personifying dangerous threats to established order and morals. They stood for new rights for new constituencies, the breakup of established power, a new identity for the nation, and the aggressive use of the executive branch to achieve those aims. And since, given the very nature of their proposals for innovative programs, these presidents had to act politically, shifting and twisting, they were especially vulnerable to charges of disorder and dishonesty.

The opposition to progressive presidents historically resists their attempts to forge a new consensus, but paradoxically, it also helps bring that consensus about and define it. Any new consensus comes after conflict, and the forces that oppose it cannot but defend what they see as their own superior morality and order. Conflict is necessary to break the bonds of the past, making possible the new arrangements. In the most sanguinary instance, there would have been no "new birth of freedom," as Lincoln put it, without the Civil War. Rage and vituperation, whipped to an irrational frenzy and even provoking constitutional crises, are signs of the grand dimensions of change.

And the issues over which Americans have actually disagreed have always been central to our politics. Who should govern the country? What is the relationship of the federal government to the people? These questions run from the beginning, from the Revolution and the battle over the Constitution, through the Civil War, down to the present time.

Clinton was moderate, charming, and embracing. He listened to every side, attempted to soothe the angry and include everyone who was willing to sit around his table. Unlike the aristocrat FDR, who reveled in his enemies, especially the "economic royalists" of his own class, once proclaiming, "I welcome their hatred," Clinton sought "common ground," the theme of many of his speeches. His story, moreover, could be considered a classic of the American Dream, in the tradition of log cabin presidents—the poor boy who rises by dint of hard work, merit, superior intelligence, and character. When he became president, the United States was emerging as the most powerful nation in the history of the world, since after the Cold War no other great power could challenge it. Yet, from the start, the new president became an object of hatred, and so did anyone who supported or associated with him in almost any way.

Clinton had power and his enemies did not. They did not think he was supposed to have it. His standing as a professional who had succeeded through merit and his marriage to a woman who had done the same aroused their scorn. In the way that he opened up so many questions about government, social equality, race, class, gender, the common good, and the American identity, he seemed to be associated with the movements and causes of the 1960s. Yet at the same time, he was advocating a political agenda that was intended to overcome the debilities of the 1960s that still afflicted the Democratic Party. Both for being of the 1960s and for trying to transcend the 1960s, he was hated and feared.

Clinton explained in countless campaign speeches and his book-length plan, *Putting People First*, that he was embarked on a strategy of immense difficulty. He wanted to reposition a disparate political party, then rebuild the inert executive branch and restore it as a progressive force, in order to turn the national government into an agent of change for American society as a whole. All these institutions were like bent, rusty tools that needed hammering and recasting. The dilemma was that he had to move forward while engaging in inevitable compromises, retreats, and expedients. Practical politics dictated ragged means to achieve imperfect goals. By necessity, he had to shift and tack.

Whenever Clinton faltered, his failures were not interpreted in the context of his strategic plans but imputed to his persona. To the right, he was satanic; to the left, a betrayer; to the media, a target whichever way he moved. He was seen as elusive, impulsive, mercurial, fluid, and both addicted to risk and fearful of it. Political miscalculations and shortcomings were cast as character flaws, which became ingrained political images even when supposed miscalculations turned out over time to be roaring successes—like his economic policy. Clinton's overall strategy, present from the start, was rarely acknowledged. Not only did he have to navigate the vessel of state in a vast sea through unpredictable storms, but he had to build a safe harbor. His political ability to tack with the wind was usually interpreted as his being rudderless. Even long-term policy gains—whether on the economy, crime, or trade—were obscured because of short-term political losses. And Clinton himself, caught in the midst of the howling winds, could not know whether and how much he was succeeding.

In the absence of an easily identifiable crisis—a Great War or a Great Depression—the internecine warfare, blinding rage, and sheer destructiveness that converged on Bill and Hillary Clinton suggested an elemental political clash. The conflict eventually led to a constitutional crisis, but its course and outcome could hardly have been foretold. All of Clinton's political art and craft would be demanded. "It's lucky," Hillary told me, "that Bill deals with ambiguity better than most of us."

II

The President-elect's economic conference was his last cloudless moment. Even before the inauguration, the patterns of light and darkness had rolled in. The sharp contrasts were not opposites, but elements of the same dynamic. Personality and freakish accident came into full play, but the President's effort to create a new national consensus was what set the political drama in motion.

The paradoxes were unparalleled: an activist president of a new generation elected with 43 percent of the vote; the clear end of not only Republican rule but the Cold War; the obvious anachronism of policy and politics; and the lack of a national emergency that would force change. Almost every incident of Clinton's presidency was perceived as a turning point and provoked an outcry. Even modest proposals were perceived as major tremors, obscure skirmishes hailed as signs of Manichean struggle foreshadowing the end of days. The President's gestures toward common consent triggered new polarizations.

Early in the campaign, Clinton had told a gay rights group that he favored overturning the policy that excluded gays from serving in the armed forces. Our NATO allies had armies that included open gays, yet thousands were drummed out of our armed services in sexual discharges. Despite its incendiary potential, the issue remained latent until a week after the election, when a reporter asked the President-elect if he would make good on his campaign pledge. "Yes, I want to," he replied. He assigned the issue to a national security aide to work out. All parties should be consulted, especially the Joint Chiefs of Staff and the Senate Armed Services Committee. Perhaps there should be a presidential review board. Perhaps there should be a presidential directive. Careful attention should be paid to timing.

Colin Powell, still the chairman of the Joint Chiefs, a holdover from the Bush administration, publicly rebuked his new commander in chief's plan, declaring his opposition. Powell took umbrage at any suggestion that discrimination was involved. "Homosexuality is not a benign behavioral characteristic such as skin color," he said. Senator Sam Nunn, chairman of the Armed Services Committee, reinforced Powell's resistance and threatened to add amendments on this subject to proposed new legislation on health care. After a tumultuous meeting with the Joint Chiefs (including the Marine Corps Commandant, who was circulating lurid homophobic videotapes), an impasse was reached. Nine days after the President took office, he announced a compromise policy of "don't ask, don't tell," which quieted Nunn and Powell.

The resolution settled the immediate controversy, but it opened an issue that had never before been a matter of national contention, least of all involving a president. Many gays and their sympathizers did not grasp why, if Clinton had raised the issue, he then appeared to crumple. To the military, the fact that they had a commander in chief drawn from the ranks of bearded anti–Vietnam War protesters was now doubly underlined, and Clinton consequently felt off-balance with them and unable to gain executive control over the Pentagon. For middle-class voters, this first presidential act was baffling. Clinton had campaigned as their champion, a president who would relieve them from economic and social pressures, but instead he seemed obsessed with gays, not with their concerns. The Washington players, for whom the game was to fill the power vacuum ruthlessly, grabbing influence quickly for the rounds to come and never allowing Clinton to preempt them, the President was seen variously as compromised and unprincipled, overly committed and weirdly principled, immoral and inept. Clinton's poll numbers fell twenty points in his first two weeks almost entirely on the basis of this one issue.

And then there was his candidate for attorney general. Zoe Baird was the brilliant, accomplished general counsel for Aetna Insurance, a protégé of the new secretary of state, Warren Christopher, and married to a Yale Law School professor. She would be the first woman in the job. However, soon after her name was put forward, it was discovered that she had overlooked paying Social Security taxes for a live-in baby-sitter. Soon, she was criticized as cutting corners of the law, seeking special privileges, and being greedy. For critics of the President, Baird was also a symbolic stand-in for the lawyer who was first lady. Here there seemed to be yet another example of Clinton's heedless abandonment of the middle-class values he had promised to respect, his generational selfishness. Two days after the inauguration, he withdrew Baird's nomination.

On February 23, 1993, agents of the Bureau of Alcohol, Tobacco and Firearms surrounded a compound outside Waco, Texas, housing a cult group called the Branch Davidians. Its leader, Vernon Howell, who called himself David Koresh after the biblical King David and Cyrus the Great, preached to his small band of followers that the federal government was the source of evil in the world and that they themselves represented the forces of goodness. All women were sexually shared with him as his "wives." Apocalyptic war must be waged against the government to bring about the reign of peace on earth and the second coming of the Messiah, who was himself. He stockpiled an arsenal of weapons. There were reports of sex abuse of children. In their effort to storm the compound, four federal agents were killed. The FBI took the place of the ATF and returned on April 19, lobbing tear gas and bulldozing into the building. Suddenly, a fire consumed it. Eighty-nine people were killed, including Koresh and the children.

The very recently appointed attorney general, Janet Reno, assumed responsibility for the operation that had ended in this firestorm. But Republicans charged that the government was at fault in some way, that there had been a cover-up, and eventually, in 1995, they held full-scale congressional hearings on the subject. Witnesses choreographed by lobbyists from the National Rifle Association suggested that dark conspiracies had occurred, which might lead to Clinton's impeachment. Not until July 2000, when former senator John Danforth, a Republican, acting as a special counsel for the Department of Justice, issued a report, was the government exonerated of all charges; Koresh and his followers bore the responsibility for their own demise.

But while the embers of Waco were still burning, the incident became a rallying point for the right wing and a signal for its radicalization. While not sharing in Koresh's revelations, some saw the event as evidence of a coming Armageddon with the federal government. Gun groups claimed to fear that the ATF and FBI action might lead to a government sweep against all gun owners—an armed attack on liberty. Since April 19 happened to be the date of the battle of Lexington and Concord, which began the American Revolution in 1775, it was taken to have special significance as the start of a new revolution against oppressive authority. Black helicopters were said to be sighted as the first wave of an invading UN army. Clinton stood at the head of the Beast of Babylon.

Just as the right was galvanized, the left was becoming disillusioned. On June 3, Clinton withdrew his nomination of Lani Guinier, a black University of Pennsylvania law professor and an old friend, to be assistant attorney general for civil rights. Right-wing groups had leveled a well-funded, coordinated attack against her for months. Leading it was a professional operative named Clint Bolick, who had worked in the Reagan Justice Department and now headed one of the proliferating groups devoted to raining havoc on the Clinton administration, benignly called the Institute for Justice. Bolick, who was encouraged by Abigail Thernstrom, an increasingly familiar political type—a former radical leftist turned rightist whose accusatory polemical style had not altered in her ideological switch—kicked off the campaign with an article on the opinion page of *The Wall Street Journal* labeling Guinier "the Quota Queen." The label echoed "welfare queen," a reactionary label used for unemployed black women. Then, in tandem with other conservative groups and working out of various Republican congressional offices, Bolick kept up the drumbeat. He distorted Guinier's views about racial quotas and other matters, too, but establishing the facts was not his intention. The campaign against Guinier showed early on how the right-wing gears meshed and turned.

The problem was not solely what the professional conservatives were saying about her, but that Guinier's academic writings argued for reconfigured voting arrangements based on race and challenged the fundamental idea of one-man–one-vote democracy. What's more, she approvingly cited John C. Calhoun, using his notion of concurrent majorities in defense not of racial privilege, as he had himself, but of racial parity. One could call her arguments mere speculation and academic musing, but politically one could not dismiss them. Opposition to her mounted in the Senate, and twenty-five Democratic senators, including liberal lions like Ted Kennedy, came to Clinton and asked him to withdraw her nomination. Guinier was doomed; he had no options. But she refused to grasp the obvious situation and pull herself out (as Baird had done). Clinton himself, in a squeamish meeting with her, had to tell her he was withdrawing her name, and her fury turned on him personally. Believing until the end that the White House legal counsel's office had had the Guinier nomination under control, Clinton had allowed it to simmer until it boiled over. He had not anticipated the organized malice of the right, Guinier's obstinacy, or the speed with which squalls develop in Washington. The storm made him seem politically maladroit, uninformed about the record of his own nominee, a false friend, and, in the eyes of some liberals, unprincipled. As he had chosen her, his withdrawal of support under pressure made him seem like a president who could be rolled. It would have been better politically had he stood by her, regardless of the outcome, to send a signal of his firmness.

And by now he was inundated with yet another debacle: the abrupt dismissal of the White House Travel Office staff. The travel staff at the White House is responsible for, among other things, the creature comforts of the press corps that follows the president, and reporters perceived the firing as a direct attack on themselves. They responded accordingly, inflating the dismissals into a full-fledged scandal. The initiative for dismissing the travel staff had come from Harry Thomason, a television and movie producer who, with his wife, Linda Bloodworth-Thomason, was a close friend of the Clintons from Arkansas and had helped to stage their campaign appearances. Thomason's business partner had an interest in a charter airline, but Thomason learned that the White House Travel Office did not put out contracts for competitive bidding, and there were rumors of corruption. A distant fifth cousin of the President was subsequently assigned to reorganize the office. The media onslaught produced bungled explanations of what was going on, which only fed suspicions. Nepotism, cronyism, and poor judgment looked like the modus operandi of the Clinton White House. Hillary was spotlighted as the villainous mastermind.

Two years later, the White House Travel Office director who had been dismissed, Billy Dale, was indicted for allegedly depositing $54,000 in media funds in his personal bank account and stealing $14,000 in cash withdrawals from a Travel Office bank account. He had offered to plead guilty to one count of embezzlement and pay a fine, but the Justice Department had rejected the offer. Dale was acquitted, and he went on to a minor career as a Clinton martyr, working the circuit of assorted right-wing groups. In 2000, the Independent Counsel, after years of investigation, finally issued a report clearing Hillary and everyone else of wrongdoing. But by then it was much too late. The event itself was a cynosure of early disorganization and self-inflicted damage in the Clinton administration.

After the marker of Clinton's First Hundred Days, the notion that energy, talent, and merit could burst through the obstacles appeared a fallacy. The energy of his administration seemed misdirected and diffuse. It even seemed to be the cause of trouble, there being too much of it without any strategy. Some observers argued that the presidency after the Cold War was diminished in its ability to affect events, especially economic ones, and that Clinton was getting involved in public relations to deflect attention from his essential powerlessness. *Time* ran a cover story on "The Incredible Shrinking Presidency."

Clinton had campaigned on the promise that he would focus on the economy "like a laser." But congressional rejection followed congressional rejection. His proposal for a $16 billion stimulus package failed in the Senate, blocked by Republican filibuster, a failure that sent his poll rating into a tailspin yet again; the event was seen as another token of high expectations dashed. Clinton also advanced and then withdrew a BTU tax, a novel idea proposed by Gore that would raise revenue by taxing measures of energy, a policy which would have the simultaneous effect of encouraging conservation and shifting consumption from oil and coal to natural gas.

By the spring, Clinton's cabinet, staff, and political advisers were at war with each other over the budget. Some argued for an emphasis on deficit reduction, others for massive public investments. The President's political advisers labeled those on the deficit reduction side "princes of pain." Clinton himself was upset that the Congress had put a cap on spending and thwarted investment in social programs, lamenting in private that he would wind up presiding over an "Eisenhower Republican" administration. But he pushed ahead on reducing the deficits.

On August 10, his plan for deficit reduction passed without a single one of the 167 Republicans in the House or the 44 Republicans in the Senate supporting it. Republicans had uniformly attacked the program as nothing but a tax increase (it did increase taxes marginally on the top 1 percent) that would cause economic disaster. "Clearly, this is a job-killer in the short-run. The impact on job creation is going to be devastating," pronounced Representative Dick Armey, the House Republican whip. "The tax increase will . . . lead to a recession . . . and will actually increase the deficit," predicted Representative Newt Gingrich. And pressure on individual Democratic members from swing districts had been intense. The President and cabinet secretaries lobbied directly and hard. When Representative Marjorie Margolies-Mezvinsky, a Democrat on thin ice in her Pennsylvania district, cast her vote in favor of the bill, the Republicans burst into a chant of derision: "Goodbye, Marjorie! Goodbye, Marjorie!" (Indeed, she lost in the next election.) The House Republicans could feel power flowing toward them. In the Senate, Vice President Gore had to break a 50–50 tie.

The 1993 budget, outlined in this August legislation, was the foundation of the successes to come with Clinton's reduction of the federal deficit. Already in his first year he was cutting the deficit in half, which caused a fall in interest rates and set off a boom in private investment. This led eventually to the lowest unemployment rate in the nation's history and to an unprecedented expansion of home ownership, and it provided the conditions for a radical decrease in crime—exactly the reverse of what the Republican doomsayers predicted at the time. The first Clinton budget also contained other dramatic shifts in policy, among them an increase in the earned-income tax credit, giving a tax cut to 15 million people and lifting 4.1 million more out of poverty by 1999; a childhood immunization initiative, raising the percentage of preschoolers immunized against mortal diseases from a shockingly low 60 percent (the third lowest in the western hemisphere) to more than 90 percent, the highest in American history, and leading to the lowest infant mortality rate ever; the creation of nine Empowerment Zones and ninety-five Enterprise Communities, which combined tax incentives and $900 million in investments targeted to poor areas; and extension of the Medicare Trust Fund's life by three years.

To his impatient distress, Clinton did not receive credit for these initiatives for years. In the time between when a law is enacted and when its policies have an impact and people can identify positive changes in their own lives lies a political no-man's-land. So Clinton's fumbles in 1993 were more decisive in the public's early assessment of him than these positive programs, whose consequences were then still uncertain. The public had voted for change but also wanted security. Clinton's emphatic talk of change excited doubt when there was no immediate evidence of improvement; his insistence on moving past the familiar heightened unease. Increasingly, the public wasn't sure that the changes Clinton would bring about would benefit them. He appeared overwhelmed and his administration in disarray. How could clarity emerge from such confusion?

Clinton's earnest efforts to work productively in Washington sometimes undermined him. From the start, he deferred to the Democratic Party's congressional leaders, and this deference encouraged them to believe they could get their way with him. He listened closely to those of his staffers whose careers had been rooted in the Democratic culture of Capitol Hill, and he would have been neglectful if he had not. But they had been trained during a period when Democrats on the Hill thought of the House as a bastion against Republican presidents, and they had had no experience with a Democrat in the White House except Jimmy Carter. They knew that business was done through committee chairmen, whose power over the rules and over constituency largesse enabled the patching together of programs based on the fragmented demands of the

House members. They tended to think of the president as a kind of super–Speaker of the House or Senate majority leader, and they advised Clinton that his fate was dependent upon this or that chairman, which was true but also less than true. It reduced the role of the president to that of a superlobbyist and spokesman; it thoroughly identified him with the Congress. He was seen as indistinguishable from its haggling and direct representation of discrete interests. The fate of the stimulus bill, which Clinton had initially wanted as an overall Keynesian spur to the economy, expressed this problem well: many on his staff perceived it as inevitably a captive of the House Ways and Means Committee.

Whenever there was a failure, Clinton was blamed for not understanding Washington's peculiar byways. In the case of Congress, he was blamed for neglecting it, which was the very opposite of what he was doing. Every member of Congress, having won with a majority, had a greater percentage of the vote than the 43 percent president, so he worked the Hill hard. But whether they admitted it or not, many of the congressional barons had been quite happy without a Democrat in the White House looming over them. They had been content with the undiluted power of unchallenged legislative primacy, meeting a Republican president, as they saw it, as an equal. Generosity was not a dominant feeling in Washington. Every misstep of Clinton's reverberated through the marble labyrinth, the sound giving people on Capitol Hill the feeling that they were more important than ever.

The divisions and rivalries within the White House staff did more than paint a picture of youthful indiscipline and self-indulgence. The factionalism contributed to the idea that Clinton was not gaining control of the presidency. Most of those who had worked on Capitol Hill saw issues from the congressional end of Pennsylvania Avenue, and they preferred the stimulus package to deficit reduction; they could not see, as Clinton came to see, that fiscal discipline would create the basis for social investment. They tended to present the budget triumph of August in orthodox Hill terms as a tax increase on the wealthy, rather than as the foundation stone of a new economy. Clinton's imagination did not run in a straight line, and few of them really followed him while discomfiture on the Hill resonated with them.

As early as April, Clinton became agitated that he was not getting cogent enough strategic advice. It was not simply that irritating incidents occurred with the media that might have been handled better. For example, it was widely reported in May that air traffic at the Los Angeles airport had been held up while he was getting a haircut on *Air Force One*;

only later was it made clear (and not much reported) that there had been no such delays. The underlying difficulty, Clinton came to feel, was that the nature of his innovative presidency was not being communicated. He demanded new strategic memos, then rejected what he got and asked for fresh ones. A change in communications directors, from the youthful George Stephanopoulos to the experienced Washington hand David Gergen, did not solve the problems.

Clinton believed from the start that he would be a domestic policy president. This illusion was not novel among new presidents. "It would be an irony of fate if my Administration had to deal chiefly with foreign affairs," said Woodrow Wilson in 1913 as he left Princeton, New Jersey, for his inauguration. But, like all presidents since Wilson, Clinton was to discover that the world would find him. And taking charge of American foreign policy was no simple matter. For Clinton it was not principally a psychological problem, even though he was the first president since the Second World War who had not served in the armed forces. Despite his youthful record against the Vietnam War, he had no inhibitions about the use of force. Yet his relations with the Pentagon were uncomfortable, given the jagged start on the gay issue and, worse, that the chairman of the Joint Chiefs of Staff, Colin Powell, viewed him essentially as an interloper who had deposed the benefactors of Powell's sterling career. Clinton's initial plan to focus on domestic affairs and to depend upon his national security team for guidance in foreign affairs proved naïve and counterproductive. The end of the Cold War had ushered in not an end to history but, rather, a host of unexpected threats, some new and others ancient. Clinton's key national security advisers were not bureaucratically strong in their respective departments and agencies, and some of them lacked practical strategies for the new international politics or failed to carry themselves with authority vis-à-vis American allies and others. Their absence of presence allowed Powell to dominate meetings with his smooth PowerPoint presentations.

On October 3, 1993, acting on an intelligence tip, U.S. Rangers descended by helicopter into a neighborhood of Mogadishu, the capital of Somalia, to capture the elusive warlord Mohammed Farah Aidid. In the closing moments of his administration, President Bush had sent U.S. forces on a humanitarian mission to feed the starving Somalians, whose country was a battlefield of contending warlords and chieftains. Since then, Somalia had become a de facto UN protectorate, and the humanitarian mission had turned into a nation-building exercise in a country where there was no state and into a hunt for the fugitive Aidid. The

United Nations then issued a warrant for his arrest for killing peacekeepers. In Mogadishu, the U.S. Rangers were surrounded by four hundred of Aidid's troops, and in a ferocious firefight eighteen Americans were killed. Gleeful crowds dragged the corpses of American soldiers through the streets and burned them before television cameras. Within days, Clinton announced a U.S. withdrawal. At the time, no one had any intelligence that Osama bin Laden's al-Qaeda was operating within Aidid's army. In a telling performance, after the Somalian carnage, Secretary of State Warren Christopher and Secretary of Defense Leslie Aspin trooped before a congressional hearing to present no policy at all and beseech the legislators for ideas: the Congress as suggestion box.

A week after the Somalian firefight, the USS *Harlan County* steamed into Port-au-Prince, Haiti, to land the first wave of a UN mission there, a lightly armed contingent of American and Canadian engineers, to help restore to power Jean-Bertrand Aristide, the democratically elected president who had been ousted the year before by a military junta, and to reform the Haitian armed forces. But an anti-Aristide group had organized a mob of thugs as a greeting party at the pier. "Somalia!" chanted the unruly crowd. Eventually the ship was ordered by Washington to turn around.

Meanwhile, U.S. inaction in Bosnia was a glaring factor in the continuing war of ethnic cleansing there being waged under the ultimate direction of the Serbian strongman Slobodan Milosevic. The former Communist Party official had staged a coup in Belgrade in 1989, transforming himself into a resurgent Serbian nationalist, appealing to ancient hatreds to forge a new dictatorship in the remnants of the old Yugoslav federation. Slovenia declared its independence; its physical distance and mobilized army dissuaded Milosevic from invading. Then Croatia broke away, and a disastrous war followed, ending in Serbia's defeat. In 1992, Bosnia was the next to declare its independence. The majority of Bosnians were Muslims, not Arabs or Turks but Europeans whose ancestors had converted to Islam during the years when the Ottoman Empire had extended to the Balkans. Many of them were more Western and secular than their Serb counterparts. Their capital, Sarajevo, was the fateful city where the First World War had been triggered by the assassination of Archduke Franz Ferdinand by Serbian terrorists—a center of pluralism, tolerance, and cosmopolitanism. Now, thanks to Milosevic, Bosnia's Serbs, funded and armed by his regime, had ringed the mountains encircling Sarajevo and were subjecting the city to a siege.

From the start, the Bush administration had adopted a policy of deliberate indifference to this Balkan carnage. Despite the plea of British Prime Minister Margaret Thatcher for Western intervention and the revelation by the press of brutal concentration camps, President Bush had stalwartly done nothing. "We don't have a dog in that fight," Secretary of State James Baker had remarked. In the new administration, General Powell remained behind to argue this position.

During the campaign Clinton had criticized Bush for his inaction, but once in office he found himself stymied. The NATO allies were adamantly opposed to lifting the arms embargo earlier imposed on Yugoslavia or to helping the Bosnian Muslims in any way. French president François Mitterand sided with the Serbs, and British prime minister John Major's government was also de facto pro-Serb. The British position was draped in world-weary conservative pessimism, but it expressed not a recurring strain of postimperial fatigue but a sharper, more profound cynicism. "There is no such thing as the international community," Foreign Minister Douglas Hurd explained, when widespread public horror was expressed at Serb atrocities. (After he left office, Hurd, now a director of NatWest, visited Milosevic to discuss lucrative privatization contracts.) The British military commander in Bosnia, General Sir Michael Rose, declared that a "powerful Jewish lobby behind the Bosnians" was responsible for calls for intervention. French and British peacekeeping troops operating under the United Nations Protection Force that had been deployed in Bosnia (UNPROFOR) were strictly curbed from aiding the Bosnians. Yet their presence on the ground gave the French and British governments the trump of any U.S. demand for action from the air. Only if the United States had troops in harm's way could its proposals be taken seriously; in other words, Clinton's protests were ruled out of order. It was in this closed box that the NATO allies stifled Clinton's wished-for policy of both lifting the arms embargo in Bosnia and bombing the Serb emplacements that were threatening Sarajevo.*

Even before Clinton assumed office, Powell, in his first briefing, had told the President-elect that if he should decide on a change in policy on Bosnia, a commitment of at least half a million U.S. troops would be necessary, and it would be the first in a series of escalating steps. In other words, Bosnia was like Vietnam. In briefings of Congress, he justified his opposition to the President's case. "I haven't changed my views," he boldly told one group of House members. Powell recommended to the

---

*See Brendan Simms, *Unfinest Hour: Britain and the Destruction of Bosnia*, Allen Lane/Penguin Press (UK), 2001.

President that he read Robert D. Kaplan's book *Balkan Ghosts*, which describes the hatreds and troubles there as age-old and intractable. Only Madeleine Albright, U.S. ambassador to the United Nations, directly challenged him within the cabinet. "What's the point of having this superb military that you're always talking about if we can't use it?" she asked. Powell wrote his response in his memoir: "I thought I would have an aneurysm. American G.I.'s were not toy soldiers to be moved around on some sort of global game board." But the riposte to Albright at that moment came not from Powell but from Anthony Lake, President Clinton's national security adviser, who had been a foreign service officer in Vietnam and like a number of others on his national security team didn't regard Albright as one of the boys. "You know, Madeleine," Lake said, "the kinds of questions Colin is asking about goals are exactly the ones the military never asked during Vietnam."*

Powell left the administration in September 1993 and was replaced by General John Shalikashvili. Shali, as he was called, was a Polish immigrant with a European orientation, empathy for refugees, worry about the future of NATO, and a disposition to face the problem. Though Powell, even out of office, argued that Bosnia was "baffling" and not worth American military commitment, the shift in the chairmanship was one of several crucial ones that began to move the frozen U.S. position. Meanwhile, there were no air strikes, and the siege of Sarajevo went on.

In all these international situations, Clinton appeared irresolute, unsure about the use of force, whether in deploying it or refusing to deploy it. He seemed to have miscalculated or, worse, blundered. But the positions for which Clinton was later criticized were advocated by a powerful figure within the administration. Colin Powell was guided, moreover, by a theory. The Powell Doctrine was based on his understanding of the Vietnam War. Only "invincible force," as he put it, and a clear "exit strategy" could justify the commitment of U.S. forces internationally. Without meeting his extraordinary standards of absolute certainty—no war in U.S. history, after all, had ever had a certain outcome—there should be no deployment of American soldiers overseas. During the Bush administration, Powell had favored sanctions rather than war with Iraq when it invaded Kuwait, but he had been overruled.

Until his departure in September 1993, Powell dominated Clinton's foreign policy councils. Neither Secretary of State Christopher nor Lake

*Bill Keller, "The World According to Powell," *The New York Times Magazine*, November 25, 2001.

openly challenged his positions to his face. And on the issue of gays in the armed forces, he had wrong-footed the President at the start. Clinton had little room for maneuver. Powell was an African-American icon, a military hero, and due to leave his post before the end of the year in any case. But as long as he was there, he refused to make the case to Congress for lifting the embargo in Bosnia and making air strikes. On Somalia, he publicly asked for patience. On Haiti, he opposed the commitment of U.S. troops. At no other previous time in his career did Powell have as much influence as he had in 1993. The first year of Clinton's presidency provided the clearest test of the Powell Doctrine.

Even as Clinton groped through the fog of diplomacy, he was striding assuredly on another related issue: free trade. He insisted on moving up on his agenda the North American Free Trade Agreement, which would create a low-tariff zone comprising the United States, Canada, and Mexico. Clinton believed that the programs he was proposing for education, the economy, and worker retraining were essential in raising U.S. standards in the global economy. If the United States withdrew behind protectionist walls, the world would continue to turn but U.S. commerce would be punished; from Asia to Africa, from Latin America to Europe, American influence would wane and U.S. productivity would necessarily fall as well.

Most of the congressional Democrats did not share this interpretation, particularly those from the Midwestern manufacturing states who were strongly linked to labor, which had gone from being for free trade in the 1960s to being protectionist by the 1990s. Fear of losing industrial jobs to factories in Mexico still haunted the factory towns, which were not yet experiencing an economic updraft. Congressional Democrats had learned to use protectionism as a political weapon in 1986, a midterm election in which voters had shifted away from the Republicans. And now Ross Perot, unheard from since the 1992 election, suddenly bounded onto television again denouncing the "great flushing sound" that he claimed were the American jobs flowing down to Mexico. Vice President Gore, however, debated Perot on *Larry King Live*, presenting him as a gift a framed portrait of two grim characters in sepia, Smoot and Hawley, the congressional architects of the tariff-raising bill that had deepened the Depression. Perot's defeat in that debate helped quicken public support for NAFTA. In the end, after another nail-biting campaign, a majority of Democrats in the House voted against NAFTA, but the bill passed with Republican votes added to a minority of Democrats. Its ratification in December did not augur a new age of bipartisan cooperation, though. The Republicans had been responding to their business constituencies, just as the Democrats were mostly reflecting labor. NAFTA was a great exception to the rising partisan tensions.

After NAFTA's passage, Clinton thought, as he would periodically, that the ravages of the preceding months were an aberration. Now the opposition would return to politics as usual and the calm would extend to the White House. He felt that his way forward to progressive legislation would be much clearer. In November, he had signed the Brady Bill, which required a background check for handgun purchasers; its enactment prevented more than six hundred thousand felons, fugitives, and other criminals from buying handguns, and the crime rate involving guns fell by 40 percent. He had gotten the National Voter Registration ("Motor Voter") bill passed, allowing people to register to vote when getting a driver's license; more than 28 million new voters registered this way. The reinventing-government initiative had begun, with Gore at its head; thousands of needless federal rules and regulations were done away with and the federal workforce was reduced, reaching its lowest level since the Kennedy administration. The Family and Medical Leave Act, giving employees twelve weeks of leave to care for a new child or sick family member, was passed; more than 20 million took advantage of the new law. New executive orders overturned restrictions that President Bush had placed on international family-planning grants; on clinics' receiving federal funds to counsel low-income women on the option of abortion; on stem-cell medical research; and on the importation of a new birth control pill, RU-486.

But just as the Christmas season began, the media harkened to new cries of scandal about Whitewater. The latest outburst was not about some momentary screwup. Claims were made of profound and systematic criminality, larceny, obstruction of justice, and cover-ups. What gave this scandal its lurid fascination and seriousness was the suicide of the associate White House counsel, Vincent Foster, who happened to be Hillary Clinton's former law partner. The old question from the Watergate scandal was reposed: What did he know and when did he know it? And a new question: Was it really a suicide?

III

There was never anything to Whitewater. There was never anything to it in the beginning, middle, or end. But the Clintons' early exoneration by

two professional reports, whose factual conclusions were never contradicted, did not satisfy the media or stifle the right wing, whose agendas
became enmeshed.

Whitewater was a pseudoscandal that began before Clinton was
elected and ended on the day before his second term concluded. There
was no precedent for its length, number of investigations, or utter trivial-
ity. In a political campaign, of course, it is expected that the media will
report on a candidate's record. The initial article by Jeff Gerth in *The
New York Times* about the Whitewater real-estate dealings in Arkansas
was error-ridden in fundamental aspects, but it was nonetheless valid, at
least theoretically, in approaching the subject. Yet never before had a sitting president been so assiduously investigated about a matter that had
occurred before his election.

In 1974, during the impeachment inquiry of the House Judiciary
Committee into Richard Nixon's constitutional abuses of office, John
Doar, the committee's counsel, sought a historical perspective. At his request, the distinguished historian C. Vann Woodward assembled fourteen historians to comb the record of each presidency. In *Responses of the
Presidents to Charges of Misconduct: Including Accusations of High Crimes and
Misdemeanors from George Washington to Lyndon Johnson*, the historians excluded charges involving private behavior, from Thomas Jefferson's affair
with Sally Hemings to Grover Cleveland's illegitimate child, which were
political controversies in their day; none of them rose to the level of a
constitutional issue. Observing that Nixon had engaged in new, historically unfamiliar abuses, putting him in a special category, Woodward
wrote:

> It would . . . be misleading to form any firm impressions of the relative
> health or virtue of presidential administrations on the basis of the num-
> ber of allegations of misconduct filed against them. . . . On that basis,
> some of the most virtuous administrations, those of Washington and Jef-
> ferson, for example, and some of the more vigorous, such as those of
> Theodore Roosevelt and Harry Truman, would come off very poorly in
> comparison with some administrations that were exceptional for neither
> virtue nor vigor. Warren G. Harding had few critics. . . . Allegations are
> not proof, and the volume of allegations may be more an index of the
> strength of congressional opposition, or the zeal of critics and the auster-
> ity of their standards than of the culpability of the accused. . . . An equi-
> table judgment would also seem to require assessment of the positive

achievements of an administration against the weight of charges of misconduct.*

Of all the early pseudoscandals surrounding Clinton, Whitewater became the biggest of all. And it had the most concentrated transforming effect on those who pushed it. It accelerated the radicalization of Republicans in the Congress. It gave the conservatives a cause. It transfixed many of the media. Whitewater was the alleged scandal that made all subsequent ones possible and to which previous ones became attached. Without it, there would have been no momentum or justification for the events that eventually led to Clinton's impeachment trial.

Six months to the day after the inauguration, on July 20, 1993, the deputy White House counsel, Vincent Foster, ate a hamburger and some M&Ms in his office, told his secretary he'd be back later, and drove to Fort Marcy Park, in Virginia. Always fastidious, he removed his jacket and tie before positioning himself near a Civil War cannon, put the barrel of a 1913 Colt revolver in his mouth, and pulled the trigger.

Foster had grown up with Bill Clinton in Hope, Arkansas. He had been Hillary's law partner and friend at the Rose Law Firm in Little Rock. An exacting lawyer, he had never lived outside the South or in a large city, nor had he had any previous political experience before coming to Washington. He cared about his reputation with his family and friends, which included the notables of Little Rock. Once in Washington, he was immediately submerged in the controversies that enveloped the Clintons. The *Wall Street Journal* editorial page identified him as a subject for flaying—one of "the legal cronies from Little Rock," "the Clinton crew"—and attacked him for "legal corner-cutting that leads to trouble." In June, the *Journal*'s lead editorial, "Who Is Vincent Foster?" accused him of "carelessness about following the law." He complained to friends about the *Journal*'s demonization and how it hurt his reputation. *The Wall Street Journal*, after all, was read by the business community in Little Rock. He lost weight, couldn't sleep, and blamed himself for the pressure he felt—classic symptoms of depression. He thought of seeing a psychiatrist and collected some names, but he never called any of them. Then he committed suicide.

*C. Vann Woodward, ed., *Responses of the Presidents to Charges of Misconduct: Including Accusations of High Crimes and Misdemeanors from George Washington to Lyndon Johnson*, Dell, 1974, pp. xi–xiii.

The Wall Street Journal published an editorial on the day of his funeral in Hope, headed "A Washington Death":

> We had our disagreements with Mr. Foster during his short term in Washington, but we do not think that in death he deserves to disappear into a cloud of mystery that we are somehow ordained never to understand. The American public is entitled to know if Mr. Foster's death was somehow connected to his high office. If he was driven to take his life by purely personal despair, a serious investigation should share this conclusion so that he can be appropriately mourned.

The *Journal*'s signal to its readers that Foster should not be "appropriately mourned" until his suicide was investigated was needless, for rumors had started before the funeral. They were fed by the fact that Foster's office files had been removed, under the supervision of White House counsel Bernard Nussbaum and in the presence of Justice Department officials and FBI agents, and one file was labeled "Whitewater." In time, numerous investigations revealed that nothing in Foster's files incriminated the Clintons in any wrongdoing, the Whitewater file contained nothing of consequence, and nothing inappropriate had been done by Nussbaum or any White House staff. But the rumors had far more impact than factual truth.

The rumors were omnipresent: Foster had killed himself because he couldn't bear the burden of covering up unnamed Clinton crimes. He was a closeted gay. He had had an affair with Hillary and couldn't deal with her rejection. Eventually, the Reverend Pat Robertson, leader of the Christian Coalition, broadcast on his Christian Broadcasting Network that Foster might have been murdered and that the Clinton administration had covered up the murder. "Suicide or murder?" he asked viewers. "That's the ominous question surfacing in the Whitewater swell of controversy concerning Vincent Foster's mysterious death."[*] Rush Limbaugh, the conservative radio talk-show host with the largest nationwide audience, who coordinated his information and program daily with the Republican National Committee, claimed that Foster may have died in a secret Clinton "safe house" and that his corpse had been deposited at Fort Marcy Park to make his death appear a suicide.

A report about the existence of a torn-up note found at the bottom of

---

[*]Cited in Russell Watson with Mark Hosenball, "Vincent Foster's Suicide: The Rumor Mill Churns," *Newsweek*, March 21, 1994.

Foster's briefcase excited more rumors. But its contents depicted a man under strain. The note was a list that read, in part:

> I made mistakes from ignorance, inexperience and overwork.
>
> I did not knowingly violate any law or standard of conduct.
>
> No one in the White House, to my knowledge, violated any law or standard of conduct, including any action in the travel office. There was no intent to benefit any individual or specific group. . . .
>
> The public will never believe the innocence of the Clintons and their loyal staff.
>
> The WSJ editors lie without consequence.
>
> I was not meant for the job or the spotlight of public life in Washington. Here ruining people is considered sport.

This sad note led to a concerted political effort to cast doubt on the terrible reality of Foster's depression and suicide. The chief drumbeater, in column after column, was William Safire. Safire had been an advertising account manager and promoter, a Republican operative who became one of President Nixon's speechwriters and also wrote some of the most partisan attack lines delivered by Vice President Spiro Agnew. (His trademark had been the alliterative insult, such as Agnew's dismissal of the press corps as "nattering nabobs of negativism.") After Nixon's fall in Watergate, he became a columnist at *The New York Times*, where some of his energy was devoted to rendering the Watergate affair an ordinary event by showing that Nixon's successors were scandal-ridden in the same ways. Safire, who also wrote a column on language usage in *The New York Times Magazine*, cleverly applied to subsequent events phrases that had come into parlance as a result of Nixon's abuses—for example, attaching "—gate" to a post-Nixon incident. This rhetorical legerdemain was intended to establish moral equivalence. No matter what the circumstance, Nixon's actions remained Safire's frame of reference.

For months after Foster's suicide, or what Safire insisted on calling "the apparent suicide," he wrote columns on the supposed enigma. In one attempt to establish his evenhandedness, he happened, gratuitously, to exonerate Nixon: "I believe Mr. Nussbaum's assertion that he did not notice the note torn into bits at the bottom of the briefcase. . . . (I also believe that 18½ minutes were erased from the Nixon tapes by inadvertence.)" Safire posed Foster's dilemma as having been created by his knowledge, on the one hand, of the Clintons' guilt or, on the other hand, of the Clintons' guilt: "Was Vincent Foster irrationally morose because of criticism of his office's abuse of the FBI in Travelgate—or was the President's closest legal confidant dreading the exposure of malfeasance yet unknown?" He cast himself as an intrepid investigator, speaking truth to power, like the reporters who had uncovered Watergate: "Journalists have a job to do, and cannot pull their punches at wrongdoing on the assumption that high officials may be mentally ill."*

After the contents of Foster's note were revealed, Safire weighed in. "Who tore up Foster's note?" he asked. (It had been Foster.) "Was dread of further scandal a triggering cause of the apparent suicide?"† In another column, he asked this question: "What terrible secret drove Vincent Foster, the Clintons' personal lawyer, to put a bullet in his head?" He had the answer, evidently: "We subsequently learned that there was indeed a scandal brewing that involved the Clintons, a go-go banker crony who financed their Whitewater real estate deal and an S&L failure, now under criminal investigation, that cost taxpayers $60 million." Then, the coup de grâce: "Vincent Foster improperly kept the potentially damaging records of that deal in his White House office." (As all investigations later showed, Foster had not acted improperly and the records were not damaging.) "When the existence of the hidden file came to light, the Clintons stonewalled." (The file had never been hidden; it was simply one of Foster's files.) From these suppositions, Safire deduced a new "—gate": "The Clintons' pattern of behavior in Whitewatergate is that of wheeler-dealers with something serious to hide."‡ Another column dragged in Nixon's chains and wrapped them around the Clintons: "What will the President do? With Hillary's professional reputation at risk, full disclosure is not a realistic option. Expect the limited, modified hangout route."§

By the time this last column appeared, the notion that Foster's suicide was linked to Whitewater was ubiquitous. *The Wall Street Journal*, for its part, took umbrage that any reasonable reader might infer that its editorials had had any effect on Foster. "Naturally, those who resent our unapologetic views grabbed the occasion to beat up on us," the *Journal* opined.‖

---

*William Safire, "When an Aide Dies Violently," *The New York Times*, August 2, 1993.

†William Safire, "The 28th Piece," *The New York Times*, August 12, 1993.

‡William Safire, "Foster's Ghost," *The New York Times*, January 6, 1994.

§William Safire, "What's the Charge?" *The New York Times*, January 13, 1994.

‖Editorial, "Re Vincent Foster," *The Wall Street Journal*, August 6, 1993.

The storms electrifying the political atmosphere prompted Adam Gopnik and me to try to put it into perspective at *The New Yorker*, where I was working. We co-wrote a draft for a "Comment" that we never quite completed, and it went unpublished. We called the piece "The Malicious Style." Part of it read:

> The sins of American liberalism are many, and they have often been cat-alogued. But Foster's death points to a plague that is, in plain fact, largely located in the American right. The ideological right has, over the past decade, evolved and exploited a style of extraordinary personal ill-will, a style that might be called, as a complement to Richard Hofstadter's dis-covery of a "paranoid style" in American politics, the malicious style.
>
> One of the problems with American liberalism is that it tends to be high-minded and abstract to the point of opacity; or else, as in the neo-liberal journals, it lacks backbone and is willing to go half the way toward conservatism, and is shocked at the unwillingness of the right to make any move in the opposite direction. But the American right, for a variety of reasons, is out for blood, velociraptors in bowties. This malicious style, whose pop embodiment is the Rush Limbaugh program, finds its most respectable embodiment in the *Wall Street Journal*'s editorials. What strikes one about their editorials devoted to Foster is their unreal mea-sure of free-floating hostility. . . . Vincent Foster was not being criticized. He was being demonized.

There was no pause for self-doubt or self-reflection either on the right or among the journalists who spilled ink over Vincent Foster. By now the idea that his suicide was the sign of an immense conspiracy within the Clinton administration had caught on. Nearly every major news organization sent reporters or producers on a short car ride to an indistinct office in suburban Washington, just off the highway in Fairfax, Virginia, to receive the hot information. At this tiny center of bustling activity were two fringe conservative operatives, packaging the allega-tions of a con man who, in turn, was being handled by an old-style segre-gationist. Working together, this strange gaggle had managed to cross the wire of Foster's suicide with the moribund Whitewater story and bring to life a monster of a scandal.

Almost all those who had been writing about the Whitewater scandal set off to Fairfax as though they were seeking the source of the Nile. They envisioned themselves on an exotic dark continent called Arkansas, in a humid environment thick with corruption, presided over by the

Clintons. *Newsweek*, for example, presented this version of Arkansas and the Clintons in an article by its chief political correspondent, Howard Fineman:

> In Arkansas, the place was Little Rock and the year was 1985. . . . In 1985 the Whitewater characters had the run of the city. . . . The Clintons were close to them all in 1985. . . . Little Rock was susceptible to the seamy side of the decade. . . . But if Whitewater has shown anything so far, it's the danger inherent in all of this coziness. For years, it's now clear, the Clintons were too comfortable to consider how their behavior might look later in another, less intimate place—Washington, D.C.*

The source of Whitewater, however, was located much deeper in the past than the arbitrary year of 1985. And it was not about anything as ephemeral as a real-estate deal or a savings-and-loan bank. The weightlessness of Whitewater belied its gravity. The accusations, which were never true, were the latest by-product of an enduring struggle: Whitewater was traceable to conflicts in Southern history over race and power.

In 1954, after the Supreme Court overturned legal segregation in the schools with its decision in *Brown v. Board of Education*, a movement calling for "massive resistance" sprang up across the old Confederacy. The movement to preserve Jim Crow laws was spearheaded by an organization called the White Citizens' Council, whose Arkansas branch was headed by a young state senator and lawyer named Jim Johnson. He traveled the state like a circuit rider, delivering a hellfire speech: "Don't you know that the Communist plan for more than fifty years has been to destroy Southern civilization, one of the last patriotic and Christian strongholds, by mongrelization, and our Negroes are being exploited by them to effect their purposes?"

Two years after *Brown*, having built up a base, Johnson decided to challenge the incumbent governor, Orval Faubus, whose policies had been relatively liberal. Arkansas was among the more moderate Southern states, with a lower percentage of blacks than any other, but Johnson's attack on Faubus as "a traitor to the Southern way of life" changed the governor. Faubus was not about to be "out-niggered" and lose. "No school district will be forced to mix the races as long as I am governor of Arkansas," he now proclaimed. With this campaign pledge, Faubus fended off Johnson and won the Democratic primary in 1956, the only

*Howard Fineman, "Big Times in Little Rock," *Newsweek*, January 24, 1994.

election that really counted, since Republicans were not strong then in the South. But Johnson placed an initiative on the ballot giving the state legislature the authority to nullify federal law—a gambit used by Southern reaction ever since John C. Calhoun had attempted it in 1832 and was struck down by Andrew Jackson. It was, Johnson said, "damned near a declaration of war against the United States." And Johnson's initiative won with 56 percent of the vote, emphatically underlining the anti-integration cause.

In 1957, a federal court nonetheless ordered the integration of Little Rock's Central High School. Johnson created a scare campaign, raising the specter of columns of armed whites descending on Little Rock. "There wasn't any caravan," he said later. "But we made Orval believe it." And Faubus became the leader of the South's resistance. President Eisenhower had to send in U.S. Army troops to integrate the school. Johnson led the White Citizens' Council in support of Faubus.*

In 1958, he got himself on the ballot as a candidate for the Arkansas Supreme Court. "Justice Jim" ingratiated himself with Faubus, becoming his liaison with the national conservative movement and proposing to his circle of contacts that they back Faubus in an independent campaign for president on the issue of states' rights. (Eventually, this small network launched the "draft Goldwater" movement that succeeded in securing the Republican nomination for Senator Barry Goldwater in 1964.†)

When Faubus retired from the state house in 1966, a moderate but unexciting judge, Frank Holt, announced his candidacy to succeed him. Holt attracted a group of college students to his campaign to lend him some dynamism—he called them "the Holt generation," after the popular "Pepsi generation" ad—and among them was Bill Clinton. Holt was shocked when "Justice Jim" defeated him in the Democratic primary.

Winthrop Rockefeller, a New Yorker and one of John D. Rockefeller's sons, who had come to Arkansas to reconstruct his life after a failed third marriage, was the Republican candidate for governor. Johnson had flayed him in the newspaper of the White Citizens' Council, *Arkansas Faith* ("Justice Jim" Johnson, editor and publisher), for favoring "race-mixing." Now he attacked Rockefeller as a "prissy sissy," a homosexual with a preference for black men, and a pornographer. Rockefeller,

*Roy Reed, *Faubus: The Life and Times of an American Prodigal*, University of Arkansas Press, 1997, p. 213.

†Rick Perlstein, *Before the Storm: Barry Goldwater and the Unmaking of the American Consensus*, Hill and Wang, 2001, pp. 14–16.

with unlimited funds and the support of moderates and newly registered black voters, became the first Republican elected governor in the state's history—and the first open racial liberal.*

From his home, which he called White Haven, Justice Jim continued his campaigns. His dream of an independent states' rights presidential candidate appeared in the form of Governor George Wallace of Alabama, who in 1968 ran on the American Independent Party ticket. In Arkansas, Johnson was the head of Wallace's campaign, and he was always at Wallace's side when he stumped the state. At the same time, Johnson ran for the Senate against J. William Fulbright, the long-time incumbent, chairman of the Foreign Relations Committee and a leading critic of the Vietnam War—"the pinup boy of Hanoi," according to Johnson. Fulbright's driver was Bill Clinton. (During the campaign, Clinton, in order to see for himself, went with a college friend to a Johnson rally in a rural county. After Justice Jim spoke, Clinton decided to confront him. "You make me ashamed to be from Arkansas," Clinton said.)

Wallace carried the state, but it was a last hurrah for overt racist populism. More racial liberals followed Rockefeller in the governor's office. The old Dixiecrat constituency transmuted into the religious right and melded into the Republican Party. Battle lines were redrawn. But the past had hardly been rubbed away. As William Faulkner wrote, "The past is never dead. It's not even past."

In 1988, during the Republican primaries, which pitted Robert Dole of Kansas against George H. W. Bush of Texas, Dole's campaign hired a conservative organizer, Floyd Brown, the former national vice chairman of Young Americans for Freedom, to run five Midwestern and Southern states. In Arkansas, Brown hired the daughter-in-law of Justice Jim. When Dole was defeated, Brown moved on to create an independent expenditure committee called Americans for Bush. In this capacity, he produced the famous television commercial featuring the fearsome black visage of Willie Horton, the murderer in Massachusetts who had committed a rape while on prison furlough, a program begun under a Republican governor but blamed on his successor, Michael Dukakis. "When we're through," Brown bragged, "people are going to think that Willie Horton is Michael Dukakis's nephew."†

---

*Conason and Lyons, *Hunting of the President*, pp. 70–71.

†James B. Stewart, *Blood Sport: The President and His Adversaries*, Simon and Schuster, 1996, p. 313.

In 1992, Brown and his sidekick, David Bossie, who had dropped out of college to work as Brown's "investigative reporter" (a self-selected title), published a little book called *Slick Willie: Why America Cannot Trust Bill Clinton*. The bill of particulars against Clinton included "blasphemy" for his use of the phrase "new covenant." "Special thanks," in the acknowledgments, were offered to Justice Jim Johnson.* During the 1992 campaign, it had been Johnson who arranged for Colonel Eugene Holmes, from Clinton's draft board, to sign an affidavit denouncing him.

After Clinton's election, Justice Jim appeared in Washington in 1993 at a Conservative Political Action Conference, presenting his expertise as an Arkansan on the new "president of the United States, who is a queer-mongering, whore-hopping adulterer; a baby-killing, draft-dodging, dope-tolerating, lying, two-faced, treasonist activist."† In the inferno of Clinton haters, a special ring of haters like Johnson, the subterranean remnants of the segregationist South, saw Clinton as an exemplar of everything that had overthrown their world. He was Northern-educated, liked blacks, was married to an uppity woman, and was white trash to boot. He was a race traitor.

In July 1993, FBI agents seized the records of a Little Rock municipal court judge named David Hale, who operated an investment company, Capital Management Services, funded by the Small Business Administration, that claimed to lend money to minority-owned businesses. Hale, in fact, had taken $3.4 million in federal funds and distributed it to himself through a series of dummy corporations. (Later, he was successfully sued for swindling his mistress's grandparents out of their family farm.) Besieged, Hale, whose brother had been a longtime supporter of Jim Johnson's, sought refuge at White Haven.

Justice Jim telephoned the office of a conservative group called Citizens United, which consisted of Brown and Bossie. Johnson had "a friend" who needed help. He put Hale on the line with Bossie. For hours, Hale spun an elaborate story in which he was "the fall guy" for Clinton. He claimed to have had many meetings with Governor Clinton, and at one of them Clinton, like a Mafioso, had pressured him into a corrupt scheme, demanding that Hale pay $300,000 from Capital Management to a company owned by Jim and Susan McDougal, Master Marketing; the money would be spread among leading Democrats, the

---

*Floyd G. Brown, *Slick Willie: Why America Cannot Trust Bill Clinton*, Annapolis-Washington Book Publishers, 1992, p. x.

†Stewart, *Blood Sport.*, p. 314.

"political family." In exchange, McDougal would loan Hale $825,000 from the Madison Guaranty Savings and Loan Company, enabling him to leverage $1 million from the SBA.

Hale's story about Clinton was in every particular a fiction. No investigation, no court, ever found a scrap of truth to it. Somehow, he hoped it would get him off the hook.

Justice Jim now telephoned another Clinton enemy, Sheffield Nelson. Nelson's campaign finance chairman's partner, Randy Coleman, became Hale's attorney. Coleman tried to plea-bargain on behalf of Hale with the new U.S. attorney in Arkansas, Paula Casey, down to a misdemeanor charge in exchange for information on "elite political circles." Instead, Hale received a four-count felony indictment in September 1993.

Nelson called Jeff Gerth of *The New York Times*, who heard Hale's tale, but Hale had no corroborating evidence, so Gerth could not get his allegations into the paper. (Hale later claimed that a large file of documents proving his charge had been destroyed by the FBI, a charge that the responsible FBI agents derided under oath.) Still, Gerth called the FBI office in Little Rock to inform an agent there of what Hale was saying about Clinton. The agent sent a teletype to Washington: "Gerth alluded that this was why the United States Attorney Casey would not deal with Coleman when he was attempting to work out a suitable deal for his client."*

Meanwhile, Coleman was accusing Casey of having a conflict of interest because she had once been a law student of Clinton's at the University of Arkansas Law School. This was irrelevant, of course, since Clinton had had absolutely nothing to do with Hale's case, but Casey, on advice from the Justice Department, recused herself.

The fervently Republican investigator at Resolution Trust, L. Jean Lewis, was communicating new messages. First, she sent out a mailing offering for sale T-shirts and mugs featuring a picture of Hillary Clinton and embossed: "Presidential BITCH." She used her RTC office as the address. Then, having reworked her criminal referral, she sent it to U.S. Attorney Casey, who rejected it on the same grounds as her predecessor had. Lewis's superiors ordered her not to have any more dealings with the U.S. attorney's office and removed her subpoena power. Almost instantly, news of her referral implicating the Clintons appeared in a front-page article in *The Washington Post*: "U.S. Is Asked to Probe Failed S&L." For three days, the story about Hale's fictitious $300,000 loan to the

*Conason and Lyons, *Hunting of the President*, p. 93.

McDougals led the newspaper. Gerth at the *Times* jumped into the fray, reporting about the secret referral and the mysterious loan. A competitive scandal race was launched. Still, this arcane story had not yet broken through in the broadcast media as the instigators hoped.

In Arkansas, Brown and Bossie were acting as Hale's exclusive talent agents. They got him bookings with journalists eager to hear the only witness against Clinton, a witness whose story became embroidered with more detail about the closeness of their relationship as time went on. No one spoke to Hale who didn't go through Brown and Bossie. In the first week of November 1993, versions of Hale's allegations appeared in many newspapers. And Bossie became a news consultant to an NBC News producer, Ira Silverman, guiding his crew in a helicopter over Whitewater and granting access to Hale.

On November 11, NBC *Nightly News* for the first time flashed David Hale's picture on the television screen: "This man, a former local judge under indictment on an unrelated case, has told NBC News that Clinton asked him in 1985 to make a loan to the McDougals, who were in financial trouble." Then an image of Vincent Foster's body appeared: "Before his death in July, former White House lawyer Vince Foster also got involved, helping the Clintons sell their share of the land company. . . . Now questions are being raised about a possible link between the growing Arkansas investigations and Foster's death." A new mystery was introduced—telephone calls between Foster and James Lyons, the professional forensic accountant whom the Clintons had hired during the campaign to issue a report on Whitewater. One of those calls, the correspondent intoned, was on "the day Foster died." The narrator added, "But the White House said Lyons didn't get through." The mystery only deepened. "That same day, in Little Rock, a judge signed a search warrant for the FBI to raid David Hale's offices." Then the denial, raising even more accusations: "White House officials insist that Foster could not have been tipped off about the impending raid, and they correctly point out that the Clintons are not the targets of any of these investigations. Andrea Mitchell, NBC News, at the White House."

Brown and Bossie had made a long-shot bet on the media that paid off spectacularly. They were used to railing against the "liberal" media, but now their schedules were filled with importuning journalists hoping to get the real dope from them. Raising money from conservative donors, they assembled packets of documents from title and real-estate transaction searches in Arkansas. Any piece of alleged information they had almost instantly found its way into a published article. Whatever they whispered in the ears of news producers was heard far and wide. Their experience was turning them into what they had never expected to be: reliable sources.

I decided to made the trek to their Fairfax, Virginia, office myself, to hear what Brown and Bossie had to say. They were beside themselves with disbelief and merriment, candid and gleeful, eager to claim authorship.

Brown explained how it had all begun with Justice Jim: "In August of 1993, we got a call from Judge Jim Johnson. He's a former associate supreme court justice in Arkansas who was one of the guys who helped us with the book. He's one of the patriarchs. And he calls us up and he says on the phone, basically, 'Floyd and Dave, got this good friend down here, his name's Judge David Hale, and he's about to be railroaded, he's gonna be railroaded, you need to check into this, you need to look into this Judge David Hale. They're family friends.' "

Brown put his hand on a stack of photocopied papers: "Judge David Hale—and we have all the documents in here—we start with the original subpoena, subpoenaing all the records of Judge Hale from Capital Management Services." He paused for effect. "Which was issued the day Vince Foster died."

He continued: "And so Judge Hale comes under the scrutiny of the U.S. attorney's office in Arkansas. He, over the course of the late summer, talks to an assistant U.S. attorney in the office and meets with him and his lawyer meets with him and this is what Judge Hale says: 'I know I've done things that are wrong, but I'm just a small fish in this pond, and I would like to turn state's evidence. Please negotiate a plea with me, and I will do a couple of things. Number one, I'm going to provide you with documentary evidence to show that people much higher than me on the political ladder are involved in financial fraud. Also, would you please tap my phone and put a wire on me? Tap my phone and I'll make telephone calls. And you can even put a *wire* on me, and I'll go into the *White House* for you.' Because you have to realize, before he's indicted, none of it's public, he's still a part of this clique that ran Arkansas." But it was no dice: "The indictments become public. Any currency Judge Hale might have as an asset in a government investigation is blown."

Then Justice Jim called Brown and put Hale on the phone. "So we meet Judge Hale, and as a result of our relationship with him and as a result of our relationship with others that helped us write this book, we assembled these documents, which we call the Whitewater-related documents."

Were they hidden?

"Well, a lot of these are actually out of the public record, honestly."

"Nobody had this stuff," Bossie piped up. "We provided this to most people."

"You know what it really is?" said Brown. "It was just a lot of work. Well, we went around and we worked hard at collecting them. We have the two of us."

"If you can believe it, yup," Bossie added.

"We've met with a lot of people," said Brown. "About a hundred. We've met with all the major networks, we've met with all the major news magazines, all the major newspapers. There's just not many people we haven't met. The key is, what we've done is a lot of the basic research that saves them a lot of time. This is the actual FBI subpoena of Judge Hale's documents." He held up another document.

"The early bird gets the worm!" said Bossie. "If they stay in good touch—look, we talk to these guys every day. It's not like a once-a-month thing."

"I personally think the best coverage comes out of *The New York Times* and *The Washington Times*," said Brown.

"And let's not forget *The Wall Street Journal*!" added Bossie.

"Well," said Brown, "the *Journal*'s editorial page does a good job. The news people are picking it up. We talk to everybody. We talk to *The New York Times*. We talk to *The Washington Times*. We talk to *The Washington Post*. There is basically not a publication that's major—"

"Anybody who calls," said Bossie. He boasted about how often he talked to Michael Isikoff of *The Washington Post*. "I talked to him, what, Friday. But I would say Jeff Gerth is the very best."

"But the key for us," said Brown, "was the November 11th NBC piece, which I think was the most significant piece of news coverage that this thing got, and I can show it to you." Bossie put a video cassette in a VCR. "This, I think, was the most significant report because"—Brown's voice fell to a whisper—"*this* does something nobody else had ever done. It links the death of Vince Foster to *Whitewater*. And that, I think, was the key to kicking the story up. See, no one ever felt comfortable with it before."

He pointed at the television screen, as Hale's and Foster's pictures appeared. "We consider this the seminal piece. This is the one that got it all started. This moves the story to TV. This was significant because it linked Foster's death. That's it. That's the first link. If it hadn't been for this piece, this story would've died—in my opinion."

Brown explained their technique for creating the impression that the White House was forever denying and covering up. "We would sit down with reporters and we would say, 'OK, here're the questions, a, b, c, and d,' and they would go back to the White House, and they would say, 'OK, how do you respond to a? How do you respond to b? How do you respond to c?' and Bruce Lindsey would say, 'Well, I don't know, I'll have to get back to you.' Lindsey is the guy who everybody has to go to to answer these questions."

"And he doesn't know any answers!" exclaimed Bossie.

"And he doesn't know the answers himself," said Brown. "So we just keep asking questions," he went on. "And we just keep asking and asking and asking, and Lindsey provides no answers. So all of the sudden the reporter is like, 'Man, what the heck does this guy have to hide, that he's acting like this?' "

Brown confided that Clinton had been connected to a cocaine-smuggling ring through a small airport in Arkansas called Mena. "That's the next wave," he said, giving me a heads-up. "Why don't you ask Bruce Lindsey that question?" Brown and Bossie burst into laughter.

I left with a sheaf of documents, including a transcript of a telephone conversation between Sheffield Nelson and Jim McDougal filled with rambling hostility toward Clinton. A producer for ABC News was waiting in their lobby.

IV

Whitewater induced a delirium. Within the conservative movement, it created the giddy sensation that accusations about Clinton would restrict him to nothing but denials, which would stall his reform program and fatally damage his presidency. Scandals became the greatest conservative cause. Untold millions of dollars from right-wing donors were invested in fabricating accusations and giving them to the news media—a scandal industrial complex. Each group tried to outdo the other in making claims about Clinton's criminality and to get a portion of the money.

Within the Republican Party, the marketing of the stories had the immediate effect of shifting the center of gravity to the right. By demonizing Clinton, the right made it heresy to express anything other than hatred for him. In the absence of anticommunism, the glue that had held conservatism together for so long, Clinton was the enemy who now served that purpose. Party publications assailing Clinton as corrupt and morally deranged barraged Republican rank-and-file voters. Every conservative magazine turned itself into a scandal sheet. Talk-show hosts receiving daily faxes from the Republican National Committee broadcast their contents around the clock, covering every inch of the country. The party base hardened.

It was nearly impossible for a Republican politician to suggest that Clinton was a legitimate president and that reasonable political deals might be struck during his administration. The only Republican politician who refused to march in lockstep was Barry Goldwater, increasingly disenchanted with the orthodoxy of the conservatives. He called a press conference in early 1994 to declare about Whitewater, "I haven't heard anything yet that says this is all that big of a deal." He told Clinton's adversaries to "get off his back and let him be president." When Republicans criticized Goldwater for daring to say this, he fired back, "I don't give a damn."* Not a single Republican stepped forward to stand with Goldwater. Working constructively with Clinton would subject any Republican congressional leader to contempt or worse. Moderates worked with Clinton at their peril. Congressmen who thought of acting independently could always be forced to pay a penalty by having to face a conservative challenger in a GOP primary.

Floyd Brown had been right when he predicted that Mena would become a story. Following the now well-grooved pattern, the allegation was first cobbled together in conservative publications, in a right-wing book entitled *Compromised*, and on the talk-show circuit. Here the elaborate paranoid fantasy included a mysterious murder, political links to Clinton, and full accounts of his conversations with cocaine smugglers. The *Wall Street Journal* editorial page published two articles encouraging investigation: "After all, as we have come to learn, Bill Clinton's Arkansas was a very strange place."† CBS *Evening News* devoted two segments to this fantasy, discovering nothing but a series of unhinged accusations. Other mainstream media investigated as well—*Time* called it a "smear"—reaching the same dead end. The method of injecting Mena into the media bloodstream was more or less the same as it had been with Whitewater. The difference was not that the first was true and the second false; they were both false. It was that the Whitewater fantasy could be sustained by Hale's story, by Lewis's efforts, and by a plethora of arcane real-estate

*Editorial, "Barry Goldwater: Still a Maverick," *Chicago Tribune*, April 2, 1994.
†Micah Morrison, "Mysterious Mena," *The Wall Street Journal*, June 29, 1994.

documents used to raise unending questions and to prompt official investigations. Whitewater was now a permanent industry.

On February 9, 1994, a new round began. *The Washington Times* published a front-page story citing anonymous employees who claimed that Whitewater files "showing President and Mrs. Clinton's involvement" had been fed into a shredder at Hillary Clinton and Vincent Foster's old law firm.*

The Washington Times is a self-consciously right-wing newspaper, financed by the Reverend Sun Myung Moon, the self-proclaimed Korean messiah, and if it has cost him at least $1 billion in losses, he is willing to incur these in order to have a platform in Washington, which he uses as a base for his U.S. activities. The paper is published heedless of profit or any hope of gaining a return. Its editor is Wesley Pruden, Jr., whose father, the Reverend Wesley Pruden, was chaplain of the White Citizens' Council in Little Rock and one of Justice Jim Johnson's associates. *The Washington Times* has the look and feel of a real newspaper, but it is a newspaper in the sense that the Communist Party's *Daily Worker* was a newspaper. It is read for its representation of an ideology and dogma; mostly, it is useful as a Republican tip sheet. Almost every lurid allegation about Clinton found its way into *Washington Times* pages reported as fact. Justice Jim found a home here for his op-ed pieces ranting against the "corruption" of Clinton and his "cronies"—who happened to be, of course, those public figures most responsible for racial integration in Arkansas.

On March 4, *The New York Times* had a front-page article evoking Watergate: "Grand Jury Is Reportedly Told of Shredding at Little Rock Firm: One Box Had Initials of Aide Who Killed Himself." The article noted only in its twenty-eighth paragraph that the shredding (described in testimony from a courier at the Rose firm), which had occurred in January, "appears to be unrelated" to Whitewater. On the same day, a censorious editorial accompanied this scoop: "White House Ethics Meltdown." On March 9, a more ominous article appeared on page 1: "Courier at Little Rock Firm Recalls Shredding After the Inquiry Began." With this supposed revelation, the idea of a cover-up analogous to Watergate became startlingly vivid. Yet, on March 13, the *Times* reported that the Rose law firm spokesman had clarified that the shredded documents were merely "miscellaneous papers collected when a lawyer

*Jerry Seper, "Rose Firm Shreds Whitewater Records," *The Washington Times*, February 9, 1994.

changed offices," and the couriers later explained that the material had nothing to do with Whitewater. Nothing more ever came of this line of inquiry in any investigation. Nevertheless, William Safire weighed in with a column on March 28, "Reading Hillary's Mind," claiming to represent her internal thinking, whose rhythms bore an uncanny resemblance to Nixon on his White House tapes: "What did Vince or Web or Bill or I bill Whitewater or McDougal? Were those records shredded? God, I hope so."

The voice of David S. Broder, the sober and determinedly moderate columnist for *The Washington Post* who was often referred to as the dean of the Washington press corps, was accepted as that of prudence itself. He wrote serious books on the political parties and how the media's new low standards were undermining them. Now even he expressed his sorrow that Clinton's White House was repeating Nixon's errors:

> From Watergate to Whitewater, the men and women who work behind the gates at 1600 Pennsylvania Ave. have shown stunningly little ability to learn from the mistakes of their predecessors. They go on doing the same dumb things, over and over, and they are perennially shocked when trouble results. How many times do we have to read about such things as erasing tapes, shredding documents, bugging phones, setting up back-channel communications, going outside the loop, and other manifestations of hunkering down and covering up, before someone gets the message?*

In this catchall last sentence, Broder elided charges from the Watergate story about erased tapes and tapped phones with the Whitewater story, where they had not previously been made.

On the same March 9, Rush Limbaugh entertained his listeners with a fascinating new tale about Vincent Foster. He had really been "murdered in an apartment owned by Hillary Clinton," and then his body had been moved to Fort Marcy Park. Instantly, the rumor sparked a major sell-off, particularly in the bond market. According to *The Bond Buyer*, traders "seized on the rumors and liquidated long positions."† Limbaugh explained that he had got the rumor from a financial newsletter pub-

---

*David S. Broder, "When Will They Ever Learn?" *The Washington Post*, March 9, 1994.

†William Pesek, Jr., "Whitewater Tales Roil Market; Bond Plummets 1½ Points," *The Bond Buyer*, March 11, 1994.

lished by Johnson Smick International, a small firm operated by two former Republican operatives who, in turn, claimed they had heard it from
a source in Senator Daniel Patrick Moynihan's office, which heatedly
termed that claim "breathtakingly untrue." Undeterred, Rupert Murdoch's *New York Post* contributed an article headlined "Foster's Secret
Apartment Hideaway Revealed." There was no secret hideaway.

The next week, *The New Republic*, historically the most important liberal magazine in Washington but then under the editorship of a Tory
Briton, Andrew Sullivan, published a nine-page article detailing an all-
encompassing conspiracy. Illustrated with drawings of spider webs, the
article, by a freelance writer, L. J. Davis, purported to uncover a cabal
involving virtually everyone of interest in Arkansas, as well as "sinister"
and "shadowy" Asians. It concluded by suggesting that a fire at the
Worthen Bank, which had once arranged a loan to Clinton's campaign,
had been mysteriously set, perhaps to destroy records incriminating the
Clintons.

Then the *Wall Street Journal* editorial page broke what it thought was
an even bigger story:

> Earlier in the week we commended L. J. Davis' *New Republic* cover story
> on Whitewater and the culture of Arkansas. But Mr. Davis modestly
> omitted a fascinating part of the tale, namely his personal misfortunes in
> reporting his article. . . . He was returning to his room at Little Rock's
> Legacy Hotel about 6:30 after an interview on the evening of Feb. 13.
> The last thing he remembers is putting his key in the door, and the next
> thing he remembers is waking up face down on the floor, with his arm
> twisted under his body and a big lump on his head above his left ear. The
> room door was shut and locked. Nothing was missing except four "signif-
> icant" pages of his notebook that included a list of his sources in Little
> Rock. . . . Editors and reporters have to grapple with a flood of stories,
> charges and rumors of violence and even deaths in Arkansas. The state
> seems to be a congenitally violent place. . . . We believe Mr. Davis.*

Rush Limbaugh followed by broadcasting that "journalists and others
working on or involved in Whitewatergate have been mysteriously
beaten and harassed in Little Rock. Some have died."

A previously overlooked witness stepped forward to describe what
had happened on that perilous night—the bartender of the Legacy Ho-·

*Editorial, "Censored in Arkansas," *The Wall Street Journal*, March 23, 1994.

tel, who remembered pouring four or five or six straight gin martinis for Mr. Davis. Davis admitted he didn't really know why he ended up on the floor of his hotel room. And, he added, the notebook pages weren't missing, just crumpled. A Worthen Bank spokesman announced that the fire, caused by a space heater, had been quickly put out by the sprinkler system; only fax paper had burned.

The same week, *Time* featured a cover story: "Deep Water: How the President's Men Tried to Hinder the Whitewater Investigation." The black-and-white cover photograph depicted Clinton holding his head in his hand, apparently overcome with anxiety, with George Stephanopoulos hovering impassively but darkly behind him. *Time* reported that "the story brings up the dread words of obstruction of justice."* The charge, it turned out, was that Stephanopoulos had complained about the Republican background of Jay Stephens, who had been appointed to head the investigation of Whitewater for Resolution Trust. And the photograph had been taken six months earlier, during a scheduling meeting.

Simultaneously, *Newsweek* competed with the revelation that in a "sweet deal" Hillary Clinton had not put up any money of her own in commodities trading in 1978 that earned her $100,000. The identity of *Newsweek*'s expert source seemed doubly damning because it was Marvin A. Chirelstein of the Columbia University Law School, who had been asked by the White House to review the Clintons' tax returns of 1978–79, the period of their Whitewater investment. But Chirelstein disputed the *Newsweek* article, saying that "I never said anything like that," and that he was "outraged" and "humiliated."†

In this electrified atmosphere, almost any charge caught fire. Right-wing media now widely broadcast stories about strange murders. A former Republican congressman, William Dannemeyer, formed a group, Californians for America, to promote these tales, and he called for congressional hearings, declaring, "The number of people who have died, under other than natural circumstances who hold a connection to President Bill Clinton, has reached a total that can only be described as frightening." In a list of "those who have died" provided in a press release, Vincent Foster was only one of twenty-four victims. The dead included

---

*George J. Church and Michael Kramer, "Into the Line of Fire," *Time*, April 4, 1994.

†Rich Thomas, "Hillary's Cash Cows and Other Sweet Deals," *Newsweek*, April 4, 1994; Howard Kurtz, "Newsweek Source Disputes Its Story Questioning First Lady's Investments," *The Washington Post*, March 29, 1994.

Clinton's campaign finance cochairman, Victor Raiser, and his son, who had died tragically in a plane crash, and Paul Tully, the Democratic National Committee's shrewd political director, an overweight heavy smoker who had died of a sudden heart attack in the middle of the 1992 campaign. Clinton had delivered the eulogies at both funerals. (He had appointed Raiser's widow, Molly, as White House chief of protocol.) Dannemeyer's press release noted Tully's cause of death as "unknown."

All of this coincided with the release of a video, *Circle of Power*, produced by the Reverend Jerry Falwell, a hard-shell leader of the religious right, and promoted through a front group, Citizens for Honest Government. Larry Nichols of Little Rock, who had been making ludicrous charges about Clinton since 1988 and had now found a way to support his calling, was the narrator, telling the folks about the "countless people who mysteriously died." The same team then produced a blockbuster, *The Clinton Chronicles*, marketed by Falwell on his television show, *The Old-Time Gospel Hour*. This video was introduced by Justice Jim and concluded with a plea by Dannemeyer for Clinton's impeachment. It asserted that Clinton, to cover up his role in cocaine smuggling at Mena, had appointed corrupt judges and officials and then embarked on a reign of terror, having witnesses killed. To the farrago of scandals such as Whitewater, the draft, Vincent Foster, L. J. Davis, and the Worthen Bank were added new charges: the murder of an Arkansas private investigator because he had files of Clinton's sexual dalliances; the murder of the wife of a state trooper who knew too much, labeled a suicide. More than 150,000 copies of the video were sold, and about $200,000 was paid out to the people telling stories about Clinton. Sandwiched between a tale about a neighbor of Gennifer Flowers who had been mysteriously beaten up and the one about the murdered PI, two new figures appeared, especially for this video: Paula and Steve Jones.

Paula Jones had first been mentioned as "Paula," a character with no further identification, in an article by David Brock entitled "His Cheatin' Heart," published by *The American Spectator*, a right-wing magazine, in January 1994. In this unveiling Paula appeared as having a tryst with then-governor Clinton and offering to be his "girlfriend." Taking issue with this account, she was to claim that on May 8, 1991, Clinton had invited her to a hotel suite, exposed himself, and asked her to perform oral sex—a charge Clinton vehemently denied.

Jones had been a secretary in the Arkansas state government, called "Minnie Mouse" by her co-workers because of her flirtatious, giggling manner. She claimed in her suit that she had been denied raises as a result of her encounter with Clinton—though she had, in fact, received several raises despite bad reports by her supervisors. Her sister and brother-in-law, Charlotte and Mark Brown, both told me when I interviewed them for *The New Yorker* that Jones was pursuing the lawsuit for "the money." "Paula's suing over a stupid lie, and she knows it," he said. "Paula hasn't done this on her own—shit, no, by no means. Paula didn't think up this all by herself."

Jones, for her part, claimed that her sense of propriety had been offended by the alleged incident, that she wasn't a "girl like that" (though after the impeachment she happily posed nude for *Penthouse*). Her notorious claim that there were "distinguishing characteristics in Clinton's genital area," as her complaint put it, was false, according to Clinton's doctors. In any case, her lawyer's first move was to contact a minor Clinton fund-raiser in Little Rock, tell him that Jones's case was "weak," and ask that Clinton pay her $25,000 or get her and her husband Hollywood jobs, in exchange for which the suit wouldn't be filed. Eventually, Paula Jones did indeed receive an apartment, a Mercedes, and a nose job, but they came from unnamed political donors.

Paula's husband, Steve, handled the couple's business, which was now this famous litigation. He cut the political and financial deals and adamantly stood in the way of any settlement. Steve Jones had been a Northwest Airlines ticket agent who once appeared as the flickering ghost of Elvis in an offbeat film, a role that nurtured his unshakable belief in his destiny as a movie star. His fellow workers remembered him as an angry, rude, occasionally out-of-control Clinton hater, who made lewd remarks to female co-workers and showed nude pictures of his wife to the men. In 1993, he asked for a transfer to California to pursue his movie career. Usually vociferous, especially about Clinton, he did not mention Paula's allegation to anyone before the suit was filed, and shortly after it was tossed out, the Joneses divorced.*

Cliff Jackson, Paula Jones's early impresario, who recruited a motley cast of characters and brought them to the stage, could not have imagined he would ever handle a production this grand. Jackson himself was an improbable figure because of his perfectly banal yet vicious dimensions as a Clinton doppelgänger, like a minor villain in a Dumas novel. Like Clinton, he was a golden boy, a Fulbright scholar while Clinton was a Rhodes scholar, and they became friends in England, bonded by the equally bright futures awaiting them at home. But as Clinton's touch

*David Ellis et al., "The Perils of Paula," *People*, May 23, 1994.

lifted him into the governor's mansion, Jackson's wilted everything he reached for. He lost the only political race he ever ran, for county prosecutor, and was relegated to a corner of Little Rock with a shingle advertising his one-man law firm. At last, when Clinton ran for president, Jackson discovered an identity as his nemesis. He created front groups to run negative ads about his old friend, leaked to the media Clinton's youthful correspondence to him about the draft, and assisted Sheffield Nelson in spreading rumors.

Jackson's reputation attracted several Arkansas state troopers, who telephoned him in 1993 to propose that he sell a book of their sex stories about the Clintons. Jackson signed two of them, Larry Patterson and Roger Perry, to a contract, promised them $1 million apiece from a book advance and royalties, and called David Brock and also Bill Rempel, a reporter with the *Los Angeles Times* whom he had already dealt with over the story about Clinton and his draft board; Jackson wanted to create competition. The troopers regaled Brock and Rempel separately with the same stories, including one about Hillary and her affair with Vincent Foster. Foster had even publicly fondled her at a Rose law firm party, they claimed. Perry was fixated on a racial angle: "Bill Clinton was infatuated with the black women. He loved black women." There were no witnesses to the two troopers' stories; they had no corroboration. The one about Hillary at the law firm party referred to a party that had never happened; the few incidents that could be fact-checked all turned out to be false, which did not prevent them from being published in the first place. Jackson assured both Brock and Rempel that the troopers were not being paid.

During the 1992 campaign, David Brock had been paid secretly by Peter Smith, the finance chairman of Newt Gingrich's political action committee, to write stories about Clinton's sex life. He had suspicions that the troopers were being paid for their talk but was glad to accept Jackson's denial. Brock had first gained prominence as a vilifier of Anita Hill, the law professor who in 1991 had accused Clarence Thomas of sexual harassment during the Senate hearings on the confirmation of Thomas's appointment to the Supreme Court. In an article in March 1992 in *The American Spectator*, a precursor to his book *The Real Anita Hill*, Brock had called her "a little bit nutty and a little bit slutty." (He admitted later in his 2002 memoir, *Blinded by the Right*, that he had been fed false information by Thomas and his surrogates.) Conservatives trusted Brock with the job of tarring Clinton. So the publication of "His Cheatin' Heart" in *The American Spectator* in late December 1993 triggered the publication of Rempel and Douglas Frantz's in the *Los Angeles Times*. Jackson's game of using right-wing media to goad mainstream media worked expertly. Then the troopers were each paid $6,500 out of funds disbursed by Peter Smith. Smith wrote Jackson a check for $5,000.

On February 11, 1994, in the ballroom of the Omni Shoreham Hotel in Washington, before batteries of television cameras and reporters, Jackson took the microphone as the master of ceremonies, introducing the troopers and Paula Jones. He had brought them to the fourteenth annual Conservative Political Action Conference, at which he also appeared on a panel with David Brock. Jackson handed out Jones's affidavit and asked for questions. Reporters demanded details about the "sexual act."

"Was this something that could have been performed without you taking your clothes off?" asked one.

"Did the governor ask you to perform fellatio?" a reporter shouted at Jones.

"Excuse me?" she replied.

"Fellatio!"

"Thank you," announced Jackson, ending the press conference. With this theater of the absurd, Jones's case began to wend its way through the legal system.

The troopers, to their disappointment, never got their book deal. They did, however, sign a contract with Larry Nichols, acting as a producer for the Falwell front group, and appeared in *The New Clinton Chronicles* casting doubt on Foster's suicide. They received one dollar for every video sold. Larry Patterson, who was living rent-free in a house owned by Jackson, collected lecture fees from conservative audiences, including militia groups, by touring with Nichols. Together, they opened a joint bank account and paid witnesses to tell tales about Clinton. One woman, Jane Parks, was paid to say she personally saw Clinton snorting cocaine.*

Eventually, the supervisor of these Arkansas policemen, Buddy Young, testified that Patterson knew nothing of Clinton's personal life, that his stories were speculation, and that his "mentality and objective in life was to sleep with as many women as he could." As for Roger Perry, he owed $270 "to the state to pay for long-distance telephone calls on our security telephone to his girlfriends." It seemed likely that the troopers had used their position as Clinton's security detail to pick up

---

*Murray Waas, "The Falwell Connection," *Salon.com*, March 11, 1998.

women.* Another trooper, Ronnie Anderson, testified, "From what I heard the other troopers say and from what I . . . read in *The American Spectator*, the stories that were provided were nothing more than old fish tales, with little if any basis in fact."† But none of this came out until 1998, long after the damage had been done.

The troopers' initial story about Clinton and women had the initial perverse effect of accelerating the press corps' obsession with Whitewater. Many journalists made a mental calculus that divided the alleged scandals, and the one about sex made the one about money seem more pristine: follow the money, just as in Watergate. For many conservatives, however, sex was the heart of the matter—sex because it could humiliate and sex because it was dirty. A special appeal of the Jones case for them was revenge: they wanted to get even for Clarence Thomas. They wanted to embarrass feminists. They wanted to demean the Democratic president by having him face charges of sexual harassment.

Even before David Brock's article about the troopers was published, there was extraordinary excitement about it at *The American Spectator*. The anticipation sparked an inspiration. Board members decided to use the magazine and its tax-exempt nonprofit foundation as a factory for concocting more allegations and articles about the crimes or misdeeds of the Clintons. Based on encouraging recent experience, they were confident that the mainstream media would amplify them.

In December 1993, the *Spectator*'s new counsel, Theodore B. Olson, senior partner at Gibson, Dunn, and Crutcher, convened a meeting in his downtown Washington office. In conservative circles, Olson was quietly emerging as a central player with many strings attached to his fingers. When he had been an assistant attorney general in the Reagan administration, he had been accused of lying to Congress on environmental decision making and investigated by an independent counsel—not indicted, but embittered. His clients included major companies—and Ronald Reagan. He had argued cases before the Supreme Court. For years, his law partner had been the former solicitor general, Kenneth Starr. They were both close friends of Robert Bartley, editor of the *Wall Street Journal* editorial page. The threesome were active in the Federalist Society, a group devoted to filling law schools, firms, and the judiciary with a network of

---

*See Jeffrey Toobin, *A Vast Conspiracy: The Real Story of the Sex Scandal That Nearly Bright Down a President*, Random House, 1999, pp. 153–54.

†Murray Waas, "Arkansas Trooper Considered Demanding Money from President Clinton," *Salon.com*, April 9, 1998.

conservatives. Olson became the president of the Washington, D.C., chapter. Like some other groups he was involved with, including the Washington Legal Foundation and the *Spectator*, the Federalist Society was subsidized by the philanthropy of the reclusive millionaire Richard Mellon Scaife. Olson, in Washington, was the man to see, not least to open those purse strings.

Scaife, the heir to one of the largest dynastic fortunes in the country, rarely made an appearance outside his perch atop the Mellon Bank Building in Pittsburgh, his closely guarded suburban estate, or his secluded Nantucket beach house. He was avidly interested in skullduggery, though, especially if it involved manipulating the media. In 1970, he had acted as a private funder for a misbegotten CIA media operation, Forum World Features, which spread smears about British prime minister Harold Wilson and other Labour Party members. Nixon, in one of his schemes against "the establishment," had tried to get Scaife to wrest *The Washington Post* from Katharine Graham, whom both men detested. Scaife owned the *Pittsburgh Tribune-Review*, a daily published like a living monument to Colonel McCormick's long-buried reactionary *Chicago Tribune*. (When Mrs. Graham died, its obituary smeared her while eerily echoing its coverage of Vincent Foster's "alleged" suicide. Philip Graham, her husband, who suffered from manic depression, the unsigned obituary stated, "built the paper but became estranged from Kay. She had him committed to a mental hospital, and he was clearly intending divorce when she signed him out and took him for a weekend outing during which he was found shot. His death was ruled a suicide. Within 48 hours, she declared herself the publisher."*) After Nixon's fall, Scaife steered clear of funding politicians until he became enamored of Newt Gingrich. But, from the 1970s on, his foundations poured tens of millions into conservative groups, many of which would have had no existence without his munificence.

Scaife took a direct interest in the *Spectator* as he did in few of the right-wing institutions dependent on him. He inserted two of his agents, whom he had used in the early 1980s when he funded most of General William Westmoreland's $3 million failed libel suit against CBS News, directly into the magazine's operation: neither Stephen Boynton, an antienvironmental lobbyist and lawyer, nor David Henderson, a public relations man who was a fishing buddy of Boynton's, had any publishing background. But they were not there to edit articles. When they formally

*"Katharine Meyer Graham: 1917–2001," *Pittsburgh Tribune-Review*, July 18, 2001.

presented to Scaife the proposal that he fund work to prepare more stories about Clinton scandals, he was enthusiastic.

Boynton and Henderson, after having met in Pittsburgh with Richard Larry, president of the Sarah Scaife Foundation, came to Olson's office with the good news. The decision was made to underwrite scandal coverage and to defend David Hale. Olson would serve as Hale's attorney in helping him to avoid appearing before congressional investigations into Whitewater, where he would certainly have been exposed to probing questions from Democrats—an effort that was successful. (Hale later testified that one "Senator Hollingsworth" had referred him to Olson. This fictional personage is not to be confused with Senator Fritz Hollings, Democrat of South Carolina, who said he was certainly not David Hale's "Hollingsworth.") According to an attendee at Olson's office, "The subject of this meeting was Bill and Hillary Clinton and the need for the *Spectator* to investigate and report on numerous alleged Clinton scandals."* It was called the Arkansas Project. Scaife invested $2.4 million in it from the time of his first meeting with Olson through 1997. Olson himself was paid $18,000 from this kitty for articles in the *Spectator* published under the pseudonym of "Solitary, Poor, Nasty, Brutish & Short." By his "partial" reckoning, Bill Clinton should serve 178 years in prison and Hillary Clinton 47 years.†

The Arkansas Project paid not only writers but some of their sources. It was a fail-safe method. Sources would claim to have been present at events that never happened or circulate rumors for which they had no proof but about which they asserted special knowledge. Two private investigators with dubious backgrounds were hired to dig up circumstantial "evidence" to buttress these rumors; they wound up inventing rumors about the rumors. Then Rush Limbaugh and the other right-wing talkshow hosts broadcast the charges, citing the authority of the printed articles. Almost overnight, from the launch of the Arkansas Project, the *Spectator*'s circulation shot up to more than 250,000.

Stephen Boynton acted as paymaster, disbursing the checks. David Henderson ensured that everyone stayed in line. They also hired the Arkansas part of the Arkansas Project in the person of a longtime friend, Parker Dozhier, a fur trapper and bait-shop owner operating on the

*Letter to Senator Orrin Hatch, chairman of the Senate Judiciary Committee, from Robert Ray, independent counsel, May 21, 2001.

†See Solitary, Poor, Nasty, Brutish & Short, "Criminal Laws Implicated by the Clinton Scandals: A Partial List," *The American Spectator*, February 1994.

banks of Lake Catherine. Boynton had been Dozhier's personal lawyer and Washington lobbyist for Dozhier's fur trappers' group; Henderson had gone along on their fishing trips. And through Dozhier, Boynton and Henderson came to know Justice Jim Johnson. Dozhier, after all, had been Justice Jim's aide in his 1966 gubernatorial campaign against Winthrop Rockefeller—and had remained in close touch with him. They shared an antagonism toward blacks and toward Bill Clinton—to which Dozhier added hostility to environmental regulation. The Arkansas Project paid him $48,000.

Dozhier set up a "safe house" for David Hale—a veritable witness protection program run by the Arkansas Project, though presumably Hale was in the care of the FBI. Dozhier gave him use of his car and fishing cabin as well as pocket money. (When Hale crashed the car, he gave his name as "Parker Dozhier.") Anyone who dealt with Hale after December 1993, from the Office of Independent Counsel to reporters, was in effect dealing with the Arkansas Project. With the only putative witness against Clinton often on his grounds, Dozhier was also fixed to serve as a source for visiting journalists who were sent his way. Finding themselves in the wilds of deepest Arkansas, they lighted upon the self-proclaimed "mountain man" as a fount of authenticity. He held forth for a traveling crew of the right: Ambrose Evans-Pritchard of the London *Sunday Telegraph*, who put many rumors into print, and Micah Morrison of the *Wall Street Journal* editorial page's new "Whitewater investigative unit," who wrote piece after piece on Mena, an Arkansas Project obsession. Other reporters, too, paid calls on Dozhier seeking information. Dozhier even allowed some of his visitors the thrill of playing with his semiautomatic weapons.

There is no way of knowing how many articles or reporters were directly or indirectly influenced by the Arkansas Project. Consider the strange case of L. D. Brown. Brown had quit in anger as a trooper when Governor Clinton declined to name him assistant director of the state crime laboratory in 1985. His wife, who had been a baby-sitter for the Clintons, had separated from him. Still enraged a decade later, he volunteered to be a source for the *Spectator*. He began by telling sex stories, including tales about Hillary's made-up affair with Vincent Foster, all reported as though credible by Daniel Wattenberg in the *Spectator*. When Brown was paid $10,000 by the Arkansas Project, he ramped up the charges, telling yarns about his adventures with the Mena smuggling operations and accompanying Clinton to cocaine parties. He also offered himself as a witness about Whitewater, insisting that he had overheard

Clinton pressure Hale to make the $300,000 loan to Susan McDougal. Brown was called to testify about this by the Office of Independent Counsel investigating Whitewater. In October 1994, *The Washington Times* reported on his testimony—at last, another witness to support Hale. *The Washington Post* followed suit with an article by Susan Schmidt headlined "Partial Support Offered on Whitewater Allegation." Brown couldn't nail down specific dates and places; he wasn't precise enough to be debunked. He had fabricated his story to try to make the frame-up fit. The *Post* could not have known he was being paid, but even publishing his accusation lent it credence.*

The moment seemed ideal for a moderate Republican to step forward to cast some perspective on the manic conformism, a person of demonstrated principle who was unafraid to reflect on whether the wild chase was a snark hunt. Congressman James Leach was prudent, courteous, and careful with his words. He was a moderate in all things, having been a moderate leader of moderate Republicans as president of the moderate Ripon Society. He was born to inherit a family fortune in the propane gas business, but he had a sense of public service. Trained as a foreign service officer, he had resigned in protest against Richard Nixon's firing of Attorney General Elliot Richardson during Watergate's "Saturday Night Massacre." Whenever I interviewed Leach, I had to lean in slightly to hear his soft voice. He worried constantly about the right's effort to dominate the Republican Party. After the 1992 convention, he said, "If the Republicans become the party of their platform, it may become nonviable as an institution."† In Iowa, the religious right, which had seized control of the state party committee, threatened him to abandon his ambition to run for the Senate. In 1993–94, from his seat as the ranking Republican on the House Banking Committee, he seized on Whitewater and legitimized everything he was against.

Leach made a series of stinging accusations and promised a "blockbuster" revelation. He charged that the Clintons had made money, not lost it; hadn't declared income; had used the bank funds to pay personal and campaign debts. He claimed that David Hale's fraud had been committed at Clinton's request. Leach denounced the Clintons' "hide and shred" standards and raised the specter of "obstruction of justice." Trying

---

*Jerry Seper, "Trooper Recalls Clinton Seeking Loan 'Help,' " *The Washington Times*, October 19, 1994; Susan Schmidt, "Partial Support Offered on Whitewater Allegation," *The Washington Post*, October 20, 1994.

†Leach remark in *The Washington Post*, August 8, 1992.

to connect Whitewater to Watergate, he drew "some analogies" between his own resignation in 1973 and Vincent Foster's suicide. "Foster knew these people [the Clintons]," Leach said, "and he came to the conclusion that he had to resign from life." Given his reputation, the media treated Leach's accusations with great gravity. When he delivered his much-heralded "blockbuster" speech on the House floor on March 24, 1994, he had no new revelations, only frightful descriptions of Clinton as a would-be American dictator, a "Huey Long": "In a nutshell, Whitewater is about the arrogance of power—Machiavellian machinations of single-party government."

Leach's office now became a major source of leads, suggestions, and documents for all the reporters on the expanding Whitewater beat. His press secretary, Joe Pinder, was suddenly a fount of information. Behind the scenes, Pinder was working closely with David Bossie, Floyd Brown's sidekick, who provided much of this material. Because it bore Leach's imprimatur, the media received it as spun gold. Later, after the congressional Whitewater hearings produced not a shred of evidence to support his charges, Leach was silent.

In the tumult, Leach was a singular type, the moderate as demagogue. The oddity was all the greater because he was not after glory or power. To be sure, he was offended by Clinton's victory over his friend George Bush, with whom he had worked when Bush was ambassador to the United Nations. And Leach was trying to mend fences in Iowa with the Christian Coalition. But his motives were never narrowly partisan. His Whitewater moment gave him a national platform he had never enjoyed before, from which he preached an unbridled self-righteousness. Manipulated, self-deluded, and erratic, Leach was for a short while acclaimed as the most ethical man in Washington. This peculiar episode of a character who turned himself inside out had far-reaching political consequences. By drawing a moral line on Whitewater, Leach greatly undermined the ability of moderate Republicans to act as an independent force on substantive issues with the Democratic president. He ended up clearing the ground within his party for the right wing.

The soft-spoken Leach soon gave way to the vulgarian Senator Alfonse D'Amato, ultimate product of Long Island's Republican political machine. The ranking Republican on the Senate Banking Committee and, after the 1994 elections, its chairman, he decided in the summer of 1995 to hold hearings about Whitewater, and these were to last, off and on, for three years. The special Whitewater committee heard 159 witnesses, 20 of them more than once, took 281 depositions, and processed more than 35,000 pages of documents provided by the Clintons. No charge against them or their staff was lodged, let alone proved. But every day the newspapers previewed a new breathless story that the committee would be investigating: Hillary would be shown to be a perjurer, and the President to be obstructing justice, and hitherto secret files of Vincent Foster would be revealed—a "smoking gun," claimed D'Amato.

The only significant disclosure achieved by D'Amato's committee was to discredit L. Jean Lewis. She debuted as a witness in August 1995, with Leach hailing her "uplifting and indeed heroic story" and Jeff Gerth interviewing her for a front-page *New York Times* article, in which she made charges of obstruction of justice with no names attached. (The "obstructions" happened to be delays in her work caused by RTC and Justice Department lawyers reviewing it.) *The Washington Post* reported her vague accusations as a "detailed description of how [her] investigation . . . was thwarted by [RTC] and Justice Department officials after Bill Clinton was elected president."* Months later, on November 29, Lewis appeared before the committee again. This time, Senator Paul Sarbanes, Democrat of Maryland, read her U.S. Attorney Banks's letter refusing to move forward with her referral because it would constitute "prosecutorial misconduct." He pointedly demonstrated that Lewis had no basic understanding of federal banking law. Her response was to have a kind of collapse on the stand: she cried and fainted on the spot. Taken away, she never returned. It was the most dramatic scene in the entire sequence of hearings. Neither the *Times* nor the *Post* reported this spectacular ending.†

One immediate effect of the hearings was to lock Washington journalists into a virtually daily cycle of dependence on Republican sources. The principal one was the new investigator on the staff of Senator Lauch Faircloth, Republican of North Carolina: David Bossie. From this position, Bossie, now cloaked in the mantle of senatorial prestige, continued to peddle his material. A long-term effect of the hearings was to undermine the popularity of D'Amato. He had reveled in his nickname of "Senator Pothole," the one who got basic things done for his constituents, but his constant and incongruous public involvement with pushing a scandal seemed to leave little time for filling potholes. Most

---

*Kevin Merida and Susan Schmidt, "Witness Says Probe Was Blocked," *The Washington Post*, August 9, 1994.

†Conason and Lyons, *Hunting of the President*, pp. 177–78, 196–97.

New Yorkers came to feel he wasn't doing his job. It was a great irony that what started with Whitewater hearings intended to tarnish the Clintons ended with Hillary Rodham Clinton being elected a U.S. senator from New York in D'Amato's place. But that was years away.

V

To settle the Whitewater affair, Attorney General Reno chose Robert Fiske to investigate the matter as an independent counsel. White House counsel Bernard Nussbaum, who had once hired Hillary as a young lawyer on the House Judiciary Committee staff to work on Richard Nixon's impeachment, argued vociferously with the Clintons against this appointment of an independent counsel. "I warned them, I warned them," he told me later—warned them that an independent counsel's resources could be used politically to ransack their lives and those of everyone else around them. But the political pressure was so great that first the President and then the First Lady acceded. Clinton made his decision while burying his mother, who had died of cancer in January 1994. He later felt that, consumed with mourning, he was not really thinking properly and that it was the worst decision of his presidency. Hillary listened closely to Nussbaum but she finally conceded to the White House political advisers, who were arguing that having an independent counsel was the only way to close the controversy. She was never comfortable with the decision because she knew the scandal was utterly false, and while she thought that at least an independent counsel would dispatch the matter, she worried that any investigation and the media uproar surrounding it would have a bad effect on the administration's new proposals for national health insurance.

Reno had not wanted to be in the position of having to name an independent counsel, but she exhibited surety about her choice of Fiske, announced on January 20, 1994, one year after Clinton's inauguration. He was "the epitome of what a prosecutor should be," Reno said. The responsibility had been thrust on her because the Senate Republicans, who had allowed the Independent Counsel Act to expire two years earlier, were now, with a Democrat in the White House, reversing themselves.

Republicans had felt that the Independent Counsel Act, which had evolved out of Watergate and was Nixon's great monument in Washington, was simply used to tarnish Republican presidents. A seven-year investigation of the Iran-Contra scandal of Reagan's presidency, conducted by Lawrence Walsh (a Republican lawyer from Oklahoma), had resulted in eleven convictions of high Reagan administration officials and their accomplices. (Two of the convictions were overturned on appeal because the officials had been previously immunized by the Congress, and as he left office, President George H. W. Bush granted six Iran-Contra pardons, including ones for two officials who had been indicted but had not yet gone to trial.) Republicans also believed that the Office of Independent Counsel was potentially a constitutional menace. They were rightly concerned that it assaulted the institution of the presidency as a general matter of principle. The office was an aberration, a veritable fourth branch of government that, unlike the executive, legislative, and judicial branches, was ultimately unaccountable. Once appointed, an independent counsel had unlimited powers and funds. Technically, he could be removed, but any attempt to dislodge him would be seen as a self-protective reflex to shield serious wrongdoing. Perversely, American law had created an office that, if abused, could be operated on the principle of the Spanish Inquisition.

In 1988, the Supreme Court had ruled in favor of the constitutionality of the Independent Counsel Act by a 7–1 vote. In *Morrison v. Olson* (Olson being Theodore Olson), the lone minority voice was that of Justice Antonin Scalia. In his dissent, he argued that the law violated the separation of powers, undermined the presidency, and created an irresponsible, unconstitutional office. He did not hesitate to say that the law was about the disposition of political power: "That is what this suit is about. Power. The allocation of power among Congress, the President, and the courts in such fashion as to preserve the equilibrium the Constitution sought to establish—so that 'a gradual concentration of the several powers in the same department,' Federalist No. 51, p. 321 (J. Madison), can effectively be resisted." By making the president, his staff, and officers of his administration vulnerable to constant investigation, the law fostered vicious, relentless political struggle:

> Besides weakening the Presidency by reducing the zeal of his staff, it must also be obvious that the institution of the independent counsel enfeebles him more directly in his constant confrontations with Congress, by eroding his public support. Nothing is so politically effective as the ability to charge that one's opponent and his associates are not merely wrongheaded, naive, ineffective, but, in all probability, "crooks." And nothing so effectively gives an appearance of validity to such charges

as a Justice Department investigation and, even better, prosecution. The present statute provides ample means for that sort of attack.

Then, uncanny in his prophecy, Scalia described how an extraordinary train of events might gradually but ineluctably lead to an inquisition against a president:

An independent counsel is selected, and the scope of his or her authority prescribed, by a panel of judges. What if they are politically partisan, as judges have been known to be, and select a prosecutor antagonistic to the administration, or even to the particular individual who has been selected for this special treatment? There is no remedy for that, not even a political one. Judges, after all, have life tenure, and appointing a surefire enthusiastic prosecutor could hardly be considered an impeachable offense. So if there is anything wrong with the selection, there is effectively no one to blame. The independent counsel thus selected proceeds to assemble a staff. As I observed earlier, in the nature of things this has to be done by finding lawyers who are willing to lay aside their current careers for an indeterminate amount of time, to take on a job that has no prospect of permanence and little prospect for promotion. One thing is certain, however: it involves investigating and perhaps prosecuting a particular individual. Can one imagine a less equitable manner of fulfilling the executive responsibility to investigate and prosecute? What would be the reaction if, in an area not covered by this statute, the Justice Department posted a public notice inviting applicants to assist in an investigation and possible prosecution of a certain prominent person? Does this not invite what Justice Jackson described as "picking the man and then searching the law books, or putting investigators to work, to pin some offense on him"? To be sure, the investigation must relate to the area of criminal offense specified by the life-tenured judges. But that has often been (and nothing prevents it from being) very broad—and should the independent counsel or his or her staff come up with something beyond that scope, nothing prevents him or her from asking the judges to expand his or her authority or, if that does not work, referring it to the Attorney General, whereupon the whole process would recommence and, if there was "reasonable basis to believe" that further investigation was warranted, that new offense would be referred to the Special Division, which would in all likelihood assign it to the same independent counsel. It seems to me not conducive to fairness. But even if it were entirely evident that unfairness was in fact the result—the judges hostile to the administration, the independent counsel an old foe of the President, the staff refugees from the recently defeated administration—there would be no one accountable to the public to whom the blame could be assigned.*

The new independent counsel, Robert Fiske, was confident, careful, and experienced. He came from an old New York family, a Republican in the moderate tradition of Nelson Rockefeller and a senior partner in the white-shoe law firm of Davis Polk and Wardell. He was at the top of his profession; he was wealthy; he had no political or social ambitions. In the 1970s, serving under first a Republican and then a Democratic president, he had been U.S. attorney for the Southern District of New York; before that, he had been an assistant in the same office. His colleagues invariably described him as fair, cool under pressure, and consummately professional. He hired a completely professional staff, but its members deferred to his judgment and vast experience. He was also experienced in Republican politics and was neither intimidated nor distracted by sniping from ideologues.

Fiske moved briskly. Five months after taking over, on June 30, he issued a definitive report clearing up the Vincent Foster suicide and the obstruction-of-justice matter. Foster had committed suicide because he suffered from depression, Fiske's report stated. "We found no evidence that issues involving Whitewater, Madison Guaranty, CMS or other personal legal matters of the President or Mrs. Clinton were a factor in Foster's suicide." However, Foster had been deeply upset by the attacks on his reputation, in particular "distressed by editorials written about him in *The Wall Street Journal*." The report quoted from these editorials at length and from Foster's note: "The *WSJ* editors lie without consequence."

Was there obstruction of justice because of contacts between White House aides and Treasury Department officials on the appointment of Jay Stephens to conduct the RTC investigation into Whitewater? The answer was no.

Fiske's investigation efficiently debunked two central myths of the supposed scandal. Having decoupled Foster from Whitewater, he expeditiously moved on to the other charges. He had already indicted Webster Hubbell, who resigned as associate attorney general, and Arkansas governor Jim "Guy" Tucker for bank-fraud schemes having nothing to do with

---

*U.S. Supreme Court, *Morrison v. Olson*, 487 U.S. 654 (1988), decided June 29, 1988, Justice Scalia dissenting.

Whitewater or the Clintons. (Indeed, Hillary Clinton turned out to be a victim of Hubbell, who had embezzled money from the Rose law firm to cover his exorbitant personal expenses and had lied to her about it.) Perhaps in a year or less the entire scandal would be over.

Conservatives rose up in a rage against Fiske. After his report, *The Wall Street Journal* angrily tried to defend its besmirched honor and revive the Foster-Whitewater link. Its attacks on Fiske had, in fact, begun with his appointment. Editorial after editorial tarnished his name with Watergate innuendo: "The Fiske Coverup," "The Fiske Hangout." Now it demanded that the panel of three judges in the Special Division, who were authorized to choose a special counsel, find a way to replace him. The *Journal*'s crusade was echoed across the right. The Scaife-funded Western Journalism Center, for example, purchased full-page newspaper ads denouncing Fiske. William Safire demanded Fiske's head: "What's with this non-independent counsel who helps Democrats avoid oversight? Find a way to get rid of him."*

From the vehemence of these denunciations it might have seemed that the conservatives' complaint was with what Fiske had done as independent counsel. But in truth they had been locked in conflict with him for a decade. The immediate stakes—control of the Office of Independent Counsel investigating the Clintons—were no small matter, but there was another prize at contest: control of the federal judiciary. In the battle over appointments to the federal bench, the right had fought with Fiske over and over again.

During the Reagan administration, Fiske had been chairman of the American Bar Association's standing committee on the federal judiciary, which reviewed nominations and issued ratings in a procedure that had been virtually an official part of the process since the Eisenhower administration. Among the criteria to which Fiske had paid special attention were a candidate's record on women's and civil rights. By these and other traditional measures, the ABA committee had viewed a number of Reagan's more conservative nominees as unqualified—and ruled them as such.

In 1987, when Reagan nominated the extremely conservative Robert Bork to the Supreme Court, Fiske was no longer chairman of the ABA committee but was still a member of it. The committee issued a mixed report on Bork, and conservatives howled. The committee interviewed Bork three times but still refused more than the mixed report. Fiske par-

*William Safire, "Chorus Line," *The New York Times*, August 1, 1994.

ticipated in one interview, questioning Bork about the most controversial act of his career: in 1973, after Elliot Richardson and William Ruckelshaus had resigned in principle rather than carry out Nixon's orders to fire the Watergate special counsel, Archibald Cox, Bork had accepted Nixon's appointment as attorney general and done the job. Bork's nomination to the bench was defeated, and conservatives held Fiske responsible, though he said he had not opposed Bork. (Fiske's tenure on the ABA judicial review committee provoked conservatives to evict it entirely from the federal judiciary nominating process and to replace it, de facto, with their own organization, the Federalist Society. One of President George W. Bush's first acts as president in 2001 was to cancel the ABA's participation.)

In 1989, when George H. W. Bush's attorney general, Richard Thornburgh, nominated Fiske to be his deputy, the right was enraged. Fourteen conservative senators signed a letter denouncing him. The Scaife-funded Washington Legal Foundation led the attack, charging that Fiske had undermined right-wing nominees even before their names had been officially advanced. "He leaked the names so liberal groups could do a hatchet job on good conservatives," WLF Senior Executive Counsel Paul Kamenar said. Then the right tried to discredit Fiske personally, claiming that he was corrupt. (Four years earlier, a tax court had ruled that he owed $14,000 on a piece of property, but the details were less than incriminating: Fiske's family had been a longtime part owner of a fishing club in the Catskills which, when transferred to a nonprofit nature conservancy, had underestimated the land's value.) And the Bush administration, sensitive to disturbances on the right, was rattled enough to give up on Fiske's nomination. To avoid trouble, Bush withdrew Fiske's name.

The same day that Fiske issued his report on Whitewater—his first, he thought—President Clinton signed the reauthorization of the Independent Counsel Act. The three-judge Special Division was reinstated as the authority for appointments. Attorney General Reno sent Fiske's name to the Special Division as a routine matter. The next day, on the floor of the Senate, Senator Lauch Faircloth called for "a new, truly independent counsel," pointing to what he insisted was a terrible conflict of interest: Fiske's sprawling law firm had once represented the International Paper Company on a matter, he said, and years before, International Paper had sold land to the McDougals.

A little more than a month later, on August 5, the Special Division released a brief statement: "It is not our intent to impugn the integrity of the Attorney General's appointee, but rather to reflect the intent of the Act, that the actor be protected against perceptions of conflict." With that, Robert Fiske was fired.

It was soon reported that the chief judge of the Special Division, David Sentelle, had been spotted having lunch in the Senate Dining Room with his political sponsor, Senator Faircloth, and his colleague, Senator Jesse Helms. Judge Sentelle claimed at the time that "nothing" had been said among them about the independent counsel, but, in 1999, testifying before the Senate, he allowed that maybe there had been "some discussion."* (In the same hearing, he assailed the ABA, saying he "distrusted" it. "I'm one of the judges and I'm by far not the only one who has disassociated from the American Bar Association because it has taken political positions.")

Chief Justice William Rehnquist had chosen Sentelle in 1992 as chief judge of the Special Division, replacing Judge George MacKinnon, a Republican who had supported Walsh's investigations on Iran-Contra and whom Republicans therefore branded as an outcast. A former county Republican chairman and a member of Helms's Congressional Club, Sentelle was such a devout conservative that he named one of his daughters Reagan. In a law review article, he accused "leftist heretics" of trying to turn the United States into "a collectivist, egalitarian, materialistic, race-conscious, hyper-secular, and socially permissive state."† Five months after Sentelle dismissed Fiske for the appearance of a conflict of interest, his wife got a job in Senator Faircloth's office.

The new independent counsel selected by the Special Division was Kenneth Winston Starr. One of his first acts was to assemble Fiske's professional staff. "I love this man," Starr told them. But almost all of them quit. They were outraged, as Jeffrey Toobin reported, because "at the same time that Starr was negotiating with Fiske about handling appeals, Starr was also talking with the Special Division about taking Fiske's job. Starr had never disclosed to Fiske that he had been approached by the Special Division, and Fiske's staff regarded this omission as a particular betrayal." It was only one of Starr's concealments.‡

Lloyd Cutler—the White House counsel, a pillar of Washington so-

---

*Roberto Suro, "Starr Blames His Accusers," *The Washington Post*, April 15, 1999.

†Sentelle's article in the *Harvard Journal of Law and Public Policy*, Winter 1991, cited by Robert Parry, " 'Politicized' Prosecutors," *Consortiumnews.com*, December 5, 1998.

‡Toobin, *A Vast Conspiracy*, p. 73.

ciety, and the senior partner at Wilmer, Cutler and Pickering—had assured the Clintons that in his opinion Fiske's position was secure. And
when Fiske and his staff took testimony from Hillary herself, she had
found them precise and completely professional. So from their own encounters, the Clintons believed that Fiske was moving efficiently to a
fairly swift resolution. When he was removed and Starr put in his place,
they felt that the change was politically inspired. People tried to reassure
them that Starr would not be too different from Fiske, but they did not
believe it. They treated Starr with elaborate courtesy, personally showing
him around the White House, but they did not trust his intentions—a
skepticism they kept to themselves.

In Washington, Starr was widely considered an eminently respectable
choice. He preferred to be called "Judge" Starr, even though he was no
longer sitting on the U.S. Court of Appeals for the District of Columbia,
as he had in 1983–87. He cultivated the appearance of judicial disinterest-
edness and the image seemed consistent with the man.* He seemed to be
in a special Washington category in establishment circles: a Republican
who could be trusted to rise above partisanship. In 1993, he had been
given an assignment that burnished his standing. Senate Democrats on
the Ethics Committee investigating Senator Robert Packwood, Republican of Oregon, for sexual harassment asked him to review Packwood's diaries, which were replete with explicit material. Starr never leaked a word
of the material. His manner was cordial, civil, and soft-spoken.

But the Washington establishment, while it admired Judge Starr,
knew only the face he wished to present to it. Contrary to some later
claims, he didn't attend their parties, send his children to the same
schools, or even live in Washington, but in a largely Republican suburb in Virginia. And there was another Starr: the Starr who was active
not only in the traditional legal associations, but in a host of conservative groups where his true friends and allies congregated. This was the
Starr of the Federalist Society. This was the Starr who, hired by the
right-wing Bradley Foundation, a funder of the *Spectator*, filed suit for
publicly financed vouchers for private academies in Wisconsin—a cause
of the religious right. And there was also an aggressively political Starr,
who in 1994 was cochairman of the campaign of Kyle McSlarrow, a
right-wing Republican running for Congress in Virginia, who was contemplating a U.S. Senate run himself, and who contributed thousands of

---

*Ben Bradlee, *A Good Life: Newspapering and Other Adventures*, Simon and Schuster, 1995, p. 464.

dollars to six different Republican campaigns. This Starr passed incognito in Washington; only Judge Starr, exalted above the grime of politics, was seen.

But there were not two Starrs, judge and partisan. The two aspects of Ken Starr were joined by ferocious ambition, which had attracted him to Washington and fixed his desire on the highest honor of all: the Supreme Court. Starr used the assiduously cultivated parts of his judicial persona to orchestrate his rise to his Olympus: the preacher's son had become Judge Starr; Judge Starr would become Justice Starr.

Raised in Vernon, Texas, Ken Starr was the son of a Church of Christ minister, inculcated in biblical literalism and the sinfulness of drink, dancing, and fornicating. He attended Harding College, an obscure evangelical school in Searcy, Arkansas, which excluded blacks and whose president promoted the John Birch Society and other far-right causes. When Starr was a student there, the school was described by an Anti-Defamation League study as "the academic seat of America's Radical Right."* Starr was a politically active student, campaigning for Nixon and Goldwater. He left Harding after two years for George Washington University and then the Duke University Law School. He was a good older man's younger man, with talent as a protégé. He clerked for Chief Justice Warren Burger, then joined the law firm of William French Smith, who brought him into the Justice Department when he became Reagan's attorney general.

Reagan's Justice Department deployed its resources to support racial discrimination. When it argued for the restoration of federal funds to private schools that discriminated against blacks (the Bob Jones University case), more than half the lawyers in the Civil Rights Division signed a protest, and administration officials told them that if they didn't agree with the policy, they should quit. At that very moment, the Justice Department was arguing against equal voting rights in another case. In 1980, in *Mobile v. Bolden*, the Supreme Court had upheld the system in the Alabama city that since 1874 had stymied the election of blacks for local offices, ruling that "proof of discriminatory intent" was lacking. The Senate and House sought to amend the Voting Rights Act to eliminate this problem, but the Reagan Justice Department actively supported the existing standard. With so many professional attorneys in the Civil Rights Division considered unreliable, Ken Starr was tapped to work on

*Arnold Forster and Benjamin R. Epstein, *Danger on the Right*, Random House, 1964, p. 87.

the case, as a lawyer who had worked closely with him told me. He pitched in on *Mobile v. Bolden* without a murmur of complaint. The Congress, however, fixed the law and wiped out the discriminatory voting system.

Within three years, Starr's work in the department and his relationship with Smith led to his nomination to the Court of Appeals for the D.C. District. He was a prodigy there at thirty-eight. Starr's biggest decision was in the *Washington Post* case.* But Starr was lured off the court by an appointment as President George H. W. Bush's solicitor general, arguing briefs before the Supreme Court (where he earned the sobriquet the Solicitous General for his unctuous manner). Though he was said to be on the short list when a vacancy appeared on the Court, he was passed over in favor of Clarence Thomas. When Bush lost the presidency in 1992, Starr joined the firm of Kirkland and Ellis, taking on major corporate clients. He was wealthy but was dissatisfied in private practice. He joined political campaigns and worked for conservative causes. He yearned for a return to public life.

Many leftovers from the Bush administration had impressive credentials, but none had quite Starr's reputation. The right understood his opportunism, and they believed they could use his standing with the Washington establishment for their own ends. Some conservatives, especially his erstwhile colleague on the D.C. Circuit Court, the influential judge Laurence Silberman, found him too opportunistic and weak to be entirely trustworthy. When Sandra Day O'Connor had been nominated for the Supreme Court, it was young Starr, eager to please, who had advised her on how to finesse her pro-choice position on abortion. And when he was solicitor general, he had quirkily taken up the case of whistle-blowers against military contractors, angering President Bush.

---

*In 1985, *The Washington Post* appealed a libel judgment against it for an article about the Mobil Oil Corporation president's giving no-bid contracts to his son. The newspaper's reputation hung in the balance, especially after the Janet Cooke affair, in which a reporter had won a Pulitzer Prize for an article about a nine-year-old heroin addict that was subsequently revealed as a fabrication. For two years, the paper anxiously awaited a judgment in the Mobil case. When the court ruled, the *Post* was vindicated in a decision stating that there was "overwhelming evidence that the *Post* defendants published the article in good faith" (Bradlee, *A Good Life*, p. 464). Bob Woodward, the editor of both the Janet Cooke and Mobil articles, believed that the decision was "a more important watershed in the history of journalism than was Watergate," according to a historian who interviewed him (Michael Schudson, *Watergate in American Memory*, Basic Books, 1992, p. 121).

Conservatives thought Starr had engaged in these small betrayals out of a desire to please and to rise. They thought he would become unsteady in outlook if he were on the Court, perhaps turn into an Anthony Kennedy or, worse, a David Souter.

But Starr was unaware of this reputation. He did not imagine that people who didn't trust him might be found among his friends and supporters and were a crucial factor in his not having been chosen for the Supreme Court. Naïveté was a fundamental part of his weakness. Anyone who understood the Office of Independent Counsel would have understood that no further public career lay beyond it. Starr would exonerate Clinton or savage him; either way Starr would be a figure of controversy.

Starr had no prosecutorial experience, so he was in over his head from the start. And taking the job demonstrated that he had scant political skills. Therefore he was doubly dependent—first on his staff, and then on the politics. His softness of mind led him into a situation where his natural reflex was to become ever more rigid, expressing his dogmatism less in prosecutorial precision than in self-justifying piety. Starr eventually became a figure in a passion play—one out of Nathaniel Hawthorne, being a cross between two characters in *The Scarlet Letter*: Roger Chillingsworth, the vengeful persecutor, and Arthur Dimmesdale, the weak Puritan. But Starr lacked Chillingsworth's iron, just as he lacked Dimmesdale's redeeming conscience.

As many on Fiske's staff made clear when they resigned, Starr had been personally duplicitous with his predecessor, and there were other duplicities. He joined the advisory board of the Washington Legal Foundation, which had spearheaded the successful campaign to smear Robert Fiske, and in 1994, he was working on an amicus brief on behalf of Paula Jones for the Independent Women's Forum, funded by Scaife and headed by Barbara Bracher, Ted Olson's girlfriend and soon to be his wife. At the same time, Starr's law firm was negotiating a settlement for a bankrupt savings and loan with the RTC officials he was now obliged to question; Kirland and Ellis also represented International Paper, the very company whose representation by Fiske's firm had been cited as the reason he had to be replaced. He revealed none of these conflicts at the time. If he had, Starr would very likely not have been appointed.

VI

Throughout the eight years of his presidency, little social pressure was exerted in Washington against the virulent partisan attacks launched on Bill Clinton and his wife. The absence of a countervailing influence against his enemies is one of the paradoxical mysteries of the capital during his presidency. And Washington's social response to Clinton was a significant factor in fostering the hostile, corrosive environment.

One of the first dinner parties for President-elect Clinton was given by Katharine Graham, publisher of *The Washington Post*, who had just retired but remained a continuing presence at the *Post* and *Newsweek* and at her mansion on R Street. Before the assembled notables she had invited, Mrs. Graham observed that she had met every president since Calvin Coolidge. "These occasions have value. They create relationships beyond the office," she said.

The President-elect was fresh from a campaign in which President Bush had desperately attacked Washington (where he had spent much of his life), and a third candidate, Ross Perot, had run on populist paranoia and dark suspicions of the capital. So Clinton had the question of Washington in the forefront of his mind. "Washington is a better place than most Americans think it is," he told the guests at Mrs. Graham's dinner in his reply to her toast. And as a newly elected political leader, he thought Washington should "calculate less what is best for all of us" and focus instead on "what is best for all of those who sent us here."

In his inaugural, Clinton honed the line he had used at Mrs. Graham's. "This beautiful capital, like every capital since the dawn of civilization," he said, "is often a place of intrigue and calculation. Powerful people maneuver for position and worry endlessly about who is in and who is out, who is up and who is down, forgetting those people whose toil and sweat sends us here and pays our way." In the CBS studio in Washington, Sally Quinn, who was serving as a commentator, turned to a producer. "That's a terrible mistake he's made, attacking Washington. He said the same thing the other night at Kay's and everyone reacted very negatively. I have to go on the air to say that," Quinn said, according to the producer.

Clinton's rhetoric was a trope echoing back to Andrew Jackson. And he was speaking not of social Washington, but of politics. He was thinking about the two branches of government running from one end of Pennsylvania Avenue to the other. To Quinn, however, Washington meant Washington society—and society meant the cream of the media.

Sally Quinn began as a party reporter for *The Washington Post*, became a clever, irreverent writer of profiles, married the *Post*'s editor, Ben Bradlee, and moved into a large house in Georgetown, where she became an avid participant-observer in the capital's social life. Even before Clinton took his oath of office, Quinn began telling the Clintons what to do and what to say, how to shed their provincial habits and learn the ways of Washington. In an article in the *Post* published on November 15, 1992, with a telling subhead, "Welcome to Washington, but Play by Our Rules," she informed the new president that the capital was a jungle: "Think of it this way: Your plane has crash-landed in the middle of Brazil and you find yourself surrounded by a curious and possibly hostile tribe. Instead of giving them beads and eating the monkey tongues they offer you, you decide that you don't need their help. Fine, but don't be surprised if you end up with poison darts in your backside. Like any other culture, Washington has its own totems and taboos. It would serve the newcomers well to learn them and abide by them."* A month later, in *Newsweek*, an article by Quinn entitled "Beware of Washington" advised the new first lady on etiquette and the proper use of pronouns: "Hillary Clinton was not elected president. . . . Those who've known Hillary for years say that she has always used 'we,' that the Clintons have always operated as a team. But Little Rock is not Washington."†

Mrs. Graham had known the simple rule that to make a friend in Washington, one must be a friend. She had gone out of her way to invite a beleaguered Nancy Reagan to lunch, which became a regular event, "either at my house or hers," Mrs. Graham wrote in her memoir.‡ There was no one like that for the Clintons.

Clinton made concerted efforts in his first year to woo the Washington social elite. He held half a dozen intimate dinners at the White House, tried to charm them, and made personally kind gestures to individuals. I attended one of these dinners, and every amenity available to the White House was laid on: drinks on the Truman Balcony, small round tables in the Green Room, engraved menus, musicians and singers from the Marine Corps Band, tours of the residence, the uninterrupted presence for hours of the President and the First Lady. Quinn, one of the guests, reported in the *Post* how another guest "laughingly remarked"

---

*Sally Quinn, "Making Capital Gains: Welcome to Washington, but Play by Our Rules," *The Washington Post*, November 15, 1992.

†Sally Quinn, "Beware of Washington," *Newsweek*, December 28, 1992.

‡Katharine Graham, *Personal History*, Knopf, 1997, p. 612.

that accepting the Clintons' invitation to a White House dinner made him feel "cheap and used."*

By July 1993, Quinn reported that animosity toward Clinton was widespread among her social group—and that they considered Clinton entirely to blame for their feelings against him: "People who have been here and who have attained a certain social or political position do not want to be 'dissed.' They want the new team to respect them. Because these tribal rituals were not fulfilled, many people were virtually gleeful when Clinton went into free fall in the polls. You reap what you sow, was the attitude."†

There did not seem to be anyone of authority in Washington who might perform the socializing political function, who had a sensibility that sympathized with Clinton's presidency. The problem wasn't just a matter of friendship, decency, or sympathy. The truth was that the inner life of Washington had fallen to pieces decades earlier, during the Vietnam War, when Bill Clinton was a Georgetown student clipping newspaper articles for Senator Fulbright's Foreign Relations Committee. The conceit that "Georgetown," a neighborhood once inhabited by many of the capital's elite, represented a permanent Washington, like a lordly class, was an invented tradition.

The rise and fall of Georgetown is a largely hidden chapter in the history of liberalism. The New Deal had made Georgetown. Before it, Georgetown was a small, busy port town on the Potomac River that had become a rundown, unfashionable neighborhood where mostly black people lived in its very small houses. But many New Dealers, including Franklin Roosevelt's aide Harry Hopkins when he wasn't living in the White House, moved there. What made the Georgetown set a distinct group was not its old school ties or old money but the shared experiences of the New Deal and the war. Few of them were wealthy, and as a group, they respected competence, intelligence, education, and tolerance; believed in government; and loved politics. The Georgetown set disliked the rigid and gilded New York society as Edith Wharton had depicted it, the claustrophobic gloom of Washington's "Cave Dwellers," and high Republicanism. Joseph Alsop, the columnist who personified this group, wrote in his memoir:

*Sally Quinn, "To the Couch, Mr. Clinton! On Therapy, the Presidential Press Corps and the Sudden Need to Be Nice to Bill," *The Washington Post*, July 18, 1993.
†Ibid.

I am glad every day that the WASP Ascendancy collapsed when it did—
essentially at the beginning of the 1930s, when the Great Depression totally demoralized most of its members—and that Franklin Roosevelt and
those who believed in him seized the leadership of this country with almost no opposition. If the ascendancy had hung on to anything like its
old leverage, I cannot imagine this country achieving what seems to me
to have been its greatest single feat in the twentieth century. It is almost
unknown for any other country to include as citizens with an equal share
the members of excluded minorities.*

Georgetown lives were complicated and they were never subjected to
facile judgments, nor did the Georgetown people seek to judge others.
Many of the famous among them had had affairs, been divorced, or been
in depression. There was no conspiracy of silence to cover up these matters or to keep silent about the sexual lives of politicians. But it was not
considered decent to ferret out such material. Blackmailing or smearing
people because of their private lives was a dirty trick practiced by the
contemptible likes of J. Edgar Hoover or Joseph McCarthy. Indeed, Senator McCarthy targeted Georgetown people and went out of his way to
float false rumors about them. Alsop wrote that in the early 1950s "it was
difficult to find a corner of government in the city of Washington free of
intimidation from Joe McCarthy and his vile crowd."†

This Georgetown was torn apart by and never recovered from the
Vietnam War. Many people who lived in Georgetown ran the war, many
of them tried to end it, and the strife was devastating. Then Watergate
and Nixon, which transformed *The Washington Post* into a major national
force, marked the beginning of a different Washington and a very different Georgetown.

Watergate was a serious and far-ranging assault on the Constitution
by President Nixon. To begin with, it was a crime to conceive and carry
out in the White House a plan to undermine democracy by creating a secret investigative unit intended to destroy political opponents—the
"Plumbers' " unit that broke into Democratic National Committee headquarters to secure political intelligence. Nixon also suborned the perjury
of witnesses by paying hush money and counseling false testimony; obstructed justice by withholding, concealing, and destroying evidence; in-

*Joseph W. Alsop with Adam Platt, *I've Seen the Best of It: Memoirs*, Norton, 1992,
pp. 36–37.
†Ibid., p. 343.

terfered with the probes of the FBI and the Department of Justice; abused the CIA, the FBI, and the IRS against political opponents; and wiretapped members of the press and other citizens for political purposes. From the arrest of the White House Plumbers during their second break-in at DNC headquarters on June 17, 1972, to Nixon's announcement of his resignation on August 8, 1974, took a week less than two years and two months.

Under the strains of Vietnam, the old establishment represented by the Georgetown set had by then disintegrated, and its vacuum was mostly filled by people working in a constantly shifting media pecking order, subject to intense status anxieties. Meanwhile, changes within print journalism and the growth of right-wing institutions were radically altering life in the capital—and in Georgetown. The advent of cable television in the 1980s remade the rewards system for all journalists. Talk shows modeled on the *McLaughlin Report*—a very noisy one hosted by John McLaughlin, a bellicose former Nixon aide and former priest—proliferated. Status and income among journalists were increasingly based on television performances, not on felicity of prose, knowledge of government, intellect, or broad experience. The status system that had put Walter Lippmann, Joseph Alsop, and James Reston in the front ranks was passé. To have access to decision makers, as they had had, was deemed corrupt except for conservative commentators, to whom no rules applied—and that was the rule. Media became society people, and this happened while the Republican right was funneling hundreds of millions of dollars into think tanks, foundations, institutes, and magazines. Starting in 1996, the Fox News television channel powerfully influenced the way Americans heard about what was going on in Washington.

For the new media, however, the Watergate story remained a template. Yet Whitewater in 1994 was Watergate turned on its head. The Watergate scandal had moved forward rapidly to a conclusion because piece by piece the rumors kept being proved. The obscure, convoluted, and unproved nature of the alleged Whitewater scandals, by contrast, sprawled across the entire Clinton presidency because none of them could not be proved. Leak by unsubstantiated leak, from the Republican congressional staff or the Office of Independent Counsel, the stories proliferated. The technique was comparable in some respects to the "multiple untruth" perfected by Senator McCarthy:

> The "multiple untruth" need not be a particularly large untruth but can
> instead be a long series of loosely related untruths, or a single untruth

with many facets. In either case, the whole is composed of so many parts that anyone wishing to set the record straight will discover that it is utterly impossible to keep all the elements of the falsehood in mind at the same time. Anyone making the attempt may seize upon a few selected statements and show them to be false, but doing this may leave the impression that only the statements selected are false and that the rest are true. An even greater advantage of the "multiple untruth" is that statements shown to be false can be repeated over and over again with impunity because no one will remember which statements have been disproved and which haven't.*

The right understood that the media's implicit antipolitical bias worked in its favor, since they always cast the difficult tasks of government and politics in the worst possible light. They could dismiss the unfolding of a political personality as largely sham and show, not the heart of the matter. The real scandal was politics itself.

Within a number of news organizations, reporters who had access to the Republicans' staff or the independent counsel's office were elevated as budding Woodwards and Bernsteins. "Everybody is on bended knee to David Bossie for crumbs," a producer at the CBS News bureau told me, when Bossie got to the Senate Whitewater committee staff. "All these reporters are begging him for stuff." A correspondent for ABC News described the situation in the Washington bureau. "I have to be really careful. My entire career hangs in the balance. I never say one word about David Bossie. ABC's Whitewater producer, Chris Vlasto, is Bossie's best friend. He's very close to Hick Ewing [Starr's deputy]. There's a war within ABC World News on this subject. The Whitewater team are believers in *The Clinton Chronicles*."

On March 18, 1994, *The New York Times* held a party for the elite of the Washington press corps at the Army-Navy Club, located in the building housing its bureau. There was no other subject but Whitewater. A prominent network correspondent held forth: "Clinton's a phony. He's an inch deep. People say he has a great mind, thinking about all sorts of things all the time. I don't believe it. He's a phony."

"Of course we all believe that," a newspaper correspondent with a famous byline chimed in. "That he's a phony."

An editor in the Washington bureau of an important newspaper piped up: "What's the difference between being president of Arkansas and pres-

*Richard H. Rovere, *Senator Joe McCarthy*, Meridian Books, 1960, p. 110.

ident of the United States? That's what Clinton was—president of
Arkansas. Would it be all right if he made an investment through a friend
now? So why was it right when he was president of Arkansas?"

"It's a hunt," an executive editor of one of the nation's most influential
newspapers told me. "If they hadn't acted like prey, we wouldn't treat
them like prey."

THREE

First Blood

I

When President Clinton arrived in office with his promise "to make health care affordable for every family," almost 40 million Americans had no health insurance at all, 22 million lacked adequate coverage, and 63 million, for one reason or another, were to lose it over the next two years.* His idea was to base the delivery of medical services on a public–private partnership between government agencies and the existing structure of the health care business.

Just days after being sworn into office, on January 25, 1993, the new president announced the formation of a task force on national health reform and its chief: Hillary Rodham Clinton. She had been indispensable to her husband's political career from its beginning and was his closest adviser on strategy and policy. They had met at the Yale Law School, where she received better grades and, when she graduated, bigger offers. But after serving as a staff counsel to the House Judiciary Committee conducting the impeachment of Richard Nixon, in 1975 she chose to accept Bill's proposal of marriage, to leave Washington, and to move to Arkansas. He appointed her to shepherd the state education reform program he planned through the hazards of the Arkansas state legislature, the teachers' union, and the hostile press, and she succeeded. She also became the principal family breadwinner as a senior partner at the Rose law firm, the most important in Little Rock. And she kept her hand in

*The White House Domestic Policy Council, *The President's Health Security Plan*, Times Books, 1993, p. 3.

national public policy by serving on the board of the Children's Defense Fund. During the campaign, she had been a lightning rod from the start, when she declared she would not be the kind of political wife who just stays home and "bakes cookies." Through every scarifying gyration in the campaign, she was stalwart and shrewd. She was to Bill even more than what Robert Kennedy had been to his brother during the 1960 campaign. Clinton trusted her implicitly and respected her abilities. "Two for one," he said on the campaign trail.

Hillary Clinton never had any intention of standing in the background and attending solely to the traditional tasks of first lady. She hardly neglected them—overseeing the preservation effort at the White House, for example. But her idea of her activities in Washington was that she would play a public political part in her husband's administration, just as she had done in Arkansas.

Many first ladies, in one way or another, have been informal advisers to their husbands. Dolley Madison first established the White House salon as a place for female presence. Louisa Catherine Adams was the motor of ambition driving her husband, John Quincy, to become president; so was Helen Taft for her husband, William Howard. Edith Wilson was, in effect, acting president for her invalided Woodrow after his stroke, but she hid her actions just as she disguised his condition from the public and from most of his staff. Eleanor Roosevelt was her husband's eyes and ears among the working class and poor during the Depression. She championed civil rights, wrote a daily newspaper column, and constantly pressed Franklin on social legislation. During the war, she was the initiator of what became the G.I. Bill, which granted veterans access to higher education and low-cost housing and led to their becoming the heart of the post-war middle class. After FDR's death, President Truman appointed her the first U.S. ambassador to the United Nations. Eleanor's great accomplishments were a personal triumph over her privileged but restricted upbringing; she was, after all, Theodore Roosevelt's niece, but she had no profession and had not been raised to do useful work in society. It was only after the crisis in her marriage that she carved out a life and work of her own.

Hillary Rodham Clinton was the first first lady who had the essential credentials to serve as a cabinet-level official. The proper comparison is not to any previous first lady but to Robert F. Kennedy, President Kennedy's brother, who was named as JFK's attorney general. Hillary was raised in a middle-class suburb of Chicago (her father sold draperies) and went east to attend college, at Wellesley, from which she graduated with honors as valedictorian, and then the Yale Law School. She was the first wife of a president who had a profession, and that made her even more novel in her position than her husband was in his; together they were the first meritocratic couple ever in the White House. (Nancy Reagan, a socialite from Chicago, had been an actress, but she dropped her career shortly after marrying Ronnie, and though she was influential in his political rise and presidency, she always remained behind the scenes.) For both Hillary and the President, her assumption of a prominent responsible post seemed obvious and natural.

In appointing his wife to head his most ambitious and innovative governmental initiative, President Clinton also declared that she would submit the health care plan to the Congress in a hundred days, a deadline that rang with the symbolism of Franklin D. Roosevelt's First Hundred Days. But in less time than that, health care reform had become beleaguered.

The Health Care Reform Task Force, like internal policy-making councils in every administration, met in private to formulate its plan. A conservative group, the National Legal and Policy Center (NLPC), sued to have the task force's proceedings made public, and *The Washington Times* and then other publications amplified the issue of its secrecy, which created a wave of criticism. Hillary was cast as "Imelda Marcos," a dragon lady wielding secret power. In one publication, the NLPC was thrilled at the conservatives' ability to shape the news coverage: "Hillary's critics were eventually so successful in making the secrecy issue stick that in July of 1994 *The Washington Post* made reference to the 'administration's secret Health Care Task Force' in a straight news article."* Eventually, all papers of the task force were released—a half-million documents, an archive of dull policy memos. But the first blood had been drawn.

The task force was disbanded in May after a summer of fine-tuning the plan, and in early September Hillary briefed members of Congress on its basic elements. The writers of the document had compiled what they hoped was a politically flexible document, seeking the center, under the rubric of "managed competition." Hillary had tried to steer a course that would avoid arousing antigovernment sentiment and would gain Democratic support. Instead of a "single-payer" system of medical insurance with a centralized control, which many Democrats favored, it recommended a more market-oriented structure, and featured alliances of

---

*Peter and Timothy Flaherty, *The First Lady: A Comprehensive View of Hillary Rodham Clinton*, Vital Issues Press, 1996, http://www.nlpc.org/hctf/tfl-09.htm.

health care units that could bargain for prices. From the left the report was criticized for not favoring "single-payer" insurances, and from more conservative Democrats for its insistence on universal coverage and for its advocacy of "employer mandates." Neither of these opposing positions could muster majorities, but they chipped away at the President's support. Senator Daniel Patrick Moynihan, chairman of the Finance Committee and an authority on social services, let it be known that he thought the Clinton plan was based on "fantasy numbers" and that there was "no health care crisis" in any case.

On September 22, the President addressed a joint session of the Congress to introduce his proposed health care reforms. A week later, Hillary gave several days of congressional testimony, winning rave reviews for her precision, command of the material, and composure. Public support was running high.

At this point the Health Insurance Association of America (HIAA) launched ads featuring actors playing a middle-class, middle-aged couple named Harry and Louise. "This plan forces us to buy our insurance through those new mandatory government health alliances," complained Louise. "Run by tens of thousands of new bureaucrats," said Harry. "Having choices we don't like is no choice at all," replied Louise. "They choose, we lose," they concluded. The first television buy cost the HIAA $4 million; eventually, the group spent a total of $30 million in the campaign against the Clinton health care program. Against this, too little, too late, the Democratic National Committee spent $150,000.

The grueling battle over NAFTA, which split the Democrats badly, made it impossible to put health care forward on the legislative agenda in late 1993. Then David Brock's gothic tale in *The American Spectator* appeared in December, about the Arkansas troopers and someone called Paula, and the recrudescence of Whitewater enveloped the White House. The media were in a frenzy; Republicans could scent Clinton's wounding. William Kristol circulated an influential memo among them arguing that any and all health care proposals should be opposed "sight unseen." House Republicans, led by Newt Gingrich, saw their chance for power in thwarting Clinton.

At his State of the Union address in January 1994, Clinton held a pen aloft and said: "If you send me legislation that does not guarantee every American private health insurance that can never be taken away, you will force me to take this pen, veto the legislation, and we'll come right back here and start all over again." That very night, Republican Senate Minority Leader Robert Dole laid out the new line of attack against him. There was "no health care crisis," he said. "But we will have a crisis if we take the President's medicine—a massive overdose of government control." In early March, at the Republican Senate retreat, the speakers' list was swelled with corporate lobbyists against health care reform, and Gingrich warned the senators against making any compromise. Just in case there might be backsliding, conservatives began to demonize Dole's chief of staff, Sheila Burke, whom they thought to be a potential deal-maker. "Our No. 1's No. 1 is a liberal Democrat," scolded *The Washington Times*.

The House Republicans had been growing bolder in their attacks throughout the spring and early summer of 1994. "Whitewater and Health Care" read a memo sent to every Republican member by Representative Lamar Smith, Republican of Texas, urging them to tie the two together. Smith, a Christian Scientist whose first wife died after refusing medical treatment, was chairman of Gingrich's Theme Team. "Democrats cannot get past Whitewater and to health care until they admit that full disclosure and congressional hearings lie in front of them," he wrote in a letter to his colleagues.

"Whitewater is about health care," Rush Limbaugh announced on April 19. Limbaugh's daily radio talk show was broadcast on 616 stations and had about 20 million listeners. He was the id of the angry white conservative males, the "Leader of the Opposition," according to a cover story in *The National Review*. Supreme Court Justice Clarence Thomas, who officiated at Limbaugh's wedding, said he taped Limbaugh's show and listened to it in his chambers. Limbaugh offered screeds against "feminazis," minorities, and the Clintons that were peppered with "facts" which often turned out to be fictions. On his television show, he joked: "Everyone knows the Clintons have a cat. Socks is the White House cat. But did you know there is a White House dog?" And he held up a picture of twelve-year-old Chelsea Clinton. He declaimed about the 1948 Dixiecrat candidate for president who had run on a platform of racial segregation: "If you want to know what America used to be—and a lot of people wish it still were—then you listen to Strom Thurmond." When a caller remarked that blacks should have a greater voice in public issues, he shot back: "They are 12 percent of the population. Who the hell cares?" About the oldest organization in America devoted to advancing the rights of blacks, he commented: "The NAACP should have riot rehearsal. They should get a liquor store and practice robberies." And he kept returning to the subject of Chelsea

Clinton: "Chelsea Clinton must write a paper titled 'Why I Feel Guilty Being White.' "*

The President was on the defensive. Whitewater hearings crowded the news, health care was beleaguered. On June 24 he vented his frustration, lashing out at Limbaugh as "a constant unremitting drumbeat of negativism and cynicism. . . . And there's no truth detector. You won't get on afterward and say what was true and what wasn't. . . . We don't need a cultural war in this country." But Limbaugh and Gingrich were ginning one up.

The New York Times on July 24 published an interview with Gingrich in which he referred to the Democrats as "corrupt," said Clinton had become president in an "accidental election," and predicted that the Republicans would capture thirty-four seats and control of the House in the fall midterm elections. He was using the health care issue "as a springboard to win Republican control," the *Times* reported.†

Trying to sustain momentum for the administration's plan, Hillary decided in late July to re-create something like the bus tour that candidate Clinton had taken in the summer of 1992, when he had drawn rapturous throngs at every stop. The "Health Care Express" began in Portland, Oregon, where Hillary and her "Reform Riders" were to stage a rally. But she had provided an excuse for the opposition to mobilize: The right-wing No Name Coalition coordinated by Gingrich's office, whose members included the Christian Coalition, the National Federation of Independent Business, and Citizens for a Sound Economy, were encouraged by local right-wing talk radio and Rush Limbaugh to get their members to join demonstrations against the Health Care Express. "Whitewater! Whitewater!" the crowds chanted. In Seattle, the protesters nearly succeeded in shouting Hillary down, and one was arrested carrying two handguns.‡

Back in the capital, Senate Majority Leader George Mitchell patched

---

*Jeff Cohen and Steve Rendall, "Limbaugh: A Color Man Who Has a Problem with Color?" *Extra!*, June 7, 2000, www.fair.org/articles/limbaugh-color.html; FAIR (Fairness and Accuracy in Reporting), "The Way Things Aren't: Rush Limbaugh Debates Reality," *Extra!*, July/August 1994, www.fair.org/press-releases/limbaugh-debates-reality.html.

†David Rosenbaum, "A Republican Who Sees Himself as a Revolutionary on the Verge of Victory," *The New York Times*, July 24, 1994.

‡For a full account of the battle over the health care legislation, see Haynes Johnson and David S. Broder, *The System: The American Way of Politics at the Breaking Point*, Little, Brown, 1996.

together a "rescue" bill, and Democratic Majority Leader Dick Gephardt introduced a parallel bill in the House. But before the Democrats could muster, Gingrich attacked unexpectedly—on the Violent Crime Control and Law Enforcement bill. The Democrats were split. Bringing the crime bill to the floor for a vote required a prior vote on the rule, as it is called, and Gingrich engineered its defeat, throwing the House into chaos. No other business could be conducted.

Mitchell proposed round-the-clock sessions in the Senate until the health care bill was taken up. But the Democrats were so rancorously split that he could not move the legislation. On August 25, Democratic leaders in both Senate and House sent their members home without bringing any health care legislation to the floor of either chamber. When they returned in September, Senate Republicans threatened a filibuster. On September 26, 1994, Mitchell formally announced that the struggle for health care was over. The greatest promise of Clinton's campaign and administration was smashed.

Clinton's initial pledge to introduce a health care bill in the Congress within his First Hundred Days was naïve and feckless. His congressional speech was made in a political vacuum, for he lacked a strategy for following it up. And making Hillary the head of the National Health Reform Task Force ensured that every problem encountered would be attributed to the personal failings of both Clintons. The President could not have any degree of separation from the tribulations of health care when he had charged Hillary with the task of reforming it. And by entering into the arena, she subjected herself to a gladiatorial combat from which she could not withdraw for the entire course of her husband's administration. Her legitimacy in an unconfirmed but powerful appointed post was more tenuous than that of Robert Kennedy in his appointment to the cabinet by his brother. And when health care failed, the blame fell directly on both Clintons.

The closed meetings of the task force also made it a sitting target, and its foes were able to raise early suspicions by turning its secrecy into an issue. The length of the bill when unveiled—more than fourteen hundred pages—was a ludicrous mistake, for it made it easy to attack as a scheme for big government. The assiduous care the task force took to put together a centrist approach alienated both liberal and conservative Democrats, and the bill was depicted as a bureaucratic monstrosity by everyone.

Clinton's early missteps over appointments, the difficult battle over the budget, the fiascos in Bosnia and Haiti, and the work on NAFTA had pushed health care reform indefinitely back on the calendar for 1993 and 1994. His miscalculation on its timing meant that it reached the floor of the Congress at a treacherously dangerous stage of his term, after the Whitewater pseudoscandal was revived and very close to the congressional elections. The threat in his State of the Union address to veto an inadequate bill was gratuitous, and only aroused the ire of the opposition. In the face of extravagantly funded enemies who were dominating the airwaves with their advertising, Clinton's political response was sputtering and feeble. To their allies he and Hillary expressed their frustration that *they* were not mounting a campaign, but this beseeching gave everyone a sinking feeling that health care reform was slipping away.

The very idea of having the bill originate from an administration council rather than from within the Congress had given no one on Capitol Hill ownership of health care reform. Instead, the Democrats who favored it were cast as good soldiers sacrificing themselves for the new president. Ambition played against ambition, and personal political advantage trumped party discipline. Clinton, frantically trying to cobble together different congressional coalitions on every issue, frittered away his commanding position, and he allowed the Democrats to buffet and bully him. "I've lashed myself to Congress like Ahab to Moby Dick," he complained privately. Hillary's bus tour was poignant and pathetic, an attempt to reenact the glory days of the campaign amid the failing politics of health care.

Perhaps, then, it was not surprising that the President's policy achievements in his first two years rebounded against him as political liabilities. When an assault weapon ban was enacted, the National Rifle Association had cause to galvanize its membership and defeat many Democratic candidates in rural districts where their majority was slim. It would take years before the wondrous effects on the economy of the 1993 budget had time to be realized, and the time lag enabled the Republicans to stigmatize Democrats as tax-increasers. Clinton's victory in NAFTA alienated the AFL-CIO, which thereafter made only grudging and halfhearted efforts in the midterm elections. Blacks upset by the sentencing provisions of the crime bill declined to turn out to vote in large numbers.

Now the collapse of health care reform overshadowed Clinton's presidency. The politically gifted young president who had vaulted into the White House seemed incompetent and overwhelmed. Even his achievements seemed to produce chaos. He and Hillary were portrayed as dictatorial, inept, and venal. Clinton had deferred to the Democratic congressional leaders, beginning with his first meeting with them as president-elect, in agreeing not to press for ethics and campaign finance reform. He agreed to leave their business up to them. But after the indictment in May 1994 of Representative Dan Rostenkowski of Illinois, chairman of the House Ways and Means Committee, for embezzlement of House funds, the Republicans were able to tar the entire Democratic Party as unethical. Rostenkowski's fall also removed a player who might have helped nudge health care along at a critical moment. Now, with Whitewater, the Republicans were able to conflate Clinton with the congressional Democrats as corrupt. Going into the fall campaign, the reeling Democrats had no theme or strategy. The Republicans, meanwhile, rallied behind Newt Gingrich's Contract with America, a ten-point program the first of which was about congressional ethics. The Contract with America carefully excluded divisive social issues that the right wing had made central, like abortion and school prayer, and concentrated on procedural changes, including term limits, and on limiting taxes.

On November 8, for the first time in forty years, the Republicans captured control of the House (230–204); the Democrats lost fifty-four seats. The Republicans also gained control of the Senate (52–48), and no Republican incumbent lost in any reelection contest for the House or Senate or governorship. The day after, at a press conference, President Clinton said stumblingly, "I think [the voters] were saying two things to me. Or maybe three . . . maybe three hundred."

II

A month after Clinton's election in December 1992, Newt Gingrich gave a seminar, his favorite forum, to members of Gopac, the political action committee that was his personal instrument in his campaign to seize control of the House of Representatives by 1994. On large easels, using markers, he dashed down sentence fragments about his ambitions. About himself, like a young Jay Gatsby, spraying capitalized letters, he wrote:

Gingrich—primary mission
Advocate of civilization
Definer of civilization
Teacher of the Rules of Civilization
Arouser of those who Fan Civilization
Organizer of the pro-civilization activists

Leader (Possibly) of the civilizing forces
A universal rather than an optimal Mission*

Now, at the opening of the 104th Congress in early 1995, the triumphant Speaker of the House Newt Gingrich—"Leader (Possibly) of
the civilizing forces"—staged many celebrations, culminating with one in
the vast spaces of Washington's Union Station, where, cheered by thousands of Republicans, he bathed in a spotlight alone. Throughout the day,
he surrounded himself with signs of his power: his "revolutionaries," the
new House members who pledged their undying fealty; Rush Limbaugh,
whose presence was received like a papal appearance; and men costumed
as cartoon characters who cavorted around the Speaker doing acrobatic
stunts. Gingrich referred to the election of the Republican majority in the
House as "magical" and "mystical"† and, of course, as a "revolution." He
believed, above all, in his own magic. He had brought House Republicans
out of their wilderness—forty years in the minority—into their promised
land. He was their mystagogue, a figure who, as Max Weber wrote, pre-
sents "magical actions that contain the boons of salvation."‡

Gingrich saw himself as the equivalent of a president. He was more
than a Speaker of the House, whose job is to balance the jostling interests
of members representing far-flung districts, to oversee the committee
structure, and to keep the ponderous machinery of the lower chamber
grinding out legislation. Gingrich was an avatar, not a deliberator; a man
in search of a zeitgeist, not a compromise. He was intoxicated with the
notion that he had a "mandate." By his lights, the congressional midterm
election was a national referendum on him and his patchwork Contract
with America—and he had won.

Newt Gingrich was born Newton McPherson in Pennsylvania. His
parents' marriage was fleeting—they quickly divorced—and his mother
remarried an authoritarian army officer named Gingrich. The family was
constantly relocating from base to base in the United States and Europe,
so Newt's boyhood was rootless; he described himself as "very lonely."§
He became a devotee of Isaac Asimov's science fiction, identifying him-

*Cited in Adam Clymer, "The Teacher of the 'Rules of Civilization' Gets a Scold-
ing," *The New York Times*, January 26, 1997.

†David Maraniss and Michael Weisskopf, *"Tell Newt to Shut Up!"*, Touchstone,
1996, p. 85.

‡Max Weber, *The Sociology of Religion*, Beacon Press, 1963, p. 54.

§Quoted in Joan Didion, *Political Fictions*, Knopf, 2001, p. 185.

self as a savior of civilization from cosmic threats. He loved zoos and dinosaurs; his ambition was to be a paleontologist. When he was a freshman at Emory University he married his high-school geometry teacher, seven years older than he. As a graduate student at Tulane, he grew muttonchop sideburns, experimented with drugs, and led a campus protest against censorship of pornography in the student newspaper. But, unlike the other students, he was burdened with a marriage and children. His first political emergence, in 1968, was as a volunteer in the moderate Republican Nelson Rockefeller's quixotic presidential campaign. Gingrich took a teaching job at West Georgia College, where he languished. After losing one race for Congress, he won in 1978. Then he divorced his wife, presenting her with papers to sign in the hospital room where she was recovering from cancer. He remarried but confessed to reporters that he still wept from feelings of isolation.* He had a hatred of losers and feared being a loser. He alternated between lashing out and seeking acceptance, often at and from the same person.

"This is my campus. I'm conducting seminars," he had declared at the 1984 Republican convention.† No matter how high he rose in the political ranks, Gingrich remained that most dangerous type in politics, the failed professor. His favored phrase to define the enemy was "*theGreat-Societycounterculturalmodel.*"‡ For the right, the 1960s are pornography. Gingrich was prurient about the 1960s, but he was a closet counterculturist who resented that he'd missed the bus. His attraction to the 1960s could only be expressed as repulsion.

Gingrich practiced and perfected a politics of annihilation and brought what came to be known as the "politics of personal destruction" into the modern era. "I think one of the great problems we have in the Republican Party is that we don't encourage you to be nasty," Gingrich was to instruct a gathering of Young Republicans in 1995. Like Joseph McCarthy, Gingrich had a keen sense of the news cycle. McCarthy could walk a reporter down the hall and by the end of their conversation produce a new communist scare for an afternoon newspaper. Gingrich would call and wheedle reporters day and night, and he boasted, "We are engaged in reshaping the whole nation through the news media."§

*John M. Barry, *The Ambition and the Power*, Viking, 1989, p. 164.

†Ibid., p. 212.

‡Quoted in Fred Barnes, "Revenge of the Squares," *The New Republic*, March 13, 1995.

§Barry, *The Ambition and the Power*, p. 215.

I first met Gingrich in 1984, in his House office, where he was planning fresh assaults. Though he would instantly provide razor's-edge quotes, even slicing at Reagan, Gingrich tried to impress and gain approval as an intellectual.* He told me in 1984 that "there are very long-term rhythms of nature in Taoism" and that he was a Taoist master. "Our policies of confrontation have begun to achieve results when policies of reasonableness have not." So Gingrich routinely called Speaker of the House Thomas P. "Tip" O'Neill a "thug" and "corrupt." Just as McCarthy and Nixon had honed it for their times, Gingrich climbed to power by rubbing out those who stood in his way.

The first was Representative Jim Wright, a prickly Texas Democrat, canny, partisan, and overbearing. He pushed hard against President Bush and yielded nothing to House Republicans. Wright also had cut a corner. A kind of memoir and compilation of his speeches, *Reflections of a Public Man*, almost a vanity publishing exercise, had appeared in 1984, of which a thousand copies were purchased by the Teamsters Union. (Gingrich had struck an arrangement for a book of his, *Windows of Opportunity*, published at the same time, in which wealthy political supporters raised money to promote it and then took tax write-offs and paid Gingrich's wife to administer their limited partnership.†) Wright had not done anything illegal, just on the edge of unethical. He had been careless, not corrupt; he had not used his office to enrich himself.

Nonetheless Gingrich went after him, and began by comparing him to Mussolini. He generated a din with his distortions and then by quoting himself about distortions, which prompted other stories, followed by media investigations filled with charges that were later disproved but that were circulated under Gingrich's imprimatur to create more stories, flanked by *Wall Street Journal* editorials. He started out with half-baked allegations about Wright's finances, investigations into which produced no wrongdoing but months of newspaper coverage. A mob psychology soon prevailed in the media, and no news organization wanted to be last. All this enabled Gingrich to gig Common Cause, the nonpartisan good-government group, to demand a House investigation of Wright in June 1988. "If it wasn't for Common Cause," remarked Representative Robert Livingston, Republican from Louisiana, a Gingrich ally, "there wouldn't have been an investigation. If Gingrich hadn't manipulated the press and

*Sidney Blumenthal, *Our Long National Daydream: A Political Pageant of the Reagan Era*, Harper and Row, 1988, pp. 167–75.
†Barry, *The Ambition and the Power*, p. 623.

got all those stories, there wouldn't have been an investigation."* The combative Wright had not known how to fight against Gingrich's attacks, and he was cornered into resigning. In his farewell, in June 1989, Wright denounced "mindless cannibalism." On the basis of having torn down Wright, Gingrich was elected the House Republican whip by a narrow margin.

The new Speaker of the House was Thomas Foley of Washington state, a charming, progressive Democrat who was deeply devoted to the institution. Gingrich's aides ginned up a rumor mill, calling reporters around Washington and smearing him as a closet homosexual. "We hear it's little boys," one of them told a reporter, who reported this remark. The Republican National Committee circulated a four-page memo to state chairmen, "Tom Foley: Out of the Liberal Closet," that compared his record to that of Barney Frank, the out-of-the-closet gay liberal congressman from Massachusetts. This was leaked to reporters. To quell the false rumor, Foley was compelled to deny publicly that he was gay, in response to questions from reputable news organizations. Eventually, the communications director of the RNC, who had composed the memo, was forced to resign as the fall guy. It was reported that Gingrich ordered his staff to stop spreading the rumor that he did not admit to spreading.†

In 1990, Gingrich commissioned his pollster to test-market words that could be used to demonize the Democrats. The ensuing document, "Language: A Key Mechanism of Control," was worthy of exegesis by George Orwell. These were among the words Gingrich urged Republicans to use: "sick . . . pathetic . . . decay . . . corrupt . . . waste . . . liberal . . . traitor." The context of usage was unimportant, and so were the issues. No matter what they were, the Democrats were to be tainted as perverse un-Americans—McCarthyism without communism.

President Clinton offered a target that allowed Gingrich to consolidate and direct his vitriol. On the eve of the 1994 elections, he described to a group of lobbyists his strategy: to depict Clinton as "the enemy of normal Americans." Gingrich's turn of phrase compactly suggested treason and deviance.

Sex was on his brain a lot. In his kitsch futuristic reveries, he talked about "honeymoons in space" and speculated about the effects of "weightlessness" on sex.‡ His novel *1945*—a contribution to alternate

*Barry, *The Ambition and the Power*, pp. 630–31.
†Richard Cohen, "Foul Rumor," *The Washington Post*, June 8, 1989.
‡Didion, *Political Fictions*, p. 175.

history in which the United States doesn't go to war against Hitler until, well, 1945—is filled with silly sex scenes: "Suddenly the pouting sex kitten gave way to Diana the Huntress . . ." He also held forth on the differences between the sexes: "If combat means being in a ditch, females have biological problems staying in a ditch for thirty days because they get infections and they don't have upper body strength . . . males are biologically driven to go out and hunt giraffes." And he went out of his way to blame AIDS on "liberals who advocated free sex."* More to the point, his view of the welfare state always came down to sexual "irresponsibility." The problem was that the poor were having wanton sex, producing litters of children, and going on welfare. "Normal Americans" were being forced to subsidize "free sex."

Gingrich's team offered differing versions of this material and complemented his drive to power. Representative Tom DeLay of Texas, his whip, was punitive and bullying. A former Dallas vermin exterminator, he sneered at the Environmental Protection Agency as "the Gestapo." A fundamentalist Christian estranged from his brother and mother, he hung a bullwhip prominently on the wall of his office. His nickname, in which he reveled, was "The Hammer." He aimed to deregulate industry, making the lobbyists of K Street an adjunct of the Republican Party and creating a Niagara of campaign contributions to the GOP. Every Tuesday he ate lunch with about forty key lobbyists to coordinate this agenda. When one industry association hired a former Democratic congressman to lobby Democrats on the Hill, DeLay demanded that he be fired: "You need to hire a Republican."† Those jobs, all of them, should be reserved for Republicans to be cogs in the machine. Every lobbyist who visited his office was seated first in front of an open book showing a list of other lobbyists who had contributed to the Republican Party. "See you're in the book," DeLay ordered.‡

Richard Armey of Texas, the Republican majority leader, was the dogmatic bishop. A defender of the one true faith of conservative Republicanism, he was inquisitorial, blunt, and insulting. Like Gingrich, he was a failed professor, forced out of the economics department at North Texas State University, to which his response had been to blast "Take This Job and Shove It" at his colleagues from a boom box he brought to campus.

---

*Hal Straus, "Gingrich Urges Ad Campaign to Fight AIDS," *The Atlanta Journal-Constitution*, October 15, 1985.

†Maraniss and Weisskopf, *"Tell Newt to Shut Up!"*, p. 117.

‡Ibid., p. 110.

In the Congress, Armey taunted Democrats, calling President Clinton "your president." He labeled Barney Frank "Barney Fag." He termed Social Security a "rotten trick."* And he insulted Hillary Clinton—"All her friends are Marxists"—also telling her, "Reports of your charms are overrated." Armey employed the wife of Supreme Court Justice Clarence Thomas on his staff, and she helped him target Democrats who they thought should be investigated. He was proud of his narrowness, believing it to be true Americanism. When he was asked why he refused to vote for funding of the International Monetary Fund, Armey answered, "I've been to Europe once—I don't need to go again," adding that he didn't need to go to Asia either.†

Gingrich, Armey, and Delay presided over a Republican Party more tightly rooted in special interests than ever. It was less a seminar than GOP, Inc. Industries that considered themselves under attack from Clinton had contributed tens of millions of dollars to Republican candidates and now they demanded legislative protection: tobacco, pharmaceuticals, insurance, guns. (The $4.5 million advance that Rupert Murdoch's publishing house, HarperCollins, planned to pay Newt Gingrich was a loss leader, an easy indirect investment in the telecommunications legislation pending before the Congress. But Gingrich returned the money after the deal was criticized.) Gingrich's coalition comprised groups that wanted government removed: the National Rifle Association wanted no more gun control; the National Federation of Independent Business wanted no more health or safety regulations and no more increases in the minimum wage; the Wise Use movement groups in the West wanted untrammeled access to federal lands for mining and logging and a rollback of environmental rules. Every week, their leaders in Washington met at the office of Grover Norquist, a lobbyist close to Gingrich, to coordinate activities. During a debate on a terrorism bill opposed by the NRA, one Republican congressman, who voted against it, summarized the sentiment: "I trust Hamas more than I trust my own government."‡

Though Gingrich, the student of history, presented himself as an original, he and his views were only the latest version of a recurrent pattern. With the end of the Cold War, it has become a commonplace to observe that the morbid fears and hatreds that had been suppressed by

*Maraniss and Weisskopf, *"Tell Newt to Shut Up!"*, pp. 78–79.

†James Kitfield, "A Return to Isolationism," *National Journal*, October 8, 1999.

‡Thomas L. Friedman, "House GOP Madness," *The New York Times*, April 3, 1996.

communist regimes in Eastern Europe, especially in the Balkans, were flourishing again. But the Cold War's end also lifted a rock in the United States, and the 1994 election marked the beginning of the return of the repressed. The old right resurged in newly virulent forms, and its politics of interest went hand in hand with its antipolitics. Now, in the 1990s, the apocalyptic struggle would be waged with the federal government, the enemy of the American right long before there was a Soviet Union.

In the last decade of the twentieth century, many conservatives felt that it was nightfall in America, a premillennial time. If government was the Behemoth from the Book of Revelation, Clinton must be Lucifer. His ability to soothe was nothing but a guise, a telltale sign of his demonic nature, for the devil assumes many identities—"the enemy of normal Americans."

The threat was coming from the sky, in black helicopters flown by secret UN agents preparing for invasion. Representative Helen Chenoweth of Idaho held hearings in her district, inviting the leader of the local militia movement to testify about these helicopters. Most of the United States, she declared, was under "the control of the New World Order." It was coming in the door, spearheaded by a phalanx of Alcohol, Tobacco and Firearms agents. "Kill the sons of bitches. They've got a vest on . . . head shots, head shots," shouted G. Gordon Liddy, the Watergate felon, now a popular conservative talk-show host. The National Rifle Association, with 3.5 million members, a major contributor to Republican campaigns at every level, sent out a fund-raising appeal warning that "jack-booted government thugs" in "Nazi bucket helmets" had "the government's go ahead to harass, intimidate, even murder law-abiding citizens." More than eight hundred private militias, operating in twenty-three states, were training with automatic weapons, according to the Southern Poverty Law Center.* The threat was even infiltrating the bedrooms, a battlefield against feminists—"femi-nazis," according to Rush Limbaugh—and gays. "They Want Your Children" read a letter warning against gays, mass-mailed by the Traditional Values Coalition, a right-wing religious group that supported Republicans.

By 1994, Pat Robertson's Christian Coalition claimed 1.2 million members and closely coordinated its activities with the Republican Party. Its political director, Ralph Reed, a protégé of Lee Atwater who had also been a campaign aide to Gingrich, depicted himself as a murderous sur-

*Southern Poverty Law Center, "False Patriots: The Threat of Antigovernment Extremists," 1996.

vivalist: "I want to be invisible. I do guerrilla warfare. I paint my face and travel at night. You don't know it's over until you are in a body bag. You don't know until election night."* Robertson insisted that the constitutional separation between church and state was a "lie." Flag and cross were one and the same. He conjured immense conspiracies against Christian America. In his 1991 work, *The New World Order*, he wrote that "European bankers and money lords," Illuminati and Freemasons, had manipulated communism and liberalism to create "one-world government." He gave special emphasis to the Rothschilds—a staple of anti-Semitic literature.† The Christian Coalition's influence with the new Gingrich-led Congress seemed indisputable: 26 senators and 114 members of the House achieved perfect ratings on its "Congressional Scorecard"; another 58 members had scores of higher than 85 percent.‡

Politically inspired violence—in the West against U.S. Park Rangers, against the federal Bureau of Land Management and Fish and Wildlife Service, and especially against clinics that performed abortions—was mounting. Domestic terrorism had been in abeyance since the mid-1960s, when it had been directed against the civil rights movement. But vicious, extreme rhetoric fostered an ever more extreme climate. Thirty antiabortion activists signed a letter in 1994 calling the murder of doctors and clinic workers "justifiable homicide." One of them then killed a doctor and his guard in Florida. With President Clinton's signing of the Freedom of Access to Clinic Entrance Act in 1994, law enforcement against these activities began to pick up, but so did the violence. More than half of America's clinics experienced an act of violence; more than one quarter received death threats.§ In December, an antiabortion fanatic, dressed in black and wielding a semiautomatic rifle, murdered two young women and wounded five staff members at two clinics in Brookline, Massachusetts.

On April 18, 1995, President Clinton held a news conference in primetime, but only one network saw fit to broadcast it. With the Gingrich "revolution" running at full throttle, Clinton had to argue that the presidency mattered. He was asked pointedly, "Do you worry about mak-

*Sidney Blumenthal, "Christian Soldiers," *The New Yorker*, July 18, 1994.

†See David H. Bennett, *The Party of Fear: From Nativist Movements to the New Right in American History*, Vintage, 1995, pp. 423–24.

‡William Martin, *With God on Our Side*, Broadway Books, 1996, p. 340.

§Feminist Majority Foundation, "1994 Clinic Violence Survey Report," www.feminist.org/gateway/cv_meth.html.

ing sure that your voice is heard in the coming months?" "The Constitution gives me relevance," he said. "The power of our ideas gives me relevance. The record we have built up over the last two years and the things we're trying to do to implement it give it relevance. The president is relevant here." The next day, April 19, was the 220th anniversary of the battle of Lexington and Concord—and the second anniversary of the battle of Waco.

At 9:02 that morning, a truck packed with explosives, like a gigantic bomb, exploded in front of the Alfred P. Murrah Federal Building in Oklahoma City. One hundred sixty-eight people were murdered and six hundred wounded: the worst incident of domestic terrorism in American history. Two days later Timothy McVeigh, spouting slogans and phrases of the extreme right-wing Christian Identity movement, was arrested. His accomplice, Terry Nichols, who had provided matériel for the bomb and urged McVeigh to "go for it," had once "renounced" his American citizenship. Before setting off his bomb, McVeigh had been a close reader and promoter of a book entitled *The Turner Diaries*, written by William Pierce, a neo-Nazi, which describes the overthrow of a Jewish-controlled federal government. Scenes of violence from the book closely resembled McVeigh's actions, and he appeared to have followed them like a script.

President Clinton went to Oklahoma City four days later. At a prayer service, he honored the federal employees who had been killed, those "who served the rest of us," and he urged Americans to take a "stand" against "the forces of fear," against "talk of hatred . . . talk of violence." Clinton's homage to the positive contributions of federal workers transformed them from faceless bureaucrats. Showing the relevant powers of the presidency, he brought to bear on the blasted city the resources of federal agencies and the federal funds for recovery. Then, in a speech at Michigan State University, he disputed that anyone could proclaim to love America but hate the government: "There is nothing patriotic about hating your country or pretending that you can love your country but despise your government."

If Clinton had been halfhearted in his political response and had acted only as a sympathetic consoler, he would have seemed weak himself and would have encouraged his opposition. But he gave the outrage its larger meaning, and his framing of the event was a turning point against the Republican right. The bombing had tragically clarified the consequences of the incendiary atmosphere they had helped to create. The federal government ceased to be a rhetorical trope and became instead the very distinct individuals who had been murdered. Clinton's "stand" set the terms of the coming conflict with Gingrich and secured the President's reelection in 1996. Ultimately, it forced the Republicans to seek radical measures beyond politics to destroy his presidency.

After the bombing of the World Trade Center in February 1993, President Clinton had included antiterrorism measures in his proposed new crime bill: new deportation laws and a federal death penalty for terrorists. Parts of that bill had been passed, but neither the memory of the World Trade Center attack nor the bombing at Oklahoma City made the 104th Congress receptive to Clinton's new omnibus antiterrorism bill, which contained what had not previously passed as well as new proposals: for roving wiretaps, already used against mobsters; taggants for explosives; new laws against money laundering; a ban on fund-raising by terrorist organizations; and even more stringent deportation powers.

The Republican right, supported by the NRA and the Gun Owners of America, opposed the bill, forging an alliance of convenience with liberals worried about civil liberties. Less than a month after the Oklahoma carnage, Gingrich defended this opposition by remarking that people living in rural areas had a "justified fear" of the federal government. The antiterrorism bill went down to defeat. (It took an entire year, until April 1996, to pass the Antiterrorism Act. Even with passage the Republican Congress deleted crucial provisions advocated by the President: it forbade the FBI to use further powers to track suspected terrorists' hotel and transportation records; to install roving wiretaps so that separate warrants didn't have to be issued for each phone used by a suspect, including cell phones; and to put tags ["taggants"] in smokeless and black explosives so their source could be traced—this last measure was opposed as an insidious form of gun registration.)

Despite the Republican majorities in both houses of the Congress, Gingrich's Contract with America encountered rebuffs. A balanced-budget amendment to the Constitution failed in the Senate. A draconian welfare bill also went nowhere in the Senate. Term limits lost in the House. The President vetoed a bill extensively cutting social programs. By the autumn of 1995, the Republicans had formed their main line of battle against Clinton: they would work for a $245-billion tax cut heavily favoring the upper brackets to be paid for with a $270-billion cut in projected Medicare spending. Before the Republican House Conference, Gingrich declared: "In the next sixty to ninety days we're going to prove whether or not we're worthy of truly being historic."

The Republicans were certain that in the end, under immense pressure, Clinton would crumble and they would march forward to victory. But the longer Clinton negotiated with Gingrich, the shakier the Speaker became. Clinton appealed to his internationalism and brought him in as a partner on various important measures. In February, Clinton invoked his executive authority to extend $20 billion in loans to Mexico, whose currency reserves had dropped to $3.5 billion, setting other Latin American economies on the edge of disaster.* Hooted at by Rush Limbaugh—"giving away our money and taking away our rights"—Gingrich broke ranks by supporting the President. And when finally the United States bombed the Bosnian Serbs and forced Milosevic into attending the Dayton peace talks, Gingrich backed Clinton again.

One evening at the White House, at a state dinner, seated next to a member of the administration, Gingrich held forth, unprompted, on the "unreconstructed" attitude of Senator Trent Lott on civil rights and race. His point was that he was not like Lott—he was more like Clinton. Gingrich regularly traveled up Pennsylvania Avenue filled with bravado and returned confusedly explaining Clinton's logic to his cohorts. "I melt when I'm around him," he admitted to his wife.† Soon the Jacobins no longer trusted their Robespierre. They insisted that he never meet with Clinton alone. Dick Armey went with Gingrich on every trip to the White House to ensure that he did not lose his will. Clinton told me later that the only House Republican leader he felt he could not "reach" on some level was the hardwired Tom DeLay.

In early November 1995, President Clinton went to Israel for the funeral of Prime Minister Yitzhak Rabin, who had been assassinated by a Jewish right-wing extremist. Clinton had a special regard for Rabin as a leader and a kind of surrogate father figure, and he was deeply grieved. He took Republican leaders on *Air Force One* with him to Israel. Back in Washington, with the clock ticking down on the budget, Gingrich held a press conference to announce that the President had demeaned him by not allowing him to ride up front with him. "You just wonder, where is their sense of manners? Where is their sense of courtesy?" The New York *Daily News* put a picture of him as a gigantic baby wearing a diaper on its front page, which the House Democrats enlarged and exhibited on the House floor.

For months during 1995, Gingrich made threats about the Republi-

*John Greenwald, "Don't Panic: Here Comes Bailout Bill,' *Time*, February 13, 1995.

†Quoted by Evan Thomas, "A Heroic Failure," *Newsweek*, August 19, 1996.

can House majority forcing the administration to do its bidding. He boasted that the President "will veto a number of things, and we'll then put them all on the debt ceiling. And then he'll decide how big a crisis he wants." He was setting off a kind of budgetary doomsday device: by blocking Clinton's budget, he would make it necessary for the Congress to pass a debt-limit bill and the President to sign it in order to continue the operations of the federal government. Who was going to be in charge? The President "can run the parts of the government that are left or he can run no government. . . . Which of the two of us do you think worries more about the government not showing up?" As the congressional term wore on, it became more and more urgent to agree on a budget, but Gingrich said, "I don't care what the price is. I don't care if we have no executive offices and no bonds for sixty days—not this time."

On November 13, the President vetoed the Republicans' debt-limit bill because of its unacceptably severe cuts in funds for Medicare, education, and the environment. For the first time ever—even including during the War of 1812, when Washington was burned and occupied—the federal government shut down. All services stopped. National monuments and museums on the Independence Mall, as well as national parks and all federal facilities in all fifty states, were closed. Public opinion overwhelmingly blamed the Republicans in general and Gingrich in particular for this crisis. After three days, Clinton and the Congress agreed to a temporary spending bill and the government reopened. A month later, the Republicans sent Clinton another budget they knew was unacceptable to him, and he vetoed it. For more than two weeks, through Christmas, the government was again shut down. The Republicans had achieved the dystopian goal of antipolitics—twice. These willful acts appeared as a strange, if nonviolent, reenactment of the belligerence toward government demonstrated at Oklahoma City.

Two-thirds of the Contract with America, which had been Gingrich's platform in the 1994 election campaign, was never enacted. Even the most ardent "revolutionaries" tried to ignore it. Republicans never mentioned it again. Almost all the congressional representatives elected in 1994 would break their pledge for term limits and run repeatedly. Gingrich spent his energies fighting internal wars against House Republicans who wanted to depose him. With his politics rapidly depleted, he attacked. His vision of one branch of government devoted mostly to investigating another branch became reality, with more than twenty committees engaged in various investigations, as he had promised before the election. It was government by revenge.

President Clinton had not anticipated that Gingrich would become his foil or that Gingrich's ascent would turn to his advantage so quickly. The Oklahoma City tragedy was a shock, but Clinton emerged from its whirlwind as a commanding figure for the first time in his presidency. The government shutdowns not only broke the momentum of the Republicans but established a ground for him to remake the Democratic Party and modernize government.

FOUR

Clinton's Strategic Offensive

I

The transformation of politics in Washington from mid-1994, when President Clinton decisively lost control, to early 1996, when he decisively regained it, could not have been more striking. By August 1994, with the defeat of the health care bill, cynicism about government prevailed. It took nearly another year and a half before the public psychologically registered the economic gains that President Clinton's program had made. Clinton's promise meanwhile became his enemy. He had a plan but seemed to be without a strategy. Congressional Democrats were battling each other and the President while the Republicans appeared to be united and on a clear course. Only about 15 percent of the public had been aware of the Contract with America, but the Republicans' self-confidence made them seem like an alternative to disorder and gridlock, even if they had deliberately been much of the source. Democrats had been in the majority in the House for forty years, and they were exhausted. Their factional opposition to various parts of Clinton's program—from NAFTA to health care to crime—was sowing despair among Democratic voters, who were prepared to stay home, sullenly disenfranchising themselves. Republicans, who were angry at everything about Clinton, galvanized themselves. The GOP systematically stressed the worthlessness of government, but their party was preparing for a maximum turnout to gain control of it.

Yet, right after the Democratic defeat in 1994, Clinton tried a new approach. Just a month after the election, he proposed a new platform, which he dubbed the "Middle Class Bill of Rights," inspired by the idea of the GI Bill of Rights (advocated by President Roosevelt and initiated by Eleanor Roosevelt) and intended to demonstrate that Clinton's focus was fixed on the middle-class voters who had expected so much from his presidency.

The Middle Class Bill of Rights was a series of tax credits—for college education, child exemption, an expansion of Individual Retirement Accounts, and a "GI Workers' Bill of Rights," which provided funds for veterans' retraining—that Clinton could set against the regressive GOP tax cut. At a Christmas party at the White House, he was upbeat about his program but anxious about its reception. He wanted nothing more than to discuss it, even surrounded by hundreds of guests. He was not about to wait for an unforeseen turn of events to rescue him. The Middle Class Bill of Rights was his first bid in the urgent new politics. And, in contrast to the Contract with America, all of its provisions were eventually enacted.

Still, Clinton faced seemingly unsolvable problems. He had to duel with the Republican majority in the Congress, which believed its election had righted the wrong of Clinton's victory in 1992. He had to handle the bitterness in his own party about its minority status. Left to its own devices, it seemed incapable of rising above a self-defeating politics of complaint. He had to force his own White House staff to create and implement strategies that worked. He had to develop a policy agenda that gave him political leverage and moved him forward. He had to communicate through media that had become captivated with scandal coverage, their cynicism easily manipulated by the right. Finally, he had to start to reverse the public's deep-seated mistrust of government.

Clinton might have become a James Buchanan–like figure—feckless, dawdling, weak, making deals with the devil. Or he might have been like Jimmy Carter—pessimistic, moralizing, increasingly isolated and overwhelmed. After the crushing rejection of his party and his first programs, his defeat might have been thorough. But he had lost an election, not his nervous system. And he needed a jump-start.

It was Hillary who telephoned Dick Morris, a political consultant who had worked closely with Clinton in 1982 in his first comeback—as governor. Using Morris's polling and stratagems, Clinton had figured out how to integrate policy and politics in Arkansas, and he had outplayed many rivals and the leading political men of his state and party. In the White House, however, Clinton had been acting as though he had unlearned many of those earlier lessons. Bringing back Morris in late 1994 was Hillary's effort to return the President to his political senses.

Dick Morris was an unlikely person to represent the restoration of sanity. Short and tightly wound, he was egotistical, controlling, and compulsive. He cloaked his insecurity with a manner of absolute certainty, except that his hands quaked as he spoke. He often had keen insight into the shifting public mind, but little understanding of individual people's emotions or psychology. He combined high levels of intelligence and obliviousness. His self-importance could not be disentangled from his politics, and both led him into baroque schemes to finagle himself into the center of the universe. He used the unusual moment and circumstance of the election of 1994 to thrust himself into the center of the White House.

Morris was a child of New York City politics. His father was a real-estate lawyer, his mother a left-wing writer on medicine and psychiatry, his uncle a stalwart of the Bronx Democratic Party clubhouse. A first cousin was Roy Cohn, Joseph McCarthy's counsel and later an influential lawyer and fixer in New York. After youthful antiwar protests, Morris moved into New York's arcane electoral campaigns, often finding himself at sword's point with Harold M. Ickes, who was to become Clinton's deputy chief of staff. Their battles on Manhattan's Upper West Side were eventually carried into the White House. Through the 1980s, Morris advised Clinton in his gubernatorial races, but he also drifted into working for Republicans, including Senator Jesse Helms. Morris and Clinton had a falling out in 1990 when the latter accused the former of exploiting and ignoring him. But now, with Clinton in crisis, Morris was summoned back.

At first, Morris's presence in the White House was a secret. He even had a code name that he used when he left messages for the President: Charlie. Eventually, he was found out, for it is impossible to operate in the White House for long without the knowledge of the staff, who have the political equivalent of sensory motion devices. And Morris in the open actually served Clinton better than Morris as a behind-the-scenes adviser. Clinton realized he could use Morris to keep the staff at bay, reorganize it, and redirect it. Clinton had been looking for order from the beginning, an order that he could not impose himself and that his habits often confounded. The absence of strategy had invariably produced disarray. His chiefs of staff had tried in vain to create a managerial structure. David Gergen, a moderate Republican and communications expert, brought in for his reputation as an entrenched Washington figure, had only momentarily calmed the elites in the capital. Other longtime Washingtonians inducted into service, like the lawyer Lloyd Cutler, had brought their competence to bear but could not stem the tides rolling in against Clinton.

Younger members of Clinton's communications and political-operations staff had enraged their elders in the press corps simply by existing, by their impertinence in being in a place where they had authority over the press and could deny or grant access. But some of these aides who had closed the door of the pressroom began to learn the survival skill of leaking out of the back door. These staffers were tacticians, operating week to week, and they found themselves immersed in relationships with the daily reporters that became central to their mentality and self-esteem. They were criticized for being spinners, but they spent much of their energy responding to the media story line, a spin in itself that changed every day, often more than once a day, to fill the accelerating news cycle. The kind of story the press liked was about conflict, scandal, and process, and its highest form was the ticktock story—who said what or did what to whom. This was always a partial and tilted account which could never be independently checked.

These aides also learned that the media covered not so much stories as sources. If one ceased to be a source, one got punished in the next story. The emphasis on process overshadowed policy and even politics, highlighting which personality was ahead on a given day. Being swallowed up in this rapidly moving, enervating game made it virtually impossible to devise a strategy. The deeper the political trouble Clinton found himself in, the greater this dysfunction.

After the 1994 election, his exhausted aides had no new strategy. Some of them had a hard enough time defending themselves from the accusations of defeated congressional Democrats, who wanted to treat them as scapegoats. In their desolation, the Democrats remaining in the Congress blamed Clinton for everything and now also wanted him to act like the leader of a minority in opposition. They were angry about what they considered his misbegotten positions—on NAFTA, on health care, on hard issues like the budget. He was either too compromising or not compromising enough—with them. Now they wanted to set the terms, and wanted him to be their voice. The congressional Democrats would use the President's bully pulpit and vetoes to make them the equal of the majority Republicans. Then they could take back the Congress in 1996. Their scenario posited an American version of a parliamentary system. The truth was, many Democrats in the Congress preferred to have the party in a majority there than to have a Democrat in the White House. And Clinton now knew this all too well.

Most of the White House staff just kept going on, like characters in a Samuel Beckett play. They plodded on but were increasingly fraught. And some of them didn't really know what to think about all the so-called scandals swirling around. The onslaught by respected news organizations couldn't all be driven by falsehoods, could it? They developed a self-protective view of themselves as principled people working for a larger-than-life politician who demanded all sorts of compromises to get ahead. Were they themselves responsible now? Had they been seduced? Was it worth it? Who were they in the end?

Dick Morris didn't think he was trapped in an existential drama. He believed there was a way back from the brink. And for all his political campaigns, Morris was an outsider in Washington who had no desire ever to become a permanent fixture. He was there for the politics and was enticed by nothing else. He lived in Connecticut and thought of Washington as a business opportunity, not a likely home. He didn't schmooze at long lunches with pundits or socialize at dinner parties. He was one-sided, impervious, and oriented toward New York. He came to Washington to do his work just as he parachuted into other cities. Only this time his client was the President. Morris insisted he would leave after the 1996 campaign.

In 1994, Morris was like a deus ex machina descending to assist the embattled forces in the White House. He wanted none of the usual perquisites. If he was kept out of certain meetings, he was indifferent. He was used to working directly with his clients and no one else. He wasn't jockeying for favor. He didn't really care if others on Clinton's staff liked him. He wasn't trying to be genial to fit in, though he made a few gestures. He wasn't burdened by a sense of fairness. The chief of staff, Leon Panetta, a former congressman, privately remarked that Morris was Clinton's "flavor of the week" and would soon be gone. But it was the White House staff who had to accommodate to him, not the other way around. Clinton used Morris to subdue the others, and Clinton gave Morris the assignments that the others had failed at attempting.

Every president and especially every progressive president has had his hardened political operatives—Jefferson's John Beckley of Pennsylvania; FDR's Louis Howe; JFK's RFK. Every president needs someone who will tell him the brutal political truth and how to turn it to advantage. Of course, Clinton always had Hillary, and in 1992 he had the able James Carville. Now he had Morris. A number of White House aides were depressed by this development and increasingly focused on securing their own reputations with the media as liberal and moral. This was an antipo-

litical drama of good government in which they cast Morris as Mephisto
with a supernatural hold over the Faustian Clinton. Both the Clintons
were aware of and had disdain for these postvirgin poses, though of
course they had to keep their feelings to themselves. Hillary coined a
phrase she used whenever this syndrome appeared: "naïve surprise."

Dick Morris was an unbalanced person who helped Clinton to
achieve a political equilibrium. He was tumultuous, but he helped to restore Clinton's composure. He was egomaniacal, but he gave new authority to the White House staff. He had no regard for old patterns but did
have a sense of political history. He would consider almost any idea on its
own merits. He had neither humility nor embarrassment about proposing seemingly outlandish schemes. He broke through the crust of ortho-
doxies and paralysis. He could think in long-term frames but act
immediately. Despite his rapid-fire cynicism, he had an earnest streak
that he did his best to hide. In his own way, he was awed that he was advising the President.

Clinton's mind needed the sort of constant political calculations that
Morris naturally produced in abundance. Morris was always trying to figure complicated bank shots that Clinton liked to think about, even if he
declined the maneuver. Clinton's options had seemed to be a series of
narrowing choices; now Morris gave him an ever-widening selection. Before the 1994 election, Clinton had groped his way across treacherous
terrain, and the more advisers he had surrounded himself with, the more
he had floundered. His impulse had been to synthesize their different
points of view as though they were representative of an actual political
situation. Morris neutralized this cacophony, enabling Clinton to decide
for himself. Some people in the White House, who appreciated Morris's
effect, called it "the madman theory."

Most important, Clinton used Morris to try to do what he had intended in the first place. Morris had an idea of the presidency. He did not
think being president was to be a prime minister. He didn't really care
what congressional subcommittee chairmen thought. He understood that
the president stood above any other elected official. He believed the
president should use his bully pulpit to get the nation's other political institutions to support his program. Though Morris never saw anything in
gray, his adamancy was not absolutism. He was an opportunist who
helped Clinton to be pragmatic for good ends.

Clinton still stubbornly wanted to be acknowledged for his economic
program, but most voters didn't believe that the American economy was
improving or that the federal deficit was decreasing, despite the statistics

that showed that both were happening. He was quickly persuaded that he should not await gratitude. And he had no hesitancy in setting his own course, independent of the Democrats in Congress. Indeed, he had no choice but to do so. If he deferred to them, he would relinquish his will and diminish his office. Morris called this new strategy "triangulation"— with Clinton occupying ground separate from both the Republicans and the Democrats in the Congress. It was an ex post facto rationale for accepting the reality of the situation. Triangulation was the politics that had to be practiced in a system that separated executive and legislative powers.

If triangulation had any precedent, it was in recent French politics. Morris had worked for Jacques Chirac and his party, and had helped the conservative Chirac eventually to defeat the socialist François Mitterand for control of the National Assembly. With Talleyrand-like adroitness, President Mitterand had allowed Prime Minister Chirac to enact parts of his conservative program and thereby to exhaust his political momentum; Mitterand was reelected in 1988, defeating Chirac. Morris learned the lesson. He now proposed that Clinton play Mitterand, with Gingrich as Chirac. The strategy would be to "fast-forward the Gingrich agenda," which would make it "less appealing," Morris wrote in a memo, while offering a "Democratic way of achieving this agenda."* Clinton studied the Mitterand example, reading a political biography, and thought about ways to outfox conservatives within a divided government.

But it was not foreordained that this strategy would work in the United States. Some liberals saw Clinton's actions in 1994–95 as a sharp turn to the right. They understood his three-dimensional politics on a one-dimensional ideological plane, especially when Clinton began carving out positions on issues that had previously been wholly occupied by Republicans, notably on welfare reform and the balanced budget. His sharp movements caused misapprehension and consternation. Liberal Democrats in the Congress thought he was making compromises and betraying the party. They wanted him to adopt a program that had no chance of passage but that set up a conflict with the Republicans which, they hoped, would return them to the majority. Their perspective tended to be immediate, reactive, and overtly partisan. Republicans thought that, on the one hand, Clinton was weak, compromising, and could be rolled. On the other hand, they were startled by his new political aggression, which left them suddenly cornered just when they thought they had

*Dick Morris, *Behind the Oval Office*, Renaissance Books, 1998, pp. 37–38.

triumphed. Their message became very confused: Clinton was more Republican than Republican, yet still a dangerous liberal; he was weak *and* powerful; he had proved their points *but* was deviously undermining them. His refusal to play by the received political rules confounded them.

The Republicans dug into their trench first: they favored massive cuts in Medicare, Medicaid, and environmental and social programs—and a tax cut. But they couched these preferences in terms of achieving a balanced budget, a popular rubric that disguised the specific damage they wanted to cause. At last, they believed, they had arrived at the moment when they could begin to unravel the Great Society and even the New Deal. Their intent was to destroy the universal basis of entitlement programs. Social Security, the achievement of the New Deal, and Medicare, that of the Great Society, had been and were for everyone, rich and poor alike. Once the wealthy were removed from the programs, which provided services the affluent could easily afford themselves, the middle class would be pitted against the poor. Then Medicare and even Social Security would be underfunded and begin to crumble.

Through May and June 1995 a battle royal was fought within the White House over the strategy that would oppose these Republicans. Morris became the point man, arguing that Clinton should adopt a balanced budget—posing his own version against the Republicans'. Most of the White House staff considered this position heresy. George Stephanopoulos, in his memoir, wrote that he and other staff members, "insulted by a charlatan" (Morris) and "the assault on the integrity of our policy-making process," talked of resigning in protest. He also wrote that he had joked with others about running in the primaries against Clinton.* Many of the President's economic advisers did not favor a balanced budget either; they viewed it as an imposition of politics on economics and, as economics, a potential straitjacket. Democrats in the Congress were overwhelmingly opposed, seeing a balanced budget as Clinton's craven capitulation. But Morris's position was actually Clinton's, and it was supported by Vice President Gore as well as Hillary. In a speech of June 13, 1995, the President argued for both balancing the budget and defending social programs; the popularity of this speech gave him leverage in public opinion to outmaneuver Gingrich in the months to come. Balancing the budget established a basis for trustworthiness, overcoming public suspicion about activist government.

Along with his balanced budget proposal, Clinton put forward a plan

*George Stephanopoulos, *All Too Human*, Little, Brown, 1999, pp. 351, 347.

to "end welfare as we know it," a promise he had made in the 1992 campaign. It was on these issues that Clinton pushed back the GOP. Clinton agreed to a time limit on welfare aid, but leveraged that to obtain broad social provisions—day care, a contingency fund in case of recession, school lunches, health care for children, and food stamps. But the Republicans' refusal to budge from their plan to drop legal immigrants from all federal welfare coverage became a sticking point. Clinton didn't want to sign such a bill and agonized over it. Morris, who had been serving as the middleman with Senate Majority Leader Trent Lott, a former client, argued that signing the bill would help the Democrats capture the Congress. Much of the staff and cabinet opposed the bill as a betrayal of principle because of the time limit on welfare. Morris's relation to Lott only heightened their misgivings.

The person who carried the day for the welfare reform bill was Bruce Reed, then deputy director of domestic policy, formerly with the Democratic Leadership Council, whose expertise and integrity were respected by everyone in the White House. Reed made the case to Clinton that welfare reform was a process, not just one bill. The current bill, he said, was a good welfare reform measure wrapped in a bad budget gimmick about immigrants. In light of the health care failure, Reed's incremental and pragmatic approach appealed to Clinton.

Hillary was initially uncertain. She didn't want to interfere in the deliberations or put herself into the story. Still, she spoke with the relevant policy players, with Morris, and, most intently, with the President—hesitantly at first but then grappling with the subject wholeheartedly. She reached her own judgment, which was that he should sign the bill.

This was not an easy decision, especially considering the unwavering opposition of her friend Marian Wright Edelman, chairman of the Children's Defense Fund, on the board of which Hillary had sat. When she lived in Arkansas, that had been her chief Washington connection and the means by which she had expressed her national interest in family and children's issues. Peter Edelman, Marian's husband, was equally committed to these issues, and he was now serving as assistant secretary of Health and Human Services. He was equally opposed to the welfare reform bill, arguing in public against it. HHS even released a report stating that one million children would be forced into poverty, which HHS Secretary Donna Shalala hand-delivered to the President.

When Clinton signed the welfare reform bill in September 1995, Marian Wright Edelman denounced it as a "moment of shame." She compared Clinton's act to Hitler's method: "Everything Hitler did was legal, but it was not right." Peter Edelman resigned in protest and wrote an article about "The Worst Thing Bill Clinton Has Done."* The press interpreted the Edelmans' rupture with the Clintons as another instance of the Clintons' discarding old friendships out of ambition.

One publicly unstated factor in the President's decision was his belief that the welfare reform law would remove race as an issue from the up-coming presidential campaign and beyond. For decades, conservative politicians had exploited race by using the New Deal's and Great Soci-ety's welfare programs as a bludgeon against Democrats, whom they ac-cused of coddling the undeserving (black) poor at the expense of the hardworking (white) middle class. Ronald Reagan had made a mythical "welfare queen" driving a Cadillac a staple of his speeches. But with wel-fare reform, this coded issue, the easiest and most accepted tactic of racist politics, was mostly erased from the politics of 1996.

Clinton went on to fight to remove from the law the objectionable strictures against immigrants—and eventually he succeeded. Welfare rolls dropped by 60 percent, to the lowest level in a generation, and that decrease was almost all accounted for in increased employment. In addi-tion, Clinton fought for and won a doubling of funding for federal child care, a doubling for the Head Start preschool program, an increase in the minimum wage, and tax cuts for 15 million working poor, lifting them above the poverty level. He also launched the Welfare to Work Partner-ship, with twenty thousand companies involved, resulting in the hiring of 1.1 million former welfare recipients. According to the Census Bureau, poverty fell by 25 percent and child poverty by 30 percent under Clinton. This was the greatest decline in poverty since the Great Society had es-sentially wiped out poverty among elderly Americans. It was concen-trated among blacks, Hispanics, and female-headed households—the truly poor. (Clinton also doubled the amount of child support money collected from wayward fathers.) The number of poor dropped by 8.1 million. When the expanded government benefits were added in, the rate of poverty as measured by the Census Bureau dropped another 25 per-cent.† This effective and coherent war on poverty was deliberate; the consequences were not unintended. Only the politics seemed to be para-doxical, though not to Clinton.

*Peter Edelman, "The Worst Thing Bill Clinton Has Done," *The Atlantic Monthly*, March 1997.

†Ronald Brownstein, "From Clinton, a Promising War Plan Against Poverty," *Los Angeles Times*, October 1, 2001.

Welfare reform and the balanced budget were the two issues that decisively allowed President Clinton to undercut the Republicans and begin transforming politics. But it was not just those large questions, or even his response to the Oklahoma City bombing, that enabled Clinton to shift direction. Morris set up an operation both outside and inside the White House that fostered a new dynamic. It worked relentlessly, day by day. The central political principle was to accelerate policy. Morris, the impresario, proposed that Clinton give him five issues a week to consider. "Ten," said the President. There would be more.

The main generator of action was a brilliant, soft-spoken young lawyer, Tom Freedman, who had worked on hunger relief in Somalia and been chief of staff to Representative Charles Schumer of New York. He was a one-man think tank, generating and analyzing policy ideas. Joined with him were pollsters Mark Penn and Doug Schoen, who had begun as Harvard political science whiz kids and gone through dozens of political and corporate campaigns. Penn was quiet, methodical, factual, logical, even academic in manner. He had none of Morris's Sturm und Drang. This group meshed with Bruce Reed of the Domestic Policy Council and Donald Baer, Clinton's communications director, and became known as the "issues group."

Almost every day, beginning in 1995, the President proposed a new initiative. These were discrete, compact, and concrete ideas. Each had a definable, measurable effect and appeal; in their limited but precise nature they were the antithesis of a grand plan like universal health care. They were often criticized as "small-bore," but their impact could be dramatic. The piecemeal programs also had a cumulative effect, because added together, like pieces in a mosaic, they created an overarching design in policy area after policy area.

As the pieces were put into place, the image of Clinton as a failure was replaced by one of his effectiveness. Part of the strategy was intended to insulate Clinton from oscillations in the perception of his personality. He had been liked and disliked, and he preferred to be liked, of course. But that was not a stable basis for a presidency. He would always be a polarizing figure. So long as he made progress on issues that mattered to most voters, however, they would support him whether or not they liked him personally. By fixing on the issues, Clinton focused the public perception of him on his job performance. The public, observing the positive changes that Clinton's programs were making in their lives, gradually began to credit the idea that a new sort of active government might work. Their hostility to government was being overcome by specific actions.*

Now the President turned his attention to the 1996 campaign. He was intent on taking his case directly to the people. Rising above the din of scandal coverage and exorcising the nightmarish ghost of the health care fiasco required complete control of the message. There was only one environment for that: television advertising.

At Clinton's request, Morris assembled a team of political media specialists in 1995, and they were harnessed to the "issues group." Clinton's advertisements began running seventeen months before Election Day on November 5, 1996—an unprecedented move. Every ad, without exception, was centered on issues, comparing and contrasting the President's stance with Gingrich's and the Republicans'. By the end of 1995, on the eve of the second government shutdown, nearly half the electorate, especially in strategically important states, had seen the commercials, and almost a third had seen thirty of them. Because they were not broadcast in Washington, these early ads went almost completely unnoticed by the media. The entire country was below their radar. But Clinton was already beginning to win the election.

I began my conversations with Dick Morris sporadically at first, in late 1995, and then more regularly in 1996. We talked about all manner of politics, always meeting in his suite at the Jefferson Hotel on Sixteenth Street, a few blocks north of the White House. Morris would sit in a wing chair, occasionally falling into a breathless caricature of himself— "We're advertising in 44 percent of America and the numbers are unchanged." Around him, it was a beehive. Other people were almost always working in the suite—Tom Freedman, Mark Penn, Douglas Schoen. His fax machine was constantly receiving and spewing out memos. He would occasionally leap up to his computer to check for an e-mail or to take a note. Even when the reelection campaign began, Morris never occupied an office at the campaign headquarters in downtown Washington. He preferred to operate from his suite and never held meetings or conducted interviews anywhere else. He handed out keys to Freedman and others to come and go whenever they needed to work. It was a nerve center with room service.

President Clinton considered preparation of the State of the Union address as a central organizing experience for his staff, pulling together

*See Richard Stengel and Eric Pooley, "Masters of the Message," *Time*, November 18, 1996, pp. 81–82.

and synthesizing all the strands of his politics and policy. The address for January 1996, coming immediately after the government shutdowns, took on additional seriousness because it would set the terms for his re-election campaign that fall. Morris had suggested to the President that he organize his ideas as "challenges" to the nation—a simple technique for rolling out his policies. Morris and I discussed how to counterpose Clinton's vision of what the United States could be against the negative Republican view of how it should be governed.

We talked about the upcoming millennium. I told Morris that people always greet the end of a century with anticipation. Just as the impingement of time can spur an urge for a final battle, it can have the opposite effect: the coming of the millennium could also be a time of possibility, ushering in a new era. Rather than running out, time could be starting over. Reconciliation and renewal could overcome the forces of chaos. Things weren't falling apart but coming together. Society wasn't decaying but discovering new sources of energy. Against the Republican gloom, Clinton could, once again, offer hope. He would monopolize optimism about the future. I pointed out that by happenstance the Olympic Games would be taking place in Atlanta during the election year—an opportunity to highlight millennial brightness and confidence and American teamwork meeting new global challenges.

Three days before the President was due to deliver the State of the Union, he and I discussed his thinking for about an hour. He felt he had failed adequately to communicate a lasting message during his battle for his economic plan. Voters didn't think that anyone could do anything about wages and family income, and they were flat wrong, Clinton said, but how could he dismiss their skepticism? He believed he had to speak to their fears and mistrust. He had to present "the paradigm of what I represent," he said, in terms of a balanced budget, a smaller federal government—and new programs. Then these voters would begin to give credence to an activist government and Democratic policies that were working on their behalf.

I thought he could capture the idea of the American union in one phrase: one America. After their 1994 congressional victory and the way in which they had forced the government to shut down, Gingrich and the Republicans represented divisiveness and extreme partisanship; their contempt for the federal government obviously wasn't abstract; and they could not easily claim to stand for the whole country. To use "One America" as the guiding theme was a way for President Clinton to set himself as the leader of the nation, heading a federal government serving all sections of the country. It also suggested the importance of forging a unified country out of an increasingly diverse people. "One America" was an updating of "E pluribus unum."

I had thought of the phrase as deriving from the British Tory idea of "one nation," a paternalistic method of providing for social welfare to trump class appeals, an approach Benjamin Disraeli expressed in his novel *Sybil* and practiced as prime minister. But "one-nation" politics could be American politics. Clinton had to reclaim a liberal position against both the antigovernment right and the fractious identity politics of the left.

Clinton began his State of the Union address in a no-nonsense way, reciting economic figures: "We have the lowest combined rates of unemployment and inflation in twenty-seven years." This was, in fact, the first time the vast majority of the American people had ever heard this plain truth, and the President's presentation of the statistics changed public perception of the economy. Clinton went on to evoke "an age of possibility"—a new industrial revolution based on "information and global competition." He posed three great "challenges": to create opportunity for everyone, to reconcile Americans' "enduring values" with the demands of the future, and to meet "these challenges together, as one America."

Clinton wasted no time in speaking to the polarizing question of government: "The era of big government is over," he declared. It became the most famous line in his speech. To some liberals, this seemed like a dismaying break with Democratic Party tradition, but they should have remembered the lines immediately following: "But we cannot go back to the time when our citizens were left to fend for themselves. Instead, we must go forward as one America, one nation working together to meet the challenges we face together. Self-reliance and teamwork are not opposing virtues; we must have both." By retiring the image of government from a generation ago, Clinton was trying to give people a chance to see activist government in a new light. He was making political space for his presidency by setting it as the fresh alternative to a one-sided Republicanism at war with the old liberalism. In a stroke he made the Republican ferocity seem overwrought and even ridiculous.

He then proposed a blizzard of new programs: college tax credits and student grants, connecting every school to the Internet, portable health insurance, community policing, job training, an increase in the minimum wage and the earned-income tax credit for the working poor, and more environmental protection.

Clinton waited until near the end of his speech to trump the Republicans' ace: the general issue of government. He pointed out that the size of the federal workforce had shrunk by two hundred thousand on his watch and that the number of government employees was the smallest in thirty years: "Most of our fellow Americans probably don't know that." The reason, he said, was that those employees were "working harder and working smarter." He gestured to the First Lady's box above the Congress, where she sat with invited special guests. The President singled out one of them, an exemplary federal worker named Richard Dean: "He is a forty-nine-year-old Vietnam veteran who's worked for the Social Security Administration for twenty-two years now. Last year he was hard at work in the Federal Building in Oklahoma City when the blast killed 169 people and brought the rubble down all around him. He reentered that building four times. He saved the lives of three women. He's here with us this evening, and I want to recognize Richard and applaud both his public service and his extraordinary personal heroism." The entire Congress, Democrats and Republicans alike, gave him an ovation.

But this was only half the story. Having gotten the Republicans to applaud Richard Dean, he told the rest:

> But Richard Dean's story doesn't end there. This last November, he was forced out of his office when the government shut down. And the second time the government shut down he continued helping Social Security recipients, but he was working without pay. On behalf of Richard Dean and his family, and all the other people who are out there working every day doing a good job for the American people, I challenge all of you in this Chamber: Never, ever shut the federal government down again.

The Democrats roared; the Republicans silently glowered.

Then the peroration. The President pointed again to the First Lady's box, and also to two people sitting with her who would be the first to carry the Olympic torch across the country to Atlanta. The Olympics became a metaphor for him to draw Americans together, to recast progressive politics:

> Now, each of us must hold high the torch of citizenship in our own lives. None of us can finish the race alone. We can only achieve our destiny together—one hand, one generation, one American connecting to another. There have always been things we could do together—dreams we could make real—which we could never have done on our own. We Americans have forged our identity, our very union, from every point of view and

every point on the planet, every different opinion. But we must be bound together by a faith more powerful than any doctrine that divides us—by our belief in progress, our love of liberty, and our relentless search for common ground. America has always sought and always risen to every challenge. Who would say that, having come so far together, we will not go forward from here?

And then he hit the last note: "God bless the *United* States of America."

II

President Clinton lost and then gained his footing in both domestic and foreign policy at roughly the same times. The tracks ran parallel. Just as he had hit a low point with the failure of health care in 1993, he had also reached the nadir in foreign policy with the humiliating retreat of the USS *Harlan County* from Port au Prince. Similarly, just as he began to recover at home with the battle over the budget, he also started to gain control internationally, first in Haiti and then in Bosnia.

The situation in Haiti after the withdrawal of the USS *Harlan County* had continued to be fraught with danger and violence. The military strongmen massacred their countrymen and refused to acknowledge the international opprobrium. Clinton had finally settled on September 19, 1994, as the certain deadline by which time General Raoul Cedras had to leave Haiti and turn it over to its elected president, Jean-Bertrand Aristide. A delegation was dispatched to deliver the news: Jimmy Carter, who had contacts in Haiti through his peripatetic peacemaking ventures; former senator Sam Nunn; and the recently retired Colin Powell. They arrived with less than two days to convince General Cedras and his retinue of the President's seriousness, and Cedras stalled. The deadline passed. The diplomatic trio believed they were on the verge of getting Cedras's assent when the President called from Washington to inform them that an armed force of American troops was under way and would shortly land. In total panic, Cedras collapsed and fled into exile. Fifteen thousand troops landed without incident. This turnabout in the Caribbean preceded the midterm elections in the United States, and it had no effect on their catastrophic outcome for the Democrats. But the making of Clinton's recovery in foreign policy was already developing its own momentum, next accelerated by inescapable pressures in Bosnia.

The Serbs were determined that 1995 would be the last year of the war and the effective end of Bosnia as an independent entity. They invaded the so-called safe areas supposedly protected by UNPROFOR and engaged in a concentrated war to eliminate the Bosnian Muslims: a massive ethnic cleansing. Clinton insisted that air strikes should be targeted on the Serb positions. When a few were made in late May, the Serbs held UNPROFOR troops hostage, even chaining some of them to trees and telephone poles. Eventually the troops were released, and the Allied command decided to stop the bombing and issued a statement proclaiming that UNPROFOR would return to "traditional peacekeeping." Now nothing stood in the way of the Serbs. In July, the Bosnian Serb army, working with the Serbs, captured Srebrenica, a town filled with tens of thousands of refugees from the region. UNPROFOR troops were pushed aside; women and children were bused out; and 7,079 men were systematically killed within a week. This was the greatest act of mass murder in Europe since the end of the Second World War.

Clinton angrily demanded that the Allied command adopt a new policy. In August, after the massacre at Srebrenica, UN Ambassador Albright sent him a frank memo that he took to heart. "Fairly or unfairly, your entire first term is going to be judged by how you deal with Bosnia," she wrote. (Clinton had also been reading a new book—Noel Malcolm's *Bosnia*, which argued that the problems there were caused by Milosevic's political manipulations—that was a bracing antidote to Robert Kaplan's fatalistic thesis in *Balkan Ghosts*.) At the same time, President Jacques Chirac, affronted by the dishonor visited upon the French soldiers in UNPROFOR and the Serbs' massacres, wondered aloud if there was a true leader in the Western alliance. With U.S. encouragement, the Croat army in August launched an invasion of Serbian Krajina, and NATO began a full-scale bombing operation to drive the Serbs off the hilltops above Sarajevo, where they were heavily invested.*

Milosevic sued for peace. Clinton sent Richard Holbrooke, a skilled and tough diplomat who was then assistant secretary of state for European affairs, to implement an agreement. Holbrooke was an aggressive player who threw elbows on the field.

At Dayton, Ohio, where the NATO negotiators met with the Serbs, Croatians, and Bosnians to work out a treaty with Milosevic, Holbrooke succeeded against considerable odds in brokering an agreement. NATO replaced UNPROFOR in the Balkans, and Clinton sent twenty thousand

---

*Ivo H. Daalder, "Decision to Intervene: How the War in Bosnia Ended," *Foreign Service Journal*, December 1998.

U.S. troops to join its forces there. American public opinion did not favor this commitment, and the House Republican leaders, with the exception of Newt Gingrich, refused to support it. But with the signing of the Dayton Peace Accords, peace was enforced. Clinton had arrived at a workable, coherent strategy using U.S. leadership to gain Allied cooperation; airpower; an army (largely provided by others, in this case the Croats and the Bosnians); and hard diplomacy. It was a formula that would work again in the Kosovo war.

Various earlier attempts to define Clinton's foreign policy had fallen flat. Albright had used the term "multilateralism" to describe the Somalia expedition, but although its tragic ending had hardly meant that multilateral cooperation was dead—it was essential to U.S. policy—it was temporarily discredited. National Security Adviser Tony Lake had proposed "neo-Wilsonian internationalism," an awkward phrase, academic and abstract, that, while seemingly high-minded, failed to explain anything beyond America's good intentions, a vague aspiration to morality, and U.S. engagement.

The actual difficulties encountered during Clinton's first term punctured this rhetoric and also provoked dismissive criticism. Michael Mandelbaum, a friend of Clinton's going back to his days as a Rhodes scholar, when Mandelbaum had been at Cambridge University (he had turned down offers to serve as director of policy planning at the State Department and was a professor at the Johns Hopkins School for Advanced International Studies), in early 1996 wrote an influential article in which he said, "President Clinton's foreign policy, rather than protecting American national interests, has pursued social work worldwide. Three failed interventions in 1993—in Bosnia, in Somalia, and the first try in Haiti—illustrate this dramatically. . . . With his domestic policy stalled, Clinton's opponents may end up painting him what he never wanted to be: a foreign policy president."* Mandelbaum's disdain expressed the views of a certain slice of elite opinion, but by the time his article appeared it had been outpaced by events. U.S. troops were now patrolling the peace in Bosnia. Still, Clinton's actions lacked a larger, easily graspable explanation.

In 1993, at the first summit meetings that Clinton had attended of the Group of Seven nations and of the Asian Pacific American Council, other leaders had lectured him about the drag that the U.S. economy was on

*Michael Mandelbaum, "Foreign Policy as Social Work," *Foreign Affairs*, January/February 1996.

the rest of the world. By 1996, the turnaround of the U.S. economy and the decline in the federal deficit had silenced those complaints. The platform that prosperity now gave Clinton was global.

And the position of the United States was unique in world history. With the collapse of the Soviet empire, there was no competing power. No European nation equaled the United States, nor did the European Union. If anything, the disgraceful behavior of Britain and France in dealing with the Bosnian crisis had made it clear that Europe could not assume military responsibilities without the United States. And in every respect, the power of the United States was greater than any of the empires of the nineteenth century had been, which had competed with each other in a global struggle that was an extension of the European balance of power. And in any case the U.S. wasn't an empire in the old sense: it was not a mother country with colonies that exported their raw materials to it. Under Clinton, it was a power for free markets, democracy, and development. "Now, at the end of the twentieth century," Clinton was to say in 1999, "we face a great battle between the forces of integration and the forces of disintegration, the forces of globalism versus tribalism, of oppression against empowerment. And the phenomenal explosion of technology, including that of advanced weaponry, might be the servant of either side—or both." But he had not yet reached that concise, even prophetic formulation.

In thinking about foreign policy, especially after the Bosnian war, I talked about the problem of U.S. power in the post–Cold War world with my friend James Chace, who was writing a biography of Dean Acheson. The architect of U.S. policy after the Second World War as Truman's secretary of state, Acheson had been, as he entitled his memoir, "present at the creation" of a new global order. Once again, we were at a moment when something new could be created. And again, we had to arrive at policies that fused America's national values and its interest. In my conversations with James, I hit upon a phrase: the indispensable nation. Only the United States had the power to guarantee global security: without our presence or support, multilateral endeavors would fail. I mentioned the phrase in 1996 first to James Rubin, Albright's aide, who had been a friend since 1986, when he came to Washington to work at the Arms Control Association and then as an aide on the Senate Foreign Relations Committee. Soon, "indispensable nation" began appearing in Secretary Albright's speeches. (In 2000, the French foreign minister Hubert Védrine started referring to the United States as the "hyperpower," by which he meant a United States that, he presumed, would be an overbearing power dictating to others. This French version, more theoretical and with an edge of ironic resentment and hauteur, was a backhanded tribute to the same concept.)

In July 1996, the Khobar Towers, where U.S. armed forces at the Dharhan military base in Saudi Arabia lived, were bombed; nineteen people died. No group claimed responsibility, and the Saudi government blocked FBI men sent to investigate the crime, though years later it conceded that Osama bin Laden's al-Qaeda had been involved. Then on July 27, at the Olympic Games in Atlanta, Georgia, a pipe bomb exploded in Centennial Park, killing two. (The FBI arrested Richard Jewell, a guard who had identified a bag as the bomb and moved people to safety. After a two-month trial by ordeal in the media, Jewell was completely exonerated. Eric Rudolph, an antiabortion terrorist, was eventually charged, but he escaped arrest while Jewell was held.)

Clinton had spoken many times to the country about terrorism. In 1995 he had also discussed it at the General Assembly of the United Nations and in 1996 at the G-7 summit at Lyons, and he had convened a Summit of Peacemakers in Egypt, a meeting of regional and world leaders devoted to counterterrorism and Middle Eastern peace. But the Republican Congress still had not passed crucial pieces of Clinton's antiterrorist legislation. So Clinton decided to give another speech about terrorism, a major address on the subject at George Washington University on August 5, 1996. "Fascism and communism may be dead or discredited," he said, "but the forces of destruction live on." Terrorists could turn our technology against us: "We must recognize that modern technologies by themselves will not make for us a new world of peace and freedom. Technology can be used for good or evil." But to eliminate it required U.S. leadership:

> The fact is America remains the indispensable nation. . . . There are times when America, and only America, can make a difference between war and peace, between freedom and repression, between hope and fear. Of course, we can't take on all the world's burdens. We cannot become its policeman. But where our interests and values demand it, and where we can make a difference, America must act—and lead. . . .
>
> But I want to make it clear to the American people that while we can defeat terrorists, it will be a long time before we defeat terrorism. America will remain a target because we are uniquely present in the world . . . and because we are the most open society on Earth. . . . In this fight, as in

so many other challenges around the world, American leadership is indispensable.

In his peroration, he called on the country "to stand strong against the moments of terror that would destroy our spirit, to stand for the values that have brought us so many blessings, values that have made us, at this pivotal moment, the indispensable nation."

"One America" had been Clinton's assertive answer to the danger of national division after the tragedy of Oklahoma City. "Indispensable nation" was his response to foreign threats after Bosnia and the Khobar Towers bombing. These phrases were not mere slogans. The words mattered. They expressed the mastery the Clinton presidency was exerting over policy and politics. They were ideas that only he could express from his experience in office. And they struck basic chords.

III

After a Christmas party in the White House in December 1995, the President asked me up to the residence for a nightcap. The Clintons and I discussed the upcoming campaign for the Republican presidential nomination. Colin Powell's memoir had just been published, and Clinton wondered if he would run even though he had announced a month earlier that he wouldn't. Hillary, for her part, feared that Lamar Alexander, former governor of Tennessee, would emerge as a front-runner. Both Powell and Alexander were moderates who could challenge Clinton for the center. But the Clintons' concerns about either Powell or Alexander were rooted in a rational hypothesis that misjudged the nature of the Republican Party. The dignified and self-protective Powell, in any case, had no stomach for the depredations of a long political campaign; he also knew that his liberal positions on social policy were contrary to Republican dogma. The suggestions that he might run for national office, which he encouraged by his smiling nondenials, were a special boost for his book. The President had mistaken a publicity campaign for a political one. Lamar Alexander, meanwhile, was running an issueless campaign, trying to finesse the GOP's ideological rightward tilt through sheer image. He eventually won no primaries and was an early casualty. The Clintons' fears about the President's having to run against a moderate Republican were based on a logical but strangely nonpolitical belief that the Republicans would come to their senses.

Deference often has an effect in Republican Party presidential selection as great as ideology. The question of who is next in line looms large. For a long time, Senator Robert Dole had felt he was next. His strongest political feelings were reserved for those who had thwarted his rise within his party. He referred to himself constantly in the third person. As far as he was concerned, Bob Dole had earned the nomination the only way he knew: the hard way.

Dole grew up in Russell, Kansas, during the Depression, living in the basement of his own house while the upstairs was rented out. His father ran a cream and egg station; his mother sold sewing machines. Young Bob and his brother arose every morning at four to do the chores. Dole was a star high-school athlete and went to the state university; but then he found himself wounded, near death, on an Italian battlefield. He spent about a year in a rehabilitation hospital trying to regain the partial use of his shattered right arm. He never disguised his eternal bitterness. His sardonic sense of humor, which could assert itself at any moment, often led to a surprising, dark punch line.

Dole was a politician's politician. He was a Midwestern conservative of a very particular time—a postwar isolationist of the pre-Reagan period. He was a harsh partisan who would cut deals. And his resentments allowed him to identify with the less favored in life. With George McGovern, he cosponsored legislation that established food stamps (not a startling move for a senator from an agricultural state), and on civil rights he remained under the impression that the GOP was still the party of Lincoln. He didn't want to create a movement; he wanted to be stamped acceptable by his party. He didn't want to be new or different; he wanted seniority and the powers that came with it.

Richard Nixon had been the dominant Republican of his generation, and Dole aspired to Nixon's position within the party, leveraging each against all to advance himself to the top. Nixon had raised Dole up, appointing him as chairman of the Republican National Committee, had used him as a hatchet man, and had then abruptly replaced him with the fresh, innocent face of well-born George H. W. Bush, who had not, in Dole's estimation, earned his position.

In 1976, when President Ford named Dole his running mate, Dole distinguished himself in the vice-presidential debate by bitterly railing that "1.6 million Americans" in the twentieth century had been killed in "Democrat wars." In 1980, he thought that he was entitled to preference for the presidential nomination, having been number two on the ticket four years earlier. He ran against Reagan and finished eighth. Dole held

President Reagan's supply-side tax cuts in contempt, for they produced deficits that offended Dole's deeply ingrained agrarian revulsion to debt. Reagan's sunny California temperament rankled him. Dole dismissed his politics as "the easy way" that only "bitter medicine" could cure.

In 1988, Dole, encouraged privately by Nixon, ran against Bush. Commending himself to the crowds, he said, "Nobody gave him [Dole] anything." He urged "pain" to overcome Reagan's happy-pill deficits. A desperate Bush, falling behind in the New Hampshire primary, placed his fate in Lee Atwater's dirty hands and hit Dole with a barrage of negative ads. After Bush had eked out the win, Dole was interviewed on NBC News; he glowered and said, "Stop lying about my record."

As soon as Bill Clinton was elected in 1992, Dole had a new joke: "The good news is he's getting a honeymoon in Washington. The bad news is that Bob Dole is going to be his chaperon." This punch line had it all: the banality, the third-person self-reference, and the sharp careen into bleakness. But Dole really didn't dislike Clinton, who, unlike Bush, had done nothing against him. Clinton was just there.

In 1996 Dole was caught between his ambition to gain the Republican nomination, to which he believed he had been long entitled, and his senatorial instinct to get laws enacted. He had agreed early on with the new president that the health care "crisis" needed attending to. (Years before, under Nixon, Dole had favored a similar health insurance plan.) But when the whole Republican Party swiveled against Clinton to deny him any victory, Dole rushed to get to its head. He had prided himself on being a master of the Senate, and now he turned his legislative skills to the purpose of blocking everything. His weapon was the filibuster.

For decades, the filibuster had been the tactic of choice of the Dixiecrats to stop civil rights bills. Dole adapted it for use against everything. Before the 1994 elections, Dole had the Republicans filibuster forty-eight times to stop legislation on campaign finance reform, on crime, on the creation of economic stimuli, and anything else Clinton proposed. He even invoked filibusters to stop bills moving to conference, an unprecedented action. "There has been total obstruction," said Senator George Mitchell, the Democratic majority leader. The point was to frustrate Clinton's goals. Whether Bob Dole might agree with them on the merits didn't enter into it.*

---

*Sarah Binder, "Going Nowhere: A Gridlocked Congress?" *The Brookings Review*, Winter 2000; Dan Goodgame, "The High Price of Gridlock," *Time*, October 10, 1994.

Elevated after the midterm elections of 1994 to majority leader, Dole was once again moving up the party ladder, and he was eager to get to the next rung. But the success of his filibusters had also helped to bring in a Republican House and another Republican leader: Newt Gingrich. There was nothing Dole liked less than a Republican rival, and Dole had held Gingrich in contempt ever since he had appeared on the scene. Gingrich possessed many of the traits Dole despised: he was a talker, not a doer, an egotist who hadn't earned the right to be so proud. The contempt was mutual. "Bob Dole is devoid of any vision," said Gingrich. And "Bob Dole never met a tax hike he didn't like." And "The tax collector for the welfare state." After he became Speaker of the House, Gingrich suspected Dole wanted to act like a politician and pass laws. Dole believed he was in charge, but he was at Gingrich's mercy. He hated being in meetings with him. "I don't want to sit there for an hour and listen to his 'worldview,' " he complained to other Republicans when he skipped the meetings.

Clinton was also a practical politician like Dole. And during 1995 he finally figured out how to bond with him. He would joke with him about which one would have to talk to Gingrich: "You talk to him," said Clinton. "No," replied Dole. "You talk to him."* Shutting down the government had not been anything that Dole would have imagined, much less approved. But his earlier filibusters had been minishutdowns and had prepared the path for Gingrich. Now Gingrich dragged Dole along with him. Dole couldn't deal his way out of being chained to Gingrich.

Still, Dole thought that at last the presidential nomination he deserved was his. He was the oldest candidate ever to run for the presidency, but that meant he had earned it. But just when his obvious rivals collapsed, the farouche Pat Buchanan, calling for a "peasant revolt," upset him in New Hampshire. Humiliated by a candidate who stood no chance of winning, Dole stumbled from victory to victory. In Arizona, he sought the endorsement of Barry Goldwater, eighty-seven years old. In 1994, while the Gingrich Republicans were gaining strength, Goldwater had denounced the new right-wing zealots of the Republican Party. "The radical right has nearly ruined our party," he said. "Its members do not care about the Constitution and they are the ones making all the noise."†

*Sidney Blumenthal, "Don't Ever Change," *The New Yorker*, February 12, 1996.
†Sidney Blumenthal, "Pitchfork Rebellion," *The New Yorker*, March 25, 1996; Michael Murphy, "Conservative Pioneer Became an Outcast," *The Arizona Republic*, May 31, 1998.

He despised their intrusions into personal liberty and their absolutism. Now Goldwater bestowed his blessing on Dole and remarked, "We're the new liberals of the Republican Party." "Barry and I—we've sort of become the liberals," Dole stammered, uttering the forbidden "L" word. "Can you imagine that?" cracked Goldwater.

Having secured the nomination in a needless bloodletting (his own), Dole returned to the Senate in the spring of 1996 and tried to wage his presidential campaign on the floor, where he was presumably master, by proposing to repeal a gasoline tax. Democrats simply tacked a minimum-wage increase to his bill, which they knew many Republicans would not support. Dole's tactic of gridlock was turned against him, and the legislative gears were grinding his candidacy to dust. On May 15, Dole quit the Senate. But the end of his congressional career was not like the loss of another primary. He had misplayed what mattered most to him. Something large had ended on something small. Dole had run for vice president twenty years before. He had campaigned three times for the presidential nomination. No longer surrounded by the institution of the Senate, where he had spent much of his adult life, and alone on the pedestal, he had no idea what he wanted to say. He had brokered himself into a deal that wasn't susceptible to legislative maneuver.

He found himself, a month after leaving the Senate, campaigning in Bakersfield, California, where he was trying to develop a stump speech.* "My wife was here six days last week, and she'll be back next week, and she does an outstanding job," he began. "And when I'm elected, she will not be in charge of health care. Don't worry about it. Or in charge of anything else." The crowd noticeably gasped. "I didn't say that," Dole continued. "It did sort of go through my mind. But she may have a little blood bank in the White House. [Elizabeth Dole was head of the Red Cross.] But that's all right. We need it. It doesn't cost you anything. These days, it's not all you give at the White House—your blood. You have to give your file." He was referring to the pseudoscandal of misrouted FBI files. "I keep wondering if mine's down there." Then he digressed further. "Or my dog. I got a dog named Leader. I'm not certain they've got a file on Leader. He's a schnauzer. I think he's been cleared. We've had him checked by the vet, but not by the FBI or the White House. He may be suspect, but in any event, we'll get into that later." Dole decided to let his audience know that he knew that what he was saying was inane: "Animal rights or something of that kind. But this is a very serious election."

*See Blumenthal, "Pitchfork Rebellion."

One of Dole's favorite butts of contempt over the years had been Representative Jack Kemp, an insistent advocate of supply-side tax cuts, whose career as great right hope was constantly promoted on *The Wall Street Journal's* editorial page. Kemp was a former Buffalo Bills quarterback, secretary of housing and urban development in the Bush administration, and a congressman. "Played without a helmet," said Dole. "A bus filled with supply-side economists went off a cliff," he began one joke. Then the punch line: "That's the good news. There were three empty seats. That's the bad news." Lagging far behind Clinton and lacking an issue, Dole needed something to create interest. So he named Kemp as his running mate. Not only that, he picked up the supply-side banner he had besmirched for decades and claimed it as his own. Suddenly, he announced that his platform was a 15 percent flat tax cut.

In his acceptance speech at the Republican convention, Dole tried to turn his age into an asset. "Age has its advantages," he said. "Let me be the bridge to an America that only the unknowing call myth. Let me be the bridge to a time of tranquility, faith, and confidence in action. And to those who say it was never so, that America has not been better, I say, you're wrong, and I know, because I was there. And I have seen it. And I remember." But what time he was remembering he never made clear. Was it the Depression? Or when Democrats held the White House, including the president who commanded one of those "Democrat wars"? This golden-hued nostalgia was new to Dole's rhetorical repertoire. The past, after all, had damaged and disfigured him. Heartfelt calls for "bitter medicine" and "pain" came more naturally to him. Whatever nostalgia he intended to elicit, he called attention to a new figure of speech: a bridge.

This was an invitation to Clinton. He now had a metaphor to make his millennial theme: he would "build a bridge to the twenty-first century." If Dole wanted to go backward, Clinton would take the country forward. If Dole were imprecise, Clinton would reel off program after program.

Nothing Dole did during his campaign against Clinton gained him an inch. The 15 percent tax cut was unwanted by the public, beginning to bask in a long period of prosperity. Kemp also failed to act as a hatchet man, as Dole had done for Gerald Ford; he was a rare figure on the right who spoke without vituperation. He could not be shaken from his good nature, a happy-go-lucky jock tossing his panaceas around like practice passes. On issues, he was barely distinguishable from Gingrich, but in temperament he was his opposite. When Kemp debated with Al Gore without indulging in angry accusations, conservative Republicans were furious. *The Washington Times*, on October 11, headlined its editorial "Civility, the Loser's Virtue." Dole and Kemp were severely taken to task: "Of course, Mr. Clinton and Mr. Gore want the campaign to be fought on the issues. . . . What we need is not civility, but a higher standard of vitriol. . . . [The Republican candidates] should remind themselves that the phony 'civility' they have been laboring under is the virtue of losers."

"Where's the outrage?" Dole demanded. His befuddlement became his slogan, repeated every day. The "outrage" he wanted the American people to express was about possibly irregular contributions to the Democratic campaign by Asian donors and fund-raisers. But Dole was hardly a perfect vehicle to carry the Republicans' righteous message about campaign finance. In 1993, the Federal Election Commission had levied the largest civil penalty ever imposed on a presidential campaign against Dole's 1988 effort. (His campaign had had to admit its extensive violations of electoral law, such as taking contributions from corporations, illegally using corporate jets, and violating state-by-state spending limits. It paid a fine of $100,000.) And in October 1996, Dole's vice chairman for campaign finance pled guilty to seventy-four counts of violations of campaign finance law and he and his company were fined $6 million for illegally funneling money to Dole's campaign. Yet Dole was unabashed in attacking Clinton's "public ethics." (This issue gave a last-minute cause to Ross Perot's bedraggled Reform Party campaign.)

Clinton had encouraged the Democrats in an aggressive fund-raising effort in 1995–96—in private he would disdainfully insist the party did not believe in "unilateral disarmament"—in great part in response to the defeat in the health care battle in which the imbalance in television-ad spending was a factor. He never wanted to be outspent again. He never wanted to rely on the media, which were driven by their own agenda, to carry his message. The Republicans' campaign doctrine was to go negative early, spend the most on late advertising, and insulate themselves from attack by blaming the opponent for violations they had committed themselves. Clinton revolutionized presidential campaigning by starting with paid advertisements that were always pegged to issues, and to do this more than a year before the election. His commercials never presented a negative message without first presenting positively his own position.

"Where's the outrage?" Dole's grasping at the campaign finance issues was a protest against Clinton's superior campaign. Clinton himself parried the charge. "No attack ever created a job or educated a child or helped a family make ends meet," he said in his second debate with Dole. He also supported campaign finance reform, which Dole and the Republican Party leaders opposed.

The late claim of "outrage" was of no help to Dole's chances. He failed to move a single point from Clinton's column to his. "The entire Dole campaign, in other words, did not drop Bill Clinton's vote at all," Dick Morris wrote.* But it had an immediate and continuing effect, in that it contributed to the Democrats' narrow failure to regain the House of Representatives. In the closing days of the campaign, Clinton rearranged his itinerary to campaign for House and Senate candidates, but his efforts fell short and ended up slightly driving down his own overall final vote total to 49 percent. If he had kept to his schedule, he would have unquestionably raised himself to above 50 percent.

"Where's the outrage?" Campaign finance was a proximate cause for reinventing the "character issue." Though Dole ended up being badly beaten, Republicans clung to the notion that Clinton was still an illegitimate president. Bored with the predictable outcome, the media seized upon the Republicans' charges and avidly pursued them. Congressional Republicans launched numerous investigations into Democratic (but not Republican) practices and fed them to the media, which were insatiably hungry for scandal. The pseudoscandal cycle was renewed. A handful of people who had helped to raise Democratic funds, all of Asian background, were eventually found to have violated laws, but no quid pro quo or violation of any kind involving Clinton or any official in the administration was ever involved. All the charges were revealed to be empty. Soon the focus was turned on Vice President Gore, the next in line.

Dole's campaign was the last hurrah of the Nixon wing of the Republican Party, and his removal from the scene left all factions other than Gingrich's headless. Dole's defeat was also the coda for Republican triumphalism. Within two years, from Election Day 1994 to Election Day 1996, the GOP had gone from political intoxication to depletion. "Where's the outrage?" was a slogan that well expressed the Republicans' anger at their squandered situation. They made no mention of the discarded and discredited Contract with America. Dole's loss confirmed the party's political bankruptcy and inflamed the right's zeal. Gingrich's career, in contrast to Dole's old-fashioned regular Republicanism, was based on scandal-mongering, and now, with Dole gone, Gingrich and his Southern fire-eaters were largely unrestrained.

*Morris, *Behind the Oval Office*, p. 277.

On election night, Hillary Clinton telephoned me from Little Rock as she and the President prepared to go before the crowd there to acknowledge his victory. She told me that with his triumph she believed the pseudoscandals would recede and the business of governing would be conducted on a more rational basis. We had reversed roles. Usually I was the optimist and she the pessimist. But swept up in the emotion of the evening, she thought, at least momentarily, that reason would now prevail. "It's going to be all right," she said.

FIVE

Hillary Under Siege

I

I first met Hillary the same time I met Bill Clinton in 1987. But I did not come to know her until we had lunch together during the Illinois primary in March 1992. We shared very similar backgrounds: only a year apart in age, from entrepreneurial middle-class Chicago families, and college in the Boston area. At that lunch, she spoke candidly about how difficult it was to present herself as a professional woman on the campaign trail. Afterward, I gave her a copy of a biography of Franklin D. Roosevelt, *A First-Class Temperament* by Geoffrey C. Ward, describing the emergence of his and Eleanor's personalities as the people we recognized. We talked about that book and many other subjects throughout the campaign. And then in mid-1994, around the time of the demise of the health care initiative, we became genuine friends. Hillary had not taken up another large domestic issue after health care's defeat, but that had not diminished the attacks on her as a political figure. The machinery of scandal, tripped into motion long before, had revved up, especially during the election campaign. Hillary privately divided the scandal-mongering into phases as though it were a disease—"acute" and "chronic."

The incident that began the most recent "acute" phase had been the authoritative exoneration of the Clintons in the Whitewater affair in December 1995. The looming shadow of their innocence had provoked the Office of Independent Counsel into hurried media manipulations, which created a wall-to-wall explosion of screaming headlines, newsweekly covers, and television specials. These animadversions of Hillary were of a scheming lawyer, liar, and crook. Her greed for money and power, so it went, was the driving force behind the Clintons' rise. Now she had to protect and hide the corrupt deals, including the deal that was her marriage; follow one lie with another and then another; face the next revelation that would cause her stonewalling to crumble on her; and deal with the final exposure that would reveal the sheer ambition and lack of principle at the core of the Clinton presidency. Not even an official exoneration had an effect on the symptoms, nor, incredibly, would an utterly clear statement about the President's innocence from the Independent Counsel in open court. It would be wrong to say that conjecture in the media swamped the basic facts because those facts were not reported. The facts would have upset the way they were telling the story, so there were no facts.

On December 13, 1995, the Resolution Trust Corporation released its long-awaited and dreaded supplemental report on Whitewater. This was the result of the inquiry directed by the Republican Jay Stephens, a former U.S. attorney, and his law firm, Pillsbury, Madison and Sutro. Stephens's appointment had led to a round of anxiety within the administration and then a round of investigation by the Congress and the Office of Independent Counsel about the anxiety. But all fears from the White House turned out to be misplaced. The report completely and categorically absolved the Clintons—and answered all outstanding questions about Whitewater.

The RTC report stated that it had in its possession "essentially all of the documents regarding Whitewater" relevant to the Clintons. It dismissed "speculation" that had appeared in the press about Clinton's supposed conversation with Jim McDougal: "There is no basis to assert that the Clintons knew anything of substance" about the McDougals' Whitewater actions. On the question raised by "the press and others" as to whether the Clintons had been passive investors, the report said this was "not the issue" and had no "legal" content whatsoever. It concluded emphatically, "On this record, there is no basis to charge the Clintons with any kind of primary liability for fraud or intentional misconduct. This investigation has revealed no evidence to support any such claims. Nor would the record support any claim of secondary or derivative liability for the possible misdeeds of others."

The report made a point of puncturing the conspiracy theories: "There are legal theories by which one can become liable for the conduct of others—e.g., conspiracy and aiding and abetting. On this evidentiary record, however, these theories have no application to the Clintons. . . . There is no evidence here that the Clintons had any such knowledge or intent. Accordingly, there is no basis to sue them." And its final words were addressed to the independent prosecutor and all other government agencies: "It is recommended," said the report, that apart from the cases being pursued by the prosecutor against the McDougals and Arkansas governor Jim Guy Tucker (on a matter unrelated to Whitewater), "no further resources need be expended on the Whitewater part of this investigation."*

In brief, every one of the accusations against the Clintons was false. The facts as laid out in the report confirmed Hillary's account and discredited the manufactured theories about the Clintons' guilt. The investigation had studied more than two hundred thousand documents and interviewed forty-five witnesses, including the Clintons. The report contained hundreds of documents and thousands of footnotes. And the facts were irrefutable. Moreover, Jay Stephens had no motive to go soft. If he put his stamp of approval on the Clintons' exoneration, he must have been certain.

Understandably, the Clintons had been pleased. At last, they were vindicated. The White House sent out copies of the report to more than 150 news organizations. Then, nothing happened. If the report had been launched into outer space it would have received more coverage. *The Wall Street Journal* ran a straightforward article in its news pages. But days passed and nothing appeared in *The Washington Post* and *The New York Times*. No network broadcast any report. As it happened, the *Post* never mentioned it, and almost two weeks later, in an item in the Sunday "News of the Week in Review," the *Times* published only a few lines, and somewhat misleading ones at that.†

During an earlier "acute" phase, editors and reporters had clamored for more than a year that the Clintons, especially Hillary, were stonewalling. They had said the Clintons' refusal to release documents to the media only proved the accusation and justified the conjectural cover-

---

*Pillsbury, Madison and Sutro, "Madison Guaranty Savings & Loan and Whitewater Development Company, Inc.: A Supplemental Report to the Resolution Trust Corporation," December 13, 1995, pp. 76–78.

†The *Times* wrote that RTC had decided not to sue the Clintons but omitted the report's conclusion that the Clintons had had no control over Jim McDougal's illegal actions. It also wrote that the RTC had not interviewed "a number of important witnesses," an unspecified remark that cast aspersions, when in fact the RTC had interviewed David Hale and Jim McDougal, dismissing their charges against the Clintons. This was not mentioned. See Stephen Labaton, "Savings and Loan Bailout Agency Will Not Sue the Clintons," *The New York Times*, December 24, 1995.

age; they had brought it on themselves. "The mystery surrounding records not produced would cause greater damage than revealing whatever they contained," wrote Bob Woodward. But in the media's confusion of their work with that of actual government investigation, they made a false analogy between the Clintons and Nixon, who had withheld crucial information, documents, and tapes from government investigators looking into Watergate.* The Clintons, on the other hand, had given every document they were aware of to all investigative governmental bodies: the RTC, the Office of Independent Counsel, and the Senate Special Committee, as well as other congressional committees. Now the RTC had made publicly available the significant documents that had been so hotly contested. And the media did not report on their contents or existence.

Lars-Erik Nelson, who had been a correspondent for Reuters in the Soviet Union, wrote, "And now the secret verdict is in: There was nothing for the Clintons to hide. . . . So, in a bizarre reversal of those Stalin-era trials in which innocent people were convicted in secret, the President and First Lady have been publicly charged and secretly found innocent."†

Then, on December 19, *The New York Times* did report that the independent counsel investigating Whitewater was building a case to indict Hillary for perjury and obstruction of justice. The article zeroed in on supposed discrepancies between her testimony and that of a former colleague involving an obscure wrinkle in the supposed case. A predictable rise in the temperature followed, with heated television special reports and accusatory punditry. The notion that Hillary might be indicted was electrifying for the media.

The source for that article was certainly the Office of Independent Counsel and, in particular, deputy counsel Hickman Ewing. Ewing was countering the RTC report by leaking this alleged "indictment" not only to reporters but also to paid agents of the Arkansas Project. (An invoice filed with the Arkansas Project by a Little Rock private investigator on its payroll named Tom Golden, who sometimes tried to pass himself off as a movie producer named "Tom Spielberg," read, "Dinner and Drinks with Independent Counsel Source regarding Hillary Clinton possible indict-

*Bob Woodward, *Shadow: Five Presidents and the Legacy of Watergate (1974–1999)*, Simon and Schuster, 1999, p. 252.

†Lars-Erik Nelson, "Whitewater Probe Finds the Clintons in the Clear," New York *Daily News*, December 20, 1995.

ment [No receipts were obtainable]: $110.00.") One journalist, Dan Moldea, later swore in an affidavit that Ewing had told him that "those writers receiving most-favored status were those who were judged to be in agreement with the OIC's positions. Ewing said he spoke more freely with writers 'when we heard where they're coming from.' "*

Ewing pioneered for Starr's office the practice of capturing select reporters by becoming an indispensable secret source for them. What he was doing appeared to be a clear violation of Rule 6(e) of the Federal Rules of Criminal Procedure, which forbids prosecutors to give the press any information that has been or might be presented to a grand jury. He also developed mutually beneficial relationships with reporters who shared their information with him in exchange for publishing his. In the precise lexicon of the prosecutor, they became his informers. And because they were benefiting from his leaks, they would not expose him as the source. They rationalized shielding him as sound journalistic ethics. Exposing him would also have required self-disclosure.

Hickman Ewing was a driven figure with a deeply personal motive and a bent view of the law. Unlike the weak, ambitious, and inexperienced Starr, Ewing was in the mold of Inspector Javert, but with a Southern Gothic twist. His father, Hickman Ewing, Sr., had been a famous football coach at South Side High School in Memphis, where football is taken very seriously. Young Hick had played for his father. But the father had been indicted and convicted of stealing $43,000 from the county government and spent a year and a half in jail. Even late in life, the son declared himself "ashamed."

In the 1980s, Ewing became a fearsome prosecutor in Tennessee, specializing in politicians he thought were corrupt. As U.S. attorney in Memphis his office twice indicted Representative Harold Ford, Sr., Tennessee's most prominent black politician, and pursued cases against him that lasted for a decade; both prosecutions ended in Ford's acquittal. Ewing operated on a presumption of his target's guilt and openly said so. He veered far to the political fringe, becoming an adherent of various groups of the religious right. He made defendants and their attorneys pray in his presence before trials, according to a Tennessee public official and lawyer. Ewing's wife became an antiabortion activist who stood out-

---

*Dan Moldea, Affidavit, filed August 24, 1998, U.S. District Court for the District of Columbia, In Re Grand Jury Proceedings, Misc. No. 98-55 (NHJ) (consolidated with Misc. No. 98-177 and Misc. No. 98-228). To view on the Internet: http://www.moldea.com/aff4.html#HickmanEwing.

side clinics trying to stop women from seeking counseling inside. Eventually, his zeal undid him even with the local Republican Party, which had got him appointed U.S. attorney: he ran afoul of the most powerful Republican in Tennessee, Representative Don Sundquist, and the Bush administration replaced Ewing in 1991. The religious right staged a campaign to restore him to his post and gave a farewell dinner for him. He said he might work with the Rutherford Institute, a right-wing religious group that believes that the law should be based on Scripture. In his car, Ewing entertained himself by playing tapes of a Clinton-hating "comedy" that had been advertised on Rush Limbaugh's radio talk show.*

It was this figure on the farther shores of the right that Starr had hired to conduct his Whitewater investigation. Ewing quietly sought help from, among others, his longtime friend Rex Armistead, the old Mississippi segregationist and crony of Justice Jim Johnson who was on the payroll of the Arkansas Project.† Ewing's leaking of Hillary Clinton's alleged future "indictment" set the stage for an episode that Hillary herself referred to privately as "Kafkaesque." In this updating of *The Trial*, Joseph K. was Hillary C.

On January 4, 1996, billing records that had been subpoenaed were discovered in the White House and forwarded to the OIC. The person who found them was a family retainer, Carolyn Huber, who had performed domestic tasks in Arkansas for the Clintons and had come to the White House along with them. She assisted guests staying at the White House and helped straighten out gifts and other such matters with the First Lady's staff. In 1996 she was still unpacking the more than a thousand boxes of personal effects, books, and papers the Clintons had carted from Little Rock. She first found the billing records in the "book room" in the White House residence in August 1995, didn't look at them, and rediscovered them months later in a box she had packed. The room was a chaotic jumble of boxes, knickknacks, sports equipment, CDs, and piles of unsorted books. Almost certainly, Huber had found the papers while unpacking, had never bothered to look at them, and had then misplaced them.

The records dealt with an obscure, minor piece of Hillary's work for the Rose law firm on behalf of a brewery project that wanted to run pipes outside its property lines. Its effort had been unsuccessful. In fact, the

*On Ewing, see Toobin, *A Vast Conspiracy*, pp. 190–92, and Conason and Lyons, *Hunting of the President*, pp. 200–202.

†On Armistead, see Conason and Lyons, *Hunting of the President*, pp. 170–72.

records exonerated Hillary in Whitewater matters because they provided material support for her previous statements and testimony about her work at the Rose law firm. Indeed, the OIC already had a version of these very records, and so did the House Banking Committee—and they were in the public record. What these records contained was the Rose firm's hourly billing, not just overall totals. Curiously, given the subsequent firestorm, they were legally insignificant except insofar as they vindicated Hillary. And the RTC had already issued a separate report in 1995 backing her account: "The circumstances of the work point strongly toward innocent explanations, and the theories that tie this option to wrongdoing . . . are strained at best"—a conclusion that was consistently ignored in the ensuing storm, a perfect storm in that it was perfectly removed from any actual evidence while it was presented as being all about key evidence.*

The revelation that previously unknown billing records had been discovered hit like lightning. "Smoking gun," proclaimed Senator Alfonse D'Amato, ginning up his Whitewater committee for new investigations. Those in the media who wished to believe that the Clintons had been covering up something felt triumphant. These old hourly billing records were reported as though the document were a lurid artifact in a latter-day version of the diamond-necklace affair that damaged the reputation of Marie Antoinette. William Safire led the pack with a column in *The New York Times* on January 8, 1996, "Blizzard of Lies": "Americans of all political persuasions are coming to the sad realization that our First Lady—a woman of undoubted talents who was a role model for many in her generation—is a congenital liar." He concluded that no one should wonder about her pattern of deceit: "She had good reasons to lie; she is in the longtime habit of lying; and she has never been called to account for lying herself or for suborning lying in her aides and friends." He advised President Clinton to retain "separate defense counsel."† His use of "congenital" suggested that Hillary had inherited an inability to tell the truth. Safire was invited on NBC's *Meet the Press* to demonstrate his expertise at precise language. "The first word I had in mind was 'prevaricator,' which means 'liar,' and the second one was 'dissembler,' which also means 'liar,' " he explained.

After two weeks of media firestorm, Ken Starr's OIC subpoenaed Hillary Clinton to appear before the grand jury at the federal courthouse.

---

*RTC report cited in Conason and Lyons, *Hunting of the President*, p. 205.
†William Safire, "Blizzard of Lies," *The New York Times*, January 8, 1996.

In the past they had interviewed her at the White House, but now they wanted her to perform what prosecutors call a "perp walk," a public humiliation before the flashing lights of the media on her way in and out.

Ewing's theory about Whitewater, according to Jeffrey Toobin of *The New Yorker*, was that Hillary was trying to cover up an affair she had had with Vincent Foster, a fantasy that included the even wilder belief that her aides were "worried that Foster had left behind something about his relationship with Hillary, such as a suicide note saying something like 'We can't sleep together anymore.' " This speculation had been bandied about before, at the time of Foster's death in 1994, "mostly in the more extreme elements of the Clinton-hating press," as Toobin wrote.* In private, Ewing was contemptuous of the First Lady, as journalists who dealt with him told me. He referred to her not by her name or title but as "the little woman."

On January 26, 1996, Hillary testified at the courthouse. Afterward, she came out to a bank of microphones and cameras and declared that she was "glad" the billing records had been found and really didn't know where they had been, and now she was going home. In private, Hillary said it was clear to her from the prosecutors' questioning that they already had all the essential records. The hourly notations had added nothing new. The controversy in one sense was "laughable," though she saw it for what it was, an effort at smearing. "The whole thing," she said, "is bizarre."

Then another tale supposedly exposing Hillary's grasping and dishonest character began to be told. Simon and Schuster had just published her book *It Takes a Village*, a mixture of autobiography and advocacy of family and children's policy. In March, NBC News claimed a scoop about it: the First Lady had used an unacknowledged ghostwriter. The ghostwriter who had first worked with her on early drafts of the book happened to be Barbara Feinman, whom Sally Quinn and a number of *Washington Post* writers had used over the years on their books. The facts were that Feinman had been hired at the beginning of the project, but then Hillary had decided to write the book on her own, which she did by longhand, not being accomplished on a computer. Feinman was in any case paid $120,000, as earlier promised, though she had no part in the final composition of the text. In the book itself Hillary gave no acknowledgment to her or to anyone else who had worked on the book because, she decided, no matter how endless the list, some of the many, many people

*Toobin, *A Vast Conspiracy*, p. 192.

who had helped her were bound to feel that they had been left off. Nonetheless, talk about Feinman was filtering through Washington and wound up being broadcast on NBC as a shocking revelation. Hillary's deputy press secretary, Neal Lattimore, told *The New York Observer*: "It was clear that she [Sally Quinn] was doing it, but she wasn't putting her name on it."* It takes a village, indeed. Hillary's aides offered to show her handwritten manuscript to Tim Russert, the NBC News Washington bureau chief, but he declined and stood by the original broadcast. *The Washington Post*, however, did view the pages and publish an article reporting that Hillary had apparently written her book herself.

It Takes a Village became a best-seller. Hillary donated all her royalties to charity. But within the Washington village, the din against her became louder. Elaborate tales were spread about Hillary's use of the White House as a lesbian demimonde, and editors were pushed to publish them. People insisted to me that the rumors were true, and editors at major media organizations told me that whether to publish them had been seriously discussed. *The Washington Post* ran a long article headlined "Ambition and Suspicion in First Year Are Redounding on Hillary Rodham Clinton," and said that "her way" was in conflict with "the Washington way."† At the end of February, *The New Yorker* published an article by Henry Louis Gates, Jr., about the phenomenon of "Hating Hillary," in which he quoted Sally Quinn as representative of a certain slice of local opinion. "There's just something about her that pisses people off," said Quinn.‡

On February 25, the Resolution Trust Company issued an additional report about Whitewater, dismissing the issues involved in the billing records. There was, the RTC stated, no consequential discrepancy between Hillary's testimony and that of her associate about what had been billed when. The RTC blamed only the garrulous Jim McDougal, whose "purported recollections . . . are inconsistent with those of the others and upon analysis make little sense." In an implicit rebuke to the latest speculative round ascribing pernicious motives to the First Lady, the report added, "Most significantly, the alleged economic motivation makes no sense. . . . Even if all the retainer had been earned in fees, Mrs. Clinton's

*Mary Jacoby, "Sally Quinn, D.C. Society Queen, Gives Hillary the Old Heave-Ho," *The New York Observer*, March 11, 1996.

†John F. Harris and Ann Devroy, "Ambition and Suspicion in First Year Are Redounding on Hillary Rodham Clinton," *The Washington Post*, February 9, 1996.

‡Henry Louis Gates, Jr., "Hating Hillary," *The New Yorker*, February 26–March 4, 1996.

share would have been less than $20 a month."* The media ignored this report's conclusions.

In April, a book by James Stewart entitled *Blood Sport* appeared, an account of the Whitewater affair that accepted Jim McDougal's version at face value and contended, contrary to the RTC report (which was not cited), that the Clintons had not been "passive" investors and had been "reckless." Hillary Clinton was described as dishonest, manipulative, and covering up. Stewart's book was featured as the cover story in *Time* on March 18. The cover photograph of Hillary was positioned so that the "M" in "TIME" hung above her head like a devil's horns. On ABC's *Nightline* on March 11, Ted Koppel devoted the whole show to Stewart and his book, which he solemnly presented as "the truth." On television, Stewart added a new charge of Hillary's dissembling: a supposedly false loan application, which raised "a question for a prosecutor and a jury to decide." Unfortunately, the document he was talking about contained a warning: "Both sides of this statement must be completed." Stewart had neglected to turn it over, and on the other side the information he claimed Hillary was hiding was written in her own hand. Weeks later, Joe Conason, columnist for *The New York Observer*, disclosed Stewart's error, but his correction received little play, while the original charge was broadcast on national television.

Hillary was not bewildered by these controversies. She thought that what was being done on Whitewater was obvious and political. Contrary to what later books and articles claimed, the Clintons did not suddenly transform their view of Starr and his investigation after Hillary had been subpoenaed. His abuse only confirmed their suspicions. Hillary had given a press conference on Whitewater and a host of interviews to magazine profilers, as well as a televised interview to Barbara Walters. They had had no effect. She increasingly protected her dignity through an assertion of her natural reticence. She stopped reading most newspapers regularly. She was frustrated at the barrage of misinformation and at the futility she felt about correcting it. She also disliked how she felt, and she tried to resist it by focusing on what she called "the ethic of gratitude," trying to outweigh her negative feelings with positive ones about having been given the opportunity to work at the White House. And yet she was discouraged. She did not recognize the picture that was being painted of her. She was revolted by the creation of her false persona. She believed it would be a long time before she could ever restore her reputation. She was at a low ebb.

*Conason and Lyons, *Hunting of the President*, p. 207.

I suggested to Hillary that she escape the stifling atmosphere of Washington by going to two places that would understand her and her concerns. The first was cosmopolitan New York City, a city of opinion makers who paid little deference to capital punditry; their place in the world owed nothing to the media pecking order of the Washington village. The second would be Chicago.

On March 19, 1996, in an upstairs dining room at the venerable Century Association in New York, a luncheon for Hillary took place, which I helped to arrange, where she met a few dozen influential editors and writers from magazines and book-publishing houses. Among them were editors from *The New Yorker* (including Tina Brown), *The New York Review of Books* (Barbara Epstein), and *The Nation* (Katrina vanden Heuvel); writers such as Frances FitzGerald and Gail Buckley; and book publishers, including Harold Evans and Elisabeth Sifton. My friend James Chace, editor of *The World Policy Journal* (on whose board I sat and to which I contributed an occasional essay) at the World Policy Institute, was the event's host.

Hillary was seated at the center of one side of a large square table. She had no prepared statement but immediately welcomed questions. The guests drew her out, encouraging her to talk on policy and politics in a way she did not and could not in Washington. They wanted to use this unusual opportunity to understand her, to elicit a full articulation of her views, to probe her commitments and seriousness. They wanted to carry on a conversation; they didn't have a need to produce a lead for a next-day article. Many subjects were discussed, but no one raised the issue of the scandals raging around Hillary. I felt it was crucial to air the subject, so I asked her direct questions at the end of the lunch. She spoke frankly, explaining Whitewater's emptiness.

Later that same day, Hillary delivered a speech at the Council on Foreign Relations, the leading private group in New York concerned with international affairs, whose members included many New York elite financial and corporate leaders and other opinion makers. The response among the members to the invitation to hear her was so great that the council had to arrange to use the auditorium at Rockefeller University instead of its usual meeting rooms. Hillary was generally associated with the health care program, but she had been traveling worldwide over the previous four years, promoting an agenda of women's rights and economic development, and these were the subjects she talked about. In her speech, she derided the notion that this agenda represented some well-meaning but ineffectual Lady Bountiful "social work." She argued that one of the most significant factors in the advancement economically of underdeveloped societies was the education of their women. She also talked about microeconomic programs of loans to poor women, which had become a special cause of hers and had proved especially successful. She then fielded a range of questions. This crowd, like the group at lunch, had not seen her in person before, making her own case, brandishing foreign policy credentials. The reception was overwhelmingly positive.

For Hillary, the day in New York was more than a passing relief from the bubble of Washington. She presented her ideas to serious people who considered them and her on the merits. They were eager to engage her, rather than rely upon stereotyped images. The foray had an even more important effect: it was the beginning of her involvement in New York on her own, a step on the road that led her eventually to decide to run for the Senate there. Hillary's impression of New York from the hazing in the 1992 primary had been very negative, but now she saw New York from another angle. She discovered broad-minded, expansive, and vital aspects of New York that she had not encountered before.

II

In now-distant Little Rock, the month-long trial of Jim and Susan McDougal and Governor Tucker for bank fraud schemes reached its climax. President Clinton had testified at length by videotape, answering all the Whitewater questions that so bedeviled the media. On May 15, 1996, Ray Jahn, the prosecutor from the OIC, finished his summation to the jury. His closing argument was the clincher—and the revelation of the trial. The facts of the case and his legal strategy compelled him, by an inescapable logic, to insist upon Clinton's innocence of any involvement in the wrongdoing. McDougal had victimized and smeared him as a sleazy gambit to escape responsibility for his crimes:

> The President of the United States is not on trial. Why isn't the President of the United States on trial? Why isn't he on trial? Because he didn't set up any phony corporations to get employees to sign for loans that were basically worthless. He didn't get $300,000 from Capital Management Services like Jim and Susan McDougal did by falsely claiming their use. . . . The President didn't backdate any leases. He didn't backdate any documents. He didn't come up with phony reasons not to repay the property. He didn't lie to any examiners, he didn't lie to any investigators. It's another act of desperation, ladies and gentlemen. The defen-

dants are trying to drag the President of the United States into this courtroom and set up a defense, hide behind the President. . . . The office of the presidency of the United States can't be besmirched by people such as Jim McDougal!

Jim McDougal was found guilty on nineteen of the twenty-one counts of conspiracy and fraud. Susan McDougal was guilty on four counts. Tucker, too, was found guilty. The trial destroyed the credibility of McDougal and of the principal prosecution witness, David Hale. After-ward jurors told local reporters that they were convinced, as one of them put it, that Hale was "an unmitigated liar. . . . We all felt that way."*

Once again, the reportage on this verdict was colored by the omission of essential information. Not a single major news outlet reported Jahn's words to the jury exonerating Clinton. Instead, the verdict was greeted routinely as "a blow to the White House," a "setback" that "portends trouble for Clinton," as *Time* put it.† Republicans seized on the news to tar Clinton further. Congressman Leach, chairing the House Banking Committee investigating Whitewater, held forth on CNN: "I have never suggested a legal context needed to be applied to the President. But in terms of the ethical aspects of this whole Whitewater circumstance, it's going to be very serious for him."‡

But the target was really Hillary. Senator D'Amato's Whitewater committee was on the eve of releasing its report. In anticipation, on June 2, *The Washington Post* published a front-page article, which ran on for an extraordinary four full pages within the paper, headlined "Hillary Clinton and the Whitewater Controversy: A Close-Up." The article, by David Maraniss and Susan Schmidt, portrayed her as someone engaged in a mysterious cover-up, and much was made of the *Post*'s request for Whitewater documents in early 1994. But the RTC report, based on those documents, and its conclusion that the Clintons were innocent of wrongdoing, went unmentioned, as did Ray Jahn's summation in the McDougal trial. The newspaper never reported them. Instead, the *Post* homed in on the billing records as though there was more to learn from them. In the end, it questioned Hillary's religion, her professionalism, and her character:

*Conason and Lyons, *Hunting of the President*, p. 245.
†Eric Pooley, "Guilty, Guilty, Guilty," *Time*, June 10, 1996.
‡R. H. Melton and Michael Haddigan, "Three Guilty in Arkansas Fraud Trial," *The Washington Post*, May 29, 1996.

The image is of a mere bystander, a good person victimized. But an examination of Hillary Clinton's public statements suggests someone less passive in her behavior, less consistent in her answers, and less committed to full disclosure than the figure in her own self-portrait. . . . When considered in isolation, many of the questions to which Hillary Clinton has had to respond—especially those involving small-time transactions in provincial Arkansas more than a decade ago—might appear minor. . . . But when the questions and answers involving her are viewed in their totality, they appear more significant. . . . Does it add up to anything? Is it just a series of meaningless mysteries, as her lawyer said? . . . What she did in Arkansas did not live up to her own ideal as an earnest Methodist doing "all the good you can, by all the means you have," nor did it match her public image as one of the nation's leading lawyers.*

The *Post* offered no facts to refute Hillary's account of Whitewater. To them, her inability to prove a negative only showed that she had something to cover up, though the answers and documents the *Post* claimed it needed were already in the public record.

Years later, in 2000, in an online *Washington Post* chat room, a reader asked the newspaper's chief Whitewater reporter, Susan Schmidt, why the paper had never published the results of the RTC-Pillsbury Report. She replied, "The Pillsbury Report was incomplete. Information that surfaced after its release—notably Mrs. Clinton's Rose Law Firm billing records—rendered it irrelevant."† Unfortunately, this was not factually true. The billing records had no relevance to any legal issue addressed by the Pillsbury Report, and the RTC had issued its February 25 report subsequent to the discovery of them, making that very point and vindicating Mrs. Clinton. In any case, this incorrect ex post facto defense cannot explain the newspaper's decision not to publish the contents of the original report in the first place. Though the *Post* has published lengthy internal reviews of its errors in the past, Schmidt's was the only explanation ever offered by anyone there involved in its Whitewater coverage.

In mid-June, the Republicans on the Senate's Whitewater committee leaked in advance their majority report, and it was splashed across front pages and on the network news. The outcome of the longest-running

*David Maraniss and Susan Schmidt, "Hillary Clinton and the Whitewater Controversy: A Close-Up," *The Washington Post*, June 2, 1996.

†See http://discuss.washingtonpost.com/zforum/00/freemedia092100_schmidt.htm.

congressional investigation of a sitting president in history, it ran to more than seven hundred pages. "We have witnessed a pattern of deception and arrogance that undermines the fundamental core of the American democratic system," proclaimed Senator D'Amato. The report rehearsed every possible charge against the Clintons, but focused mainly on Hillary. It ignored the findings of the RTC and contained not a single piece of new, relevant information.

Richard Ben-Veniste, who had once been the deputy counsel on the Watergate committee, was now the Democratic counsel on the Whitewater committee. Applying the rigorous standards he had used in Watergate, he oversaw the minority report on Whitewater:

> The central question that faced the Special Committee is: Did Bill Clinton misuse the powers of the Presidency? The answer is a clear and unequivocal "No." A secondary question is whether, prior to his election as President, Mr. Clinton used his official position in the State of Arkansas improperly to provide favored treatment to business associates or others. In its exhaustive review of various allegations extending back to the 1970's in some instances, the Committee examined in excruciating detail a number of matters in Arkansas ranging from the handling of water and sewer legislation to state regulation of the sale of alcoholic beverages. Again, the clear conclusion is that then-Governor Clinton did not abuse his office.
>
> Having failed to tarnish the President, the Majority turned its attention to Mrs. Clinton's private law practice in Arkansas more than ten years ago. The Majority launched a massive hunt for some way in which to contradict statements made by Mrs. Clinton during the last four years. Again, no credible evidence has been put forward to show that Mrs. Clinton engaged in any improper, much less illegal, conduct.

The Democratic minority report, using all the evidence and documents available to the committee, reached the same conclusions as the RTC report. Systematically, it dispensed with every charge. It also presented for the first time a carefully detailed account of how the Whitewater accusations had been promoted and manufactured by L. Jean Lewis and David Hale. The Republicans had protected Hale from being subpoenaed, but the minority report nonetheless documented his pattern of falsehoods. And it noted the final abuse:

> The game of leaking information has marred the Committee's credibility throughout these proceedings. Often, distorted or even baseless

charges have been disseminated through faceless leaks. The recent, well-orchestrated leak of the Majority report is but part of a pattern. The supposed short-term benefits of leaking will be offset by the longer-term diminution of credibility that the Majority must suffer for these blatantly political and unfair tactics. The Minority report was not leaked. It was released according to the rules.

The minority report, with its careful adherence to the rules, was not reported in the media. The evidence it gave about how the Whitewater story had been concocted went completely unnoticed, and the media continued to fixate on the billing records, which credited the notion of the Clintons' guilt and burnished the standing of Ken Starr. *The Washington Post*, for example, wrote:

> The partisan bickering tended to diminish the fact that the Whitewater hearings indeed disclosed curious patterns of behavior by the Clintons and the people around them, and put them out for public consideration. If not for the hearings, these patterns would have gone undetected or at least unknown to anyone but Kenneth W. Starr and his assistants in the independent counsel's office, who have been conducting a separate investigation on a more secretive track.*

The "curious patterns of behavior" the *Post* cited were only about the whereabouts of the billing records, a matter the RTC had already resolved, a resolution that went unmentioned. Innuendo replaced fact; vague suspicion was substituted for skepticism; a bias toward the Republican version was presented as objective.

At the same moment that the Republicans were leaking their Whitewater report, Starr indicted two small-town Arkansas bankers for concealing and misusing campaign contributions to Clinton's 1980 gubernatorial campaign. Ewing was in charge of the case and he had a theory—a sex theory. It was that Bruce Lindsey, Bill Clinton's former law partner and now deputy White House counsel, was the keeper of Clinton's sexual secrets.† Lindsey, who had been a campaign treasurer in 1980, was named an unindicted coconspirator with the bankers. Ewing wanted to convict the bankers and flip Lindsey, who presumably

---

*David Maraniss, "The Hearings End Much as They Began," *The Washington Post*, June 19, 1996.

†Toobin, *A Vast Conspiracy*, pp. 192–93.

would tell all about Clinton, but on August 1 the jury acquitted them. For all intents and purposes, the OIC's Whitewater case was at a dead end.

Still without anything to link the Clintons to Jim McDougal's chicanery, except for a story without evidence or witnesses told by the discredited David Hale, Ewing put the screws on Susan McDougal. She refused to cooperate and was shackled and transported to the first of seven prisons, where she was mostly held in solitary confinement for twenty-one months. In September, she telephoned *The Arkansas Times*, a weekly paper in Little Rock, to say that her former husband was preparing to support Hale's story. "He told me he was going to lie, and he wanted me to lie too," she said. She declared that she was determined to defy Starr. "I'll never talk to the independent counsel," she said.* She refused to go before the grand jury because she was sure she would be indicted for perjury when she didn't say what Starr wanted her to.†

When she was not confined alone, she was "housed on the same row with murderers, molesters, abusers and psychotic prisoners, one of whom attempted to stab her with a sharpened pencil," according to a brief filed almost two years later by her attorney.‡ Still she refused to testify before the grand jury. (Her mother had been a member of the Belgian resistance to the Nazis, which she later cited as a source of inspiration.) A story was leaked—from where?—that she had had an affair with Bill Clinton. This rumor, without any corroboration and denied by both parties, was published in *The New Yorker* in an article by James Stewart.

Starr, through Ewing, had drawn up an indictment of Hillary Clinton ("the little woman"), leaked it to the media, forced her to do a "perp walk," and subpoenaed her aides. But lacking evidence, he was unable to indict her. Susan McDougal, down on her luck, became the woman he imprisoned. After eighteen months behind bars, and after President Clinton's impeachment, McDougal finally had her day in court in 1999. She testified that her husband had told her that if she claimed she had had an "affair," which would allow Ewing to "get Clinton with a sex charge" before the 1996 election, she would be released. (Ewing denied

---

*Michael Haddigan, "Seeking Susan? After 5 Months in Jail, McDougal's Holding Firm," *The Arkansas Times*, September 20, 1996.

†See Susan McDougal, *The Woman Who Wouldn't Talk*, Carroll and Graf, 2003, especially pp. 347–76.

‡Robert Scheer, "Talk or Face the Starr Treatment," *Los Angeles Times*, May 12, 1998.

that he had done this "at the time frame she's talking about.") She testified that she knew of no wrongdoing by the Clintons. She was acquitted
of all charges against her.* Shortly afterward, I encountered her in Washington at a White House correspondents dinner. "I wonder how many
people understand how insane Starr and Ewing are," she said. "Insane.
Insane." But in 1996 she was only at the beginning of her ordeal.

In almost every one of the tens of thousands of Whitewater articles
published in 1994–98, Hillary was depicted as emerging from a primeval
Arkansas swamp of corruption. I suggested to her that she reclaim her
identity as a Chicagoan, and after the 1994 election she began traveling
to Chicago. She had kept up with her old friends, and now she saw them
more often. She went to her old high school. She developed a relationship with Mayor Richard M. Daley and his wife, Maggie. If her accent
was flat, her manner direct, her ambition clear, it was because of where
she was from: striving middle-class Chicago. It was right politically and
important psychologically for her to remind herself and others of this
background.

The Democratic convention was held in Chicago in 1996. The second night of the convention was Hillary's, for she, even more than the
keynoter, was the most prominent speaker. It was her best and only
chance to present herself on her own terms to a national audience. The
last time she had been seen live on television was after her grand-jury appearance, when her comments to the press were broadcast. Now she
would be speaking to assembled Democratic delegates there to nominate
her husband. She would stand alone on the podium, a singular opportunity and a terrifying one.

Hillary wrote and rewrote her speech. As she rehearsed the evening
before, she was receiving whole new draft sections submitted by Dick
Morris. Earlier that day I had run into several consultants working on
Clinton's campaign who described Morris's behavior as increasingly
manic. He was attacking some of his campaign colleagues, trying to force
them out of meetings, and he seemed consumed with his own image. For
its convention issue, *Time* had a cover story on Morris and his influence
with the President: the cover image was a montage, which Morris had
negotiated himself, showing Morris perched at the President's ear. But he
seemed more and more untethered. Everyone who ever had contact with
Dick knew that he was compulsive. But the Clintons also knew that he

*Michael Haddigan, "McDougal Says Ex-Husband Urged Her to Lie, Admit a
Clinton Affair," *The Washington Post*, March 25, 1999.

had his purposes. Hillary discarded Morris's last-minute demands—he was becoming more of a distraction than a help—and kept working on her own draft.

I planned to watch the speech with my wife, Jackie. As she was director of the White House Fellows program, she and I had seats in a box graciously made available that evening by Peter Knight, the campaign's director (and husband of Jackie's deputy and friend Gail Britton), for the members of the White House fellowship commission.

Just as Hillary was about to speak, Dick Morris burst into our box. He grabbed me and pulled me into a corner. He was dripping sweat and his hands were shaking worse than usual. He held his beeper, which was constantly going off, in his hand.

"Do you know how to stop a story from being printed in *The New York Post*?" he asked me.

"No," I said.

"Are you sure?"

"Yes."

"Do you know anyone who might?"

I didn't have an answer for him.

"There's a bad story coming out about me," he said. "It's about me and a woman." He looked at me and then at his beeper and then at me again.

I didn't know what he was talking about.

"The *Star* is going to print it," he said. "*The New York Post* is going to report it tomorrow. Are you sure you don't know anyone?"

The lights dimmed. Jackie came over and we sat down. Morris sat down, too. Tipper Gore introduced Hillary, and she began:

> Chicago is my kind of town. And Chicago is my kind of village. One friend suggested that I appear here tonight with Binti, the child-saving gorilla from the Brookfield zoo. [Binti was in the news for sheltering a child who had fallen into the gorilla pit.] You know, as this friend explained, Binti is a typical Chicagoan, tough on the outside but with a heart of gold underneath. Another friend advised me that I should cut my hair and color it orange and then change my name to Hillary *Rodman* Clinton.

She was a Chicagoan. She was like Binti. She was like the Chicago Bulls' bad boy, Dennis Rodman. "But, after considering these and countless other suggestions, I decided to do tonight what I've been doing for more than twenty-five years. I want to talk about what matters most in our lives and in our nation, children and families."

Morris rose from his seat and left.

Hillary was warming up. For the ten minutes allotted she spoke about the Family and Medical Leave Act, about the need for health care and education programs. Quickly, she got to her closing: "It takes all of us. Yes, it takes a village. And it takes a president!"

Backstage, after the speech, Hillary was surrounded by some of her oldest friends and her childhood pastor, the Reverend Don Jones, who had first introduced her to the world of social issues. Her speech had been a great success, and the next morning, at a brunch for her friends, it seemed as though a burden had been lifted from her. She wore a large button featuring her face topped with a multicolored fright wig. It read, "Hillary Rodman Clinton, Bad as She Wants to Be."

By now, the article about Morris had been published. It said he had been paying a prostitute, who had sold details of their liaison to the *Star*. Morris had to resign. Truth to tell, even the people whom he had brought in to the White House were not unhappy to see him go. His megalomania had been alienating everybody around him, and his contribution had already been made. Some people on the staff wanted the White House and the Clinton campaign office to make statements condemning him. But others, including Hillary, prevailed against that. His public humiliation was sufficient punishment. And Morris, after all, had helped Clinton. He should be dealt with humanely. He should not be treated as an antagonist. And he was gone.

III

The interregnum between the election and the inauguration appeared to mark the start of a new period of calm. Or was it? Clinton's victory, it was hoped within the White House, had brought about an anticlimax for his opponents. The pseudoscandals had failed to dent him politically. Attacks on Hillary and Gore had not moved any voters, except those already inclined to vote Republican. But many on the right refused to accept Clinton's reelection as legitimate. "A Stolen Election" read the headline of a column in *The Wall Street Journal* by Paul Gigot. And events that might have appeared either minor or left over from the past now became scene setters for turmoil to follow.

On January 17, 1997, the House Ethics Committee issued a well-documented 214-page report on flagrant violations committed by Speaker of the House Newt Gingrich. Abusing various laws governing nonprofit institutions at taxpayer expense for his partisan activity, his action was either "intentional or it was reckless," the report stated. "The violation does not represent only a single instance of reckless conduct. Rather, over a number of years and in a number of situations, Mr. Gingrich showed a disregard and lack of respect for the standards of conduct that applied to his activities." The report also concluded that Gingrich had tried to deceive the committee by providing it with "inaccurate, incomplete and unreliable" information.*

Gingrich was punished with an official reprimand and a $300,000 fine. In the 208-year history of the House it was the most severe penalty ever levied against a Speaker. Gingrich's abuses were worse than anything he had accused any Democrat of having committed, including Jim Wright, whom he had driven from the Speakership.

"Somehow on the left," Gingrich told a public meeting, "you can do anything you want, and nobody seems to notice. But if you are a conservative and you want to follow the law and you hire lawyers and you do what you can—if you make a single mistake, you better plan to be pilloried because you're politically incorrect."†

Gingrich's favorable rating hovered below 30 percent—a hard core of Republicans. He was not seen and could not stand as an alternative to Clinton. His fellow "revolutionaries" no longer trusted his leadership. Whenever he broke from their party line—for example, in backing an amendment that opposed government shutdowns—they regarded him as a betrayer. He was embittered and weak. His gyrations became wilder and his impulse to strike out greater.

Among the documents and memoranda released by the House Ethics Committee was one written in 1995 by Joseph Gaylord, Gingrich's chief political operative. It revealed a Gingrich strategy for making any inquiry look partisan and trying to short-circuit it: "Bring back to life Dems' ethical problems." Gaylord listed eleven House Democratic leaders for

---

*Ruth Marcus and Charles R. Babcock, "Gingrich Actions 'Intentional' or 'Reckless,'" *The Washington Post*, January 18, 1997; Katherine Q. Seelye, "Report Describes How Gingrich Used Taxpayers' Money for Partisan Politics," *The New York Times*, January 18, 1997.

†Eric Pianin, "Combative Gingrich Is Cheered at Home," *The Washington Post*, January 26, 1997.

targeting. "Indict the Clinton administration." "Get the Clinton administration under special prosecutor problems and have Clinton administration get the House Dems to back down."*

"Oyez! Oyez!" On January 13, 1997, four days before Gingrich's ethics violations were reported, the U.S. Supreme Court heard oral arguments in *Jones v. Clinton*. The Arkansas judge in the case, Susan Webber Wright, had delayed taking depositions until the federal appellate court had ruled on Clinton's objection, which was that the civil suit should be postponed until after his presidency because it could interfere with the discharge of his duties. In January 1996, the appellate court had handed down a 2–1 decision denying Clinton's motion, and Clinton had appealed again. Now the case was in the Supreme Court.

Jones's attorneys were two small-time Virginia lawyers, Joe Cammerata and Gil Davis, hoping to get a cut of a large settlement and publicity that might attract other clients. Davis also had political ambitions. But they were merely the attorneys of record. Behind the scenes operated a crew of high-powered conservative lawyers who framed the arguments for them, wrote their briefs, prepped them, and helped undermine them when they strayed toward settlement. The Supreme Court brief was written principally by two lawyers not of record and eager to keep their roles secret. They were George Conway III and Jerome Marcus, partners in largely Democratic law firms: Conway at New York's Wachtell, Lipton, Rosen and Katz; Marcus at Philadelphia's Berger and Montague. Against their firms' rules, they hid their involvement in the Jones case. Yet another conservative lawyer, Richard Porter, a partner at Kirkland and Ellis, Ken Starr's firm, was also involved. As an aide to Vice President Dan Quayle, he had worked with Starr on a panel of Quayle's Competitiveness Council. During the 1992 campaign, Porter had accepted an assignment digging up sexual rumors about Clinton; in 1994, he had helped the Chicago businessman Peter Smith, who paid off the troopers, to get Brock to do the article that led to the Jones case; and then he had played talent agent, searching for legal help for her.

Porter, Marcus, and Conway were part of a political circle, a small, tight-knit group of friends with ties going back to their law-school and clerkships days. All were members of the Scaife-funded Federalist Society. The immediate circle included prosecutors in the Office of Inde-

*Eric Pianin and Kevin Merida, "Agreement Was Violated, Counsel Says," *The Washington Post*, January 18, 1997.

pendent Counsel and partners of Washington law firms, including
Starr's. Eventually, this secret group, which came to call itself "the elves,"
brought Linda Tripp and her story about Monica Lewinsky to Starr's
door.

Davis had never argued before the Supreme Court. So Conway and
Marcus, authors of the Jones brief, organized an unusual moot court in
early January 1997 for him to practice in. Ted Olson and Robert Bork,
the conservative jurist whom the Senate had rejected for the Supreme
Court, prepared him. When Olson and Bork had served Republican presidents they had argued in favor of executive prerogatives, but now they
prepped Davis to argue the other side against a Democratic president.

The Washington Post and *The New York Times* editorialized that President Clinton was not "above the law." But that was not the argument his
attorneys made to the Court. They stated merely that the civil case
should be held off until after his term in office. Robert Bennett, the President's personal lawyer, made the point to the Supreme Court that failing
to postpone the case would violate the doctrine of separation of powers.
Walter Dellinger, acting solicitor general, argued, "The public interest in
the president's unimpaired performance of his duties must take precedence over a private litigant's interest in redress."

Justice Antonin Scalia ridiculed the idea that such a suit would consume
valuable presidential time and focus. "We see presidents riding horseback,
chopping firewood, fishing for stick fish, playing golf. . . . Really, the notion that he doesn't have a minute to spare is, is just not credible." To
which Dellinger replied with a quote from President Reagan, who had
said, "Presidents don't have vacations. They have a change in scenery."

Chief Justice Rehnquist shot back, "Surely that may be true of an individual with an ordinary job, but with all the pressing concerns that the
President has, one would think it would be less true of him." His logic
was upside down.

Scalia made another sarcastic remark: if the President had the "intes-
tinal fortitude to say I am absolutely too busy so that he'll never be seen
playing golf for the rest of his administration, if and when that happens,
we can resolve the problem."* On that frivolous, dismissive note, the
Supreme Court took the case under advisement.

---

*Toobin, *A Vast Conspiracy*, pp. 114–17; Vincent Bugliosi, *No Island of Sanity: Paula
Jones v. Bill Clinton: The Supreme Court on Trial*, Ballantine, 1998, pp. 98–100.

IV

About two weeks before the inauguration the President asked me to come over to the White House. It was a Sunday night. Clinton was dressed in jeans, sneakers, and a sweater with an American flag stitched across its front. He led me to the family kitchen, in a part of the residence I had never seen. It was unlike the large White House kitchen on the ground floor, with its long steel counters and huge refrigerators and sinks, where presidential meals, including state dinners, are prepared. This kitchen was indistinguishable from any kitchen in an ordinary suburban house: Formica surfaces, chairs around a small table, a range, wood cabinets. Clinton set out mugs, boiled some water, and made tea.

Now we had a chance to discuss his inaugural address. I suggested to the President that he use the occasion to deliver a valedictory to the twentieth century. He would be the president presiding at the turn of the century. He had campaigned on millennial themes, and he should continue to develop them. From the vantage point of the end of the century, he could describe the transformation of the country and then swivel to describe the demands of the twenty-first century. He could define the progressive unfolding of the American experience and set himself and his program within it. Gertrude Stein had remarked that America was the oldest country in the world because it had been the first to enter the twentieth century. It was always seeking to become a new nation, its oldest identity.

We reviewed the campaign and how it had ended: his frantic but failed efforts in its closing days to help Democrats win the Congress. Clinton wasn't angry, just disappointed, not particularly by his own result, but by the Democrats' lacking the majority. He still had to maneuver his way through a Republican Congress to reach his goals. But his demeanor was of one who felt far more secure and knowledgeable about wielding his power than he had in 1992.

Clinton was frustrated but almost philosophical about the pseudo-scandals. He knew that the Republicans knew they had been ginned up for political effect—and the Republicans knew that he knew that they knew. He related a conversation he had had with Senator Alan Simpson, the Republican from Wyoming, who was retiring.

"You know there's nothing wrong that Hillary and I did in Whitewater," Clinton told him.

"Of course," Simpson replied. "We all know there's nothing there. It was just politics. And it just got out of hand."

Clinton shrugged. He told me another story. He and Dole had become even friendlier after the campaign than they had been before, when they bonded over Gingrich's antics. They were two veterans, no longer competitors, who had a love and respect for politics.

"Let me ask you this," Clinton said he told Dole. "Do you think that politics are dirtier or cleaner since you came in?" Here Clinton was the younger man asking the older one about gritty reality before his own time.

Dole, during the race, had billowed clouds of smoke about campaign finance scandals at Clinton. Now the race was over. "Much cleaner," said Dole. "No comparison." He related that politicians literally used to stuff their pockets with payoffs. He recalled long-forgotten Senator Herman Talmadge of Georgia, who had had the misfortune of getting caught.

Clinton wondered why politics was depicted as dirtier. "What accounts for the difference?" he asked.

"The media," Dole replied. He explained his view that campaign finance laws gave the media endless grist for their mills, and the details were mostly blown out of proportion. So even if politics were cleaner, they were reported as dirtier.

Clinton shrugged again. The scandals were not going to disappear, but they were more an undercurrent than an engulfing wave. In Hillary's terms, they were more "chronic" than "acute."

After we reviewed the inaugural address one more time and rummaged across the political scene, he posed a question. "Do you want to come work with me?" the President asked. He wanted me to help him develop and communicate his political ideas and policies. His ambition was not necessarily confined to domestic affairs, for he thought there might be an international influence for the kind of progressive politics he was pioneering. Clinton was renewing a political party that had been considered hopelessly encrusted in the past. Within the last year I had introduced him to Tony Blair, who was engaged in a similar project with the Labour Party in Britain. There would be an election there in the coming year. We discussed Blair's prospects.

Then Clinton brought the talk around again to his question. "What do you want to do?" he asked.

I accepted his offer to join his staff. "Leave it to me," he said.

On January 20, at the Capitol, overlooking Independence Mall, Bill Clinton took the oath of office again. And then he spoke: "At this last presidential inauguration of the twentieth century, let us lift our eyes toward the challenges that await us in the next century." He reviewed the progress of America to put the moment in perspective:

> It is our great good fortune that time and chance have put us not only at the edge of a new century, in a new millennium, but on the edge of a bright new prospect in human affairs—a moment that will define our course, and our character, for decades to come. We must keep our old democracy forever young. . . . We began the nineteenth century with a choice, to spread our nation from coast to coast. We began the twentieth century with a choice, to harness the industrial revolution to our values of free enterprise, conservation, and human decency. Those choices made all the difference. At the dawn of the twenty-first century, a free people must choose to shape the forces of the information age and the global society, to unleash the limitless potential of all our people, and, yes, to form a more perfect union.

The progress of the last four years had proved not that change simply runs its course, but that it can be directed. He folded in the history the political conflict over the role of government during his first term. "As times change, so government must change."

As it happened, this inauguration day was also Martin Luther King, Jr.'s birthday.

> The challenge of our past remains the challenge of our future: Will we be one nation, one people, with one common destiny—or not? Will we all come together, or come apart? The divide of race has been America's constant curse. Each new wave of immigrants gives new targets to old prejudices. Prejudice and contempt, cloaked in the pretense of religious or political conviction, are no different. These forces have nearly destroyed our nation in the past. They plague us still. They fuel the fanaticism of terror. They torment the lives of millions in fractured nations all around the world. . . . Our rich texture of racial, religious, and political diversity will be a godsend in the twenty-first century. Great rewards will come to those who can live together, learn together, work together, forge new ties that bind together.

Clinton, whose father had died before he was born, often reflected in public on mortality. He had done so in an inaugural address as governor.

Now he quoted Joseph Cardinal Bernardin of Chicago, who had recently died: "It is wrong to waste the precious gift of time on acrimony and division."

Those on the podium shook his hand and offered their congratulations. Chief Justice Rehnquist, however, had been chilly and inexpressive toward the President throughout the morning. He was grim while swearing in Clinton to his second term, with Hillary holding the Bible. Now Rehnquist turned to speak to him. "Good luck," he said. "You'll need it."

"They're going to screw you on the Paula Jones case," Hillary said.

The President waved to the crowd.

SIX

A Political Education

I grew up in Chicago on Birchwood Avenue, a tree-lined street, in a brick and stone house like almost all the other houses in the neighborhood, inhabited by middle-class families like mine. I was the oldest of three children. My best friend lived next door. We played baseball in the spring and summer and touch football in the fall in the street. I collected baseball cards, played board games about military battles that went on for weeks with a friend who had had polio before there was a vaccine, rode a Schwinn racer bicycle, and endlessly read history books and biographies.

We lived on the North Side. My mother had lived there her whole life. I attended the same high school that she had—Roger C. Sullivan High School (named after a local politician). My father had grown up on the West Side, the old Jewish neighborhood encompassing the peddlers' Maxwell Street (where my grandfather sold shoes), Jane Addams's uplifting Hull-House (where Benny Goodman was taught to play the clarinet), and Colonel Jake Arvey's clubhouse (where he became chairman of the Cook County Democratic Party). Paul, my father's father, had left Russia alone at the age of eleven, became a traveling auctioneer, and owned a shoe store that went bankrupt during the Depression. He was meticulous in his dress, always wearing a white shirt and a tie. One of my earliest memories is of watching television westerns with him. His favorite was Hopalong Cassidy. When our family moved from an apartment to a house, my grandfather learned that an older bully was picking on me and the other little boys on the street. He and my father taught me how to box. The next time the bully confronted me, I knocked him down. Paul could not have been prouder. Emma, his wife, doted on her grandchildren and on her two sons, my father and my uncle, who were known in

the old neighborhood as the Baer brothers, after two famous Jewish boxers of the time. They were brawny, energetic, and inseparable. So far as I
knew they talked or saw each other almost every day of their lives. They
grew up together and worked together. They introduced each other to
the women who would be their wives. They turned down job offers from
Benjamin "Bugsy" Siegel to set odds at the Flamingo Hotel in Las Vegas
(my mother thought it was no place to raise children), double-dated with
Jack Ruby ("He couldn't stop crying when Roosevelt died. He was very
emotional," according to my father), and broke up German Bund meetings in the 1930s with their friends (not followers of Gandhi or Stalin).
None of this was urban legend. They were optimistic, exuberant, and ir-
repressible. Eventually they settled down and started selling things. They
sold steel, corrugated boxes, and plastic inflatable toys. In 1956, my father drove up to our house in a brand-new pink Oldsmobile.

I was named for Sidney Stone, my mother's father. He was born in
Cincinnati and raised in Columbus, Ohio. His mother, Alice, came from
Russia, and his father, Moses Stone, came from Cardiff, Wales. When I
was a child, we spent part of our summers at the home of my great-
grandmother in Columbus. She always regretted that her husband had
not bought real estate on High Street when he had had a chance. Moses,
however, was a successful restaurateur. My great-aunt Rose, who graduated from Ohio State University and was the personal secretary of Mr.
Wolfe, the most important banker in town, was a rock-ribbed Republican
who believed as an article of faith that having Republicans hold political
office was good for business. My grandfather Sidney was one of the first
Jews admitted to the U.S. Naval Academy at Annapolis, but despite the
urging of the Jewish community of Columbus, he decided he did not
wish to endure the expected anti-Semitic hazing. Instead, he attended the
University of Ohio at Athens. During the First World War, he served as
a quartermaster for the General Staff of the American Expeditionary
Force in France, and afterward started up a sheet metal factory in
Chicago, which went bankrupt during the Depression. (He promised my
grandmother he would not vote again for Hoover, but for Roosevelt, in
1932.) My mother, Claire, went to Ohio State for a year but dropped out
after the outbreak of the Second World War, attended Katherine Gibbs
Secretarial School, and then worked in businesses around Chicago. After
the war she expected to travel in Europe with her father as he established
a new business: Sidney had plans to become a wine and beer importer.
His contacts included French vintners and the Heineken brewery in the
Netherlands. Unfortunately, he died suddenly in 1945 at the age of fifty-

five from an infection of his heart lining that he had contracted in the First World War.

When I was seven, my grandmother, Minnie Stone, moved in with us—the den became her bedroom—and lived with us for twenty-six years. She lived to be nearly one hundred years old. Minnie had been brought as a six-month-old baby to America by her parents, well-educated urban people who fled Odessa after a wave of anti-Semitism there. Her father, Louis Finkelstein, came to Chicago to work in the Columbian World Exposition of 1893. (I still have his pass to the exhibits.) He was restless and eventually moved on to California, where Minnie was enrolled in advance at Mills College. But both her parents were stricken with tuberculosis and died in a sanitarium in Denver. Minnie's younger sister, Lily, was placed in an orphanage, and Minnie hit the open road as a showgirl for the Schubert organization. She danced in vaudeville troupes across the country, using the stage name of Leslie Gardner. When she married her first husband, Harry Meyer, a Pinkerton agent and sportswriter for the *New York Sun*, she was able to get Lily out of the orphanage. They traveled to Buenos Aires, where Harry became a promoter for the exiled Jack Johnson, the black heavyweight champion, who was fleeing trumped-up sex charges. Possibly Harry was also spying on Johnson. Minnie showed me pictures of herself with Johnson and his white wife, Lucille, who, she said, was nothing like the character in the play *The Great White Hope*. She said Johnson was generous and gentlemanly and Lucille was a "bitch" who treated him poorly. The years in Argentina came to an end when Meyer caught a tropical disease and—it was now during the First World War—they had to take a "dark" ship, avoiding German U-boats, back to the States. Harry Meyer died in New York, and Minnie returned to Chicago, where she was introduced to Sidney Stone. Turning down an offer to dance in the Ziegfeld Follies, she married him instead.

Minnie was always plucky in the face of adversity. On the ship from Buenos Aires, she had worked as a manicurist to help pay for the passage, and when Sidney went broke during the Depression she worked as a telephone operator and receptionist to keep the family in their North Side apartment. My mother told me that Sidney often remarked in the 1930s, "We should think of ourselves as only temporarily without funds." On both sides of my family, going back as far as I know, there was inveterate optimism, a belief not necessarily in happy endings, but in relentless striving.

The world has looked radically different to me at different times.

Sometimes a change in the angle of vision has been responsible. Sometimes I've found myself overtaken by happenstance and sudden offers, and I have moved under my own steam to unexpected places. You can never predict where events will take you, but I have never felt a severing of continuity. My experience has accumulated.

Two days before I was twelve and four days before the 1960 election, my political education began. I would soon get as a birthday present the two hardcover volumes I had asked for—Carl Sandburg's *The Prairie Years*, about Lincoln. Lincoln was the god of Illinois, the Prairie State. My grandmother's first cousin, a traveling salesman, would later take me downstate with him on one of his swings; in Springfield I toured Lincoln's house and tomb, and in New Salem, a reconstructed frontier village, I saw where he studied law and courted Ann Rutledge. The Sandburg mythology was a boy's poetic truth and it was touchable.

It was November 4, 1960, and John F. Kennedy was winding up his campaign with a visit to Chicago. For me it was the beginning of the world. My Virgil was an unlikely figure living on the next block—a short, bald, feisty man named Danny Spunt. He had been a boxers' corner man, one of those who hung out with fighters, wore shirts with their names stitched on the back, handing them the water bottle between rounds. He showed me his collection of boxing photographs and gave me one of Floyd Patterson, then the heavyweight champion. Danny worked for the city. I didn't really know what he did, but he came around our house from time to time and my parents liked him. He helped them get some maple trees planted in the front yard. He was our Democratic Party precinct captain. Since election day was coming up he wanted to know if I would like to work for him after school. He'd tell me which of our neighbors hadn't voted by late afternoon; I'd leave them a palm card of Democratic candidates and ask them to come to the polling place. It was worth five dollars to me, he said. Sure, I'd do it. Oh, and by the way, Danny offered, he'd be glad to take me along to the Democratic workers' parade and rally. My father said Danny was a sport. Sure, I'd go.

Every day my father brought home four newspapers—the *Chicago Tribune*, a partisan Republican paper that used to be filled with anti-Semitic undertones that Sidney had banned from his household; the *Chicago Sun-Times*, then the liberal paper owned by the Marshall Field family; the *Daily News*, a moderate-liberal paper; and the *American*, a Hearst tabloid. I had read them avidly for sports news—once even writing a letter about the Cubs to a *Daily News* columnist that he answered publicly, which made it my first publication, as it were—and I was now consuming the political reports with the same intent interest.

Besides Boston, perhaps no other city was more electrified by the Kennedy campaign than Chicago, which like Boston was struggling to renew itself. There was talk of a new Chicago as there was talk of a new Boston. The campaign provided a unifying experience in a place where cleavages of race and class threatened to split the city apart. In an ethnic city of patchwork wards, Kennedy drew together the blue-collar and middle-class constituencies, whites and blacks. His Catholic background made him a redemptive figure not only for Irish Catholics but for Italian and Polish ones as well, and his wealth made him seem like the last political grandee, FDR. Within the Democratic Party, Kennedy was a higher synthesis of Harry Truman, the party regular, and Truman's antithesis Adlai Stevenson, the patrician whom the party had slated for governor of Illinois in 1948 as the "Blue Ribbon" candidate and who had been the losing candidate for president twice against Eisenhower. Chicago was also familiar Kennedy territory. It was the family's principal business base, where they owned the mammoth Merchandise Mart, managed by JFK's brother-in-law Sargent Shriver, who was chairman of the Chicago board of education then. Crucial events in the campaign swept through Chicago: the Republican convention and the first televised presidential debate. Mayor Richard J. Daley exerted every sinew of the party organization on Kennedy's behalf, finally having the Cook County party purchase a half hour on national television to broadcast Kennedy's November 4 speech in Chicago. In every respect the rally would be a mixture of the new and the old.

From time immemorial Democratic presidential campaigns in Chicago reached their climax with a torchlight parade of precinct captains. Danny Spunt took me to a bus that deposited us at a downtown site, and we marched up Madison Street to the ancient Chicago Stadium. I pinned a Kennedy button to my jacket and carried a "Kennedy for President" placard stapled to a wooden stick. There were men holding torches aloft as far as I could see, an endless trail of fire. In the stadium everybody was standing, bellowing, and whooping. This was more exciting than Ernie Banks winning it with a home run for the Cubs in the bottom of the ninth. Suddenly, Kennedy emerged with the mayor holding his arm, rushing him along. The half-hour television time slot had already begun.

Through a blizzard of banners, I could see Kennedy step onto the platform. He appeared immediately separate from every other politician clustered around him. He was better-dressed, more polished, and younger. There was something diffident about the way he smiled and gestured; he didn't wave his arms or shout. Yet he was engaged; he drew the crowd toward him. He was the first cool candidate. The thousands of men gathered before him were prosaic men, paid city salaries, who thought they had seen it all, but they became a deafening voice of earthy enthusiasm. They weren't just doing young Kennedy up there a favor; they meant it. "You have all seen elephants in the circus," Kennedy began to rising laughter, "and you have seen how they grab the tail of the elephant in front of them, and they pull themselves around that way." The crowd applauded in anticipation. "Mr. Nixon grabbed that tail in 1952 and 1956, but now he is running, not President Eisenhower, but Mr. Nixon." And the crowd let loose an animal roar.

Four days later, I did just as Danny instructed. After school, I met him at the polling place, Temple Menorah on California Avenue, received a pocketful of palm cards, and knocked on the neighbors' doors. Upon my return, Danny gave me five dollars. When I woke up the next morning Kennedy had been elected president by a few votes in Illinois. A change of one vote per precinct would have moved the state into Nixon's column. I knew I had made my contribution.

Politics, as I grew to understand it, was just there. There was no distance in Chicago between politics and getting a driveway widened, having a tree planted, getting garbage picked up, having a kid get a summer job. Many small aspects of life and many large aspects of business required connections. It was impossible to grow up politically innocent. That didn't mean that you were going to become a ward committeeman, but simply that you couldn't avoid the reality. The schism between politics and daily life that emerged in the suburbs did not exist. There were political representatives and representations of politics everywhere you turned.

I had no memory of any other president before Eisenhower. He was just there, too. Ike was like a large piece of Victorian mahogany furniture. He reminded me of my great-grandmother's house. I never heard any adult utter a disrespectful word about him. It was not just that he had been the commanding general in the Second World War and was being given deference. It was that he was president, and while people might say something about the economy going sour or the U-2 spy plane being shot down, they never made personal remarks about the president. Vice President Richard Nixon, however, was another case altogether. Every adult I knew had an intense visceral distaste for him. Adlai Stevenson had called him "Joe McCarthy in a white collar," and he was being polite. "Strictly a medicine man" was how my father put it. My grandmother had a friend who occasionally visited us and was under doctor's orders not to watch Nixon on television because of her heart condition. When, for some reason, old clips of Roosevelt would be broadcast, I noticed everyone warming and drawing to the source of his voice. But whenever Nixon appeared, people cringed and pulled back.

My seeing Kennedy at that rally left a deeper imprint with me than my initial encounter with the political process. Chicago politics had little romance. Its operations were daily, not just about Daley. They were routine and about ordering routines. But Kennedy unveiled my first vision that there was such a thing as national politics and that a president could also be a leader of American society. For my parents' generation, Kennedy was someone their age who himself had every advantage but was also overcoming ethnic and religious prejudice. For me, he stood for the future. Kennedy valued intelligence, he wrote a book—*Profiles in Courage* is a fine introduction to politics for a young person—and he surrounded himself with his own brain trust, people who simply had talent and skill. You didn't have to be a precinct captain to be in politics, and you didn't have to be rich. You could get there by reading and writing. Kennedy's administration, for people my age, gave us a glimmer of the idea of meritocracy. When he spoke about passing the torch to a new generation, I had a feeling that that torch was being passed all the way down the line to us, the children of the American Century, the largest generation in the country's history and the first that would attend college in the millions. We would be the first meritocracy. My early perceptions of modernity, about the relevance of intelligence, of the expanse of the country and the world, about what politics means, about social mobility and social inclusion, all stem from Kennedy.

Political parties are living organisms, not machines, though they are called that. Like the parties in bloody British civil wars organized around kingly and princely figures, they take on the characteristics of the personalities leading them. Just as those who grew up during the New Deal saw politics as divided between the Roosevelt party and the Hoover party, my formative experience caused me to see politics as a contest between the Kennedy and Nixon parties. And I still see politics as a continuation of the clash between those forces.

My identification with Kennedy sparked me to try to understand the crises that were cascading upon the United States. We had air-raid drills in grammar school and practiced hiding under our desks or crouching near our lockers in the hallways. During the Cuban Missile Crisis, everyone I knew at Sullivan High School discussed what we would do if we knew that there was going to be a nuclear war in ten minutes. (For girls, the most common answer was: run home. For boys, it involved the girls.)

The immediacy of danger from foreign affairs awakened in me a new interest and made me search for more detailed information. One thing I discovered about Kennedy was that as a boy he read *The New York Times* and he read it every day as president. I had never seen that newspaper. In the Middle West, it was possible to be completely unaware of it. The sources of news were local papers and network television broadcasts, which had just expanded from fifteen to thirty minutes. One day I found that *The New York Times* was sold at a newsstand underneath the tracks of the Howard "L" station, so I went out of my way coming home from school to take the "L" and then a bus to be able to get the *Times*. I also read William L. Shirer's mammoth *The Rise and Fall of the Third Reich* and all eleven volumes of Upton Sinclair's political novels about Lanny Budd, President Roosevelt's secret agent.

In my senior year in high school, I was prepared to go downstate to the University of Illinois at Urbana-Champaign. But then my mother mentioned that the son of a friend of hers went to Brandeis. Out of curiosity I wrote away for the catalog. Three features about it impressed me: it was near Boston (which I associated with Kennedy), it was intellectually serious, and it was the only Jewish-sponsored secular university in America. I applied, had an interview with a Chicago alumnus, and forgot about it until I received a letter of acceptance.

Brandeis was founded in 1948, when Jews were still subject to a quota system at the Ivy League schools. By 1965, when I was admitted, quotas were a thing of the past and Brandeis was thriving in its own right. Located ten miles outside Boston, the campus was a self-enclosed jewel on the banks of the Charles River, at the edge of the depressed industrial town of Waltham. It was the most New York–oriented school in Massachusetts. The buildings were mostly named after New York immigrant businessmen who had not graduated from any university but had adopted Brandeis as their own. Many New York intellectuals had taught or were teaching there: Philip Rahv, Irving Howe, Lewis Coser, and Max Lerner. Herbert Marcuse had just departed, one of the survivors of the Frankfurt School, a group of German thinkers on the left who had developed a cultural critique to undermine what they called "vulgar Marxism" and many of whom had come to America in the 1930s. Also on the faculty was

Abraham Maslow, the psychologist who originated the theory of self-actualization and the author of *Toward a Psychology of Being*. The place had a cosmopolitan kind of parochialism. Orthodoxy of any kind was the only forbidden category. Modernism was the classic canon. Notions of complexity, ambiguity, and contingency were the truisms.

I was sixteen years old when I graduated from high school and had never been east of Columbus, Ohio. I hung my Kennedy poster in my dorm room. By the end of my freshman year, my roommate and I had turned our room into a gallery of surrealist art, with furniture hanging from the walls and mobiles from the ceiling. In the space of those few months, the relative quiescence of politics had cracked. I attended an anti–Vietnam War rally on campus. The bohemian, beat atmosphere changed, too. At Cholmondeley's, the campus coffeehouse, which had featured jazz and folk music, rock bands now played. The dormitory quads could be ranked according to the music wailing out the windows: from Ridgewood (Cream) to East (Four Tops), from Hamilton (Byrds) to North (Beatles). A spring arts festival, a cross between a countercultural and an Elizabethan fair, became the biggest annual campus event—called Bronstein Day, in honor of an older art professor rumored (falsely) to be a cousin of Trotsky (né Bronstein).

I studied political theory with Isaac Kramnick, social conflict with Coser, classics with Aileen Ward. I became an American studies major. My favorite course was American literature, and my favorite professor was Sacvan Bercovitch, whose particular specialty was Puritan jeremiads. I took the "Sociology of Consciousness" course with Maurice Stein, who produced huge, detailed posters tracing the influences of modern thought in politics, sociology, and psychology that I and other students hung on our walls. I read as much as I could across these charts.

Student politics as such barely existed, as the line between politics and culture was blurred. I participated in Students for a Democratic Society, which held discussions and chartered buses to go to Washington for antiwar marches. Two members of the Maoist Progressive Labor Party (both short-haired graduate students) tried to foment a sectarian politics, but they were rejected. The rest of us were anticommunist, mostly antithetical to organization of any kind, and had no use for their stupid rigidities. (At Harvard and Tufts, by contrast, PL had sizable contingents of privileged students who believed in their superior purity and advocated a make-believe version of Marxism-Leninism.) In my own case, no matter how adamantly opposed I was to the war, I never ceased to regard myself as a Democrat.

At Brandeis, the 1960s were a decade where inherited traditions were elaborated on, not broken with. There were no events, like the University Hall bust at Harvard in 1969, precipitating overnight radicalization. And there was no violence. When black students occupied Ford Hall on campus, demanding a black studies department, white students surged into the administration building, where our actions turned into a teach-in. Instead of shutting out the administration, everyone went to work as usual and coexisted. The head of the Black Student Union happened to live next door to me. I was elected to the strike committee and wandered back and forth to talk to him in Ford Hall. In the end, the administration found a way to meet the important demands, no one got hurt, and everyone learned something.

In 1966, I joined a crowd of about one hundred thousand at Soldiers Field in Chicago to hear Martin Luther King, Jr., launch the Chicago Freedom Movement in one of the most segregated cities in the North. Two days later, from the Central Post Office on the West Side, where I had a summer job as a letter sorter, I could see the smoke and fire rising from the nearby ghetto, my father's old neighborhood. It took days for the National Guard to restore order. King's movement foundered and he abandoned Chicago.

In 1967, I returned to the Chicago Stadium, this time to see King delivering a jeremiad against the Vietnam War. His speech was an invocation for the National Conference for a New Politics, which turned into a festival of left-wing factionalism and black nationalist posturing whose outcome was a denunciation of Israel. If anything, this inoculated me against the coming Days of Rage—the descent into violence. (As I wandered around the Breugel-like scene at the Palmer House, I encountered the person who was funding the disastrous conference, Martin Peretz, a Brandeis alumnus whom I would come to know later, after he became the owner of *The New Republic*. Peretz walked out and started backing Eugene McCarthy's primary challenge to Lyndon Johnson.)

In 1968, after King's murder in April, and just back from Brandeis, I sat alone late on a June night and watched on television when Robert Kennedy was assassinated. I remember waking my parents to say, "Kennedy's been shot." In August, I joined a childhood friend at an antiwar rally in Grant Park in front of the Conrad Hilton Hotel, where the Democratic candidate, Vice President Hubert Humphrey, who had still not taken an independent stand on the war, was headquartered during the convention. The police went wild and staged what can only be called a riot. I ran faster than my friend, who got his skull cracked.

I dragged him to a first-aid station. Politics had become a nightmare.

This breakdown of liberalism allowed Richard Nixon into the White House, as the Vietnam War was becoming more ferocious and pointless. At our graduation ceremony in June 1969, my entire Brandeis class wore stenciled red fists on the backs of our gowns. I felt I had gotten an education, but to what end I did not know. I had no notion of a profession and no resources. Politics as I had known them had evaporated. The adult world I had thought of as permanent was gone. I was twenty years old.

Soon, I moved into an apartment in a working-class section of Cambridge and got a job as a guard in the Boston Public Library. A few months later I boarded a bus in front of Cambridge City Hall headed for the South Boston Army Base for a draft physical. Every single person on that bus returned stamped with an ineligible draft status, 1Y or 4F, perhaps because they came from antiwar Cambridge. (I had asthma.) The army, too, seemed dysfunctional and disintegrating under the strain of Vietnam. On the bus, I was surprised to meet someone I knew, Paul Solman, an art student who had graduated two years before me from Brandeis. He told me that he was working at a newspaper, *Boston After Dark*, and suggested I might write for it. I asked what I needed to do to qualify and he told me just to show up. It was a lucky encounter because I was fired from the library when I was caught reading there.

I wandered over to the offices of *Boston After Dark* on Boylston Street and discovered a shabby warren of broken plaster filled with people my own age. I was soon given a press card. *BAD* had begun as a thin weekly tabloid of entertainment listings and reviews distributed on college campuses, but overnight it had turned into a new kind of newspaper. It wasn't yet called "alternative" and it wasn't "underground." It resembled *The Village Voice*, but it wasn't a product of the Beat years, and its presence in Boston actually made it a broader and more influential publication than the *Voice* was in New York. Everyone at these new papers—the Cambridge *Phoenix* had just sprung up—was just out of college, intensely ambitious, but uninterested in lockstep professional careers at that tumultuous moment. It did not occur to us that we should toil in backwater small-town newspapers and work our way up the chain until we arrived at a big-city daily. That seemed the most ridiculous notion of all.

Journalism as we understood it was a continuation of the experiment begun in college by other means, and it was politically engaged. The tone of these new publications was adversarial and eclectic. No one was slotted into covering a particular beat. Any original idea, however speculative, was welcomed. Politics could be written about like a movie review, a movie review like politics. News stories were written with literary devices and as narratives. The classic *New Yorker*–style profile was adapted as a common feature. It was a given that journalism was committed and crusading—and that David Bowie's latest album was an important statement. Investigative reporting was strong, including exposure of the racist elements in the antibusing movement and the complicity of some politicians with them, and of corruption in the legislature and City Hall, as well as stories about working-class neighborhoods trampled by leviathan bureaucracies, whether public or private. There was a lot of subjective writing, yet it adhered to basic standards of fact. (Not a single libel suit was ever filed against *BAD* or the *Phoenix*.) Being weekly gave us time and space. We were like magazines, but with propellers and edges. Journalism was how we traveled to wherever we needed to go.

We thought of ourselves as both antiestablishment and in the mainstream. We were the first wave of baby-boom graduates, leaving college and migrating to urban neighborhoods where we fashioned our postbohemian world. The Boston area had one of the highest concentrations of college students in the country, about three hundred thousand. It was also a destination city for young people throughout the Northeast. Very few writers at the papers were homegrown Bostonians. We had come from elsewhere, and we weren't rooted in Boston's endless ethnic conflict between the Yankees and the Irish. We were a new side altogether. Much of old Boston still existed physically, and we could find decent places to live at low rents. With the proliferation of bookstores and coffeehouses the place made for a congenial environment in which to live cheaply and experiment professionally. It was our moveable feast.

The papers reached hundreds of thousands of readers. They intervened in local elections, promoting the rise of antiwar, female, and gay candidates. Politicians followed the political coverage closely. When Massachusetts became the only state to vote for George McGovern, the Democratic candidate for president in 1972 against Nixon, J. Anthony Lukas, then at *The New York Times*, wrote that some of the credit belonged to the unusually influential alternative press.

The ensemble of writers at the Boston papers included, at one time or another, a fantastic array of talent: Joe Klein, now of *The New Yorker*, Bo Burlingham, who became editor of *Inc*; Paul Solman, the economics correspondent for PBS's *Jim Lehrer News Hour*; Jon Landau, a Brandeis classmate and rock critic who became Bruce Springsteen's manager and producer after discovering him in a Cambridge bar; David Denby, film critic of *The New Yorker*; Janet Maslin, film critic and book reviewer for

The New York Times; Stephen Schiff, writer and screenwriter; the documentary filmmaker Arnie Reisman; Peter Herbst, editor of *Premiere* magazine; Lynn Staley, design director for *Newsweek*; Ben Gerson, a Brandeis classmate who became an editor of the *Harvard Business Review*; Ken Emerson, an editor of *The New York Times Magazine* and biographer of Stephen Foster; Derek Shearer, U.S. ambassador to Finland and international affairs professor at Occidental College; Richard Rosen, Edgar Award–winning mystery novelist and CBS producer; Timothy Crouse, author of *Boys on the Bus*; Jim Sleeper, New York *Daily News* columnist; Joe Conason, *New York Observer* columnist; Laura Shapiro, *Newsweek*'s book critic; David Ansen, *Newsweek* film critic; Diane McWhorter, Pulitzer Prize–winning author of *Carry Me Home*; Christie Hefner, publisher of *Playboy*; Rory O'Connor, documentary filmmaker; Craig Unger, editor of *Boston* magazine; Howard Husock, director of case studies at the Kennedy School at Harvard; and James Kugel, now a distinguished biblical scholar at Harvard. The scene was memorialized in a comedic film, *Between the Lines*, directed by Joan Micklin Silver in 1977.

At *Boston After Dark*, I wrote about labor strikes, local schools, and the Massachusetts congressional delegation. I wrote book reviews and essays. I got a byline, something I hadn't paid much attention to before, and was somewhat startled to have my work be recognized. I learned to write news stories on deadline as well as long profiles, to do investigative digging, and to interview newly published authors. I turned the microphone on Studs Terkel, the oral historian of ordinary people's experiences, Chicago's de facto poet laureate, and traveled to Portugal to write a series of articles in 1975 on the revolution toppling Antonio Salazar's dictatorship there. And I wrote a political and cultural column called "Guns & Butter." My editors and fellow writers were my peers. (From one of them, Derek Shearer, son of the legendary journalist Lloyd Shearer, I first heard talk of a former roommate of his at Oxford who was beginning a political career in Arkansas.) I also wrote for any other publication that would print my writing, from *Sport* magazine to *Oui*, a skin mag, to *In These Times*, a left-wing weekly. I did political commentaries on a Cambridge radio station and news broadcasts on a Boston one. And I wrote about the Boston Red Sox, becoming friendly with the ace pitcher Bill "Spaceman" Lee. It was an antic apprenticeship that couldn't last.

The owner of the Cambridge *Phoenix* sold out to the owner of *Boston After Dark* in 1972, and the amalgam became the *Boston Phoenix*. But the staff of the original *Phoenix* refused to disband and in defiance formed a collective to publish a newspaper called *The Real Paper* to compete with the supposedly phony *Boston Phoenix*. Soon, *The Real Paper* collective collapsed because of sexual jealousies and the cunning of a few communards who bought up the others' shares and concentrated control. They sold *The Real Paper* to a group consisting of David Rockefeller, Jr.; Ralph Fine, a Boston businessman; and William Weld, who installed Martin Linsky as editor. Linsky, a *Boston Globe* editorial writer, had been the bright young man of the liberal wing of the Republican Party in Massachusetts, whose political career effectively ended when he lost a congressional race in 1972. Linsky turned out to be an excellent editor, smart, worldly, and encouraging. With the change at *The Real Paper*, I jumped from the *Phoenix*. Linsky was a superb guide for my increased focus on Massachusetts politics, though I created a slightly uncomfortable moment for him when one state senator, a former pugilist, confronted him about an article I had written entitled "The Ten Dumbest State Legislators."

A new form of politics was emerging in the 1970s—the permanent campaign. Boston had a dense political calendar with major elections every year: city, state, congressional—and in neighboring New Hampshire the first presidential primary election occurred every four years. Beginning with the successful antiwar candidacy for the Congress of Father Robert Drinan in 1970, the old Irish political establishment in Boston was supplanted by a younger generation, including Congressmen Ed Markey and Barney Frank, and Senator John Kerry, all of whom I wrote about early in their careers. Tip O'Neill, who became Speaker of the House in 1977, turned antiwar and adjusted to the new vibrations. He became a benign avuncular figure to these upstarts. The intense political schedule, the assimilation of social movements into regular politics, and the shattering of Boston's fragmented political machine led to the growth of a new kind of political figure: the consultant, who relied upon computerized polling and media campaigns to move the candidates ahead. In the late 1970s, I fell in with a group of Democratic consultants—John Marttila, Dan Payne, and Tom Kiley, who were behind many Boston campaigns—and wrote about them. At the urging of Linsky, I applied my ideas about the fundamental change in politics to Republicans as well. It became my first book, *The Permanent Campaign*, published in 1980.

I tried to show the distance from riding in a bus with beefy precinct captains to the new world of the consultants:

> The consultants have supplanted the old party bosses as the link to the voters. Consultants have the personal contact, possess knowledge of the

intimate history of campaigns, and have the voter-catching skills that party bosses once prided themselves on. . . .

For different candidates, the permanent campaign will assume different shapes; but whichever candidate triumphs, the permanent campaign will remain. The permanent campaign is not the game plan of any specific politician; it is a description of the new process of American politics.*

There was a relation, too, between the new economy and the permanent campaign. Boston had been an incubator for the high-tech shift, and as the counterculture was fading, a sort of countereconomy was burgeoning there. This was all of a piece with the political change:

Politics . . . is not a static enterprise in which faces change but institutions remain the same. A deep transformation of American society has only just begun. And the coming of . . . the information age—where white-collar workers outnumber blue-collar, computers are the archetypal machines, knowledge is a vital form of capital, much heavy industry is exported to the more dynamic Third World countries, and America becomes the home office of the world—must alter politics. The permanent campaign, which rests on the new technology, is the political form of the information age.†

I viewed the techniques of politics as inherently neither honest nor dishonest. I was not judgmental about candidates using television commercials, any more than I was about precinct captains. The new methods were available to any candidate to apply toward any end. They could be deployed in endless permutations. While many bemoaned the emptiness of image making and the lack of principle in polling, I saw these new techniques as inevitable and neutral. One could not make the new means of politics disappear by denouncing them. They could no more be waved away than could new computer and media technologies. I had little sympathy for moralistic gestures or nostalgia. Despite my agreement with his stated policies, I had disliked Eugene McCarthy's anti-Vietnam candidacy because of its moral vanity and narcissistic tone of poetic doom.

*Sidney Blumenthal, *The Permanent Campaign: Inside the World of Elite Political Operatives*, Touchstone, 1982, pp. 17, 26.
†Ibid., p. 10.

The complex imperfections of Bobby Kennedy had appealed to me, though. When he was killed, no one else appeared who remotely fit the bill. Evocations of the glorious past were like a dead spot for me. That sort of rhetoric inspired no feeling whatsoever. Whenever I heard hackneyed talk of a golden age I went numb. But I had an aesthetic appreciation of the people who approached politics as an art, regardless of their ideological complexion, including an old trouper like Ronald Reagan, who effortlessly glided from the movie making of the big studio era to the nimble politics of the small screen. I wondered when a Democrat would emerge for whom modern politics was second nature. I was waiting for the new.

I began exploring the sources of Reaganism, writing about the thinkers who had fabricated that pastiche doctrine called supply-side economics and about the neoconservatives. My wife, Jackie, and I were living in a drafty, tilted wooden house behind the police station in Brookline Village with our two young children, Max and Paul. *The Real Paper* had been sold and had then gone under in the recession. (Linsky was teaching at Harvard. When Bill Weld became governor, Linsky served as his chief of staff.) I had no job. I began to work on my book about the conservative movement, *The Rise of the Counter-Establishment*.

Michael Dukakis, a capable, articulate, and policy-oriented politician, had been defeated when he campaigned for reelection as governor of Massachusetts in 1978, swamped in the rising conservative tide by a stumbling, tongue-tied, reactionary candidate named Ed King (advised by Dick Morris). In 1982 Dukakis was going to challenge King again in what was billed as The Rematch. As an adviser on Dukakis's strategic team, I urged him to emphasize his gubernatorial record of 1974–78 when he had helped to create the new economy in Massachusetts and understood its needs. On this point, I argued alongside Ralph Whitehead, a fellow Chicagoan, former press secretary to Boston Mayor Kevin White, and a professor at the University of Massachusetts at Amherst, whose studies on the shift of blue collars into what he called "new collars" had contributed to these ideas of a changing economy and electorate. I also recruited a new friend, Robert Reich, who had arrived at Harvard's Kennedy School as a refugee from the Carter administration after the 1980 election. Reich was developing ideas about the new economy and industrial policy that became the basis of his book *The Next American Frontier*. (Reich mentioned in passing his sojourn at Oxford as a Rhodes scholar along with the governor of Arkansas.)

But Dukakis tended to be literal-minded, almost stubbornly unable to see beyond specific policies to larger ideas and themes. He was a Silent Generation liberal, a believer in civil liberties, civil rights, and civil debate (he had been moderator of a local PBS show called *The Advocates*), muted and controlled, unwilling and perhaps unable to engage in any appeal beyond the logic of his proposed policies, as though he were suspicious of moving people emotionally. Still, his performance in the debates was sharp and surprisingly aggressive, stunning his wooden opponent, and he easily won.

Out of the blue, a year later, I received a call from Martin Peretz, now owner of *The New Republic*, asking me to cover the forthcoming 1984 presidential campaign. I had written several articles for the magazine over the years (including one piece about the political ineptitude of Ted Kennedy's ill-fated race against Jimmy Carter for the Democratic nomination in 1980). I accepted on the spot and became the magazine's national political correspondent. Within a week, a producer at the NBC *Today Show* who had read *The Permanent Campaign* invited me to be a commentator during the campaign—I was supposed to be the youthful, fresh voice playing off the graybeard pundits. Through Jane Pauley, the *Today Show* host, I befriended her husband, Garry Trudeau, the illustrator and writer of the *Doonesbury* cartoon strip, and we engaged in a number of fruitful collaborations, not least interviewing the presidential candidates about their favorite Beatle.

The New Republic, founded in 1914, was the historic standard-bearer of liberalism, reflecting the history of its ups and downs throughout the twentieth century. Almost every important liberal intellectual had written for it. In the aftermath of Carter's defeat in 1980 and near the high-water mark of Reaganism, *The New Republic* became a crucial institution in which to observe the struggle over liberalism. The conflicts within the magazine differed in emphasis from those within the Democratic Party but overlapped them. The central argument was between liberals attempting to renew their politics and neoconservatives, in practice if not in name, aligned with the Reagan administration on the basis of his foreign policy. The liberals disagreed about what to retain from the past and what to advocate for the future—more a matter of nuance than harsh contention. The magazine's internal tensions infused it with electricity that attracted the attention of Washington's political class. Because it was so closely read, *The New Republic* had the ability to drive the way in which larger papers, especially *The New York Times* and *The Washington Post*, covered politics. And as for those neoconservatives whose articles appeared in it, the credential lifted them out of the right-wing ghetto.

The divisions within the magazine reflected to a degree those within its owner. Martin Peretz, a Harvard lecturer, had married an heiress to the Singer sewing-machine fortune and had bought *The New Republic* for a song in 1974. As its impresario he had a knack for assembling talented, jostling writers. His own skepticism about liberalism, much of it in reaction to his involvement in the causes of the 1960s—when he had been faculty adviser to the Students for a Democratic Society chapter at Harvard, among other things—often had a productive effect. His one consistent position was unwavering support for Israel. Marty had a contentious impulse to write pointedly sharp notes to prominent establishment figures, and to his delight he turned those figures into a pantheon of antagonists. But in arguing along with the rest of us he did not impose his fiat on those who disagreed with him.

Almost instantly, I became fast friends with Hendrik Hertzberg, the editor. Like other gifted writers and editors on the magazine—Michael Kinsley, Leon Wieseltier—Rick had been at Harvard when he first encountered Marty. For a dozen years before he became President Carter's chief speechwriter, he had written at *The New Yorker*. His political erudition came not only from his own experiences but from his genes. His parents had a long history of devotion to high political ideals and had been close to Gandhi and Norman Thomas. Rick appreciated practical politics and was an idealist without being a prig. Given his family tradition on the democratic left, there was never any question of both his liberalism and his anticommunism. He had a quick wit, immense charm, and an ability to keep political differences from turning nasty. Though I was still living in Brookline and on the campaign trail, only occasionally coming to Washington, we spent hours on the phone every day.

While I had been writing *The Permanent Campaign*, I met Lee Auspitz, a founder of the moderate Republican group the Ripon Society, and a genuinely original philosopher of American pragmatism. Auspitz had been the tutor at Harvard of Patrick Caddell, who since his work in the Carter White House as Carter's pollster had become a Boston as well as a Washington denizen, as a founder of Cambridge Survey Research. Caddell is one of those people who love to play at speculative politics all the time. By 1983, his mercurial, incisive mind was going mad contemplating the Democrats' near-hopeless presidential predicament. Like him, I believed that the certain Democratic nominee, former vice president Walter Mondale, would not be a success. Despite his deeply progressive instincts, Mondale combined the burdens of having been on the defeated ticket in 1980 and of seeing politics through the old interest-group lens of someone raised in the Minnesota Democratic–Farmer Labor Party. This marked him for overwhelming defeat, and the Democratic party as incapable of rejuvenating itself.

On the eve of the 1984 primaries, there was no really promising candidate in sight. The political isolate Caddell and I wandered around Beacon Hill, where he had an apartment, and the bars of Harvard Square, as he became more and more agitated. Finally, he decided he would invent a candidate and poll on behalf of his imaginary campaign. "Mr. Smith," he was named, was an innovative moderate liberal senator of the younger generation, unbound to the old, usual politics. "Smith" beat all the other Democratic contenders.

Without a candidate, no idea has force in politics. Caddell, the wizard of alienation, was alienated from his natural ally in the race, Senator Gary Hart, himself a remote character. Hart had been McGovern's campaign manager in 1972 when he hired Caddell, still a Harvard student, as pollster. Hart got himself elected to the Senate from Colorado in the Watergate class of 1974, making a serious and intelligent career as a reformer in military policies and economics. He was the legislative counterpart to a group of Pentagon planners who advocated a leaner armed forces in line with new strategic imperatives. Hart, working with Reich and others, proposed elements of a new industrial policy, too, foreseeing globalization, and unlike the conservative ideologues, they favored decisive government action. They eschewed protectionism, which set them off from Mondale and the more traditional Democrats. In the field, Hart was most like "Smith." Overcoming obscure personal differences, Caddell and Hart saddled up and rode into New Hampshire, routing Mondale. For a while it appeared that Hart might capture the nomination, but the constituencies within the party backing Mondale were finally too powerful. Though Hart romped ahead in California, the last primary, he was an outrider. Warren Beatty hovered offstage throughout his campaign (Beatty had been a friend since the McGovern campaign), offering advice, some of it good, some of it not so good. It was a cliché among those of us who watched this that Beatty wished he were Hart and Hart wished he were Beatty. Caddell wanted to be both at the same time.

The Democratic convention took place in San Francisco, and on its opening night the keynote speaker was the governor of New York, Mario Cuomo. Cuomo was the dream version of the dull but decent Mondale: passionate, brilliant, and unapologetic. But Cuomo did not run for the presidency that year. He remained a fantasy candidate who could never bring himself to make the leap. That night, Cuomo spoke in his commanding, sonorous voice, holding a light to the party caught in the middle of the tunnel. The problem was that he was providing illumination from the back. Cuomo attributed Reagan's popularity to "smoke and mirrors" and "illusions." The Democrats needed to recover their past to move ahead: "We can do it again. If we do not forget. . . . Please make this nation remember how futures are built." Yet Cuomo's speech was an appeal to memory.

Right after the convention's first session adjourned, I went to the party sponsored by *The Washington Post*. To my surprise, as soon as I entered the glass doors, invitation in hand, my arm was grabbed by a soft-spoken young woman who brought me to a small table, got me a glass of wine, and asked me to wait there for Katharine Graham. Mrs. Graham, who had choreographed this meeting, promptly sat down, said she had been reading my *New Republic* articles, and wondered about my opinion of Cuomo's speech. I told her that I thought it was politically wrong-headed and, especially because of Cuomo's convincing force, would help push the Democrats toward incomprehension about their coming defeat. I had no idea what her thoughts were as I blurted out mine, but she agreed with me. As her guests approached the table to pay respects, we chatted for about an hour.

Mrs. Graham was a more interesting woman than her matriarchal image suggested. Through her aristocratic diction and regal bearing she could be forbidding when she chose, but she was not Queen Victoria, self-exiled to Balmoral Castle in mourning clothes. As she wrote in her wonderful memoir, she had been treated by her parents as something of an ugly duckling and had surprised herself by attracting Philip Graham, the adventurous and brilliant young New Dealer who gradually transformed her father's staid newspaper, the perennial number two in Washington, into the capital's number one. Graham had been a force in the Democratic Party and had used the *Post* and *Newsweek* to shape the news. When he committed suicide in 1963, the victim of manic depression, she realized she had to step into his job herself, but felt insecure about her abilities and inferior about her charm. Yet she was instinctively drawn to men like Phil, of whom the principal one was Benjamin Bradlee, an aristocratic swashbuckler, a pal of Phil's, and a friend of Jack Kennedy's. Mrs. Graham enjoyed hobnobbing with world leaders and celebrities, hearing inside gossip and funny off-color stories, and cultivating literary lions and self-made millionaires. Her judgment, when the newspaper itself was at stake, was invariably right and courageous. The showdown with Nixon during the Pentagon Papers and Watergate conflicts was in its way the culmination of the Kennedy wars. It was the making of *The Washington Post*. About a week after our conversation at the Democratic convention she telephoned me and asked if I'd like to work at the *Post*. Then Bradlee called and asked me to visit him.

Bradlee was one of the most natural leaders I ever met. He made you want to wear his team's jersey and play to exhaustion. He had this quality not because he controlled his job and your paycheck but because of his personality. He was gruff and caring, freewheeling and exacting. He radiated confidence without a scintilla of insecurity in his being. No one intimidated him, least of all Nixon. He had remade the *Post*, and he had invented its "Style" section, a daily alternative newspaper within the paper that featured iconoclastic writers with strong points of view like Nicholas von Hoffman.

Before the *Post* Bradlee had had a picaresque career—going from his old Bay State origins to publishing a liberal, failed newspaper in New Hampshire, from serving as press attaché in the Paris embassy to becoming *Newsweek*'s Washington bureau chief and friend of JFK. Bradlee preferred a Redskins football game to a Kennedy Center concert, the tough-guy insider banter of the fabled attorney Edward Bennett Williams to a policy preview from a cabinet secretary. But he respected and fed off ideas. One of his closest friends, his intellectual alter ego and sidekick, was a writer on the *Post* named Lawrence Stern, a former radical with a sharp and whirring mind, constantly coming up with angles and theories and stories. When Stern died of a sudden heart attack in the late 1970s, Bradlee led a memorial tribute on the roof of the *Post*, outside Mrs. Graham's office, making a toast to Stern and shattering his glass against the wall. Hundreds of others threw their glasses, too. After that, Bradlee slowly but surely began to retire emotionally into his new N Street mansion with his new wife, the "Style" writer Sally Quinn.

The high Bradlee days had peaked, but Bradlee still presided over the *Post* as its charismatic chieftain. I was supposed to be his "impact hire," outside the normal guidelines, and he assigned the national editor, Shelby Coffey, to figure out how to make it work. Shelby was imaginative, ironic, irreverent, and solidly within the Bradlee orbit. He designed a position wherein I would write a long commentary and analysis every other week in the Sunday "Outlook" section but sit in the newsroom with the national staff, contributing news stories if and when they developed.

Before I managed to move to Washington and start the new job, however, Coffey accepted the editorship of *U.S. News and World Report*. The "Outlook" editor, Robert Kaiser, was promoted to the position of national editor—and I went with him. The carefully devised arrangement I had negotiated was gone. Though there was no "Outlook" editor for a year, I occasionally wrote pieces for the section.

The first project I undertook was a four-part series splashed on the front page about the influence of conservatives in Reagan's Washington. Outside their own precincts, the growth of the conservatives' infrastructure had gone virtually unnoticed. Their long march was like a secret history. I had spent years studying and getting to know them, which was like being a foreign correspondent in one's own country. I learned about their obscure origins, conflicting ideas, alliances with politicians, internal rivalries, sources of funding, and levels of penetration by their cadres in the agencies and departments of government. "People are policy," as Edwin Feulner, president of the right-wing Heritage Foundation, told me. Mrs. Graham was happy about the series, my editors were happy, but the most pleased of all were conservatives, who felt they had been acknowledged at last in the newspaper they hated most.

I made something of a beat out of the conservatives. My situation on the national staff was somewhat awkward because my precise function had not been defined. A few of the political reporters were guarded and jealous of their turf. They had the mentality of medieval guild members, and only those who they thought had paid their dues would be permitted into their closed ranks. These were some of the same people who had initially dismissed the Watergate story, had trusted Nixon's account, and were suspicious of Bernstein and Woodward—and Bradlee. Kaiser was supportive and handed me the political media beat. I also wrote on the Reagan administration's political uses of "the window of vulnerability" in nuclear strategy, on Rehnquist's legal philosophy when he was made chief justice, on the influence of Defense Department official Richard Perle and his decades-long opposition to arms control, and on the left-wing Institute for Policy Studies, with its withdrawal from actual politics and its romanticism about Third World revolutions. And I was part of a team that broke the story revealing Oliver North's existence and activities on the National Security Council. CIA Director William Casey strode into the newsroom to implore the editors not to publish North's name, claiming "national security" considerations. Dismayingly, for two days, the article was indeed held in abeyance. We did not know at the time that we had identified a key player in what became the Iran-Contra scandal, which undoubtedly was what Casey was trying to shield from public view.

My relations with the conservatives were mostly friendly. Many of them were eager to talk to me because I was interested in their politics, gave them coverage, and granted them the validity of their ideas. I regularly talked with Jack Kemp, the great conservative hope, and Pat Buchanan, especially after he became Reagan's communications director. I checked in with Newt Gingrich and the tight group of congressmen who were his palace guard. (They gave me my first news stories for the *Post*.) I kept up with the think-tankers at Heritage and the American Enterprise Institute, the younger writers at *The Washington Times* and the small journals.

In 1986, my book *The Rise of the Counter-Establishment* was published. It followed the idea I had posited in *The Permanent Campaign*: that conservatives were filling a "vacuum opened by the old parties' decay. . . . The realignment of policy the conservatives have wrought is a reflection, not of a realigned party system, but of a realignment of elites."* Believing, almost as if they were vulgar Marxists, that a "liberal establishment" was the ruling class, the conservatives, over decades, built an infrastructure to counter it: "By constructing their own establishment, piece by piece, they hoped to supplant the liberals. . . . Through the making of a far-flung network they attempted to conquer political society. . . . The Counter-Establishment was a political elite aspiring to become a governing elite."†

The publication of the book and my writing in the *Post* aroused a vehement reaction from only one element: the neoconservatives. Their antagonism came mainly from my having traced their methods and tactics back to their origins on the far left or in the Communist Party. They tended to think of conservatism as a Marxist-Leninist party, an inner party of those who made the decisions and an outer one of those who carried them out. There were publicists and "reliables." Those who came to disagree were treated as "splitters," to be purged and denounced. The neoconservatives were the latest in an ideological line going back to James Burnham, Frank Meyer, and Whittaker Chambers—all early editors at William F. Buckley, Jr.'s *National Review* and all ex-communists. Former Trotskyists among the neocons brought a special air of superiority and intellectuality, as though conservatism were an extension of the Fourth International. (Their Trotskyism sometimes transmuted into Straussianism, the ahistorical philosophy of Leo Strauss, at the University of Chicago, whose adherents see themselves as Platonic

---

*Sidney Blumenthal, *The Rise of the Counter-Establishment: From Conservative Ideology to Political Power*, Times Books, 1986, p. ix.

†Ibid., pp. 4–5.

omniscient tutors manipulating benighted but necessary politicians—for example, William Kristol acting as chief of staff to Vice President Dan Quayle.)

Some of these neoconservatives regarded me in any case as coming from the wrong side of the political tracks, the liberal side of *The New Republic*. (They believed they were competing for control of the magazine.) In a small neoconservative newsletter eerily reproducing the Stalinist style and appropriately called *Contentions*, which was published by Midge Decter, Norman Podhoretz's wife, every issue designated an enemy for vituperative treatment, and I became the "*Washington Post*'s hitman." A decade later, when the neoconservatives gained important positions within Rupert Murdoch's media, their smearing of enemies had wider circulation than it had had through *Contentions*. And my reporting at the *Post* on various people involved in the Iran-Contra scandal earned me enemies on the right who became even more vociferous in their attacks on me after I went into the White House. With Clinton in office, the neoconservatives could not wait for what they regarded as pure and simple political payback. Elliott Abrams, assistant secretary of state for Latin America for Reagan, had been most intimately linked to them, being the son-in-law of Norman Podhoretz and Midge Decter. His illegalities had included soliciting $10 million in aid to the Contras from the Sultan of Brunei, which he managed to deposit in the wrong Swiss bank account by confusing the account numbers. Abrams pled guilty to misleading Congress and investigators. Early in the Whitewater controversy, in May 1994, his wife, Rachel Abrams, wrote an article in *The Washington Times*, in which she laid out the neoconservatives' vindictive hatreds:

> I know something about Bill and Hillary Clinton right now. I know how their stomachs churn, how their anxiety mounts, how their worry over their defenseless child increases. I know their inability to sleep at night and their reluctance to rise in the morning. I know every new incursion of doubt, every heartbreak over bailing friends, every sting and bite the press gives, every jaw-clenching look at front-page photographs of . . . the special prosecutor. I know all this, and the thought of it makes me happy. Yet complete contentment remains just out of reach. The pleasure I take in the suffering of the Clintons isn't full, for it is clear that there is more in store for them, and I feel strongly that they haven't suffered enough. . . . I will be even happier as this unfolds. More important for me is the sense that until now the president and his first lady have been

rather too alone in their troubles, that there are others who, worms that they are, should be squirming now with discomfort and embarrassment, and have only just begun to do so. . . . What really counts about them, what binds them to one another and sets them apart from the hoi polloi, is their membership in the educated, left-leaning, affluent professional class. These are the lawyers, the columnists and editorialists, the reporters, the legislators and the executives, the aristocrats of "idealism."*

For my various ideological crimes—being a liberal on *The New Republic*, writing my books and my articles in *The Washington Post*—I became one of the class enemy, "worms that they are."

During the 1988 presidential campaign, I mostly covered the Republicans: Jack Kemp's fading; Pat Robertson's "neo-Confederate" charge; and Pat Buchanan's revenge. I traveled to Russell, Kansas, where I examined Bob Dole's background and rise. But I was also involved in another campaign. The candidate was a youthful, moderate liberal Democratic senator bearing an uncanny resemblance to "Smith." His name was Jack Tanner, and he was running for the presidency to fill the vacuum left by Gary Hart's unceremonious departure. But Tanner couldn't quite figure out his motive for running other than a need to ask "the impertinent question." Tanner stumbled from one crisis to the next, from the primaries to the convention. And it was all broadcast on HBO. Michael Murphy played Tanner's befuddled efforts at effectiveness with understated nuance. Garry Trudeau wrote the scripts, Robert Altman directed, and I was the consultant, inventing a slogan to stress the authenticity of this fictional candidate: "For Real." Garry's writing was sharp, quick, and subtle. I watched Bob Altman in action, with his creation of overflowing, seemingly chaotic scenes that were sculpted into complex narratives. But when the convention ended, so did the series. Michael Dukakis, not Tanner, stood on the platform as the Democratic nominee.

From that pinnacle of his campaign Dukakis loomed seventeen points above Vice President George Bush. Bush's manager, Lee Atwater, felt his candidate had no choice but to go negative, the dark territory where Atwater operated best. Bush could never locate what he called "the vision thing," so Atwater's night vision had to substitute. Dukakis was attacked as weak on crime, unpatriotic, and, worst of all, "liberal," marked with what Bush derided as the "L" word. Rather than rise to the occasion,

*Rachel Abrams, "When a Special Prosecutor Comes into Your Life," *The Washington Times*, March 10, 1994.

Dukakis shrank from the battle, diminishing himself. After he gained the nomination, his will retracted.

When Bush defeated Dukakis, I took a leave from the *Post* to write a book on the avoidance and denial in American politics of the consequences of the Cold War's end. Politics itself seemed to be at a dead end. Former Brookline neighbors told me that a week after the election they had seen the former Democratic candidate roaming our local hardware store—and no one approached him to tell him he had fought a good fight or even to talk with him. They felt ashamed that he had not answered the smears and slurs about "the liberal governor of Massachusetts." Their local patriotism was offended by his passivity. It was a sad coda.

In 1990, *Pledging Allegiance: The Last Campaign of the Cold War* was published. In it, I not only tried to describe the recent past but also looked forward to the political possibilities created by the waning of the Cold War. Though there were no signs of change yet, conditions for change were being established. The 1988 presidential campaign had been the political centerpiece of an anxious, confused season, roughly the period 1985–90, and it had showed a stunning failure to come to terms with the new realities of the world as it was and as it was becoming:

> There was a vast silence. Political society as a whole was stricken with aphasia. . . . The problem facing the Democrats was not the restoration of an earlier age but the invention of a political language and program for a new one. . . . Just as the Cold War's beginning had radically transformed American politics, so would its ending. If the rest of the world was changed, America would change, too.*

By the time my book appeared, Rick Hertzberg had returned to *The New Republic* as editor and asked me to come back, too. At the *Post*, Bradlee would eventually retire and write his memoir. A classic institutional succession—by which the charismatic, instinctive leader is followed by the routinizing, bureaucratic one—was beginning to take place at *The Washington Post*. And the chance to renew my collaboration with Rick was an offer I couldn't refuse.

Under Rick's editorship *The New Republic* twice won the National Magazine Award for General Excellence. But in the early spring of 1992, Rick left the magazine and was replaced by Andrew Sullivan, the unlike-

---

*Sidney Blumenthal, *Pledging Allegiance: The Last Campaign of the Cold War*, HarperCollins, 1990, p. 351.

liest editor in its history. Sullivan was a young British Tory—rightist, Catholic, and gay. His appointment was an arrangement made in bad faith against *The New Republic*'s tradition, and it signaled more than the end of the liberal-neoconservative tension that had characterized Peretz's version for the previous two decades. To Americans, Sullivan's conservatism may have seemed quirky and original, but to anyone familiar with British politics it was predictably hard-line Conservative. In any event, he steered the magazine away from politics (except for weird polemics against Hillary Clinton as an "ice queen") and toward lifestyle pieces. Still, the few months we worked together before I left for *The New Yorker* were collegial.

In January 1992, my first article on Bill Clinton's candidacy was published in *The New Republic*. "The Anointed" described his extensive connections crossing all boundaries within the Democratic Party and noted his ability to square political circles. Shortly afterward, the attacks against him began. In New Hampshire, most seasoned observers agreed that he was finished. But then in Dover, in a bandbox of an Elks lodge, I watched Clinton lift himself back to political life. "They say I'm on the ropes now," he said, "not because of anything I did in my public life, not because of anything I've done to you." His voice strained. "I'm on the ropes because people questioned my life, after years of public service." The crowd was rapt and silent. "I won't forget who gave me a second chance. I'll be there with you until the last dog dies." He was transcending the kind of media attack that had brought down Hart and the calculated negative campaign that had paralyzed Dukakis. His performance, upon which the fate of his entire campaign depended, was the most electrifying political moment I had witnessed since I was a boy in the Chicago Stadium. The issues confronting Clinton in the beginning remained until the end—and his temperament and skill rescued him throughout. A couple of nights later I drove over to the motel on the outskirts of Manchester where Clinton was headquartered. Returning from a grueling day, Clinton sat in the restaurant, jauntily telling stories to whoever would listen and ordering French fries. On election night, Jackie and I spent some time with Bill and Hillary, and while we could hear the music blaring and his supporters celebrating nearby, I observed him absorbed in thought about what he would say. That was when Clinton became the Comeback Kid.

While I was writing for *The New Republic* I also was a contributing writer to *Vanity Fair*, and in late May, Tina Brown, its editor, took a small band of writers to Britain to make a splash for the magazine. We would debate before the Oxford Union the following proposition: "This house believes that rogues make better politicians than saints." The team arguing for "rogues" consisted of the historian Michael Beschloss, Alan Clark, and me. Clark was undoubtedly the greatest rogue in British politics, a deeply untrustworthy and cynical Tory member of Parliament. Michael Beschloss, an American historian of far-ranging knowledge, wore his learning lightly and elegantly. His authority, too, was unassailable. I had thought that I would be debating alongside Christopher Hitchens, a friend of mine and Tina's, but he switched at the last minute to the "saints," joining Michael White, an estimable political journalist at *The Guardian*, and Gary Maloney, a Republican party opposition researcher and Oxford graduate student, taking the high road on behalf of virtue. Hitchens's presentation for "saints" digressed into amusing reminiscences of his glory days at the Oxford Union until he came around to making the case for purity of heart.

I argued that the Republican Party, perhaps under Mr. Maloney or some other Puritan inquisitor, should set up a Ministry of Character to try American presidents posthumously. It could begin its trials with George Washington, a self-proclaimed "votary of love." I read from his love letters to Sally Fairfax, the wife of his neighbor: "The world has no business to know the object of my Love . . . when I want to conceal it." Next, the tribunal could take up the character crimes of "Slick Tom" Jefferson. By a vote of 178–64, the rogues crushed the saints. A little American history went a long way. "Bloody hell," muttered Hitchens. The London *Sunday Times* reported that the *Vanity Fair* writers imported for the debate "completely outglammed" the Brits. It was a smash. Tina was thrilled.*

A month later Tina was named editor of *The New Yorker*, and a month after that, at lunch at the Royalton Hotel in New York, she asked me to become the Washington editor. Clinton was likely to win the presidency and she wanted me to write about him. She did not want plodding, flat, and comprehensive news stories. She wanted something more like opinionated and informed British journalism. I recommended that she hire Rick Hertzberg as her number two. She didn't know him but a week later, she hired him.

Perhaps more than any other publication, *The New Yorker*, founded in 1925, established a standard for clear, concise, and stylish writing. Amer-

---

*Rebecca Mead, "The Bedroom Ayes Have It," *The Sunday Times* (London), May 24, 1992.

ican literature and journalism in the twentieth century are unimaginable without it. It had several bright strands running through its history. There was a thread of irony, wit, and humor: James Thurber, Robert Benchley, Dorothy Parker, S. J. Perelman, E. B. White, Woody Allen. There were the novelists of the American experience: John Cheever, John Updike, John O'Hara, Richard Ford. Then there were the reports that altered fundamental perceptions on the environment, race, nuclear war, culture: Rachel Carson, James Baldwin, John Hersey, Edmund Wilson. *The New Yorker*'s politics were implicitly and profoundly liberal: open-minded, decent, reasoned, and voraciously curious. The voice of those politics ranged from E. B. White's self-consciously simple idealism to Richard Rovere's sophisticated acumen to Jonathan Schell's adversarial analytics.

Tina Brown had been brought in to shake up *The New Yorker*, and shake it up she did. Her talent was to play off what she had inherited as the bad girl rattling the stodgy. She had begun her career doing that at *The Tatler* in London. Called to the attention of S. I. Newhouse, who with his brother Donald had bought *The New Yorker* in 1985 and already owned the Condé Nast magazines, she was first hired to give bounce and buzz to a languishing *Vanity Fair*, a Condé Nast property, then made editor at *The New Yorker* and directed to purge its longueurs. Tina's sensibility was theatrical, which came to her naturally; her father had been a theatrical agent in London. Above all, she depended on what the British call "nose," her instinct. It was for what was "hot"—she handed out paperweights embossed, "Hot Is Cool!" Her aesthetic was in favor of the new, the inside, the startling. Her husband was Harold Evans, the most significant British newspaper editor of his generation, an analogue to Ben Bradlee, daring and widely read (in American history, too). Harry, who moved from England and became editor in chief at Random House, which the Newhouses also then owned, was never-failing in his buoyancy and in having an encouraging word for you, "dear poet." He was a true prince among men. When Tina began dismissing some of the old guard at *The New Yorker*, they retaliated by labeling her a celebrity-obsessed philistine. Yet her sensibility, in creative tension with the magazine's tradition, made it lively again.

In mid-October 1993, Tina took a debating team composed of David Remnick, Christopher Buckley, and me to do combat at the Cheltenham Festival of Literature with the Tories of the London *Daily Telegraph* over the proposition "This would be a better world if the Sixties had never happened." The *Telegraph* reported, "Sidney Blumenthal, the visitors' team captain, won applause by turning the guns on the British government. 'This debate is the central issue now in British politics. "What went wrong?" It's the Sixties! And 14 years of Conservative rule? George Bush attacked the 1960s and now we find the strategy has crossed the Atlantic.' " I concluded by quoting the Beatles: "All you need is love." Buckley flashed the *Telegraph* team a peace sign and Remnick, the former Russia correspondent for *The Washington Post*, recalled Lenin's revolutionary admonition: "Seize the telegraph." The Yanks trounced the Brits.* At *The New Yorker*, it was blue skies.

But back in Washington that fall the press corps had become obsessed with Whitewater. On Sunday, December 18, CNN's six o'clock broadcast led with David Brock's lubricious article about the Arkansas troopers. CNN had done no work on its own to confirm Brock's allegations; its reporter was simply repeating what had appeared in *The American Spectator*. I happened to be booked on a journalists' roundtable on CNN immediately following the news. Our discussion, supposedly a year-end look back and then forward, was swamped by the Brock story. I made the points that Brock's work was tabloid journalism, a stew of uncorroborated sex tales, and that the press should not put its credibility at risk by trafficking in them. It was too late. The AP put out a bulletin and the next morning so did *The Washington Post*. The *Los Angeles Times* then published its own version of the Brock article, relying on the same bribed sources.

Two days after the CNN report, I was invited to appear on ABC News *Nightline* opposite the *L.A. Times* reporter covering this fuss. Once again, as I had ever since Gary Hart had been driven out of politics, I made the case that the mainstream press should not turn itself into a yellow press, dealing in sexual innuendo and invading the privacy of politicians to try to get at it. I also noted that the motives and methods of the *Spectator*'s writer were dubious: "This all started with David Brock, a right-wing—well, I hesitate to call him a journalist."

This *Nightline* appearance marked me as somehow having crossed the line from the media's side to the President's. I didn't believe there were sides. I thought that the fundamental problem was that the Whitewater story as it was being retailed was wrong and that the sustained application of skepticism would have unraveled it. But there was protection in conformity, as there always is in packs, and in social panics one loses sta-

*John Gaskell, "Gallant Old Gal Swings It for the Sixties," *Sunday Telegraph* (London), October 17, 1993.

tus only by standing alone. Journalistic values were now inverted: skepticism was abolished in favor of credulity masquerading as toughness. My skepticism made me an early casualty of the pack mentality on Whitewater.

In mid-January 1994, Hillary asked me to come to her office in the West Wing. I did not know what she wanted to discuss. In great detail, she explained to me her version of Whitewater. In 1978 Jim McDougal had convinced the Clintons to make a passive investment in an Ozark land deal. He was not then the wreck he became later. Others, including Senator Fulbright, trusted him and invested in his businesses. But the Whitewater investment went bust and the Clintons lost all their money. Bill paid little attention. He left the problem to Hillary. Hillary kept after McDougal periodically about the paperwork, but he eluded her. She had no idea what he was really doing. McDougal turned into a manic-depressive drug addict, completely unreliable and evasive. At last, when Clinton was preparing to run for the presidency, McDougal's attorney, Samuel Heuer (Hillary called him "McDougal's cowboy lawyer"), dumped cardboard boxes filled with Whitewater files on her. She did not read the files, much less organize them. She only looked at them enough to see that they were thoroughly chaotic, and then left them in their boxes. When Jeff Gerth of *The New York Times* asked the Clinton campaign headquarters, as he prepared to write the first story about Whitewater, it handed over documents to him. Hillary also contacted a forensic accountant, James Lyons, to try to piece together the mess McDougal had left her with. Lyons concluded that the Clintons had sought no special tax advantages, and his conclusions were the same later reached by the RTC report. After the election, the records were packed with thousands of other boxes on moving vans in Little Rock and transported to Washington. Hillary had still not gone through their contents, but she knew that she and her husband had done nothing wrong and that the heated charges being made about presumed manipulations were false. She also knew that McDougal was mentally unbalanced and had been for several years.

Hillary said that she had invited over Leonard Downie, editor of *The Washington Post*, to tell him her account of Whitewater just as she was telling me. She had told him she didn't understand why the issue was being blown up. He demanded to see all the documents. She explained she hadn't read them and didn't know where all of them were. He asked about an obscure issue concerning the International Paper Company's purchase of Whitewater property—on a supposition that Governor Clinton had paid off the company with lax state regulation. She said she didn't know anything about it. "How can that be?" he demanded. (Clinton was to testify in the McDougal trial that he had never had a discussion with McDougal about International Paper and knew nothing of its transactions. The Clintons' account was borne out by all subsequent investigations.) Downie left abruptly. Hillary learned later that he didn't believe she had told the truth. Back in the newsroom, he ordered intensive investigations. "Len thinks this is his Watergate," said the *Post*'s national editor, Karen deYoung.*

Much has been made of the question whether the scandal would have been stanched if Hillary had turned over the Whitewater files. Both David Gergen and George Stephanopoulos insisted that if the *Post* had been handed the documents the Whitewater fuss would have effectively been ended.† But Jeff Gerth already had documents, including the long memo from the Arkansas bank commissioner Beverly Bassett Schaeffer, with the correct information. This last was not, apparently, part of his picture.

According to Clinton aides, Gergen had promised Downie he would get the files but had made the promise without gaining prior approval from the Clintons or their attorneys. It was a promise that would not and could not be kept. The lawyers gave stern advice to their clients that they should give the files only to legal authorities; otherwise they would find themselves being tried in the press, and a political atmosphere would develop that might adversely affect a special prosecutor if one were appointed. And the *Post*, for its part, had already begun publishing articles based on the premise of the Clintons' wrongdoing. The files were scattered and incomplete—nobody really knew how much—and the Clintons were unfamiliar with them. With only partial files, newspapers could keep publishing fragmentary story after story, making inexorable points day after day, and with no end, the hunt would go on.

When Downie was not given the files, he believed, perhaps understandably, that a promise had been broken. He chose to blame the Clintons and attribute to them a nefarious motive for covering up. Over time, of course, the files were released through congressional committees, the RTC report, and other governmental inquiries—there was never any

*Marvin Kalb, *One Scandalous Story: Clinton, Lewinsky, and Thirteen Days That Tarnished American Journalism*, Free Press, 2001, p. 18.

†See Stephanopoulos, *All Too Human*, pp. 227–28; see also David Gergen, *Eyewitness to Power*, Simon and Schuster, 2000, pp. 286–91.

cover-up—and were made fully available to the press. But when the RTC report with its relevant documents vindicated the Clintons, the *Post* did not report it at all.

Unlike Downie, I believed Hillary Clinton, partly, no doubt, because I was inclined to believe her, whereas he was disinclined. But I was under no obligation to believe her. Her telling of the story, however, sounded convincing; her demeanor struck no false notes. It was not the behavior of someone engaged in a cover-up. Either she was Meryl Streep playing herself or she was telling the truth. I asked her if I could quote her in *The New Yorker*. But she didn't want me to defend her, or rebut the other accounts, or tell her version. She only wanted me to understand. If anything she told me turned out to be untrue, I would find out and write about it. We were friends, but I had my own perspectives and had written criticism of the uneven early record of her husband's administration, especially on foreign policy. Over time, I tested my skepticism about Whitewater, even meeting with Floyd Brown and David Bossie, the sources behind the stories, and I was as disinclined to believe these right-wing pitchmen as much of the media was inclined to depend on them.

In mid-December I had an hour-long interview with President Clinton for *The New Yorker*. This took place before the publication of Brock's *Spectator* story but as the Whitewater furnace was starting to be stoked. Our conversation ranged over the nature of his politics, his navigation of the ragged first year, and his budget battles. Mostly I asked about presidential power and how Clinton had shaped it. I did not focus on Whitewater. About his first six months, I wrote, "Clinton was forced to demonstrate that no fixed quantity of power inheres in the office and that power can be created and multiplied under adverse conditions." He himself put it this way:

> I think you can recreate political capital continuously throughout the presidency. Change is difficult to do. If it were easy, it would happen of its own accord. If things that ought to be done were all that self-evident in terms of what should be done and how to do it, we wouldn't need much of a political system. . . . One of the things that I underestimated was the profound importance of continuing to speak about the larger issues. . . . It may look like making sausage, but it's taking us to the larger goal.

By the time the article appeared, in January 1994, the press was uninterested in reflection, even on the course of the past year, but was firmly

fixated on Whitewater. Marvin Kalb, a Harvard professor and former
CBS correspondent, recorded, "From November 1993 until early February 1994, *The Washington Post* published sixty-one articles on the Whitewater story. Sixteen were on the front page." After Downie's meeting
with Hillary, the paper created a special Whitewater team. With many
rakes being handed out, the muck to be raked increased. Downie himself
described his own attitude to Kalb as "zeal."

On January 18, a sarcastic attack on my *New Yorker* article and me appeared in the "Style" section of the *Post*:

> If any doubts remained about Blumenthal's sympathies, this week's Letter
> From Washington should obliterate them. Blumenthal returns from a
> Clinton interview with the excellent news that Clinton's "Presidential
> power has begun to flourish." The piece features long, forgettable quotes
> from the president. . . . That's a relief. . . . No question the president de-
> serves credit for the achievements of his first year, but they are not the
> whole story. . . . Maybe the column should be renamed "In the Tank."*

This was not really criticism—it grappled with no ideas at all—but simply an effort to discredit. The *Post*'s unusual publication of such a raw
attack on an individual writer showed the editors' intensifying concentration of resources on scandal. I had left the newspaper, where I had made
many friends, with no hard feelings and, so far as I knew, no bitter enemies. The article showed less about my opinions than it did about the
tightening and narrowing mentality of pack journalism. The author was
an unexceptional conservative whose celebratory banalities on Newt
Gingrich, for example, had been published at length. ("Though he said
not much of substantive interest, the man managed to come across in all
kinds of subtle ways as an easy, generous spirit, totally unlike the menace
he was supposed to be. First, he seemed utterly at home with himself, in
a way we haven't seen since perhaps John Kennedy."†)

In February 1994, I had lunch with Tina Brown in New York to clear
the air and to discuss future stories. All was affable and uneventful. When
I returned to Washington, I received a call from a friend and former col-

---

*William Powers, "Clinton's Man in Washington," *The Washington Post*, January
18, 1994.

†William Powers, "Newt Gingrich: Just Like He Says," *The Washington Post*, January 7, 1995.

league working at the "Style" section of the *Post*; this friend told me there was a campaign being conducted against me, that the "Style" piece was part of it, and that Sally Quinn, who still exercised some influence at the "Style" section, was boasting that I would soon be fired from *The New Yorker*. I called Sally up. She openly acknowledged spreading the rumor about me and wondered why anyone would make a fuss about it; that was just how Washington operated and nobody should blame anybody. Tina Brown, for her part, told me the rumor was not true. A friend of mine at *The New Yorker* suggested that I might deflate the ruckus by attacking Clinton. "That's how you can get well," he said.

A month later I went to New York again to see Tina. I had just written an article on Senator Daniel Patrick Moynihan's effort to build a restored version of the Pennsylvania Railroad Station in New York City decades after the original architectural landmark had been demolished. Tina now told me that by failing to write Whitewater scandal stories I had forfeited the game for the magazine. She wondered why the Clintons didn't just admit they had done something wrong and make the scandal go away. "I just can't take the pressure anymore," she said, referring to the journalistic pack. She explained that she was removing me as Washington editor but that I could write about anything other than the Clintons. Her manner was anxious, even solicitous, but not accusatory. She wondered if I would like to be appointed as London or Los Angeles correspondent.

My removal as Washington editor was an enactment of the law of the pack. When I did not stampede along with the herd I was punished. It was cautionary for others. (After Clinton left office, Tina apologized to me. She said that she had been wrong about me, wrong about those who criticized me, wrong about Whitewater, and wrong about Clinton. But that was many years later.)

I chose to stay in Washington and write from there. Tina told me that my replacement would be Michael Kelly. I knew Kelly slightly, having met him a couple of times, always with others and under pleasant circumstances. He had written fine dispatches for *The New Republic* on the Gulf War and had then produced colorful political coverage for *The New York Times*. I had no idea that he was drifting into a cloud of Clinton hatred. I sent a congratulatory letter to Kelly. "You'll do great," I wrote. I never got a response. Jackie called him and his wife, leaving three separate messages that we were eager to have a dinner for them and that we would like to invite guests they might want. None of her calls was returned. I decided to leave the matter there. It was better to have a congenial atmosphere, but we didn't have to relate to each other simply because we wrote pieces for the same magazine.

About six months later, the phone rang while I was eating dinner with Jackie and the children. The person at the other end did not identify himself when I answered but screamed, "You fucking asshole! You asshole! You fucking asshole!" I recognized the voice as Kelly's. "Mike," I said, "you need to get control of yourself. What is this about?" As best I could understand through his obscenities, I had received a phone message at *The New Yorker*'s office in Washington from the First Lady's office. Kelly shouted that at Hillary's direction I was spying on him: "You're a spy! You fucking asshole! Your reputation will be nothing!" Once again, I suggested that he get control of himself. He hung up.

This amazing explosion of anger had obviously been building for some time. (The next day I called the First Lady's office and learned that they had called to invite me to a social event at the White House. The idea that Hillary had enlisted someone to spy on Michael Kelly for her was simply mad.) Tina asked David Remnick, a colleague, to smooth things out, and he asked Kelly to speak rationally and lower the temperature, but a few months later Kelly shouted obscenities at me again.

In mid-1997, Martin Peretz hired Kelly as the editor of *The New Republic* to replace Andrew Sullivan. His tenure was marked by the fierce columns he wrote denouncing the alleged corruptions of President Clinton and Vice President Gore and by his promotion of an extraordinary young writer named Stephen Glass, a former researcher at the conservative Heritage Foundation. Glass fabricated startling story after story. When the subjects called to question their veracity, Kelly shrieked at them on the phone and wrote letters calling them liars. Later Glass's ruses were exposed, and nine months after his hiring, Peretz fired Kelly. "Michael is so far to the right that he's in a breakdown lane," he said. "He was controlling the material that got into the magazine in a way no editor ever did."* Peretz added, "He's not beyond fabricating."†

My friend and former editor at the *Post*, Jeffrey Frank, moved to *The New Yorker* and became my editor once again. And then, after seeing a production of Richard Sheridan's *School for Scandal* in the summer of 1994, it struck me that the most appropriate way to deal with the farcical

---

*Jonathan Broder, "Another One Bites the Dust," *Salon.com*, September 1997, http://www.salon.com/sept97/media/media970908.html.

†Dan Kennedy, "Don't Quote Me," *The Boston Phoenix*, September 11, 1997.

but venomous atmosphere in Washington was comedy. By the end of the year, I had written a play that I called *This Town*.

As the plot unfolds, in the White House press room, a small pack of archetypal, frustrated journalists compare their respective speaking agents and fees while projecting their anxieties onto the President and his staff, who are being unhelpful in advancing their careers. Suddenly a scandal materializes in the form of Scamper, the presidential First Dog, and the issue of who is paying for his dog food. Burton, a failing network correspondent, seizes upon "the crisis of perception." Loretta, another network reporter, who is trying to coax her husband, a *New York Times* bureau editor, to quit so that they can become a "media couple" on television and receive larger lecture fees, spreads rumors about the First Lady's lesbian affairs that involve Scamper's veterinarian. The scandal escalates when it is revealed that the Park Ranger who walks Scamper is a distant cousin of the President. The youthful press secretary is overwhelmed. Burton finds himself vaulted onto *Press Beat* as a commentator. The pack learns that the moderator of *Press Beat* has been promoted to become president of the News Division. The struggle to succeed him meshes with the scandal. Burton's "crisis of perception" heightens when he reports that Scamper has been breeding with a dog owned by Mary Susan Hibbert Crankshaw, the grand dame of the Democratic Party and White House chief of protocol—a sex scandal. Frank, a crusty columnist of the old school, refuses to report the sex angle, focusing instead on how the President handles the sex angle. Bill, a network correspondent past his prime, goes for the character issue: "The character of a pet is an obvious reflection of the character of a master." Mason, a writer for a New York glossy, who has inserted himself into the pack, spurs them on: "What's hot is democracy." Crankshaw resigns, while the White House tries hopelessly to end the scandal by throwing a sacrifice to the press. The Republicans demand that Scamper be fixed. At the White House correspondents dinner, to the chagrin of the competing newsmen, the new host of *Press Beat* is announced as the White House press secretary. Mason's article on "The Boys and Girls in the Shark Tank" viciously tears apart the Washington journalists, revealing their personal secrets. But the biggest agent in town asks them, now that they have gotten invaluable publicity, to star in a new political talk show called *The Shark Tank*. They all happily sign up. Burton, who has been fed his stories by an underhanded administration source with a personal agenda against the First Lady, wins the coveted Correspondent of the Year Award for his brilliant reportage on the "crisis of perception."

Throughout 1995 and 1996, the play was staged by the L.A. Theatre Works (with the cosponsorship of *The New Yorker*) from Los Angeles to Chicago to Cambridge to the National Press Club in Washington (where Secretary of Labor Robert Reich played the role of *This Town*'s biggest agent).

In mid-May 1996, Tina once again took a debate team to Britain. This time, the team—Salman Rushdie, still under the threat of the Iranian ayatollahs' fatwa; Adam Gopnik, the Paris correspondent of *The New Yorker*; and I—jousted with a threesome from the London *Times* at the Hay-on-Wye Literary Festival in Wales over the proposition "Europe should resist the culture of America." Salman dissected the transatlantic cross-migration of popular music: how American R&B had made the Beatles who made American punk rock who made Manchester's Oasis. For good measure, he delivered a peroration against cultural fundamentalism. Adam noted that his son rode a German-made musical horse on the Boulevard St. Germain to the song "Buffalo Gals" by way of pointing to the complex, yet prosaic, entanglement of European and American culture. I argued that America was the expression of Europe's own dreams, the flowering of the European Enlightenment, and even an expression of its erotic imagination. I cited John Donne's "To His Mistress Going to Bed": "License my roving hands, and let them go, / Before, behind, between, above, below. / O my America! my new-found-land . . ." *The New Yorker* defeated the London *Times* handily.

The Hay-on-Wye debate was a last hurrah for me at *The New Yorker*. The President had asked me after the reelection to join the administration—which for three years I had not written about—as a senior adviser. The decisive moment had arrived when I could become a wholehearted political participant. It would be the chance to work closely with the first two-term Democratic president since FDR and the most influential first lady since Eleanor Roosevelt. I would be able to see firsthand how policy was created, how a president made decisions, and how a White House responded to crises. And I would be able to do more than see; I'd be part of the presidential operations. I could gain unparalleled understanding. Leaving late the night President Clinton asked me to join the staff, I knew that I would be returning to the White House every day but that it would never be commonplace. There would surely be slings and arrows, but I could only speculate as to what these would be. And I could not anticipate an impeachment, a war, a political campaign by the First Lady herself, or an election decided by the Supreme Court.

Henry Kissinger, in his memoir, offers the view that in the White House ideas reach their limit and the experience of working there has a narrowing effect: "High office teaches decision making, not substance. [It] consumes intellectual capital; it does not create it." Much of the truth of this proposition depends upon what is meant by "intellectual capital." If it means theories about the world, they are likely to be altered and enlarged, but that is not the same thing as being consumed. Only with presidents who have arrived at inflexible certainties are ideas consumed and not replenished. The presidency, I was to discover for myself, is open to American life in all its diversity, expansiveness, perplexity, and fury, and the White House offers a political education like no other. As for me, I had an inexhaustible source of energy to draw upon. As the opening words of Saul Bellow's *Adventures of Augie March* put it, "I'm an American, Chicago-born."

SEVEN

Mine Canary

On the night before my first day at the White House, I shined my shoes. It reminded me of shining a new pair of shoes on the night before I started high school more than thirty years before. I had expected then to enter a large building filled with hundreds of people I had never met and to be swept up into a new life. But in high school one is a member of a class, all of whom share the same experience and are starting at the same time. Now, the entering class consisted of two: Paul Begala and me.

Begala had been heavily involved in Clinton's 1992 campaign as a War Room veteran and a political adviser during the first two years of Clinton's first-term administration. A spirited partner of James Carville, he had worked in Dick Gephardt's office on the Hill and had a gift for phrasemaking and tactics. Our impending entrance into the White House naturally provoked a round of conservative punditry. Paul Gigot, the *Wall Street Journal* columnist, wrote that we were "the bash brothers," hired for scandal, and that Republicans should be "alert for foul balls."* Gigot's column was an excuse to raise the then-receding specter of Clinton scandals and to tarnish us a bit even before we turned up for work. Jokingly, Begala and I called each other "Bash."

Begala and I talked a lot before we went in about how the months after Clinton's reelection differed from the first term's uncertain beginning. We had no interest in being pulled into the operation dealing with so-called scandals; that was a small outfit, consisting basically of one lawyer, Lanny Davis. We were gearing up to work on the main politics of policy.

*Paul Gigot, "New Clinton Recruits Know How to Smite," *The Wall Street Journal*, June 20, 1997.

Paul even wanted to be engaged in space policy. We were hopeful, but agreed we didn't know where this new venture would lead us. Paul said he felt that we were like Butch Cassidy and the Sundance Kid standing on a cliff, holding on to the ends of a belt and jumping into the rushing river below.

Coming to the White House was not exactly like entering an unknown land. I knew many people in Clinton's White House—some friends, some of whom I had interviewed on various political campaigns, and some friends of my wife. But knowing them was not the same thing as being one of them. Being on the outside in whatever capacity was never the same as being in. Glimpses behind the curtain could not give the unobstructed view of being there day after day.

My title was Assistant to the President. Within the formal rankings of the White House, this is the highest level. The national security adviser, the chief of staff, and the legal counsel, for example, are assistants—and everyone at that rank is also considered a senior adviser. About a couple of dozen people held this title in the Clinton White House. Franklin D. Roosevelt began the institutionalization of presidential aides, and when asked what was required of those in the position, he remarked, "A passion for anonymity." In a gesture toward this sentiment, I asked to have the title with nothing added to it, such as "for communications." "Assistant" was traditional, clean, and succinct. In anticipation of the day when I would enter public service, there were long conversations with friends. Those already in the government whose advice I sought warned me about the contrast between being a presidential aide and being anything else. They wanted me to accustom myself to the strange rituals of the staffer without too much abrasion. Obviously, I wanted to be accepted by my new colleagues, to learn quickly how to operate within the government, and to be effective. When anyone new is introduced, anxiety over turf and the question of one's proximity to power always arise. I was intent on doing nothing to provoke petty competitions. Having been in the press, I was not interested in its further attention. I had no need to be quoted or to appear on television. (During my tenure in the White House, I accepted only one invitation to appear on television, on CNN, to discuss the growth of progressive politics in the United States and Europe.) The less visibility outside, I thought, the more impact inside.

I came to the White House with high expectations of being able to contribute. I was eager to work on government policy and to help create a new political consensus around it. The Clinton presidency was the culmination of a generation of struggle to reorder national priorities, and I knew that its early harsh battles and setbacks reflected the difficulty of achieving these goals. This opportunity and moment would not appear again.

Of course, I expected static. Like Gigot, the conservative columnist Robert Novak attempted to foment a little mischief. Several months before I was scheduled to start work he wrote that Clinton's press secretary, Michael McCurry, was "particularly depressed by the prospect of Blumenthal joining him in the White House mess."* But the last thing I wanted was to set myself up as a kind of rival press secretary. The conflict Novak wanted to provoke was more grist for his column than anything real. McCurry and I respected each other, worked well together, and never had any clashes. Gigot's and Novak's columns were predictable programming from conservative pundits, a constant low-level drone in Washington that one could ignore.

Jackie, my wife, had joined the White House more than a year earlier as the director of the White House Fellows program. When I had met her in 1974 she was an editor at a division of *Yankee Magazine* in Boston, and she had gone on to run a community-based foundation. When we moved to Washington, she became the media director for People for the American Way, an advocacy group devoted to promoting tolerance and separation of church and state. Then she became a direct-mail marketing strategist for nonprofit groups ranging from Planned Parenthood to Amnesty International to Habitat for Humanity. At PFAW, she had worked with Melanne Verveer, who became Hillary's chief of staff, and through that connection she was recruited to run the White House Fellows program. Started by President Johnson in 1964 as something like Rhodes scholars for public service, the program annually selected fewer than twenty extraordinary people, mostly in their late twenties and thirties, to work in the executive branch with cabinet secretaries and senior White House officials. The alumni were a remarkable group, including then–CNN president Tom Johnson, the historian Doris Kearns Goodwin, and Colin Powell.

For the first time in twenty-one years of marriage, the next morning, Jackie and I would go to the same place of work, or at least nearly the same. I didn't yet have an assigned parking space. So she would drive me to her office, a townhouse on Lafayette Park across from the White House, to get me there in time for my first meeting at 7:30 a.m.

*Robert Novak, "Probe of Burton Brings Backlash Against Lobbyists," *Chicago Sun-Times*, June 15, 1997.

We had spent a lot of time discussing what might happen when I went to work in the White House. Jackie was rightly concerned about the constant attacks and worried about my becoming a target. We had watched many people we knew as they were burdened with legal bills, had to cope with stress and depression, and became exhausted. We had few resources to fall back on. In fact, with these two government jobs we would be earning more income than we ever had before. Jackie cautioned, half-jokingly, "The minute you have to get a lawyer, you're out of there." But we were encouraged, for the storms seemed to be subsiding as my start date of August 11 approached.

It was about 10:30 at night on August 10, and Jackie was already in bed reading. I was still tinkering around. I had developed a habit of checking e-mails and surfing the news on the Internet before I turned in. I checked CNN.com, the Associated Press's latest stories, and the *Drudge Report*. Drudge was a real person, not just an ideal Dickensian name. His site wasn't quite the news, but a romper room of right-wing phantasmagoria.

On the blank screen, in inch-tall block letters, a headline slowly formed:

CHARGE: NEW WHITE
HOUSE RECRUIT
SIDNEY BLUMENTHAL
HAS SPOUSAL ABUSE
PAST

I blinked. The cliché "I couldn't believe my own eyes" suddenly came true for me. I was astonished and bewildered. I put the cursor on the headline and clicked to try to get to the underlying story. Nothing. I clicked again and again. Nothing. There was just the headline.

"Jackie!" I called out.

"What?" she replied, slightly irritated. "What is it?"

"Come here!"

"Why?"

"Just come here."

"Just stop playing on the Internet and come to bed."

Reluctantly, a bit exasperated, she came into my study. Wordlessly I pointed to the screen.

"Is this a joke?" she asked.

"No, I don't think so."

She peered behind my computer. "Did one of your friends put it in there?"

"No."

"It's a joke. Are you sure one of your friends didn't do this? Come on." She asked me to click on the headline.

"I've done that already." I did it again. Nothing.

It seemed to me that this was not an attempt at humor, but a smear timed to my first day in the White House. I imagined that Drudge had no idea who I was. It was probable that he had never even heard my name before. He must have been fed this lie. I knew he was a Clinton hater, an unreliable scandalmonger living on the fringes of Los Angeles. He would be a perfect channel for others with a political agenda.

"I'm going to have to sue him," I said.

"Nobody sees this," Jackie said. "It's a joke. Just try to forget about it. Come to bed. You have to get up early."

For a last time, I clicked on the headline. Nothing. I shut down my computer and went to bed. The next morning, driving to the White House, we talked about what my day would be like and what meetings I would have. The *Drudge Report* was forgotten. It was a weird headline without a story. What was that about?

Jackie parked at her office and I walked down Jackson Place, which runs alongside Lafayette Park, crossed an empty Pennsylvania Avenue, and passed through the Northwest Gate, where I was given a pass with a large "T," for "Temporary." It would take two months before I was issued my permanent badge, the blue pass, with my picture on it, which would arrive after an FBI investigation into my background. Soon, I was in the West Wing.

I made my way to my office, a small windowless room on the ground floor, across the hall from the Mess and the Situation Room, and near a short flight of steps up to the Oval Office. One entire wall was covered with mirrors. Like every nook and cranny in the White House, this room had a history. I would soon befriend the curator, Betty Monkman, who showed me the secret hieroglyphic signs chiseled into the foundation stones by the original masons and the blackened inner archway charred when the British torched the building. I came to know where all the burn marks were in the White House. My office had once been the barbershop. It once had a chair nailed to the floor in the middle of the room on which the presidents had gotten shaves, haircuts, and manicures. Michael Beschloss, working on a three-volume series based on the Lyndon Johnson White House tapes at the LBJ Library in Austin, Texas, dug up for me a photograph of the tiny room as it had looked in Johnson's glory days. It resembled the famous scene of the crowded stateroom in the Marx Brothers' *Night at the Opera*. LBJ had a barber and manicurist in attendance, while his aides, Jack Valenti and Joe Califano, hovered. But now the room was barren. There was a desk, a table, a computer, a couch, a chair, and a television. On the desk lay a copy of the White House News Summary, a thick collection of articles from the morning's newspapers assembled overnight by the press office.

I walked up the stairs to the Roosevelt Room for the senior staff meeting held every morning. Under its skylights in the center of the West Wing everyone clustered around a long table. The Roosevelts— TR in his Rough Rider uniform, on a rearing horse, over the mantel; FDR, pen in hand, on the wall; and a bust of Eleanor (added by the Clintons), perched on the mantel below her uncle—gazed down.

Erskine Bowles, the chief of staff, called the meeting to order. He was a courtly North Carolinian, a banker with a long lineage in Tarheel state politics—his father had nearly been elected governor in 1972 and had inspired a cadre of New South reformers. Bowles had supported Al Gore in 1988 and came to the Clinton administration through that avenue. He was a negotiator, a manager, and a New South Democrat. The President had hired him to wrangle with the Republicans in the Congress, organize the staff efficiently, and represent his own views. Behind his seemingly remote, pin-striped demeanor, Bowles was compassionate and decent. He cared a great deal about policy outcomes. While he negotiated a balanced budget, at the same time he pushed for children's health insurance for the poor and for health care programs. (His own son suffers from juvenile diabetes.)

Erskine crisply swung around the room. The President's schedule for the day was laid out. Every department presented what it would be doing that day—the Domestic Policy Council, the National Economic Council, the National Security Council, the Press Office, Communications, the Science Adviser, the First Lady's Office. Then Bowles introduced Paul Begala and me. We were now on the team. "Anyone else? Anything else?" Erskine asked. Everyone bolted. Erskine quietly took Paul and me aside and asked us in the future to join the early-morning senior staff meeting in his office that preceded this one.

Then there was the message meeting. This took place across the narrow hall in the office of John Podesta, deputy chief of staff. Mostly, we discussed the policies that the President would propose before he departed on his summer vacation: an announcement on tobacco, a welfare-to-work event in St. Louis, new labeling on pediatric dosages. The political atmosphere was unusually calm, while people spoke up as it was decided what messages the White House would issue that day. Podesta closely assessed what others said and quickly made his own arguments. He was constantly alert, his points invariably incisive and lawyerly. He had, after all, been a law professor at Georgetown University. But he also had a long history in political campaigns; had worked on the Hill, notably for Senator Patrick Leahy; and had previously been the White House staff secretary. His brother, Tony, had been president of People for the American Way and a Democratic campaign consultant; he now ran his own consulting firm, of which the original partners were Tony, John, and, through its first year, Jackie.

By now it was a little after nine in the morning and I had to rush to a third meeting, a staff meeting, presided over by Ann Lewis, director of communications, a seasoned political veteran, sister of the voluble Congressman Barney Frank of Massachusetts, and a prominent feminist. Her office was decorated with posters highlighting women's history, and some staffers referred to it as "Suffragette City," as in, "We're meeting in Suffragette City." I had six other meetings scheduled that day, including one I had called myself to help prepare for the President's announcement of the White House Millennium Program on Friday. In addition I had to figure out when to take my drug test and be interviewed by the FBI. I had also scheduled meetings for the next day on global warming and with the communications operation of the National Security Council, and I'd been asked to participate in other meetings—on Fast Track trade negotiating authority, a divisive issue among Democrats, and on the State of the Union address.

I had been in the White House less than two hours. It was a typical day, untroubled by any crisis, but it was also like being at the receiving end of a fire hose. The torrent never stopped and, to change the watery metaphors, like everyone else I was always swimming upstream. Events happened swiftly, but affecting events would require patience. Nobody could do everything. One had to perform an essential triage. I had to decide where to put my energies. I had the luxury of moving around fluidly since I had no bureaucratic line responsibility. My job was to be free-ranging. With just a dip into the pool, I was already paddling away and preoccupied.

I dropped by my office on my way to the next meeting. Jordan Tamagni, a friend and speechwriter, was adjusting a picture she was hanging

on the blank wall, the first decorative touch. It was a large framed photograph of Bill Clinton shaking hands with Tony Blair in the Rose Garden
of 10 Downing Street, which she had expropriated from its old place in
the corridor. These big photos of the President were hung throughout
the West Wing and changed every week or two, as though it were a
gallery. "Perfect in here," Jordan said, alluding to my having brought
Blair and Clinton together, and then she dashed off.

I noticed that paper had begun to materialize on my desk: the President's schedule; the draft of a speech he was to deliver, requesting that
my comments be directed to the speechwriters by a certain deadline; and
a card listing my meetings on the left side and the President's on the
right. There was also a sealed manila envelope. I opened it and read a
cover note written by Jackie. "Read this and call me," it said. One of my
assistants told me that Jackie herself had dropped it by and seemed upset.

I lifted up her note and read the sheet underneath:

DRUDGE REPORT (8/11/97 12:30 AM)
GOP: THE BLUMENTHAL OPTION?

Exclusive

Republican power player Don Sipple was blinded last week when *Mother
Jones* magazine reported that he had knocked a few of his wives around.
Sipple, who has helped top GOP candidates like Bush, Dole and Wilson
take on the gender gap with attack ads that exploit women's fears of violence, is alleged to have beaten two ex-wives himself, the magazine
roared. As word of the story spread, Sipple began losing face and losing
clients. He immediately quit the congressional race of New York Republican Vito Fossella—the Molinari seat—telling the campaign in a letter
that he did not wish this to be a distraction for Vito. The Bush Boy
[George W. Bush] and San Diego's [Mayor Susan] Golding are now likely
to take a pass on Sipple's media advice.

But more importantly, the wife-beating revelations in *Mother Jones* by
George magazine senior editor Rich Blow could be unsettling long held
establishment secrets in the capital city. Some are calling it the "Sipple
Effect."

The *Drudge Report* has learned that top GOP operatives who feel
there is a double-standard of only reporting republican [*sic*] shame believe
they are holding an ace card: New White House recruit Sidney Blumenthal has a spousal abuse past that has been effectively covered up.

The accusations are explosive.

"There are court records of Blumenthal's violence against his wife," one influential republican [*sic*], who demanded anonymity, tells the *Drudge Report*.

"If they begin to use Sipple and his problems against us, against the Republican Party . . . to show hypocrisy, Blumenthal would become fair game. Wasn't it Clinton who signed the Violence Against Women Act?"

(There goes the budget deal honeymoon.)

One White House source, also requesting anonymity, says the Blumenthal wife-beating allegation is pure fiction that has been created by Clinton enemies. "(The First Lady) would not have brought him in if he had this in his background," assures the well-placed staffer. "This story about Blumenthal has been in circulation for years."

Last month President Clinton named Sidney Blumenthal an Assistant to the President as part of the Communications Team. He's been brought in to work on communications strategy, special projects, themeing [*sic*]— a newly created position.

Every attempt to reach Blumenthal proved unsuccessful.

Blumenthal is married to Jacqueline Jordan Blumenthal. Mrs. Blumenthal is also employed at the White House as the Director of the President's Commission on White House Fellows.

I read this and reread it. Here was the story I couldn't access the night before. Once again, I was astonished. But now I was angry, too, at the sheer brazenness of the elaborate lies.

I was familiar with the allegations about Don Sipple because I had read the *Mother Jones* article. Two of his former wives had testified in court documents that he repeatedly beat them, and the magazine had published photos of the battered women, their faces marked by blood and bruises. His second wife, Deborah Steelman, a Republican policy expert and Reagan administration official, had been especially forthcoming with the reporter. Democrats were not using the story politically and were not even interested in a minor figure like Sipple. It was far more a subject of conversation and concern among Republicans, who knew the people involved.

It was immediately apparent to me that the Big Lie about me was another matter. The fabricated detail about hidden "court records" slyly conveyed the false impression of factuality and of my covering something up. It wasn't just that there were beatings, but that there were "records" about them and I was concealing them. The quote from the "well-placed staffer" in the White House was patently contrived; so was the staffer. No "well-placed staffer" would be handing out blind quotes to Drudge, and none would take potentially damaging information about a new White House hire and fail to pass it on to others, and to the legal office. If a "well-placed staffer" had received such a call the inquiry would have necessarily gone through an established chain and I would have known about it. The fillip that the story "had been in circulation for years" was another detail to suggest a damning accumulation of facts when there were none. Not a single person I knew in Washington, almost all of whom make it a habit of learning as much about each other as possible, had ever heard this lie about me before, even as a lie. Finally, Drudge had lied about trying to reach me for comment. My telephone number was listed in the Washington, D.C., telephone directory. Anyone could get it from directory assistance. (Later, Drudge said he had mistakenly called the Maryland directory assistance because he thought I lived in Takoma Park, Maryland. But I myself did that to see what happened. I was told my number wasn't available in Maryland, so I asked the operator for other listings for that name in the region, and I was given my own. "Every attempt?") Drudge's mention of "one influential republican" as a source suggested that this was obviously a political operation. He must have been given the libel with all its pieces carefully assembled for him.

An assistant told me a reporter from the *New York Post* was on the phone to speak to me about the *Drudge Report*. I rerouted the call to the press office. I could see how this might unspool across the next week or two. The conservative media would be filled with stories about Blumenthal's "spousal abuse past." I would deny it, of course, but what proof did I have that it hadn't taken place? How could I disprove a negative? It would be a he said/he said story. And weren't the "records" hidden? Whatever Jackie said would be discounted. After all, she was still living with a wife-beater, wasn't she? The stories would continue and turn in the direction of the Clintons. Why, as Drudge intimated, was the President—and Hillary—complicit in hiring someone who was violent toward women? The intent was political; the means were personal.

I called Jackie. She told me that the Drudge story had been waiting for her on her office fax machine when she arrived at work—faxed in the middle of the night. The cover sheet had markings showing that at 1:11 a.m. Nick Thimmesch II had sent it. I knew the name as that of a small-time Republican operative. (He had been the press secretary for the right-wing Congressman Steve Largent of Oklahoma.) Jackie sounded distressed and angry, and said she was going to leave work early. I told her I thought I would have to sue to try to stop the defamation from being accepted in any way.

Then James Carville called me. James called almost every morning to ramble on about politics, always responding to my "Hello" with "Whazup." I had first encountered Carville at a Democratic Party retreat after the 1988 defeat. Virtually unknown, wearing tight, short jeans, white socks, and sneakers, the Ragin' Cajun had lectured the party leaders and related a long story about an old spinster schoolteacher in Louisiana who had a pet parrot she had taught eight languages. She left the parrot in the care of Old Joe, her neighbor, while she tended to her sick sister, only to discover, upon her return, that during a poker game Joe had put the bird in the gumbo. The schoolteacher cried, "And I taught him eight languages!" To which Joe responded, "Well, why didn't he say something?" Carville turned to the Democratic leaders and yelled, "They've put you in the gumbo! Why don't you say something?" In Clinton, Carville had found his candidate. More than anyone else in 1992, besides the Clintons, he had held the campaign together and pushed it forward. Shrewd, superstitious, and loyal, he did not like to see his friends in the gumbo.

When I explained the situation to him, he gave me the name of his lawyer. In between meetings, I called William A. McDaniel, who had left the big Washington firm of Williams and Connally to start his own in Baltimore. McDaniel succinctly walked me through the law and my options. He said he would begin by writing a letter to Drudge. But I could not make a decision to sue him until I had consulted with my new colleagues. I did not yet know what I could or couldn't do in the White House.

One person told me I should "suck it up." That was what one did in the White House: you were smeared and you acted stoic. This was a fairly conventional approach, but not to my mind satisfactory. While the object of the attack might feel that he was sustaining a code of honor by not descending to the level of the attackers, ignoring an attack also had the unfortunate effect of leaving a shadow of a doubt about the original smear. That was something I felt I couldn't afford, especially on a charge so personal. If the accusation were only political I would have ignored it, just as I had the Gigot and Novak columns. But what Drudge had contrived and published was character assassination; a political jab would have attracted no interest, and he wouldn't have bothered with it. I believed I was operating in the very short run, the span of one daily news cycle—witness the call from the *New York Post*. If I didn't stamp the libel for what it was right away, I would be on the defensive about the smear for days—and years—to come. With conservative media like the *New York Post* ready to spread the story, undoubtedly to be picked up by Rush Limbaugh, his imitators, and *The Washington Times*, I couldn't simply call up professional reporters, deny the accusation, and expect that they would even write up my denial. The *Drudge Report* would circulate, and the denial wouldn't be news. Newspapers aren't in the business of correcting the record of allegations that have appeared elsewhere, especially when the elsewhere is an online gossip site. If they felt compelled to correct the errors of online gossips and talk-radio hosts there would be little room in their pages even for baseball scores. There was no viable platform for refuting the lie except a lawsuit. I felt I had little choice but to do something dramatic to underscore the falsity of the smear. I was also aware of my own natural emotions, the instinct for self-defense, especially when it was not just me but my family that was defamed.

John Podesta sympathetically examined the question from a variety of angles. With my interest in mind, he laid out a few cautions. Wouldn't this turn me into a story that would, as he said, "bounce endlessly around in the press"? Did I want to get entangled with "a guy who is an asshole"? On the other hand, the story was hurtful. It was my decision. He'd support me whatever I did.

I showed the *Drudge Report* to Paul Begala as we raced between meetings. At first, he thought it was "a joke." Then he said, "It's up to you. But if it were me, I'd sue their ass."

I sought the opinion of Cheryl Mills, the deputy counsel. She was young, experienced in the law, from a military family, and battle-hardened by the scandal wars. She was outraged on my behalf. She said that it was my decision to sue or not. The White House could have no official position on the decision. It was a personal libel and would have to be answered personally. She explained that the law would treat the case as one involving a public figure, which might make things difficult, even if the smear was obvious. But she and the others would understand completely if I were to sue. Several days later, when I attended a political strategy meeting, both Clinton and Gore offered me sympathy and moral support. Begala told me that the story had been the talk of the White House on our first day but that no one believed a word of it. Even those who didn't know me thought it was a dirty trick. He added, "It's hurt you outside. No question."

Before the end of my first day in the White House, I had retained

the services of McDaniel and he composed a letter to Drudge. It concluded:

> Your action in disseminating these outrageous falsehoods across the
> country was despicable. You acted with actual malice in that you knew
> that these allegations were false, but published them anyway. You took no
> steps to verify your allegations: even the most rudimentary check by you
> would have revealed that no court records exist which document your ac-
> cusations. Indeed, in your cowardice, you never even bothered to check
> with Mr. and Mrs. Blumenthal before scattering your lies across the In-
> ternet. (Your statement that you did so being yet another of your lies.)
>
> Your falsehoods have defamed both Jacqueline Blumenthal and Sid-
> ney Blumenthal. The Blumenthals demand that you remove your con-
> temptible drivel from the Internet immediately. Before proceeding
> against you, Mr. and Mrs. Blumenthal want to give you an opportunity to
> disclose to them the following: the names of the "top GOP operatives
> who feel there is a double-standard" and who believe "they are holding
> an ace card"; the name of the "influential republican, who demanded
> anonymity"; the court records which you claim document Mr. Blumen-
> thal's act of domestic violence; and the name of the "White House
> source" whom you purported to quote.
>
> If you have not provided this information to my office by 5:00 p.m.
> E.D.T., tomorrow, August 12, 1997, the Blumenthals will take the appro-
> priate action against you.

I called Jackie, who was at home by now, and read the letter to her. Then
I told McDaniel to fax it to Drudge.

I went to the meetings about the upcoming announcement of the
Millennium Program, a direct result of conversations I had had with Hillary. I would draft the speech for the President to give then. I sat in my
chair in my office and gazed at the mirror that had once reflected the
groomed presidents. Comb it wet or dry? During a brief, calm moment,
the door had burst open and a Secret Service agent, head down, had
walked in and pulled down his zipper. He looked up, realizing he was not
in the men's room, which was next door, and turned quickly on his heel.
Now the door suddenly flew open again.

"Guess who I brought!" shouted Jamie Rubin. In danced Madeleine
Albright and Hillary Clinton, laughing.

"We want to see your new office," said Madeleine.

"That mirror is your window," said Hillary.

Just as suddenly they were gone.

At home, at the end of day one, Jackie and I compared notes. We had received many phone calls from many people, mostly journalists, who had read the *Drudge Report*. Jackie was especially disturbed by a friend who asked, "Are you sure there aren't any court records? There aren't any records about something else that could be misinterpreted?" This friend couldn't quite believe that a claim of court records would be mentioned unless there were some. I got a call from a friend of two decades who had vacationed with us and our children and who asked the same question.

Our sons—Max, then a nineteen-year-old student at the University of Pennsylvania, and Paul, a sixteen-year-old high-school student—were on the spot. At first, they thought the charge was a joke, a ridiculous stunt. They were shocked that anyone might take it seriously. Then they were angry that their family was being described by such an outrageous lie. Living in Washington, where even the children know the latest political news, they had to explain things to their friends. My mother and father, a thousand miles away, living a retired life on the street where they had lived for more than forty years, where I had grown up, found themselves facing friends and acquaintances asking about the *Drudge Report*. One neighbor remarked to my mother, "I hope there are no court records, but you know what they say: where there's smoke there's fire."

Almost everyone thought of the Drudge story as being about me, but it was equally a smear of Jackie. She was the woman who was supposed to have been repeatedly beaten, to have filed complaints with the police, but to have continued to live with a brutal man and then to have cooperated with her abuser in shielding the evidence, presumably out of a combination of ambition and self-loathing. She, too, had a career. Her position at the White House Fellows program placed her in daily contact with the fellows themselves; with members of the executive branch, including cabinet secretaries; with commissioners and past fellows; and with prominent figures from the President to Colin Powell. On August 12 she met with the leaders of the White House Fellows Alumni Association to plan a commissioners' meeting the following month. They arrived to find her watching Greta Van Susteren on CNN talking about her. (Most offices in Washington keep CNN on all day long.) She had to explain the *Drudge Report* and the story about "wife-beating" to these people she didn't know very well. The thought of millions of other viewers watching along with them made her physically ill. She was a professional who felt her own life was beginning to spin out of control.

For me August 12 began with the 7:30 morning meeting in Erskine's office, followed by the senior staff, message, and communications meetings. Then there was a meeting called by Todd Stern, who was in charge of the global warming initiative, to discuss, among other things, a suggestion I had made to invite local weathermen from across the country to be briefed by the President and the Vice President on the issue. And then came a Millennium Program meeting called by Hillary and three more meetings on presidential matters. My office was besieged by calls from reporters and friends about the Drudge smear, and I spent the time between meetings answering them.

Two news articles that morning reported strange, contradictory statements by Drudge that were simultaneously evasive and revealing. Drudge was trying to get himself out of the situation—but he never offered an unqualified, straightforward apology. My threat to take action prompted him to sound defensive in *The Washington Post*: "I apologize if any harm has been done. . . . The story was issued in good faith." He explained his notion of "good faith": "It was based on two sources who clearly were operating from a political motivation." He seemed to be evoking the two-source rule demanded by professional news organizations on investigative stories, rather than making a truthful statement that he had "two sources" with a political axe to grind. He continued, "Someone was trying to get me to go after [the story] and I probably fell for it a little too hard." He had done no checking, and had simply repeated what he was told. "I can't prove it," he said. "This is a case of using me to broadcast dirty laundry. I think I've been had."* He confirmed that he had acted at the instigation of others. If he was "had," he had been eager to be "had."

Drudge's tone was still accusatory in the *New York Post*. Here he presented himself as a diligent reporter still working on the story, even though he had in fact already pulled it from his website. "Page Six," the *Post*'s gossip column, wrote, under the headline "Old Wives' Tale Axed from Web":

When did you stop beating your wife?"
    That's the classic question we wanted to ask a certain White House advisor yesterday after the infamous online Drudge Report named him as a spouse-abuser.

*Howard Kurtz, "Net Result: Blumenthals Get Apology," *The Washington Post*, August 12, 1997.

Matt Drudge, 30, the one-man gossip clearing house who operates out of his apartment in Los Angeles, included a big story on the allegation yesterday in his cyber-column. . . .

[But he] not only expunged the copy from his web page, but also recalled a news flash that had been wired to several thousand regular readers.

When we asked Drudge about the sudden edit, and if someone in high places had spooked him, he was surprised that we had the premature story in our possession.

"I just wanted to make it as solid as possible," he told Page Six's Braden Keil, "plus, I have a major addition that just came to my attention."

. . . A White House spokeswoman later told The Post: "It's a lie."

But Drudge says no one called him to complain: "When they don't call, that's when you got something," he said.*

The mysterious "major addition" Drudge claimed never materialized, nor did he ever refer to it again. His statement that "they don't call" was false, if the faxing of my lawyer's letter to him counted. If he hadn't received the fax before his interview with the *Post*, he had had many hours to call back to correct his comment after he did get it. But he chose to let the impression stand that he stood by his story. Adding to his confusion, but obviously in response to my threat of legal action, he posted on his website that day, in the smallest possible type, a single sentence about his previous report:

I am issuing a retraction of my information regarding Sidney Blumenthal that appeared in the *Drudge Report* on August 11, 1997. Matt Drudge.

Meanwhile, Drudge was adding new details to his "information." According to *The Washington Post* on August 15, "Drudge told a reporter there *were* court records; he just didn't have them. He said he believed the allegation had surfaced in the FBI background check of Sid Blumenthal, which . . . had not yet begun."† The nugget about the FBI file was a new one. Had Drudge invented it himself or had it been whispered by a "source"?

---

*Richard Johnson with Jeanne MacIntosh and Sean Gannon, "Old Wives' Tale Axed from Web," *New York Post*, August 12, 1997.

†Howard Kurtz, "Cyber-Libel and the Web Gossip-Monger," *The Washington Post*, August 15, 1997.

Drudge never responded to my lawyer's letter. And he continued to spread the defamation. Mark Miller, then an ABC News producer and later chief of correspondents for *Newsweek*, told me that within hours of Drudge's posting his oblique "retraction," he spoke with Drudge: "He said, 'I'm still working on a story that will blow the roof off the White House and will force a staffer to resign.'" Miller was sure Drudge was referring to me. Drudge had been gleeful, even boasting. "This is such a great job," Drudge had told Miller. "I have no editors. I just press a button." At the end of day two it was clear that suing Drudge was the only way to counter the defamation. Jackie and I told McDaniel to prepare a complaint.

Drudge basked in the widespread publicity he had generated by the defamation. For a *USA Today* photographer, he donned a straw fedora and posed with a computer beside a pool, claiming to be the Walter Winchell of cyberspace—his very own sweet smell of success. This was a far cry from his suburban Maryland childhood, which by every account, including his own, had been that of a misfit with near-failing grades. His only published writing before he began the *Drudge Report* had been an entry in his high-school yearbook:

I, Matt Drudge, being of sound mind and body, do hereby leave the following: To my only true friend Ms. thing, Vicky B, I leave a night in Paris, a bottle of Chaps cologne and hope you find a school with original people—And to everyone else who has helped and hindred [sic] me whether it be Staff or students, I leave a penny for each day I've been here and cried here. A penny rich in worthless memories. For worthless memories is what I have endured. It reminds me of a song, "The Funeral Hyme [sic]."*

After high school, Drudge had lived as a loner on the margins of the Dupont Circle neighborhood of Washington, without holding a job. He had drifted to Hollywood, where he worked as a sales clerk in a CBS Entertainment gift shop for seven years. Then he set up a website, attracting attention for gossip he claimed to have gleaned from gift-shop customers. Soon he was posting political stories. He was a self-proclaimed "Clinton crazy," whose postings attracted conservative activists—stories in 1996 about Hillary's imminent indictment, for exam-

*Eddie Dean, "Hard Times and Jalapeño Bologna: Internet Rebel Matt Drudge's Early Years," *Washington City Paper*, March 13, 1998.

ple. His celebrity gossip stories, true or not, particularly the ones with wild mistakes, boosted his visibility. He called himself an "information anarchist." "The First Amendment," he informed *The Washington Post*, "doesn't require you to call people." He proudly admitted that only 80 percent—his estimate—of his postings were accurate.* At a forum at the Annenberg School of Communication at the University of Southern California, he declared, "I'm not a journalist!" One reporter trying to verify his work concluded that only ten of thirty-one stories Drudge had touted as "exclusive" were found to be true. "Screw journalism!" Drudge told the reporter. "The whole thing's a fraud anyway!"†

For years, I had observed others being demonized, having distorted images created and cast as their true selves. Once a false persona was projected, it was built upon, and the gaudier the image, the more it was said to reveal the real person. Now I was being subjected to the same process. The false Blumenthal persona that Drudge proposed was a primitive and fearful stereotype, a fantasy of omnipotence and helplessness, aggression and victimization. In the Clinton White House, it suggested, lurked a punitive, harsh, and secretive power. If this aggressor would beat his wife and hide records about it, what else would he do? It was not simply one brutal individual who must be exposed and destroyed, but the president who would choose such a beast as an adviser.

The use of the Internet was a groundbreaking technique in political character assassination. Its instantaneous impact, available to hundreds of millions of people around the globe (unlike a newspaper published in one city), and the free-floating permanence of material on the web and in databases made it ubiquitous and indelible. Neal Gabler, the biographer of Walter Winchell, described the alternate reality that the Internet could provide for millions: "In a world where the purpose of news is no longer to provide knowledge but to provide excitement, verifiable facts don't seem to mean as much as they once did. Did Blumenthal beat his wife? Drudge had said yes, the Blumenthals no, but even though it didn't happen in physical reality, all that mattered for many readers is whether it happened in their collective imagination."‡

---

*Howard Kurtz, "Out There," *The Washington Post*, March 28, 1999.

†David McClintick, "Town Crier for the New Age," *Brill's Content*, November 1998.

‡Neal Gabler, "Why Let Truth Get in the Way of a Good Story," *Los Angeles Times*, October 26, 1997.

Drudge himself was frivolous about the hostility he generated. His self-presentation as a new incarnation of an old type—the yellow journalist or gossipmonger as Internet pioneer—gave him an image to fit the new medium. That he was nobody with no profession, no career, and no achievements only underscored his novelty. The more he identified his having no qualifications with the new technology that promoted him, the more he justified his lack of responsibility.

Suddenly Drudge was sought out by new "friends" confiding "information" that he could make something of. Lacking articulated politics of his own, he turned himself into the servant of his political manipulators. To continue receiving their "friendship" and publicity, he had only to publish whatever they gave him. They were his "sources," but of course not in any remotely journalistic sense. His "sources" found him and poured their "information" through him unfiltered. They could, moreover, hide behind him, since his limitless subsidies ensured that he would maintain silence. The self-styled iconoclast was bought and paid for. His reliance on his sources enchained him. His so-called Defense Fund was a facade. The funding for his defense, through a conservative group called the Individual Rights Foundation, came to him from Richard Mellon Scaife.

At the time that he posted his defamation of me, Drudge was not completely on his own but was being paid contractually by America Online. AOL was his principal source of income. He was heavily promoted to its members, who were given a special keyword for his site. A month before Drudge smeared me, AOL had issued a press release calling attention to his hiring and approving of his reporting:

AOL HIRES RUNAWAY GOSSIP SUCCESS
MATT DRUDGE

Dulles, VA, July 15, 1997—Maverick gossip columnist Matt Drudge has teamed up with America Online to reach a potential audience that is 160 times bigger than he has drawn to his web site. At the age of 28, Drudge established himself as the Walter Winchell of the electronic age, a contrarian who lives to break show business and political news stories ahead of all competitors. Now a seasoned 30, Drudge makes his successful Drudge Report available to AOL members.

The Drudge Report, solely created by Matt Drudge two years ago and still a one-man operation, found success on the World Wide Web with his take-no-prisoners newsbreaks. . . . Giving the Drudge Report a home on America Online (Keyword: Drudge) opens up the floodgates to an audience ripe for Drudge's aggressive brand of reporting. By giving Drudge both a home on AOL and an AOL keyword all his own, AOL has made Matt Drudge instantly accessible to members who crave instant gossip and news breaks.

"Drudge fits the AOL style and demographic," said AOL Networks President and CEO Bob Pittman. "You can't help but draw a parallel between Drudge and AOL. The Internet has fostered the success of a few players who have established a strong editorial voice. Matt Drudge and AOL share the same ingredients—instant, edgy information—that enable them to be among the very few standouts in cyberspace."

Under the Telecommunications Act of 1996, Internet providers were exempt from liability for what was transmitted by those using their services. In effect, they were the equivalent of a telephone company that laid out the technology but was not legally responsible for what people said through its wires. In June 1997, the U.S. District Court for Eastern Virginia upheld that law in the case of *Zeran v. AOL*. Before filing my suit against Matt Drudge, I tried to learn as much as I could about the law and sought out the opinions of established authorities. And I had to think hard about attaching AOL to his suit.

Our case was markedly different from *Zeran*, which had concerned an anonymous AOL subscriber posting a defamation. Drudge had been hired and paid by AOL, which touted him as a "runaway gossip," was familiar with his methods, and even hailed them. Drudge was anything but an unknown user, as in *Zeran*, and AOL was hardly acting as a passive provider of his material. If AOL were immune from prosecution, then any news organization could publish anything it wanted to on the Internet without ever having to bother about its truthfulness. A newspaper, for example, would have to adhere to basic standards in its printed version but could abandon them in a web edition. *The New York Times*'s standards, say, could be one thing in print, another online.

I did not take lightly the thought of including AOL in my suit against Drudge. I had been a journalist for twenty-seven years, often writing controversial articles but always working closely with editors. When I made inadvertent factual errors, as all journalists do, I corrected the record. Given my journalistic background, my strong interest was in bolstering the First Amendment.

In suing Drudge and AOL, I would have to accept that I was a "public figure," which meant that the burden was on me to prove the defamer's "actual malice"—that is, his knowledge of falsity or his reckless disregard of the truth. (As a private person I would have had only to demonstrate "negligence.") Unquestionably, Drudge had demonstrated that he was unconcerned about publishing falsehoods; his disdain for fact was shown in the whole defamation and in its parts. By paying, distributing, and marketing Drudge, AOL should bear the same responsibility that print or broadcast news organizations would for someone they had hired.

The libel law governing public officials had been established by the case of *New York Times v. Sullivan*, decided in the newspaper's favor by the Supreme Court in 1963. In 1960, sixty prominent Americans, including Eleanor Roosevelt, had taken out a full-page ad in *The New York Times* for the Committee to Defend Martin Luther King and the Struggle for Freedom in the South. The Montgomery, Alabama, city commissioner in charge of the police, L. B. Sullivan, sued the *Times* for libel, even though he had not been mentioned in the ad. As Anthony Lewis wrote in his history of the case:

> The aim was to discourage not false but true accounts of life under a system of white supremacy: stories about men being lynched for trying to vote, about cynical judges using the law to suppress constitutional rights, about police chiefs turning attack dogs on men and women who wanted to drink a Coke at a department-store lunch counter. It was to scare the national press—newspapers, magazines, the television networks—off the civil rights story.*

A diehard segregationist state judge ruled in Sullivan's favor and fined the *Times*, which appealed up to the Supreme Court. Justice William Brennan's magisterial opinion was a landmark in strengthening the First Amendment: "Thus we consider this case against the background of a profound national commitment to the principle that debate on public issues should be uninhibited, robust, and wide-open, and that it may well include vehement, caustic, and sometimes unpleasantly sharp attacks on government and public officials."† The Court made only one exception:

---

*Anthony Lewis, *Make No Law: The Sullivan Case and the First Amendment*, Random House, 1991, p. 35.

†Cited in ibid., p. 143.

one could not publish with a reckless disregard for the truth and actual malice.*

Sullivan was the Magna Carta for reporters covering the civil rights revolution in the South and the war in Vietnam, and doing battle royal with the Nixon administration over publication of the Pentagon Papers and during Watergate. The emboldened press in the 1960s and early 1970s felt, as never before, that its work was protected by the Constitution. But Drudge's caper raised new issues, unforeseen before the Internet. And in my case, I had been defamed about my private life, not criticized for my public conduct, though I would have to pursue the suit as a public official. Also, AOL's culpability was more complex than Drudge's. When I filed papers against it, AOL sought refuge under Section 230 of the Telecommunications Act: "No provider or user of an interactive computer service shall be treated as the publisher or speaker of any information provided by another information content provider." But was someone hired, marketed, and paid by AOL just "another content provider"?

Before proceeding with the suit I consulted those I respected most on these issues: Anthony Lewis, the historian of *Sullivan*, who had taught law at Harvard and Columbia and was a columnist for *The New York Times*, whom I considered a model in the journalism profession; and Floyd Abrams, who had been cocounsel for *The New York Times* in the Pentagon Papers case. It was Abrams who suggested to me that my suit was in essence a defense of *Sullivan*, and that I should present it as such. I was not demanding new law or asking to be treated as other than a public figure subject to the standards of *Sullivan*; I would be trying, he said, to extend to the Internet well-established constitutional law defining protected speech. I hoped, perhaps naïvely, to be doing a service for journalism.

*Speech about public affairs might still be punishable, as the Supreme Court's 1942 decision in *Chaplinsky v. New Hampshire* made clear: "That speech is used as a tool for political ends does not automatically bring it under the protective mantle of the Constitution. For the use of the known lie as a tool is at once at odds with the premises of democratic government and with the orderly manner in which economic, social or political change is to be effected. Calculated falsehood falls into that class of utterances which 'are no essential part of any exposition of ideas, and are of such slight social value as a step to truth that any benefit that may be derived from them is clearly outweighed by the social interest in order and morality.' " Justice Frank Murphy, in *Chaplinsky v. New Hampshire*, 1942, cited by Justice Brennan in the Meikeljohn Lecture at Brown University in 1965, cited in Lewis, *Make No Law*, p. 155.

But rather than disgracing and quarantining Drudge, the press corps lionized him. He was profiled in glossy magazines, given access to newsrooms, invited to be a panelist on NBC News *Meet the Press*, asked to address the National Press Club. Fox News hired him to host a half-hour weekly show, promoting him with full-page advertisements reading, "The Country's Reigning Mischief Maker." As the anti-Clinton crusade continued, Drudge was able almost systematically to drive standards down to his level. The speed with which he posted his "exclusives" riveted entire newsrooms. His wildings were the scandal-obsessed media's fantasies. Other scandal reporters had, of course, long been doing what he did, depending on unchecked information often from the same "sources" that fed Drudge. But Drudge succeeded in influencing the tenor and level of journalism far more than professional journalists succeeded in isolating him.

Through filing a lawsuit against him I tried to gain a measure of control at least of my own situation. It was essential to make a forceful statement in order to be believed. Neither Jackie nor I felt we could let the lie stand. For the moment, this strategy worked. But I had not reckoned on Drudge's posting of the libel being just an opening shot, that his "sources" and others on the right would go on to tarnish me further. For some conservatives the opening salvo was just a drive-by shooting with no consequences. For others it was the beginning of a long campaign. *The Wall Street Journal*, for example, would launch repeated attacks on me.

The real work of the government, back at the White House, never stopped. At constant meetings we discussed what the President might say publicly about various policy matters during his upcoming vacation, and we continued to plan the State of the Union address, five months away but already the subject of intense activity. Even while moving into the lazy days of summer holidays, the White House was preparing for the next round of activity.

On August 17, five days after I began work, an article appeared in *The New York Times* about Begala and me. It started without incident: "President Clinton, searching for new intellectual energy and vigor for his White House, has brought two longtime partisan loyalists into his inner circle and given them broad latitude to work on political strategy and Presidential themes." It went on, tick by tick, and then ran off the cliff:

Mr. Blumenthal—who is expected to work on speeches and high-profile projects like the White House's newly announced emphasis on the millennium—is a more controversial figure. He is friends with Mrs. Clinton and his hiring caught several high-ranking White House officials by surprise. Some of his new colleagues express skepticism that a career in opinion journalism is the requisite background for a White House staffer.

One thing Mr. Blumenthal will not be is a Gergenesque image polisher. A former writer for the *New Yorker*, Mr. Blumenthal has had notoriously bad relations with many of his former colleagues in the Washington press who saw him as too close to the Clintons. When his job was announced by the *New Republic*, for whom he used to write, the magazine sniffed that perhaps "he'll get his back pay."

"A beat is just an assignment but a slut is who you've become maybe," the magazine said.*

The New Republic was now being edited by Michael Kelly, whose politics consisted of Clinton-hating and who frequently spewed invective in my direction. I was not startled by his vituperation; that was his style. But the last quoted line in the *Times* made me laugh out loud. I called the newspaper and asked for a correction. They published it the next day, at a length of more than the usual maximum:

An article yesterday about President Clinton's search for new intellectual energy and vigor in the White House focused on the recent hiring of two political advisers, Paul Begala and Sidney Blumenthal.

The last paragraph, a quotation that appeared to be a cynical and uncomplimentary allusion to Mr. Blumenthal, a former journalist, was truncated and misattributed because of an editing error. One word was incorrectly transcribed, compounding the misimpression.

The quotation, as it appeared in *The Times*, said, "A beat is just an assignment but a slut is who you've become maybe." It did not appear in *The New Republic*, which wrote about Mr. Blumenthal's appointment.

It was, in fact, a line from a play by Mr. Blumenthal that lampooned the White House press corps in which a reporter is bemoaning his career, and should have read, "A beat is just an assignment but a slot is who you've become maybe after being on a beat so long it becomes your life."

The article made the point that Mr. Blumenthal has had tense relations with some of his former colleagues, and the quotation was intended to serve as an illustration of the author's observations about some White House reporters.

*Alison Mitchell, "Clinton Looks for Inspiration from the Left," *The New York Times*, August 17, 1997.

The word "slot" was incorrectly transcribed from an audio tape of the play as "slut."*

The week that had begun with Drudge ended in farce. Life parodied art. I was transported into my own play.

For months afterward, wherever I went, I was asked about the Drudge defamation. It was inescapable. I had to talk about it in a cool, even tone, but having to do this endlessly made me angry, and then made me redouble my effort not to sound angry.

Being smeared produces different effects on different people. Avoidance is one natural reaction, an impulse to retreat, not to read, see, or hear anything about what is being done to you. Denial might have helped Vincent Foster, who spiraled into a fatal depression while being repeatedly smeared. One healthy response for coping was dissociation. I came to see the false persona being constructed by malicious enemies and called by my name as an alien being. Recognizing that even the most personal assault was in one sense impersonal enabled me not to be overwhelmed by anger, humiliation, or avoidance, but to function. My conversations with Hillary Clinton, who had also had to work through this problem, were particularly helpful. She joked that perhaps my job description should include "mine canary." She had been one herself.

Toward the end of August, with the President and his wife away on Martha's Vineyard and the White House on a holiday schedule, Jackie and I sat at the kitchen table editing our 136-page complaint against Matt Drudge and America Online. "Who would have thought I'd be in the White House doing this?" I said.†

---

*Editors' Note, *The New York Times*, August 18, 1997.

†The complaint, *Sidney Blumenthal and Jacqueline Jordan Blumenthal v. Matt Drudge and America Online, Inc.*, can be found on the Internet at http://www.courttv. com/legaldocs/cyberlaw/drudge.html.

EIGHT

Inside the West Wing

I

Every day I drove down Seventeenth Street past the Old Executive Office Building on my left, then past the Corcoran Museum guarded by its sleeping lions on my right, turning left onto E Street, where I could see the Washington Monument catch the early morning sun, then taking another left, where I was stopped by Secret Service agents and a trained dog that would sniff all the way around my car and in my trunk in search of bombs. I would drive a few more yards and display my pass to another agent, and the two tall, spiked black gates to the White House would slowly open. On each were encrusted seven—yes, seven—gold presidential seals. I parked my car on West Executive Drive in front of the steps to the Old Executive Office Building, entered the West Wing, picked up the daily White House News Summary, and headed upstairs to the chief of staff's office for the first meeting of the day.

There were short-term planning meetings and long-term ones. Even though we tried to focus on one presidential action a day, literally thousands of decisions had to be made. At any one time the meetings included so-called amplification meetings of the communications staff, who had to figure out how to spread the President's immediate message on the issue of that day or of tomorrow; speechwriters' meetings; chief-of-staff meetings on the President's schedule for the next week and month; meetings on issues from trade to tobacco to race; meetings convened by the press secretary of the Gang of Four (a group larger than four) to decide which interview requests should be granted; meetings in the Cabinet Room with the President preparing him for press conferences; National Security Council meetings on speeches, policy planning, and foreign trips; and sporadic political meetings in offices throughout the West Wing.

It's a cliché that working at the White House is like living in a firehouse. Without notice, an alarm would sound and I'd be racing. But at other times the White House was like being on the floor of the Chicago Commodities Exchange. Instead of trading in the pit and shouting bids on pork bellies and wheat, I'd be trading policies with other presidential aides: Health care! Climate change! Guns! We lobbied each other to muster support before meetings: What do you feel about pushing for funding heart defibrillators at airports? Should we advocate this safe food standard this week or that environmental program? How about doubling the Peace Corps budget? Why don't you come in on African free trade? The pace never ceased. The White House was like a twenty-four-hour pickup basketball game that just kept going and going.

Shortly before I began at my post, I had a talk with Ted Sorensen, who had been speechwriter, counsel, and intellectual alter ego to President Kennedy, and who was also a commissioner of the White House Fellows program that Jackie ran. He recalled the compact staff of the Kennedy White House—no more than a couple dozen people who really mattered—which allowed him and the others not only to develop a close-knit group but also to produce memorable presidential prose. Sorensen couldn't imagine how one could manage a White House with a sprawling staff of more than fifteen hundred people. It was a different era. Yet, despite the growth of the White House staff from the age of Kennedy to that of Clinton, there was an intimate feel to the West Wing. Some of it had to do with the coziness of the physical space, some of it with the still quite small number of senior staff, and some of it with the constant proximity of a president who was deeply engaged in deciding every issue.

Staying in the game required more than reading all the news articles, more than keeping up with the constant flow of memos, talking points, and official statements. Being on point and seeing every problem whole in all its policy, fiscal, congressional, and larger political dimensions was essential for full participation in any meeting. It was crucial to know when to intervene and when to be silent and listen to others so as to understand the shape of a room. And every room on any given day had a different shape. The West Wing, like all political societies, was an oral culture, thriving on the oldest form of communication: word of mouth. There were so many swiftly moving parts that in order to keep up you had to get information from colleagues and provide your own. The contours in one area or another could change from minute to minute or remain stable for weeks on end and then suddenly be turned upside down. One issue could be topsy-turvy while another skimmed along in a straight line. There were basic facts to be learned daily. What would the Council of Economic Advisers report on the economy? What would the National Economic Council say about the projected surplus? How would it affect housing proposals? When would the Domestic Policy Council present its review to the chief of staff on the tobacco settlement, and what was the view of Treasury?

The agreement that had been struck in June 1997 between the tobacco companies and the various states that had sued them was subject to the approval of the President and the Congress. It would settle all the legal actions, establish a compensatory fund for the victims, and govern future marketing, regulation, and research of tobacco products. The big tobacco companies had become major financial backers of the Republican Party, and Republicans opposed the President with the exception of Senator John McCain, Republican of Arizona, who was our ally. (Ken Starr represented one of the tobacco companies, Brown and Williamson.) Over the next seven months, the companies spent tens of millions of dollars in a campaign to combat the President's regulatory proposals, and by April 1998 they had succeeded in killing any deal.

But inside the administration, in the fall of 1997, there were subtle variations to the arguments over the tobacco question. What did Deputy Treasury Secretary Lawrence Summers's idea of oligopoly have to do with tobacco? Quite a bit, it turned out. Summers's view was that the tobacco settlement guaranteed the companies an oligopoly, secured by the federal government, which enormously benefited them and should therefore lead to a greater settlement than the one on the table—a view that affected Treasury's position.

Constant choices were made at the staff level. For example, which outside experts should be invited to the climate change conference? (I proposed Robert Stavins, an environmental economist at Harvard—and boyhood friend from Chicago—who had devised an emissions trading system that could be used to regulate global warming, an idea the administration was already considering. He was invited and his system became a central feature of administration policy.) Or who should get the Presidential Medal of Freedom? (At a meeting in the Roosevelt Room, we pushed for and knocked off each other's candidates.)

And there were unending political problems. How could we resolve tensions among Democrats over the Fast Track trading authority, which the AFL-CIO opposed? The Fast Track bill would give the president the power to negotiate trade agreements without allowing the Congress to amend them. It was shaping up as a replay of the internally polarizing division among the Democrats over NAFTA. Even the White House staff was split.

There were constant anticipations. Who was on the Sunday morning network talk shows? The list was e-mailed around before each weekend. Would I help at a prep meeting for administration talk-show guests and come up with difficult and embarrassing questions for them?

Following the media was like following a wire ticker. Who was speaking with which reporter, giving out what information or picking up what? What news stories were coming out? Who needed to be worried about what? I swept up and down the West Wing several times a day gleaning bits and pieces. Others dropped in and out of my office. Being in the West Wing was like being in a turbocharged think tank that was also the ultimate political clubhouse that was also the office of the assignment editor for the nation's press.

If you didn't know all the answers, and nobody did, it was essential to know who did have them. Someone, somewhere within shouting distance, would possess them. Once, in making a presentation to the President in the Oval Office, I was stumped on a matter of constitutional law. The deputy domestic policy director, Elena Kagan, who had taught at the University of Chicago Law School, was summoned and succinctly answered the question. It was sort of like being Woody Allen in *Annie Hall*, being able to pull Marshall McLuhan out of nowhere at an instant's notice to settle a debate.

President Clinton's staff in the second term was different from the staff in the first. The Arkansans whom Clinton had brought with him either had left their positions or were in secondary ones. The youthful network put in place by George Stephanopoulos had lost more than its central organizer; most of those who had been close to him were gone or dispersed, and the twenty-somethings within the complex did not see themselves as a distinct corps but were layered into the operations. Many on the staff had extraordinary political histories; almost all of them had come from working- or middle-class backgrounds, having accomplished much professionally, and having wended their way up on Capitol Hill, in campaigns and public interest groups. They were like the classic cast in a war movie about a platoon on the Western Front. I worked every day with people from West Virginia, Iowa, Idaho, Brooklyn, North Carolina, Texas, Vermont, and California. Nearly half the staff were women, including some of the most seasoned political operatives in the Democratic Party, and they were as battle-tested as any of the men.

The West Wing during Clinton's presidency was the most integrated place I've ever worked in. Blacks held positions of responsibility throughout the staff. They were anything but token figures, as they had been in Republican administrations. They attained a critical mass at every level, from director of the Office of Management and Budget to deputy legal counsel to political director to chief speechwriter. Members of the first generation of black professionals made possible by the civil rights revolution, some had been activists in the struggle, and at least one I knew had witnessed firsthand as a child, like Clinton, the integration of Little Rock's Central High School. They were perhaps the greatest meritocrats of all. Their loyalty to Clinton was profound, heartfelt, and unwavering. They took the attacks on him personally, as attacks on their own progress. Terry Edmonds, the chief speechwriter, spoke for them when he wrote that Clinton was "a brother in the struggle. . . . So, in black America the question is not why we love the man so much, but why you don't."*

If there was any ethnic deficit in the Clinton White House it was of white Anglo-Saxon Protestant males, especially wealthy ones. Only Mack McLarty and Erskine Bowles qualified. At many meetings there would be none—only conglomerations of Catholics, Greek Orthodox, Jews, Hispanics, and blacks. At one such meeting, Clinton joked that he was the only WASP present. Gore made two.

Clinton had promised to appoint a cabinet that looked like America, and he did. Forty-four percent of the administration appointees were women. There were seven black cabinet secretaries. And there were the first openly gay appointees in any White House.

The White House staff included people who intimately knew every aspect of American life, from Native American reservations to investment banks. There were experts of every sort—international trade, law, welfare—and also a film producer, a historian of Jacksonian America, and a Polish-born human-rights activist, and that was just the speechwriting office of the National Security Council. There was the son of Thurgood Marshall, Goodie Marshall, director of cabinet affairs; the nephew of Lyndon Johnson, Philip Bobbitt, on the NSC; the sister of Barney Frank,

---

*Terry Edmonds, "Cotton Comes to Harlem: Why Clinton Is a Real Brother," *The Washington Monthly*, September 2001.

Ann Lewis, director of communications; and the nephew of two Nobel Prize–winning economists, Lawrence Summers, deputy secretary and then secretary of the Treasury, who sat in on senior White House staff meetings, as his predecessor Bob Rubin (former cohead of Goldman Sachs) had done. (By the time I arrived, the son of FDR's secretary of the interior, Harold Ickes, had departed for a Washington law office from his job as deputy chief of staff.) There were former aides to half the Senate and the House, veterans of every Democratic campaign for twenty years, and lawyers from virtually all the major firms in Washington. The mix made for an intellectually challenging atmosphere that ensured that almost every possible idea would receive an airing.

People from every office inserted their ideas at every stage of the process. The generic word "process" doesn't begin to describe the continuous involvement of the staff with everything from the invitation list of an upcoming presidential appearance in Detroit to what the President should say about human rights in China. "If you like laws and sausages, you should never watch either being made," Otto von Bismarck, Germany's Iron Chancellor, is said to have remarked. I have never toured a meatpacking plant, but within the West Wing I felt that what I had read about past presidencies and even ancient kingships suddenly came to life. I understood directly about the influence of personality on events, about the nature of court society (all White Houses fit the bill), and about the play of human nature, in a cramped building with only a few actors, for very high stakes.

Being inside the West Wing opened what seemed at first to be an unobstructed vista of knowledge about how presidential decisions were made. But the more I learned, the more I discovered how mysterious the White House was. Journalists, knowing one part of how an event may have been shaped, often raise their very partial information to a conceit of near-omniscience, covered by a scientific claim of objectivity. As a participant, however, I found it a delusion and occasionally dangerous to think in such terms. I learned that it must be taken as a rule that there were always political actors beyond one's knowing. I had something to do with events in ways that many others were unaware of; I discovered later the actions of others on matters on which I wrongly thought I had complete knowledge. There was no such thing as omniscience, not even for the President. Clinton himself understood the inevitability of the scattered, incomplete, and sometimes hidden state of knowledge. But dealing with ambiguity and nuance was a strong point for him. And it had to be for the rest of us, as we ran without stop through dense forests.

Still, the West Wing was a vantage point from which one could see the widest expanse of American politics. From a department or agency, the angle of vision was linear; from the Congress, the view was kaleidoscopic. While the actual West Wing is a sunken addition to the White House built in 1902, barely visible from outside the perimeter, and overshadowed by the stately residence and the ornate Old Executive Office Building, it was the locus of concentrated power.

Learning by observing others on the staff, I quickly saw that part of my function was that of a catalyst. For example, when the Senate Judiciary Committee, controlled by the Republicans, refused to confirm the highly qualified Bill Lann Lee as head of the civil rights division of the Justice Department because he favored affirmative action, in November I suggested that the President name him to the post as an interim appointment, which can be made when the Congress adjourns and its powers have expired at the end of a session. On the merits, Lee deserved the position, and there would be political consequences from his getting it. Lee was a Chinese-American from California, where Asians were about 9 percent of the electorate. In the 1980s, Republicans had usually won more than half of the Asian vote in California. But the GOP was now engaged in investigations into the Democrats' campaign finances whose chief targets were Asians, which most Asians felt was an attempt to exploit nativist stereotypes with a long history in the West. By standing up for his nominee, the President was also rebuking this nativist trend. The appointment was indeed made in December, and Lee performed admirably. By 2000, the Asian vote for Republicans had cratered in California, giving the Democrats a twenty- to thirty-point advantage among them in elections there.

In my new White House post I was susceptible to being buttonholed by friends with pet schemes, many of them worthy. One lawyer friend who had been involved in gun-control class action suits suggested in early 1999 that public housing authorities should be able to sue gun manufacturers for damages caused by gun violence. I brought up the idea with Bruce Reed, director of the Domestic Policy Council, who was enthusiastic but said we needed Andrew Cuomo, secretary of housing and urban development, to take it up. Catching Andrew as he went into a meeting, I laid out the idea, which he liked. He worked it up in his shop in conjunction with Bruce's. Finally, Cuomo announced the proposed new legislation in December 1999. From conception to birth (amid many complications because of the cities' class action suits), the process had taken almost a year.

Making policy and fending off scandals were never separate endeavors in time or space. They happened simultaneously, and the White House had to mobilize to deal with them simultaneously. Like others, I was drawn into politically generated controversies that appeared out of nowhere like twisters. When this happened it was like being in the dream sequence at the beginning of *The Wizard of Oz*, where a surreal pattern of images flashes past Dorothy as she gazes out the window of a house being tumbled into a strange fantasy.

Despite the constant affirmation of chaos theory—the slightest flapping of a butterfly wing always reached the West Wing—there was also an order to the kinetic motion. President Clinton's reelection, and the opprobrium attached to Speaker Gingrich, had given Clinton decisive momentum. In August 1997, just as I entered the White House, Clinton accelerated that momentum with his masterful maneuvering of the budget. Not only had he achieved a balanced budget, but he had altered its priorities to include the Children's Health Insurance Program, which covered 5 million previously uninsured children, the largest increase in health care for children since the creation of Medicaid in 1965. The budget also included the largest increase in college scholarships since the GI Bill, the Hope scholarships, which provided a tax credit for the first two years of college. Within two years, 10 million students had claimed its benefits.

Now every sinew of the executive branch was being flexed in the preparation of the State of the Union address to be delivered the following January, in which Clinton would lay out his next program: a budget headed toward surplus, which would put the paralyzing legacy of Reaganism to rest and establish a progressive agenda for the information age.

The West Wing—which is to say, the senior staff—was in the cockpit. Cannier cabinet secretaries scoured it, lobbying for their budgets and for the inclusion of paragraphs about their work in the speech. For example, Donna Shalala, secretary of health and human services, diminutive in stature but unflagging in energy, used every occasion of her presence in the West Wing to talk with me and others about her proposals, sometimes leaving memos. She understood that there was no such thing as cabinet government in the executive branch of the American government. The cabinet meetings I attended were almost all perfunctory affairs. It was not that the cabinet-level departments were extraneous—they were extremely active and important in developing and administering government programs—but that the final decisions were made at the center, in the West Wing.

II

President Clinton wanted to have a schematic sense of what was possible in his second term and of what he was unlikely to achieve. In sixteen policy areas, from education to science, from race to the environment, the staff in the West Wing analyzed prospective issues, and this analysis was assembled into a book simply entitled *Pillars*. The future was mapped according to a design like a management consulting chart. For example, school construction was headlined "Provide up to 50% Interest Subsidy for New School Construction and Renovation." The timeline: "4 years." The benefits: "Increase the amount of school construction by $20 billion (25%). Subsidy targeted to urban and high poverty districts that have the most significant needs. One-third of all schools facing extensive repair or replacement. New schools needed to address overcrowding caused by record enrollments." The cost/feasibility: "$5 billion grant program— part of the funds awarded by competition to local school districts and the other part by formula to states. State grants ensure that rural and suburban schools will also receive interest subsidies. Record enrollment this fall ensures that overcrowding will continue to be an issue of great concern." The political ramifications: "Strongly supported by urban constituencies. Some potential for bipartisan support, although many Republicans vocally oppose." In the end, Republicans blocked the President's proposed school-construction program more than vocally.

Pillars, the ultimate long-range planning document, internally documenting the Clinton agenda at that moment, described hundreds of policies, including the Human Genome Project and a twenty-five-year program to trace the origins of the universe. Many of its policies were proposed and enacted during Clinton's presidency, but many would have to be left to a future Democratic administration. The document was as complete as the staff could make it. Of course, it did not account for policies and strategies that Clinton was ruminating over in his head, some of which turned out to be the central driving force animating the dry plans neatly outlined for him. *Pillars* was a schema that was flat on the page, awaiting political application.

The President was in a becalmed yet unsettled place. He had vanquished Gingrich, won reelection, and balanced the budget on his terms. Deficits were banished; surpluses were on their way. The prosperity that his early policies had made possible was growing. Still, a majority of the American people were in the grip of pessimism and cynically distrusted government's ability to change the facts of life, even as it was demonstrably doing just that. Three-quarters said they didn't trust government, according to a *Washington Post*–ABC News poll in late August 1997. Only one in six believed the budget would be balanced. There was a widespread sense of denial that the present was producing the greatest prosperity in the country's history.* The public still had the mentality of the Bush presidency's recession, combined with a lingering suspicion of government from the Gingrich revolt against it. At the same time there was a feeling among politicians, including Democratic leaders, that prosperity only fostered a limp complacency. Their party remained fractious, regardless of Clinton's proven politics in the reelection campaign, and often captive to strong currents of protectionism. This literally reactionary protectionism proved how deep-seated was the grip of past political mentalities over fresh facts. Clinton had not yet built a consensus, only the foundation for one.

In the first memo I wrote to the President, dated August 28, I addressed the potential hazards contained in his fall program and how he might move beyond them:

> The old rules no longer seem to apply and their inability to describe reality is perplexing to those who claim to be its savants. . . . Neither the Phillips Curve nor monetarism work anymore; the reigning doctrines of the past appear useless.
>
> For five years, the administration has endured the harrowing ordeal of conducting the transition from the old to the new economy. . . . If Ronald Reagan was the last president to ride the old economy (just as he was the last president of the Cold War) and George Bush was thrown by the transition to the new one (just as he was the president of the transition from the Cold War), then Bill Clinton is the first president of the new economy.

I attacked the fallacy that only overwhelming crises, like wars and depressions, can enable a president to achieve great things. The twentieth-century evidence ran contrary to this assertion: "Eras of American reconstruction are products of good times, not hard times. . . . Times of promise permit people to feel expansive, positive and forward looking. It is always easier to accomplish reform in periods of relative abundance rather than in periods of scarcity." I suggested that for the first time in a

*Richard Morin, "Poll Finds Wide Pessimism About Direction of Nation," *The Washington Post*, August 29, 1997.

generation, since the collapse of the Great Society, "prosperity evokes once again a time of possibility." Clinton had had to do remedial politics in the first term; now he could be reconstructive.

Fast Track trading authority and the problem of global warming might promote a politics of pessimism, I thought. Critics would dismiss Fast Track as a game of winners and losers, global warming as a zero-sum game. The danger would be that the President would be "disconnected from prosperity," while "reactionary populism" would be revived. But it was possible to argue that "the President is at last in a position to explain how he has managed the transition to the new economy and how it can continue to progress for the benefit of the vast majority."

I defined the new economy implicitly as a political economy:

> The goal of policy is not the false choice of either increased productivity or wages but both at once. The new economy as a model is neither laissez-faire nor command control. Global in dimension and driven by high technology, the new economy is constantly increasing efficiency; yet it requires equally constant investments in education and training. Quality-of-life issues are central to quantitative performance. Greater efficiency and greater equity, in short, are not opposites, but complements.

I went out of my way to emphasize that I was suggesting neither that "inflation has disappeared for all time" nor that the "business cycle has been vanquished." The new economy was a reality, and the President should define it in order to shape a new politics.

In September, the President convened a meeting in the Yellow Oval Room in the residence to discuss *Pillars*. "Do we do a little of a lot, or a lot of a little?" asked Erskine Bowles.* Clinton spoke first about the economy and described the "paradigm shift" to the information age. He wanted to assert his economic management above all, but he also wanted to make incremental gains on health care. "Every single step we take removes the stain of having tried to do what we did," he said. Gene Sperling, the indefatigable and expert director of the National Economic Council, discussed Social Security reform in the light of the baby-boom generation's retirement about fifteen years down the line. Clinton was encouraging but noncommittal. It was obvious that he was trying to figure out a solution himself.

---

*One account of this meeting appears in a valuable memoir by the chief speechwriter: Michael Waldman, *Potus Speaks*, Simon and Schuster, 2000, pp. 180–82.

Clinton asked me to talk about my memo, and after I gave a brief summary Bob Rubin raised some objections. Rubin, an outwardly unprepossessing man with a soft voice and self-deprecating manner, almost always began a conversation with protestations about his inferior knowledge and flattery about the superior insight of the person he was addressing. Rather than deflecting attention away from himself, this tactic riveted it on him even more intently. He was crisp but engaging, a careful listener and genuinely open to others' views, even if his own were almost always proven more astute. His record as director of the National Economic Council and secretary of the treasury ranked him not unfavorably in comparison to Jefferson's Albert Gallatin, who stands just below Alexander Hamilton. Rubin was a driven man and very successful, but he did not appear overwound or preoccupied. His corporate success enabled him to pursue his deep commitment to liberal values and especially to issues concerning the cities and the poor.

Rubin was skeptical that there was a "new economy," despite technological changes. He did not believe that the business cycle had been banished. In subsequent talks I had with him, he told me he worried about the barely regulated derivatives market and its potential effect in undermining the global economy. His anxieties were well founded, but his caveats were advanced with a banker's prudence and caution.

Al Gore, who had underlined the parts of the memo dealing with the new economy in his copy, agreed that there was indeed such a thing, and he agreed, too, that the administration needed to speak about it. It demanded, he said, "a new maturity for progressives" to grasp its complexity, to understand the balance of government and markets.

The President commissioned me to write a speech on the new economy. I did so, and in the next few months, he was prepared to deliver it on several occasions, only to be deterred by a sudden, erratic downturn in the stock market. It became a running gag in the White House that such a downturn could be predicted by a scheduling of the new-economy speech. In the end, it was never given, but the President began talking freely about the new economy, even using that locution.

American economic growth continued unbroken, and surpluses grew faster than anyone anticipated. But the global economy was not on automatic pilot. It did not achieve equilibrium on its own. Rubin was right that it was subject to crises—crises both particular to and endemic in the new economy—sparked in faraway places like Malaysia, fanned into flames by new financial devices like derivatives, and spreading like wildfire. The President's understanding and action were needed to prevent these wildfires from burning out of control.

III

Clinton's reelection did not give him a sense of relief that after the storms of the first term he could let up a bit. Critics on the left continued to construe his actions as overly cautious, small-bore, or warmed-over Republicanism. A sizable contingent within the House Democratic Caucus blamed him for the Democrats' having failed to capture a majority in the House in 1996. Many congressional Democrats, writhing under Republican rule, were both passive and accusatory. They expected Clinton to rescue them without their having to do more than be lifted out of the morass. They saw him both as a deus ex machina and as the source of their afflictions. Operating by district and by constituency, they were incapable of developing a coherent national message on their own; still, they resisted presidential leadership. They had not really approved of the balanced budget, even though Clinton's solution had created solvency as a basis for new social policies, and they mostly opposed free trade. The clash over Fast Track trading authority had set off a train of events that led first to a defeat for the administration in November and then to a greater acceptance of presidential leadership by the congressional Democrats.

A harbinger of future trouble came when the President went to the Hill to lobby the House Democratic Caucus himself. The first questioner was Representative Marcy Kaptur from Ohio, a protectionist, who challenged Clinton's assertions about the benefits of free trade: "Why should I believe you?" About a month later, when it was certain that Fast Track would not pass the House, the administration withdrew the measure rather than suffer the humiliation of a vote.

On November 14 I wrote a memo to the President on the "Fast Track Aftermath," in which I observed that Fast Track, being unattached to any trade agreement in which anyone had a vested interest, "became a symbol of free-floating fear of the global economy." Analyzing our internal tally of the House Democrats opposed to it, I discovered that the greatest resistance came from Catholics: of the seventy-two Catholic representatives, only six favored it. I told the President that the campaign against Fast Track was about "more than a reaction to the global economy; it was also about a certain notion of society." Many Fast Track op-

ponents related to the labor movement precisely because of its allegiance
to that notion. "Catholics will accept the new economy, including free
trade," but it had to be presented in the terms of a new social compact inherent in a new social vision.

Clinton was not a laissez-faire free trader. He was already thinking
about how the rough inequalities of globalization might be changed—
"capitalism with a human face," he called it. He worked to lessen insecurity
by proposing environmental protection and labor-rights provisions in all
future international trade agreements. Broadly, he thought hard about how
to spread the benefits of global integration more equally. And his administration accepted that new forms of business regulation would be required
to prevent potential crises in this new global economy. But the Republican
Congress thwarted every effort to prohibit the financial and accounting
practices that permitted the corporate excesses that led to the collapse of
Enron and other companies within a few years. In 1997, Brooksley Born,
Clinton's chair of the Commodities Futures Trading Commission, proposed the regulation of derivatives, which were an instrument in Enron's
house of cards, but the House Banking Committee chairman, Jim Leach,
scolded her for hours and the Republicans killed the bill. In 2000, Arthur
Levitt, chairman of the Securities and Exchange Commission, proposed to
ban accounting firms from simultaneously auditing firms and consulting
for them, but the accountants, including Arthur Andersen, ran a lobbying
campaign, led by Harvey Pitt (later George W. Bush's appointee as SEC
chief), and the Republicans destroyed any new regulation. Also in 2000,
Treasury Secretary Summers proposed a crackdown on offshore tax havens, and once again the Republican Congress thwarted the proposal.

Within days of Fast Track's withdrawal, the House Democratic
leader, Richard Gephardt of Missouri, who had been a Fast Track opponent, delivered a barely disguised denunciation of Clinton at the Kennedy School of Government at Harvard. "This will be an era of small
issues in our politics only if fearful and calculating politicians make it so,"
he said. He argued that the party "should also have the confidence to be
who we genuinely are—not a slightly more compassionate version of the
other side, or a constantly shifting combination of tactics and momentary
calculation." He was speaking as though he were president, or a presidential candidate, forgetting that his job was to manage the Democratic
Caucus. Instantly, he found himself assailed by supporters of the President in the House and he started to retreat.* But the overall effect of his

*"Dems Criticize Gephardt," *Congress Daily*, December 5, 1997.

speech and the reaction to it were salutary. In airing some of the congressional Democrats' unstated grievances, Gephardt dissipated them, and he also discovered that they were not universally shared in the party. In the end, the President's position as the predominant Democratic voice was reinforced.

IV

In the Oval Office, President Clinton sat behind a massive oak desk, called the Resolute desk, which had been used by President Kennedy. It had been built from the timbers of a British frigate, HMS *Resolute*, and given as a gift by Queen Victoria to President Rutherford B. Hayes in 1880. Or he sat in a gold upholstered chair in front of the fireplace that was flanked by two long couches. If I was alone with him, or with just a couple of others, he might stand up and walk around while he talked, the better to gesticulate or wrap his hand around your arm as he made a point. On the wall he had hung Childe Hassam's great impressionist painting *The Avenue in the Rain*, filled with American flags fluttering above New York's Fifth Avenue. In a corner he had stationed a large Native American drum. On a table behind his desk he displayed medallions and trinkets he had received from every state. Around the room were busts of Benjamin Franklin, Harry Truman, Abraham Lincoln, and Martin Luther King, Jr. On the desk, amid pictures of Hillary and Chelsea, were busts of FDR, JFK, and a world leader Clinton revered, Yitzhak Rabin, the only non-American represented. The shelves were filled with volumes of his personal library of biographies of the presidents. On a coffee table, Clinton had placed a rock from the moon, to remind him, he sometimes told visitors, of how short was his time in this place.

When he was among his advisers he spoke directly about his views of the memos they had given him. Sometimes he played with his reading glasses and sometimes he read memos and magazines or even worked on a crossword puzzle while he was being briefed. If you thought he wasn't listening to every word, you were wrong. He'd interrupt on a nuance and ask you to clarify it. He rewrote every single speech, marked up every memo that crossed his desk, and circulated daily to his aides and friends dozens of newspaper and magazine articles he had read, almost always underlining key parts and writing comments in the margins: "Unbelievable . . . I wish . . . Good point . . . What can we do about this?" After rewriting his speeches, he would read portions aloud: "How does that sound?" Someone would make a suggestion and he'd knock off a word or add a phrase. He'd read it again: "That's better." He disliked obsequiousness, regarding it as distinctly unhelpful. He didn't mind arguing over a point and often demanded an argument. He did not like simple assent. He wanted a discussion in which all potential criticisms and pitfalls were raised.

If a speech was settled, the mood would become relaxed before it was time for him to deliver it, and he might launch into a rambling political tale from Arkansas—like the time he faced down a lobbyist from the National Rifle Association and challenged him to a shootout. He'd be laughing until the last moment before he had to step through the double French doors to the Rose Garden to speak. He liked to tell jokes and stories and laugh uproariously. But he also had an ironic sense of humor that he mostly kept hidden because it revealed a sharp edge to his observations.

Clinton's talk in private was endless but not loose. It always had an objective. He was working through some problem, testing a proposition, trying to elicit a reaction, seeing whether a particular idea would be supported or not, or expressing his frustration with a political opponent. He rarely showed off his superior knowledge. He was confident in his intelligence but never used it to appear superior. If he had any arrogance, it showed in his incorrigible lack of punctuality. Even when world leaders were kept waiting, he took his time, seeing sights, reading, and dawdling; usually he was also figuring something out. Another sign that he was in a ruminative mood was that he would start rearranging objects on his desk, moving things slightly here and there.

His humor and his cloudbursts of anger always had reasons behind them. Clinton was genuinely spontaneous and conscious that he was spontaneous. He understood his effect on people while he was having it, an unusual combination of instinct and self-awareness. Being oneself is the hardest thing to achieve in politics, and it demands an undetectable self-control. "If an actor can become a president," Clinton said, "a president can be an actor."

His preferred mode of communication was often the telephone, and his preferred call was placed around midnight. He padded around his study, sifting through memos and articles and books, fielding calls, rocking in his chair. He would talk about basketball, the intricacy of a new government proposal, the motives of this or that senator, golf, something a foreign leader had said to him about a diplomatic initiative, something that someone he had run into at a recent Democratic event had said about what he was doing, something he had just read. In the middle of this patter, he would often say, "Let me ask you a question." And then he would.

Clinton played cards for hours with the staff, Secret Service agents, and visitors. He played hearts, and also other games he picked up, like "oh, hell," which Steven Spielberg taught him one night. He liked to keep score and comment on how the other players were doing. He was a card counter, paying close attention even when it seemed he was just talking. He would take risks but not risks that endangered his hand. He would play double solitaire if he was alone. Once, at one in the morning, in a hotel room in Cologne, Germany, at a G-8 economic summit, I found him playing cards by himself, watching the news on television, reading memos, and talking to Hillary on the telephone all at the same time. He would play games to the very end. As tension built outside his presidential limousine as it pulled up, with people awaiting him, Secret Service at attention, crowds murmuring, sometimes Clinton would be finishing a game in the back seat with his staff.

Clinton's thorough knowledge of government policy was prodigious. Rarely did anyone in the room know more than he about a given policy's details or implications when it was discussed. For his aides this was a burden and a relief. If you wanted to have an effect you had to have mastered the policy, too—why else were you there?—but you could also depend on his knowledge. It was reassuring that he would make the decision. He understood that policies were politics, that they were means and ends at once. He saw them both on their own merits and as elements in strategy. But he frequently made difficult decisions on the logic of the facts, overriding his political inclination.

The first foreign policy issue I was involved in concerned land mines. President Clinton wanted to sign the international treaty banning them and receive the credit that he felt the United States was due under his leadership for being the world's principal systematic remover of land mines. From 1996 through 1998, the United States destroyed 3.3 million land mines. We had lost a team of deminers in 1997 when their plane crashed in Namibia. The way the treaty was written, antitank mines were exempted except those of the specific type deployed by the United States in its patrol of the demilitarized zone between North and South Korea, a barren, unpopulated strip of land that was heavily mined. It was an entirely arbitrary distinction. Clinton asked that the treaty include a provision granting the United States additional time to create an alternative to these mines, but the International Campaign Against Land Mines, the group spurring on the issue, influenced the international community, especially Canada, to refuse the American request. In these circumstances Clinton could not allow the United States to sign the treaty: he could not put the thirty-seven thousand U.S. troops on the other side of the demilitarized zone at risk. On September 17 I joined the group working in the Oval Office on a speech he was going to give on the subject, which included the statement "There is a line that I simply cannot cross, and that line is the safety and security of our men and women in uniform." "I like that," the President remarked, marking up the text. He reviewed the entire policy record verbally as he read.

In his speech, Clinton pledged to destroy all stockpiles of U.S. mines, besides those in the DMZ, by 1999, and all mines deployed outside Korea by 2003, and to end their placement in Korea by 2006. This was a unilateral decision. Then Jody Williams, chairperson of the International Campaign, won the Nobel Peace Prize in October and used her new prominence to attack Clinton. "I think it's tragic that President Clinton does not want to be on the side of humanity," she said. Clinton, dismayed by her grandstanding, belatedly sent her a note of congratulations. But he did not regret his decision on the treaty.*

Throughout the fall of 1997, President Clinton gave speeches and launched initiatives to advance civil rights. Racial equality was his earliest and most passionate motivation in politics. He returned to the source of his commitment on September 25 to commemorate the fortieth anniversary of the integration of Little Rock's Central High School. The nine black students who had first walked the gantlet of taunting whites once again marched up the steps, and the President opened the schoolhouse door for them. (Goodie Marshall, whose father had been the lawyer for the Little Rock Nine, accompanied him.) Clinton's political career was an outcome of the struggle at Central High. The line from Faubus to Clinton was from the Old South to the New South. And some of the segregationists who had whipped up the crowds forty years earlier, like Justice Jim Johnson, were still plotting in the shadows with the Arkansas Project. The past was not another country; it was operating differently in the present.

For Clinton, the anniversary was a moment when he could address the nation's whites, too. "Like so many Americans, I can never fully repay my debt to these nine people," he said. "For with their innocence, they

*Ginia Bellafante, "Kudos for a Crusader," *Time*, October 20, 1997.

purchased more freedom for me, too, and for all white people." He sought to restore the ideal of integration. Jim Crow had been banished, but American society still remained fractured by race and suspicion. "Segregation is no longer the law," he said, "but too often separation is still the rule." Soon he turned to another aspect of rights and separation.

In October 1997, Matthew Shepherd, a young gay man, was brutally beaten to death in Laramie, Wyoming. Shortly after, President Clinton was invited to speak at the Human Rights Campaign annual dinner, the biggest event of the main gay rights group. No president had ever appeared at a gay event, though Clinton had attended numerous private gay fund-raisers and had been the first president to welcome a delegation of gay leaders to the White House. Within the White House a position had been created for someone to be a liaison to the gay community—an important and overwhelmingly Democratic constituency. Clinton saw gay rights as akin to other rights movements. Richard Socarides, a soft-spoken and politically adroit New York attorney, was appointed director of the Office of Public Liaison. I joined him and others on the staff in advocating that the President speak at the HRC dinner.

On November 8, Clinton delivered the first presidential speech placing gay rights within the American tradition. He addressed programmatic measures—the Employment Non-Discrimination Act, increased funding for research on HIV and AIDS, and an executive order banning discrimination against gays in the federal government—but his speech was especially notable for its statement about the essential relationship between the establishment of rights and the function of the presidency:

> Our ideals were never meant to be frozen in stone or time. Keep in mind, when we started out with Thomas Jefferson's credo that all of us are created equal by God, what that really meant in civic political terms was that you had to be white, you had to be male, and that wasn't enough—you had to own property, which would have left my crowd out when I was a boy. Over time, we have had to redefine the words that we started with, not because there was anything wrong with them and their universal power and strength of liberty and justice, but because we were limited in our imaginations about how we could live and what we were capable of and how we should live. Indeed, the story of how we kept going higher and higher and higher to new and higher definitions—and more meaningful definitions—of equality and dignity and freedom is in its essence the fundamental story of our country.

The President drew an analogy between civil rights for blacks and those for gays. A progressive president could help to bring about the full realization of rights by defining them, using the bully pulpit of the office, and then by getting them enacted into law:

Fifty years ago, President Truman stood at a new frontier in our defining struggle on civil rights. Slavery had ended a long time before, but segregation remained. Harry Truman stood before the Lincoln Memorial and said, "It is more important today than ever to ensure that all Americans enjoy the rights [of freedom and equality]. When I say all Americans, I mean all Americans." Well, my friends, all Americans still means all Americans. . . . To be sure, no president can grant rights. Our ideals and our history hold that they are inalienable, embedded in our Constitution, amplified over time by our courts and legislature. I cannot grant them, but I am bound by my oath of office and the burden of history to reaffirm them.

Only two days later, Clinton convened a White House Conference on Hate Crimes at George Washington University. Three years earlier he had gotten legislation passed increasing the penalties for hate crimes, and one year earlier he had created the National Church Arson Task Force to investigate a plague of church burnings and prosecute those responsible for them. Now he proposed new laws that would make violence because of gender, disabilities, or sexual preference hate crimes. (As a direct consequence of these initiatives, the number of hate crimes reported by law enforcement agencies to the Justice Department more than quadrupled, from 2,771 in 1991 to 12,122 in 1999.) "All Americans deserve protection from hate," he said at the conference. A heckler interrupted, shouting, "If you murder Vince Foster, it is not a hate crime!" The tangled paranoia of the right wing, like underground steam building up pressure, had burst out. "We have the First Amendment, even here," Clinton replied evenly. "But I think the hate's coming from your way, not mine." This tiny, isolated incident tellingly demonstrated how Clinton's efforts at social conciliation provoked the right. It was not that he was vaguely misunderstood, but that he was seen as devious, hypocritical, and criminal—or at least that there was a political project to have him be perceived that way.

A month later, in December 1997, the President began the first of a series of town hall meetings of his One America initiative, a program that was partly inspired by the Kerner Commission's report. The National

Advisory Commission on Civil Disorders, to give the Kerner Commission its formal name, had concluded in 1968 that America was drifting toward becoming two societies, one black and one white, more separate and more unequal. The mandate for the One America initiative was broad and nebulous. It was to conduct discussions about race and ethnicity across the country, to address persistent patterns of discrimination, and then to give a final report. One America became a source of internal tension within the administration: the assigned writer for the prospective report, Christopher Edley, a Harvard Law School professor, did not agree with a number of administration policies, including welfare reform, and saw drafting the report as an opportunity to correct them, while Bruce Reed, the Domestic Policy Council director, and others on the staff resisted him. Paralysis was the natural outcome. The conflict within the West Wing expressed on a small scale schisms that would divide Democrats everywhere if allowed to spread.

Almost from the start the One America initiative was plagued by a lack of clarity as to its ultimate objectives. In a memo to the President on October 8, I suggested that it have three focus points: first, acting swiftly and effectively on discrimination issues that could be addressed by laws, such as employment and housing; second, acting on issues of "separation, exclusion, and isolation" on a "multi-issue" basis; and third, "framing the American identity so that its multicultural sources are understood as intrinsic in, not separate from, or outweighing, the whole. It must be stressed that the identity of the American nation at the beginning of the twenty-first century is neither the nativist old-stock model nor the disintegrative identity politics model." I pointed out: "The Republicans are rooted in an old-stock model of American identity, which appears today not so much as a claim to the natural order as a form of identity politics itself." I had in mind especially the white Protestant religious right wing, with its conception of the United States as a Christian nation: "For their part, the Democrats, at worst, descend into a fragmentation of identity politics accelerated by interest-group narrowness, which allows the Republicans to portray them as out of the mainstream."

But the One America initiative remained deadlocked until the end of Clinton's administration, when a brief, summary legislative agenda was released as a substitute for the promised final report. Still, the President's forums spread the message of a new national identity that was both multicultural and unified.

Under Clinton, poverty among black Americans had dropped to its lowest level in American history, homeownership among blacks had risen to its highest, black enrollment in colleges had increased from 48 to 59 percent from 1992 to 1997, and black median income had risen almost 15 percent. Moreover, the income of the poorest fifth of Americans had grown at a 5.4 percent annual rate, compared to 3.9 percent for the top fifth. Of course these gains were the result of Clinton's overall policies that encompassed minorities, not specifically as a consequence of the One America initiative, but the initiative coincided with an immeasurably important change in the American self-image, and it was an emblem of Clinton's intent. He did not want to reiterate the old debate of the 1960s or even that of his first administration, which had centered on affirmative action. He wanted to turn the discussion to the theme of the national strength that could be found in diversity. The country was receiving new waves of immigrants from Asia and Latin America as well as assimilating the repercussions of the civil rights revolution. More than his economic policies, his renovation of the welfare state, or his education programs, this recasting of the national ideal ranks as among his most lasting accomplishments. Clinton's notion of inclusion was at the root of his idea of the country.

The private President was even more adamant about this theme than the public one. In front of the cameras, Clinton used his persuasive powers for conciliation and understanding. He tried to convince, to reason, and to appeal to emotion. But when he was not on public view, when there was no chance that what he said would be reported, he was more insistent.

Once, a small group of about six senior advisers met to brief the President in the Oval Office. We presented the policy options and the political implications. We thought we had covered all the bases. Clinton waited patiently for us to finish. Then he said, "You are the dumbest bunch of white boys I have ever seen." He reprimanded us for coming into the Oval Office as an all-white, all-male group. He mentioned the names of several minority women whom he expected to have included the next time. "Don't let it happen again," said the President. It didn't.

V

When the President of the United States makes an overseas trip, the staff gathers on West Executive Drive, outside the West Wing, and fills several black vans. The vans wend their way through Washington to Andrews Air Force Base and drive onto the runway near *Air Force One* and an identical plane that is for the staff. When you board, a card with your name on it designates your seat. *Air Force One* is a series of chambers, beginning with the President's, in the front of the plane—a bedroom, complete with a shower. There is a rectangular Oval Office with an appropriately massive desk. Past the galley is a small compartment seating four people, the highest-ranked staff members on the flight, including the national security adviser. Next comes a conference room with a huge table and long benches, where meetings and presidential card games can take place. Behind it is a room for about a dozen senior staff people. In this room, to the side, is a computer and transmission center where speeches can be worked on and printed out, and faxes can be sent or received. The next compartment is for traveling dignitaries, cabinet secretaries and the codel—that is, the congressional delegation. Finally, in the last room, is the press corps. Everyone finds his or her place before the President arrives, almost always by helicopter, *Marine One*. Then *Air Force One* is cleared for takeoff.

The rule is that no one is supposed to wander forward of his or her compartment unless by request. But the staff intermingles, working, chatting, and watching movies on the screens in the conference room and the senior staff area. Unsurprisingly, a favorite was *Air Force One*. Everyone knew the dialogue, and whenever we saw Harrison Ford, playing the action hero president, kick Gary Oldman, the bad guy terrorist, out the cargo dock, we would chant in unison, "Get off my plane!"

President Clinton planned a Latin American trip for mid-October 1997. First on the itinerary would be Venezuela, a country that had been nominally democratic since 1958, where he could reinforce the growing democratization of politics that had been spreading across Latin America since the 1980s. Democratic stability was not a given in that oil-rich country, with its sharp divisions of wealth and poverty and its history of caudillo strongmen. In Brazil, the President would confer with the greatest political leader on the continent, President Fernando Henrique Cardoso, once a figure on the left, a Marxist economist who had become a subtle and effective politician trying to find a "Third Way" involving market economics and social justice. The agenda there stretched from environmental measures to help save the Amazon River basin to trade; Brazil, as the largest nation on the continent, presides over its own regional trading bloc, Mercasur, and the effect of the Fast Track defeat there especially weighed on Clinton's mind. He also raised the issue of universal education in an appearance he made in a Rio shantytown. He was beginning to speak out about the need for a global social compact concerning issues of education, health, the environment, and civil liberties. And in Argentina, only a decade earlier ruled by a ruthless junta, Clinton would discuss democracy, trade, and human rights.

I had been following the accounts of violent Argentine campaigns of intimidation against the press, which had been going on since the "dirty war" of terror conducted by the military junta in the 1970s. Argentina's civil society was underdeveloped. In circumstances where a strong judiciary and legal system should have been in place, the press was doing desperate and awkward work in its efforts to reveal corruption. The press had the power only of exposure, not enforcement, and increasingly it was exposed to retribution. Together with the dedicated leaders of the Committee to Protect Journalists—an American group founded in 1981 to call attention to attacks on freedom of the press around the world—I pushed the issue of the Argentine press within the administration, which until then had largely ignored it.

Before going to Argentina, I wrote a memo for Sandy Berger, the national security adviser, reporting that, since Carlos Menem had become president in 1989, violent attacks or threats increasingly had been made against journalists. Most recently, in early 1997, a photojournalist, José Luis Cabezas, had been brutally murdered. Menem sneered at freedom of the press, calling instead for "freedom of the stick" to beat journalists. Yet public-opinion polls showed that Argentines ranked journalists as the most trustworthy members of society and the "worst enemies of criminals." (The press's high reputation in Argentina was the reverse of the falling reputation of media in the United States, where their pursuit of pseudoscandals was radically eroding their public standing.) I argued that if President Clinton did not address this issue, a potential pall would be cast over the entire South American trip, and the seriousness and consistency of America's commitment to human rights would be open to question.

My position was initially opposed by James Dobbins, a foreign service officer who was director of the Latin America section of the NSC. He argued that my idea would provoke Menem's anger and threaten the trip. Sandy Berger brought us together in his office with others on the NSC. We each made our case. Finally, Dobbins suggested doing something with the Organization of American States about freedom of the press. (He was a creative diplomat and became the U.S. representative to the Balkans after the Kosovo war, then U.S. ambassador to Afghanistan after the war against the Taliban.) Others came up with the idea of an office to monitor abuses against the press—a rapporteur on the Human Rights

Commission of the OAS. I pressed to meet with Argentine journalists to hear their accounts firsthand—and for the President to raise the issue directly with Menem and to hold his own conference with the Argentine press, during which he would address their situation.

On the trip, the contrast between the trivial and the serious was sharply underlined in the contrasts between the performance of the traveling U.S. press corps and the predicament of their Argentine counterparts. Tony Blinken, chief speechwriter for the NSC, and I wrote remarks for the President that would invite serious questions.

Standing next to President Cardoso in the garden of the Alvorada Palace in Brasilia, President Clinton said, "The issues we face are central to the well-being of both our peoples. The fate of our hemisphere, with strong democracies, a commitment to fight crime and drugs, to work for lasting peace, the future of the new economy, preparing our people for the twenty-first century—that's what this trip is all about. These are all objectives we share, and they really matter to ordinary citizens in both our nations and throughout this hemisphere. Thank you."

"President Clinton," said Cardoso, "I'd like to ask you to begin if you don't mind." Clinton called on an American reporter for the first question.

"Mr. President, Attorney General Reno has made her decision and will extend her inquiry into your telephone fund-raising to determine whether a special counsel should be named. How do you feel about that hanging over you for another sixty days at least?"

"I feel nothing about it," Clinton replied. "There is a law and there are facts. And I feel that it would be much better if she were permitted to do her job. I know I didn't do anything wrong. I did everything I could to comply with the law. I feel good about it. But I told you yesterday, the thing I don't feel good about is the overt, explicit, overbearing attempt to politicize this whole process and to put pressure on more than one actor in it. That's wrong. There's a law. There's a fact-finding process. And I'm going to cooperate with it in every way I possibly can."

Later in the press conference, John Donvan, White House correspondent for ABC News, asked, "Sir, does it embarrass you when these questions about fund-raising follow you on foreign trips, as they have on this one, or does it embarrass the country?"

"Well," the President replied, "I can't be embarrassed by other people's judgment. I have no control over what you decide to ask about. That's your decision, not mine. That's a question you should ask somebody besides me. I didn't have anything to do with what was asked. I think other people sometimes in other countries wonder what it's all about, especially when everyone concedes that there was no request or improper public action in any way, nor did any occur as a result of whatever communications are in dispute. But that's a decision for you. You have to decide what questions you're going to ask. I can't be embarrassed about how you decide to do your job."

The White House press corps inhabited its own universe no matter where they were. They could circle the globe and never leave the mental confines of the West Wing pressroom. A year later, in Santiago, Chile, I dined with American reporters who were stationed in Latin America; they were as absorbed in the battle for freedom of the press as their Latin counterparts, and they were dismissive of and baffled by the provincial inconsequentiality of the traveling White House reporters.

When we landed in Buenos Aires, we dined at Cabaña Las Lilas, a famous steak restaurant. Before we sat down, the President pulled me aside, as he often did, to discuss his train of thought—a continuing discussion. While everyone milled around and the guests in the restaurant gawked, we talked about the notion of a "social contract for the information age." Then Clinton was presented with a gigantic plate of raw steaks, from which he chose his cut.

The following night, at La Rural Center, President Menem held a state dinner for Clinton, inviting what seemed like the entire Argentine elite, filling a vast ballroom with more than fifteen hundred people. The entertainment consisted of a native rodeo, vaqueros performing on racing and dancing horses. Afterward, Clinton said to me that over at the head table, seated above the sea of people, he could feel the social tension and anxiety. His political sixth sense was always operating.

In the Sheraton Hotel the next day, while the President met with representatives of the Jewish community, which had sustained anti-Semitic bombings of a synagogue and community center in 1992 and 1994, James Steinberg, deputy national security adviser, and I met with five outspoken and prominent Argentine journalists.

"I question whether this trip is relevant, unless there's something concrete," said Maria Luisa MacKay, a writer with *Clarin*, Argentina's largest newspaper. José Eliaschev, a columnist for the Buenos Aires *Herald*, wondered, "Who can guarantee that there will be any follow-up on a proposal for the OAS?" Martin Granovsky, managing editor of *Pagina 12*, a liberal newspaper, said, "We live in a paradox. We are exercising the right of freedom of the press, and at the same time, the government tries to restrain freedom of the press. The press is the last hope. The ghosts of the past are still struggling against this new type of freedom."

In his meeting with Menem, Clinton pressed the issue of freedom of the press, and he asked Menem to support his initiative at the OAS. Within hours of our meeting at the Sheraton, the President held a press conference with Argentine journalists. He went out of his way to bring up the issue of press freedom, even before he was asked, and the Cabezas case as well. "And I said to President Menem," he explained, "that if a civil society can maintain a vigorous, free press, an economy that works, and you can just preserve democracy, time takes care of a lot of this. That is, I believe that twenty years from now an American president will be sitting here, and either you will be sitting here or your successors will be. And I will predict to you that if democracy survives in Argentina—which I believe it will—there will be less corruption; but you could still ask a question about corruption. Do you see what I mean? You could still ask."

The very day we returned to Washington, October 18, *The New York Times* ran an editorial under the headline "Too Polite in Argentina," criticizing President Clinton for failing to speak to Menem about freedom of the press: "Mr. Clinton erred by not plainly telling Argentina's political leaders that they must not condone attacks on journalists. . . . Mr. Clinton did meet with Argentine journalists, but he should have told Mr. Menem directly that Argentina's new democracy cannot be secure so long as those responsible for informing the public run such risks."* This was not only churlish but inaccurate. After I made phone calls, the *Times* published a rare correction to an editorial: "An editorial on Saturday about President Clinton's visit to Argentina mistakenly said that Mr. Clinton failed to stress the importance of a free press in his meetings with President Carlos Menem and other Argentine leaders. The record shows that he raised the issue privately and publicly during his visit, including at his meeting with Mr. Menem."†

Creating a new office at the OAS devoted to freedom of the press was now on the agenda for next year's Summit of the Americas—a hemispheric gathering of national leaders to discuss goals for education, trade, judicial training, democracy, and human rights. Working with Mack McLarty, the former White House chief of staff, who held the unique post of special envoy of the Americas, a superambassador to the entire

---

*Editorial, "Too Polite in Argentina," *The New York Times*, October 18, 1997.
†"Correction," *The New York Times*, October 22, 1997.

continent, I worked to secure final approval of the meeting. After Clinton's talk with Menem, the violent rhetoric against the press in Argentina almost completely stopped and the number of physical incidents of intimidation of journalists fell dramatically.

Freedom of the press remained an essential item for the President in other countries where there were abuses. In December, Clinton was to meet with Prime Minister Yilmaz of Turkey. The Committee to Protect Journalists had established that members of Yilmaz's cabinet, including the foreign minister and the deputy prime minister, would welcome U.S. pressure for liberalization; meanwhile, more than forty journalists were currently in prison in Turkey. The President followed through—and many Turkish journalists were subsequently released. From Argentina onward, in country after country, from China to Russia, from Africa to the Balkans, Clinton kept raising the issue.

VI

Vice President Al Gore had begun 1997 by composing the early stages of his coming campaign for the presidency, carefully putting people and programs in place. But the Republicans had already put him in the line of fire, hoping to eliminate him from political life altogether. On the basis of Dole's desperate last accusations against Clinton in 1996 about campaign finance, the Republican Congress developed full-scale investigations, and they homed in on Gore.

A new ally joined the Republicans and the compliant, excitable media in this hunt: the Federal Bureau of Investigation. Together this conjunction of forces helped turn a string of insignificant events and falsehoods into a concatenation of scandal hanging over Al Gore: a campaign stop at a Buddhist temple, forty-six fund-raising telephone calls, and dark accusations of a stealthy plot by China to buy the American presidency.

In April 1996, Gore had made a campaign stop at the Hsi Lai Buddhist Temple in Hacienda Heights, California. Without Gore's knowledge, John Huang and Maria Hsia, two Chinese-American fund-raisers for the Democratic National Committee, had invited guests from a canceled fund-raising event in nearby Monterey Park to the Buddhist Temple event and had sent their donations on to the DNC—contrary to instructions about never mixing fund-raising and "community" events. Gore said he had believed he was at a "community event" and didn't know it had become a fund-raiser. In any case, whether it was a fund-raiser or not, it was never illegal for him to appear at it. Any culpability lay with the organizers of the event, not him. His account was confirmed, time and again. "A skeptical look at the key charges against Gore . . . reveals that they hinge on fuzzy thinking, malevolent assumptions, and the intransigent refusal to credit exonerating evidence," Roger Parloff, a lawyer and journalist, wrote in *The American Lawyer*.* Huang in 1999 and Hsia in 2000 were convicted of campaign finance violations, but Gore was never a target. At best, he was an uninformed witness. However, his defensiveness naturally stimulated aggressive media moves, which produced thousands of stories. And the Buddhist Temple, with its colorful and strangely dressed Asians, became a regular feature of the negative Republican ads against Gore throughout the 2000 election campaign.

On March 2, 1997, *The Washington Post* published an article, "Gore Was Solicitor-in-Chief," detailing his participation in raising money for the reelection campaign. The famous byline, Bob Woodward's, gave the piece the electricity of highly charged scandal. The following day, Gore held a press conference. "My counsel advises me, let me repeat, that there is 'no controlling legal authority' that says that any of these activities violated any law," Gore said. His abstract, lawyerly phrasing, intended to dispel suspicion, succeeded in setting off a political fury. Under the headline "Gore's Meltdown," Charles Krauthammer, a conservative columnist at *The Washington Post*, wrote, " 'Controlling legal authority.' Whatever other legacies Al Gore leaves behind between now and retirement, he forever bequeaths this newest weasel word to the lexicon of American political corruption."†

A month earlier, on February 13, a full-fledged communist conspiracy, something unseen since the end of the Cold War, had also been dropped into the stew of accusations—a China plot with a hint of Bill Clinton as the Manchurian Candidate. Bob Woodward, citing anonymous sources identified as "officials" and "some officials," reported that "representatives of the People's Republic of China sought to direct contributions from foreign sources to the Democratic National Committee before the 1996 presidential campaign." With this allegation, never proved but often repeated, the scandal was raised to the level of breathless dread: "The information gives the Justice Department inquiry what

*Roger Parloff, "Temple in a Teapot," *The American Lawyer*, May 2000.
†Charles Krauthammer, "Gore's Meltdown," *The Washington Post*, March 7, 1997.

is known as a foreign counterintelligence component, elevating the seriousness of the fund-raising controversy, according to some officials."* Everyone in the White House believed with certainty that "some officials" referred to the FBI.

FBI director Louis Freeh, a prosecutor and judge from New York, had been appointed by Clinton in his first year in office. "We've hit another home run," White House legal counsel Bernard Nussbaum had remarked in 1993 to his deputy, Vincent Foster, when the announcement of Freeh's appointment was made. It was considered a perfect appointment. But within the White House the bleak joke went that Foster must have understood what was going to happen because the next thing he did after that conversation was to commit suicide. Freeh soon encountered a host of problems at the FBI: turmoil at its crime lab; charges of malfeasance and cover-up against agents and officials involved in the Ruby Ridge shootout with a white supremacist, in which his wife and son were killed; and the disastrous handling of the terrorist bombing at the Atlanta Olympics. When the Republicans gained control of the Congress in 1994, the threat of his being subjected to constant hostile congressional investigation loomed over Freeh; quickly he courted Gingrich and his lieutenants, and the harassment stopped.

With the campaign finance charges, Freeh emerged as a prime mover of scandal promotion against the Clinton administration. In December 1996, the Justice Department created a Campaign Finance Task Force. By that time, the cost of the Whitewater investigation had exceeded that of the investigation into the 1993 terrorist bombing of the World Trade Center, according to Senator David Pryor, Democrat of Arkansas.† But both were now dwarfed by the campaign finance investigation (until the September 11, 2001, terrorist attacks, the largest federal investigation in U.S. history), to which more than three hundred FBI agents were assigned. It demanded the greatest document production from the White House ever: greater than Watergate, the Iran-Contra scandal, Whitewater. In the end, not a single administration official was indicted. Nonetheless, the FBI regularly leaked stories to the media. The one about the China plot and "foreign counterintelligence" helped justify

*Bob Woodward and Brian Duffy, "Chinese Embassy Role in Contributions Probed," *The Washington Post*, February 13, 1997.

†Editorial, "The High Cost of Prosecuting," *The Arkansas Times*, August 30, 1996.

Freeh's decision to drain the FBI's finite resources from counterterrorism activity into campaign finance.

Attorney General Janet Reno had almost no contact with Freeh. From his fiefdom, he seemed to be waging a war on her authority and against the President. He pushed Reno hard to recommend the appointment of an independent counsel. Neither the Attorney General nor the President could rein him in because the public would have seen this as an effort to obstruct justice. So on his own—after pointedly not getting permission from Lee Radek, the head of the Public Integrity Division of the Justice Department and of the task force—Freeh instructed his agents to conduct interviews with more than one hundred White House and Democratic Party officials who were not on the task force's list. In September 1997 he circulated a secret memo to "All Field Offices," demanding a "meticulous review of all file holdings in the FBI's possession that bear on attempts by the PRC (China) to influence U.S. political elections." The "importance" of this review, Freeh wrote, "cannot be overstated."* Repeatedly, White House aides were questioned about normal political campaign activities as though they were ipso facto criminal. Career professionals in the Justice Department privately told us they were appalled.

In this heated atmosphere, almost any charge seeming to lend credence to the China plot that Freeh had put into play received media attention. In June 1997, for example, Representative Gerald Soloman, Republican chairman of the House Rules Committee, raised a flurry when he claimed he possessed "evidence" that a Democratic fund-raiser had "committed economic espionage and breached our national security." (Only after two years did the *Los Angeles Times* report that Soloman's "source" had been gossip he had gleaned from a Republican staff member at a Capitol Hill cocktail party.†)

Initially, the White House worried that the Senate hearings might have considerable political impact. The chairman of the Senate Governmental Affairs Committee, Senator Fred Thompson, had played senators in the movies before being elected to play one in real life, and it was

---

*Larry Margasak, "Justice-FBI Animosity Detailed in GAO Study," Associated Press, June 4, 2000; Daniel Klaidman, Mark Hoseball, and Michael Isikoff, "Fumbles in High Places," *Newsweek*, October 20, 1997.

†Art Pine and Alan C. Miller, "FBI Notes Dispel 'Evidence' of Security Breach by Huang," *Los Angeles Times*, December 17, 1999.

thought he'd put on a good show. But for all the media stories, charges, and rumors before the hearings began, the Republicans' case petered out. With nothing at his disposal, Thompson, in his opening statement, portentously alleged the China plot. The FBI had briefed him beforehand. "The committee believes," he intoned, "that high-level Chinese government officials crafted a plan to increase China's influence of the U.S. political process. . . . Our investigations suggest that the plan continues today. . . . Although most discussion of the plan focuses on Congress, our investigations suggest it affected the 1996 presidential race and state elections as well." For weeks, the hearings droned on without a shred of proof. The committee's final report, 9,575 pages in six volumes, contained no evidence whatsoever of any foreign influence in Clinton's re-election campaign. Having overreached, the Republicans had nothing to offer—at great length.

But the pressure to force the naming of an independent counsel to investigate Gore was ratcheted up. The media focused on telephone calls he had made from his White House office to potential donors. His statement about how there was "no controlling legal authority" declaring these improper had made him appear clumsy and possibly deceptive, even though he had nothing, in fact, to hide.

Within the West Wing, regular meetings began to be held in September on the campaign finance problem. Lawyers, Gore aides, and a few Clinton staff members convened in John Podesta's office. The accusations of malfeasance were constant, numerous, and diffuse. So were the reactions. It was as though we were all running around with fire extinguishers.

I suggested that the defense should be staked on a specific, concrete, and, therefore, indisputable point of law. Standing on the facts would dispel unsubstantiated rumors. Since the media were insisting on the empirical facts, they would be driven at least to report this answer. The empirical point was the Pendleton Act of 1883, which was intended to prevent federal officials from soliciting funds from employees and which outlawed shaking down civil servants for political contributions. Gore had made his telephone calls to private citizens, not federal workers, so he was innocent of violating that law. Further, he was raising only "soft" money, did not know that the Democratic National Committee was handing it over as "hard" money to individual campaigns, and had no intent to break any law. On the facts, he was absolved of the charges against him. And indeed this is what began to happen.

Soon, the Associated Press reported that Ronald Reagan in his day had made fund-raising calls from the White House. The Republicans were beginning to look hypocritical with their charges against Gore. Anthony Lewis weighed in at *The New York Times*: "It is wrong to try to use the criminal law in this situation. What Al Gore did was unseemly, but it was not corrupt. It did not remotely approach the stink of the huge contributions made by the tobacco companies to Republicans last year, for example, or of Congressional committees inviting corporate lobbyists into the room where bills undoing environmental laws were being written."* With that article, the tide turned.

Yet even as Gore's defenses stiffened, the attacks on him widened to encompass people around him—Peter Knight, for example, perhaps his closest political adviser. Knight had been chief of staff to Gore in the House and Senate, had run his 1988 campaign, and, in 1996, had been director of the Clinton-Gore campaign, partly to prepare for running Gore's 2000 campaign. While waiting for 2000, Knight was working as a lawyer, taking on clients, as lawyers do, including Walt Disney and Lockheed Martin. One client was Molten Metal Technology, a company developing innovative techniques for recycling and treating toxic radioactive metal wastes. The company had won a contract from the Department of Energy, which was sufficient for the House Energy and Commerce Committee to put Knight under suspicion. Republican staff investigators uncovered layers of innocence: "nothing improper" about the DOE contract, according to their internal memorandum; no "intervention or interference on the part of the Vice President"; no political influence at all. They wondered whether to subject Knight to a hearing: "The cons of holding such a hearing are . . . there is no smoking gun, which opens us up to partisan criticism for engaging in a witchhunt or smear . . . and . . . there are documents and witnesses that undercut our case." Yet the GOP staffers emphasized, "The pros of holding such a hearing are . . . it forces the key players to deny allegations of misconduct under oath . . . and . . . will likely generate enormous press coverage."†

Given no evidence of wrongdoing on the one hand and the prospect of creating a pseudoscandal through manipulation of the media on the other, the Republican chairman, Joe Barton of Texas, distinguished by his record of hostility to environmental protection, had no hesitation in opt-

---

*Anthony Lewis, "Whose Ox Is Gored," *The New York Times*, September 15, 1997.

†U.S. House Democratic Policy Committee, "Politically-Motivated Investigations by House Committees, 1995–present," June 18, 1998, pp. 37–40.

ing for the scandal spray. Hearings were announced and the Republican staff selectively leaked documents to Bob Woodward at *The Washington Post* and reporters from *The Washington Times* and *Time*. Woodward's article ran on page one, with a headline implying sleaze and corruption: "A Lobbyist's Lucrative Ties to Gore: Ex-Aide Raised Funds from Client, Helped Its Federal Business."* When Knight was finally questioned on November 5, after being subjected to this public trial by insinuation, the committee kept him waiting all day; he was not called until the evening. The interrogation was insolent and pointless—except for its political impact. No charges were ever leveled at Knight, but the bad publicity made it impossible for him to act as Gore's campaign manager. Molten Metal was driven into bankruptcy and its stock collapsed. The "witch-hunt or smear," as the Republican staff memo put it, had achieved its aim.†

As tension built over Attorney General Reno's decision on an independent counsel, increasingly freakish stories overwhelmed the media. On November 18, the President was returning from a visit to Wichita, Kansas, where he had been highlighting the welfare-to-work program. He was briefed about an Islamic group's terrorist attack at Luxor, Egypt, which had killed sixty-three tourists. At the same time, Saddam Hussein was refusing to allow United Nations inspectors into Iraq to detect whether he was producing weapons of mass destruction. Clinton also had his eye on Israeli prime minister Benjamin Netanyahu, who was on a tour of the United States to drum up support for his stubborn opposition to the Middle East peace process and was pointedly not visiting the White House. So there was plenty of real news. But the same day, an advance copy of *Insight*, a right-wing magazine published by *The Washington Times*, was circulated to Republican operatives and radio talk-show hosts. Its cover featured an article headlined "Is There Nothing Sacred?" which claimed that "dozens of big-time political donors or friends of the Clintons" had received waivers for burial in Arlington National Cemetery. Instantly, a Republican congressman, Terry Everett of Alabama, chairman of the House Veterans Affairs Subcommittee on Oversight and Investigations, issued a press release declaring that his subcommittee had "found some questionable waivers made in recent years." Rush Lim-

---

*Bob Woodward, "A Lobbyist's Lucrative Ties to Gore," *The Washington Post*, October 17, 1997.

†Jonathan Broder, "How a Republican Smear Campaign Against Al Gore Undid a Promising Boston-Area Company," *Boston*, February 1998.

baugh and G. Gordon Liddy were immediately on the airwaves stirring up anger at the latest Clinton sacrilege. The chairman of the Republican National Committee, Jim Nicholson, declared, "This has to represent one of the most despicable political schemes in recent history." Speaker Gingrich announced there would be investigations, and Senator Arlen Specter, Republican of Pennsylvania, issued an open letter to the President demanding that he "respond personally" and announcing that Specter would hold hearings.

Three days after this uproar started, Secretary of the Army Togo West released the names of the sixty-nine people who had received waivers. Four had been made at the request of President Clinton: former Supreme Court Justice Thurgood Marshall; Elvera Burger, widow of Supreme Court Justice Warren Burger; J. W. Seale, a U.S. Army veteran killed on an undercover mission in Peru as a drug enforcement agent; and Henry Daly, a Marine Corps veteran killed in the line of duty as a Washington, D.C., policeman. The outraged Everett had known of this list for five months, it turned out. There was only one political donor on the list, M. Larry Lawrence, the former U.S. ambassador to Switzerland, who had died a year earlier from cancer and whose record listed him as having served in the merchant marine during the Second World War and having incurred injuries when his boat was sunk by a German submarine.*

One month later, it was revealed that Larry Lawrence had invented his war record; he had fooled everyone, including his own family. The mendacious story about the President had forced out a maudlin falsehood that could only reflect on a dead man's memory. The media went on talking about it for a month.

The pretense that the so-called campaign finance scandal had anything to do with actual campaign finance reform was removed on October 6, when supporters of the reform legislation could not muster sixty votes to overcome a threatened Republican filibuster in the Senate. "Dead," proclaimed a gleeful Senator Mitch McConnell, Republican of Kentucky. "Not going to pass ever!" Before the vote, reform proponents held a rally at the White House and President Clinton addressed them. Questioned by a reporter who found it hard to understand how he could support campaign finance reform while being accused of supposedly scandalous activity himself, he replied, "It may be hard for you, but I

---

*Jonathan Broder, "The Great Arlington Cemetery Smear," *Salon.com*, December 3, 1997, http://www.salon.com/news/1997/12/03news.html.

don't think it's hard for people. You know, I'm not ashamed of the fact that I did the best I could within the present system. I knew we would be outspent badly in 1996, but we weren't outspent as badly as we would have been if I had laid around and done nothing."* (Four months later, on February 26, 1998, Republicans again filibustered campaign finance reform, and Senate Majority Leader Trent Lott pulled it from the floor to prevent a vote.)

On December 2, Reno made her long-awaited decision. She announced that the President and the Vice President had not violated the Pendleton Act, and there would be no new independent counsel. Interestingly, Freeh then issued a statement of his own, as though he were an elected official and not an appointed person in a position that is supposed to be removed from politics. He declared that though he disagreed with the Attorney General's decision, he acknowledged her right to make it. It was like a statement from a Latin American generalissimo indicating he would not, at least now, throw his backing behind a coup d'état.

For days before Reno's announcement, the President raged in private about Freeh—his obvious politicking, his alliance with the Republicans, his unconscionable trafficking of innuendo to the media. At a press conference, reporters repeatedly asked him about Freeh, but the President deflected the questions. At a meeting in the West Wing, a group of us devised an answer for Press Secretary Mike McCurry to deliver in his briefing on December 4. "I think," he said, "the President thinks that the FBI is the world's greatest law enforcement agency, and I think the President has great confidence that Louis Freeh is leading that agency as best he can." The phrase "best he can" was widely understood as a vote of no confidence. But Freeh only continued his underhanded campaigns against the President and the Vice President.

The failure of the Republicans to turn their campaign finance smears into a Watergate fed their frustration. By June 1998, the Republican House had conducted fifty politically motivated investigations. Four committees alone were devoted to investigating foreign influence in the last election. "None of the completed investigations had turned up evidence of wrongdoing," the House Democratic Policy Committee stated.† Gingrich suggested a shift in rhetoric: "I want you to forget the word

---

*Helen Dewar, "Campaign Finance Overhaul Blocked," *The Washington Post*, October 8, 1997.

†U.S. House Democratic Policy Committee, "Politically Motivated," p. 7.

'scandal' and start using the word 'crimes.' "* The China plot, never proved, went underground, only to emerge in other virulent, false forms. Thompson's Senate committee transmuted into the Cox committee in the House; the investigation of phantom Chinese influence in the Clinton administration went on and on. The media and the Republicans contrived a rolling and empty scandal over a Chinese satellite. Then came the extravaganza of a Chinese-American scientist, Wen Ho Lee, falsely jailed for almost a year for downloading classified national security information. China plots proliferated.

The campaign finance imbroglio was the most vexing political incident Vice President Gore had ever encountered. He knew he was a man of integrity and prided himself on being one. He also knew he had done nothing wrong. Yet he felt tainted by the charges and felt a need to explain himself. Of course, that is a natural reaction for someone who has been muddied with falsehoods. He believed he had been unfairly caught in a game that was still somehow on the level. He behaved as if the charges and scoops and editorials had been made in earnest. He couldn't fully see the accustations as what they were—politics, pure and simple. And perception of scandal created about him became a basis for the Republican negative campaign against him in the 2000 election. The groundwork was laid.

VII

In October, Hillary Clinton turned fifty. After the defeat of health care and the Democratic loss of the Congress in 1994, she had receded from the West Wing, rarely appearing in her second-floor office there, working instead from the residence or from her redoubt in the East Wing—all hers, known generally as Hillaryland and staffed almost exclusively by a band of women. But now the storms seemed behind her. The Whitewater hearings had wound down with a whimper; the drama of the reelection was finished; the drumbeat of demonization muffled. Hillary had championed veterans suffering from Gulf War syndrome. She had embarked on a whirlwind of travel to raise the issues of women's rights, economic empowerment, and education—from Panama to Mongolia, from

*George Lardner, Jr.,"Burton Apologizes to GOP," *The Washington Post*, May 7, 1998.

tin shacks to yurts. She hopped for almost two weeks through the "Stans": Turkmenistan, Kazhakstan, Uzbekistan. She continued to advocate her oldest concerns for families and children. She conducted a White House conference on child care. (The President's resulting initiative doubled federal funding for child care and almost doubled it for Head Start's early-education program.) She pressed for an Adoption and Safe Families Act, which passed in November. (In three years the number of adoptions increased by 64 percent, the greatest increase since the creation of the National Foster Care Program.) And she went home to celebrate.

To honor her birthday, Mayor Richard M. Daley proclaimed October 27 Hillary Rodham Clinton Day in Chicago. On that day, Hillary took her friends and family on a tour of her early life. We began at her old family house in Park Ridge, moved on to the Field Elementary School, where she had been "best girl," and then to the First United Methodist Church, where the Reverend Don Jones, who was present for this occasion, had made a deep impression on her with his religion-based social commitment and intellectual vigor. A bus whisked us over to the West Side to Harpo Studios, where Oprah chatted with the First Lady. Next we went to Orchestra Hall, on Michigan Avenue, where Reverend Jones had brought her and other young people in 1962 to hear Martin Luther King, Jr. At the Chicago Historical Society, Hillary was on exhibit in a conversation with Carl Anthony, historian of first ladies. The day ended at the ornate Chicago Cultural Center, where she cut a birthday cake to the strains of a blues band. In the slough of despond of late 1995, I had suggested to Hillary that she reassert her Chicago roots, and at the Democratic National Convention in 1996, she had proclaimed, "Chicago is my kind of village." Now, waiting for her entrance with the President at the Chicago Cultural Center, the blues band played "Sweet Home, Chicago."

Earlier in 1997, Hillary and I had talked about the imminence of the millennium, the coming of the year 2000, which governments around the world were planning to celebrate, some quite elaborately, quite apart from its momentous religious significance for Christians. Unlike every other Western country, the United States had no official office, organization, or plan for 2000. Hillary had initially been skeptical, but she quickly warmed to the idea of creating some kind of initiative. Over tea one February afternoon in the Map Room, she and I and Hillel Schwartz, a visionary historian of the millennium (and my former college roommate) had discussed current thinking about the millennium in all its religious, cultural, and political dimensions.

From that teatime conversation stemmed the White House Millennium Council. Its slogan emerged from Hillel's conception of honoring the past and imagining the future. Ellen McCullough-Lovell, who had worked with Hillary to gather support for the arts in the face of intense conservative opposition in the Congress, proved an adroit administrator of this council.

On August 16, at the end of my first week of work at the White House, the President, standing before the Declaration of Independence and the Constitution in their glass cases at the National Archives, unveiled the Millennium Program:

> For centuries, people have wondered what this millennium would bring. Would it signal an Apocalypse or herald a new world, mark a time of decline or a time of renewal? . . . The millennium is no longer a distant possibility. It has arrived. We are present at the future, a moment we must now define for ourselves and for our children. . . . What of our values and heritage will we carry with us? And what gifts shall we give to the future?

Funding for the National Endowments for the Arts and for the Humanities had been frozen—a significant victory for the right, with Senator Jesse Helms and other philistines making political hay. But the Millennium Council opened up a new source of uncontroversial funding, without any partisan objections, equal to the amount of that for the NEA, and it significantly augmented subsidies for the arts and humanities.

With the Millennium Council Hillary also gained a new national platform and became responsible for the greatest American program of historic preservation ever, securing $80 million from the Congress and then raising $52 million from private sources. On its behalf she visited nearly forty-five sites around the country on "Treasures Tours." The original and tattered Star Spangled Banner that flew over Fort McHenry was restored. So were the yellowing parchments of the Declaration of Independence and the Constitution. Hundreds of invaluable artifacts of our national past were saved: the Ferry Building at Ellis Island, Thomas Edison's laboratory, Louis Armstrong's home, the only recordings of former slaves' narratives, photographic archives from Jane Addams's Hull House, the Mesa Verde cliff dwellings—and other projects in every state. The Millennium Council also saved and designated more than one thousand trails; encouraged the planting of trees and gardens through the Millennium Green; designated hundreds of communities as millennium communities, which created their own projects; and sponsored the first White House Conference on Philanthropy. The White House itself became an intellectual forum in nine millennium evenings, at which scholars delivered lectures that the President and First Lady responded to with their own remarks. The historian Bernard Bailyn, the physicist Stephen Hawking, the poet laureate Robert Pinsky, the theologian Martin Marty, the Internet inventor Vinton Cerf, and the musician Wynton Marsalis (leading a seventeen-piece band) were among those who appeared.

The climax of the millennium would, of course, be New Year's Eve 1999. The film producer George Stevens, Jr. (who also produces the annual Kennedy Center Honors), became the impresario for our plans. Hillary invited Steven Spielberg and Jeffrey Katzenberg to lunch, where they discussed their ideas. "The first thing I always do when I'm planning a big project," said Spielberg, "is get big music. I always get John Williams." Whereupon Spielberg was commissioned to produce a film for the celebration—with music composed by John Williams.

Hillary had been the advocate for the arts since the first months of her husband's first term, but her leadership of the health care initiative had obscured this advocacy, and now the Millennium Council gave her a prominent position from which to continue it, in a seemingly more traditional context for a first lady. In the meantime, she chose other lobbying efforts selectively. For example, when Republicans tried to kill the Community Reinvestment Act, which requires banks to provide capital to low- and moderate-income urban neighborhoods, effectively outlawing the insidious banking practice known as redlining, Hillary weighed in, telephoning key senators.

Her travels to more than sixty countries made her the most international first lady since Eleanor Roosevelt had been "first lady to the world." One of her most exciting trips was to Ireland in the fall of 1997, where at Dublin Castle, at a dinner hosted by Bertie Ahern, the Taoiseach (the Celtic title for prime minister), the novelist Frank McCourt, and the Nobel Prize–winning poet Seamus Heaney outdid each other in eloquence, telling stories and reciting poetry.

The peace negotiations between Protestants and Catholics in Northern Ireland were hitting a rough patch at this juncture, but Hillary's work helped push them forward a bit. The next day, in Belfast, Hillary delivered a speech at the University of Ulster in memory of Joyce McCartan, a community activist who had brought together Protestant and Catholic women on issues of common concern, and whom Hillary had befriended. McCartan called herself a "family feminist," and Hillary took up the term. Drawing from McCartan's work, she spoke of "kitchen table" issues, and developed the notion that she would eventually carry into her Senate campaign in New York, not yet imagined:

> Societies will only address the issues closest to the hearts of women when women themselves claim their rights as citizens. That message has come to life in my own country. Suddenly, the debates about politics and our future are not only about defense or diplomacy. They are also about how to balance work and family, about improving public schools, about keeping health insurance after leaving a job or sending a child off to college for an education. . . . Now, there were some observers who were perplexed that during the last presidential campaign, these kitchen table issues had become so important. They, in fact, derided the phenomenon as the feminization of politics. I prefer to think of it as the humanization of politics—because how we raise our children, care for our sick, train our workers will determine the strength and prosperity of all our people in the days to come. And how we learn to live together across religious, ethnic, and racial lines will determine the peace and security of our children's lives.

Hillary privately met afterward with the British minister on Northern Ireland, Mo Mowlam, and then flew to London and drove through the English countryside to Chequers, the country retreat of the Prime Minister. There the first meeting between high officials of the Clinton and Blair governments was held—the first such meeting ever—to discuss common politics and policies and how to further them.

NINE

Clinton's Third Way

I

The travails of President Clinton's first term were resolved by the expenditure of a good deal of blood, sweat, and tears. In Bosnia, the confused passivity of policy there during his first year in office was replaced by decisive military and diplomatic initiatives that repelled the Serbs' ethnic cleansing. And on the economic front, Clinton's policy of reducing the deficit had succeeded in lowering interest rates and ushering in a long period of prosperity. In his battle with the Republicans, moreover, he had cornered the Congress and won reelection as president.

It was not until the election of Tony Blair as Britain's prime minister in 1997 that the global imperatives of Clinton's politics began at last to come into focus. Then the Democratic president appeared no longer as a strange, isolated figure, but as a forerunner, model, and senior partner in a newly reframed transatlantic alliance. His sort of politics no longer appeared as a matter of mere chance, skill, and personality. He was not a political exception but the leader of an international movement.

President Clinton had spent two years in England as a Rhodes scholar. He was naturally antipathetic toward the British class system and naturally sympathetic with the progressive elements of his generation as they attempted to gain elective power. But what decisively shaped his attitude toward British politics was his experience in the 1992 presidential campaign.

Two months before election day, the Republicans, exhausted of ideas and foundering, enlisted the support of Prime Minister John Major's Conservative Party strategists, who recommended the negative campaign that had been used only months before with devastating effect against Labour. Sending strategists from the Conservative Central Office to Washington armed with videos, posters, and tactical gimmickry, the Tories tried to preserve the special relationship that had existed between Conservatives and Republicans throughout the 1980s. At the Bush campaign's request, John Major's Home Office ransacked its files to see if there were damaging photographs of or documents on young Bill Clinton. Flailing about in desperation as the end loomed, the Bush campaign produced television ads attacking Clinton on themes suggested by the Tories: "trust" and "taxes."

The Clinton campaign, in its characteristic rapid-response mode, sought advice from a Labour Party political consultant, Philip Gould, who flew to Little Rock and moved into the War Room for the duration. "There is absolutely no doubt that the Bush campaign is borrowing heavily from the Conservatives," he wrote in a memo. "Forget the plaudits, concentrate on the smears. Fear builds slowly, is hidden, and only shows in the vote."*

In November 1995, President Clinton delivered a speech to Parliament, praising Prime Minister Major, and then he met privately with the opposition leader. Initially, he had been skeptical about Tony Blair's political prospects. But I had stressed with him the similarities between Blair's efforts and his own. And I had encouraged him to meet with Blair.

When Tony Blair and Bill Clinton's parallel political lives finally intersected at the point of power, they had the chance to recast the alliance between the United States and Britain. They both had had to reform parties once discredited as mismanagers of the economy and mishandlers of foreign policy. They both had faced opposing parties that believed with profound certitude in their right to rule. They had the same view of society as pluralistic and inclusive, and the same view of women's equality; both had married women who were accomplished lawyers. They were comfortable with modern political technology, not intimidated by it. Perhaps their similarities were underlined most emphatically by the criticism leveled against them.

Clinton's political difficulties were often ascribed entirely to his personality. He was called seductive, overly cautious, overly reliant on polling, unprincipled, untrustworthy, compromised. Blair soon found himself subjected to the same denigrations and psychobabble. There

*Cited in Sidney Blumenthal, "The Order of the Boot," *The New Yorker*, December 7, 1992.

were plays on his name to suggest that he, too, was seductive and callow, lacked convictions, expressed only market-research-tested opinions, depended on spin doctors: Tony Blur, Phony Blair, Tory Blair.

Despite the constant criticism and the same kind of stereotypical disparagement, both Clinton and Blair secured the legitimacy of modern progressive government after a generation of discredit. They advanced programs that worked, producing more opportunities for education and reductions in poverty, among other social gains. Their politics were incremental and empirical, not defined by large ideological doctrines. Nonetheless, they achieved their successes by overcoming the twin burdens of their own parties' history and the intense opposition of their conservative foes. Clinton and Blair referred to their approach as the Third Way—neither statist nor laissez-faire. In defining this new policy approach, they had had to start almost from political scratch. In the 1960s, both the American Democrats and the British Labourites had created a new synthesis based on the mixed economy and welfare state spending. But the inflation of the 1970s and the defeats of their parties had broken that consensus, and it was left to a new generation to reformulate progressive politics.

In the House of Commons in 1983, in a small, cramped windowless chamber with room for little more than battered desks, were shoehorned two of the youngest of the newly elected members of the Parliament, from the party that had just suffered the greatest defeat in its history. One of them was already a political force in Edinburgh, a veteran of battles on the left from Red Clydeside and among the Scottish nationalists, who bore his scars as proudly as if they had been won in the Jacobite cause against English rule. Brooding, radical, and intellectual, he filled the office with mounting towers of papers, reports, and books. "Colleagues would compare him to a street-dweller whose every possession was dragged around in a moving pile," wrote one of his biographers, James Naughtie.* This was Gordon Brown, future chancellor of the exchequer. The other was bright-eyed, with a chirpy voice, carrying a barrister's leather briefcase with his initials embossed on it. In the recent election, he had echoed the Labour Party's encrusted positions, lending his youth and vigor to the loyalist rhetoric. This was Tony Blair, the future prime minister.

*James Naughtie, *The Rivals*, Fourth Estate, 2001, p. 27.

The two men had been elected by a party whose future was doubtful. Some of the most respected and experienced figures within it had broken away to form a new party, the Social Democratic Party, which had whatever momentum, innovation, and glamour existed on the left side of the British political spectrum. What remained of the Labour Party had the odor of stale beer in a gloomy workingman's pub in northern England. Defeat had followed defeat. And these were not normal defeats, routine shifts in the alternation of power, but fundamental rejections based on the widespread feeling that the Labour Party was incapable of governing, being mired in ruinous alliance with narrowly self-seeking unions, bereft of new thinking, and incompetent. On a terrace of Westminster, in his early months there, Blair stood at night, staring at the rushing dark currents of the Thames, and remarked to anyone who wandered by, "This party has about eighteen months left."[*]

In January 1993, Blair and Brown made a pilgrimage to Washington, an unlikely place for Labour politicians to be seeking enlightenment. For a dozen years it had been anathema to them, and Blair had even retained until the mid-1980s a lingering membership in the Committee for Nuclear Disarmament, the left-wing group that opposed the U.S. nuclear presence in Britain. But now a new American president was about to be inaugurated, and they came to learn the lessons of victory.

Throughout the 1992 campaign, Jonathan Powell, first secretary at the British Embassy, had traveled the campaign trail, following Clinton and filing dispatches predicting his success that were dismissed as romantic nonsense at Whitehall. (Powell was an Americanist, with an advanced degree in American history from the University of Pennsylvania. His brother, Sir Charles, had been Prime Minister Margaret Thatcher's foreign affairs adviser and was as profoundly Tory as Jonathan was a Labourite.) When Blair and Brown came to Washington, Powell arranged their itinerary and invited me to a small lunch to discuss with them why Clinton had won.

On every point, the British visitors drew instant analogies. Their tone was eager and incredulous. They could barely believe that someone like Clinton had been elected, and they seemed slightly humbled by the news. It was a very American story, with a happy ending. But the Labour Party had lost an election only months before, the fourth in a row; it would be five years before the next one. They were used to, though resisting, failure. They were on a long march.

[*]Naughtie, *The Rivals*, p. 26.

That fall, when I was in England for the Cheltenham Literary Festival, I stopped by Parliament to see Blair. We spent hours together reviewing American and British politics. At this point, he was the Labour shadow home secretary, responsible for issues of crime and justice. Labour, like the Democrats before Clinton, were tagged as soft on crime and criminals, for Labour ministers, when in power, had eased authoritarian laws on issues that ranged from divorce to abortion and had abolished the death penalty, leaving the party vulnerable to the Conservative reaction. Blair formulated a classic statement of a middle way as his response for the future: the Labour Party would be "tough on crime, tough on the causes of crime." He wanted to bridge positions that were generally taken as inherently antagonistic, and his efforts showed the difficulty of crossing the unpredictable currents of polarized politics.

I suggested that Blair come to Washington and talk directly with policymakers to explore new ideas. I did what I could to help this shadow minister, with no firsthand contacts of his own, to set up appointments with people in the White House and the Department of Justice. Jackie and I gave a dinner for him at our home. His name was virtually unknown; his status, to be generous, minor. I invited then–Speaker of the House Tom Foley and a number of other Democratic notables with the enticement that they would be meeting the future prime minister. Blair was not even the Labour Party leader, but I believed that he was likely to be so, though I couldn't describe the circumstances. They were skeptical but turned out anyway.

Blair came away from Washington more convinced than ever that the Clinton experience was a treasure trove of lessons. Most important, it contributed to direct results. In Britain's 1992 election, voters had believed that the Tories were best to deal with crime; only 25 percent believed Labour could do the job. But in 1994, Labour topped the Conservatives on the issue, a turnabout due entirely to Blair, eliciting a harsh and anxious rebuke from the Tory home secretary, Michael Howard, who said, "But now they are pretending to change course."* That charge was among the early criticisms of New Labour as cosmetic, unprincipled, and inauthentic—a common complaint voiced by the right and the left—and it was an echo of the dismissal of Clinton as a politician who engaged in little more than marketing.

In the United States in 1994, a sea of troubles was rising against Clinton, and the Republicans gained control over the Congress that autumn.

---

*Jon Sopel, *Tony Blair: The Moderniser*, Bantam, 1995, p. 165.

Clinton's hazardous experience offered another set of lessons to Blair, who was at the same time being blocked and losing influence within his own party. He believed that his efforts to alter Labour had been thwarted and that he faced years more in the wilderness.

The background of Anthony Blair, among his greatest assets, allowed him to personify the change he wished to make in Labour. He was not a social worker, or a civil servant, or of Celtic heritage. His father, Leo, was a barrister in the beautiful old town of Durham, in the north (County Durham being a famous coal-mining territory); he had been active in the Tory Party in the 1950s and slated as a parliamentary candidate, but his campaign had ended prematurely when he was felled by a stroke. Much of Leo's earlier background—his illegitimate birth, adoption by music hall actors, and youthful membership in the Young Communist League—was unknown to Tony until later in his life. The father he saw was a businessman and lawyer, who transported the family to Australia in search of opportunity in the mid-1950s. The Australian tie was important in Blair's subsequent political development, as he looked to the pragmatic Australian Labor Party as a model. Raised in an atmosphere of striving, he was also influenced by Australia's openness, not only antithetical but hostile to the presumptions of the British class system. Tony was a rebel at his boarding school in Edinburgh and at Oxford grew shoulder-length hair and played in a rock band called Ugly Rumours. He joined in demonstrations against the neofascist National Front and belonged to a New Left study group devoted to Christian socialism. After Oxford, he roamed around Paris, working as a barman and insurance agent. Then, back in London, he read for the law at the Temple office of Alexander Irvine, queen's counsel, where he met his wife, Cherie Booth, a superior lawyer in training, from a family of working-class Labour activists. Tony and Cherie were a politically minded couple, and after his defeat on his first run for the House of Commons, it was thought that she would have the successful parliamentary career. But through the link between Irvine and his best friend, John Smith, a Labour Party leader, Tony's ambition was put back on track.

By the late 1970s, the Labour Party, like the Democratic Party, was caught in the downward spiral of inflation, oil shocks, and political chaos. Britain suffered in 1979 through what was called the Winter of Discontent, a contagion of strikes that revealed not only the crisis of a failed government and of union recklessness, but also the collapse of social democracy as England had understood it. First in Britain in 1979 and in 1980 in the United States, conservatives rose to power.

Margaret Thatcher despised the establishment of her own party as effete "wets," just as Ronald Reagan rebuffed the Eastern establishment of the Republican Party. The greengrocer's daughter disdained paternalistic Tory politics going back to Disraeli. She was not a throwback to Victorian values, but more radical. Her program of tax cuts, deregulation, and privatization suggested the titanic struggle she saw herself as fighting on behalf of unvarnished capitalism against socialism. "The lady is not for turning," she declared. She was a conviction politician, and her convictions were that the state was the "road to serfdom," as her ideological mentors in conservative think tanks taught her, and that, as she famously said, "There is no such thing as society."

In reaction to its own failure and in horror at Thatcher, Labour retreated and, in 1983, was reduced to rubble, winning only 27 percent, its lowest total ever.

Neil Kinnock, the new Labour leader, radiated earnest decency; his Welsh accent marked him as decidedly not English. Indeed, Labour had become a largely regional party, driven into its redoubts in the north and the west, in Scotland and Wales. At the same time, it was concentrated in the dwindling industrial working class. Kinnock knew that radical change had to be made, and he brought evangelical fervor to the effort. But altering the party's fundamental program still ran against his grain, and he did not undertake the arduous task of reforming Labour's rules, which gave the unions dominance through block votes. Though he succeeded in saving Labour from itself, his own errors, particularly on foreign policy, helped undo Labour in 1987.

The Iron Lady regnant did not last forever. The antagonisms she had created and her own arrogance led to her downfall within her own party. Her chosen successor, John Major, lower-middle-class in origin, was a classic steward, a colorless manager. He was tenacious in a plodding way. And in 1992, his Tory campaign resorted to smears and falsehoods played through the Conservative press that rekindled the old fear of Labour as untrustworthy in government. It was given additional credence by a late rally at which Labour's leaders, feeling victory in their grasp, dropped care and discipline and regressed to celebration by waving the red banners and singing the old songs. Major won, the fourth Tory victory in succession. It was wondered generally whether Conservative rule was permanent.

The new Labour leader was the dour and decent Scotsman John Smith. He had contempt for what he called the "black arts" of modern political communications. Smith continued Kinnock's reform by forcing through a one-man–one-vote rule and reducing the unions' block votes, and he gave Blair and Brown posts in the shadow government. But he did not appreciate Blair and Brown's impatience for further reforms, and they were beginning to fall out of his favor when without forewarning, one night in May 1994, John Smith dropped dead of a heart attack at the age of fifty-five. The obvious next party leader was Gordon Brown, shadow chancellor of the exchequer, who had spent his life preparing for his chance, but he was stunned to learn that Blair had assembled the backing to win. Brown withdrew before he ever announced.

In October 1994, at the Labour conference in Blackpool, a new banner was unfurled: "New Labour, New Britain." Blair's effort to rebuild a party whose right and left had both lost politically and become intellectually anachronistic required him to respond to a global economy in which Britain still had its Commonwealth ties and where no European state alone could stanch the flow of capital by "common ownership" for social ends. And he chose to begin by abolishing Clause IV in the Labour constitution, which called for the "common ownership of the means of production," a victory that impressed his leadership on the party and set it in a new direction. But in removing Clause IV he left a vacuum, to be filled, he believed, by what he and the others called simply The Project. "I want us to be a young country again," Blair had told the Labour Party conference. "Not resting on past glories. Not fighting old battles."

At his first meeting with Clinton at Westminster in 1995, Blair had handed the President a single-page note that set out three problems which, if "left of centre" parties did not solve, would leave them not in control, "even if we are in Government." He thought there should be joint meetings on the transatlantic political project. The first problem was of "definition": "The labels the left of centre attached to themselves . . . big government, tax and spend, liberal or social issues, indifference to the family—are discredited. . . . The values are still relevant and popular. . . . We have to find radically different means of meeting traditional ends." The second problem was "differentiation": "The truth is the era of grand ideologies is over. . . . We need to colonise certain key issues as ours. . . . The right need to be seen as sectarian, selfish and, in a sense, anti-patriotic, anti-one-nation." The last problem was "dissemination": "The left of centre suffers from a chronic lack of confidence. One part is seen as pragmatic, out to win but unprincipled; the other just longs for the past to come back again. There is a dire lack of academic and intellectual backbone to sustain a modern left-of-centre project. The commentators often don't understand it. There is no sense of an intellectual movement for change. This feeds a cynicism and disillusion that is wholly unjustified."

Blair now wanted to make another visit to Washington, this time in his new capacity as Labour Party leader. Kinnock had visited in the 1980s, only to be disastrously rebuffed by President Reagan, but Clinton would welcome Blair. Blair wanted to make sure the trip, planned for April 1996, went well, and I helped him as much as I could. On April 11, my wife and I gave a cocktail party at our home for him, inviting Democratic congressional leaders, political consultants, and liberal newspaper writers. Most prominently, Hillary came, and there was a way for Blair and the First Lady to have a long conversation without any problem of protocol: the three of us simply stood in my dining room talking politics. The party created an anticipatory mood about the forthcoming British election and fostered a sense that Clinton's politics now had international resonance. The evening happened to coincide with Jackie's and my twentieth anniversary, and Hillary and Tony delivered festive toasts. The next day Blair met with the President for more than an hour, an extraordinary length of time granted to an opposition leader. "I talked with your friend," Clinton said to me later.

John Major had promised "a nation at ease with itself," but the contradictions inherent in Thatcherism were tearing at the Tories. They were ferociously split over whether Britain should join the European Union and adopt its future monetary unit, and the nation was mired in recession. Major could not resolve these tensions. Nor could the Tories figure out how to campaign against Blair. He was not the old Labour figure they had demonized in the past. This did not prevent them from plastering London with posters of Blair with the red, narrowed eyes of the devil. "New Labour, New Danger" went the new slogan.

On election night, May 1, I joined about two thousand loyal Labour supporters at the Royal Festival Hall as the results were broadcast on gigantic television screens. One after another, Tory strongholds crumbled. The Labour faithful could hardly believe it, as victory after victory was announced, and they let out huge roars. In the end, the scale of victory was beyond what anyone had dared anticipate. Labour gained 145 seats, its greatest gain ever, for a majority in the House of Commons of 179 seats, its greatest ever, and a total of 419 seats, the greatest number since the National Government's victory of 1935. The Conservative defeat was disastrous. The Tories' proportion of the popular vote was the lowest it had been since 1832; the 165 seats it was left holding were its lowest number since 1906. The party was wiped out in Scotland and Wales—and in virtually every city, especially London.

From Royal Festival Hall I notified the President of the magnitude of the Labour victory, while Blair was streaking to London in a small jet from his constituency in Sedgefield. As he was making his way south, at four in the morning, he received a congratulatory telephone call from President Clinton. They were now in business. Clinton was no longer alone.

New Labour's program was intended to make the means of upward mobility available to everyone. This was a fundamental assault on the class system, on the basis not of working-class solidarity but of classlessness—of meritocracy. In this, he was more American than any of his predecessors, just as Clinton was more of a European-style social democrat than any previous U.S. president had been. This was how they viewed each other.

II

Chequers is a brownish-red brick and wood rambling sixteenth-century house in Buckinghamshire set on a large estate reached by roads lined with beech trees. It was deeded in 1917 to the office of the prime minister and since then has served as the incumbent's official country home. On November 2, 1997, Hillary and I brought an American delegation there for a daylong meeting with British counterparts.* The President had commissioned us to begin the new transatlantic political project and, having conceived it, I was charged with the responsibility for implementing it.

---

*The U.S. delegation consisted of Hillary, myself, Don Baer (former White House communications director), Andrew Cuomo (Secretary of Housing and Urban Development), Al From (president of the Democratic Leadership Council), Joseph Nye (director of the Kennedy School of Government at Harvard University), Franklin Raines (director of the Office of Management and Budget), Lawrence Summers (deputy Secretary of the Treasury), Melanne Verveer (Hillary's chief of staff), and Morley Winograd (Vice President Gore's policy adviser). The British delegation consisted of Blair, Ed Balls (Treasury adviser), Gordon Brown (Chancellor of the Exchequer), Stephen Byers (Minister for School Standards), Anthony Giddens (director of the London School of Economics), Patricia Hewitt (Member of Parliament on the Social Security Select Committee), Margaret Jay (Minister for Health), Peter Mandelson (Minister Without Portfolio), David Miliband (director of the Prime Minister's Policy Unit), and Geoffrey Mulgan (deputy director of the Policy Unit).

Chequers is organized around a main hall with a vaulted ceiling, and Tony Blair was there in blue jeans to greet us. Once our delegation had assembled, we climbed the ancient stairs around an inside balcony and into a narrow, rectangular room, where we sat at a long table and began the first of four day-long sessions on every important policy area. In a nearby room where we took our tea, the artifacts informally lying around included Napoleon's briefcase, captured at Waterloo, which still contained his handwritten order of battle.

In the meeting, Blair said about our respective political parties: "The similarities are more striking than not. But something is missing from the picture. We win power, but not the battle of ideas. The right wins, even though they're not in power. Unless we define our new type of politics, people will become disillusioned with us. They apply the wrong tests to us." The center-left was being judged by the standards either of the old left or of the right. "We must be for progress and justice, but in a different world, economy, and political context."

Hillary responded: "We must move beyond the personality-based politics that have broken past the considerable resources of the right."

Al From remarked to Blair: "We would die for your kind of discipline."

"We may yet," Blair joked.

The Chequers meeting was the beginning of an international "Third Way." The Anglo-American special relationship had never before been politically parallel. This parallel gave Clinton's presidency a new sense of coherence and depth, and ratified his course. Moreover, Blair's success dramatically altered the international stage on which Clinton operated. The Prime Minister was an ally like no other through all sorts of difficulties and challenges, from foreign crises in the Balkans to the domestic one over Clinton's possible impeachment. With Blair's election in 1997, Clinton felt that he himself was leading an international movement. That encouraged him as he planned the next stage of his own Third Way politics at home.

III

On September 13, 1997, President Clinton called a meeting to discuss his State of the Union address for 1998. It was held in the room known as the Yellow Oval, on the second floor of the residence. Clinton wanted to talk about his fall agenda and his January speech as the beginning of a political strategy to establish the Democrats as the majority party for more than a generation.

"How can what we do last beyond us?" he asked. "I would like to remove all arguments from the Republicans and conservatives. I want to have the next election fought on a progressive agenda." Vice President Gore, sitting next to Clinton, nodded. "Why can't we change patterns of thought?" Clinton continued. "If we want to win, we have to change patterns of thought." He wanted to move public opinion past "false choices." "All elections, all politics, are about the future," he said.

Then he itemized the various immediate issues facing the country. He wanted to press ahead on raising education standards and expanding health care insurance coverage. It was important to show that the 1994 defeat on health care had not stopped progress. He had been reading extensively about global warming, at Gore's instigation, and he believed the administration had made "a good faith beginning." Increased child care funding, he said, was necessary for welfare reform. Welfare reform couldn't be achieved in isolation, but only with more social services.

But the Democratic Party was split over trade. "There's still a war in our own party," as Clinton said. And public opinion remained unconvinced that the federal deficit was actually being eliminated. Scandal-mongering was a constant distraction.

"This is a terrible, stupid system," Clinton said about the campaign finance laws, but he knew that the Republicans would defeat any effort to reform them, while the media, relying on Republican sources, would continue to exploit stories about alleged Democratic misdeeds.

"The good news is they're trying to put me in jail now," Gore joked.

"This is a goddamned jungle, a sick perverted place," said Clinton.

Yet the President's approval ratings were up: "That enables us to do things," he said. And the battle over the real function of government was shifting favorably. "Government was totally discredited," Clinton said. "But it's not now."

It was at this meeting that we also debated my memo on the new economy, when Bob Rubin was skeptical and Gore vigorously countered his views. Clinton agreed with Gore that the administration should speak publicly about the new economy in terms of the "interdependence" that globalization created. "The world we're living in will present individuals with more choices," he said, "but make them more interdependent. Some of those choices may be illusions." The ultimate choice, he concluded, was "integration or disintegration."

After the meeting, Clinton and I had a long discussion—the first of many over the next few months—about the relation of the political agenda to his understanding of the presidency as the one national office that must articulate the national purpose. He had been reading a biography by the historian Jean Edward Smith of John Marshall, the chief justice of the Supreme Court who first propounded a jurisprudence of federalism. The President understood the growing success of his programs and the emergence of the budget surplus as a platform for a new progressive turn in politics. And he was searching for a way to express national purpose above and beyond the terms used by the Republican right. He grasped, as perhaps only a Southern progressive of his generation could, the destructiveness of the antinationalist strain. The slogans about states' rights, "interposition," and "original intent" had all been watchwords of massive Southern resistance to Washington's federal power and to its enforcement of civil rights. These still virulent beliefs, sometimes whipped up into a new jingoism by the imaginative and incoherent Gingrich, were at the heart of the Republican Party.

The only authentic American conservatism is that of John C. Calhoun, who laid the political arguments for the Confederacy. Other arguments masquerading as "conservatism" are forms of self-interest expressed on behalf of concentrated private power. Calhounism, a frankly antinationalist ideology that presumes the supremacy of states' rights over both the federal government and the individual, argues that the states created the union and that therefore there is no nation beyond this minimal construct. In the 1960s as in the 1860s, Calhounism was confronted and defeated by the national government. But the Republicans who gained control of the Congress in 1994 well understood the power of this old secessionist language—virtually all its leaders were Southern conservatives—and their Contract with America was a poll-driven antinationalist manifesto.

After the 1994 election and in an effort to transcend what he thought of as the platitudes of an older liberalism, Clinton had adopted a rhetoric of retrenchment, which meant that he sounded more conservative than he was. Reagan had said, "Government is the problem," and the Republican right had so demonized the federal government that Clinton thought he had to use certain phrases in order to puncture its balloon: for example, "The era of big government is over." But that was a first step, just at the beginning of the battle. Once he had outmaneuvered the Republicans during the government shutdowns and won reelection in 1996, he wanted to move the country beyond Reagan's debilitating simplifications.

By reasserting a progressive nationalist vision, Clinton wanted to accomplish two political goals: First, he wanted to remind the country of its own national imperatives and of conservatism's undermining of them. (Once, when Mississippi suffered hurricane damage, and Senator Trent Lott was among those appealing for federal aid, the President jokingly remarked to me, "Maybe I should just tell them to go it alone, just be true to their ideology, that it's just a matter of states' rights.") Second, he wanted to create a political language that transcended the traumas that had scarred post-Vietnam liberalism. He wanted to speak positively about the nation, about both its public and private resources, about the energies to be summoned.

On October 27, the President began testing his new State of the Union themes at the annual conference of the Democratic Leadership Council, laying out a new "social compact," a new formulation of liberalism for the globalized age. From 1992 onward, when he spoke of a "new covenant," Clinton had been reaching for a new social settlement, as the British put it. Now, amid a renewed prosperity, his effort came into clearer focus.

Clinton described the struggle of coping with those who insisted government could do "nothing" and those who claimed it could do "everything": "We had to go area by area to abandon those old false choices, the sterile debate about whether you would take the liberal or the conservative position." Now he located his presidency in the stream of history:

> In the industrial age, the progressive movement and the New Deal forged a social compact in which the success of the economy was premised on the security of working people. The twentieth-century social compact served us very well. It built our middle class. It embodied the American Dream. But it is not adequate to deal with the rapid change and energy of the information economy.
>
> Therefore, it is up to us—to all of us—the generation of the computer evolution, to craft a new social compact for a new economy, a new understanding of the responsibilities of government and business and every one of us of what we owe to each other. . . . We can master this new economy, but we have to do it as one America.

In a meeting in the Cabinet Room about the State of the Union address, on December 1, Clinton held forth for almost an hour about the cycles of American history. He made two salient points about the progressive position: the importance of the nation, as opposed to its parts, and the importance of extending the Constitution and the Bill of Rights to meet new challenges. "From RFK in Indiana (during the 1968 primary, where he won liberals, blacks, and conservative whites) to Carter to Gary Hart to me, there has been a constant attempt to redefine the party. We took what Bobby Kennedy was trying to do in Indiana in 1968, and we pulled it off."*

Shortly after, the President and I met in the Oval Office to talk more about the State of the Union, and as we spoke he wrote out a seven-page outline.

"All the balls up in the air," he wrote at the top. "Catch easiest ones. Prob: hard ones." Then: "Quest for power over unifying vision." A scrawled paragraph encapsulated American history from Washington and Lincoln to Theodore Roosevelt and Woodrow Wilson through FDR. Each one had helped forge "one nation." "But, by 1992, the Cold War" had ended, and "science, technology, and information presented the world with a whole new prospect—new winners and losers, new possibilities and new threats." It was "necessary to strengthen our union." And: "For five years I have struggled to redeem the promise of America. . . . Because the road has not always been clear, because neither I nor anyone has all the answers, I have embraced the path of bold, persistent experimentation that has served us so well in the past." He laid out "three principles: opportunity for all, responsibility from all, and American community of all. To make these principles real in this time it has been necessary to change our perception of the role of government, going beyond the debates of recent years." He wrote, "It has also been necessary to change the view Americans hold of our relations with the rest of the world."

From late December through much of January, before the Republican Congress returned to Washington from its recess, the President had the political stage to himself. It was a time of holiday parties in the White House—and previews to the press about the upcoming State of the Union address. We coordinated which policy proposals to publicize each day. "The State of the Union isn't just a speech," my colleague Rahm Emanuel remarked. "It's a month." But one issue remained unmentioned publicly: what to do with the growing federal surplus.

For the first time, at the September meeting in the Yellow Oval, the prospect of there being a budget surplus was discussed. Its appearance

---

*For an extended account of this meeting by another participant, see Waldman, *Potus Speaks*, pp. 188–89.

would be a transforming event. If there were no plan for its use or deployment, though, the Republicans would soak it up with big tax cuts, heavily tilted to the wealthy, leaving nothing in reserve for investment in new programs: Reaganism redux. But the surplus could alternatively provide the basis for progressive government, a fair outcome for years of sacrifice and skepticism. Secret meetings, called "special-issue" meetings, now began to decide how to handle the surplus. They were chaired by Gene Sperling, director of the National Economic Council, an agency of the White House created by Clinton to coordinate economic policy throughout the government.

Sperling was the very opposite of an absentminded professor, which all too many people imagine economists are. To begin with, he was not absentminded, having complete command of arcane economic details and a grasp of their political utility. He was also not a professor, though he had been Robert Reich's research assistant at Harvard. Before becoming NEC director, he had served as Bob Rubin's and Laura Tyson's deputy. Sperling famously worked the longest hours of anyone in the White House. He once interviewed someone for a job on his staff at one in the morning, and didn't act as if that were unusual.

Sperling pointed out that linking the surplus to Social Security would thwart any move to make regressive tax cuts. The President weighed in, insisting that the meetings focus on Social Security solvency since the huge baby-boomer generation was soon going to retire. The Vice President's chief of staff, Ron Klain, suggested that perhaps not all the surplus should be devoted to Social Security because that would tie Gore's hands in future political debates: if there were Democratic rivals in the 2000 primaries, they could propose many programs but Gore would be shackled. The political team (of which I was a part) and the economic team agreed on Sperling's linkage concept.

After the New Year, when the staff had returned to the White House, Clinton presided on January 5, 1998, at a meeting in the Cabinet Room about the surplus. Sperling impishly began his presentation, "Now that we've balanced the budget—" "Now let's spend some money?" cracked Clinton. Sperling laid out various formulas for dividing the surplus. "Just recognize," said Gore, "that the decisions we make are going to affect the future of progressive government for decades into the future." He took the position that the surplus should be, above all, dedicated to making Social Security solvent. This was also Clinton's position. The beauty of that option was that Social Security would receive the growing surplus funds first, a move forestalling Republican tax cuts, while reserving money beyond the solvency for other programs. The exact percentages didn't have to be stamped in metal.

"Save Social Security First," as this proposal became known, redefined America's political debate. Before the State of the Union address was given, in both the House and Senate the Republicans proposed tax cuts that would completely soak up the surplus, including any funds for Social Security. But once Clinton made his proposal, they were thrown off balance and put on the defensive, where they remained for the rest of his presidency. Everything they did thereafter was in reaction.

Two days later, on January 7, the President hosted what we called a thinkers' dinner, which I helped to organize. It brought together many different kinds of thinkers to discuss the ideas framing the State of the Union address, which was now two weeks away. Over dinner, I divided the conversation into three parts: the first about nationalism and progressivism; the second about "values," family policy, and multiculturalism; and the third about globalization and interdependence. Clinton had had thinkers' dinners in his first term, but they had been diffuse affairs by all accounts. I wanted this one to focus, so that the President could receive the benefit of thought that would stimulate his own. I also wanted the participants to join in the ongoing discussion that was so central to the evolution of Clinton's presidency.

The guests gathered around one long table in the Blue Room, the room in the center of the first floor of the White House that Dolley Madison had decorated with French Empire furniture; it offers a view of the statue of Andrew Jackson on a rearing horse in Lafayette Park in one direction and of the Jefferson Memorial in the other. Hillary and I arrived shortly before the President and the Vice President. Other aides— Sandy Berger and Michael Waldman—were also present. The guests included Benjamin Barber, then of Rutgers University, author of *Jihad v. McWorld*; Samuel Beer, a Harvard University emeritus professor of government, author of *To Make a Nation: The Rediscovery of American Federalism*; Albert Camarillo, director of the Stanford University Center for Comparative Strategies in Race and Ethnicity; William Galston, a University of Maryland professor of philosophy who had been on the staff of the White House Domestic Policy Council in the first term; Harvard Law School professor Randall Kennedy; Michael Lind, a contributing editor at *Harper's Magazine* and author of *Up from Conservatism*; Paula Rayman, director of the Radcliffe Public Policy Institute; Dani Rodrik, professor of international political economy at Harvard's Kennedy School; Richard Rorty, the University of Virginia philosopher known for his study of pragmatism; Michael Sandel, another Harvard professor of government, author of *Democracy's Discontent*; Cass Sunstein of the University of Chicago Law School; Barbara DaFoe Whitehead, codirector of the National Marriage Project at Rutgers; Patricia Williams of the Columbia University Law School; and Daniel Yergin, Pulitzer Prize–winning author of *The Prize: The Epic Quest for Oil Money and Power* and *The Commanding Heights*.

As moderator, I opened the discussion by inviting the participants to identify "the kind of transformation we are in." But I asked the President to speak first, and he set the tone by comparing the present moment to the progressive era: "This, too, is a time of reform. I have to be able to tell the story of America in a progressive way."

Samuel Beer, the most notable intellectual exponent of the national idea, a tall, erect octogenarian with a shock of white hair and a bristling white moustache, recalled being a boy in Ohio and watching parades of Civil War veterans. His venerable presence brought the sweep of history into the room. He connected Clinton's prospect to the national tradition, and stressed that the struggle for racial equality was intrinsic in it: "The nation is more than the government. It encompasses the very citizens who feel excluded." And he spoke to the President's comparison to the Progressive era: "Then, as now, Americans were struggling with the fact that the economy had outrun the capacity of political institutions to hold it to account." He argued for an emphasis on decentralized, local institutions of civil society.

Rorty defended the progressive and pragmatic model, citing the bible of Theodore Roosevelt's New Nationalism, Herbert Croly's *The Promise of American Life*, which argues for Hamiltonian means to achieve Jeffersonian ends. Camarillo raised the widespread public fear of globalization, while Rodrik argued that globalization was not new and that governments were capable of action nonetheless: "There's too much sense of impotence."

Barber thought that Rodrik was too complacent, saying, "Government needs to be as large as it needs to be to deal with the problems it faces."

Yergin responded, "Markets are a very effective way of getting things done. They shouldn't be treated as threatening."

Lind, a former conservative, argued for a more Hamiltonian emphasis on strong government and for going beyond "the neo-Progressive bromide." This comment provoked Sandel to defend Jefferson's ideals: "If we look out this window here, there is a memorial to Thomas Jefferson. There is no memorial to Alexander Hamilton. And the reason for that is that he didn't need one." The task, Sandel said, was to make democracy vibrant in a commercial society.

"Let me say something about the [Supreme] Court," said the President. "Have you noticed, every decision the Court passed this year was an assault on the presidency, and thus an attack on government? Well, we're the only ones still fighting for a belief in a role for government. The Court, the Congress—they're on the other side. But sixty-five percent of the American people support us." He continued: "Today the Republicans want to tear down government to liberate private power and private interest. Democrats, though sensible to the need for change, still believe government can serve justice and remedy inequality. It's ironic, isn't it? Because the difference today between Democrats and Republicans inverts the nineteenth-century model Sam Beer was talking about. Then the Republicans stood for national government. What's happened today is the reflection of a two-hundred-year-old struggle, starting with the Federalists and coursing down through Lincoln's battle for Union. Yes, it's this legacy of Lincoln the modern Republicans have betrayed. And then, in the twentieth century, the Democrats, once champions of disunion and confederation, began fighting for a national government capable of rectifying injustice."

The room was silent.

"Yes," he said, "I pronounced big government finished. But that's been misconstrued. . . . We won't make war on government. We will make it a lean and efficient instrument of justice."

The President asked Sam Beer to make concluding remarks, and Beer invoked national union and racial justice once again. The formal event was over, but the evening was not. Clinton lingered for almost an hour, regaling his guests with political stories and discussing his recent reading of presidential biographies (one of Grant was on his nightstand). Hillary disappeared and returned with Buddy on a leash. But Clinton talked on, and Hillary and Buddy went upstairs. Finally, after midnight, I said, "Thank you, Mr. President."

"Put those ideas on paper for me by Monday," he told his departing guests.*

*For various accounts of the thinkers' dinner, see Waldman, *Potus Speaks*, pp. 193–95; Benjamin R. Barber, *The Truth of Power: Intellectual Affairs in the Clinton White House*, Norton, 2001, pp. 238–48; and Martin Kettle, "White House Wise Guys," *The Guardian*, January 19, 1998.

Michael Waldman now coordinated the writing of the final draft of the State of the Union. The early drafts, one on January 10, another the next day, contained long paragraphs tracing the progressive tradition through every phase of our history. But we knew that the speech must be boiled down or else Clinton would be speaking for two hours.

On January 14, at the evening residence meeting—the political meeting in the Yellow Oval where polls and strategy were thrashed out—we all noted that the trends were moving in Clinton's direction. His numbers were up in public-opinion polls, and the policies he would propose were popular. Afterward the President asked Waldman, Al From, Mark Penn, and me to stay behind. We formed a semicircle around him as he sat in the large chair where he presided. Outside the lights blinked atop the Washington Monument. Clinton told us that he believed that the poisons of antigovernment hatred were being drained. "FDR saved capitalism from itself," he said. "Our mission has been to save government from its own excesses so it can again be a progressive force." He commissioned us to work hard on the speech to make sure it expressed that idea. As we walked out of the residence through the West Wing and into the night, we continued talking about the State of the Union.

At 10:18 p.m., Deputy Attorney General Eric Holder received a call on his cell phone as he was leaving a Washington Wizards basketball game. It came from Jackie Bennett, Ken Starr's deputy independent counsel. "We are sort of into a sensitive matter," read Bennett's notes of the conversation. "Breaking. Paying close attention to jurisdictional limits—confident sufficient jurisdictional nexus. Involves people at and associated with White House."* Starr's office wanted from the Justice Department—and the next day received—an expansion of its Whitewater probe on the basis of its allegations that Monica Lewinsky and Vernon Jordan were suborning perjury and that the President was obstructing justice in the Paula Jones case.

*Toobin, *A Vast Conspiracy*, p. 200.

TEN

Seven Days in January

I

President Clinton's deposition in the Paula Jones case went well. That's what I was told. It was Monday, January 19, 1998. Hillary was told the same thing. The media had been building up the tension leading to this moment for months, and now it seemed that another would-be scandal had turned into another nonevent. It was more than an anticlimax: it was a triumph for the President. "They didn't lay a glove on him," Robert Bennett, his lawyer, told me. "On a scale of one to ten, it was a fifteen."

Clinton had testified on Saturday, January 17. I had gone to Chicago for the weekend. On television network news, I watched the presidential limousine drive to Bob Bennett's office at the Skadden, Arps law firm, a short distance from the White House, and then, when the deposition was over, depart. Nothing amiss was reported. Bennett prided himself on his street-smart Brooklyn origins—he had been an amateur boxer—and, unlike his brother, the conservative ideologue William J. Bennett, the pragmatic Bob was a consummate Washington player, who shuttled from his corporate clients to the Hill, from media interviews to the White House. His manner was more jagged than silken, but that was how he liked to project his aggressive, savvy defense. He knew his way around the city's Byzantine mazes and cleverly led his clients to safety. Bill Clinton would be only the latest to be rescued. Yet Bennett confided to me that the President seemed "down" to him after the deposition. He didn't know why. Bennett said he told him, "You did a magnificent job. The worst is over."

I had been speaking to Bennett fairly often about the Jones case, especially since the Supreme Court ruling in January 1996 that the President could not postpone depositions until after his term of office was over. Regardless of the media attention and publicity, it appeared that Clinton would win the case without complicating judgment. Jones had spurned Bennett's reasonable effort in August to settle it, despite the urgings of her lawyers, Joe Cammarata and Gil Davis. Her husband, the underemployed Steve, had believed he could make a much bigger killing. He demanded $1.2 million and began chasing a lucrative book deal. Their lawyers warned the Joneses, "A perception of greed and hatred on your part will lose the public relations battle for your good name which your lawyers have worked long and hard to build up."*

At Steve's instigation, Paula Jones fired these lawyers in September and hired new ones from the Rutherford Institute, a tiny organization on the far shores of the right wing founded by people who advocated a literal interpretation of biblical scripture as a replacement for civil law. One of the members of the small founding board, R. J. Rushdoony, was a Holocaust denier who favored the death penalty for homosexuals and doctors performing abortions. The person responsible for recruiting the Rutherford Institute to the case was Jones's new adviser and makeover consultant, Susan Carpenter-McMillan, a conservative antiabortion activist from suburban Los Angeles whose full-time occupation was to appear on radio and television talk shows. She managed to gain control of Jones's legal defense fund—and rewarded Jones with a nose job and a white Mercedes. (In 1999, Steve left Paula and they divorced. Carpenter-McMillan also divorced her husband at the same time, fantasizing on a TV talk show about having an affair with John F. Kennedy: "I know he's dead, but if I could raise him from the dead . . ."†) Meanwhile, Jones's unofficial lawyers, the right-wing "elves," as they came to be known, worked behind the scenes to destroy any settlement efforts and to continue the case as a political weapon against Clinton. Jones's lawyers relied on the elves to write their briefs, but they never knew of these secret and successful maneuvers to derail the settlement.

From the moment in 1994 when Jones was introduced at the Conservative Political Action Conference, she had time and again altered her story about her encounters with Governor Clinton to make it more salacious. Her shifting account, undoubtedly not of her own invention, was

---

*Cited in Toobin, *A Vast Conspiracy*, p. 128.

†Ann Gerhart and Annie Groer, "The Reliable Source," *The Washington Post*, February 4, 1999.

fuel for her hidden handlers in their media campaign against Clinton. They would load stories in right-wing media from the *Drudge Report* to Murdoch-owned outlets like the *New York Post* and Fox News to the Moonie-owned *Washington Times*. Then the rest of the media would clamor after the unproved but irresistible tales, justifying coverage by their prior circulation. One *Newsweek* reporter, Michael Isikoff, was an exception to the rule in mainstream news organizations in that he carved out a special beat on the sexual folderol swirling around the Jones case. As he darted from sex rumor to rumor, competing news organizations felt increasingly obliged to follow or risk losing an edge.

When in October 1997, Jones added a new twist to her evolving charges, now claiming that Clinton had "distinguishing characteristics" on his genitals, George Conway, a key elf, rifled this bit of imagined pornography by e-mail to Matt Drudge, who promptly posted the story on his website for days. It was soon widely reported elsewhere. "This was just an effort to humiliate and embarrass the President, and at the appropriate time we will show that it is absolutely baseless and without merit," Bennett declared. And Clinton's doctor signed an affidavit stating that it was completely false.

For months Jones's legal team had been trolling for women who had supposedly had sexual relations with Clinton. The women's stories were uncorroborated; some were contradicted; and according to the President, Dolly Kyle Browning, a former high-school classmate of Clinton's, explained to him at their class reunion, in the presence of a witness, that she had felt compelled to make her claims because she was in dire financial straits and seeking a book contract. (She denied making this statement and sued for libel, but her case was dismissed.) In May, after Jones had filed her complaint with the Arkansas court, Bob Bennett had said, "In a single term, this complaint is tabloid trash with a legal caption on it,"* and he made it clear to me that, though there might be a season of "tabloid trash," Jones would lose. He had affidavits that proved that Jones's claim of sexual harassment on the job, the only legal basis of her claim, was dismissible on its face. (She had, in fact, been promoted despite her evident absence of ability.) The case would very likely never even come to trial; it would be tossed out.

January 19, 1998, Monday, was Martin Luther King, Jr., Day, and not much went on at the White House. I came back from Chicago and spoke with Bob Bennett, and the next day I went to staff meetings where we

---

*Toobin, *A Vast Conspiracy*, p. 51.

worked on drafts of the State of the Union address. I met with the President in the Oval Office about it; I met with members of the National Security Council; I attended meetings to prepare for the next political strategy session with the President. Also on that day Israeli prime minister Benjamin Netanyahu, a prickly character whom Clinton was trying to handle, came to the White House. Yasser Arafat, an even more difficult customer, was due on January 22.

I had not a glimmer of knowledge that several members of the legal counsel's office were already responding to Ken Starr's expanded probe from Whitewater into the sex tapes of Monica Lewinsky. I learned later that a few of the lawyers, less than half a dozen, were aware that a story was coming soon about the President's sexual relationship with a White House intern, a rumor whose dimensions they weren't sure of.

The first portent had come from a *Drudge Report*, posted late Saturday night, January 17:

NEWSWEEK KILLS STORY ON WHITE HOUSE INTERN,
BLOCKBUSTER REPORT: 23-YEAR OLD FORMER WHITE HOUSE
INTERN, SEX RELATIONSHIP WITH PRESIDENT

The next night, Drudge posted Monica Lewinsky's name. His sources for his stories were the elf George Conway and Lucianne Goldberg, Linda Tripp's Linda Tripp, the goad to the goad, whose role was still masked.

On January 20, Drudge posted:

CONTROVERSY SWIRLS AROUND TAPES OF FORMER
WHITE HOUSE INTERN, AS STARR MOVES IN!
World Exclusive
Must Credit the DRUDGE REPORT
Federal investigators are now in possession of intimate taped conversations of a former White House intern, age 23, discussing details of her alleged sexual relationship with President Clinton, the *Drudge Report* has learned.

On January 18, on the ABC Sunday morning program *This Week*, the conservative commentator William Kristol had been the first to broadcast this material, sending it out to a national television audience. Kristol had learned of the latest Drudge posting from Richard Porter, who had been one of Kristol's aides in Vice President Quayle's office and was now Ken Starr's law partner at Kirkland and Ellis.

"The story in Washington this morning," Kristol said, "is that *Newsweek* magazine was going to go with a big story based on tape-recorded conversations, which a woman who was a summer intern at the White House—" George Stephanopoulos, who had become a commentator on the panel, interrupted him. "And where did that come from, Bill? The *Drudge Report?*" "There were screaming arguments at *Newsweek* magazine yesterday," Kristol went on. "They finally didn't go with the story. There's going to be a question of whether the media are now going to report what are pretty well validated charges of presidential behavior in the White House."

Though I later learned that some people in the White House were reading the *Drudge Report* with growing trepidation, I had only rapidly skimmed it while I was away from Washington. From what I gleaned superficially, I simply thought this was just another Drudge story, like the "distinguishing characteristic" one. It was enough for me to hear the name "Drudge" to dismiss it. I did not even read it closely enough to see the name "Lewinsky." Paul Begala told me about Stephanopoulos's rejoinder to Kristol, and I thought George had reduced the item to its proper place. Eerily, most of the President's political team was working without any sense that the legal team was frantically scrambling. That brief division of labor would abruptly end.

On Wednesday, January 21, I woke up to a blaring headline in *The Washington Post*: "Clinton Accused of Urging Aide to Lie." The article began:

> Independent counsel Kenneth W. Starr has expanded his investigation of President Clinton to examine whether Clinton and his close friend Vernon Jordan encouraged a 24-year-old former White House intern to lie to lawyers for Paula Jones about whether the intern had an affair with the president, sources close to the investigation said yesterday.
>
> A three-judge appeals court panel on Friday authorized Starr to examine allegations of suborning perjury, false statements and obstruction of justice involving the president, the sources said. A Justice Department official confirmed that Attorney General Janet Reno had forwarded Starr's request to the panel that oversees independent counsels after Starr had asked her for "expeditious" consideration of his request.

The article identified Lewinsky as the intern and Linda Tripp as the informant. It was the first time I recall reading those names. The article continued:

The expansion of the investigation was prompted by information brought to Starr within the past few weeks by a former White House aide who surreptitiously made tape recordings of conversations she had with the former White House intern describing a relationship with Clinton.

The former intern, Monica Lewinsky, began work in the White House in 1995 at age 21 and later moved to a political job at the Pentagon, where she worked with Linda R. Tripp, who had moved there from an administrative job at the White House.

Sources said Tripp provided Starr with audiotapes of more than 10 conversations she had with Lewinsky over recent months in which Lewinsky graphically recounted details of a year-and-a-half-long affair she said she had with Clinton. In some of the conversations—including one in recent days—Lewinsky described Clinton and Jordan directing her to testify falsely in the Paula Jones sexual harassment case against the president, according to sources.

Bob Bennett was quoted as saying, "This story seems ridiculous, and I frankly smell a rat." The article ended with a description of Starr's mandate:

A Justice Department official said there was no question about approving Starr's request.

"Starr made it clear that he needed this," the Justice source said. "We did not want to look like we were slowing down the process." As a result, Reno made her decision "right away."*

The obvious was immediately apparent: Starr's stalled investigation had broken through to an entirely new plane that now threatened the President. This was not just another wrinkle in the tangled fabric of Whitewater. The charges were linking personal and allegedly criminal actions. They involved both Clinton and Vernon Jordan. But the cold type was hieroglyphics in need of translation and elaboration. It was unclear what an "affair" with the President meant. Was it past or current? What had been said on the tapes? Who was Lewinsky? Who was Tripp? The sparse information in that story was all I knew at the moment. It contained twenty-four anonymous sources. It was impossible to know who they were, but the heart of the piece—the notion of criminal allega-

*Susan Schmidt, Peter Baker, and Toni Locy, "Clinton Accused of Urging Aide to Lie," *The Washington Post*, January 21, 1998.

tions against Clinton and Jordan—clearly came from Starr's deputies.
The main reporter, Susan Schmidt, had for years been a reliable outlet
for Republican congressional staffers in the Whitewater investigations
and the Office of Independent Counsel, the reporter most likely to accept what they said and transmit it most directly. It did not take Sherlock
Holmes to deduce that her usual source remained intact.

What the *Post* presented was Starr's maximum case as he wished it to
be understood. "Allegations" were claimed but not factually supported—
neither in this article nor in any subsequent one. These were charges
lined up into a plausible logic from a prosecutor's point of view. I wondered if one thing followed another. My initial instinct was more than extreme skepticism that the President and Vernon Jordan were locked in a
criminal conspiracy. I could not imagine that such careful political men
would be reckless lawbreakers. An affair? I had no idea. But obstructing
justice? Suborning perjury? This seemed impossible. In fact, every criminal allegation reported in this first article was eventually disproved—first
on the very next day and then again repeatedly over the course of more
than a year. Yet the frenzy was at its literal dawn and facts would not
quell it.

It was about 6:45 a.m. when I bolted from my house for the West
Wing. I arrived before almost anyone else. Fewer than about a dozen of
us filed into Erskine Bowles's corner office for the regular early-morning
meeting and sat around his long table. We all turned to the *Post* in our
White House News Summary. Bowles's face was pale, his voice subdued.
Just a week before, he had agreed reluctantly to serve for another year.
He had wanted to return to North Carolina, where his wife and children
spent most of their time. For him, negotiating the passage of the balanced budget the previous fall had been a crowning achievement. During
the Whitewater investigation, he had been subpoenaed before the grand
jury and had not liked it a bit. Now everything about his body language
and tone conveyed that he wished he were anywhere but where he was.
He said that the White House staff would focus on the work at hand and
avoid distraction. At the senior staff meeting in the Roosevelt Room, he
repeated his stricture to maintain focus and just do our work. But he was
clearly upset.

Erskine worked hard and was respectful of everyone around him, encouraging, well organized—and wealthy, therefore independent. He was
neither censorious nor particularly judgmental about people's private
lives. He had become a regular golfing buddy of the President's and
shared in humorous banter with him. As information began to pour out,

we learned that he had played a tangential role in trying to get Monica Lewinsky a job. Perhaps the revelations about her and Clinton came as less of a surprise to him than to others. Nonetheless, the impact swept him off his feet. After a mid-morning meeting with lawyers and the political staff, he remarked, "I think I'm going to throw up." Later that day— or was it the next day?—I went to see him alone. I told him I would support him in any way I could. I knew that others had also gone to talk to him. He replied that he wouldn't have anything to do with managing the scandal and he didn't want to hear about it. I understood, without his mentioning it, that he expected to be subpoenaed. I was sympathetic to his reticence and even withdrawal, but I didn't have the same feelings. By the end of the week and through the weekend, Erskine took time off. He was coping with his emotions, as everyone was, and in his case he wanted to be able to get back to work on the President's legislative program. But his absence on those first few days created an instant vacuum at the center.

By the time the senior staff meeting finished, at about eight o'clock, the last semblance of regular order had departed. Pandemonium descended. The television morning shows were preaching apocalypse. On ABC's *Good Morning America*, Sam Donaldson held forth: "If Kenneth Starr can mount sufficient evidence that the President of the United States told this young lady to lie, that's a federal crime, that's suborning perjury. And, clearly, a serious impeachment investigation would begin on Capitol Hill." George Stephanopoulos adopted that scenario as his own: "If the allegations are true, it could lead to impeachment proceedings."

George had already talked that morning to Begala and Rahm Emanuel; they had all worked together in the Little Rock War Room during the 1992 campaign. The trio had gone through ups and downs in the first term, Begala leaving for a sojourn in Texas after the 1994 midterm defeat, Rahm going in and out of various posts, and George losing favor, then inching himself back, only to depart for television punditry after the reelection victory. Whenever a crisis had struck Clinton, Stephanopoulos's impulse was to turn doomsayer. In difficult situations, his pessimism invariably overcame him. He had once been a vote counter on the House floor for Dick Gephardt (in whose office he had worked side by side with Begala) and was, by his own admission, more a tactician than a strategist. During the New Hampshire primary, at a particularly low ebb, George had believed that Clinton would have to quit the race. And now, once again, pessimism gripped him. He believed the charges against Clinton and was doomsaying to friends and acquaintances on the phone. Since he was Clinton's best-known former aide, his uttering the word "impeachment" on television was treated as a news event in itself. Some on Clinton's political staff were furious at him as a betrayer for using what quickly became known as "the 'I' word." But the problem wasn't Stephanopoulos.

Tensions were already developing within Clinton's staff. The political aides thought the lawyers were withholding information. The lawyers, both those in the counsel's office and Clinton's outside attorneys, believed that information had to be guarded and dispensed according to the best interests of the President's legal situation. But nobody had much information to begin with. The political people tended to think the lawyers lacked political sense, while the lawyers tended to think the political staff lacked legal understanding. Each believed that the other side might create a catastrophe if given control and left to its own devices. But neither side really had a strategy. Out of the early meetings among all these people, a consensus emerged to issue a statement on behalf of the President denying the charges. Almost everyone in the White House was swamped with phone calls from the media, demanding responses, tidbits, hints, anything to feed the story that was the only story. Charles Ruff, the legal counsel, wrote a draft statement in which the President, through the press secretary, Michael McCurry, would say that he was "outraged by these allegations" and "never had a sexual relationship with this woman." Someone in the meeting suggested a word change: from "sexual" to "improper." McCurry, with Clinton's concurrence, released the statement. "Improper" became the other "I" word of the day.

In anticipation of the State of the Union speech, three news interviews with President Clinton had been scheduled for that day. Their cancellation would constitute a tacit admission of guilt, so that was out of the question. The interviews went on. The first one was with Jim Lehrer, the careful and fair-minded host of Public Broadcasting's *News Hour*.

Lehrer: The news of this day is that Kenneth Starr, independent counsel, is investigating allegations that you suborned perjury by encouraging a twenty-four-year-old woman, former White House intern, to lie under oath in a civil deposition about her having had an affair with you. Mr. President, is that true?

Clinton: That is not true. That is not true. I did not ask anyone to tell anything other than the truth. There is no improper relationship. And I intend to cooperate with this inquiry. But that is not true.

Lehrer: "No improper relationship"—define what you mean by that.

Clinton: Well, I think you know what it means. It means that there is not a sexual relationship, an improper sexual relationship, or any other kind of improper relationship.

Lehrer: You had no sexual relationship with this young woman?

Clinton: There is not a sexual relationship; that is accurate.

At his morning briefing, McCurry was asked 113 questions about the Lewinsky story.* In the White House press room, the reporters now whooped and hollered about Clinton's use of the word "is." Was he trying to avoid an admission of past events by using the present tense? Clinton tried to preempt the "is" controversy in the other two interviews of the day, one with Morton Kondracke of *Roll Call*, a Capitol Hill newspaper, and one with two reporters from National Public Radio, by determinedly using the word "was."

The television network anchors were all in Havana that day to report on the unprecedented visit of Pope John Paul to Castro's Cuba. By midafternoon, they were breaking into their regular programming with reports from Havana about Monica Lewinsky. By nightfall they had packed their bags and crews and headed back to the United States for the big story. Cable television was booked solid with wall-to-wall discussion, free association, fantasy, and rumor. Talk radio had no other subject. By the next morning, it was obvious the news cycle would crank up again and again—scandal without end.

By the late afternoon of the first day, hardly anyone inside the White House had new information that had not already been reported in the morning. Details began to dribble out about Lewinsky and Tripp. Lewinsky was a twenty-four-year-old former White House intern who had transferred to the Pentagon in 1996, where she met Linda Tripp, who had also worked in the White House—a secretary held over from the Bush administration. Tripp had gained her position at the Bush White House through Republican connections, and in the Clinton White House she had been part of an informal group of remaining conservatives, including Gary Aldrich, an FBI agent. Working in the legal counsel's office, Tripp had managed to insert herself into the investigations into Whitewater and Vincent Foster, and had become a witness before the Special Senate Whitewater Committee. She was almost certainly the "inside White House" source, given the pseudonym "Deepwater," whom two conservative writers had quoted as doubting "the authentic-

*Kalb, *One Scandalous Story*, p. 138.

ity" of Foster's suicide note.* Shuttled to a well-paying Pentagon job in August 1994 after her congressional appearances, Tripp became determined to expose the Clintons, whom she saw as interlopers, usurping the presidency from Bush. She was already in touch with Isikoff. Tony Snow, a former Bush speechwriter and now a Fox News anchorman, put her together with a literary agent, Lucianne Goldberg. In 1996, she encountered Monica Lewinsky, recently employed at the Pentagon, and they discovered their common recent past at the White House. Tripp, twenty-four years older, became Lewinsky's confessor.

The circumstances under which Starr had expanded his investigation, however, were largely unknown. Almost all the ceaseless television commentary was speculative, and it turned on whether the President would have to resign. "The next forty-eight to seventy-two hours are critical," intoned NBC's Washington bureau chief, Tim Russert, on an afternoon segment.† Characters like Lucianne Goldberg who had been lurking in the shadows still remained undetected. The contents of Linda Tripp's conversations with Monica Lewinsky, except that they revealed some kind of affair, were undisclosed. Clinton's actual relationship with Lewinsky remained a mystery.

Within the White House, there was no organizing focus, no strategy, no one calling meetings, and we had a growing sense of standing on a beach waiting for a tidal wave. Some felt near panic. Normally poised political people believed they faced potential personal ruin. They correctly thought that Starr's power was limitless and his motive to destroy the President relentless. They convinced themselves, even if they had no reason, that they, too, would become Starr's targets. Their fear was stark and it was seeping out to reporters.

From the *Post*'s report, an early ABC News bulletin, and calls from certain reporters, many of us could see that Starr's prosecutors were directing the story, fanning the flames, leaking material to favored correspondents and producers. It was impossible to second-guess what he would leak next. After the debacle of "is" and "was," almost all the political aides wanted Clinton to clarify his denial again, while the lawyers wanted him to be silent.

The plague that had gone through chronic and acute phases from the

---

*She was interviewed by Deborah Stone and Christopher J. Manion for their book *Slick Willie II: Why America Still Cannot Trust Bill Clinton*. See Conason and Lyons, *Hunting of the President*, pp. 281–83.

†Kalb, *One Scandalous Story*, p. 143.

beginning of Clinton's administration was now extremely acute. But as sudden and all-encompassing as the crisis was, its elements were not unknown to us. For years there had been accusations, congressional hearings, and Starr's grand juries. There had been prosecutorial leaks and raging firestorms over Whitewater, with Hillary herself dragged past the klieg lights to testify. The entire scandal system was already in order. All the actors, from Starr to Gingrich, from the reporters to the talking heads on television, were on their well-rehearsed marks. The plague now arrived in full force and the whole political city was consumed by delirium.

Lewinsky was Starr's salvation. He had been flustered by the dead ends he kept encountering in his Whitewater investigation. He had wanted to escape and had tried to resign; he had been humiliated into going back into this thankless case with no leads. His pride was injured, the last of Robert Fiske's judicious, skillful prosecutors were gone, and his office was being run by fiercely partisan Republicans who had embarked on a sexual fishing expedition before Lewinsky ever appeared on the witness list. Starr's invasion of the Jones case showed the culmination of his frustration. It was his only way out.

A veteran journalist who had firsthand contact with *The Wall Street Journal*'s editorial board told me the story went back to 1996. He had learned then that Starr had approached Robert Bartley, the *Journal*'s editor, "seeking help" for "a mutual exchange of information on Whitewater." Starr and Bartley were old political and personal friends. Both were active in the conservative movement, especially the Federalist Society, and they shared a social circle, among whom was Ted Olson. (Within the conservative movement, Bartley and Olson belonged to what George Orwell would have called the "Inner Party.") Starr was getting nowhere in his investigation. The *Journal*'s editorials and op-ed articles insisted that a great scandal was there. Starr asked Bartley for assistance, which would of course never be publicly acknowledged: the *Journal* would dig up information for Starr, and he would continue to serve as a primary news source for it. Starr soldiered on; the *Journal* continued to thunder and publish wild accusations—Clinton at the center of an international cocaine smuggling ring!—but the arrangement yielded only fool's gold. Starr was still stuck. And Clinton was reelected.

After Clinton's reelection, in January 1997, Pepperdine University, perched near the surf in Malibu, California, announced the dean of its new public policy school (funded by Richard Mellon Scaife): Kenneth W. Starr. The school would allow its dean to continue with his lucrative private law practice. Starr declared that the Office of Independent Counsel—a "mini-Justice Department," he called it—would have no problem carrying on without him. Ted Olson admitted that he didn't think his friend would be quitting "if he was about to embark on a prosecution of historic proportions."* Conservatives were enraged, however, since Starr's leaving would foster the impression that there wasn't really any case against the Clintons. "The Big Flinch" ran the headline on an angry *New York Times* column by William Safire, who lashed the "craven" Starr for his "warped view of duty," a "wimp" bringing "shame on the legal profession,"† and a chorus on the right denounced him. Finally he crumbled under the pressure, reversed his decision, and declared that he had been "personally humbled."

Three weeks later, a gossip column in the *New York Post* ran a buried item saying that FBI agents assigned to Starr's investigation were "closely question[ing]" Arkansas state troopers "who guarded Clinton when he was governor" about his "personal life." Four days earlier, a news article had appeared in the *Arkansas Democrat-Gazette* noting that Starr's investigators were asking troopers about the President's "alleged sexual encounters." Neither of these articles attracted much attention. In June, Woodward and Schmidt used essentially the same material, which was splashed across *The Washington Post*'s front page: "Starr Probes Clinton's Personal Life." The explanation given by the Independent Counsel was that "the extensive interviews were part of an effort by Starr's office to find close Clinton associates in whom he may have confided and who might be able to provide information about the veracity of sworn statements Clinton has made in the course of the Whitewater investigation."‡ Somehow investigating sex would divulge what could not otherwise be proven in Whitewater.

Mark Tuohey, the deputy counsel to Fiske and then to Starr during his first six months in his post, thought that Fiske, had he not been replaced, would have finished the Whitewater investigation and report by the spring or summer of 1996, and that he would have found no wrongdoing by the Clintons. He told me he was sure the report would have concluded the matter once and for all. Tuohey, who directed Starr's only

*Susan Schmidt, "Starr Will Stay with Probe," *The Washington Post*, February 22, 1997.

†William Safire, "The Big Flinch," *The New York Times*, January 20, 1997.

‡Bob Woodward and Susan Schmidt, "Starr Probes Clinton's Personal Life," *The Washington Post*, June 25, 1997.

successful prosecutions, became aware after he left the independent counsel's office for private practice that Hickman Ewing, the deputy in charge of the "Arkansas phase," was leaking grand-jury material, or what purported to be grand-jury material, to the press. This was, of course, most improper conduct, and Tuohey told me that his successor, John Bates, had reprimanded Ewing and demanded that he stop—to no avail. Ewing, who had once considered seeking a job with the Rutherford Institute, the base for Jones's lawyers, kept up the leaks. Long before the Monica Lewinsky story, the Office of Independent Counsel had developed relationships with reporters who came to depend on its unacknowledged leaks.

Tuohey told me that Starr himself never believed the Clintons were innocent, though the Independent Counsel's closing argument against Jim McDougal in his trial had pointedly stated that the President was innocent. As for Ewing, he had a particular animus against Hillary Clinton, and he also believed that the deep secret of Whitewater was that she was covering up an illicit affair with Vincent Foster. Thus, sex charges against *both* Clintons seemed to be an obsession for the Office of Independent Counsel.

Long before Lewinsky, I knew from reporters that the other chief leaker at the OIC was the other deputy, the one in charge of the "Washington phase," Jackie Bennett. Then, after the Lewinsky story broke, I learned about his record and reputation. As a federal prosecutor in south Texas he had crusaded against Democratic politicians and contributors with uneven results. He had convicted one former congressman, Albert Bustamante, for racketeering and bribery. In another case, against a Democratic businessman and party donor named Douglas Jaffe, Bennett had tried to get Jaffe to wear a wire to incriminate Representative Henry Gonzalez, a prominent Democrat, in exchange for immunity. Jaffe refused and was acquitted. The judge, Lucius Bunton, rebuked Jackie Bennett for bringing a "rinky-dink" case before him and told him not to conduct another "witch hunt." Judge Bunton later said about his prosecution, "This was strictly a political thing." Bennett's tactics, including subpoenaing reporters to disclose their sources, earned him, even among his colleagues, the sobriquet "The Thug."[*]

In 1997, a reliable and respected investigative reporter in Washington for a major daily newspaper had told me at length of his relations with

---

*Maria Recio, "Ken Starr's Heavy Hitter," *Salon.com*, July 17, 1998; Toobin, *A Vast Conspiracy*, p. 193.

Jackie Bennett—and it wasn't only about the leaks. The reporter had been present at a meeting of Bennett with the inevitable David Bossie—a major source for scandal beat reporters who was by now working for Representative Dan Burton on the House Government Operations Committee. He observed Bennett and Bossie coordinating their politics, the Office of Independent Counsel planning tactics with the House Republicans. The reporter surmised from their familiarity that this was a regular practice—and he also thought it was a violation of the Federal Rules of Criminal Procedure. But the reporter did not want to write an article about the meeting and get it published. He was sure Bennett and Bossie would just deny it, and he wanted them as sources.

So, at daybreak on January 21, I knew about the OIC's penchant for leaks, the obsession with sex, Starr's weakness and inexperience, the simmering anger over the dry hole of an investigation, the rough record of his deputy, the prosecutors' partisanship and even zealotry, the spreading of innuendo, the loss of perspective, and the lack of proportion.

What I didn't know was anything factual, only what was alleged in *The Washington Post*'s article. But I knew about the right-wing conservative movement: its players, institutions, dogmas, beliefs, factionalism, relationships, hatreds, campaigns, sources of funding, and methods, both overt and covert. I sought facts about its involvement in roiling this scandal. In midmorning, after the early rounds of breathless meetings, I telephoned David Brock.

David Brock had dropped the pebble that started the avalanche. His article in *The American Spectator*, in December 1993, where he mentioned "Paula" as a woman who had been sexually harassed by Clinton, had prodded Paula Jones into filing her suit. Brock prided himself on being a "right-wing hit-man," as he described it. He was advised and coddled and partied by the most prominent Republicans in Washington, becoming a fixture at their conferences and meetings, and at the dinner table of Ted Olson. Republican elders, including U.S. federal judge Laurence Silberman, lent him their wisdom on how to throw his darts. He was the sorcerers' apprentice. Editors at the Free Press lavished a munificent advance on him for his book on Anita Hill, which became a best-seller. With that success, the Free Press gave him a $1 million advance to produce a biography of Hillary Clinton; they anticipated that, during the 1996 election campaign, he would expose her as a lesbian. He also defamed two friends of mine, Jane Mayer and Jill Abramson, then reporters for *The Wall Street Journal*, in a review he wrote of their accurate and telling book about the Thomas-Hill controversy, *Strange Justice*. (Brock later acknowledged that he had lied in his review to make it appear they had lied.)

In July 1996, a book had appeared entitled *Unlimited Access*, by a former FBI agent who had worked in the Clinton White House, Gary Aldrich (Linda Tripp's friend). He claimed such imaginary revelations as Hillary hanging pornographic ornaments on the White House Christmas tree and the President sneaking out, under a blanket in the back seat of a car, for sexual assignations at a nearby Marriott hotel. Aldrich's exposé had been touted in a front-page story in *The Washington Times*, excerpted on *The Wall Street Journal*'s editorial page, and its salacious stories gained general circulation. When pressed on his sources for the Marriott hotel details, Aldrich pointed to Brock, but he, in turn, denied he had said any such things. Aldrich lost all credibility overnight.

Three months later, just before the election, Brock's book, *The Seduction of Hillary Rodham*, was published. It offered a mostly sympathetic, mildly critical view of the First Lady. His research had led him to conclude that the scandalous charges against her were all false. He seemed to be emotionally withdrawing from the right, feeling used. Brock's refusal to back up Aldrich's tales and to trash Hillary Clinton infuriated the right. He had been paid, but he had not delivered. Like a heretic, he was excommunicated. On the day his book on Hillary was published, Barbara Olson, Ted's wife, withdrew an invitation to a dinner party she was giving with Justice Thomas's wife. Conservatives in Washington, led by a lobbyist, Craig Shirley, bruited it about that Brock, who is gay, was failing the cause because he was upset at Aldrich's gay bashing. In July 1997, *Esquire* magazine published his "Confessions," in which he announced his resignation as a "road warrior of the right." Still, he remained employed by the *Spectator* and maintained ties with a number of his old right-wing friends who hadn't cut him off. His disenchantment was growing, but he was between worlds.*

In 1997 I met Brock through a mutual friend. I had learned from Stephen Rivers, who was active in Democratic politics in California, that, improbably, he knew Brock. After I was defamed by Matt Drudge, Rivers suggested that in his current state of disillusionment Brock would probably have some information about Drudge's sources, and he gave me Brock's telephone number. I called him up. Without hesitation, he told me of conversations he had had with Drudge and others in which he had

*See David Brock, *Blinded by the Right: The Conscience of an Ex-Conservative*, Crown, 2002.

learned how Drudge had been prompted by a small group of right-wingers to post the libel about me on his website. I was stunned by his detail and his eagerness to assist me. But I was aware of his past and I was wary. I suggested that we meet face-to-face.

We met on August 26, 1997, at the Tahoga restaurant in Georgetown. Brock was a short, good-looking young man with fashionably spiky hair, and somewhat nervous. He told me he believed that Whitewater was a hoax. That had contributed to his change of mind about Mrs. Clinton. After the incident with Gary Aldrich, his mentors told him they knew that what he had written in his book on Anita Hill was false, but that they supported it nonetheless. Now he wanted to expose their hypocrisy and cynicism. And he had become contemptuous of mainstream reporters he had encountered on the same slippery trails; he named some names.

Brock's disgust with his conservative scene was thorough. His confessions to me were part of an effort to separate himself from his past, which was hardly remote. I told him about how I had been harshly attacked for failing to adhere to the general media line about Whitewater and for having criticized his trooper story. Our far-apart but parallel tracks became a personal connection. Brock's stories had the ring of truth, though I had no way of checking them. I didn't doubt his hurt feelings about the right-wing people who had made his career, but where the apostate would turn next remained uncertain. He had suddenly lost faith in the total worldview; fallen from the world of believers, he had to find his own way.

Over the next few months our talks became an ongoing conversation. I seemed to be someone he could confide in about his continuing disillusionment. He told me about his meetings, parties, and encounters with conservatives, once his political soul mates, but now engaged in activities that, he said over and over again, were "so crazy." He remarked, "I'm so out of sync with them. It's so apparent to me now. It's just appalling."

In late October, Brock described a dinner he had attended the night before. It was the Saturday Evening Club of the *Spectator*, held at an upstairs room at La Brasserie on Capitol Hill. The assembled guests were from *The Washington Times*, the *Wall Street Journal* editorial board, Regnery Publishing (Aldrich's publisher), radio talk shows, and the *Spectator*. That evening's business was to develop ideas to help the featured speaker, Representative Bob Barr, Republican from Georgia, on his resolution for the impeachment of the President. Barr's proposal had no specificity, citing only "systematic abuse of office." Barr complained he was having "limited success" rounding up cosponsors. John Fund, a *Wall Street Jour-*

nal editorial writer, piped up, "When Congress shows spine, there will be indictments." He said impeachment was a question "not of law, but of political will." There were gestures of assent, according to Brock. "They're down to the knuckle-dragging crowd," he told me. "It's so crazy."

Whenever Brock learned something new, he made it his mission to tell me. Our relationship was becoming important to him in disentangling himself from the right. The more we talked, the more disabused he became of the conservative mythologies. In November, he told me for the first time about the Arkansas Project. He noticed that someone had left a check for $50,000 on the copying machine at the *Spectator*. That discovery prompted him to tell me what he had long known: the Arkansas Project had started after publication of his trooper story in 1993.

Brock described to me how the *Spectator* was wracked with turmoil over the Arkansas Project. The publisher, Ron Burr, had started to question it in the summer of 1997, raising the issue of financial irregularities and demanding an independent audit. He was fired in October 1997 at a meeting presided over by Ted Olson, a member of the magazine's board.

So, on January 21, I thought Brock might know something. His phone, he said, had been ringing off the hook. Drudge, boastful, was "spilling his guts. Drudge is flying high, out of control. He called several times last night." Brock had also been constantly on the phone with Laura Ingraham and Ann Coulter, who, like him, had come to Washington to promote their careers as professional conservatives. They were young, blond, miniskirted lawyers whose outrageous opinions, name-calling, and antifeminist poses had gotten them gigs as featured talking heads on television. Ingraham and Coulter were part of a clique consisting of the elves around the Jones case, younger members of the Federalist Society, and some of Starr's independent counsel staff. In recent months, Ingraham and Coulter had made a special friend of Drudge, their new playmate. His carefree malice and easy manipulability suited their idea of fun. Both women regarded Brock as a confidant, telling him of romantic pursuers and of being squired about town by famous older conservative men. The breaking of the Lewinsky story had Ingraham and Coulter in a state of high excitement; they were thrilled to be inciting the people who were stoking the fires.

By the end of my conversation with Brock that morning, I knew many of the essential elements. And he had described what happened the night before at *Newsweek*. Drudge had already claimed that *Newsweek* editors could not bring themselves to run Isikoff's article about Lewinsky. "Isikoff listened to a tape, but that section was left out of the story," said Brock. "*Newsweek* wasn't sure of it." How had Isikoff gotten the tape? Both Starr's office and the elves appeared to be involved. "There's no question it came from Starr," but, Brock added, "the tape was leaked to *Newsweek* by [George] Conway." (Starr repeatedly denied that he had given *Newsweek* a tape, which would have been an illegal act. But Starr's successor, Robert Ray, admitted in late 1999 that the prosecutors had given the tape to Tripp's attorney, James Moody, at a midnight rendezvous at a Holiday Inn on January 17. Jackie Bennett and Bruce Udolf were the prosecutors who passed the tape to Moody, who was with George Conway, and then they drove to *Newsweek*'s office. The purpose of this secret transfer, which had to be arranged carefully beforehand, was to get the tape to Isikoff.*)

Brock then explained to me about the elves Conway and Moody. Conway was an attorney at the New York law firm of Wachtell, Lipton and a Federalist Society activist, and he was doing most of the legal work for Jones's lawyers; he had met Linda Tripp in the course of the Jones case. When Tripp told her then-attorney, Kirby Behre, that she had made tapes of her phone conversations with Lewinsky, he instructed her to stop, and that was when she had sought a new lawyer: Conway recommended Moody, who apparently had no compunctions about the illegal taping of phone conversations. He was friendly with Ann Coulter, Brock said, and had worked with the Scaife-funded Landmark Legal Foundation that had helped Paula Jones in 1993.

Conway also "suggested that Tripp go to Starr," Brock told me. Since Conway and Moody and Richard Porter and the Federalist Society members on Starr's staff were all friends, there was no trouble making contact. "Tripp has been trying to do this"—put herself in Starr's service—"since the Willey thing," said Brock. (Kathleen Willey was a Democratic contributor from Virginia who had once worked as a volunteer in the White House social office; as a witness in the Jones case, she had claimed that Clinton had groped her in the Oval Office—a charge he adamantly denied.) "But," said Brock, "the Willey thing didn't work out right."

For hours at *Newsweek*, Isikoff and his editors played the tape. "But *Newsweek* doesn't go with the story. So Conway gives the story to Drudge. Starr's people panic because it's out on the *Drudge Report*." Coulter has heard one of the tapes. "She says Monica's a little crazy, con-

*Joshua Micah Marshall, "Midnight Rendezvous," *Salon.com*, December 16, 1999.

fused," Brock told me. "At one point on the tape, she's asked about lying, could she be lying, and the girl responds, 'My family is a lie,' and talks about her broken family." Brock said there were seventeen tapes. "There's no Clinton on these tapes. He's not recorded saying anything. Monica, I heard, has tapes of Clinton returning her calls. She loves the President. She's infatuated with him. He's only interested in oral sex, no penetration. It's incredibly graphic." Brock continued, "The girl supposedly kept a dress that supposedly has Clinton's semen stains on it. It sounds wacky to me. But Drudge says that."

Drudge also told Brock that one of his sources was Linda Tripp's book agent, Lucianne Goldberg: "Goldberg thought she could sell the book that wasn't written yet by going to Isikoff. She thought she could get publicity. She was interested in the book deal."

Lucianne Goldberg prided herself on her gossipmongering, usually about sex, an interest she combined with visceral right-wing politics. In 1972, she had posed as a reporter on George McGovern's campaign plane; she was being paid as a political spy by the Nixon campaign. She hinted at having had an affair with Lyndon Johnson when as a young woman she had worked at a low-level job in the White House. She had written a novel entitled *Madame Cleo's Girls* about prostitutes and their high-paying johns as told on tape by the fictitious madam. One of Goldberg's clients, Kitty Kelley, had successfully sued her for breach of contract, winning a judgment of $41,407 in 1983. Before latching onto Tripp, Goldberg had tried to sell a book by the Arkansas troopers, but the project fell apart. Then she helped Tripp construct a proposal for a book tentatively titled *Behind Closed Doors*, which included a chapter called "The President's Women."

Goldberg seemed to enjoy leading people into trouble for its own sake. At every step, she pushed Tripp along. "Tripp was working with Jones's lawyers while doing those tapes," Brock told me. Then Tripp went to Starr. And then the Independent Counsel, with her help, staged a sting against Monica. "They were trying to blackmail her to blackmail Clinton," Brock told me. He didn't know more than that. In due course we all learned that Starr's prosecutors had pressured Lewinsky to wear a hidden wire to tape conversations with the President and Vernon Jordan—an offer she refused.

It was only day one, but Starr was already nervous about the weakness of the Lewinsky material, according to Brock. Conway had told Ingraham and Coulter that "if Monica holds firm against him, he doesn't think Starr will indict her." Starr's staff, Brock said, was also "worried" that someone would discover that Lewinsky's mother, Marcia Lewis, had "invented, falsely claimed that she had a romantic relationship with Pavarotti or Placido Domingo. Sounds crazy, but we're in crazy land." (Profiles of Lewis subsequently noted that her 1996 book, *The Private Lives of the Three Tenors*, included a three-page passage about a fantasized affair with Domingo.*) By extension, Starr was worried about Lewinsky's credibility. All he had were tapes about a purported affair. From what Brock had heard, Starr's claim about obstruction of justice was also unproved: "All he knew was that there were these other tapes between Monica and Tripp. Was that what he was investigating? He couldn't have gone after the obstruction charge."

Thus, in this one conversation, I learned about the collusion between Paula Jones's legal defense team and Starr's office; about Isikoff's activism, Goldberg's prodding, and Drudge's sources; about Starr's attempted "blackmail" of the President, the content of the tapes between Monica Lewinsky and Linda Tripp, the nature of the affair, the semen-stained dress, the prosecutor's thin case—all of which were later made public. But I could not substantiate any of it myself. To find out more, I could hardly make calls myself as though I were a reporter. But whatever Brock had told me would have to be proven by other sources.

If sex was all Starr had, he was in a bad corner even though he had the White House reeling. From Brock, I gained a sense that while Starr seemed to have the upper hand for the moment, he was not on solid ground. He had carefully leaked the story about Monica Lewinsky, editing it to his specifications, to compliant media. But if what Brock told me were corroborated, Starr's investigation would appear as what it was: the work of an overreaching prosecutor in league with conservative opponents to remove the President of the United States. If a light were shone on Starr's shadows, the nature of his effort would become clear.

II

On January 21, Hillary went to speak at Goucher College in Baltimore at the invitation of an old friend, Taylor Branch, the biographer of Martin Luther King, Jr. She was chipper in her remarks to reporters who asked her if she believed her husband: "Absolutely."

---

*Blaine Harden, "Ex-Intern's Mother Put the Soap in the Opera," *The Washington Post*, January 25, 1998.

Upon her return to the White House that afternoon, she called me. She explained that this story involved Clinton's concern for a person with personal problems, a common occurrence since she had known him. His empathy, she went on, came from his relationship with his mother, an open, compassionate woman, and from Clinton's own difficult experiences growing up. I knew, of course, what she was referring to: being fatherless and poor, the often terrifying battles with his alcoholic, abusive stepfather. She had always known her husband to befriend people in trouble, and as she saw it, this was another example. I knew myself of people Clinton had gotten close to and helped, privately and without publicity. Anyone who knew him would encounter this unusual ability of his to connect. In explaining what had happened, she relied upon her understanding of her husband. I assumed that she had spoken with him and that what she was saying reflected their conversation.

For her, the stakes were greater than for anyone. They encompassed not only everything she had worked on politically for a lifetime, but her marriage. She had to defend both. Over the years, I had had many separate conversations with the Clintons, and especially with Hillary, during which they spontaneously talked about each other. They were, of course, a team. They talked to each other several times a day, and each thought the other was the smartest person he or she knew. They were always warm about and toward each other and, in each other's presence, touching. They were also extremely caring about their daughter, Chelsea. I saw the three of them together fairly frequently. They seemed to me to be a close family.

I didn't presume to have superior insight into the deep, dark secrets of other people's marriages. I had had friends who I thought were happy but suddenly divorced. And I had married friends whose marriages, which appeared less than ideal, endured everything. I had many friends in second and third marriages. I had friends who had committed adultery and loved their wives. I had friends who had never strayed, to my knowledge, and complained constantly about their spouses. A marriage belongs only to those in it. As a friend, I didn't believe it was an act of friendship to second-guess a marriage from the outside. Had Clinton had an affair with an intern? I just didn't know. I had no reason to doubt Hillary's sincerity in her version of events, and whatever my doubts, I wanted to believe her—to believe along with her.

Above all, though, she and I had no doubt we were confronting a supremely political crisis. Starr's investigation was a daring political venture that used dubious accusations of criminality as a justification. The notion that President Clinton and Vernon Jordan had criminally conspired struck me as ridiculous. Whether Starr would succeed in making this charge stick would depend on the politics. Could he foster enough hysteria and momentum? Neither of us was panicked. This was politics, perhaps a greater crisis than ever, but politics nonetheless. She said that the President had remarked to her, "Well, we'll just have to win."

I related to Hillary my conversation with Brock. I had been telling her about him all along. His revelations filled in the details of what was driving this new "acute" scandal phase. Having knowledge restored a sense of normality, even amid the storm. We could see the lines of influence underlying the scandal, the cause and effect, intent and action—and they were political and familiar. Thus, on the first day, both Hillary and I knew about what she would soon call the vast right-wing conspiracy.

Hillary laughed and told me that as a matter of fact, the Daddy Warbucks of the conspiracy, Richard Mellon Scaife, was coming to dinner that night at the White House. Of all the gin joints in the world, why was he showing up at this one? It turned out to be a long-scheduled dinner to honor the donors to the White House Preservation Society. Those who had contributed since the 1980s would be present, including, for a rare excursion, the reclusive Scaife. But who should sit next to him? Hillary thought maybe I should, or maybe my wife, Jackie. For the rest of the afternoon, while the President was giving his three dreaded interviews, Hillary and I were back and forth a couple of times on the phone joking about Scaife and the seating arrangements.

At about six that evening, Betty Currie, the President's private secretary, called me in my office and asked me to come up to the Oval Office. I found the President alone, standing, his gaze distracted. He started pacing slowly behind his desk and then in front of it. He rearranged knickknacks, touching some and slightly moving others. He wanted to explain to me about Monica Lewinsky. He told me he had been trying to help her. I said I had spoken to Hillary and that she had told me the same thing. Before he could elaborate, I said that I understood his feeling of wanting to counsel a troubled person. I knew he was compassionate. I knew he had helped many people. Then, I said: The problem with troubled people is just that, that they're troubled. These troubled people can get you into incredible messes, and I know you don't want to, but you have to cut yourself off from them. He replied: It's very difficult for me not to want to help. That's how I am. I want to help people. I cut in: You can't do that at this point, whatever you've done in the past. The reason is that you have to be self-protective. You can't get near anybody who is remotely troubled. You don't know how crazy people may be. You are the president.

He shifted the discussion. He told me that he had spoken that day to Dick Morris. I wasn't surprised. I knew he maintained some contact with Morris. Most of the people on Clinton's staff despised Morris, and I was one of the few who didn't. I had had no history of conflict with him; I thought his political intelligence deserved a hearing, which should not be confused with accepting his advice. And Clinton knew I thought that. He told me that Morris had said to him that if Nixon, at the beginning of Watergate, had delivered a speech on national television explaining everything he had done wrong, making it all public, he would have survived. I thought this was one of Dick's wacky ideas, a complete misreading of history and a false analogy. The Plumbers who broke into the Democratic National Committee headquarters had committed crimes at Nixon's behest and were being paid from a secret fund he had authorized. I asked Clinton: What have you done wrong? Nothing, he replied. I haven't done anything wrong. Then, I said, that's one of the stupidest ideas I've heard. Why would you do that if you have done nothing wrong?

He launched into an account of an incident involving Lewinsky. He said that she made a sexual demand on him and he rebuffed her. He said: I've gone down that road before, I've caused pain for a lot of people and I'm not going to do that again. He said she responded by threatening him. She said she would tell others they had had an affair. She said that her name among her peers was "the Stalker," that she hated being called that. If Clinton had sex with her and she could say she had had an affair, she wouldn't be known as the Stalker anymore.

I repeated to Clinton that he had to avoid troubled people. You need to find some sure footing here, I said, some solid ground, some traction.

I feel like a character in a novel, Clinton said. I feel like somebody who is surrounded by an oppressive force that is creating a lie about me and I can't get the truth out. I feel like the character in *Darkness at Noon*.

I knew the novel well. *Darkness at Noon* is a fictional portrait by Arthur Koestler of one of the original Bolsheviks facing a purge trial and execution for political crimes. I did not respond to this literary reference. Instead, I asked a series of questions about reports I had read or heard about Lewinsky. Were you alone with her? I asked. I knew that the Oval Office had outside peepholes at its doors. I had looked in through them myself many times. The President was surrounded by a host of watchers, by aides, secretaries, valets, waiters, Secret Service agents. If he were ever alone, he would have to arrange it carefully. I was within eyesight or earshot of someone, he said.

You know, I said, there are press reports that you made phone calls to Monica Lewinsky and that you left voice-mail messages on her machine. Did you make phone calls to her? He said he recalled calling to tell her that Betty Currie's brother had died in a car accident. He explained that Monica had been friendly with Betty, that Betty had been kind to her.

I repeated myself again. You need to find some solid ground here, I said. You need to find some traction. I mentioned that I had heard a report that Vernon Jordan had scheduled a press conference the next day. Maybe, I said, that will provide some traction. Clinton didn't say anything. Our extraordinary meeting ended.

I had seen him upset before, wandering around the Omni Center in Atlanta at the Democratic National Convention in 1988 after he had delivered a disastrous nominating speech for Michael Dukakis. But I had never seen him this off-balance before. I was used to him in the Oval Office as a master of policies, facts, and ideas, the judge of arguments, always in control. Now he described himself as being at the mercy of his enemies, uncertain about what to say or do.

In that Oval Office encounter I saw a man who was beside himself. He told me a story that was basically the story I had heard earlier that day from his wife. Part of me wanted to believe him as a friend. Part of me wondered if his story could be true. That was why I repeatedly asked him probing questions. I wanted an explanation. Part of me had nagging doubts. I was a friend separately and together of the President and the First Lady, though closer to her. And I was also the President's aide. Both of them wanted me to believe the story as he told it, because he wanted her to believe it and she wanted to believe him. In any case, I felt awkward even being in the middle. I felt it should be between the two of them. But this was a personal crisis that affected my job in the White House and how I would do my work in the future. Even if he was lying about Lewinsky, I could understand. He wouldn't have been the first man to lie to me about sex. More than one of my friends (including well-known journalists) had done so and then asked for my help afterward, and I was happy to give it, and the friendships lasted. These are the terms of a mature friendship, what friends expect from friends, freely given. I did not believe that President Clinton and Vernon Jordan had obstructed justice or suborned perjury. Nor, in my wildest dreams, did I imagine that my listening to his telling me what he did was, as the House Managers later claimed, part of an obstruction of justice. That was absurd.

I did not mention this conversation to anyone except my wife. I did not tell other people on the staff. Not until later did I learn that this was the most detailed story the President had given to anyone, including his lawyers. To several other aides that day he had denied having an affair with Lewinsky, I learned later, in uncomplicated, brief denials. It was only then that I realized he probably had told this elaborate story only to me because of my relationship with Hillary. He knew we would share information and develop our politics together. There was no reason for him to think I would ever be subpoenaed. After all, I had never heard of Lewinsky until that very day. I never knew her, spoke with her, or met her. To my knowledge, I was never even in the same room with her. But I was close to Hillary and there was nothing more important to him at that moment than protecting his marriage.

Much much later, after the release of the Starr Report, I learned that almost everything he had told me was true. Almost. He *had* spoken with Morris, who had run a poll. (When I saw the poll reproduced in the Starr Report it struck me as mostly worthless as a political document, because all the key questions had the word "crimes" attached to them, ensuring negative responses. The statistics indicating the public's inclination to forgive incidents that were just sex, Morris misinterpreted.) Clinton *had* called Monica about Betty's brother's death—one of several calls. Lewinsky *had*, in fact, demanded that he engage in sexual intercourse with her, which he refused. It was when he broke off with her, according to the Starr Report, that she made her demand for intercourse and her threat to expose him.

Had he done anything "wrong"—the word I used with him? He had committed no crimes; he was innocent of Starr's accusations. But he had acted recklessly, and in doing so he had given ammunition to his enemies and endangered everything he believed in. Later, I told him and Hillary that that was what I thought he had done wrong. Infidelity was between them, but this was the error that pulled the rest of us in.

Clinton was a man who came from nowhere; overcame all obstacles by virtue of his own intelligence, skill, and attractiveness; and then, having achieved his goal, gave in to his weakness. It was a mundane weakness, a most ordinary weakness. He did not give in to it for money, power, status, or fame. He did not do it out of mean-spiritedness, resentment, or cruelty. What he did was not a crime. It was part of the same personality that got him to the White House, with his need for affirmation, attention, and affection. He was a character with large appetites and desires, and a surplus of human nature, not unlike Henry Fielding's Tom

Jones, the good-natured, life-loving figure who falls into follies of his own making as he tries to fend off the vicious connivances of others. The tragic aspect, the inexorable drama, was that this least unconscious president knew that what he had done was stupid. He understood that he had given in to his weakness. He had known that it was a mistake, but he made it anyway. It hurt his wife, Lewinsky, and himself. He knew, moreover, that this was not like the Kennedy era, when private lives had been kept private. He knew hateful pursuers were seeking to hurt him, and he knew he had the Jones case before him. Yet with this self-centered act he set himself up. And he knew it. Stunned by the situation, he did what most husbands would do: he tried to protect his wife, his daughter, and his own privacy. He acted as a man, not as a president. But the collision of roles could not be avoided.

Hillary, in her conversation with me, was not wrong in her assessment. She knew Bill Clinton, loved him, and worried about him—more than anyone. Understandably, she didn't want to believe that his empathy had extended into an affair. Whatever the truth of that situation, it was entirely her business—and no one else's. No matter what, she would defend her marriage, her privacy, her husband, and his presidency.

Even though Clinton had momentarily lost his equilibrium, he was not deprived of his political sense. His reference to *Darkness at Noon* indicated that he was anticipating that a certain kind of spectacle was about to take place. The impeachment trial, when it came, was in one respect the very opposite of a Stalinist purge trial, where countless people were called to account for public crimes they had not committed; it was a special inquisition only for Clinton—and everyone around him. And he knew why: it was because he had won the presidency. Whatever the animosities against him, his ultimate offense was that he was in the White House. That was the truly unforgivable crime. The additional crime was that he had survived previous would-be scandals.

In the book, at noon the accused is forced into a dark inquisition chamber and can give no right answer. His position is always that of a guilty party. The fact of being named is a certificate of condemnation. Just raising the question of innocence means it is a moot question. Rubashov is indeed guilty—of seditious thought—and he confesses, agreeing with his prosecutors that, given his loss of faith in the revolution, he should have rebelled against Number One. If that text was not apposite for President Clinton, then another notable novel about totalitarianism, George Orwell's *1984*, perhaps was. In it, Winston commits the "thoughtcrime" of having an affair with Julia, which is a crime against the state, which trains young people through compulsory membership in the Junior Anti-Sex League. The Ministry of Love tortures him into betraying Julia and loving Big Brother. He is reduced to terrified obedience.

But, then, the Starr inquiry was not operating in a totalitarian state. Clinton knew how it was. He understood the Republicans' ruthlessness and unscrupulousness. He had been through years of Whitewater, years of the Independent Counsel's grand jury, years of endless congressional hearings. Now everything came down to a sheer political struggle. Clinton may not have known where to find "traction" on the first day, but he knew the score: "We'll just have to win."

That night, the White House Preservation Society dinner was a glittery event. The President shook the hand of Richard Mellon Scaife, who waited in line for the honor, and they posed together for the official White House photographer. At dinner I was seated not next to Scaife, but next to the wife of the chief executive officer of the Philip Morris tobacco company, Mrs. Bible. Mrs. Scaife was at our table and seemed delighted to be present, applauding when the President delivered gracious remarks. After dinner, Clinton and the First Lady mingled with the guests as though they didn't have a care in the world.

III

The next morning, January 22, NBC's *Today Show* featured Matt Drudge. "I go where the stink is," he said, and began chattering about Lewinsky's semen-stained dress, freely admitting he had no proof except "what I've just heard."* And *The Washington Post* that morning reported:

> The FBI last week secretly tape recorded former White House aide Monica Lewinsky saying that President Clinton urged her to lie about having a sexual relationship, then confronted her with the tapes to persuade her to cooperate with their investigation of Clinton, sources familiar with the investigation said yesterday.
>
> Lewinsky, 24, was recorded while meeting at an Arlington hotel with a former colleague, Linda R. Tripp, who was cooperating with authorities and wearing a "body wire" recording device, the sources said. The FBI operation helped corroborate other tapes made earlier by Tripp on her

*Kalb, *One Scandalous Story*, p. 151.

own and was used to help persuade Attorney General Janet Reno and a three-judge panel to authorize a new investigation into Clinton, according to sources.*

The article, coauthored by Susan Schmidt and based on "sources," was like a thunderclap, stating conclusively that the President's guilt was proven by evidence already in the hands of the prosecutors. It drove the rest of the media to perceive inevitable doom. Democrats on the Hill wondered if they would soon have to send a delegation to ask the President to resign, and many on the White House staff wondered about that, too. There was no way of knowing that the article's flat assertions that Lewinsky had said that Clinton "urged her to lie" and that it "helped corroborate other tapes" were false.

The Independent Counsel demanded documents and issued subpoenas, and the White House legal counsel office began to cooperate. In their conversations with the OIC prosecutors, the White House lawyers encountered an extraordinary truculence and arrogance. The prosecutors acted as though the President were a criminal, as though their case were airtight and he would soon be toppled. The White House lawyers concluded that Starr's strategy was to stage the Lewinsky story as a political shock wave that would force Clinton to resign.

Now, on this day, the President was meeting with Yasser Arafat in the Oval Office, continuing his attempt to end the seemingly intractable conflict between the Israelis and the Arabs. Before their meeting, the press was brought in. A reporter asked, "Could you clarify for us, sir, exactly what your relationship was with Ms. Lewinsky, and whether the two of you talked by phone, including any messages you may have left?" The President responded:

> Let me say, first of all, I want to reiterate what I said yesterday. The allegations are false and I would never ask anybody to do anything other than tell the truth. Let's get to the big issues there, about the nature of the relationship and whether I suggested anybody not to tell the truth. That is false. . . . I'd like for you to have more rather than less, sooner rather than later. So we'll work through it as quickly as we can and get all those questions out there to you.

*Peter Baker and Susan Schmidt, "FBI Taped Allegations Last Week," *The Washington Post*, January 22, 1998.

Clinton no longer had to say anything further that day. His statement was a placeholder.

An hour later Ken Starr appeared before a bank of microphones in front of his office to declare three times that his conduct had been proper: "We use appropriate investigative techniques that are traditional law enforcement techniques." But his illegal leaks were holding virtually the entire press corps in his thrall. At the top of his hierarchy of status were his favored reporters and producers: Susan Schmidt of *The Washington Post*; correspondent Jackie Judd and her producer, Chris Vlasto, at ABC News; and Michael Isikoff at *Newsweek*. Below them, the others scrambled for access. Starr granted it immediately to the networks and newsweeklies, but regional newspapers had to scrape by on leavings. *The New York Times* was second-best in his eyes to the *Post*. Cutouts emerged—conservative lawyers close to the investigation—who fed scandal-hungry reporters. A survey conducted by the Committee of Concerned Journalists on the reporting done during January 21–27 revealed that of the 1,565 statements and allegations repeated by major television programs, newspapers, and magazines, only 1 percent were based on two named sources, 41 percent had no claim of factual reporting at all, and 40 percent were derived from anonymous single sources. Drudge was simply a trendsetter.*

Susan Schmidt's method was to reproduce what was given her, and her reports were valuable to readers who understood that they accurately presented what Starr wished people to know. Jackie Judd was the stand-up on-camera talent mostly for the work of her producer, Chris Vlasto, a new type of journalist peculiar to the period. Vlasto had the intensity of a true believer but no real political ideas. He wasn't an ideologue himself, just someone who relied on ideologues for his information. Scandal and Clinton hatred, not politics, animated his work. David Bossie became Vlasto's friend and source. "Dave Bossie has never lied to me, and the Clinton White House has lied to me," Vlasto told a reporter from *The Washington Post*. "If it comes down to a question of whom do you believe, I'd believe Bossie any day."† He wrote articles for the *Wall Street Journal*

---

*Committee of Concerned Journalists, "The Clinton Crisis and the Press: A New Standard of American Journalism?" February 18, 1998, http://www.journalism. org/resources/research/reports/clinton/standard/default.asp

†Lloyd Grove, "A Firefighter's Blazing Trail: David Bossie Is Throwing Sparks on the GOP Campaign Finance Probe," *The Washington Post*, November 13, 1997.

editorial page and *The Weekly Standard*, insisting portentously that Whitewater had darker secrets yet.

If Vlasto was an apolitical scandalmonger at ABC News, Dorrance Smith, producer of *This Week*, was ultimately political. Smith had been President Bush's communications director, and his secretary in the White House had been Linda Tripp. "The Washington bureau was like an outpost of *The American Spectator*," an ABC News correspondent told me. "Dorrance was in constant touch with Tripp. He was calling the shots. He kept opposing views off the air and put views supportive of Starr on the air." (One of the Smith-promoted commentators, Jonathan Turley, a George Washington Law School professor with a specialty in environmental issues, testified before the House in favor of impeachment, and another, Brad Berenson, was to become an associate counsel in George W. Bush's White House. Jeffrey Toobin, the regular *ABC News* legal analyst, was not permitted to appear on *This Week*.)

But the reporter most indispensable to the advancement of the scandal from the moment Paula Jones appeared at the conservative conference in Washington in 1993 to the breaking of the Lewinsky story in 1998 was Michael Isikoff. He was an avid participant who rushed to the center of the scandal, wrapped in the raincoat of intrepid detective. He was used at every turn by everyone from Jones's lawyers to Lucianne Goldberg to Starr. "The players in this saga—the accusers, the conspirators, even the President—had all at times calculated their actions in response to what they thought I might do," Isikoff boasted in his book.* But his peregrinations through the fragrant alleys of the scandal made him a useful man to many he found there.

Isikoff never hesitated in plunging himself excitedly into a wilderness of sex rumors. Through pursuit of the Kathleen Willey story, he met Linda Tripp, and through Tripp, Lucianne Goldberg. In mid-1997 Isikoff asked Tripp to verify Willey's testimony about how she had repelled an alleged sexual advance made by Clinton in 1993. But Tripp told him Willey was not telling the truth, that she had sought an encounter. (The Independent Counsel's final report dismissed Willey as a witness whom a jury was not likely to believe.†) Tripp claimed that Willey's clothes had been disheveled and her lipstick smeared after the alleged

---

*Michael Isikoff, *Uncovering Clinton*, Crown, 1999, p. ix.

†*Final Report of the Independent Counsel, in Re: Madison Guaranty Savings & Loan Association, Regarding Monica Lewinsky and Others*, March 6, 2002, pp. 90–94.

incident. How and when could that have that happened? Willey would have had to go from the Oval Office into a waiting area packed with White House officials and pass unnoticed. Tripp's version of Kathleen Willey's story was never substantiated by anyone else—and of course Willey denied it. But it became crucial in the unfolding of the Lewinsky scandal.

Isikoff's wild-goose chase to confirm Willey's tale continued through the summer of 1997. For support of her story, Willey sent Isikoff not only to Tripp but to another friend of hers, Julie Hiatt Steele. According to Isikoff, Steele told a graphic tale—and also told him she had once driven Willey to check into a mental hospital. And according to Steele, Willey had telephoned her moments before Isikoff showed up at her suburban Virginia home, telling her the Clinton sex story for the first time and telling her to lie and say she had heard it from Willey on the very day it had supposedly occurred.

"In late August," Isikoff wrote, Ann Coulter, with whom he had appeared on a cable TV talk show, "kept dropping hints suggesting inside knowledge about Jones's legal strategy. I remarked on this. Oh yes, she said with a laugh. 'There are lots of us busy elves working away in Santa's workshop.' " Isikoff wrote:

> Busy elves? I remembered hearing something about George Conway in New York. Now Coulter. Who else? And what were they doing?
> The next day I looked up Conway's number at Wachtell, Lipton in New York and caught him off guard at his desk. How did you get my name? he answered, sounding startled.
> Well, I just did.*

But Isikoff had not gotten the idea of telephoning Conway from Coulter, as he implied. He had been meeting secretly for years with David Brock, and during the summer of 1997, it was Brock who suggested that he call Conway and Brock who gave him Conway's phone number—according to Brock's account. When *Newsweek* withheld Isikoff's article about Willey for a week, in late July, Conway leaked the story to Drudge—"to screw Isikoff," as Brock put it. Drudge was Isikoff's punishment, administered by the elves for not doing what they wanted when they wanted. Isikoff blamed Drudge's "scoop" on Tripp and never mentioned Conway. By this time, Brock said, Conway and Coulter knew about the tapes.

*Isikoff, *Uncovering Clinton*, p. 182.

Isikoff wrote that he had first learned of the Tripp-Lewinsky tapes on October 6, 1997, when Lucianne Goldberg and Linda Tripp invited him to the Washington apartment of Goldberg's son, a conservative writer named Jonah, where Tripp offered to play one of them. Isikoff claimed he didn't want to hear it. "I just knew it didn't feel right. And I was in a bit of a hurry to make it to *Hardball*"—a cable television talk show. He told Tripp, "If the White House was going to arrange to get the President's girlfriend a job she didn't deserve, that might make the subject of a story in *Newsweek*. Tripp nodded knowingly."* Goldberg had hoped that playing the tapes would get Isikoff to write something that would provide publicity so that she could sell Tripp's book.

By November 13, Tripp was beside herself with aggravation. Nothing was working out for her: no Isikoff story, no book contract, and the Jones case headed into a ditch. She called Goldberg to suggest that Jones's lawyers subpoena her to testify about Lewinsky. A round-robin of calls lit up the conservative network. Goldberg telephoned Alfred Regnery, the right-wing publisher, who suggested that she call Peter Smith, the Chicago banker who had financed the search for sex stories in 1992 and 1993. Smith advised Goldberg to call Richard Porter, at Kirkland and Ellis, who sent an e-mail about Lewinsky to George Conway. Conway forwarded Goldberg's phone number and Porter's e-mail to Jones's lawyer.

On November 21, Tripp was contacted by one of Jones's lawyers, whom she told about Lewinsky. Tripp and the attorney agreed that she would receive a subpoena, would keep her own lawyer in the dark, and, when the subpoena was served, would act shocked.

On December 22, Goldberg and Tripp were still plotting to sell Tripp's book. Isikoff scolded Tripp that "such a move right now, under the circumstances, was insane." She would "undermine her own credibility" in the Jones case. "You're also going to muck up my story, you idiot. . . . My advice was right, of course."†

Three days earlier, Monica Lewinsky had been subpoenaed by Jones's lawyers. She immediately telephoned Vernon Jordan, who had been helping her to find a job in New York, and he arranged for her to meet Francis Carter, a defense attorney, on December 22.

On November 23, Goldberg arranged a conference call with Richard Porter and Jerome Marcus, a lawyer in Philadelphia who had been Porter's classmate at the University of Chicago Law School. He was an-

*Isikoff, *Uncovering Clinton*, p. 206.
†Ibid., p. 253.

other one of the elves. She told them, falsely but assuredly, that Jordan had ordered Lewinsky to lie in her deposition and that Tripp's lawyer—the one who had told Tripp to stop her illegal wiretapping—had to be replaced. Conway promptly found James Moody.

On January 7, Monica Lewinsky signed an affidavit prepared by her attorney saying that she had not had a sexual relationship with President Clinton. The next day, at a restaurant in Philadelphia, Jerome Marcus, Richard Porter, and George Conway dined with a friend, Paul Rosenzweig, another classmate of Marcus's and Porter's at the University of Chicago, a fellow member of the Federalist Society, a law partner at Kirkland and Ellis, and a staff member at the Office of Independent Counsel. Over dinner, Rosenzweig was invested with knowledge of Lewinsky. The next day, he told Jackie Bennett.

On January 12, Starr gave Jackie Bennett the nod to accept information from Linda Tripp. Word of this approval traveled from Rosenzweig to Marcus to Goldberg to Moody, Tripp's new lawyer. The report by Starr's FBI investigator that was used to justify relying on Tripp stated: "TRIPP believed that [Robert] BENNETT and the White House would try to destroy her based on what she had seen them do to other people who got in their way. That belief ultimately motivated TRIPP to begin tape recording telephone conversations TRIPP had with MONICA LEWINSKY."* This statement, factual in tone, was a totally false representation of Tripp's motives. It neglected her prospective book, the presence of Lucianne Goldberg, Isikoff's advice on what would constitute a publishable *Newsweek* story, and Tripp's own animosities, including her political hatred of Clinton. Tripp was no stranger to the independent counsel's office, having testified as a witness in four separate investigations: Vince Foster's suicide, the Travel Office firings, the FBI files, and Whitewater. The prosecutors had been familiar for years with her sudden appearances amid nearly every scandal and her avid hostility to the Clinton White House. But on the basis of Tripp's fiction that her safety was in peril, Starr granted her immunity from prosecution.

On January 13, Tripp, wearing a wire furnished by Starr's office, met with Monica Lewinsky and taped their conversation. At best, it was a confused one, in which Monica contradicted herself repeatedly while Tripp tried to lead her on. But it did make clear what Monica thought of the content of her affidavit. "I did not have a sexual relationship," she insisted to an exasperated Tripp, who challenged her. "I never

*Toobin, *A Vast Conspiracy*, p. 194.

had intercourse," she explained. To her, a "sexual relationship" meant "intercourse."

On January 14, Moody obtained Linda Tripp's tapes of her telephone conversations with Lewinsky from Kirby Behre, Tripp's dismissed attorney. He played the December 22 one, supposedly the crucial incriminating one, for his friends Coulter and Conway. If anything, the tape revealed Tripp finagling to incriminate Lewinsky. "Look, Monica," she said, "we already know that you're going to lie under oath." But Lewinsky wondered how the Jones lawyers could possibly know about Clinton's gift to her of a hatpin. "Someone has told them something," said Tripp, who knew that she was that "someone." The elves were "crestfallen," Coulter told Isikoff, when there was nothing on the tape about the President or Jordan telling Lewinsky to lie.*

On January 15, Jackie Bennett met with Deputy Attorney General Eric Holder to demand authority to expand the Whitewater investigation. He claimed that the Independent Counsel had clean hands: "We've had no contacts with the plaintiff's attorney. No contacts w/Paula Jones lawyers." This was, of course, a deliberate deception.

Starr rushed a letter to Holder asserting that he believed Linda Tripp was "being urged to perjure herself"—a false claim based on the as yet unrevealed Talking Points memo. His letter also claimed that Jordan's helping Lewinsky find a job was like the help he gave Webster Hubbell, the former associate attorney general, after he had been indicted for larceny, in hope of silencing his testimony. Starr believed that Hubbell held secrets of Whitewater and more. "Ms. Lewinsky's statements suggest that the very same individuals are using the very same tactics [as] in the [Jones] case," Starr wrote. In neither the Jones case nor in the Lewinsky matter, however, did he ever prove any obstruction of justice, though his unfounded claim of analogous conspiracy provided the tenuous legal argument that helped win him authorization for his expanded probe. Starr did not tell the Justice Department that Jordan had begun his job search for Lewinsky long before she was subpoenaed and before signing an affidavit—prima facie proof that he was innocent of the trumped-up charge.

Nor did Starr tell Justice that he had already invaded the Jones case without authority: James Moody had faxed him a copy of Lewinsky's affidavit. All parties in the Jones case were under a court gag order not to disclose important information, a ruling that made Starr a party to Moody's contempt of court. Starr's copy of the fax, reproduced in the

*Isikoff, *Uncovering Clinton*, p. 306.

Starr Report, bore the court stamp showing it came originally from Jones's lawyers. If the Justice Department had been informed of this fax, it would have clearly seen the collusion between Starr's office and the Jones team.*

There was one more thing. Jackie Bennett gave Eric Holder an additional bit of information: "A seriously complicating factor came to our attention this evening. Mike Isikoff is on to this. He has been receiving information from a friend of Tripp's." (In fact, Lucianne Goldberg's notes, later subpoenaed by Starr, read, "Isikoff told me PJ lawyers told him about the feds coming in.") Bennett continued, "We met with him and he is disturbingly far along. So we have a very short window of opportunity to try to move this along."† In other words, Isikoff might, by publishing an account of the plan to expand the Whitewater investigation in the Lewinsky direction, prevent the "crime" from happening, since a *Newsweek* article would alert the President, who was about to testify. That was what the Independent Counsel feared. By telling the Justice Department about Isikoff, Bennett was putting Attorney General Reno on notice: if Starr did not get his expanded authority, she would certainly be blamed for acting to protect the President politically, as she had been before. Starr used Isikoff as a threat to get what he wanted.

Tripp had urged the OIC prosecutors to let her wear the wire she'd used to tape her confused conversation with Lewinsky on January 13, the tape that Starr had taken to the Justice Department to force the expansion of his investigation. Now, on January 16, Tripp arranged another meeting with Lewinsky at the Pentagon City Mall's food court. When the two met, Starr's prosecutors surrounded Lewinsky and took her to Room 1012 of the attached Ritz Carlton Hotel. There they told her she faced twenty-seven years in prison for obstruction of justice, subornation of perjury, perjury, and witness tampering. The prosecutors asked her to wear a wire to tape conversations with President Clinton and Vernon Jordan. "What if I want to call my attorney?" she asked. They told her to listen to them instead. They promised her immunity if she cooperated. Then they wouldn't prosecute her mother, they told her. She asked to call her mother. Jackie Bennett told her, "You're twenty-four years old, you're smart, you're old enough, you don't need to call your mommy." She was allowed to call. Marcia Lewis got on a train in New York. When

*Isikoff, *Uncovering Clinton*, pp. 200–202; Conason and Lyons, *Hunting of the President*, pp. 356–58.

†Toobin, *A Vast Conspriacy*, p. 202; Isikoff, *Uncovering Clinton*, p. 304.

she arrived, she telephoned Lewinsky's father, Dr. Bernard Lewinsky, who got a lawyer friend, William Ginsburg, to call back. He informed the prosecutors that Lewinsky would not agree to their terms. Twelve hours after she had been grabbed, they let her go. Even though she was understandably terrified, she had refused to buckle under.

If Lewinsky, alone, scared, sobbing, had been told as law requires that of course she had a right to an attorney, and if she had been able to call Frank Carter promptly when she asked about her right to do so, two things would undoubtedly have happened: First, Carter would have told Bob Bennett about her predicament, and the President would have known about it before he gave his deposition, which might well have been postponed under the circumstances. Second, Carter would have called the court in Arkansas and recalled Lewinsky's affidavit: it had been mailed that morning to Arkansas but was not officially registered there until the next business day, January 20. It never would have been filed. But Starr wanted to entrap the President.*

Isikoff, meanwhile, was scrambling with the tape that he had gotten from Jackie Bennett via Moody and Conway. But his editors were unconvinced by Lewinsky's and Tripp's circuitous yammering, and his article did not run. Conway and Goldberg once again screwed him and gave the story to Drudge. Starr's office, for its part, leaked it to Susan Schmidt of the *Post* and Jackie Judd of ABC News. But Isikoff received a consolation prize.

On the evening of January 21, *Newsweek* posted an article by Isikoff on its website, recounting his uncovering of the scandal (without any mention of Goldberg or the elves) and exposing an electrifying new document—the "Talking Points." This was his big scoop. Lewinsky had given the Talking Points to Tripp on January 14 to coach her in her testimony about Kathleen Willey. "It's not clear who prepared these talking points," Isikoff wrote, "but Starr believes that Lewinsky did not write them herself. He is investigating whether the instructions came from Jordan or other friends of the president."† Here was a smoking gun—the possibility that Lewinsky was suborning perjury and that behind her lurked a chain that led to the President.

The Talking Points memo had been written as a script for Tripp. It challenged Kathleen Willey's story and labeled Lewinsky a stalker—the first time that description of her appeared in print. It read:

*See Gene Lyons, "Mistakes Were Made," *Salon.com*, October 5, 1998.
†Michael Isikoff, "Diary of a Scandal," *Newsweek*, January 21, 1998.

Your first few paragraphs should be about yourself—what you do now, what you did at the White House and for how many years you were there as a career person and as a political appointee.

You and Kathleen were friends. At around the time of her husband's death (The President has claimed it was after her husband died. Do you really want to contradict him?), she came to you after she allegedly came out of the Oval and looked (however she looked), you don't recall her exact words, but she claimed at the time (whatever she claimed) and was very happy.

You did not see her go in or see her come out.

Talk about when you became out of touch with her and maybe why.

The next you heard of her was when a Newsweek reporter (I wouldn't name him specifically) showed up in your office saying she [Willey] was naming you as someone who would corroborate that she was sexually harassed. You spoke with her that evening, etc., and she relayed to you a sequence of events that was very dissimilar from what you remembered happening. As a result of your conversation with her and subsequent reports that showed that she had tried to enlist the help of someone else in her lie that the President sexually harassed her, you now do not believe that what she claimed happened really happened. You now find it completely plausible that she herself smeared her lipstick, untucked her blouse, etc.

You never saw her go into the Oval Office, or come out of the Oval Office. . . .

You want [Robert] Bennett's people to see your affidavit before it's signed.

Your deposition should include enough information to satisfy their questioning.

By the way, remember how I said there was someone else that I knew about. Well, she turned out to be a huge liar. I found out she left the WH because she was stalking the P or something like that. Well, at least that gets me out of another scandal I know about . . .

I have never observed the President behave inappropriately with anybody.

With the publication of the Talking Points, finger-pointing began—finger-pointing at the President, Vernon Jordan, Bruce Lindsey, and others in the White House—and it went on for months. William Safire, for example, wrote in February that the Talking Points—"the smoking gun"—"explains the existential dread palpable in the White House today.

. . . The author of the talking points will likely be found, is in real danger of going to jail, and may not want to go alone for long."*

Isikoff never explained how he happened to receive the Talking Points, which was in the possession of only Starr and Tripp, whose immunity agreement placed her under Starr's control. Nor did he note that the document supported the story Tripp had told him about Willey. In fact, as Jeffrey Toobin wrote, "Every word in the talking points was *true*; thus, regardless of its authorship, there was no way the document could be evidence of a plot to obstruct justice."† Isikoff also forgot to report something else. In August 1997, after his article about Willey had appeared in *Newsweek*, Tripp had faxed him a long, angry letter that *Newsweek* never published, a letter that expressed precisely the same arguments made in the Talking Points. After President Clinton's impeachment, Isikoff acknowledged, "In the excitement of the moment, I simply forgot about Tripp's August 1997 letter and the underlying similarities to the 'talking points.' "‡

In August 1998, Lewinsky was conclusively to resolve the mystery by testifying that she had written the Talking Points, based on her discussions with Tripp. In them, she had simply given Tripp's own ideas and language back to her. But Starr had Tripp all along, as a witness who knew from the beginning how the document had been created. Starr's leaking of the Talking Points as a mysteriously authored work was intended to set in motion a speculation that somehow Clinton and Jordan were guilty and there was a White House cover-up. He leaked the document not because it was proof but because he didn't have proof.

"May I have your attention? My name is Vernon Jordan." In the midafternoon of January 22, Jordan appeared at a packed press conference he had called at the Park Hyatt Hotel. With his dignified bearing, his height of six feet four inches, his characteristically well tailored suit, and his resonant baritone voice, Jordan expressed a masterly, measured control over the bizarre situation.

The targeting of Vernon Jordan by Kenneth Starr was one of the most curious recent episodes in the political sociology of Washington and of race in America. Jordan was the most influential, respected, and prominent black man in the capital. His success story was a modern clas-

---

*William Safire, "On the Trail of the Smoking Gun," *The New York Times*, February 12, 1998.

†Toobin, *A Vast Conspiracy*, p. 199.

‡Isikoff, *Uncovering Clinton*, p. 383.

sic. The grandson of a sharecropper, educated in segregated schools in the South, he had become a civil rights leader, a field director for the NAACP, and then the president of the National Urban League. For anyone who had lived through the civil rights movement, Vernon Jordan was a major figure. He had joined the Washington law firm of Akin, Gump; had been named to eleven corporate boards; and had become a social friend of almost everybody in Washington's establishment. He had a close bond with Bill Clinton, another Southern boy made good, and Clinton appointed him cochairman of the transition team after his first election; he vacationed with the President on Martha's Vineyard, playing golf and, at a party with summering Washington and New York eminences, belting out with him the Negro National Anthem ("Lift Every Voice and Sing"); and he was regularly relied upon for his confidential advice. Now, having risen perhaps higher than anyone in Washington except for his friend the President, renowned for his accomplishments, prudence, and generosity, Vernon Jordan stood accused of a criminal conspiracy.

"Jordan Was Justification to Widen Probe" ran a later headline in *The Washington Post* over an article that stated, "Most of the evidence presented to the Justice Department on Jan. 15 by Whitewater independent counsel Kenneth W. Starr in seeking to expand his inquiry focused on the president's close friend and adviser, Vernon E. Jordan Jr., rather than President Clinton, according to officials familiar with the deliberations."*
Anyone who knew Jordan would know that he had helped many young people get jobs. He had promoted others for jobs in the government. He had given job advice to others freely. His search on behalf of Lewinsky had begun before she had any inkling she would be subpoenaed in the Jones case. His effort had consisted of a telephone call to one of his wide network of friends in the corporate world, the chairman of Revlon's board, Ronald Perlman. The notion that a crime had to be committed for him to get Lewinsky hired at Revlon was patently absurd.

Almost everyone knew Jordan. Katharine Graham knew Jordan, of course, and had him as a frequent guest to her dinners and parties. Everyone in the city's cultural circles knew Jordan—his wife, Ann, sat on the Kennedy Center's board of trustees. And Jordan knew the political press corps, the columnists, pundits, and bureau chiefs, with whom he regularly exchanged political gossip.

*Roberto Suro, "Jordan Was Justification to Widen Probe," *The Washington Post*, January 28, 1998.

But not *everybody* knew Jordan—not most of the scandal reporters or their editors, including those at *The Washington Post*. This was not Mrs. Graham or Ben Bradlee's *Washington Post* any more. Their function at the paper was largely ceremonial; their presence in their suite of offices above the newsroom blessed what was presented below as an unbroken tradition. But in the newsroom itself there was now a sense of superior morality in *not* knowing someone like Jordan personally. It was believed that he could thereby be written about more objectively; knowing him would only compromise one's independence.

Not knowing who Vernon Jordan really was, however, had the effect of transforming him into a one-dimensional cardboard figure. The less the press knew about him, the more susceptible they were to questionable assumptions about him. What they knew was that Jordan was close to President Clinton, whom many of them considered guilty of everything from Whitewater to accepting secret Chinese government funds for his reelection campaign. Why should Jordan be treated differently than the President? If they were pals, they must be partners in crime.

The fallacies in how Jordan was written about, and how the articles were read, were based on astounding leaps of faith and imagination. First, while Jordan was unknown to most of those writing articles about him as an alleged criminal, they presumed that their information was solid because it came from Starr, whose motive of heartfelt truth-telling they believed in. Second, the reporters and editors operated under the self-delusion that they were donning an antiestablishment mantle. In attacking Clinton and those close to him, they imagined they were heroically taking on a Nixon-like government—a "culture of concealment" run by a "psychologically disturbed individual," in Isikoff's words.* In fact, they were manipulated by an unaccountable instrument of government, the Office of Independent Counsel, animated by partisan Republicans, whom they treated as sources of objective and unimpeachable information. The third and perhaps strangest fallacy emerged when a number of Jordan's friends came forward to offer testimonials to him. For example, Robert Strauss, an establishment pillar in Washington legal and political life and Jordan's law partner, told the *Post*: "He offers judgment and integrity and confidence in himself. He has a manner about him that is warm and attentive."† Indeed. But if Jordan were a man of in-

---

*Isikoff, *Uncovering Clinton*, p. 168.

†Marc Fischer, "First Friend Vernon Jordan Is a Man Comfortable with Power and with Himself," *The Washington Post*, January 27, 1998.

tegrity, then his integrity must have extended to his dealings with the President and with Monica Lewinsky. If that were so, then it was likely he hadn't committed crimes, and if he were innocent, it followed that the President was, too. According to Starr's scenario, Jordan's guilt would prove the President's. They were either both guilty together—or both innocent.

"May I have your attention? My name is Vernon Jordan." On the second day of the scandal, Jordan spoke:

> I did two things for Ms. Monica Lewinsky. I assisted her in trying to find employment in the private sector in New York City. I referred her for interviews at American Express and at Revlon, where I am privileged to serve as a director. I also referred her to Young and Rubicam, a New York advertising agency.
>
> Secondly, when she was served with the subpoena and—at her request, I recommended a very competent Washington lawyer, Mr. Frank Carter. I actually took her to Mr. Carter's office, I introduced them, and I returned to my office.
>
> I want to say to you absolutely and unequivocally that Ms. Lewinsky told me in no uncertain terms that she did not have a sexual relationship with the President. At no time did I ever say, suggest, or intimate to her that she should lie.
>
> Throughout my professional career, I have been privileged to assist people with their vocational aspirations. I have done so for two reasons. First, I stand on the shoulders of many individuals who have helped me. And second, I believe to whom much is given, much is required. And so I believe in giving a helping hand . . .
>
> I was pleased to be helpful to Ms. Lewinsky, whose drive, ambition, and personality were impressive. Ms. Lewinsky was referred to me by Ms. Betty Currie, a secretary to the President.

Every point Jordan made was true, and over the next year Starr never produced evidence to the contrary. He had gotten renewed investigative authority from a misled Justice Department; he had a compliant news media, a pile of tapes from Tripp, a presidential deposition in a civil suit of a humiliated husband trying to hide his foolishness, and, eventually, a stained dress. But the criminal case as he revealed it on January 21 on the front page of *The Washington Post* never materialized. It took only twenty-four hours for Vernon Jordan to deflate it. Yet the frenzy was just beginning.

IV

Early on the evening of January 22, the working draft of the State of the Union speech took precedence over the turbulence outside. Four of us—Michael Waldman, who was the chief speechwriter; Bob Shrum; Mark Penn; and myself—holed up in Waldman's office in the Old Executive Office Building to write and polish every line. We had to have a text ready that the President could use in his rehearsals, which were going to begin the next day. Shrum, a political consultant, was the most artful Democratic speechwriter, and he was especially close to Ted Kennedy and Dick Gephardt. He had written Kennedy's memorable "The dream will never die" speech delivered at the 1980 Democratic convention. Penn, Clinton's pollster, had a keen sense of nuance as well as of every word's political dimension. Gene Sperling and Bruce Reed, the policy directors, came in and out. Slowly, we labored over every phrase, reading it aloud, writing, and rewriting. We broke for Chinese food that we ordered in while Penn drove over to CNN's studios to appear on *Larry King Live* to defend the President. We critiqued his performance over spring rolls. Then he returned and we went back to the writing. Finally, after two in the morning, we had a draft ready.

On January 23, the *Post* headlines blared, "Starr Appears on Solid Ground," and "Flowers Feels Vindicated by Report." In his Jones deposition, Clinton had admitted to a one-night stand in 1977 with Gennifer Flowers, though she had been claiming, during the 1992 campaign, a twelve-year affair with him. Apparently relying on Jones's lawyers as sources, the *Post* reported:

> Flowers said she feels vindicated by President Clinton's reported acknowledgment of their affair and sees parallels between their liaison and the president's alleged relationship with former White House intern Monica Lewinsky. In a telephone interview from Dallas, Flowers said Clinton's use of a close political operative to help her find a job and his request that she cover up their affair reminds [sic] her of the Lewinsky case. Investigators are trying to determine whether the president instructed confidant Vernon E. Jordan Jr. to assist Lewinsky in her job search or urged her to lie about their relationship.

There was no reportage about Clinton's exact testimony, but Flowers was further quoted saying that Clinton had asked her "to engage in a conspiracy of cover-up to protect him, to lie to anyone if necessary to protect him."*

That morning, the President held a cabinet meeting to discuss the State of the Union speech. The cabinet secretaries suggested the principal policies they wanted to see in the speech. Clinton briefly remarked that the charges being made against him were false. Upon leaving the meeting, the cabinet was met by a phalanx of reporters and TV cameras. "I believe the allegations are completely untrue," Secretary of State Madeleine Albright said. "I'll second that. Definitely," said Secretary of Commerce William Daley. "Third it," said Secretary of Health and Human Services Donna Shalala. They were all unhappy later that the President's comment had prompted them to make these statements, but they were not publicly asked again about the scandal. Clinton's decision to tell everyone that every accusation was untrue was his alone. He was obviously going to continue saying that until Starr proved otherwise.

President Clinton was scheduled to begin rehearsing the State of the Union in the family theater, but at a meeting in the Oval Office, he said he wanted more time to work on the passage about the Asian economic crisis. The tension over another aspect of the speech became enormous, however, as the scandal roared outside. Should the President mention the scandal? I and everyone else on the political staff were against his doing so. Separating what Clinton was doing as president from the scandal became a basic strategy. It helped the public to keep the two spheres in perspective and to judge the relative importance to their own concerns.

Over time, this strategy also clarified a basic truth: what Clinton had done was a personal indiscretion that had no bearing on his conduct of public policy. And once the strategy was adopted at that early moment while we were working on the State of the Union, the President adhered to it with great discipline. In private, he railed against Starr and his investigation, but he also kept himself focused on the policy aims of his administration. It wasn't that he compartmentalized but that he was aware of both things at once. Everyone on the staff believed that the scandal was intended to halt the political agenda of the administration, and that concentrating on the speech and its contents not only confounded that effort but emphasized our reason for being there. "Load me up, boys," Clinton would say, referring to policy initiatives.

*Lorraine Adams, "Flowers Feels Vindicated by Report," *The Washington Post*, January 23, 1998.

Throughout the day, several of the senior staff members received calls from reporters asking them if they wanted to resign in protest against the President. These reporters explained they would be happy to receive and publish the resignations. Universally, these offers were refused. Meanwhile, no reporters seemed to be gathering information to publish or broadcast about how Starr had managed to attach himself to the Jones case and to its strange cast of characters.

That night, on Geraldo Rivera's cable TV talk show, Ann Coulter volunteered that Clinton had used Lewinsky to "service" him "along with four other interns." This invention, like almost every other invention, assumed a life of its own and was repeated endlessly.

During the day, I talked to David Brock. George Conway, he explained, had pulled the strings of Paula Jones's case without being her attorney of record. He had needed to operate in the shadows because he would never have received the permission of his firm to take on Paula Jones as a client, and he had never informed them about his informal work. Remaining in the background, he wasn't covered by the judge's gag order, like the other lawyers, and therefore he could act as a cutout to Drudge, Coulter, and others. "Conway *has* to be secret," said Brock.

It occurred to me that without having attorney-client privilege, Conway had no shield to prevent him from being subpoenaed to testify. So I called Bob Bennett. The window of opportunity, he told me, was closing fast. There were only several more days in the period in which depositions could be taken. He said he would have Conway served with a subpoena right away.

With Starr's launch of the Monica Lewinsky story, the prevailing atmosphere in Washington became more Roman than American. The capital may be the center of the world, but it is also a political cloister, filled with small groups, clubs, and exclusive societies. Yet the cliques responsible for fomenting this new round of scandalous allegations were of a fundamentally different nature than these.

The prosecution of the Lewinsky matter seemed to be dressed in the high moral garb worn by the Puritan judges at the Salem witchcraft trials. But the Salem magistrates believed in the factual truth of their charges on the basis of spectral evidence, and they followed a strict code as they understood it; they ultimately halted the hysteria, some acknowledging that the "evidence" had been unreliable.

The Starr investigation and the subsequent impeachment, however, though they had some roots in puritanical ground, were triggered by an Italianate conspiracy—an intricate, covert, amoral operation bent on power. The plotters brandished the law as a stiletto to try to destroy a president they considered illegitimate. For them the law was not a resource for justice but a lethal political weapon. Their claim to represent the rule of law was a subterfuge for subversion. They were single-minded in abusing the law to bypass and cancel the democratic process.

In Washington, intrigue supplanted debate. Accusations against people who were in or close to the administration became the order of the day. Fear of the subversion of the republic by powerful plotters who might manipulate the law, politics, and society—a Cataline conspiracy—was a political idea at the forefront of the thinking of America's Founding Fathers. It was part of the shared classical political instruction that informed them in the Revolution, in their work on the Constitution, and in the early years of the republic. All the founders had read Cicero, particularly his speech exposing the plot of Cataline, a powerful former praetor who had sought to overthrow the Roman Republic. Having destroyed Cataline's plot, Cicero was called by the Roman orator Cato "the father of his country," the origin of the phrase. Jefferson recommended Cicero to his younger aides. John Adams read Cicero's orations against Cataline aloud to himself repeatedly. Throughout American political history the prominence of the Cataline analogy endured. Hamilton decried Aaron Burr as an American Cataline. Senator Charles Sumner, in 1856, decried the slave powers in Kansas as creating a Cataline conspiracy.

In the scandal of 1998, many figures were operating in the shadow of Cataline—the elves, Starr and his prosecutors—but none more fully than Speaker of the House Newt Gingrich, next in the presidential line of succession after the Vice President. Gingrich believed that the Monica Lewinsky business would destroy both Clinton and Gore, and he prepared for that eventuality. In April 1998, Elizabeth Drew, the former Washington correspondent of *The New Yorker*, spoke about Gingrich's scenario:

Speaker Gingrich is talking to, and has been talking to over a period of time, close associates about the idea of impeaching both Clinton and Gore. It goes as follows: Gingrich expects that the Starr report will be very tough and that the House will have no choice but to proceed with hearings looking toward an impeachment.

Gingrich believes that the report will be so tough that Clinton will be impeached. The thinking then goes that Gore, as his successor, will pardon Clinton. This, of course, leaves Gore in place as the incumbent president, which is not something the Republicans wish to have happen. So

once Gore has pardoned Clinton, Gingrich's thinking goes, the Congress
will impeach Gore for having pardoned Clinton. As one of these close associates of Gingrich said to me, "You can't have a Clinton strategy without a Gore strategy."

I know this seems wild. . . . I'm simply reporting what the Speaker of
the House has been talking about.*

The Founding Fathers would have seen the plotters against Clinton
as what they themselves knew was the most dangerous kind of threat of
faction to any republic. The last thing Jefferson, Hamilton, Madison, and
Adams would have done would be to dismiss the obvious design of a
Cataline-like conspiracy as a ridiculous fantasy.

In the White House, I tried to be the loyalist, not merely to the President and to Hillary, to them as friends, but to the progress being made
in his administration and by the country, and, most important, to our
democracy. Eventually, I believed, the facts would be established. An illicit sexual relationship and the illicit subversion of democracy were
hardly morally equivalent in my mind. If the overthrow of the President
could be achieved by these conspiratorial means, it would deface the
Constitution and damage for a long time the ability of the executive to
advance the general welfare of the whole nation.

Part of my duty as good soldier, first knight, was to try to get the right
story out. I felt I had to go into a journalistic mode, but I couldn't be a
journalist myself. I could suggest information, ideas, and leads to writers
willing to examine them rather than follow the story line as Starr set it
out. But some of the reporters and editors I called brushed me aside.
They were polite, but they didn't want a narrative that differed from the
one that advanced the scandal. Understandably, they were all trying to
lay their hands on Tripp's tapes. (Lucianne Goldberg's son, Jonah, announced that the *National Enquirer* tabloid had offered $2 million.) They
were seeking witnesses to the sexual act. Sex was conflated by implication
with the obstruction of justice allegation; every new sexual detail was
breathlessly presented as though it were proof of the criminal case. I
quickly learned that most of the major media were dependent on and
protective of their relationships with Starr and his prosecutors. More
than a few said so to me matter-of-factly.

But independent-minded and skeptical journalists could be found—

*Cited by Jonathan Broder, "Gingrich's Impeachment Scenario," *Salon.com*,
April 29, 1998.

some in Washington, others all over the country, and in every medium. When they began to publish or broadcast their early reports on the elves or opinion columns that were critical of Starr, the part of the press that was joined to Starr became enraged. Reporters and editors who were close to the Independent Counsel took criticism of him or contrary reporting about him as attacks on themselves as well as on their invaluable source.

The development of a different narrative about the burgeoning scandal had a significant political impact. To begin with, it created a debate where there had been almost none before. Starr, his methods, his prosecutors, the political character of his case, and the activities of the right wing properly became subjects of controversy.

The right-wing politics that had forced the scandal were alien and unknown to much of the White House senior staff. To them, what the right was doing seemed so far-fetched, so impossibly convoluted, that they couldn't quite credit it. The self-enclosed hothouse nature of the right-wing world made it difficult to explain what was going on to those who lacked contact with it. Many had never even heard of people like Scaife. So I had to convince people in the White House, too. Good-naturedly, they took to calling me "Grassy Knoll" after the site near where President Kennedy was assassinated. That was all right. The nickname didn't bother me. In a short time, they, too, understood.

At the same time, I had no problems at all conveying information to the President's lawyers. I developed a close relationship with the White House legal counsel, Charles Ruff, in whom I confided everything I knew and who let me know that he approved of my efforts. I never acted without consulting Chuck. Ruff was a person of great integrity and intelligence with vast legal and political experience. He had been the last Watergate prosecutor; had served in the Justice Department; had been a partner in Covington and Burling, a famous Washington law firm; and was the corporation counsel of the city of Washington. As a young man, before he had begun his storied career, while on a Ford Foundation grant in Africa, he contracted a tropical disease that left his legs paralyzed. In his wheelchair he moved deliberately through the West Wing. Chuck had very sure and principled ideas about what he was doing, was anything but an ideologue, and operated on the notion that almost all matters could be resolved through good-faith efforts that reached common ground.

On assuming his post in 1997, Chuck had believed that he could establish a trusting and reasonable relationship with Starr. By then Starr had already made a point of subjecting the First Lady to humiliation in her grand-jury appearance, had resigned and then returned, and had allowed his deputies to embark on a sex hunt. Still, Chuck believed Starr would make every effort to put matters on a thoroughly professional basis. To his surprise, he found Starr to be poorly prepared, halting, unsteady in his grasp of the material, and deferential to his deputies, whom Ruff assessed as second-rate and strangely hostile. Chuck thought Starr had little concept of how to behave as a prosecutor—he had certainly had no prior experience, unlike Ruff himself. Momentarily, during those first confusing January days, he hoped that somehow he and Starr might work out some arrangement to prevent a constitutional crisis. He was privately uncomfortable with Clinton's relationship with Lewinsky, as were many on the White House staff, but he never believed that any criminality was attached to it. It seemed wildly irrational to him that Starr had expanded his investigation in this direction. Ruff very swiftly realized that his desire to reach some accommodation was just a wish on his own part. He could see, better than almost anyone else in the White House, the ways the President's enemies were manipulating the law for their own purposes.

Lewinsky's attorney, William Ginsburg, a specialist in medical malpractice law in Los Angeles, was the opposite of a seasoned Washington lawyer who could discreetly and skillfully smooth things over. Ginsburg—while negotiating with Starr about the terms of a proffer from Lewinsky in which she would provide information in exchange for immunity from prosecution—declared to the media that the prosecutors had tried to "squeeze" his client to turn against the President. Ginsburg's publicity was not good for Starr, who put out another story. On January 24, the *Post* reported (in an article coauthored by Schmidt) that Lewinsky herself was to blame for her ordeal: "Sources close to Starr described a far different episode that dragged on mainly because Lewinsky insisted her mother be present."* Also on that day, Lucianne Goldberg unveiled her relation with Linda Tripp.

That same morning, the President at last came to rehearse the State of the Union address. The family movie theater is a small private screening room in the East Wing, decorated with orange and brown curtains, and filled with about fifty cushy leather armchairs. For the rehearsal, a podium was set up facing the audience. Speechwriters sat behind their computers on a long folding table in front to take down every alteration

---

*Susan Schmidt and Peter Baker, "Ex-Intern Rejected Immunity Offer in Probe," *The Washington Post*, January 24, 1998.

in the text. A speech coach, Michael Sheehan, offered advice on pacing and which words and phrases to emphasize. Clinton's Georgetown roommate, Tommy Caplan, a novelist, joined the team just for these occasions. Harry Thomason, the television producer, also turned up, as he had for every State of the Union, to notice any problems in presentation. Harry was a loyal friend, a bulwark of support.

In the windowless theater, as the President began to read his speech aloud to about twenty of us, the world outside seemed to disappear. His concentration was riveted on the text and on his policies. He read and reread. He stopped to change words here and there. We would interrupt at the end of a paragraph to suggest improvements. No, he'd say. Good idea, he'd say. He'd write the changes himself on his draft, while the speechwriters tapped away on their computers. Did you get that? they asked each other. Clinton would hit a line hard: Minimum wage! Yah! He'd cheer himself. And now the Democrats all cheer! he said. Is this right? he asked about a statistic. Check it, he told an aide. How about if I talk about it this way? Then he'd read a few lines. He'd reread it, changing a phrase.

He got to the section on Social Security. "What should we do with our surplus? Social Security first!" He tried it again. "What should we do with our surplus?" His arm came down with a karate chop. "Save Social Security first!" We applauded. "See, I haven't totally lost it," he said.

We took a break. Clinton pulled Shrum, Penn, and me aside. He asked us if we thought he should mention the scandal in the speech. We were uniformly against that. "That's what I think," he said. "I'm not going to."

During the break, I went to see Hillary in her study in the residence. The day before she had been calling Democratic leaders, shoring up their support. She told me she wished she still had her notes from the Nixon impeachment inquiry, when she had worked on the staff of the House Judiciary Committee. Those notes had been ruined in storage. She was certain that Starr and the Republicans would drive his investigation to its ultimate political limit. She envisioned step by step the train of coming events: Starr would write a report and refer it to the House, calling for impeachment; the Republicans would force through a vote for an impeachment; and then there would be a Senate trial of the President. Nobody could predict its outcome, how firmly the Democrats would be behind the President. She wanted to know if I would help her. I replied that I'd be there all the way through.

I returned to the State of the Union rehearsal. The staff had transferred itself to the Roosevelt Room, haggling on the next draft over lunch.

Afterward, I went to my office and called David Brock to see if he had any news. He had had dinner the previous evening with Laura Ingraham and Alex Azar, a lawyer who worked at Wiley, Rein and Fielding and was part of the clique of elves. He had worked on the staff of the independent counsel and remained close to those who were still there. "He's playing some role as an intermediary between what's going on and Starr's office," Brock told me. According to Azar, he said, Starr didn't have a case: "They thought they had Monica to tape Clinton and Jordan. Now they think they won't prove the crime. They'll just have an affair story." Under the circumstances, Starr was pressing the politics. Azar told Brock, "They want a public uproar," but Azar himself was skeptical. "Alex doesn't think the OIC will get perjury or obstruction. The sex stuff is graphic and convincing." Brock and Azar had discussed the likely scenario: "Starr goes forward with the investigation. There's a big uproar. Congress gets the guts to ask Starr to turn over everything. The tapes are released. There are impeachment hearings." And then? The scenario faded to black.

If Azar was to be believed, both Hillary Clinton and Starr's office foresaw the same broad outline of events that would take place over the next year. Both thought that evidence of criminality was lacking. Both viewed the struggle as a political one. But only one had the power to bring the scenario to pass: Starr.

Late in the afternoon a small group of the President's political and legal aides met to prepare Paul Begala and Rahm Emanuel for Sunday morning television interviews. Everyone agreed that both of them should harshly criticize Starr. At the same time, some of the political team worried that Clinton's denial had been unconvincing. We wanted him to repeat it forcefully, unlike the erratic denials he had given on the first day. We discussed the articles we knew were being prepared in the media. Suddenly, the television that was always droning in the background flashed on its screen: "BREAKING NEWS." We stopped, stared, and waited. Wolf Blitzer, CNN's White House correspondent, was introduced as having "an exclusive report." Standing on the White House North Lawn, less than a hundred yards from us, Blitzer said, "Despite the President's public and carefully phrased public denials, several of his closest friends and advisers, both in and out of the government, now tell CNN that they believe he almost certainly did have a sexual relation with . . .

Lewinsky, and they're talking among themselves about the possibility of a resignation."

Startled, we looked at each other in silence. He was speaking about us. But we had said nothing like what he reported. Perhaps someone who was not on the staff had made such a remark at some dinner party. It was impossible to tell from Blitzer's vague and blanket report. Despite the tensions and pressures of the past few days, despite our own disagreements, we had hung together as a team. We had all agreed that, whatever we privately thought, we would tell those outside the White House that we believed the President. If we allowed the slightest doubt to creep into any of our talk, it would be instantly blown up by the media. Now, we were watching a broadcast claiming exactly what we had been disciplining ourselves to prevent. Each of us picked up the telephone, one after another—myself, Begala, Emanuel, Bruce Lindsey—and rebuked Blitzer. But the effect of our action was less to temper the media in their race for the sensational story than to bind us more tightly together as we faced the storm. We went back to preparing Begala and Emanuel, now to answer questions about resignation rumors.

On Sunday, January 25, on ABC's *This Week*, Jackie Judd offered "new revelations": "ABC News has learned that Ken Starr's investigation has moved well beyond Monica Lewinsky's claims and taped conversations. . . . Several sources have told us that in the spring of 1996, the President and Lewinsky were caught in an intimate encounter in a private area of the White House." Then the panel of pundits held forth. "His presidency . . . is dead," said George Will. "I think his presidency is numbered in days," predicted Sam Donaldson. "He cannot survive," said William Kristol. Donaldson burst out that "corroborating witnesses have been found who caught the President and Miss Lewinsky in an intimate act in the White House."

On NBC's *Meet the Press*, Tim Russert introduced Matt Drudge: "There is talk all over this town [that] another White House staffer is going to come out from behind the curtains this week. . . . There are hundreds, hundreds, according to Miss Lewinsky. . . . We're in for a huge shock that goes beyond the specific episode. It's a whole psychosis taking place in the White House." Isikoff was on the panel, too, and he, promoting *Newsweek*'s publication of new tape excerpts, sympathized with an "anguished Linda Tripp."*

That afternoon, we met in the Map Room for another State of the

---

*Steven Brill, "Pressgate," *Brill's Content*, July/August 1998, p. 139.

Union rehearsal. (The theater was being readied for the televising of the Super Bowl that evening.) Once again, it was as though the clamor had been shut out as Clinton read and reread. Later, some of us discussed whether he should issue another denial. The lawyers were furiously opposed. They did not want him making any more public statements about Monica Lewinsky. Harry Thomason, though, weighed in on the side of making a strong denial. Clinton had told him, as he had told most of his senior staff, that he hadn't had a sexual relationship with Lewinsky, so Harry argued that if that were so, he should want to underscore it. I asked Hillary if she would favor another statement and she said she would. Her sentiment was not insistent, just assenting. I relayed her view to the others. It may well have been the decisive vote.

On January 26, both the tabloid newspapers in New York, the *Daily News* and the *New York Post*, used the same headline: "CAUGHT IN THE ACT." *The Washington Post* headlined its story: "STARR SEEKS WITNESSES":

> Investigators working for prosecutor Kenneth W. Starr searched aggressively yesterday for any independent evidence that President Clinton had a sexual relationship with former White House intern Monica S. Lewinsky and then urged her to lie about it. . . . On some of the tapes, Lewinsky reportedly is heard saying that Clinton and his friend, Washington lawyer Vernon E. Jordan Jr., wanted her to deny the relationship to Jones's lawyers. . . . Word that Starr is looking for witnesses to alleged White House sexual activities in spring 1996 was first reported on ABC News yesterday and later confirmed by The Washington Post. But details of what, exactly, is alleged to have been seen by whom were sketchy and sometimes conflicting.*

This article was like a purloined letter. Lying out in the open, it revealed how Starr was prosecuting his problematic case through the press. "Reportedly" having proved his criminal case on obstruction and perjury, he was now devoting his resources to exploring the sexual angle. Starr was the protagonist of the story he himself dictated, claiming at once to have evidence on the tapes and also to be seeking evidence.

*Peter Baker and Susan Schmidt, "Starr Seeks Witnesses," *The Washington Post*, January 26, 1998.

That same morning, in the Roosevelt Room, President Clinton presented a new federally financed program for after-school care, a new educational initiative that would affect a half million youngsters. After about an hour of speeches from others, the President stepped to the podium. At first, he talked about day care, class size, education standards, and the success of his policy to link schools to the Internet. Then he took questions. In answer to one, he said, "I want you to listen to me." He raised his left hand and pointed. "I'm going to say this again. I did not have sexual relations with that woman, Miss Lewinsky. I never told anybody to lie, not a single time—never. These allegations are false. And I need to go back to work for the American people." And he did. We rehearsed in the theater all afternoon.

Clinton's statement had been made at the instigation of anxious staff aides who wanted reassurance and support in fending off the media. However, that statement caused him more lasting damage than any other of his presidency. It was not true. It did not mollify the media, which were in great part driven by Starr. And it did not help him with the Congress, which would be his court of justice. It would have been better for him to let his earlier equivocal statements stand without trying to dress them up again. With those brief, defiant remarks Clinton lost more in credibility over the long run than he gained in political space in the short run.

From the first day of the scandal, the media had reported extensively about Monica Lewinsky. With their voracious appetite for sexual details, they dredged up every scintilla they could about her private life—her boyfriends, her parents' divorce, her therapists. Beginning with Isikoff's publication of the Talking Points on January 21, in which Lewinsky called herself a "stalker," newspapers across the country and all the television networks and cable stations expanded upon the stalker theme. On January 25, Kathy Sawyer and Susan Schmidt co-wrote an article in *The Washington Post* based on "information" about the contents of the tapes received from "sources": "Lewinsky also acknowledges that she had become known around the White House as 'the Stalker' because she was always trying to get close to Clinton."* On January 26, Deborah Orin wrote in the *New York Post*, "Lewinsky told her friend, Linda Tripp, that she believed [then–deputy chief of staff Evelyn] Lieberman had derisively

---

*Kathy Sawyer and Susan Schmidt, "On Tapes, Lewinsky Describes Alleged Trysts with Clinton," *The Washington Post*, January 25, 1998.

dubbed her 'The Stalker' because of her eagerness to get close to Clinton, a source told The Post."* (Lucianne Goldberg had a contract with the *New York Post* to serve as a source.)

These reports proved to be accurate. None of them originated with anyone I knew at the White House, and certainly not with me, since I had never known Lewinsky. There were some young people in the White House who knew Monica and told unflattering stories about her. I and others heard them—but none of these were ever published, though it would have been easy enough to arrange that. Having learned about Lewinsky's ordeal at the hands of Starr's prosecutors and her refusal to wear a wire to spy on the President and Vernon Jordan, I gave her credit for being more than the silly person depicted by the media and some of her former co-workers. And I was keeping to myself my conversation with the President about her. Like everyone in the White House, I explained to people outside that I believed the President. That was our code. I chatted with journalistic friends whom I had known for years about the articles that appeared, written mostly by White House antagonists. In Washington there is always an area involving friendship and acquaintanceship among those in the press and those in politics and government where informal, personal, and off-the-record opinions are expressed. Whatever views, theories, and conjectures journalists imparted to me, I held in confidence, and they also respected this custom with political figures.

Meanwhile, reporters in hot pursuit of the phantom witness to an intimate act between Monica Lewinsky and President Clinton were marching into uncharted territory. On the night of January 26, *The Dallas Morning News*, in an article for its next day's paper but posted instantly on the Internet, reported, " 'There is at least one witness who saw them together in a compromising situation,' a source said, declining to elaborate."† The Associated Press moved this item onto its wire immediately, and Larry King broke into his patter to read the dispatch on CNN. Then Ted Koppel, the host of ABC's *Nightline*, began his program heralding the "tomorrow edition of *The Dallas Morning News*, not only citing sources confirming Jackie Judd's report of yesterday, but adding new details."‡

---

*Deborah Orin, "Hillary's Pal Knew Monica Was Trouble," *New York Post*, January 26, 1998.

†David Jackson, "Source Affirms Clinton Affair," *The Dallas Morning News*, January 26, 1998.

‡Kalb, *One Scandalous Story*, p. 245.

Within an hour of its posting on the Internet, the article was re-tracted, and it was never published in the paper. The problem was that it had no real sources at all. Its provenance was a Republican lawyer and television talk-show regular, Joseph diGenova, who had conveyed to the reporter the gist of a half-overheard phone conversation of his wife, an-other Republican lawyer and television talk-show frequenter, Victoria Toensing. As Steven Brill described the sourcing, "DiGenova (1) heard his wife (2) talking to a friend (3) of someone (4) who had talked to some-one (5) who said he'd seen Lewinsky with Clinton."* With this incident, the scandal press set itself on the defensive.

January 27 was the day of the State of the Union address. Hillary had long scheduled an interview on the NBC *Today Show* and she intended to keep the appointment. She was the most important person in the drama who had yet to make a public statement. We discussed her appearance for several days beforehand. I made notes that I shared with her. In them, I pointed out that the key question was whether the President had tried to "suborn perjury and obstruct justice in a network of conspiracy," not whether he had engaged in a sexual relationship. Hillary also had to walk a fine, difficult line in her personal presentation, coming off as neither a warrior nor a wounded bird. I suggested that she say, "There are profes-sional forces at work whose only purpose is to sow division by creating scandal." About ten minutes before the *Today Show* began, we talked again.

"On Close-Up this morning," said the host, Matt Lauer, "the first lady of the United States, Hillary Rodham Clinton." He asked her about Lewinsky and what she knew. She gave the audience the description she had given me seven days earlier: "He is kind, he is friendly, he tries to help people who need help, who ask for help." Then, she began to move the interview in another direction: "So I think everybody ought to just stop a minute here and think about what we're doing. I'm very concerned about the tactics that are being used and the kind of intense political agenda at work here."

"I want to ask about Ken Starr in a second," Lauer interjected.

After a few more questions, Hillary turned the interview back to the investigation: "This is what concerns me. This started out as an investi-gation of a failed land deal. I told everybody in 1992, 'We lost money.' People said, 'It's not true, you know, they made money. They have money in a Swiss bank account.' Well, it was true. It's taken years, but it

*Brill, "Pressgate," p. 143.

was true. We get a politically motivated prosecutor who is allied with the right-wing opponents of my husband, who had literally spent four years looking at every telephone—"

"Spent $30 million," said Lauer.

"—More than that now. But looking at every telephone call we've made, every check we've ever written, scratching for dirt, intimidating witnesses, doing everything possible to try to make some accusation against my husband."

"We're talking about Kenneth Starr," said Lauer, "so let's use his name, because he is the independent counsel."

"But it's the whole operation. It's not just one person. It's an entire operation." Asked about James Carville's remark that there was a "war" between the Independent Counsel and the President's friends, Hillary replied:

> I do believe that this is a battle. I mean, look at the very people who are involved in this, they have popped up in other settings. This is the great story here, for anybody who is willing to find it and write about it and explain it, this vast right-wing conspiracy that has been conspiring against my husband since the day he announced for president. A few journalists have kind of caught on to it and explained it, but it has not yet been fully revealed to the American public. And, actually, you know, in a bizarre sort of way, this may do it.

For years, most of the press had given short shrift to the dynamic behind the political attacks on the Clintons. Now Hillary made it front and center. Her phrase—"this vast right-wing conspiracy"—had an electrifying effect. For our adversaries, it became a point to deride and dismiss as though it were fiction. But it galvanized those who wanted to defend the Democratic president, it forced the media to respond to her challenge, and it stunned the right and Starr. Immediately, the "vast right-wing conspiracy" entered the political lexicon and debate. A week later, a Washington Post/ABC News poll showed that 59 percent believed that "Clinton's political enemies are conspiring to bring down his presidency."*

Starr released a written statement hours after the interview: "The First Lady today accused this Office of being part of a 'vast right-wing

*Richard Morin and Claudia Deane, "President's Popularity Hits a High," *The Washington Post*, February 1, 1998.

conspiracy.' That is nonsense. Our current investigation began when we received credible evidence of serious federal crimes. We promptly informed Attorney General [Janet] Reno, and she determined that the allegations merited further investigation."

Michael Isikoff and Evan Thomas, a few weeks later, compared Hillary's charge to McCarthyism. "Hillary Clinton's conspiracy theory has a familiar echo," they wrote. "It is a reminder of the postwar years, when many Americans feared that the United States was being undermined by a communist plot. 'A conspiracy on a scale so immense,' in the famous words of Sen. Joe McCarthy, the right-wing demagogue who led a nationwide witch hunt in the early 1950s."*

George Conway, for his part, went temporarily on the lam. As soon as he learned that a process server with a subpoena had turned up at his law office, he disappeared for a while without a forwarding address or telephone number. He knew he had only to remain hidden until January 28, when the discovery period in the Jones case closed, and he needed to avoid testifying about his covert activities.

On January 28, the day after Hillary made her remark about the "vast right-wing conspiracy," the reporting began. Conway's identity was unmasked in two articles: Joe Conason, in *The New York Observer*, detailed Conway's role in the Jones case and had Drudge naming Conway as one of his sources.† Jill Abramson and Tim Weiner wrote in *The New York Times*:

> While no proof has been offered to support Hillary Rodham Clinton's allegations that a "vast right-wing conspiracy" is behind the accusations of sexual impropriety imperiling her husband's Presidency, several figures in the case against President Clinton have common ties in conservative groups and causes.
>
> Monica S. Lewinsky's alleged account of a sexual relationship with the President were steered to the Whitewater independent counsel, Kenneth W. Starr, by two lawyers, George T. Conway 3d of New York and James A. Moody of Washington, who have been active in conservative causes. Mr. Starr himself has been active in some of the same causes and groups. . . . Mr. Conway, a behind-the-scenes figure in Paula Corbin

---

*Michael Isikoff and Evan Thomas, "Monica Isn't the First Skirmish," *Newsweek*, February 29, 1998.

†Joe Conason, "What Did Kenneth Starr Know About the Lewinsky Tapes," *The New York Observer*, February 2, 1998.

Jones's sex harassment case against the President, referred Linda R. Tripp, who tape-recorded Ms. Lewinsky's accusations against the President, to Mr. Moody on Jan. 9. Three days later she went to Mr. Starr, who himself has been active in conservative legal causes and once considered writing a brief in support of the Jones lawsuit.

Like Mr. Starr, Mr. Moody and Mr. Conway are members of the Federalist Society, a legal organization in Washington that is composed of a few hundred conservative lawyers and judges.*

The President rehearsed his speech for the final time. Sections were rearranged, words polished. Then there was nothing more to do. That night, the staff gathered in the Diplomatic Reception Room before we raced out into the freezing rain to clamber into the vans for the motorcade to the Capitol. Red lights whirring, flags fluttering on the President's car, we slowly drove up Pennsylvania Avenue. The last I saw of the President before we went into the House, he was preternaturally calm. We hustled in a long line through the corridors and up staircases. Rather than sit in an anteroom, watching on television, I preferred to stand on the floor of the Congress, at the rear, behind the rows of foreign ambassadors, to see for myself. The nervousness of the Democrats milling in the chamber was palpable, just as was the smugness of the Republicans. Then they all took their seats. The sergeant at arms flung open the door at the back and shouted, "The President of the United States!" I felt like a Union soldier on Little Round Top before the battle of Gettysburg.

Clinton marched down the aisle to respectful applause. He mounted the podium, shook hands with Speaker Gingrich, faced the Congress, and spoke:

For 209 years, it has been the President's duty to report to you on the state of the union. Because of the hard work and high purpose of the American people, these are good times for America. We have more than 14 million new jobs, the lowest unemployment in twenty-four years, the lowest core inflation in thirty years, incomes are rising, and we have the highest home ownership in history. Crime has dropped for a record five

*Tim Weiner and Jill Abramson, "The President Under Fire: The Actors; In the Case Against Clinton, Some Links to Conservatives," *The New York Times*, January 28, 1998.

years in a row, and the welfare rolls are at their lowest levels in twenty-seven years. Our leadership in the world is unrivaled. Ladies and gentlemen, the state of our union is strong.

The achievements were undeniable. The Democrats clapped loudly. Clinton set the scene:

Rarely have Americans lived through so much change in so many ways in so short a time. Quietly, but with gathering force, the ground has shifted beneath our feet as we have moved into an information age, a global economy, a truly new world.

For five years now, we have met the challenge of these changes as Americans have at every turning point in our history, by renewing the very idea of America, widening the circle of opportunity, deepening the meaning of our freedom, forging a more perfect union. . . .

We have moved past the sterile debate between those who say government is the enemy and those who say government is the answer. My fellow Americans, we have found a third way. We have the smallest government in thirty-five years, but a more progressive one. We have a smaller government but a stronger nation.

Then:

For three decades, six presidents have come before you to warn of the damage deficits pose to our nation. Tonight, I come before you to announce that the federal deficit, once so incomprehensively large that it had eleven zeros, will be simply zero.

The Democrats' applause was tumultuous. Then:

Now, if we balance the budget for next year, it is projected that we'll then have a sizeable surplus in the years that immediately follow. What should we do with this projected surplus?

Clinton paused, and then:

I have a simple four-word answer: Save Social Security first.

The Democrats roared, an animal roar.

Tonight, I propose that we reserve 100 percent of the surplus—that's every penny of any surplus—until we have taken all the necessary measures to strengthen the Social Security system for the twenty-first century.

The Democrats kept cheering and even Speaker Gingrich, seated behind the President, slowly rose to join in the applause so that the Republicans wouldn't become isolated and damaged by the President's proposal. Following in perfect sequence, Clinton then said:

In an economy that honors opportunity, all Americans must be able to reap the rewards of prosperity. Because these times are good, we can afford to take one simple, sensible step to help millions of workers struggling to provide for their families. We should raise the minimum wage.

The Democrats were on their feet, clapping and shouting and laughing. And Clinton went on, issue after issue—education (new college scholarships for all), making the difficult case for free trade, for child care (a tribute to Hillary), for a patients' bill of rights, demanding support for the U.S. mission in Bosnia, for paying our United Nations dues, calling for inspection of Saddam Hussein's weapons of mass destruction, for clean water, a program to deal with global warming, more funding to combat racial discrimination, more funding for medical research against diseases—and a tribute to the upcoming space flight of Senator John Glenn—"Godspeed, John Glenn!" Then, the peroration, an invocation of the original Star Spangled Banner, being preserved through the White House Millennium Program: "A tattered flag, its broad stripes and bright stars still gleaming through the smoke of a fierce battle."

We burst back into the White House and ran up the stairs to the State Dining Room, where the rest of the staff and a couple hundred supporters welcomed us. The President clasped his hands above his head to raucous cheering. The polls were already rolling in: Support for the President's speech was above 80 percent.

Across town, David Brock was watching the State of the Union at Laura Ingraham's, along with Alex Azar and Bret Kavanaugh, a conservative lawyer who had served on Starr's independent counsel staff and would soon return to coauthor the Starr Report. (He would become deputy legal counsel to President George W. Bush.) When the camera focused on Hillary, Kavanaugh muttered at the television screen, "Bitch."

"Both Bret and Alex are talking to Starr's office constantly," Brock told me. "Bret said Monica is not singing. Whatever proffer was made is not what they want." Lewinsky was refusing to state that the President or Vernon Jordan had asked her to lie. "Starr is very mad at Hillary Clinton. They're concerned from seeing the polling," said Brock. "There are twenty lawyers in his office. He's huddled with four of them, who know nothing about the case, who are worried about the public relations."

By now, the White House legal counsel's office had received subpoenas for Bruce Lindsey, a deputy counsel and the President's oldest and closest friend on the staff, and Lanny Breuer, a lawyer from Covington and Burling whom Ruff had recruited to the White House staff. It was a signal that Starr would invade the President's inner circle, trying to strip him of protection of his attorneys, and that he would give no quarter. Ruff now believed that the assault on the White House would be total. Starr would wage war to the end.

The next morning, daily meetings in Chuck's office commenced with the political and legal teams synchronizing strategy. Lewinsky's immunity talks with Starr were continuing and subpoenas were flooding in. I was also preoccupied with preparations for another imminent event: Tony Blair was to arrive at the White House. There were many decisions to be made, many messages to send, not all of them political and diplomatic. Capricia Marshall, the social secretary, asked me what I thought of Stevie Wonder playing with Elton John at the state dinner.

ELEVEN

In Starr's Chamber

I

Starr's grand jury was convened on the day of the State of the Union address. His office shot off subpoenas to White House officials, including the President's lawyers, and to Secret Service agents on the President's detail, and to Vernon Jordan, and to Monica Lewinsky's girlfriends, former boyfriends, former lawyer, therapists, and mother.

The grand jury was developed in England in the fourteenth century as a legal proceeding that would take the place of the secret and repressive royal star chamber, which was finally prohibited in 1641. But grand-jury abuse by prosecutors led to its abolition in Britain in 1933. In the United States, the federal grand juries were enshrined in the Fifth Amendment as a protection against governmental coercion. Through this intervening form of citizen authority, the hand of arbitrary government was to be stayed. Yet, though intended as a check on unlimited prosecutorial power, the grand jury, as in Britain, became the prosecutor's instrument. It can function as his arena, cockpit, bandstand. It receives only the information the prosecutor selects, which does not have to be confirmed or proved according to the rules of evidence obtaining in a courtroom. The grand jury hears only witnesses called by the prosecutor, and no lawyers for the witnesses are allowed in the room. There is no judge. The grand jury decides whether to bring indictments only at the prosecutor's prompting, on the reasonable suspicion that a crime may have been committed—the level of suspicion being within the prosecutor's adjustable control. If the prosecutor doesn't like his grand jury, he can convene a new one. He can use the grand jury to indict a ham sandwich, as the courthouse expression has it.

Ken Starr had been granted his authority for an expanded investigation. He had a budget of unlimited funds. He had prosecutors, FBI agents, and private investigators. For all intents and purposes, he had no authority exercising oversight over his work. That was why he was the *independent* counsel.

He also had a retinue of reporters at his call. Of course, it is against the law for a federal prosecutor to leak information that is or might be used in a grand jury. The Federal Code of Criminal Procedure 6(e) strictly forbids that sort of disclosure by a prosecutor or anyone associated with his apparatus. Witnesses are free to speak about their own testimony, but this is rare because they fear punitive retribution. They can always be turned into ham sandwiches. But Starr's men had been leaking for years in their slog across the marshes of Whitewater. Starr's grand-jury chamber became an echo chamber by virtue of his influence over the press. Within the grand-jury room his prosecutors ruled unchallenged, and by using the grand-jury process—dragooning witnesses and leaking information or surmise about them—Starr now dominated Washington.

Starr had believed that Clinton would be gone within days of the story about Monica Lewinsky breaking. He was unprepared for any response other than swift capitulation. And he was enraged at the First Lady for labeling him political, for urging the press to cover the "vast right-wing conspiracy," and for remaining loyal to her husband. He was incensed that the President's popularity had increased rather than collapsed after the State of the Union address, and he was exasperated by news articles that described him as anything other than righteous. He still had no evidence to prove the criminal case he had trumpeted through *The Washington Post* on January 21—no evidence that Vernon Jordan had obstructed justice or suborned perjury, nor that the President had done so. Nonetheless, he believed he would somehow prevail. After all, Starr had the grand jury.

The Office of Independent Counsel was opaque to us at the White House. What little we knew we gleaned from the spare contacts the President's lawyers had with the prosecutors—and from press accounts, which Starr's office leaked. It was like looking into a black pool. As I was writing this book, however, I encountered a prosecutor from Starr's office who explained to me what happened within it: its personnel, its political complexion, its operations, its conflicts, and Starr's actions. The firsthand account of this participant verifies much that many of us in the White House only supposed about Starr's office and contradicts published accounts of various crucial episodes written by reporters to whom Starr leaked partial information.

I also had extended on-the-record conversations with Samuel Dash, who was Starr's ethics counselor until he quit during the impeachment. Dash had been the majority counsel for the House Judiciary Committee during the Watergate investigation and a principal proponent of the Independent Counsel Act. He was a professor at the Georgetown Law Center when Starr asked him in late 1994 to act as ethics counselor. He spent perhaps a couple of days a week at the office, attended staff meetings, and spoke regularly with Starr; though he was not there every day, he had access to all the prosecution memos on all matters from the beginning.

Starr established an atmosphere that was contemptuous of the President. Some of the prosecutors were professional lawyers who regarded sex as irrelevant to their work. They believed they were there to investigate white-collar crime. But those in charge regarded Clinton as morally unfit to hold his office. For them anything to get at Clinton was fair game. "There was a general animosity toward Clinton," I was told. "This was fueled by frustration by not getting anywhere, dead ends on other investigations. So we had to see who he is screwing." Their moral indignation and Republican politics could not be disentangled from their prosecutorial work. "I saw decisions made on moral grounds that had nothing to do with criminal grounds," Dash told me. "They believed that someone was a bad person, a sinful person, who ought to be punished for it. They distorted their judgment. Ken allowed his personal concepts of morality to interfere with the role of a prosecutor."

According to Sam Dash, Starr "could have rounded up" his initial investigation within two years of his appointment, "by 1996 or 1997. On all the issues involving the White House, fairly early he had enough information to conclude." Dash carefully reviewed the prosecution memos in each and every case: Whitewater, Susan McDougal, Webster Hubbell, the White House Travel Office, the FBI files. "They had nothing," he told me. "But they were under the impression that there was a lot of lying and cover-up and they couldn't put their finger on it. That was why they pursued Susan McDougal and Web Hubbell. They pursued McDougal I think unfairly. I was vehemently opposed." But Starr did not listen to his ethics counselor. "Even with Hubbell, it was wrong constantly to pursue him." Once again, Starr ignored Dash's advice. "Even though early on they knew they didn't have enough evidence, they believed they would get those facts. It was furthered by this assumption that there was crime here. They continued to believe it. The delay, the time it took for them to finish up their job was really because they believed that we didn't have the evidence. My view was, Why don't you announce it and close shop?"

Far from closing shop, Starr's office was expanding its work. The prosecutors' sense of mastery after they broke the Monica Lewinsky story became an almost intoxicated belief in their own omnipotence. Swagger and supremacy were raised to ultimate virtues. Within the office, Jackie Bennett, Starr's deputy, promulgated a cult of toughness. He and his closest allies called themselves the "Likud faction," after the hard-line, right-wing Israeli political party, and dubbed others who did not always share their unbending fervor "commie wimps." They posted a chart in the office with "Likud" written above their names at the top and "Commie Wimps" at the bottom, beneath which were listed those who had not attained their plateau. In staff conferences, the soft-spoken Starr made a point of stressing the word "toughness."* He would not be a "commie wimp."

Jackie Bennett was "a crazed hard charger," according to my source, and "fascinated with the President's sex life." He had grabbed onto sex as a means of getting Clinton and had been using private investigators to conduct sex hunts for almost a year. "It was whatever worked." When Bob Woodward's article about Starr's sexual pursuit of Clinton was published in *The Washington Post* in June 1997, a prosecutor who was not privy to Bennett's work asked Starr if it was true. "He said it was not happening." Yet Starr publicly admitted at the impeachment hearing before the House Judiciary Committee that it had been happening. Reading Woodward's article, Sam Dash also asked Starr about it: "The response I got was, 'We're not looking into the sex life of the President. We're looking into persons who may have information. We're trying to identify them on Whitewater and things of that nature.' I accepted that."

Bennett was the chief leaker—"leaking to reporters constantly," a prosecutor told me—and had a hierarchy of favorites in the press whose careers had become reliant on him. He was especially "sweet" on Susan Schmidt at *The Washington Post*. Starr assured Dash that he was investigating for the source of the leaks and asked Dash if he wanted to do so as well. Dash explained that that was not his job. "I was constantly told by Ken and his staff that they weren't leaking," he told me. The leaks went on.

*Toobin, *A Vast Conspiracy*, p. 271.

Jackie Bennett also acted as a secret liaison to the Republicans in the Congress, and he met regularly with David Bossie, now working for Representative Dan Burton. A prosecutor who was present told me that under a gigantic poster in Bossie's Capitol Hill office, which showed members of the Clinton administration with a red "No" sign slashed through their photographs, Bennett and Bossie coordinated congressional Republican politics and investigations with Starr's work: "Bennett and Bossie talked a lot. They seemed to know each other very well." Starr was kept informed, but Dash was in the dark.

Around Bennett formed a tight group that included another deputy, Bob Bittman, nicknamed "Bulldog" and "Maximum Bob." Perhaps the most partisan Republican in an office filled with partisan Republicans, Bittman was Starr's pet. "Ken loved Bittman," I was told. A "shameless self-promoter," he had never prosecuted a case before. (His father, William Bittman, had been E. Howard Hunt's attorney in the Watergate affair and had accepted the money from Nixon's slush fund for the Plumbers.) Sol Wisenberg, who had worked for the Justice Department in Washington under Attorney General Edwin Meese and in Texas (with Bennett) during the presidency of George H. W. Bush, claimed to be the head of his own political organization, which he called Southern Agrarian Reactionary Jews. His colleagues termed him "the most conservative Jew in America." He was gruff, unyielding, and hostile when challenged.

The chief of the "Arkansas phase" of Starr's investigation, Hickman Ewing, the avenging rider of the Gothic South, was still in Little Rock. For years, Starr had allowed Ewing a long leash to run rampant through Arkansas. Some other prosecutors working on Whitewater came to believe that Ewing was prolonging his investigations because he had no other viable career. There was "nothing there, just dead ends," one prosecutor told me. The "sad case" of Webster Hubbell was just "a guy spending to impress his wife and father-in-law." Starr kept filing charges against Hubbell in an effort to flip him against the Clintons, but the career prosecutors believed he was not being "bribed" to remain silent on Whitewater; the fact was that he knew "nothing." Though Starr had used Vernon Jordan's financial support of Hubbell as a key argument in winning an expansion of his probe into Lewinsky—the argument on which he had rested his new authority—prosecutors in his office working on the Hubbell case believed that the point had no merit. Hubbell, they had concluded, was "a charity case." Pursuing him was "going nowhere," and indicting him the second time was "stupid and unfair." Yet going after

Hubbell sustained the fiction that there were still unresolved Whitewater matters and the Clintons might be obstructing justice.

Ewing joined the OIC team on the speakerphone from Arkansas and occasionally came to Washington meetings; he was always taking an "aggressive" stance, according to Dash. But even Starr came to recognize his "limitations," a prosecutor told me. Starr's inexperience and Ewing's antagonism to Clinton had combined to give Ewing free rein in Arkansas after Robert Fiske's lawyers had left the independent counsel's office, but now Starr's trust resided with Jackie Bennett, Bittman, and the others like them in Washington.

The career prosecutors, however, saw things narrowly as just another case and did not grasp the Independent Counsel's political agendas. They were unaware—and kept unaware—of the clandestine dinner meeting in Philadelphia on January 8 between their colleague Paul Rosenzweig and his old college chums the elves—Conway, Porter, and Marcus—about Lewinsky. Nor was Dash notified of these connections. "I didn't know about the elves," Dash told me. "I knew about some allegations that some of these lawyers and Ken's staff were together and conspiring about this. I raised those issues. They insisted that they had no contact with them, that Linda Tripp came to them without prior knowledge. Those were the answers I got—right around that time. That's what I was told." But Starr's office later admitted that it was at this secret meeting that arrangements began for Tripp to walk in their front door.

And that, too, may have been a cover story for collusion. "Jackie Bennett told me a few weeks beforehand that something was in the works, something big brewing—two to three weeks before," one prosecutor told me. "He had to be referring to this. On the ninth, they went to Tripp's house in Maryland. I remember Bennett saying it more than once. I heard it twice—from Bennett himself."

The career lawyers were aware that Starr had filled the office with men who were former clerks of conservative justices on the Supreme Court and members of the Washington chapter of the Federalist Society. Within the office, these young conservatives openly held forth, "pontificating on things that had nothing to do with the practice of criminal law," as my source said.

Ken Starr's manner was earnest, courteous, and deferential. "One of Starr's problems was that he had never been a federal prosecutor," Dash told me. "He lacked the judgment and even the understanding of the role of the federal prosecutor. So he delegated to these very aggressive prosecutors. Part of my role was to tell him that he was going too far or inappropriate. I said they were not relying on any code of ethics. They wanted to win. They don't have the brakes on them that prosecutors ought to have. His very innocent response was that he was relying on his federal prosecutors."

When Dash took the job, he received an assurance from Starr. Dash said, "He was a partisan Republican. I really believed him when he said when he undertook it he said he could push that all aside."

"It was clear," said a prosecutor, "that this was a mean-spirited, politically motivated investigation. Was Ken naïvely manipulated? Now I don't think he was naïve at all. He was just prolonging the pain to keep Clinton on the ropes. To that degree he was enormously successful. He was incredibly political. Ken is capable of saying anything so long as you don't have him on tape."

Starr was "usually indecisive," and under pressure from those who claimed to be tougher and more resolutely conservative, he would usually cave in. He was often on the phone with Republican politicians. "He used to talk to the governor of Oklahoma"—Republican Frank Keating—"all the time." And he spent much of his time with his door closed, which to the prosecutors meant that he was on the phone.

He prized his reputation above all. When Starr found himself suddenly a subject of criticism, he "felt he was trapped," a prosecutor told me. "He was obsessed with public relations." Every day the prosecutors were given a packet of media accounts of the investigation from around the country—"three inches thick." "He read a great deal of it. He was very conscious of how it would impact on his career."

On January 29, Starr filed a motion before Judge Wright in Arkansas to stop Paula Jones's lawyers from subpoenaing OIC witnesses. In the motion he reduced the Jones case to insignificance in comparison to his own work: "The criminal matter raises issues of the gravest concern, and their resolution may moot many of the discovery questions pending." In short, he believed that the President's criminality would quickly be proved. What would be "moot" was Clinton. Judge Wright thereupon severed Monica Lewinsky—who up to now had been a potential witness in a potential Paula Jones trial—from the Jones case. This certainly proved her irrelevance to it, but her fate was now entirely up to Starr.

For two weeks, Starr's office had been negotiating a proffer from Monica Lewinsky—an offer of what she would testify to in return for immunity from prosecution—and how Starr mishandled this negotiation determined the course of events over the year to come. He discarded a swift, professional resolution, which would have concluded there would be no charges of criminality, in favor of a politicized sexual dragnet.

Face-to-face, Starr authorized two prosecutors, Bruce Udolf and Michael Emmick, to secure Lewinsky's proffer. On January 19, in the prosecutors' first meeting with Lewinsky's lawyer, William Ginsburg, Lewinsky refused to say that the President and Vernon Jordan had asked her to lie. Udolf suggested subjecting her to a lie detector test. Jackie Bennett shouted, "No! I don't trust her. . . . She needs to fear us."*

On February 2, Emmick and Udolf concluded a final agreement for Lewinsky's proffer in exchange for immunity. It stipulated that she would have to take a lie detector test, and Udolf had already lined up an expert to administer it. Lewinsky's proffer stated that she had had an "intimate" relationship with Clinton and that neither he nor Jordan had ever asked her to dissemble. The first point read, "Ms. Lewinsky had an intimate and emotional relationship with President Clinton beginning in 1995. At various times between 1995 and 1997, Ms. Lewinsky and the President had physically intimate contact. This included oral sex but excluded intercourse." Point 10 read: "Ms. L had a physically intimate relationship with the President. Neither the Pres. nor Mr. Jordan (or anyone on their behalf) asked or encouraged Ms. L to lie. Ms. L was comfortable signing the affidavit with regard to the 'sexual relationship' because she could justify to herself that she and the Pres. did not have sexual intercourse."

Were he to accept this proffer and grant immunity to Monica Lewinsky, Starr would also be accepting that the criminal actions which he had alleged in order to expand his probe, and which now had the entire nation in suspense, were chimerical. He would have nothing but a sad little sex story.

The draft of this proffer was faxed to Lewinsky's lawyer on February 2. Under usual circumstances, the draft would constitute what the prosecutor was agreeing to. But now, though Starr had authorized it, he reversed himself. Bennett and the others had gotten to him with talk of "toughness." He sent Bittman to sit with Udolf and Emmick while they concluded their negotiation with Ginsburg by speakerphone. Bennett and Wisenberg also eavesdropped. Bennett exploded. Agreeing to the proffer was "a sign of weakness," he said dismissively, and Wisenberg threatened to resign if Starr accepted it. "You knew what your marching

---

*Susan Schmidt and Michael Weisskopf, *Truth at Any Cost: Ken Starr and the Unmaking of Bill Clinton*, HarperCollins, 2000, p. 52.

orders were," Bennett yelled at Udolf and Emmick, "and you went beyond it because you didn't give a rat's ass. We're not going to do it."

For an entire day and night a battle royal raged among the OIC prosecutors over the proffer. Udolf and Emmick believed there was nothing more to be gained from Lewinsky. She was a "little girl stupidly in love" who would not implicate Clinton and Jordan. Udolf and Emmick were both experienced prosecutors; they had seen many cases, including cases that had gone awry. According to my source, they did not think there was a case against the President; they both vehemently opposed prosecuting Lewinsky; and both gave long, passionate speeches. Lewinsky could be charged only with a technical crime, and the prosecutor would lose. By granting her immunity, the prosecutor could determine within days if there was any evidence to support a broader case; if there wasn't any, as it seemed there wouldn't be, he could and should drop it. Udolf said, "The prosecution of Monica Lewinsky would be ridiculous." Starr took offense. Udolf went on, "In Communist China they have show trials. In the United States of America we don't have show trials." Starr was even more offended. Udolf argued that what Starr was going after was not an indictable offense, not a case that could be won. It would create months of adverse publicity but be only destructive. It would tear the country apart. It would lead to a failed impeachment. Udolf and Emmick made plain that they were not there to investigate the private life of the President. They appealed to professionalism and honor: What was important was how the prosecutors spoke to each other as lawyers. When you give your word, you have a deal. Giving your word conveys a legal and moral obligation.

Starr, assuming his mantle as judge, issued his decision: "Different cultures esteem different values. In the Japanese culture, honor is the most important virtue. If you are dishonored, that's the end. In my Christian culture, faith is the highest value. But in my professional life, the value I esteem above all is truth. Honor or not, this statement isn't the truth."*

But it *was* the truth. Starr, however, was looking for a different truth. He had faith that there had been obstruction of justice. Therefore he could not believe the truth. In the conflict between truth and faith, his faith won.

---

*Schmidt and Weisskopf, *Truth at Any Cost*, p. 85. *Truth at Any Cost* is a semi-authorized account based on interviews with Starr and Bennett. It does not report Starr's authorization of Udolf and Emmick's negotiation or his denial to them afterward that he had done so.

Udolf was so disgusted that he refused to sign the letter rescinding the proffer. Bittman was left to perform the task. Bennett screamed invective at Udolf. Then Starr said to Udolf and Emmick that he had never authorized their negotiation of a proffer. With that, they were set adrift. Having claimed that he had never commissioned them—a falsehood that must somehow have redeemed his notion of his own integrity—Starr continued to pursue the President with his other assistants. The "Likud faction" was triumphant.

That same day, Charles Ruff and Lanny Breuer visited Starr in his office in a final effort at reason. Ruff asked Starr to respect executive privilege and not to subpoena the President's lawyers. (Subpoenas had already been issued to Breuer and to Bruce Lindsey.) The next day, Starr sent a letter saying that he intended to subpoena the White House staff. Less than an hour after receiving this document, Ruff was telephoned by a reporter at *The New York Times* asking about it; he seemed to have full knowledge of the letter's contents. Ruff had not solicited the call, so only Starr's office could have leaked the letter. Ruff filed a complaint with the FBI. Soon Starr hauled Breuer before the grand jury.*

Within the White House, none of us, neither the political staff nor the legal team, knew about the acrimony within Starr's office. Nor did any of us know the actual content of Lewinsky's proffer. We would not know it until September, when it was made public after she had made her later proffer, which did not differ from the earlier one except that it did not require a lie detector test—despite the misleading publicity put out by Starr's office that it had been wrung out of her at last. In other words, Starr tossed out in February what he then received in July, 176 days later.

The news reports in July made it seem as if it had been not the outlander Bill Ginsburg but the two seasoned Washington lawyers, Plato Cacheris and Jacob Stein, with their canny understanding of the way things really work, who finally got Lewinsky to cooperate. In fact, her story remained unchanged from what it was in February. She stood her ground on what she knew to be the truth. She wasn't to be bullied by Starr's threats against herself or her family.

Monica Lewinsky was stronger than anyone around her—and she had a stronger sense of justice. But when Starr accepted her proffer in July, unveiling it as a revelation, she was compelled to give humiliatingly intimate testimony that could only be demeaning—graphic details that

*Schmidt and Weisskopf, *Truth at Any Cost*, pp. 90–91.

satisfied, if not gratified, the prosecutor, but that lacked legal necessity.

In the White House, we were operating on bits and pieces of information—half-truths, rumors, tips—and it was difficult if not impossible to sift the facts from the fiction. The press serving Starr presented disinformation without a grain of skepticism. On February 5, Susan Schmidt wrote in the *Post* that "according to sources with knowledge of the investigation," Lewinsky's proffer was "not solid enough to form the basis of an agreement because it contained inconsistencies and contradictions. Lewinsky acknowledged having a sexual relationship with President Clinton in the statement, the sources said, but she gave a muddled account of whether she was urged to lie about that relationship to lawyers in the Paula Jones sexual harassment suit."* In fact, Lewinsky's proffer was not inconsistent or contradictory, and her account that neither Clinton nor Jordan had asked her to lie was not muddled but straightforward, precisely why Starr rejected it.

A little more than three months later, on May 16, Schmidt reported a supposedly new wrinkle in the rejected proffer story: it had been rejected "because the offered testimony contained no information about a central piece of evidence in the Lewinsky probe—the so-called talking points she allegedly gave to Linda R. Tripp, the erstwhile friend who secretly taped hours of conversation with Lewinsky. The three pages of talking points coached Tripp about what to say to lawyers for Paula Jones when she gave a deposition in Jones's sexual harassment suit against the president."† But the prosecutors had not asked Lewinsky to explain Tripp's note in her proffer. Instead, Starr used the Talking Points to mesmerize the press into suggesting that the guilty composer of them was hiding in the White House. The Talking Points were a recurring prop in his shadow play.

On February 5, Starr held a press conference to justify his rejection of Lewinsky's proffer. "We want the truth," he said. "We want all the truth. We want it completely, accurately. And we will satisfy ourselves that we're getting the truth. And that is the absolute, bedrock point. We want the truth."

Starr and his office clung to the belief that the Clintons were devious criminal conspirators. "I think it was consistent throughout the office,"

---

*Susan Schmidt and Peter Baker, "Starr Rejects Proposal on Lewinsky Testimony," *The Washington Post*, February 5, 1998.

†Susan Schmidt, "Appeals Court Rejects Lewinsky's Immunity Pact Claim," *The Washington Post*, May 16, 1998.

Sam Dash said to me. "Ken ultimately believed it himself. They said, [the Clintons are] powerful, they can cover up, they're pressuring people to lie. We're going to stay on it until we get it. It was a hypothesis." But Starr had no evidence that the Clintons were obstructing justice. "From time to time," said Dash, "I would sit at a staff meeting, and a prosecutor would present all the evidence. I would get a copy of it before the meeting, and they were talking it up as though they had something of value. They had nothing. I said, 'Zero plus zero plus zero equals zero.' I was advising they didn't have it. My view constantly was that if you don't have it, it may not be there, and your job is over." But Starr didn't listen. And when his investigation expanded to Lewinsky, his methods and assumptions remained the same.

Starr's assumption of the Clintons' guilt was not different fundamentally from that of other Clinton haters or, for that matter, from that of the scandal-beat press corps. What separated him from the unwashed masses of Rush Limbaugh's Dittoheads was not that he was prim rather than vulgar, not that he believed that his integrity and piety could not be challenged, but that he controlled a grand jury. Starr had the instrument to compel his logic.

From the beginning, Starr hurtled toward the President's impeachment by using the grand jury to prosecute symbolic offenses. He was his own runaway train. He claimed to be throwing up caution signs while he was stoking the engine with coal. Starr believed that Susan McDougal was lying, Web Hubbell was lying, and Monica Lewinsky was lying. But he had no legal strategy beyond a hope that somehow, someone, somewhere, would materialize to prove his case against the President. He would subpoena witnesses, tell the story as he wished it to be told by leaks to the press, mobilize public disgust and anger at his target, drive his target into a corner, instigate the filing of articles of impeachment, and *then* hope there was a case. "They thought they'd have this daily show of people coming in and out of the grand jury, milking it for all it was worth," I was told. "The case wasn't going to get stronger."

Robert W. Gordon, professor at the Yale Law School, observed about Starr, the unstoppable prosecutor:

He cranked up the machinery of the criminal process, spent millions of taxpayer dollars, fed a major national scandal, and hauled the President of the United States before a grand jury, in order to catch a civil party in a lie that was not central to Paula Jones's case but so peripheral to it as to be almost completely irrelevant, and which concerned underlying conduct that is not criminal at all. . . . It is a sure bet that no other prosecutor in the history of the republic has spent millions on a criminal investigation of an offense like Clinton's, a lie in a civil deposition about a consensual affair that was totally collateral to any issue of importance in the case.*

Ruff told Starr on February 3 that he assumed he was driving toward an impeachment, and Starr did not disagree. The outcome was foreordained. Once Starr managed to expand his probe, impeachment was inevitable. Anything less than an impeachment would be failure. Committed to a maximum legal case he did not have, he committed himself to the maximum political case. And it was inevitable that the Republican majority in the House would have to approve his referral, the report he would send to the House Judiciary Committee, and this would force a Senate trial. The political logic was ironclad. Starr engineered a process in which he was required to advance an unfounded criminal accusation against President Clinton in the brown-paper wrapper of a sex story. To gain leverage, he had to use the grand jury to squeeze from his witnesses information about sex. And the more Clinton was vindicated of criminal wrongdoing, the deeper Starr sank into sex in search of his "truth."

"He lacked a lot of judgment," Sam Dash told me. "Starr didn't see the difference between sin and crime. His judgments were distorted." Once on the sex trail, Starr sentenced himself to presenting sex from a certain angle through the peephole. Without proof of anything else, it became Starr's only way of making Clinton's position foul. It is the easiest and basest pornographic technique to depict sex—any sex, even between the happiest of married couples—as sordid by using graphic detail. Microscopic, clinical documentation removes the human element as it distances and alienates the viewer (or voyeur). Starr used this method to excite and repel simultaneously. Though he did not himself question a single witness before the grand jury, he personally dictated the compilation of sexual question upon sexual question.

Sex had been a label to explain a cluster of ideas and values that had upset Clinton's enemies for decades. He had always been a screen on which were projected conservative feelings about the 1960s, the counterculture, and race. Through it all, sex had been a tracer, a code. Clinton had been accused of miscegenation—an ancient and recurrent theme in

---

*Robert W. Gordon, "Imprudence and Partisanship: Starr's OIC and the Clinton-Lewinsky Affair," *Fordham Law Review*, Vol. 68, 1999, pp. 665–67.

racist Southern politics—from the start of his career. In politics, sex is rarely just about sex. The prudish and pedantic Starr was setting off cultural depth charges.

Immediately after Hillary Clinton made her televised remark about the "vast right-wing conspiracy" on January 27, Starr negotiated to appear on CBS's *60 Minutes* to counterattack, but advisers convinced him he shouldn't expose himself on television and instead create favorable stories about himself and his office in the print media. "Deeply Christian Starr Starts Day Jogging, Singing Hymns" ran a front-page headline in *The Washington Times* on February 2. The paper held him up as a moral exemplar communing with God, but tarnished by immoral villains:

> "My favorite is going on a morning jog—real early," Mr. Starr told the Christian Business Men's Committee during a 1995 speech in Washington. "A two- to three-mile run which happily takes me—by my customary route—to a little park called Pimmit Run. . . . And I sing a hymn. And I sing it aloud. Sometimes I'm"—Mr. Starr pretends to be huffing and puffing—"but I sing it aloud. And then I offer a prayer. . . .
>
> "I was fortunate enough to be brought up in a Christian household that was very much committed to Christ as Lord and Savior," said Mr. Starr, who was raised in San Antonio, Texas. "My father a minister, a household that was quite devout."*

February 3, the day when Starr rejected Lewinsky's proffer and Ruff's entreaty, *The Washington Post* ran a long article headlined "Starr Warriors," about his unified squad. "In the eyes of many prosecutors, they are an all-star team," said the article. They were depicted as being held in "awe," proud of being called "unrelentingly aggressive" and "rough-and-tumble prosecutors." Hillary Clinton's suggestion that politics was involved in Starr's investigation was ridiculed: "Inside Starr's office and out, among prosecutors and defense lawyers alike, first lady Hillary Clinton's notion of a 'right-wing conspiracy' at the root of Starr's investigation strikes lawyers as laughable. Because with rare exceptions, criminal lawyers say, what drives prosecutors is not ideology but the hunt." The article went on to say that Starr's office was scrupulous, too, about leaking to the press: "Virtually all prosecutors' offices leak—prosecutors and the press have a quietly symbiotic relationship. Reporters covering the

*Bill Sammon, "Deeply Christian Starr Starts Day Jogging, Singing Hymns," *The Washington Times*, February 2, 1998.

Starr probe say the office is a typically difficult but sometimes forthcoming source. 'It's like chipping rocks,' says one reporter who covers the office."*

II

At four in the afternoon on February 4, the Washington bureau chief of *The Wall Street Journal*, a staid journalist named Alan Murray, pressed the button that put a report for the next day's paper onto the *Journal*'s Internet website. It asserted that the President's steward, Bayani Nelvis, had testified to the grand jury that he had seen Clinton and Lewinsky alone in the private study off the Oval Office and that he had discovered tissues with "lipstick and other stains." Within the hour, Murray was on CNBC to tout the scoop. *The Wall Street Journal*, as it happened, had just concluded an agreement with the network to provide on-air reporting talent. This pooling of media resources was called "synergy." Unfortunately, the paper had neglected to get a comment from the White House or Nelvis's attorney for its exclusive sex "sighting."

The *Journal*'s story, now electrifying the television-watching public, was untrue in every particular. Nelvis had not told it to the grand jury—and he had not told it at all. The next morning White House press secretary Michael McCurry denounced it as "the sleaziest episode in the history of American journalism." Nelvis's lawyer called it "absolutely false and irresponsible." A week later, the *Journal*'s managing editor issued a retraction and apology: "We deeply regret our erroneous report."†

Into this lightning storm flew Tony Blair. I had been working with 10 Downing Street and the National Security Council to organize an extended three-hour discussion on policy and politics between the President and the Prime Minister and members of both governments. The work had been going on ever since Hillary's visit at Chequers the previous fall, and it was a juggling act. I was also helping to choreograph Blair's visit to the FDR Memorial; write a joint radio address on Iraq to be taped in the Map Room, where Roosevelt and Churchill had planned strategy in the Second World War; brief the British team on the current

---

*Marc Fischer, "Starr Warriors: Behind the Special Prosecutor, a Battle-Hardened Brigade," *The Washington Post*, February 3, 1998.
†Kalb, *One Scandlous Story*, pp. 248–51; Brill, "Pressgate," p. 146.

political situation and help Blair for his joint press conference with Clinton; and assist Clinton's social secretary in compiling the list of guests for the state dinner. In between, I attended meetings in Ruff's office on the scandal.

Blair and his entourage landed in the afternoon on February 4. That evening, I hosted a dinner at a restaurant in Dupont Circle for the respective British and American policymakers. We had convivial conversations on serious subjects that only a gathering of dedicated wonks could manage. Our side was delighted to welcome our counterparts—at last, another government like us. The British were immensely pleased to be part of a Labour government paying its first visit to Washington and receiving such a warm reception. If anything marked the end of their wilderness years, this was it. From their own bitter experience, they were hardly naïve about being the targets of the slings and arrows of a scandal-obsessed press. Nonetheless, they were stunned by the ferocity of the struggle accelerated by a twenty-four-hour news cycle.

While we were all still dining at the restaurant, the media was quickening its scandal coverage. A report on NBC *Nightly News*, citing "sources in Starr's office" eight times, wheeled out the Talking Points to demonstrate that the prosecutor was closing in on his prey: "Sources in Starr's office and close to Linda Tripp say they believe the instructions came from the White House. If true, that could help support a case of obstruction of justice."

On February 5, the welcoming ceremony on the South Lawn—a twenty-one-gun salute, a march of soldiers in Revolutionary War uniforms to the music of bagpipes and fifes, preceded the one-on-one meeting—"the bilat"—between Blair and Clinton in the Oval Office. Much of their meeting was devoted to the delicate condition of negotiations and a potential settlement in Northern Ireland. Then, about twenty or so members of each government gathered in the Blue Room for an afternoon-long conference that we called White House I and the British called Chequers II.

At that conference Blair argued that through "one nation" and "one America" the center-left in Britain and the United States was redefining patriotism. Clinton proposed that the center-left had to win elections on more than economics; we needed to win on a concept of a new social contract. By stressing the web of connections among people, the cultural warfare of the right could be countered, though the right would use its media power to exploit every subtle cultural difference among various groups. The right, he said, was "mad for power," but we were "mad to achieve things and make them better." The President and the Prime Minister were equally determined to expand our new brand of center-left politics beyond the Anglo-American relationship. I and my counterpart, David Miliband, were charged with organizing a public conference that would draw in other governments. We set to work immediately.

For the state dinner that evening, we entered the White House through the East Gate, passing television cameras filming the arriving guests. Each guest, even those from the White House staff, was led up the marble staircase to the main reception room, where we all waited in a long line to greet the President and the First Lady, the Prime Minister and Cherie Blair. With handshakes, hugs, and quick jokes, the photographers snapping our pictures, we were ushered into the East Room to our seats beneath the portraits of George Washington and Theodore Roosevelt. The after-dinner toasts concluded, the guests moved to a tent specially constructed atop the walkway beside the Rose Garden, where Stevie Wonder and Elton John serenaded. Sometime before Stevie sang "You Are the Sunshine of My Life," a whisper passed through the rustling crowd, as the journalists among the guests—the ABC News anchor Peter Jennings, for example—received messages on their pagers that a major story would break the next morning in *The New York Times*. It would describe how the President, after his deposition, asked questions of his secretary Betty Currie about whether he had been alone with Lewinsky. As the guests buzzed about the impending scoop, the Marine Corps Band cranked up some Motown music and the President took to the dance floor with the First Lady. They rocked until one in the morning.

The article about Currie the next morning reported that the President's secretary had "told investigators" of her meeting with the President after his deposition on January 17. The article implied that he had asked her to lie, and that this might be part of his obstruction of justice and subornation of perjury. (At the time of their conversation, however, Starr had not yet expanded his probe, Currie had not been subpoenaed, and in any case Clinton did not ask her to do or say anything.) The details in the article, based on Currie's grand-jury testimony, did not come from Currie, her attorney, or the White House. They could have come only from the Office of Independent Counsel.

The afternoon of February 6, the President and the Prime Minister held their joint press conference. The first questioner asked the President not about Ireland and not about Anglo-American relations, but about what he had to say about Monica Lewinsky. "That's good. That's very good," said Clinton, and he turned to the next reporter. He was asked if he intended to resign. He replied, "Never!" Asked if he had tried to get Betty Currie to lie, he said he had not. Blair, when given the chance to say something, offered his support, calling Clinton "someone I could trust, someone I could rely upon, someone I am proud to call not just a colleague but a friend." Ten of the sixteen questions were about what the press saw as an unstoppable scandal. When he was asked about the "vast right-wing conspiracy," Clinton answered, "Now you know I've known her for a long time, the First Lady. And she's very smart. And she's hardly ever wrong about anything"—the reporters laughed—"but I don't believe I should amplify on her observation in this case."

Afterward, Clinton and Blair taped their joint radio address. The contrast between what the press was interested in and what the two heads of government wanted to talk about could not have been stronger. The speech was a warning to Saddam Hussein that he must permit United Nations inspectors into Iraq to determine whether he was building weapons of mass destruction, and that if he did not, the Allies would use armed force against him. The din about the scandal grew ever louder, even as President Clinton's deadly serious work on Iraq headed toward a possible military confrontation later in the year.

That same day, David Kendall, the President's attorney, sent a letter to Starr documenting fifty-two examples of illegal leaks from his office (seventeen of them to *The Washington Post*), and telling him that Kendall had filed a motion in federal court to find Starr in contempt. "In the past four years," wrote Kendall, "I have written you in confidence about the various leaks that have occurred from your office. I am making this letter public today because of the calculated tactic your office is now employing of selectively releasing both information and falsehoods, in an attempt to pressure, manipulate, and intimidate witnesses and possible witnesses, affect public opinion in your favor, and cause political harm to the President."

Within hours, Starr issued an angry rebuttal. He claimed that the press was "often misleading," that it had misattributed its sources, and that the stories in question might well have been leaked by the "President's defense attorneys," and he accused Kendall of making "reckless accusations," "media grandstanding," and "smearing" him.

Starr well knew that his office was a sieve, and he knew the precise identities of those doing the leaking. In his reply to Kendall, he had claimed that leaking was a "firing offense," but Starr was protesting what he encouraged. The utter silence of the press about this issue was a telling aspect of this mounting battle. If any party could report conclusively on the veracity of Kendall's complaint, it was those news organizations he cited as recipients of Starr's leaks. Understandably, the press does not willingly reveal its sources. But in this case the silence was especially noticeable. *The Washington Post*, for example, adopted a vague, passive voice: "Leaks happen, particularly in high-profile cases . . . there are so many potential sources of information."*

Numerous reporters, editors, and news producers freely told me of leaks they had received from Starr's office. Once, when I gave some information to a television network correspondent, explaining that of course she'd have to verify the material on her own, she said to me, "That's not how Starr's people do it. They give us everything. We don't have to do any work at all."

Starr's rejection of an immunity deal with Monica Lewinsky prompted more charges and countercharges. Her lawyer, William Ginsburg, claimed that on February 8 Starr leaked false stories that the prosecutors had witnesses who would contradict her on the obstruction of justice and subornation of perjury charges, and had tried to intimidate her family. (Dr. Bernard Lewinsky received threats that his tax records and medical practice would be investigated if his daughter didn't cooperate, I learned at the time from California friends who knew him and from the President's lawyers, who had been told independently.†) "They want us to say things that we can't say," said Ginsburg. "This is an orchestrated campaign." Starr had begun the campaign with the suddenness of a coup, but within weeks the struggle was being drawn out. Kendall's complaint threw Starr's method into turmoil, and his control over the story itself was being contested.

When Hillary Clinton had called for reporting on the "vast right-wing conspiracy," she was speaking with the knowledge of certain facts, and they were about to become public—the subpoenaing and temporary disappearance of George Conway being just one among them. "Persecuted or Paranoid?" read the headline in *Time* over a chart of "Hillary's Unified Theory."‡ "Conspiracy or Coincidence?" read the headline in *Newsweek* over a graphic depiction of the "tangled web" of what it labeled "Lewinsky players"; it showed a "conservative universe" that included Conway, James Moody, Lucianne Goldberg, Scaife, Drudge, Judge

---

*Ruth Marcus and Roberto Suro, "Punishing Leaks Is as Hard as Plugging Them," *The Washington Post*, February 7, 1998.

†See also Toobin, *A Vast Conspiracy*, p. 272.

‡Walter Kirn, "Persecuted or Paranoid?" *Time*, February 9, 1998.

David Sentelle, the Federalist Society, and the Rutherford Institute, all revolving around Starr. White House aides were spreading "ever more elaborate theories," it claimed, and were "busy adding baroque new details and retailing them to reporters. One White House insider, a colleague of his says, 'is over there on the grassy knoll.' "*

During the writing of the State of the Union address, Bob Shrum had mentioned to me that a former classmate of his from Georgetown University had called him to say he had valuable information about the Arkansas Project. So I telephoned Ralph "Bud" Lemley on January 31 at his office in Chicago. What I now learned from Bud Lemley confirmed everything David Brock had previously told me about the project.

Bud Lemley had inherited a financial management business from his father. Among the clients passed on to him was *The American Spectator* magazine, a small conservative publication produced in Bloomington, Indiana; the parents of its editor, R. Emmett Tyrrell, had been friends of Bud's father. So Bud took over the account, handling it for twenty years, even after the magazine moved to Washington, and he became a close friend of the publisher, Ronald Burr. In 1997, Burr confided in him a story of fiscal mismanagement and ideological mania. He told him about what had happened after the publication in 1993 of Brock's article about the Arkansas troopers, the one that had mentioned in passing a woman named "Paula," and what happened after Rush Limbaugh's hyping, which drove the magazine's circulation to more than 350,000. Burr told Bud about Richard Mellon Scaife's investing millions through his foundation to replicate Brock's success, about his agents, David Henderson and Stephen Boynton, being inserted into the magazine to direct the Arkansas Project and handle the money payments. Tyrell had been a passive player, more interested in leisure than editing, and he had been paid off as a front man—half of his mortgage on a house in Virginia, an apartment in New York, club fees, credit cards, posh vacations.

Burr was a staunch conservative, but he had become anxious when the magazine published articles he believed were false. His worry was heightened by his growing knowledge of large but unknown sums of money sloshing around. Feeling responsible for the magazine's financial state, he had sought an independent audit. With that, Richard Larry, the head of the Scaife Foundation, accused *him* of misallocating the Arkansas Project funds. Burr was shocked that his earnest efforts had put his own position in jeopardy. So in late 1997, on Lemley's advice, the two of them began

*Howard Fineman, "The Counterattack," *Newsweek*, February 9, 1998.

documenting the abuses. That was when they discovered that $2.4 million of Scaife funds had been spent over four years.

Burr, in naïve good faith, gave Tyrrell a memo of their findings. Two weeks later, Theodore Olson presided at the meeting at which Burr was fired. He was told that he would receive no medical insurance and no severance unless he signed a confidentiality agreement that stipulated his silence on the magazine's internal affairs. With young children to worry about, he signed. But he kept his documents in a bank safety deposit box—with copies stashed in two other places.

In January, Brock was fired.

Lemley did not share the politics of the *Spectator*, but he had worked diligently and professionally on its behalf for decades. When his friend Burr tried to do an honest job about the financial abuses and was unjustly accused of misappropriating the money, then fired, he became increasingly distressed and angry. He decided the outrage should be exposed.

Bud Lemley told me, as Brock had, that Henderson, Boynton, and Richard Larry had spent time with the convicted con man David Hale in Arkansas—officially in the custody of Starr's FBI agents—and had given him money and other gifts. It seemed extremely peculiar and irregular that the only "witness" against President Clinton would be so loosely controlled that he would be permitted to hang out with anti-Clinton conservative activists and accept payments from them.

While Ron Burr was keeping his documents under lock and key, Lemley had copies of Burr's letter demanding an audit, of Larry's accusation against him, and of Olson's instructing him to turn over all "notes and other documents in your possession" when he left the magazine. Lemley also had an accounting record of payments, carefully noting the precise amounts alongside names and dates: the Arkansas Project had paid Ted Olson for helping to defend David Hale; writers on the *Spectator*; an Arkansas trooper, L. D. Brown; and Dozhier's Bait Shop, numerous times.

On February 9, *The New York Observer* published an article by its political columnist Joe Conason (with Murray Waas) that revealed these payoffs to writers and sources. Olson now claimed he was conducting an "internal analysis." Boynton admitted to being a "friend" of David Hale, said that Henderson "is an old friend of Mr. Hale's," but denied giving Hale money. Conason wrote, "Questions have arisen about how Mr. Hale has paid his enormous legal bills—including those to Mr. Olson, whose fees are estimated to be in the range of several hundred dollars an hour."*

Lemley did not disgorge all his documents at once. He distributed them over time. His evidence did more than verify Brock's account; he had irrefutable documentation—the bank account numbers, the internal letters, the lists of payments and recipients. Everything Brock had said was true—to the dollar. Lemley was never cited or publicly acknowledged, but his work was essential as a corroborating second source.

I tried to interest other journalists in these developments, but I met rejection as swiftly as a door-to-door salesman does. The news organizations were not buying because they were already buying from a competitor: Starr. They were not going to alienate their big supplier and be left at a disadvantage in the scandal marketplace. As one news-magazine editor explained, he was hoping to get his hands on Tripp's tapes in Starr's possession. I was in an embattled White House that many reporters imagined would soon dissolve, and I had no incentives to offer.

And yet criticism of Starr mounted. Lars-Erik Nelson of the New York *Daily News* accused the Washington press corps of being "gullible" and printing Starr's "slander"; Anthony Lewis of *The New York Times* charged Starr with "an alarming abuse of power"; Robert Scheer of the *Los Angeles Times* wrote that Starr was conducting a "witch hunt"; the Internet magazine *Salon* in San Francisco, with solid journalistic standards and hardly frightened of Washington pressures, ran daily bulletin after bulletin; two reporters from the *Minneapolis Star-Tribune* wrote a series on the Arkansas Project; and the Associated Press, ever professional, began assigning reporters to new subjects like the Arkansas Project.†

I realized that these writers, critical of Starr, would not necessarily see each other's work, so I developed a list of their fax numbers, and every morning I'd fax them each other's articles. I also began to work with the research department of the Democratic National Committee, and soon it began producing informational faxes that it sent out to the entire press corps. After Conason's *New York Observer* article appeared, for example, the DNC sent out two single-page faxes headlined "Ken Starr & Richard Mellon Scaife" and "Did Richard Scaife Tamper with Ken Starr's Number One Whitewater Witness?" The faxes, with their credibly docu-

---

*Joe Conason with Murray Waas, "Richard Scaife Paid for Dirt on Clinton in 'Arkansas Project,' " *The New York Observer*, February 9, 1998.

†Howard Kurtz, "Independent Counsel Draws Increased Scrutiny," *The Washington Post*, February 4, 1998.

mented facts and figures, became a general source of information. I also talked with many reporters every day, of course, about the stories they were hearing. Within the White House, our morning and evening strategy meetings in Ruff's office continued.

Starr's grand jury was a gaudy spectacle of coercion and pity. Betty Currie cowered as she ran the gantlet of media cameras and microphones outside the courthouse. Robert Weiner, press attaché to the Office of Drug Policy, was subpoenaed by the OIC because he had called to congratulate local Democrats in Howard County, Maryland, where he lived, for issuing a press release asking local officials there to prosecute Linda Tripp for violating Maryland's wiretap laws. Starr's office claimed it was trying to determine if the White House was obstructing its investigation. "It's Big Brother," said Weiner.

Starr also subpoenaed Marcia Lewis, Lewinsky's mother, to testify on her daughter's confidences to her on February 10 and 11. On her second day on the stand, Lewis broke down in the grand jury, sobbing, "I can't take it. I can't take it." She left the courthouse looking ashen. In the meantime, Starr generated more sex stories.

Bruce Udolf was the prosecutor who questioned Mrs. Lewis in the grand jury. When she collapsed, I was told, he felt it was "too cruel" and simply stopped the proceeding. He was not supported by his superiors and sensed that the investigation had careened into callousness and mendacity. Jackie Bennett told him that the FBI agents in the office no longer trusted him; stories were spread that "powerful drugs" he was taking "made him depressed and paranoid," as Susan Schmidt reported in her book.* Udolf got pneumonia, and after his illness he never returned to the independent counsel's office.

On February 11, *The Washington Post* published its own "sighting" story: a retired Secret Service agent, Lewis Fox, was reported to claim that "Lewinsky, then a White House intern, spent at least 40 minutes alone with Clinton while Fox was posted outside the Oval Office door. . . . Fox is the first person to publicly say that he saw the president and Lewinsky alone together. As a result, his statement could be critical to independent counsel Kenneth W. Starr's attempt to determine whether Clinton did have a relationship with Lewinsky and then attempt to conceal it."†

---

*Schmidt and Weisskopf, *Truth at Any Cost*, pp. 104–105.

†Susan Schmidt, "Clinton, Lewinsky Met Alone, Guard Says," *The Washington Post*, February 11, 1998.

I surfed the Internet and discovered that Fox had granted an interview a week earlier to his hometown newspaper, *The Observer-Reporter* of Washington, Pennsylvania, in which he said he "noticed nothing unusual about Lewinsky's visits," that he had no knowledge about what had transpired between the President and the intern, and that he couldn't "imagine" an affair.* None of this had appeared in the *Post* article. My colleague Paul Begala and I called around to news editors to tell them of the *Observer-Reporter* piece and faxed it to them. The *Post* story died; Fox testified the next day before the grand jury, but his appearance was an anticlimactic event, for he had no information—and he was Starr's only direct witness of a "sighting."

Now, instead of receiving plaudits, the *Post* attracted criticism. The newspaper, wrote Thomas Oliphant, a columnist for *The Boston Globe*, "joined the *Wall Street Journal*, *The New York Times*, the *Dallas Morning News*, ABC News, and *Newsweek* in the dubious distinction of having significantly overreached the facts in mad pursuit of an actual or circumstantial witness to White House sex." Oliphant added, "By putting a Starr Spin on its story, the *Post* furthered the prosecutor's effort to enhance the value of Secret Service agents as potential witnesses, their sensitive duties notwithstanding."†

The *Post* followed the peculiar Fox episode with a most curious article about itself as the victim of a White House conspiracy. According to it, in 1996 I had had a conversation with a member of the White House legal staff urging that it concoct a denunciation of Susan Schmidt's coverage of Whitewater. Hillary Clinton forced this polemic to be prepared, it went on, though it was then killed by Press Secretary McCurry. I was described this way: "Administration colleagues jokingly call Blumenthal 'G.K.,' or grassy knoll, for his fondness for conspiracy theories. He is one of the strongest proponents in the White House of attacking Starr over what the administration views as illegal leaks in the Lewinsky case. Kendall also has been outspoken in his criticism of the leaks, and earlier this week asked for an official investigation."

Indeed, I had heard constant complaints about Susan Schmidt's reporting from the legal aides in the White House who dealt with Whitewater. I had suggested that rather than carp about her articles they

*Bob Niedbala, "Greene Man Witnessed Lewinsky Visits," *The Observer-Reporter*, Washington, Pa., February 4, 1998.

†Thomas Oliphant, "The Witness Who Wasn't," *The Boston Globe*, February 17, 1998.

should present the facts to the *Post* to correct any errors. The editors could run these as corrections, which they do every day. Beyond that, I never knew about a study of Schmidt's reporting. I asked Hillary and she had no memory of anything either. The *Post* had failed to mention that David Kendall had written letters to the editor that the paper had chosen not to publish. But the article did give its executive editor, Leonard Downie, an opportunity to praise Schmidt for "extremely hard reporting work" that was "able to find things out that I felt were significant for our readers to know." He blamed the Clintons for the Whitewater saga: "It never ended because we never got the truth fully."*

Sally Quinn now attempted to rally her society behind Starr by drawing social, political, and even diplomatic distinctions that defined the President and the First Lady as outside the charmed circle. On February 8, writing in the *Post*, she discerned a crisis of American foreign policy through the scene in the Oval Office on the day the scandal broke, when the President was about to negotiate with Yasser Arafat. "As Arafat stood by," Quinn wrote, "reporters bombarded Clinton with questions about matters most undiplomatic. It was deeply humiliating to Arafat and, in the view of some Palestinian officials, at least temporarily damaging to the Middle East peace process."† She was solicitous of Arafat's sensibility as a means of invidious comparison to the President's.

Two weeks later, in another article, she explained who belonged and who, emphatically, did not: "At a black tie dinner at the British Embassy not long after the Lewinsky scandal broke, you could sense the distinction Washington makes between one of its own—Vernon Jordan—and the president he serves, who is not of this town and who will be gone in less than three years, if not sooner." Ah, "this town." She continued:

> From the point of view of many who are entrenched in Washington, Hillary and Bill Clinton are not seen—nor are many presidents—as actually part of the city. They are viewed as having some sort of alien status, as being outsiders. Some in the permanent Washington establishment even view presidents and those they bring with them as being like occu-

*Howard Kurtz, "First Lady Ordered 1996 Critique of Coverage," *The Washington Post*, February 14, 1998.

†Sally Quinn, "When Foreign Policy Is Driven by Distraction," *The Washington Post*, February 8, 1998.

pying armies, rather than as welcome participants in the process of government.*

In this A-list utopia, society was elevated above government and excluded the executive branch, particularly the only Democratic president twice elected since Franklin D. Roosevelt, as well as his wife. Having status based on election must mean impermanence and therefore second-class rank. This effort to assert an exclusive "We, the People" of Georgetown seemed fretful rather than self-assured.

On February 17, David Brock telephoned to tell me that Conway had emerged from hiding. "Conway called Laura Ingraham," Brock said. "He's figured everything out. He couldn't believe I would speak to someone like you." With the press articles now appearing that described him, the other elves, and the Arkansas Project, Conway had deduced my relationship with the disenchanted Brock. Ingraham told Brock that this shocking news was spreading among conservatives. She didn't really care, she confided to Brock. It sounded exciting to her.

Two days later, the president of the American Bar Association, Jerome Shestack, delivered a harsh rebuke to Starr:

> Does prosecutorial zeal justify sting operations and unauthorized wiretapping in order to leverage the hiding of non-criminal, sexual indiscretion into a criminal obstruction of justice? . . . Is the special counsel a fourth arm of government lacking any meaningful accountability and realistically immune from removal? . . . Are prosecutors entitled to ignore ethical prescriptions on the grounds that their pursuit of truth or common practice justifies departure from professional standards?†

III

On February 18, Bruce Lindsey appeared before the grand jury. He testified that he didn't write the Talking Points and didn't know who had. The next day, the prosecutors' questions to him revealed an obsession

---

*Sally Quinn, "Crisis as Ritual: When the Alarm Sounds, Washington's Establishment Knows Just Where to Stand," *The Washington Post Magazine*, February 22, 1998.

†Associated Press, "ABA Head Questions Starr's Tactics," February 19, 1998.

with their self-image and public relations. They asked Lindsey if he had talked to eight different news organizations, by name. He had not. "How many times did you talk to Claire Shipman?" he was asked about an NBC News correspondent. He was read a list of names of members of the White House staff and asked if they "talked to news reporters":

"Sidney Blumenthal?"

"Sidney talks to the press."

"Who does he talk to?"

"I don't know."*

For months afterward, articles would periodically appear suggesting that Lindsey, the President, or even I had written the Talking Points. Three days after Lindsey testified, Fox News cited "sources" saying that Starr was "considering the possibility that President Clinton helped Monica Lewinsky write the so-called Talking Points memo." On May 18, *The Washington Times* claimed that Starr, "according to lawyers and others close to the grand jury probe, wants to know what White House deputy counsel Bruce R. Lindsey and senior aide Sidney Blumenthal know about the source of the summary, or 'talking points' . . . which prosecutors are convinced was not written by Miss Lewinsky."†

Under the duress of the scandalmongering and with the explosion of modern communications that made "news" an instantaneous cycle that went on twenty-four hours a day, I realized I could not simply respond to daily events or give answers to questions from the White House press corps. I had to bring to reporters' attention the facts that otherwise might elude them. One paradox of the new information age is that the Washington press corps, encapsulated at the center in the capital's small bubble, are often so blinkered. I was using the Internet and the fax machine to burst that bubble as best I could, expanding the range and context of the stories the press covered. I provided documents and sources for journalists to check, but much of what I did was simply to distribute already published but neglected news articles and columns. The effect was to help shatter the phalanx of certitude surrounding Starr's investigation. This activity enraged Starr and his prosecutors, of course, for they believed they had had and deserved total control. They and their sup-

---

*Communication from the Office of Independent Counsel, Kenneth W. Starr, "Supplemental Materials to the Referral to the United States House of Representatives . . . , September 9, 1998," U.S. Government Printing Office, 1998, p. 2,393.

†Quoted in Howard Kurtz, "Report Faults Lewinsky Coverage," *The Washington Post*, October 21, 1998.

porters demonized me. To the right wing, I was the focus of evil in the White House. To the scandal-beat press, as a former journalist I was a traitor, a Lucifer-like figure who had leaped from grace to serve the devil. Having crossed over, I was supposedly capable of any betrayal and therefore worthy of any.

On February 15, the columnist Robert Novak claimed that a number of scandal-beat reporters had "privately" accused me of maintaining an "enemies list," like Nixon's: "Other White House aides deny that Blumenthal or anybody else has made up an enemies list reminiscent of the Nixon era. Several of the journalists say the White House has criticized their work to their superiors, leaving the reporters apprehensive. Blumenthal, who is close to Hillary Rodham Clinton, is credited with giving birth to the concept of a vast right-wing conspiracy against the president."* Of course, there was no "enemies list" or any other secret document or register; nor were there any punitive plans—unless efforts to correct the public record were considered dirty tricks.

Among the many articles I faxed around were several about two misbegotten legal cases involving Bruce Udolf and Michael Emmick, the two prosecutors who were outcasts from Starr's office for having negotiated Lewinsky's now repudiated proffer. One article had been sent to me, unsolicited, by Stanley Sheinbaum, former president of the Los Angeles Police Commission, an old friend of mine and the Clintons, long active in Democratic politics, and a widely respected figure, moving knowledgeably from L.A. police precincts to Hollywood (Betty Warner, the daughter of Harry Warner, is his wife) to the Middle East. The article he sent was from a local daily legal newspaper called the *Los Angeles Daily Journal*. "Starr Aide No Stranger to Sex Tapes Inquiries," ran the headline.

Michael Emmick, when he had been an assistant U.S. attorney in Los Angeles and chief of the public corruption and government fraud section, had prosecuted an L.A. detective, Stephen Polak, for allegedly skimming drug money; the defendant wound up being fined fifty dollars on unrelated misdemeanors. It turned out that the old story included elements— wiretapping, sex, and a perjury trap—that were resonant with the Lewinsky case.†

*Robert Novak, "Colleagues Cool to Gingrich," *Chicago Sun-Times*, February 15, 1998.

†Martin Berg, "Starr Aide No Stranger to Sex Tapes Inquiries," *Los Angeles Daily Journal*, February 6, 1998. Polak's former wife, Christina Townley, had offered no

At about the same time that I received the faxed article from Shein-baum, I was also sent, unsolicited, something from Jack Bass, another old friend, a journalist and professor at the University of Mississippi and the author of several books on Southern politics. A column in the *Atlanta Journal-Constitution* by Martha Ezzard, a member of the paper's editorial board, recounted a 1985 case in Atlanta of a carpenter, wrongly held in jail for five days on a stolen-gun charge in an attempt to turn him into a witness in a drug case about which he claimed to know nothing. The car-penter filed suit in federal court and won a $50,000 judgment against Bruce Udolf for having violated his civil rights. Udolf was voted out of office and moved to Florida to start over, working for the U.S. Justice Department there before being hired by Starr. Ezzard wrote, "The ques-tion for Starr is, why didn't he investigate his investigators?"*

The *Los Angeles Daily Journal* and *Atlanta Journal-Constitution* articles had appeared because Starr's sting operation against Lewinsky had sud-denly vaulted his prosecutors into prominence, making them natural sub-jects for journalistic inquiry in the places where they were known locally. When I faxed these articles out, they generated interest from other jour-nalists, who produced their own pieces. Soon Starr's office was fielding calls from a press corps it had believed just days earlier was its completely pliable instrument.

On February 20, Lanny Breuer asked me to stay after the evening strategy meeting in Ruff's office. I learned that Starr had subpoenaed both Lanny and me to appear before the grand jury. Mickey Kantor, the former U.S. trade representative, who was one of the President's pri-vate attorneys, had received a subpoena as well, as had Terry Lenzner, who headed the Investigative Group International, a private investigating

---

evidence against him in the trial, but in 1994, a sheriff's deputy secretly wiretapped her to prove she had lied on the witness stand about having an extramarital affair. Confronted with the tape, Townley refused to flip, so a prosecutor under Emmick's supervision indicted her for tax evasion. The judge dismissed the charges, saying that the prosecutors in the U.S. attorney's office had used "threats, deceit and harassment . . . to compel her to cooperate" and were "callous, coercive and vindictive." Emmick, interviewed by the *Los Angeles Daily Journal*, said, "We had a completely legitimate theory. It's always distasteful. But you have to do what you have to do." Emmick later complained to reporters that he had been the victim of an unfair campaign because a prosecutor under his supervision, not he himself, had handled the Townley tax case, and because the judge in the case afterward wrote a commendation for him.

*Martha Ezzard, "Ken Starr's Tainted Lieutenant," *Atlanta Journal-Constitution*, February 14, 1998.

With President Clinton in the hallway of Franklin D. Roosevelt's Hyde Park, New York, home, February 19, 1993. James Roosevelt, FDR's grandson, is on the stairs in the rear.

After signing the Oslo Peace Accord on the South Lawn of the White House, President Clinton joins (from left to right) Israeli Foreign Minister Shimon Peres, Prime Minister Yitzhak Rabin, and Palestinian Authority President Yasser Arafat in promoting the Seeds of Peace initiative, a program involving Israeli and Palestinian young people, September 13, 1993.

above: With President Clinton and Vice President Al Gore outside the West Wing, just after the congressional vote approving the North American Free Trade Agreement (NAFTA), November 17, 1993. (I was then Washington correspondent for The New Yorker.)

below: On April 23, 1995, President Clinton speaks at the memorial service for those who died in the bombing of the federal building in Oklahoma City. COURTESY OF THE CLINTON PRESIDENTIAL MATERIALS PROJECT

*President Clinton negotiates with Senator Bob Dole in the Cabinet Room during
the second government shutdown over the budget, December 29, 1995.*

With Hillary Rodham Clinton, next to a bust of George Washington, before the luncheon in her honor at the Century Association in New York City, March 19, 1996.

Jackie and me with Tony Blair and Hillary Clinton at our house on April 11, 1996, the evening before Blair, then Labour Party leader but not yet prime minister, had his first long meeting with President Clinton.

above: On my first day of work in the White House, August 11, 1997: Hillary Clinton, Secretary of State Madeleine Albright, and Assistant Secretary of State for Public Affairs James Rubin drop by my office.

below: With President Clinton in the Oval Office, September 15, 1997.

The U.S. and British delegations to the first Third Way meeting, at Chequers, November 1, 1997. From left to right: Andrew Cuomo (Secretary of Housing and Urban Development), Lawrence Summers (deputy Secretary of the Treasury), Gordon Brown (Chancellor of the Exchequer), Melanne Verveer (the First Lady's chief of staff), Ed Balls (Treasury adviser), Geoffrey Mulgan (deputy director of the Policy Unit), Patricia Hewitt (Member of Parliament on the Social Security Select Committee), Cherie Blair, David Miliband (director of the Prime Minister's Policy Unit), Prime Minister Blair, Sidney Blumenthal, Hillary Clinton, Anthony Giddens (director of the London School of Economics), Stephen Byers (Minister for School Standards), Al From (president of the Democratic Leadership Council), Margaret Jay (Minister for Health), Joseph Nye (director of the Kennedy School of Government at Harvard University), Franklin Raines (director of the Office of Management and Budget), Don Baer (former White House communications director), and Peter Mandelson (Minister Without Portfolio).

On January 27, 1998, President Clinton delivers his State of the Union address before a joint session of Congress, the culmination of "Seven Days in January." Vice President Al Gore and Speaker of the House Newt Gingrich are seated behind the President.

Briefing the President,
January and February 1998.

Speaking to the press after my grand-jury appearance at the federal courthouse on February 26, 1998. I am with my lawyers, Bill McDaniel and Jo Bennett.

On Air Force One, *returning from* Time's *seventy-fifth anniversary dinner in New York City, the President joins the conversation Jackie and I are having with Senators Edward Kennedy and Daniel Patrick Moynihan (facing us but not in the picture), March 3, 1998.*

above: At Jackie's surprise fiftieth birthday party in the Diplomatic Reception Room at the White House, President Clinton regales a group of White House Fellows, March 21, 1998.

below: After an introduction from First Minister David Trimble, President Clinton, along with Prime Minister Tony Blair, addresses the Northern Ireland Assembly in Belfast on September 3, 1998. The President had negotiated the Good Friday Accord early that year.

On December 19, 1998, the day President Clinton was impeached in the House of Representatives, this picture was snapped in the White House offices immediately after the Democratic support rally in the Rose Garden.

My office was the old presidential barbershop, its mirrors still in place.
By 1999 I had on the wall a framed front page of The Washington Post from
the day after President Clinton's Senate impeachment trial. Under the
headline "Clinton Acquitted" and above the picture, the President wrote:
"To Sid, Thanks, Bill Clinton."

On the President's visit to Slovenia, Betty Currie and I reenact the impeachment
drama: I am rescuing her from a stuffed bear and other wild beasts in Brdo Castle,
Marshal Tito's hunting lodge, June 21, 1999.

*After the allied victory in the Kosovo war, the President visits the Stenkovic I
refugee camp near Skopje, Macedonia, where he is greeted
by Kosovar children, June 22, 1999.*

*With Hillary, now a candidate for the U.S. Senate in New York,
after her speech to the Democratic National Convention,
August 14, 2000.*

*At the Third Way Progressive Governance Conference of fourteen world leaders, at
the Waldorf-Astoria Hotel, New York City, September 6, 2000. At the far right,
Prime Minister Goran Persson of Sweden, and on the left,
President Thabo Mbeki of South Africa.*

With President Clinton at Princeton University, October 5, 2000.
PHOTOGRAPH BY DENISE APPLEWHITE

In the Oval Office after President Clinton delivered his Farewell Address, with Bruce Reed, his domestic policy adviser (to the President's left), Jeff Shesol, a speechwriter (on my left), and other aides, January 18, 2001.

firm. I was told that I should not tell anyone, including any staff members, that I had been subpoenaed. Kantor was trying to get his subpoena withdrawn. I must maintain strict silence.

I was stunned and also puzzled. I had played no part in the events Starr was investigating, and I had never met Lewinsky or even heard of her before January 21. I could not imagine any legal reason to subpoena me. It was all too obvious that Starr, beleaguered and besieged, was lashing out politically. He would try to prove an evil conspiracy: Kantor would be cast as the chief organizer, doing the President's bidding, of efforts to destroy Starr's reputation and undermine his truth commission; Lenzner would be the digger of dirt; and I would be the disseminator.

The subpoenas were a way for Starr's office to kill two birds with one stone. Udolf and Emmick could be further marginalized while Starr rose up in righteous anger in defense of their honor against a malevolent White House. "They were playing both ends against the middle," I was told by my source in Starr's office. Starr's control over the press coverage could also be reestablished; thus dissidence from within and without his office could be suppressed. According to what Susan Schmidt later wrote, Jackie Bennett believed the White House "was using its might to try to intimidate prosecutors. . . . He wasn't alone in his frustration. Sam Dash advised: 'Subpoena the S.O.B.'—meaning Blumenthal. The next day, February 21, Bennett did."* But the date is wrong and Dash has denied that version.

"I don't remember ever being asked or stating that," Dash told me. "I was not in favor of that. It had nothing to do with the investigation. I was not asked for my opinion. I was aware that they were highly incensed by the criticism and by the strategy in the White House to discredit them. Their job was to ignore it and do their job professionally." He went on: "People have a right to express their opinion, and the White House has a right to defend itself. If the Independent Counsel is acting unfairly, let the public know about that. Their view was that by contacting reporters and letting them have stories you were attempting to undercut their prosecution. They saw it as an obstruction of justice, which obviously it was not. I would disagree with their collateral attacks on you, [with] even calling you to the grand jury. People would say, 'Why don't you stop it?' I'd say, 'I'm not Ken's mother.' I didn't see myself as the ultimate independent counsel."

Indeed, Dash had made clear to me at the time that he disapproved of

*Schmidt and Weisskopf, *Truth at Any Cost*, p. 104.

my being subpoenaed. At the White House Correspondents Dinner on
April 25, he pulled me aside and said, "I was against what they did in issuing you a subpoena. I sympathize with you."

That night of February 20, Lanny told me that Starr's office was faxing over the subpoena. We waited to read it as it arrived, page by page.
Part A of the subpoena rider seemed predictable and absurd: "Produce
any and all documents referring or relating to Monica Lewinsky." Of
course I had none, except newspaper clippings from the past month. But
Part B was something that the vastly experienced Ruff had never seen before. It was not just extraordinarily intrusive but ominous and repressive:

> B. Produce any and all documents referring or relating to the Office of
> the Independent Counsel Kenneth W. Starr ("OIC"). These documents
> should include, but not be limited to, the following:
>   1. all documents referring or relating to attorneys and other staff
>   members of the OIC;
>   2. all documents referring or relating to any contact, directly or indi-
>   rectly, with a member of the media which related or referred to the
>   OIC, or attorneys or other staff members of the OIC; and
>   3. all documents referring or relating to any communications which
>   relate or refer to the OIC, or attorneys or other staff members of
>   the OIC.

Five pages followed of "Definitions and Instructions" of documents
and how to turn them over to the prosecutor: "correspondence, calen-
dars, daytimers, datebooks, telegrams, facsimiles, telexs, telefaxes, electronic mail, memoranda, records, reports, books, files (computer or
paper), summaries or records of personal conversations, meetings or interviews, logs, summaries or records of telephone conversations and/or
telefax communications . . ."

No constitutional shield protected me as it would a journalist in such
a situation. I would have to surrender to the prosecutor every record of
every contact with "a member of the media." Starr was using the powers
of his office to suppress criticism by making an example of me. His politics was floundering, his own office was in disarray, and his uniform dominance over the press was shattered. So he would stamp out opposition
through intimidation.

According to Schmidt's later account, Jackie Bennett "regretted giving in to his anger. Coming now, the subpoena looked retaliatory. Bennett tried to call it back, but Blumenthal's lawyer, William McDaniel, had

already begun to turn it into another First Amendment cause célèbre."*
But in fact the subpoena remained secret for days except to the reporters
to whom Bennett leaked most of it, and McDaniel did not remark upon
it until after I did. Bennett may have wished to withdraw the subpoena,
but he made no effort to do so and did not contact anyone about it. On
the contrary, when I made a motion to quash it, Starr's office accused me
of obstruction of justice.

In essence, I was being accused of speaking to the press, which was
part of my job. If I was under investigation for talking to as many journalists as I could about Starr's abuses, I was undoubtedly guilty. Starr was
not mistaken there, and he was directly targeting my offense: speech.
Everything I had said, every article I had faxed, every phone call I had
made to reporters or they had made to me, was now subject to prosecutorial questioning. This was a way to threaten the President's other aides,
letting them know they would be ruined if they persisted in defending
him. But I could not let my colleagues know of this assault on the White
House, aimed at them as well as me. I had to wait for events to play
themselves out before I could utter a word.

I already had the burden of legal fees incurred in suing Matt Drudge.
I knew that this cold, clinical, and terrifyingly weird subpoena would
mean tens of thousands of dollars more in legal fees—and I had no savings, having spent them all on school tuition for my two children, one in
college. I was on a government salary; so was my wife. There was no reserve: her parents were dead and we had given what little they left to her
siblings; my parents were retired, living on Social Security and savings. I
also knew that the glaring klieg lights would swivel in my direction. For
those on the right and in the press who reviled me as demonic this would
be a brightly lit, gleeful danse macabre.

The next day, Saturday, I met with those few members of the White
House legal team who were privy to the subpoenas. I also conferred with
my lawyers, Bill McDaniel and his partner, Jo Bennett Marsh, who were
representing me in the Drudge case. I was grateful to have them as aggressive advocates. Bill had been a law clerk to Supreme Court Associate
Justice Harry Blackmun and a protégé of the fabled Edward Bennett
Williams before setting up his own practice with Jo, a Texas tornado
who had extensive experience with criminal cases. The first thing they
drilled into me was how to respond in the grand jury to the prosecutor's
questions: Don't give information you're not asked for, and don't give

*Schmidt and Weisskopf, *Truth at Any Cost*, p. 104.

elaborate answers. The best answers are yes, no, I don't know, I can't recall. Tell the truth. And you must always presume that the prosecutor is out to get you.

While I met with the White House lawyers, one of them passed on a message from the press office. Chris Vlasto, the ABC News scandal-beat producer, was claiming he knew I had been subpoenaed and wanted me to explain my relations with Terry Lenzner, Jack Palladino, and Anthony Pellicano—all private investigators who at one time or another had worked for Clinton's lawyers. I had never had dealings with or met any of them, but that wasn't the point. Vlasto's call seemed more like a taunt than a genuine request for information, and I was counseled not to respond. Vlasto was merely taking dictation, but this phone call was valuable in helping to confirm the prosecutor's new line of attack: to prove that there was a conspiracy against Starr. I maintained silence.

On Sunday, on NBC's *Meet the Press*, Joseph diGenova—who, with his wife, Victoria Toensing, was now a regular on the television talk-show circuit defending Starr (they had been the sources of the "sighting" rumor that had embarrassed *The Dallas Morning News*)—made a new and startling accusation: the President had hired Lenzner to investigate diGenova's and his wife's private lives, or so he said. DiGenova claimed he had learned about this from a magazine reporter, whom he declined to identify. He suggested that the investigators were going after Starr, reporters, and the President's critics. It was, he went on, "truly a frightening, frightening development."

"Blatant lies," said McCurry.*

After *Meet the Press*, David Brock telephoned me to convey his conversation with Alex Azar, the former prosecutor in Starr's office and unheralded member of the elves' clique. "Alex says the thing is to shift the subject from collusion"—that is, collusion between Starr's office and Paula Jones's lawyers and the elves—"to the Nixonian White House."

On Monday, February 23, at the Clinton White House, tensions grew between McCurry and the lawyers, who acknowledged that they had hired Lenzner—Bob Bennett had used him for years on the Jones case—and that he was collecting public records. But he was not investigating anyone's private life. Kendall and Bennett said they'd issue a clarifying statement to that effect the next day.

After that evening's strategy meeting, Ruff told me that Mickey Kan-

---

*John M. Broder, "White House Denies Using Investigators to Go After Starr," *The New York Times*, February 23, 1998.

tor had succeeded in quashing Starr's subpoena. In withdrawing it, Starr, through Jackie Bennett, had claimed he had had no idea that Kantor was one of the President's private attorneys. (Al Hunt of *The Wall Street Journal* wrote, "If Mr. Bennett said that, he's lying."*) Ruff said that now I was free to speak, that I should break the story of my own subpoena as soon as possible.

It was after seven in the evening, after the network news programs and close to newspaper deadlines. I called Adam Nagourney, a reporter at *The New York Times*. I explained the extraordinary nature of my subpoena, Kantor's subpoena, and Starr's leak. Then I called my lawyers, who told me that under the key passage of the subpoena demanding "documents referring or relating to any contact directly or with a member of the media, which related or referred to the OIC," my conversation with Nagourney would have to be reported to the prosecutor.

On February 24, the *Times* ran Nagourney's article on page 1. "In a further escalation of the battle between the White House and the independent counsel Kenneth W. Starr," Nagourney wrote, "a senior White House adviser said today that he had been subpoenaed to testify before a Federal grand jury about any conversations he had with journalists about Mr. Starr's office." I was quoted as saying, "His subpoena demands that I name journalists that have talked to me about Ken Starr. And it demands any records of conversations I have had with journalists about Ken Starr." And, "This is seeking to create a chilling effect among reporters. It is an outrageous attempt to intimidate public opinion and to silence all reporting that might be skeptical or critical of Ken Starr and his methods."†

That morning, after the senior staff meeting at the White House, where we discussed Iraq, Social Security, and the budget, a black Chrysler limousine drove me from the West Wing down Pennsylvania Avenue to the E. Barrett Prettyman Federal Courthouse. Hundreds of reporters and television technicians were encamped in front of the building, as they had been for weeks. The car took me to the side entrance. I passed through the metal detectors and took an elevator to the chambers of Judge Norma Holloway Johnson. After a conference with Jo Bennett Marsh and several prosecutors, she decided she would hear arguments on

*Albert R. Hunt, "The Inspector and the Jock," *The Wall Street Journal*, February 26, 1998.

†Adam Nagourney, "President's Adviser Ordered to Divulge Contact with Press," *The New York Times*, February 24, 1998.

my motion to quash Starr's subpoena. There were only four of us in the large courtroom. The black-robed judge was perched behind her high bench.

My motion, written by my lawyers, stated: "The Subpoena is being used by the Independent Counsel for an improper purpose: to stifle any and all criticism of the Independent Counsel himself. Such an action is unheard of in the United States of America and should not be countenanced." It underlined this point: "Counsel is aware of no previous reported instance in which a prosecutor has ever attempted to use the power of the grand jury to investigate what an individual may have said, written, or transmitted—including to members of the media—about the prosecutor himself." My lawyers noted that the subpoena was so broad that it encompassed all my communications when I had been a journalist, and they argued that the subpoena was "designed to intimidate and chill" my rights:

> Prior to his employment at the White House, Mr. Blumenthal was a journalist. Mr. Blumenthal has developed many friends and acquaintances among the media. Partly for this reason, Mr. Blumenthal, as part of his job, is responsible for communicating various Administration positions and opinions to the media. And Mr. Blumenthal has every right to do so. . . . The Independent Counsel has no right to learn whether this has occurred—much less to gain access to any information that may have been gleaned as a result of any such efforts.

Bittman rose to argue in opposition. His words were dull and his expression dull, but his argument was spectacularly original. I listened intently to his monotone as he claimed that anyone—not just someone working for President Clinton, but anyone—who for whatever reason spread what he called "misinformation" about the Independent Counsel and anyone in his office was obstructing justice. I was astonished. This argument went far beyond the subpoena. Starr's deputy was making a case that I was in jeopardy of being indicted for obstruction of justice merely for criticizing him. He was trying not just to intimidate but to promulgate a doctrine for suppression of speech. Starr was advocating a new Sedition Act.

The judge's ruling was not unexpected but still shocking. Johnson was known as a prosecutor's judge and she seemed well disposed toward this one. She decided that my years as a journalist were excluded from the reach of the subpoena, but she otherwise ruled in favor of the prosecutor;

she offered no reasoning. It took a lot more of Starr's abuses, flouting her sense of rightness, for Judge Johnson to turn against him, which she eventually did.

Now my lawyers would have to hand over to the prosecutors everything they had demanded in the subpoena: phone logs, articles, letters, e-mails. Starr now had the names of dozens of reporters who had telephoned me.

I was led to the fourth floor, past a tall barricade set to mark off a long, dimly lit, windowless corridor with seats lined up against one wall. At one end was a pay phone; at the other, around the corner, unseen, was the grand-jury room. It was, I thought, Kafka's waiting room. A few witnesses were there with their lawyers. I identified one young woman from the White House, subpoenaed because she had known Lewinsky, and she was obviously distressed, her attorney trying to calm her before she was called in.

I was about to sit down when I noticed that Terry Lenzner was sitting there, impassive. I went up to him and said, "Terry, we've never met." I introduced myself.

"Of course," he said.

"We have a lot of friends in common," I said, "so it's strange we've never met." We shook hands. "Starr believes we're in a conspiracy together," I said.

Lenzner pointed to the far end of the corridor and explained that he had already been in the grand jury and was waiting to be called back. "They're insane," he said. "Stupid and insane."

In his case, there was a bitter irony. Lenzner had been a deputy counsel on the Watergate committee. He had been the lawyer who questioned William Bittman about the secret payoffs to Nixon's Plumbers. Now Lenzner was accused of being at the center of a "Nixonian" plot, and Bittman's son would get to question him. For these Republicans, it was payback time.

For hours I waited in the nondescript corridor. Other witnesses came and went. I was never called. No one came out to tell me when I might be. I read the newspaper several times, chatted with my lawyer, paced, and just sat. Finally, a prosecutor told my lawyer that I would not be needed that day. I was to return on Thursday.

The media had positioned themselves like a Roman square at the courthouse's front door. No one from the White House had yet said anything to them about his or her experiences in the grand-jury room. I welcomed the chance to explain my position. I had been a reporter, and my subpoena related to the fact that I had talked with the media. But I had not yet testified, so my lawyer spoke instead. Jo explained that I had been kept waiting for hours and had not been called to testify. She said Starr was "out of control" and "unprofessional from the beginning." And, she said, addressing the press corps, "This is all so Mr. Starr can just find out which of you guys Sidney has been talking to lately and what he said."

Back at the White House, I had racked up a yard of messages from reporters. I telephoned first those whose names I had had to turn over to Starr. When I told them about this, some responded with silence and many with anger. I read everyone the key portions of the subpoena pertaining to "members of the media." I told them about the fantastical legal argument made by Bittman that "misinformation" constituted an obstruction of justice.

When I woke up the next morning and went downstairs, I opened the blinds in my living room and gazed out onto a street filled with reporters, satellite trucks with huge dishes, and TV cameras pointed at me. My son Paul, seeing the array, shouted, "Media!" When I left for work I was in a cone of lights literally beaming down. It was like being at center stage in a theater, a high-pitched, tightly organized space, with its own rules and time frame, removed from the rest of society. Reporters shouted questions—"What will you say to the grand jury?"—as I drove away.

That morning's editorial in *The New York Times* began by calling Starr "bone stupid." Subpoenaing Blumenthal was

an attack on press freedom and the unrestricted flow of information that is unwarranted by the facts and beyond his mandate as a prosecutor. This latest blunder fits a pattern of chronic clumsiness and periodic insensitivity to his public responsibilities. . . . The effort to collect the name of every journalist who talked with a White House communications specialist amounts to a perverse use of the prosecutorial mandate to learn what the Nixon White House attempted to determine through wiretaps. Like any newspaper, we have an obvious selfish interest in the confidentiality of the reporting process. But you do not have to be a journalist to see that Mr. Starr has committed an ignorant assault on one of the most distinctive and essential elements of American democracy.*

Meanwhile, a campaign of invective cranked up. An editorial in the *New York Post* called me "Sid Vicious," the first time that label was affixed

*Editorial, "Ken Starr's Misjudgments," *The New York Times*, February 25, 1998.

to me. Conservative websites immediately spread it. The vilification intensified over time in proportion to the crisis surrounding the President. These personal, false attacks were occasionally but not always instigated by Starr's office.

Many serious journalists were shocked and dismayed as they assessed Starr's damage to the First Amendment. "What Sidney Blumenthal was doing is called politics," said Doyle McManus, Washington bureau chief of the *Los Angeles Times*. "The independent counsel has already been accused of criminalizing the political process. This looks perilously close to taking that one step further and potentially criminalizing the journalistic process." "Here's a guy whose job it is, in part, to talk to the press," Nina Totenberg, National Public Radio's legal correspondent, remarked. If I were to be charged in the Lewinsky case, she added, "we really are living in a police state." Jane Kirtley, executive director of the Reporters Committee for Freedom of the Press, said, "If Ken Starr is serious about finding out where leaks are coming from, he ought to start by investigating his own office. It's disgraceful to do investigations of this nature that appear to be founded on the notion that Blumenthal criticized Ken Starr."*

Now Starr walked down the driveway to his suburban Virginia home to expound publicly on his understanding of the First Amendment. "Our office in recent weeks has been subjected to an avalanche of lies," Starr told reporters. "The First Amendment is interested in the truth. Misinformation and distorted information have come to us about career public servants. . . . The grand jury has a legitimate interest in inquiring into whether there is an effort to impede our investigation."†

Starr's doctrine was nothing less than a recapitulation of the Sedition Act of 1798, the most infamous attack on free speech in American history. The Federalists had passed the act to harass and jail political opponents associated with Thomas Jefferson and James Madison. Starr's statement could have been copying the Sedition Act's notorious sections criminalizing speech that would "excite" opposition as a "conspiracy" to "impede the operation of any law." In 1798, the Federalist Congress had enacted this law and President John Adams had signed it; in 1998, Starr alone proclaimed his own version.

Starr had felt beset and misunderstood almost from the start, when

---

*Howard Kurtz, "Prosecutor Lobs a Grenade," *The Washington Post*, February 25, 1998.

†Peter Baker and Toni Locy, "Prosecutor Decries 'Avalanche of Lies,'" *The Washington Post*, February 26, 1998.

his scandalmongering had failed to force Clinton from office. Now, he was donning a new identity: the prosecutor as victim. He claimed to be daunted by those subject to his capricious and unlimited powers. A sense of grievance increasingly propelled his aggression. The more he felt victimized, the more self-righteous he became. He was not a bully, but being bullied. He was not entrapping, but being ensnared. Starr's doctrine could only be taken as a precedent to repress political opposition under the guise of the rule of law.

On February 26, I went again to the courthouse, accompanied by my lawyers and Cheryl Mills, the White House deputy legal counsel. We had coffee in the basement cafeteria, where the media pack discovered us. I chatted nonchalantly with them for about ten minutes, to the consternation of my attorneys, but I wanted the reporters to get the sense that I was not fearful and that important issues involving them were at stake. Then we took the elevator to the fourth floor. In the Kafkaesque corridor, my attorneys told me that while they could not be present with me, I could come out to talk to them whenever I wanted to clarify any question. After a short wait, Sol Wisenberg emerged. He explained that I was being questioned as a witness, not as a target. With that, I was escorted into the room.

The grand-jury room was a windowless, fluorescent-lit chamber, antiseptic and shabby. It reminded me of the cell within the Berlin Wall where, as a reporter for *The Washington Post*, I was detained for an hour by the Volkspolizei after meeting with dissidents in East Berlin in 1986. ("And whom did you meet with?" the East German interrogator asked me. "What did you say to you? Did you take notes? Where are those notes?") I sat on an old, armless aluminum chair at the end of a battered table. Two prosecutors were seated to my right—Bittman and Wisenberg. To my front and left, in raised stands, were arrayed twenty-three grand jurors in rows. Behind me in a box—the owner's box—sat other prosecutors, including Jackie Bennett. It was impossible to tell what the grand jurors were thinking. They were expressionless. About two-thirds of them were black, most of them women. One juror was reading a newspaper; another appeared to be dozing but suddenly came to life. Most, however, seemed to be paying careful attention. The grand-jury room was the setting not for a histrionic hearing but for a shabby police procedural.

Bittman began by reading from paragraphs from the extension of Starr's authority in the Lewinsky matter, citing particularly passages about obstruction of justice. "These are the matters that we're inquiring of today, Mr. Blumenthal," he said. Even though I was technically a witness, under Starr's doctrine of free speech as obstruction, I could become a target.

From the start, the prosecutor wanted to establish that I worked with the media. I explained that this was "part of my job." He asked for the names of those on the White House staff I consulted with regularly. I gave them. He asked if I had "any role in the Monica Lewinsky matter." I answered that I attended twice-daily meetings. He asked the names of staff members at those meetings. I named them. He wanted to know if the President's private attorneys attended. They did not, I said.

"What occurs at these 8:30 and 6:45 p.m., these daily meetings?" I replied that White House counsel had instructed me that I could not discuss that because it was covered by executive privilege, which covers discussions between the President and his senior advisers.

"Have you received any information relating or referring to Monica Lewinsky?" I immediately thought of my private conversation with the President on January 21. I left the room to confer. Cheryl told me I had to assert executive privilege about any conversations with the President and the First Lady. Executive privilege was not mine to invoke: it was a privilege that belonged to the President, and it was being invoked.

When I returned to the grand-jury room and did invoke it, I could tell by the look on the prosecutors' faces that they were surprised. They had not asked about what the President might have said to me about Lewinsky, because they did not believe I knew anything. I was there to be questioned about a conspiracy.

Bittman wanted to know if I had spoken to the President's lawyers— David Kendall, Bob Bennett, or Mickey Kantor. I said that I had. He asked about my conversations with Kendall. "He has expressed his dismay at the grand-jury leaks to me," I answered. Bittman observed that I had turned over to the judge two copies of Kendall's letter about the leaks, which had been in my files. He demanded to know if I had helped him write it or "provide Mr. Kendall with any of the information contained in the letter." I had not.

"Have you ever spoken to a gentleman by the name of Terry Lenzner?" "No." (I had only just met him the day before, in the waiting room.) "Have you spoken to a guy by the name of Jack Palladino?" "No." "Have you ever received any information from Terry Lenzner directly or indirectly?" "No." "Have you ever received any information directly or indirectly from Jack Palladino?" "No." "Did any of the private attorneys for the President ever indicate to you that they had hired private detectives?" "No." "Did they ever indicate to you that they hired Mr. Lenzner?" "No." "Or Mr. Palladino?" "No." "Did they ever indicate to you that they were doing any investigation into the factual matters underlying the Monica Lewinsky matter?" "No."

The prosecutor suddenly digressed, trying to get me to reveal the contents of my conversations with Hillary Clinton, even though I had invoked executive privilege. Finally he gave up on that line of questioning and returned to the private investigators: "Have you ever spoken to a gentleman by the name of Anthony or Tony Pellicano?" "No." "Have you spoken to anyone who has identified himself or herself as a private investigator or private detective?" "No."

Now the prosecutor began to ask how old stories about OIC prosecutors had gotten recent coverage, implying that I had received information from private investigators and passed it on. "Have you received any information specifically about Bruce Udolf? From any source," I was asked. "From an article in the *Atlanta Journal-Constitution*," I answered. "Prior to the publication of that article, did you receive any information about Bruce Udolf?" "I believe that he was mentioned in an article in *U.S. News*." "Okay. Let me ask it this way. Prior to the publication of any news article relating to Mr. Udolf, had you received any information about Mr. Udolf?" "No."

I was somewhat surprised the prosecutor did not ask how I'd gotten the article about Udolf. I amended my last answer to explain that a reporter from *Time*, Jay Branegan, had asked about a rumor about Udolf he had heard. (All this was blacked out in the public transcript.) I was asked, "Did you tell anyone else about that story or contact with this member of the news media?" I said I'd spoken with Paul Begala, whom the reporter had also called. "And what was the purpose of the person from *Time* magazine calling you about it, if you know?" "No idea. Don't know." "Did you know anything about the facts?" "No. I had no material facts to offer whatsoever. No information." "Did you tell anyone else other than Mr. Begala about it?" "No."

"What about Mr. Emmick? You said you may have received information about Mr. Emmick. . . ." "I have." Bittman homed in: "And from what source?" "The source of my information was Stanley Sheinbaum." "Can you spell his last name, please?" "Yes. It's S-h-e-i-n-b-a-u-m." "And who is he?" The prosecutor stared hard. Perhaps Sheinbaum was a private investigator they had not yet discovered. "He is the former commissioner of the Los Angeles Police Department." There was dead silence and a long pause. (Actually, he was chairman of the L.A. Police Commission, which oversees the police department.) "Any other sources of information?" "None." "The information that you received from Mr. Shein-baum, did you relay that information to anyone else?" "I did." "To whom?" I answered at length about the article from the *Los Angeles Daily Journal*, its content, and some of the reporters and editors to whom I'd sent it. (Almost that entire page of the transcript was blacked out.) My statement concluded, "So that was on the public record in this article that had been faxed to me by Stanley Sheinbaum. He had told me that there was widespread concern among the law enforcement community in Los Angeles." With that exchange on Sheinbaum, the prosecutor's conspiracy theory crumbled.

Now he wanted to know more about my relations with the media: "And what was your purpose in disseminating this information to members of the news media?" "I believe that the public has the right to know about the character and records of public officials."

Then he asked, in a tone dripping with sarcasm, "Have you ever disseminated any information positive about members of the Office of Independent Counsel staff to the members of the news media?" Of all the bizarre questions of the day, this was the strangest.

The prosecutor then began asking oblique questions about "talking points." "I've seen talking points from the Democratic National Committee," I said. "And what was the substance of those talking points?" "Different talking points." "Do you remember the subject? Other than Monica Lewinsky, was it about the Office of Independent Counsel staff?" I explained exactly how the "talking points" at the DNC were created: "They're produced by the research department, and they are all based on published reports, and they're summaries of published reports, and obviously they expressed the view of the research department of the DNC." "And you received this from the DNC?" "Yes."

The prosecutor asked, "Did you distribute it to anyone outside the White House?" This question was aimed directly at my contacts with the media. I responded by listing the news organizations I had dealt with most recently. By grouping them together I hoped to avoid intrusive questions picking apart my relations with individual reporters: "If reporters called me or I spoke with reporters, I would tell them to call the DNC to get those talking points, and those included news organizations ranging from CNN, CBS, ABC, *New York Times*, New York *Daily News*, *Chicago Tribune*, *New York Observer*, *L.A. Times*."

"Would you, though, distribute the talking points? Would you cause the talking points to be distributed to any of these news organizations?"

In order to break the pattern of these invasive questions, I went out of the room to consult my attorney.

When I returned, the prosecutor returned to his conspiracy theory, asking a series of questions about Hillary and the President, trying to pin them down as the ultimate bosses of the obstruction of justice: "In your conversations with Mrs. Clinton about the Monica Lewinsky matter, did any of those conversations refer or relate to the dissemination of information about members of the Office of Independent Counsel to the news media?" My answer was: "No." Asked if Hillary or the President had directed me to take actions "about the Monica Lewinsky matter," I said, "None," and, "No."

Then Bittman said, "We have seen on the television that some talking point type document that at least the news reporter indicated had come from the White House." Finally, after far too much about the DNC talking points, he was being direct. The only "talking point type document" discussed on television had been the famous "Talking Points." And the report that the prosecutor passively described as having "seen"—an NBC News report—cited "sources in Starr's office" eight times. "I haven't seen that," I said. "You haven't seen that," the prosecutor mocked.

But he still pursued the question: "Have you heard about the White House disseminating to any news organization any type of document like that, any talking points, factual summaries, or anything like that to any member of the news media?" This compacted question once again demanded specific information about reporters. Bittman asked the question that I had answered several times already, and I had answered repetitively: "Has anyone at the White House received any other talking points from any other sources?" "I don't know." "Have you heard?" "No."

Sol Wisenberg took over from Bittman. His task was apparently to blame the White House for the leaks in the press that had come from the Independent Counsel's own office: "Mr. Blumenthal, do you know if anyone at or acting on behalf of the White House leaked to the press the story to the effect that Monica Lewinsky had visited the White House about thirty-seven times after losing her job there?" "I know nothing about that." "Okay. You don't know if anybody at or acting on behalf of the White House leaked that story?" "To my knowledge, no."

"Are you aware of any information either personally or just through hearsay, are you aware of any information that the White House or people acting on behalf of the White House has leaked to the press but accused the Office of Independent Counsel of leaking to the press?" Of the many cynical questions I was asked, this was the baldest. "Absolutely not," I answered. "That's all I've got," said Wisenberg.

Bittman jumped back in, once again bringing up "talking points" and launching into a last effort to prompt a new answer. "Let me ask you one other question," he said, as he extended into logical absurdity. "We talked specifically about talking points and then summaries of facts, and I had started with the question, Mr. Blumenthal, about whether you have seen any document in the White House, that is, any piece of paper on which something is written, any document that was created or believed to be created at the White House that related to the Monica Lewinsky matter." "I have not." "So as far as you know, no one in the White House has written anything down relating to Monica Lewinsky." His self-induced repetitive frustration had reduced him to sarcasm again. "I don't know," I said. "But I have not seen it."

The prosecutors asked me to leave for a moment and then they recalled me. While I was in the corridor, they had spoken with the grand jurors and elicited and shaped a question intended to cast their investigation as truth seeking. David Barger, another of Starr's Likud faction, asked the first question, about my "earlier testimony to the effect that the public has a right to know about the character of public officials. Do you recall that?" "Yes." "Is that a fair characterization of what you said?" "Yes." "I take it that your belief in that would also include the President, that the public has a right to know about the character of the President as well." "Absolutely." "All right," he said in self-satisfied triumph. "Can you tell us again—again, I'll ask you"—he paused for dramatic effect— "can you tell us about your conversation with the President concerning the topic of Monica Lewinsky?" "I've said everything I have to say on that," I replied. "The substance is covered by executive privilege."

To demand the dissemination of public information about the records of officials doing public work is not the same as to invade their privacy for political purposes, of course. The prosecutor's intention was to impugn his target, the President, by suggesting to the grand jury that the President's aide was hypocritical and uncooperative.

"That's all I have," said Barger. "Mr. Blumenthal, you're excused," said Bittman. "Thank you for appearing."

I turned to the grand jury: "Thank you all very much for taking your time." I stood and shook the hands of the surprised prosecutors at the table. Then I turned and shook the other prosecutors' hands. "Hello, Mr. Bennett," I said to a somewhat startled Jackie Bennett. "How are you?"

"All right," he said. I had been before the grand jury for about three hours.

Out in the corridor, I told the lawyers about my closing bit of testimony. Cheryl got on the phone to Ruff and Kendall to tell them. McDaniel and Marsh took notes. I sat for about ten minutes writing on a small piece of paper. The images of Betty Currie bowing her head as she escaped through the assembled press after her own grand-jury appearance, of the other women from the White House trying to protect themselves from the gaze of the media by fleeing from side exits, of Marcia Lewis photographed distraught and exhausted as she left the grand jury were in my mind. I was not fearful of the reporters. I had been one myself. Now, as a witness, I could tell what had happened inside the grand jury, and be the one to do so before they heard Starr's version from his leakers.

So I walked out the front door of the courthouse to stand before a bank of microphones and hundreds of reporters. My lawyers stood on each side of me. It was a warm, sixty-degree February day, shortly after noon. "Mr. Blumenthal faced the cameras at the peak of the Western Hemisphere's last total solar eclipse of the millennium," *The New York Times* reported.* I took out my scrap of paper and read:

> For nearly thirty years I was a working journalist and for six months I have been an assistant to the President. I never imagined that in America I would be hauled before a federal grand jury to answer questions about my conversations with members of the media. But today I was forced to answer questions about conversations, as part of my job, with *The New York Times*, CNN, CBS, *Time* magazine, *U.S. News*, the New York *Daily News*, the *Chicago Tribune*, *The New York Observer*, and there may have been a few others.
>
> Ken Starr's prosecutors demanded to know what I had told reporters and what reporters had told me about Ken Starr's prosecutors. If they think they have intimidated me, they have failed. And if any journalist here or elsewhere wants to talk to me, I'll be glad to talk to you.

I did not take questions there. I walked the length of the courthouse, got in the car, and drove back to the White House. In my office I had a long list of telephone calls from reporters to be returned. Bill McDaniel

*John M. Broder, "A Clinton Adviser Details Testimony," *The New York Times*, February 27, 1998.

and I walked across Lafayette Park to the Hay-Adams Hotel, where he had a room, and he got David Kendall on the speakerphone. Kendall asked me to tell him what President Clinton had told me. So I related the conversation in the Oval Office on January 21. Kendall said it was the most detailed account anyone had, and if I had to testify about it, I would have to tell that story. McDaniel and I spent the afternoon reviewing my testimony, based on my recollection and his notes of what I had told him. He created a kind of transcript that he could share with the other lawyers, including the White House legal counsel. While we worked, I placed calls to reporters.

The next morning, I showed up at the White House as usual. Before the senior staff meeting in the Roosevelt Room, John Podesta summoned me to sit next to the Chief of Staff. Podesta took out a brass nameplate and set it on the table: "Grassy Knoll." Everyone laughed. I sat down to raucous applause.

My brief remarks outside the courthouse had been broadcast on every network news show and reported on the front page of almost every newspaper. The *New York Times*/CBS News poll showed, as the *Times* wrote, "a plummeting public approval rating" for Starr. His favorable rating had sunk to 11 percent, one of the lowest ever recorded for any public figure, while President Clinton's rating had reached 73 percent.* Public opinion now believed that Starr was "out to get Clinton, whatever it takes, fair or unfair"—53 percent, according to the Harris Poll.† "White House officials said they believe Mr. Starr turned the public against himself, particularly when he subpoenaed White House communications strategist Sidney Blumenthal," *The Dallas Morning News* reported.‡ "Starr succeeded in undermining himself in ways the White House could have only dreamed," *Time* said. "The decision to grill Blumenthal instantly transformed a city where people have black belts in Not Taking a Stand. It sent everyone scurrying madly into one of two camps: either you were part of the vast right-wing conspiracy trying to get the Clintons or you belonged to the vast left-wing conspiracy trying to topple Starr. It made

*Don Van Natta, Jr., "White House's All-Out Attack on Starr Is Paying Off, with His Help," *The New York Times*, March 2, 1998.

†Doyle McManus, "Starr's Actions Found Wanting by Friend, Foe," *Los Angeles Times*, March 1, 1998.

‡David Jackson, "White House Keeping Heat on Starr for Inquiry Tactics; Polls Show Low Public Opinion of Investigation," *The Dallas Morning News*, March 19, 1998.

news organizations, many of which had relied on leaks to move the story along, suddenly jump off the fence and swear fealty to the First Amendment."* "Sanctimonious arrogance," wrote Al Hunt about Starr, in a column in *The Wall Street Journal*.† There was international condemnation. Article XIX, the British group devoted to free speech, issued a statement saying that Starr had violated "international law," citing the European Court of Human Rights. And the historian of the Sedition Act of 1798 Richard Rosenfeld wrote, "Independent Counsel Kenneth Starr is the first public official to attempt to criminalize press criticism without using national security as a rationale when he subpoenaed presidential assistant Sidney Blumenthal to testify before a grand jury about press criticism of Starr. Worse, Starr has no Sedition Act to define the criticism he will punish."‡

Starr's Republican allies bemoaned his political incompetence. "He is the Helen Keller of American politics. He is deaf, dumb, and blind," said Richard Galen, a political consultant and adviser to House Speaker Gingrich.§ A former Starr prosecutor was quoted: "I can't get over it. He's completely out of control. I can't begin to defend this."‖

The *Chicago Tribune* reported a turnabout of events:

> White House aide Sidney Blumenthal provided the latest personification of the rhetorical grenades when he stood righteously on the courthouse steps this week after answering questions from Starr's inquisitors and declared that nothing would silence him. Suddenly, the public discussion and news coverage were not about whether the president had an affair with a former intern and asked her to lie about it under oath. . . . Instead, they were about whether Starr would prevail in his efforts to force White House aides to divulge which reporters they had talked to and to what end. . . . Now, the case was about the 1st Amendment, and any challenge to it is certain to set off a flood of negative media reaction from the defenders of free speech.#

---

*Nancy Gibbs and Michael Duffy, "Everyone's Talking Trash," *Time*, March 9, 1998.

†Albert R. Hunt, "The Inspector and the Jock."

‡Richard Rosenfeld, "Whose Intrusive Tactics?" *Chicago Tribune*, March 4, 1998.

§McManus, "Starr's Actions."

‖Gibbs and Duffy, "Everyone's Talking Trash."

#Michael Tackett, "Starr Is Sinking Deeper into the Mudslinging," *Chicago Tribune*, February 28, 1998.

Starr never recovered his image after this. He had drawn the battle lines where he wanted them and had expected a swift, total victory, and his rout surprised no one more than himself.

Starr and his political and journalistic followers shared an ironclad self-rationalization for whatever they did—they were pursuing the truth—and they could not accept that Starr had no criminal case and that his inquisitorial tactics had generated public opposition. They instinctively sought to find a scapegoat for his failures. What I did was now turned into a myth that made me responsible for almost all the trouble that was confounding Starr and the Republicans. I was wildly overestimated as a ubiquitous, omnipotent, and spectral presence at the White House—and yet underestimated at the same time. Only those I dealt with knew how straightforward my work was—a combination of political strategy and journalism.

The attacks on me were about a contrived persona, always easier to describe than the actual person. The Sidney Blumenthal whom Drudge first conjured as a violent wife-beater became a delusional Nostradamus, a dark sorcerer, a Rasputin. (*The Weekly Standard* had published a cover story about me the week before entitled "Hillary's Brain" and calling me "Nixonian."*) "Sid Vicious" was a sex-crazed predator and drooling night crawler, as I was shown to be in an illustration in the *National Review*. "And just as real-life mafiosi often maintain Jewish consiglieri, so the Clintons have their . . . Blumenthals."†

Once I became a lightning rod, the bolts never ceased—but I tried to turn my now unwanted, charged function to political benefit.

"Starr Targets Blumenthal in Probe of Leaks" ran the *Washington Times* headline the morning after my grand-jury appearance. The article was a string of falsehoods that the writer, Jerry Seper, one of Starr's reliable outlets, had clearly been fed: that I had been brought into the White House "to fine-tune the administration's response to the expanding Starr probe," that I was in charge of an "effort [to use] a private-investigative firm hired to gather evidence in Mr. Starr's Whitewater probe and in Paula Jones' sexual-misconduct lawsuit against Mr. Clinton." I was then turned into the person who was investigating sex: "In recent days, efforts have been made to shop several unsubstantiated stories about the independent counsel and his staff, including suggestions that Mr. Starr was

---

*The article, by Carl Cannon, "Hillary's Brain," *The Weekly Standard*, February 25, 1998, was the fairest about me and the most serious about my politics.
†Michael Ledeen, "Clinton the Chin," *National Review*, April 6, 1998.

involved in an extramarital affair; that a member of his staff is a homo-sexual but has not publicly acknowledged his sexual preference; and that some members of the Starr team have been involved romantically with members of the media. Mr. Starr has called the campaign an 'avalanche of lies.' "* That I had no knowledge of these stories until I read this arti-cle was irrelevant to their publication.

If there was any doubt that this smear of me had emanated from Starr's office, a column by Michael Kelly, now at *The Washington Post*, re-moved it. He was so eager to rush an accusation into print that he did not realize he was exposing the game. Four times in his column of March 5 Kelly cited Jackie Bennett, quoting him at length. This could not have been what the prosecutor wanted; it broke with his preferred cloaked identity—as a "source close to Starr's office."

Kelly began by expressing his personal view of Sidney Blumenthal (he didn't "like" me, he wrote, in the name of "full disclosure"). Having estab-lished his sincerity, he then described an incident wherein a prosecutor had been called by a reporter about "a past episode in his private life" and then had announced he wished to "quit immediately." Kelly wrote, "The White House's smear operation had not merely attempted to in-timidate a Whitewater prosecutor; at least for a moment, it had suc-ceeded. . . . The Blumenthal subpoena went out the next day." This appeared to be a distorted and false account of Bruce Udolf, whose de-sire to leave the independent counsel's office was in fact motivated by his belief in Starr's dishonesty and by Bennett and his acolytes' lack of professionalism.

Kelly freely cited Bennett as his source that "Clinton's whisperers" had conducted a "malign campaign of personal smearing" and "sex smears," that the White House was not only "sexually smearing Starr's assistants" but also spreading a rumor that Starr was having an affair with a lady in Little Rock. Kelly quoted Bennett: " 'What you have here is a situation where somebody is peddling filth and lies about federal prosecutors, in what appears to be an attempt to intimidate those pros-ecutors, and, based on what we have been told, we believe that the somebody is the White House. If a bunch of narcotics traffickers who were being investigated tried this tactic, I don't think most Amer-icans would have a problem with the prosecutor inquiring into it.' "†

*Jerry Seper, "Starr Targets Blumenthal in Probe of Leaks," *The Washington Times*, February 27, 1998.
†Michael Kelly, "Clinton's Whisperers," *The Washington Post*, March 5, 1998.

Thus the Clinton White House as a criminal conspiracy of drug lords.

Two columnists saw fit to respond to Kelly's attack. They had reason to write because they had been personal friends of mine before I joined the White House and because I spoke with them often. They had direct knowledge and were willing to stake their credibility on it. Lars-Erik Nelson, in the New York *Daily News*, wrote:

> Starr and his band of whimpering bullies complain that somebody is spreading "an avalanche of lies" about their sex lives in an effort to intimidate them and distract them from investigating President Clinton. The only problem is that they can't point to any sex stories that have actually appeared anywhere.
>
> Another problem is that Blumenthal—who I talk to as much as anybody in the press does—never spread any such stories. And if he had any to spread, I guarantee he would have told me. Blumenthal despises Starr. I despise Starr. But I have never heard any stories about his sex life or the sex life of any of his deputies, and if I had, I would not repeat them because they are totally irrelevant to Clinton's problems. . . .
>
> Odd fact about Starr's complaint that he is being smeared by the White House: Only three print sources in the country have referred to the rumor that one of his staff is homosexual. They are the Rev. Sun Myung Moon's *Washington Times*, conservative columnist Patrick Buchanan and syndicated columnist Michael Kelly, who was fired as editor of *The New Republic* for being, in the words of his publisher, "an obsessive right-winger." Are they in cahoots with the Clinton White House? I think not.*

Gene Lyons, in a column in the *Arkansas Democrat-Gazette*, described the sex rumor about Starr as risible and my involvement as nonexistent:

> This baseless canard was first published in the semi-underground newsletter "Bullwhiz" more than a year ago. In the interim, I've personally warned at least a half-dozen national reporters not to waste their time and resources pursuing it. While I'd laugh for a month if Starr got caught with his pants down, I told them, the existence of the tale merely illustrated an Arkansas fact of life some of us have tried in vain to warn

---

*Lars-Erik Nelson, "Ken Starr Has My Name—I've Got His Number," New York *Daily News*, March 9, 1998.

them about: that as an island of relative cosmopolitanism in a sea of sex-obsessed fundamentalists, Little Rock is perpetually awash with sexual rumors, mostly false. . . .

Because I do speak with Blumenthal, I happen to know that he shares my opinion about the futility of investigating Starr's sex life.

Nor have I heard him discuss the intimate lives of Starr's investigators, nor of his retinue of pet reporters.

Because I spoke with him last week, I also happen to know that Starr's investigators never asked Blumenthal about the Starr rumor. They were too busy forcing him to name every reporter he'd spoken to since joining the White House staff and what they talked about. Right here in the United States of America.*

My lawyer wrote a letter to *The Washington Post* to establish a public record, and it was published as a letter to the editor about Kelly's column:

Sidney Blumenthal has had no involvement whatsoever at any time at any place in investigating any aspect of the private, sexual lives of Ken Starr or his staff. Mr. Blumenthal has not been involved in any way in the spreading of any of the stories that are specified in Kelly's article. Mr. Blumenthal knows of no one connected to the White House who has been so involved. . . . It also is worth noting that neither the *Post* nor Michael Kelly asked Mr. Blumenthal or his lawyers about the allegations made by Mr. Kelly. It is especially disturbing that you have published these lies from the pen of a man who admits his personal malice toward Mr. Blumenthal.†

Shortly after Kelly's column revealed the hand of the prosecutor in these leaks, I joined, along with the President and Bruce Lindsey, in a complaint lodged against Starr about the leaks. Lindsey and I were also at the center of the executive privilege case that Starr filed in March. In a sealed brief, he demanded that the federal court rule that we must speak to the grand jury about our conversations with the President, conversa-

*Gene Lyons, "Blundering Strike at Free Speech," *Arkansas Democrat-Gazette*, March 4, 1998.

†William Alden McDaniel, Jr., "Blumenthal vs. Kelly," Letter to the Editor, *The Washington Post*, March 9, 1998.

tions that Clinton believed were covered by the doctrine of executive privilege. The idea that a president can protect and keep confidential the discussions he has with his advisers derives from the constitutional doctrine of the separation of executive, legal, and legislative powers, and it goes back to George Washington.

Over the months ahead, the legal wrangling, false accusations, and raw struggle for power only intensified as Starr sought to topple the President, and I was increasingly demonized and isolated. One morning at a particularly low point, I discovered that my son Paul had handwritten a message and posted it with a magnet on our refrigerator door: "In the end we will remember not the words of our enemies, but the silence of our friends. Dr. Martin Luther King, Jr."

It stayed there for a year.

TWELVE

The Reign of Witches

I

Clinton's presidency was "deader really than Woodrow Wilson's was after he had a stroke." Thus pronounced the conservative pundit George Will on ABC's *This Week* on January 25, 1998. But in the three weeks after the Monica Lewinsky scandal broke, this sentiment, near universal among the Washington press corps and political classes, was defied by the American people. In poll after poll Clinton's ratings dramatically increased—from 60 to 69 percent job approval in the CNN/*USA Today*/Gallup poll; from 59 to 66 percent in the CNN/*Time* poll; from 57 to 72 percent in a CBS News survey—and in the NBC News/*Wall Street Journal* poll, Clinton received his highest approval rating ever, of 79 percent. The American people made the distinction between the public and private spheres more easily than the elites. And the more President Clinton was assailed, the more they supported him.

In his State of the Union address, Clinton had proposed a budget with unprecedented surpluses that would also increase investments in child care, education, the environment, and health care. Once again, the Republicans were confounded as he spent the year outmaneuvering them just as they imagined he would be swept away. Rather than being bound to the obsessions of the political capital, Clinton became a larger-than-life president, traveling farther and wider than ever. He went to Africa, China, Latin America, Britain, and Germany. He welcomed Tony Blair and more than a dozen other world leaders to the White House. Day by day, he worked toward breakthroughs in the peace negotiations in both Northern Ireland and the Middle East. He closely monitored the stealthy buildup of Saddam Hussein's weapons of mass destruction. And after al-Qaeda's bombings of the U.S. embassies in East Africa, he launched a war on terrorism that never flagged in its intensity until he left office. But in Washington all these struggles seemed to recede into the background when the assault on Clinton's presidency took center stage.

From the time Ken Starr captured Monica Lewinsky in January, through the submission of his report to the House Judiciary Committee in the fall, he maneuvered toward a show trial of President Clinton the likes of which had not been seen since the impeachment and trial of President Andrew Johnson in 1868. The complex legal maneuvers over abstract concepts like executive privilege were but skirmishes that preceded a monumental battle over very large political questions: about the Constitution, about cultural mores and the position of women in American society, and about the character of the American people. It was, ultimately, a struggle about the identity of the country. President Clinton understood that; his wife did, too; so did many people in the White House; and so did Ken Starr and the Republican leaders. It was why he and they were fighting. So the Independent Counsel drove his investigation relentlessly into open alliance with the Republican Congress. To stage an impeachment and trial, they required each other. Starr would produce the inevitable charges, the Congress the inevitable judgment.

Over the next months, Starr's storm enveloped in shadow and fog everyone standing in his path. He and his supporters needed a convenient explanation for their continued failures and Clinton's popularity. As they saw it, Starr should be acclaimed a national hero, and the President already should have quickly resigned. But the drama wasn't unfolding as they had imagined it should. Eventually, in their angry frustration, they would wind up blaming the American people.

In the meantime, I became a target that could personify their political troubles. Almost anything bad that befell Starr or the Republicans they would blame on me, whether they believed it or not. I would be their scapegoat. When I spoke out about what he was doing, I inflicted political damage on him, and thereafter Starr and his deputies tried to restore his image by trashing me. Sticking pins in me was intended to harm the President. I also became a screen on which Starr projected his own underhanded techniques: just as he had invaded the President's sex life, I would be accused falsely of invading his opponents'.

Starr had allies among reporters, editors, and pundits who had aligned themselves with his cause, and these now assailed me, a former journalist who had crossed over to being an object of their scorn. Others followed their lead in a tail-holding line of conventional wisdom, parading as bravely independent. As for the people in the conservative movement who had reviled me ever since I had started reporting on them for *The Washington Post* in the Reagan period, I was the class enemy, "the devil," as they put it (for example, in a front-page headline in the *New York Post*). In the literally thousands of attacks that were made on my character, not one mentioned a policy or even a political issue. "I don't know much about him but he's just a scummy guy," a prominent Republican operative, Ed Gillespie, was quoted as saying in *The Washington Post*.* (A former aide to House Majority Leader Dick Armey, Gillespie was the chief lobbyist for Enron.) Whenever it turned out that I wasn't who they said I was, the attacks only became nastier.

The stereotype conjured up of me was a series of contradictions: an omnipotent yet weak person, repulsive yet seductive, in a superior position achieved by unethical means. For example, Michael Kelly, in a column in *The Washington Post*, called me "Sid the Human Ferret"—a subhuman.† Not a single documented incident was cited to verify this portrait of a vile, unspeakable presidential aide, except the obvious fact that I supported the vile, unspeakable President.

On the morning of my first grand-jury appearance I had had to walk through shouting reporters and snapping cameramen just to get to my car. I did not resent them for doing their work, but I had to put on a game face to go down the sidewalk in front of my own house. All of us who worked at the White House had to gird ourselves every day. Whatever I was feeling had to be tamped down. Anger, frustration, suspicion, doubt, had to be suppressed. Sometimes when the accusations were particularly outrageous I felt compelled to respond, but usually I did not.

Self-control didn't arrive on the doorstep like the daily newspaper. I had to put on a suit of armor every morning—and keep it fastened all day long. While the blows rained down there was little to do but weather them. Inexpressiveness became the psychological order of each day, exhaustion the constant physical condition. Once, I found myself asleep standing up at a public event in the East Room. I came to think of this as a political version of trench warfare as in the First World War—occasional ferocious battles, a mile gained or lost, and no end in sight.

---

*Michael Powell, "Mud About You," *The Washington Post*, September 25, 1998.
†Michael Kelly, "Starr Wars: The 21st Century," *The Washington Post*, July 8, 1998.

Perhaps the most helpful advice I received was from Hillary. "Remember," she told me, "it's never about you. Whatever you think, it's never about you." It was about President Clinton, about his agenda, about the Constitution. At a certain point, even the President had to think it was not about him. This insight enabled you to surmount the distractions of personal attack and maintain a clear sense of what was important. The more personal the attack, the more you had to grasp that it was political.

I had decided when I joined Clinton's White House that it was worthwhile to endure the criticism that came my way. I made another decision after January 21, when I decided to fight to preserve Clinton's presidency for all that it still promised for the country. I made yet another decision after being subpoenaed by Starr. I decided not to back down when I became a lightning rod. At each point, there was no way to assess what the personal toll would be on me or my wife and sons, who became touched, too, by anger and frustration at the assaults on my integrity. But there was a toll. Jackie responded at first by writing letters to newspaper editors and reporters she knew to protest stories that trashed me, but then she gave up; it was like spitting into the wind during a hurricane. There was no way to set things straight or expect that a rational explanation would be accepted in the midst of this storm. If people thought I was opaque and icy, or a mindless follower, or self-aggrandizing, so be it. I had decided that what I *felt* was not that significant. Confidence that we would prevail was the best and only face to wear. Loyalty was the only sentiment to display. Self-denial was the price of public service that had to be paid.

On March 7, *Time* held its seventy-fifth anniversary celebration at Radio City Music Hall in New York. The event was packed with the famous people who had graced the magazine's covers over the decades. A red carpet had been laid out in front of the music hall with lines of photographers ready to snap pictures of the celebrities. My wife and I wanted to arrive before the presidential entourage so that we'd have time to chat with some friends we knew would be attending. As we walked to the door some paparazzi began shouting my name. I stopped with a startle, flashbulbs popping in my face. This was not the frenzy of renown, as the literary critic Leo Braudy called it; it was renown born of frenzy.

Escaping inside, I spotted Joe DiMaggio and became transformed into a fan, asking him for an autograph for my son, which he grudgingly granted. I was delighted to see Ted Sorensen, President Kennedy's special counsel, who offered me his warm support. Gestures like his meant a great deal, especially coming from someone who had worked in the White House. At the dinner, I was seated next to Steven Brill, the former publisher and editor of *The American Lawyer*, who told me that he was launching a new magazine devoted to the media, *Brill's Content*. In between speeches by Mikhail Gorbachev and Steven Spielberg and Bill Gates and Mary Tyler Moore, we discussed what was going on in Washington.

Each of the speakers delivered a tribute to one of the movers and shakers of the past seventy-five years. "To me," said President Clinton when it was his turn, "one man above all others is the personification of our American century: Franklin Delano Roosevelt. Now, that choice might have pained Henry Luce [*Time's* founder, a staunch Republican], but surely he would not be surprised. . . . The advance of freedom has made this the American century. . . . The embodiment of the triumph, the driving force behind it, was Franklin Delano Roosevelt. Today, with the happy outcome known to all, it is tempting to look back and say the victory was assured, inevitable—but it wasn't." Then he turned more personal:

> He was born to privilege, but he understood the aspirations of farmers and factory workers and forgotten Americans. My grandfather came from a little town of about fifty people. He had a fourth-grade education. He believed Franklin Roosevelt was his friend, a man who cared about him and his family and his child's future. Polio put him in a wheelchair, but he lifted our troubled nation to its feet and he got us moving again. He was a patrician who happily addressed the Daughters of the American Revolution as "my fellow immigrants." He was a master politician, a magnificent Commander-in-Chief. Yes, his life had its fair share of disappointments and failures, but they never broke his spirit or his faith in God or his people. Because he always rose to the occasion, so did we. FDR was guided not by the iron dictates of ideology, but by the pragmatism by what he called bold persistent experimentation. If one thing doesn't work, he said, try another thing; but above all, try something. It drove his critics crazy, but it worked.

Beyond connecting his presidency with Roosevelt's tradition, Clinton used the occasion for a specific political purpose. United Nations Secretary-General Kofi Annan was present, and the President lauded him for supporting the recent Security Council resolution that required Saddam Hussein to permit UN inspections in Iraq for weapons of mass destruction. He praised the work of the UN in general, which was, after all, in great part Roosevelt's creation, and asked that "Americans support the United Nations," a call on the Republican Congress to pay the outstanding debt that the United States owed. "Now we know what came of Roosevelt and his generation's 'rendezvous with destiny.' What will come of ours? To this generation of the millennium, in President Roosevelt's words, 'much has been given' and 'much is asked.' "

On *Air Force One*, riding back to Washington, Senator Ted Kennedy was seated across from me, and he launched into a detailed discussion of health care proposals. Senator Daniel Patrick Moynihan, next to him, noticed that Ted was monopolizing attention on these issues, so he began talking about New York's transportation needs. The President wandered by and joined in this duel of wonkery from two of the most knowledgeable and eloquent practitioners of governmental arts. Fame is short, policy long. But on our returning to the capital, it seemed as if scandal was forever.

"Too many lies are being told. Too many lives are being ruined. And, I— I think it's time for the truth to come out." Thus spoke Kathleen Willey, in public for the first time to claim that the President had made an unwanted sexual advance, in an interview to Ed Bradley on CBS's *60 Minutes* on March 15. Groomed and affluent, wearing a long strand of pearls signifying that she was no Paula Jones, Willey related sordid details to the shocked reporter. Bob Bennett, darkly lit, was permitted a brief response as the President's attorney.

A divorced former airline stewardess, Kathleen Willey had married Ed Willey, Jr., a Virginia lawyer and a prominent Virginia politician's son who rolled up enormous personal debts to maintain their extravagant lifestyle. After fund-raising for Clinton in 1992, she became a volunteer in the White House social office and, according to her friend Linda Tripp, sought a sexual relationship with the President. In November 1993, Willey said, she had gone to see Clinton about a White House job and he had groped her. Clinton adamantly denied this. The very day she was at the White House, Ed Willey, burdened with debt, had committed suicide.

There were a dozen discrepancies between her vague testimony in the preliminary maneuvers of the Paula Jones case—she couldn't even remember her own claim about Clinton having kissed her—and her graphic account on *60 Minutes*. Yet, on March 9, Starr had granted her unusual transactional immunity from all prosecution of any past offenses, including any perjury in her Jones deposition or in the messy legal suits she was involved in after her husband's death. She testified before his grand jury the next day, then appeared on *60 Minutes*, which highlighted her as a reluctant and credible witness, demonstrating the power of self-presentation, especially on television. Her television appearance had been arranged by Starr's office. Already a witness in the Jones case, which in effect he was taking over, she seemed likely to be a witness in an impeachment trial.

Willey, however, had written numerous letters to the President after her encounter, explaining her constant affection and respect for him, calling herself his "number one fan," and requesting jobs, including an ambassadorship. Some of her notes were signed, "Fondly." If Clinton had felt any need to silence her, he might have given her a plum position, but she never received one, and she was angry about it, according to one note, saying she was not to be "trifled with."* The day after her *60 Minutes* interview, the White House, after some internal debate, released this correspondence, which cast doubt on her credibility.

I was at that moment in San Juan, Puerto Rico, with Mack McLarty, helping to prepare for the Summit of the Americas that was going to take place in April. We were attending a conference of the Inter-American Press Association, hoping to gain its approval of our proposal to create a special office within the Organization of American States to report on violations of freedom of the press throughout the hemisphere. That very evening, Bacardi Rum held a party for the conference participants at a magical village made of papier-mâché and populated by a calypso band and dancers attired as colorful animals, who pulled us into an endless conga line. Carefree San Juan seemed less surreal than grim Washington.

On March 30, *Time* was the first to report that Willey had had an unpleasant breakup of an affair in 1995 with a much younger man. (She had lied to him, saying she was pregnant with "twins," had allowed him to convince her to have an "abortion," and then had backed out on the day of the "procedure," insisting she would not end her "pregnancy.") She had lied under oath to Starr's office about this sexual imbroglio and, when confronted with her lie, said, "I was embarrassed, and I was ashamed of it."† Her reason was why most people lie about sex. She had

---

*Florence Graves and Jacqueline E. Sharkey, "Starr and Willey: The Untold Story," *The Nation*, May 17, 1999.

†Toobin, *A Vast Conspiracy*, p. 397.

perjured herself, and her immunity was null and void. Starr could have prosecuted her for this perjury, but he chose instead to grant her immunity from any such thing. He hid this second grant of immunity from the public and the Congress.

On April Fool's Day, Judge Wright issued a summary judgment in the Paula Jones case, dismissing the plaintiff's case against Bill Clinton as being without merit. When her decision was announced, a small group of us danced and hugged each other in Ruff's office. "It's over!" one of my colleagues shouted. But I knew it wasn't.

President Clinton received the news in Dakar, Senegal, on the penultimate day of an eleven-day trip in Africa. When Bob Bennett reached him, he asked if it was an April Fool's Day joke. Then he beat on a drum.

Clinton's African trip, the most intensive ever undertaken by an American president, was also the most comprehensive in terms of policy. He ranged from Ghana, where he was greeted by a million people and talked of economic development; to Rwanda, where he addressed genocide survivors and promoted what was called an Africa Crisis Response Initiative; to Uganda, where he appeared at a conference on democracy and human rights; to South Africa, where he announced American-sponsored programs on diseases and education and was taken by President Nelson Mandela on a tour of the Robben Island prison where he had been jailed for decades; to Botswana, where he introduced environmental initiatives. The President promoted international trade everywhere he went—he had proposed a new trade bill opening access for African markets that was successfully making its way through the Congress—and Hillary learned more about schemes for microeconomic credits for women villagers.

On his final stop, on April 2, Clinton toured Goree Island, notorious as a slavers' trading post, and spoke:

In 1776, when our nation was founded on the promise of freedom as God's right to all human beings, a new building was dedicated here on Goree Island to the selling of human beings in bondage to America.

Goree Island is, therefore, as much a part of our history as a part of Africa's history. From Goree and other places Africa's sons and daughters were taken through the door of no return, never to see their friends and families again. Those who survived the murderous middle passage emerged from a dark hold to find themselves, yes, American. But it would be a long, long time before their descendants enjoyed the full meaning of that word.

We cannot push time backward through the door of no return.

We have lived our history.

America's struggle to overcome slavery and its legacy forms one of the most difficult chapters of that history. Yet, it is also one of the most heroic—a triumph of courage, persistence, and dignity.

The long journey of African-Americans proves that the spirit can never be enslaved. And that long journey is today embodied by the children of Africa who now lead America, in all phases of our common life.

Many of them have come here with me on this visit, representing over 30 million Americans that are Africa's great gift to America. . . .

A few hours from now, we will leave Africa and go on home, back to the work of building our own country for a new century. But I return more convinced than when I came here that despite the daunting challenges, there is an African renaissance.

That same day, Ken Starr walked down the driveway of his suburban Virginia house carrying plastic garbage bags and held an impromptu press conference. Speaking of the Paula Jones case, he said, "You cannot defile the temple of justice. You must play by the rules. . . . And if you don't play by those rules, if you lie under oath, if you intimidate a witness, if you seek otherwise to obstruct the process of justice, it doesn't matter who wins and who loses in the civil case. What matters, from the criminal law's perspective, is: Were crimes committed?" In other words, the Jones case would now go forward under his auspices—headed toward Clinton's impeachment.

Starr assumed a new identity. He explained that he was emulating a personal hero—Sergeant Joe Friday, the character from the 1950s television series *Dragnet*. "I've always been a big believer in that show . . . that Jack Webb was in, 'Just the facts ma'am.' " But his self-dramatizing metaphor only confused his image: prosecutors can be righteous gangbusters or grand inquisitors in the popular imagination, but not plodding detectives. Starr was running the wrong movies in his head.

Suddenly, Starr faced an obstacle he had not expected. On March 17, *Salon* magazine reported that David Hale, the convicted con man who was Starr's sole witness against President Clinton in the Whitewater investigation, had accepted money from a key participant in the Arkansas Project, Parker Dozhier, the virulent right-wing activist and owner of the bait shop where Hale spent time. Dozhier denied the charge. But the sources of this report were Dozhier's former girlfriend and her teenaged son, who had dozens of pages of notes in Dozhier's handwriting, detailing the comings and goings of the Arkansas Project through his shop, including conservative journalists in search of "dirt." And an anonymous source (it was Lemley, *The American Spectator*'s financial manager) was quoted as saying that the *Spectator* executives in charge of the Scaife money spoke openly of helping Hale.*

The problem for Starr was that this news suggested his Whitewater witness had been tampered with. Attorney General Janet Reno, responding to the article, said that the charge of witness tampering must be investigated. On April 9, Deputy Attorney General Eric Holder wrote Starr that the FBI had conducted a preliminary inquiry and that there was evidence that Hale "may have received cash and other gratuities from individuals seeking to discredit the president during a period when Hale was actively cooperating with your investigation." Further investigation, he stated, was warranted.† Holder pointed out that Starr might have a conflict of interest "because of the importance of Hale to your investigation and because the payments allegedly came from funds provided by Richard Scaife."‡

But Starr was desperate to hang on to this investigation. He finally renounced the deanship at Pepperdine University, paid for by Scaife, in an effort to remove his conflict of interest, and in late May, he and Reno agreed that he would appoint Michael Shaheen, former head of the Justice Department's Office of Professional Responsibility, to investigate the David Hale charges and report—to a panel of retired judges rather than to Starr. Many months later, after the impeachment trial, Shaheen reported, "There is insufficient credible evidence to show that a thing of value was provided or received with the criminal intent defined by any of the applicable statutes," but nothing else is known of what he wrote. His 168-page report reached the conclusion that Hale's testimony had not been bought, but the public has never seen that report. The New York *Daily News* reported that two of Starr's former prosecutors had been referred to the Justice Department for disciplining as a consequence of the

---

*Jonathan Broder and Murray Waas, "The Road to Hale," *Salon.com*, March 17, 1998.

†Roberto Suro and Susan Schmidt, "Justice Department Urges Starr to Probe Alleged Hale Payments to Key Witness," *The Washington Post*, April 10, 1998.

‡Quoted in Susan Schmidt and Roberto Suro, "Clinton Lawyer Renews Assault on Prosecutor," *The Washington Post*, April 14, 1998.

investigation, but at Starr's insistence, the report was sealed. Its lengthy contents remain undisclosed, a mystery.*

In late April, I traveled with the President to the second Summit of the Americas, a gathering of the thirty-four elected heads of state, in Santiago, Chile. There he signed a declaration for new education programs, economic development, human rights, and the environment, and pledged to fight the terrorism of drug mafias and to open the Free Trade Area of the Americas to include more of our neighbor nations. Among the proposals that were ratified was one that included a new office in the OAS for freedom of the press.

At Valparaiso, Clinton spoke before the Chilean Congress: "To those anywhere in the Americas who would seek to take away people's precious liberties once again or rule through violence and terror once again, let us reaffirm President Aylwin's historic words at Santiago Stadium: Nunca mas—Never again."

General Augusto Pinochet, the former dictator, still an ex officio member of the Congress, had claimed to be too ill to attend the session when Clinton spoke. And a number of right-wing military officers grumbled publicly about President Clinton's remarks, for they were an authoritative rebuke to those who had overthrown Chile's democracy. I left the Congress with Isabel Allende, the novelist and niece of Salvador Allende, the Chilean president slain in the coup, and she expressed immense gratitude for Clinton's remarks. In Santiago, I also met with high-ranking members of the Socialist Party and told them I would be organizing international conferences growing out of the Clinton-Blair meetings—a new platform for what we called Progressive Governance and the Third Way. If they won the next election, I said, they would be included. And they did, and they were.

Though I spent plenty of time discussing the new press freedom office with Latin American reporters and U.S. correspondents stationed in Latin America, I could interest the traveling U.S. press corps in this subject hardly at all. (The most extensive coverage in *The Washington Post* consisted of an ad hominem critique: "And some uncharitable folks recalled Blumenthal's libel suit against Internet gossipmeister Matt Drudge. . . . Blumenthal lacks any bona fides for his new role."†) They

---

*Joe Conason, "Why Won't Kenneth Starr Release the Shaheen Report?" *Salon.com*, August 10, 1999.

†Al Kamen, "Blumenthal, Champion of Free Press," *The Washington Post*, April 17, 1998.

were buzzing about *Brill's Content*, though, the first issue of the magazine, devoted to the press, still weeks away from publication but rumored to contain an article about Starr's leaks.

On April 30, Starr indicted Webster Hubbell again—and his wife Suzanne—on tax-fraud conspiracy. Hubbell declared, "I want you to know the Office of Independent Counsel can indict my dog, they can indict my cat, but I'm not going to lie about the President, I'm not going to lie about the First Lady or anyone else. My wife and I are innocent of the charges brought today."* (In June 2000, the indictments against the Hubbells were dismissed by the Supreme Court.)

That same day, Representative Dan Burton, chairman of the House Government Reform and Oversight Committee, released twenty-seven pages of transcribed telephone conversations between Hubbell and his wife, taped while he was in jail. The transcribed remarks strongly suggested he was covering up Hillary's involvement in Whitewater. In one excerpt of the Burton version, Hubbell was cited as saying that new claims against his law firm would "open up" Hillary. The unexpurgated tapes on which these transcriptions were based were listened to by a dozen reporters but not by any Democratic members of the committee. Three days later, the Democrats were allowed to hear them, and they discovered that the transcripts had been extensively doctored. (Edited out, for example, was this exculpatory remark: "Hillary's not. Hillary—the only thing is people say, why didn't she know what was going on? And I wish she'd never paid any attention to what was going on at the firm. That's the gospel truth. She just had no idea what was going on. She didn't participate in any of this."† Also deleted was Hubbell's statement that Hillary had "no idea" of billing irregularities at the firm.) Burton had to apologize and get the resignation of the aide who had doctored the tapes: none other than David Bossie. Bossie's long career as a professional Clinton-hater came to an abrupt conclusion, and he was exposed at last as a flimflam artist. For their part, the reporters who had written articles about the doctored tapes as if they were credible later claimed they had been working under deadline pressure. "But the press may have been more complicit in the controversy than previously understood," wrote Howard Kurtz in *The Washington*

*Susan Schmidt, "Indictment Claims Hubbell Lived Lavishly," *The Washington Post*, May 1, 1998.

†George Lardner, Jr., "Democrats Hit Burton over Hubbell Tapes," *The Washington Post*, May 4, 1998.

*Post.** The incident that led to Bossie's downfall was a cynosure of his long relationship with reporters avid to take his lead; it differed only in that this time he had been caught.

Upon his return from Latin America, in the first week of May, the President flew out to Silicon Valley in California to talk about the new economy. He observed there that although unemployment was at the lowest level in twenty-eight years, there were still inequalities. "And what we have to do now at this moment when the economy is working so well is to try to devise systems that will work for everybody. . . . We're doing what we can in our administration to create the special economic incentives to go into inner-city areas and isolated rural areas where there hasn't been a lot of new investment." Then he held a forum on the subject of global warming. As soon as he got back to Washington, he used the occasion of the opening of the Ronald Reagan Building and International Trade Center to give a speech on internationalism—an indirect rebuke to the increasingly isolationist Republican Congress—and he met with Prime Minister Prodi of Italy. Also in that week, the Senate finally passed a bill that Clinton had proposed five years earlier to improve federal support for job training.

Within the White House, I found that I had become someone whom others who felt especially injured or assailed would come to for solace and advice. This was not a role I had sought but one that had sought me. Several women quietly came to my office, shut the door, and wept and raged. False stories were being circulated about them in tabloids. Or the prosecutor had asked them humiliating questions about their sex lives. They were consumed with anger, shame, and worry. None of the sleazy charges were true. They fretted about their loved ones' reactions—one woman's husband had a heart condition. Two of the women wanted to strike back by suing their defamers, but after long, wrenching talks, they decided not to throw themselves before the tabloid press and the right wing for raking over in public. Their agonies remained private.

Throughout the months after my first grand-jury appearance, the press was filled with material attacking White House staff members but aimed at the President. He was not supposed to have defenders. In my case, one example was an insidious false rumor, first aired by *The Washington Times* and by Michael Kelly, instigated by Jackie Bennett, that I had spread stories about the prosecutors being closeted homosexuals.

*Howard Kurtz, "Some Reporters Heard Unedited Tapes," *The Washington Post*, May 11, 1998.

Doug Ireland, a left-wing freelancer, gay militant, and Clinton-basher, repeated this worn charge in *The Nation*, citing Kelly and anonymous sources.* I had denied this malicious charge emphatically when he had called me, but it wound up being broadcast on NBC and ABC, though they made no effort to substantiate anything. In this hothouse environment, any lurid charge, whatever its provenance, whatever its veracity, received full airing.

Vanity Fair, the magazine of fashionable moods, published an article in May that was a snide compendium of anonymous animosity. It wrote that if Blumenthal "turned up murdered, everyone in town would be a suspect." *The Washington Times*, under the headline "Sid the Red?" reported that *Vanity Fair* "insinuates that Mr. Blumenthal is—or at least once was—a Communist."† (The magazine had described me as "a sort of journalistic apparatchik," called my writing in *The New Yorker* "party-line propaganda," and quoted an anonymous source saying that I had "the mentality of someone who joined the Communist Party in the '30s." Drawing a full stereotype, he also wrote that "Blumenthal seems to ooze intellectual superiority" and quoted another anonymous source: "He comes from an intense family, of emotion, a certain kind of Jewish family. They don't spare your feelings. It would have taken a lot of work on his part to become a truly gracious person."‡)

My lovely mother telephoned me, very upset that she and my father had been indirectly demeaned by someone who had no idea who they were. She took the gratuitous attack personally. Why would anyone write such a nasty thing about them? I tried to explain that it was simply a falsehood that was the product of an overheated political environment. No matter how personal it appeared to be, it had nothing to do with her or my father. But this explanation only upset her further. She understood all too well the caricature of "a certain kind of Jewish family."

In April, I went to Harvard's Kennedy School of Government to give a talk, mostly about international affairs, but I added a philippic on Starr's abuses. I had written my remarks on this score with the assistance of David Kendall and Charles Ruff. In my conclusion, I said, "I am certain that in historical retrospect this perverse episode will be viewed in its

---

*Doug Ireland, "Of Closets and Clinton," *The Nation*, March 30, 1998. See also his "Whitewater Rafting," *The Nation*, April 22, 1996, and "Money Talks and Gore May Walk," *Newsday*, September 14, 1997.

†Greg Pierce, "Sid the Red?" *The Washington Times*, April 17, 1998.

‡Michael Shnayerson, "Sid Pro Quo," *Vanity Fair*, May 1998.

proper perspective, as Jefferson viewed the Alien and Sedition Acts, in his words, a 'reign of witches.' " In passing I referred to Hickman Ewing (whose connections to the religious right was just then the subject of a profile by Jeffrey Toobin in *The New Yorker*) as "a religious fanatic, who has proclaimed that he operates from a presumption of guilt." The characterization was certainly accurate, but it was a careless political mistake. Even a small phrase like this uttered in an academic setting would be picked up and amplified. I should not have been surprised when a caucus of fifty of the most conservative Republican members of the House signed a letter demanding that the President repudiate my comment. Erskine Bowles asked me to issue an apology to make this squall subside. I expressed "regret if I have offended anybody" by using the word "religious."

"Sid Vicious" screamed the headline in a lead editorial run then by *The Weekly Standard*. "Like certain varieties of venomous snakes, he is kind enough to offer physical warning cues whenever he is about to spit and bite. . . . Rattle, rattle, rattle. *Hisssssssss*. . . . Sidney Blumenthal is a creature of the dark. Nearly every word out of his mouth is a poisonous lie. . . . One of these men, Blumenthal or Starr, must go. The Constitution isn't big enough for both of them."*

In mid-May I traveled to Berlin and London with the President. It was his last meeting with German chancellor Helmut Kohl, who was facing certain defeat in the upcoming September election. Kohl was the longest-serving political leader in Europe, first elected in 1982, and his boldness after the fall of the Berlin Wall had helped to create the newly unified Germany. He had not been entirely candid about the costs of the reunification, however, which turned out to be enormous, and his role in a scandal about illegal payments to his party's treasury, as well as his lengthy incumbency, were pulling him down. He was a colossus, six feet four inches tall, weighing perhaps three hundred pounds. Backstage after one public event with the President, I observed Kohl tilting a large plate of pastries into his giant hand and virtually inhaling them in one gulp.

In Berlin, I met quietly with officials of the opposition Social Democratic Party at its headquarters, Willy Brandt House, where we discussed the campaign and the potential role of an SDP chancellor in the international Third Way–Progressive Governance process. In Bonn, President Clinton, observing the "trouble brewing in Kosovo," addressed the future of the transatlantic alliance: "We begin our common journey with

*David Tell, for the Editors, "Sid Vicious," *The Weekly Standard*, May 11, 1998.

one basic premise: America stands with Europe. . . . If Europe is at peace, America is more secure. If Europe prospers, America does as well. . . . Therefore, we welcome Europe's march toward greater unity."

Just before the speech, I met with Gerhard Schroeder, the new SDP leader. Like Blair, he was a generational counterpart of Clinton's. And like Clinton, he was fatherless—his father had been killed on the Eastern Front in the Second World War—and he had been a student leader on the left, a member of the 1968 generation, moving over time to the center, trying to realign his cumbersome, entrenched party. Superficially, Schroeder might appear somewhat formal, but I discovered from conversing with him that he had a quick intelligence, a sharp sense of humor, and political shrewdness. His ascension as chancellor that September would mark a further ratification of Clinton's brand of center-left politics in the West.

After Germany, the President's party went on to Britain. A month earlier, Clinton had helped to forge the breakthrough for peace in Northern Ireland announced in the Good Friday Accords—an agreement he had been working for ever since 1992, when during his first campaign he declared he would send a special envoy to Ireland to work for peace. This statement had infuriated John Major's Conservative government, who thought the Democratic candidate was demagogically appealing to Irish-American voters and meddling in internal British affairs. (Major, for his part, had been trying to aid Bush's campaign.) Clinton's and Major's chilly relationship got frostier in 1994 when Clinton granted a visa to Irish Republican Army leader Gerry Adams. But Clinton was pushing new diplomacy whether Major approved or not, and he had given the visa to Adams with the understanding that Adams would secure a cease-fire in Northern Ireland. In November 1995, Clinton was welcomed by rapturous crowds when he visited Belfast, where he shook hands with Adams (offending the British) and turned on the lights on the city's Christmas tree.

Then he appointed former senator George Mitchell as his special envoy, initially on economic issues. This was a herald of a promising future, for with Mitchell inserted into the process, Clinton had a lever. The week Blair was elected in 1997, the President swooped into London on an unannounced visit. Clinton now had a real British partner, and the new British government agreed to name Mitchell as chief mediator in Northern Ireland. No longer was the United States acting unilaterally. Rather than seeing him as having ulterior political motives, Blair brought Clinton into the center of the negotiations to use his skills to get the opposing parties to reach a consensus. While Mitchell held talks at Belfast's Stormont Castle, the President was summoned to speak to all sides, nudging them here and there. The entire process now rested on his credibility and good faith.

For the St. Patrick's Day party he had held in the White House in March, Clinton had invited the Northern Irish leaders on all sides of the dispute—David Trimble, John Hume, Seamus Mallon, and Gerry Adams. One by one, that afternoon, he met with them, brought them together at the boisterous reception, and afterward took them upstairs together for a pep talk. In April, he had stayed awake for nights talking on the phone to them until, on Good Friday, the agreement was announced: there would be an elected assembly in Northern Ireland, joint north-south Irish governmental bodies would deal with common issues, and violence would be renounced.

There were years of hard work ahead to secure this accord, but when we arrived in Britain on May 18, a glow surrounded both the President and the Prime Minister, for they had jointly achieved what had been thought impossible.

Another meeting at Chequers explored the political prospects common to the United States and Britain. Clinton asked the British about Schroeder's progress in his campaign. Then he explained his vision of the Third Way, not a fixed organization like the Socialist International but a political "floating opera."

"We have to be thinking the whole time of how we renew ourselves," said Blair. "It always ends in tears for the individual. There should be people coming up who should renew it."

"My biggest worry," said Clinton, "is that they figure out to be more Machiavellian by running someone who sounds moderate but has the same reactionary core. And when we're gone, the reactionaries with their built-in advantages win again. That's what I'm worried about. What are like-minded people doing to help each other? I didn't do all this work to bring the Democratic Party back from the dead to say I could do better than everybody else." He turned to Blair: "You have to help us not be some accident."

"From now on," said Blair, "we have to make this happen."

Then we flew back to Washington.

II

In early June, the President dropped his claim in the executive privilege case. The matter had been gradually working its way through the courts, and we knew that if necessary Starr would surely appeal it all the way to the Supreme Court, which would almost certainly rule against Clinton. The President decided to remove executive privilege from the controversy before that could happen. Executive privilege belongs to the president alone, and only he can invoke it, not an aide. (When I had first testified before Starr's grand jury, I was not the one to claim this privilege; it was claimed for me.) Once it was withdrawn, Starr was free to summon me once again to testify, and so he did.

On June 4, the day of my return to the courthouse, William Safire suggested that I would soon be going to prison. With his now familiar reflex of comparing everything to Nixon's crimes in Watergate, he wrote, "Blumenthal, lest we forget, may be Colson Revisited. Watergate buffs will recall that Nixon counsel Charles Colson pled guilty to disseminating derogatory information from Daniel Ellsberg's F.B.I. file to influence the outcome of the Pentagon Papers leaker's trial. Especially coming from a Federal official, such defamation was obstruction of justice. . . . I suspect Starr will charge that a defamation conspiracy is obstruction whether aimed at defense or prosecution."*

Several days later, the *Times* published a letter from my lawyer, Bill McDaniel, noting that "defamation conspiracy was a heretofore unknown crime":

> We have no crime of "seditious libel," and associate it with totalitarian regimes that jail those who criticize officials in public. Yet Mr. Safire suggests that Mr. Blumenthal has committed exactly that crime by speaking about the professional conduct and record of prosecutors who are investigating the President.
>
> Mr. Blumenthal has done what Americans have every right to do: he exercised his freedom of expression about government officials. He did so by speaking to journalists, including reporters from *The Times*, all of whom would presumably be co-defendants in Mr. Safire's "defamation conspiracy."
>
> Mr. Blumenthal has never seen, much less misused, any material from F.B.I. files, and until Mr. Safire's column, no one had suggested that he had done so.

*William Safire, "Enter the Supremes," *The New York Times*, June 4, 1998.

By suggesting that Mr. Blumenthal could be, or should be, punished for speaking to the media about public officials, Mr. Safire betrays how much of an unreconstructed Nixonian he is.*

Back inside the harshly lit grand-jury room, my interlocutors were Jackie Bennett and Sol Wisenberg, who in lowered, grim voices told me that I was not "a witness," as I had been in my previous appearance, but "a subject," one category below being a target. My vulnerability was promoted; no reason for the change was given. "You understand that we can't make a promise that somebody who is a witness or a subject will never be a target. Do you understand that?" "I do." "It's just a way of telling you what your status is at this point in time." I understood—"just a way."

For two hours, Bennett and Wisenberg rehearsed what I had already been asked in February. They wanted to know again who was in "the strategy meetings," what we discussed, and whether we acted on direct orders. "Do you ever get information at the meeting about what the President or First Lady's wishes are? As an example, would somebody ever say, 'The President wants this done,' or 'The First Lady wants this done'?" "No." They asked again about White House responses to articles in the press, asking particularly how we had handled the false story that had appeared in *The Wall Street Journal* about the grand-jury testimony of Bayani Nelvis, the President's steward. "Do you remember any discussions about Bayani Nelvis?" "Yes. I recall discussion about the *Wall Street Journal* article about him." "Okay. And tell us about that."

Only in the last ten minutes did they ask me about my meeting in the Oval Office with President Clinton about Monica Lewinsky, which I related. Instantly, upon finishing, I was asked about sex. I had used the word "minister" to describe Clinton's attention to "troubled people." I had also explained that Hillary had told me that these efforts were based on "religious conviction and personal temperament." Wisenberg asked, "The first is did the President say that part of his ministry—did he tell you that part of his ministry with Ms. Lewinsky in any way, shape, or form was in engaging in any kind of sexual activity with her?" "He told me the opposite." Then the session was over; I would be called back.

Outside, I made no public statement, but my attorney did. "What we had," said McDaniel, "was two hours of questions about, 'Up there

*William Alden McDaniel, Jr., "Starr's Tactics Endanger Us All; Aide Broke No Law," *The New York Times*, June 9, 1998.

at the White House, do they talk about us prosecutors? And up there at the White House, do you talk about Starr's investigation?' " He noted that only at the end had I been asked about what Clinton had told me, the contentious subject of the executive privilege fight.

Back at the White House, at the end of a strategy meeting in the office of John Podesta, who I knew would soon be returning to the grand jury, I remarked on a strange occurrence. I noted that both *Air Force One* and *Air Force Two* had recently disappeared for five minutes from the air traffic controller's screen at New York's La Guardia Airport. As anyone who watched the popular science fiction TV series *The X Files* knew— and John was a big fan—that signified alien abduction, I observed. So it's possible, seen in that light, I continued, that the President and the Vice President were not really the President and the Vice President. I concluded that anyone who was grilled in the grand jury on what was said in White House strategy meetings would have to answer truthfully and fully.

A few days later, on June 23, Sol Wisenberg bore down on John Podesta in the grand jury: "How close are you with Sidney Blumenthal?" "I've known him a long time. I used to work with his wife and I would say we're friendly. Friends." "Okay. Not close friends?" "We're not close friends, but we're friends. I sort of get a kick out of him. He has a new theory about all this." The prosecutor asked instead what the two of us had discussed about Monica Lewinsky, eliciting John's testimony that we had never talked about "evidentiary information." He asked John about my supposed "interaction with any private detectives," which reporters John spoke with, and how it would "affect you" if it turned out that Clinton's denial of sex with Lewinsky turned out to be false. "I believe him," John said.

Finally, the prosecutor took the hook in his mouth: "You were mentioning Mr. Blumenthal's latest theory. Tell us, if you can—well, I don't know how long it would take to go through it—" "Well, I'll do the quick version." "Okay." "He's noticed that *Air Force One* and *Air Force Two* have gone off, I think this has actually already been reported, that they've gone off the radar screen coming into La Guardia recently and that that usually precedes a claim that there's been an alien abduction and that we have a new theory or a new defense that this whole matter is somehow linked to alien abductions, but I think that's probably the result of *The X Files* [movie] being previewed this week. But with Sidney you're never quite sure whether he believes it or he's just kidding. I think he was just kidding." By now, the prosecutor realized he was entering his own twilight zone. "This is one reason why I could ask you when you come back in are you the same John Podesta." "That's what I thought you were getting at," John replied. The prosecutor continued, "All right, but, of course, if somebody had taken over your body they probably wouldn't admit that anyway." "When Agents Scully and Mulder are out in those green chairs [outside the grand-jury room], I'll really start to worry."* Thus it was that the Office of Independent Counsel investigated alien abductions. When John returned from the grand jury, he burst into my office: "I really teed it up for you."

Back in the grand-jury chamber on June 25, the prosecutor zeroed in on sex questions. He asked me, "Did you specifically ask the President whether he had received oral sex from Monica Lewinsky?" "No." "Did the President state anything to you about receiving oral sex from Monica Lewinsky?" "No." "Did you prepare the President and/or First Lady for responding to any questions that might arise because of the nature of the Lewinsky case about sexual addiction?" "No."

Only about halfway through my third session did the prosecutor elicit vital information about my relationship to and knowledge of Monica Lewinsky: "Did you have any discussions with the President about Monica Lewinsky before January 21, 1998, of any kind at all about Monica Lewinsky?" "No." "So even the fact she was an intern, a friend, nothing." "I never knew her, never met her, had no idea of her existence." In short, I was truly clueless. Yet I had been subpoenaed, appeared three times and been questioned for more than seven hours.

The day before, Ken Starr, who never once sat in on the questioning of a single witness, had made a highly unusual appearance before the grand jury. His remarks are unknown, but at the conclusion of my third session, the foreperson, an older woman, made a statement that bore the language of something that the prosecutor might have prompted: "The work that we are doing here is very serious and the integrity to our work as representatives of people of the United States of America is very important to us. We are very concerned about the fact that during your last visit that an inaccurate representation of the events that happened were retold on the steps of the courthouse. We would hope that you will understand the seriousness of our work, and not in any way use it for any purpose other than the purpose that is intended, and that you would really represent us the way that events happened in this room."

Her statement was distorted and highly inappropriate. My lawyer's

*Starr, "Supplemental Materials," pp. 3,326–33.

remarks after my last appearance had accurately described the questioning I had received. Even if she meant to criticize my remarks on the courthouse steps after my first grand-jury appearance, which did so much political damage to the prosecutors, it was wrong for the prosecutor or a grand juror to lecture a witness or subject about what he could or couldn't say outside the grand-jury chamber, or to request a witness to speak on the grand jury's behalf. I replied simply, "I appreciate your statement." As I intended, I told the press after my third appearance, in a brief statement, that my testimony "supported" what the President had said.

A few days later, I related to columnists and one reporter the questions as I recalled them—about sex addiction, oral sex, and whether Clinton's "ministry," or religion, included sex with Lewinsky. Anthony Lewis of *The New York Times* wrote, "What we have here, I think, is third-rate prosecutors full of hubris and obsessed by sex. I am sure they have pursued that obsession with other grand jury witnesses who have so far been too scared or too embarrassed to talk about it."* Lars-Erik Nelson of the New York *Daily News* wrote, "Linda Tripp has found the perfect audience for her dirty stories: Kenneth Starr and his team of federal prosecutors."†

Now Starr was beleaguered by a revelation of his office's leaking. The one who had exposed him was a talkative Ken Starr. On June 13, Steven Brill's magazine *Brill's Content* debuted, with a twenty-eight-page article, "Pressgate," that he had researched and written. "The abuses that were Watergate spawned great reporting. The Lewinsky story has reversed the process," he wrote. Brill described how the press had become Starr's "cheering section" and with "a willing, eager press corps Starr was able to create an almost complete presumption of guilt." Starr's "hubris" was "so great" that "he himself will admit these leaks when asked." Indeed, Starr was quoted as having told Brill, "I have talked with reporters on background on some occasions, but Jackie [Bennett] has been the primary person involved in that. He has spent much of his time talking to individual reporters." There was, he insisted, "nothing improper . . . because we never discussed grand jury proceedings." He rationalized the talking by saying that "what we are doing is countering misinformation that is being spread about our investigation in order to discredit our office and

*Anthony Lewis, "Questions That Degrade," *The New York Times*, June 29, 1998.
†Lars-Erik Nelson, "Tripp's Taking Us for Another Ride on Rumor Mill," New York *Daily News*, July 1, 1998.

our dedicated career prosecutors." Bennett, he went on, had spent most of January 21, the day the scandal broke, "briefing the press." Starr named the names of reporters to whom his office had talked "extensively": Susan Schmidt of *The Washington Post*, Michael Isikoff of *Newsweek*, Jackie Judd of ABC News, and Jeff Gerth and Stephen Labaton of *The New York Times*. Brill concluded that Starr's "protestation that these leaks—or 'briefings,' as he calls them—do not violate the criminal law, and don't even violate Justice Department or ethical guidelines if they are intended to enhance confidence in his office or to correct the other side's 'misinformation,' is not only absurd, but concedes the leaks. Worse still is the lack of skepticism with which the press by and large took these leaks and parroted them."*

Outraged, Starr immediately issued a statement: "Steven Brill has recklessly and irresponsibly charged the Office of Independent Counsel with improper contacts with the media. These charges are false." Two days later, he issued another such statement, stamping his foot.

Brill's article had a dramatic effect on the "leaks" case against Starr of which the President, Bruce Lindsey, and I were plaintiffs. Starr's comments to Brill were now added in our brief to the list of his other violations of Rule 6(e). On June 19, in a sealed decision, Judge Johnson ruled that Starr was guilty of prima facie violations and must "show cause" why he should not be "held in contempt." We filed another brief asking the court for discovery—the right to question Starr and his deputies under oath. On June 26, in a sealed decision, Judge Johnson granted us the power to "depose the OIC employees"—meaning Starr and his prosecutors—on their press contacts. Our lawyers could now interrogate his prosecutors, which would open them to damaging revelations of their illegal manipulations, to penalties for these, and even potentially to charges of perjury and obstruction of justice.

This was not good for Starr. If discovery went forward, his office would unravel. So he filed an extraordinary sealed motion. His main argument was that his investigation depended on its press contacts for securing secret information: "It is impossible to disclose the Government's contacts and communications with press sources without revealing confidential investigative information. . . . Disclosure of the OIC's contacts with reporters may undermine the OIC's future ability to obtain information from potential sources." Here he cited a privilege "long recognized at common law, the informer's privilege." Reporters were his

*Brill, "Pressgate."

informers! They were, in his own description, his army of spies. While they might think of themselves as independent and intrepid seekers of truth, to him they were snitches.

In desperation, Starr appealed to the District of Columbia Circuit Court of Appeals, which granted him a stay against the July 11 court date. On August 3, a three-judge panel, weighted with two conservatives, one of them, Judge Laurence Silberman, a close friend and political soulmate of Starr's—and David Brock's old mentor—issued a writ of mandamus in Starr's favor. There would be no discovery. Instead the case was sent back to Judge Johnson, who appointed a special master to investigate and issue a report to her. Thus, Starr's office was now under two investigations—one by special counsel Michael Shaheen in the Hale case, the other in the leaks case. But Starr had escaped the worst.

On July 16, Judge Silberman issued another decision: Secret Service agents must testify before Starr's grand jury. His ruling was filled with intemperate language, lashing out at Attorney General Reno for "acting as the President's counsel under the false guise of representing the United States," and claiming wildly that "the President of the United States has declared war on the United States."* Two days later, the Supreme Court, in a decision issued by Chief Justice William Rehnquist, upheld his ruling, and a parade of agents marched through the grand jury, none of them with any evidence of any consequence to offer, as Starr discovered.

While all this was going on, Tim Russert appeared on the *Today Show* on July 16 gravely to announce that Secret Service agents had "facilitated" Clinton's affair with Lewinsky, according, he said, to "people close to Starr." "Remember that code word—it was used about the state troopers in Little Rock," he instructed helpfully, neglecting to mention that the troopers had been paid for their stories and were now discredited. Russert's report was a variant of the "sighting" reports of a few months earlier. At the White House that morning, I asked a young communications aide to call NBC to get a transcript so that Mike McCurry, the press secretary, could respond to Russert's exact words, and so that we could give the transcript to other members of the press. As soon as we received it, McCurry declared Russert's report "slimy." Starr's office was angry at Russert, too, and he got a call demanding that he retract his statement that the Independent Counsel was his source. On the cable channel MSNBC that afternoon, Russert retold his story: "This morning I reported that congressional sources had told NBC News that Ken Starr

*Jonathan Broder, "The Attack Judge, *Salon.com*, July 21, 1998.

is very interested in finding out . . ." The next day, Lloyd Grove had an article in *The Washington Post* headlined "The Scoop That Slowly Melted." Russert was infuriated—at Grove and at me, though I had not spoken with Grove. In an interview with *The Hotline*, a political newsletter, Russert connected nonexistent dots, claiming that I had called for a transcript (conflating me with the communications office). "Bottom line: Lloyd Grove buys the White House spin," he said.* Like many others swept up in the hysteria, he had let his ambition to be a player at the center of the whirlwind outweigh his prudence. This journalistic comedy of errors met with an impulse to blame a scapegoat, another symptom of the mania.

On July 25, the President set off for China for nine days to work on what he called a "vital strategic relationship." He believed that China's power would only increase during the twenty-first century and that the more it was integrated into the community of nations the less its power would be a threat. Clinton's visit stirred domestic controversy in the United States on both his right and his left. Some Republicans continued to project a demonic image of China as a menace to the United States—after all, it was still a communist state. And some Democrats opposed more open trade with a country so manifestly undemocratic and marred by so many human-rights abuses.

On his trip across the expanse of China and in his meeting with President Jiang Zemin, Clinton bound China to security commitments on nuclear nonproliferation, as well as cooperation on North Korea and with Taiwan. He also discussed China's future entry into the World Trade Organization, which would require it to abide by the tenets of international property rights and thereby extend the rule of law. He raised the question of the environment—the Chinese government was hostile to the treaty on global warming, which it viewed as an effort to curb its industrial growth. And the President was frank in speaking about human rights—in a televised speech to the Chinese people, at a forum at Beijing University, and in his private and public sessions with Jiang. Clinton urged him to open a "dialogue" with the Dalai Lama, to end the oppression of Tibet and recognize its rights, and to release political prisoners. The President insisted that China's leaders come to terms with its his-

*"Blowback: Russert Says Post's Grove Buys WH Spin," *The Hotline*, July 17, 1998.

tory, especially the Tiananmen Square massacre of 1989. In his joint press conference with Jiang, he said:

> Nine years ago, Chinese citizens of all ages raised their voices for democracy. For all of our agreements, we still disagree about the meaning of what happened then. I believe, and the American people believe, that the use of force and the tragic loss of life was wrong. I believe, and the American people believe, that freedom of speech, association, and religion are, as recognized by the UN Charter, the right of people everywhere and should be protected by their governments.
>
> It was to advance these rights that our Founding Fathers in our Declaration of Independence pledged our lives, our fortunes, our sacred honor. Fifty years ago, the UN recognized these rights as the basic freedoms of people everywhere.
>
> The question for us now is how shall we deal with such disagreements and still succeed in the important work of deepening our friendship and our sense of mutual respect.
>
> First, we Americans must acknowledge the painful moments in our own history when fundamental human rights were denied. We must say that we know, still, we have to continue our work to advance the dignity and freedom and equality of our own people. And, second, we must understand and respect the enormous challenges China has faced in trying to move forward against great odds with a clear memory of the setbacks suffered in past periods of instability.
>
> Finally, it is important that whatever our disagreements over past action, China and the United States must go forward on the right side of history for the future sake of the world. The forces of history have brought us to a new age of human possibility, but our dreams can only be recognized by nations whose citizens are both responsible and free.

Back in Washington, the focus was not on China but on Monica Lewinsky. In early June, she had dismissed her lawyer, William Ginsburg, and hired two seasoned Washington attorneys, Plato Cacheris and Jacob Stein, to represent her. For almost two months, they conducted negotiations with Starr to gain immunity from prosecution for their client. Lewinsky also hired a public relations agent, Judy Smith. Suddenly, Lewinsky began to send secret messages to the White House, intended for the President. The route she used was through Smith, who was black, to a black actress in Hollywood, to a black member of the White House staff, who contacted me—an underground railroad eluding

Lewinsky's attorneys. I gave her messages to Kendall. Clinton never knew about them. They were all the same: she hated Starr, she was holding out against him. We sent no messages back. Then came a final message: I can't hold out any longer.

On July 28, she received immunity in exchange for a proffer that was virtually identical to the one she had made in February that had split Starr's office. The only news about its contents was that she now declared she was the author of the Talking Points, written on the advice of and with suggestions from Linda Tripp. The next day Tripp, finishing her eighth and last day of grand-jury testimony, emerged on the courthouse steps to present herself as the "average American" who had been "vilified for taking the path of truth." "I am you," she announced. Lewinsky's appearance before the grand jury was now being arranged. And Starr issued a subpoena to President Clinton.

The President's lawyers fought among themselves about what his strategy should be. Taking the Fifth Amendment was ruled out as politically disastrous. Bob Bennett argued directly with the President that it was crazy for him to testify at all. It would legitimize Starr's investigation. Bennett was overruled, and David Kendall negotiated a date for Clinton's appearance: August 17. The prosecutor insisted that the testimony be videotaped in case a grand juror was absent, and Kendall consented. Meanwhile the political staff at the White House was told that Clinton's story would essentially remain the same, and we were not told about the lawyers' debate. Clinton had not yet told anyone of the actual nature of his relationship with Lewinsky. On August 3, Lewinsky's blue dress with a semen stain on it was transported to the FBI crime laboratory. That night, Clinton gave a blood sample, and within hours a DNA match was made. Only Starr and his deputies knew. No one else was told.

On August 6, President Clinton went to Capitol Hill to discuss his legislative agenda with the House Democratic Caucus, which warmly greeted him with applause and cheers. No one raised the subject of the scandal, even though that was the day Lewinsky began her testimony before the grand jury.

What had begun with an investigation in 1994 into an obscure Arkansas real-estate deal, headed by the experienced and judicious Robert Fiske, had under the aegis of Starr never unearthed any wrongdoing by the Clintons. Then it had veered into an aimless sex hunt in early 1997, and so it remained until Starr swallowed the Jones case a year later. Now it turned on Starr, setting the stage for the impeachment of the President, having his prosecutors ask a distraught young woman these questions: "Then he touched your breasts with his hands?" "Did he touch your breast with his mouth?" "Did he touch your genital area at all that day?" "And did he bring you to orgasm?" "And again, just with respect with bringing you to an orgasm, did he touch you directly on your skin on your genitals, or was it through underwear?" "The ejaculation?"*

A grand juror asked for more detail about a particular sexual incident. "Uh—" said Lewinsky. "I understand—" "Oh, my gosh. This is so embarrassing." "You could close your eyes and talk." Another grand juror said helpfully, "We won't look at you." "Can I hide under the table? Uh, I had, I had wanted, I tried to, I, oh, this is just too embarrassing. I don't . . ."†

I was in Rome, having lunch at the Chigi Palace, the baroque residence of the Italian prime minister, with Romano Prodi and Ricardo Levi, his assistant and my counterpart. We were meeting to discuss Prodi's participation in a Third Way conference that would take place in September in New York. We talked at length about the convolutions of Italian politics. Then Prodi asked me to explain the scandal. "Please," he implored. I gave him a brief, factual chronicle. "No, no," he said. "I don't understand." I tried again. "No, I still don't understand." As I tried to offer yet another explanation, he interrupted: "There's a man, yes?" he asked. "Yes," I answered. "There's a woman, yes?" "Yes." "I don't understand. There's a man. There's a woman. Please explain this scandal to me." I gave up. Trying to explain Ken Starr in Italy was not a productive exercise.

Jackie and I, along with a sizable White House contingent, were in Rome on our way to the wedding of my friend James Rubin, assistant secretary of state for public affairs, to Christiane Amanpour, the CNN international correspondent, which was to take place at a medieval castle in Bracciano, just north of Rome. At the cocktail party the night before, we drank gin and tonics with John Kennedy, Jr., a college friend of Christiane's, and his wife, Carolyn, and the turmoil of Washington seemed, at least momentarily, a world away as we chatted about the bride and groom. On August 7, Secretary of State Madeleine Albright landed in Rome for the wedding, but then after five hours she suddenly returned to the United States: she had just received word that the American embassies in Kenya and Tanzania had been bombed, that about three hun-

*Toobin, *A Vast Conspiracy*, pp. 323–25.

†Sarah Pekkanen, "The Many Faces of Monica," *The Baltimore Sun*, September 30, 1998.

dred were dead and five thousand injured. The perpetrator of this dual crime was Osama bin Laden and his al-Qaeda terrorist network.

After the wedding, we drove to a small village outside Florence, Castelfranco di Sopra, where our friends John Ritch, the U.S. ambassador to the United Nations at Vienna, and his wife, Christina, lived in a villa overlooking the Arno Valley. We were moving in a pack, with Jim Steinberg, Clinton's deputy national security adviser, who had also been at the wedding, staying at the villa up the hill. A secure phone line was run up there so that he could participate in discussions to plan the American response to the embassy bombings.

On August 14, the President met the caskets of ten Americans killed in the embassy bombings as they were brought to Andrews Air Force Base, and one after another, he met their grief-stricken families. He was photographed with tears streaking down his face. "No matter what it takes," he said at the public ceremony, "we must find those responsible for these evil acts and see that justice is done." Then he drove back to the White House, where he had to prepare for his deposition. Ken Starr was demanding his attention while he was planning the American retaliation to Osama bin Laden.

Up at the villa, I wrote rough notes for a speech that the President could deliver after his deposition. It was based on the assumption that he would deny a relationship with Lewinsky. I quoted from Justice Scalia's dissent on the potential for abuse in the Independent Counsel Act and criticized Starr's intrusion into the President's privacy. Bits and pieces of this, I thought, might make their way into whatever speech was ultimately drafted. My friend John wondered if I should compose an alternative version, in case Clinton altered his account. So I wrote an additional few paragraphs.

On August 16, the day before the President's deposition, I read *The Washington Post* on the Internet, which led with an article by Bob Woodward: "President's Lawyers Brace for Change in Story." He reported that Clinton had not prepared his family. "Looks like you better send the alternative version," John said. "Yup," I agreed. After I'd made a few calls to the White House, it was apparent that the place was in a state of great confusion and consternation. Nobody but the lawyers knew what Clinton was going to say in his testimony and nobody knew what he would say afterward. Numerous drafts of a postdeposition speech were floating around, but there was no commitment from Clinton.

Absent from the scene, I was isolated and unable to participate. I was

chagrined to learn of Clinton's likely confession, and flustered, too. I had
wanted to believe him, as the rest of his staff had wanted to, whatever our
doubts might have been. But the uncomfortable truth now could not be
denied. Throughout the already long battle since January, I had suppressed whatever I felt about Clinton's behavior on behalf of the larger
political interest. What I felt mattered even less now. The battle over the
past eight months was just a preliminary to an even greater one—a fight,
it appeared to me, to the death.

If Clinton's presidency were destroyed as a result of Starr's work—a
partisan investigation targeting Clinton for alleged crimes, having failed
for years to discover any wrongdoing and now invading his private life—
the effect on the Constitution and American politics would be poisonous.
The presidency would be shattered as an institution and the devastation
to democracy would be irreparable.

I called Hillary. We dispensed with the extraordinarily difficult personal problem at the start. As her friend, I wanted to respect her privacy.
I said that whatever "issues" anyone had, and hers was worse than anyone's, we had to think about the politics. That was her reasoning as well.
She said that the President would be "embarrassed," but that was for him
to deal with. And that was all she would say about it. Even in a private
conversation with a friend, she maintained her dignity. It was my intention to help her do that, and through the next two days we kept in
constant contact.

Hillary had hoped against hope that her husband had reformed himself, that whatever agony she had gone through earlier in her marriage
had been resolved. Now she was discovering that it was not over. This
was something she would have to deal with both alone, in private, and in
the full public glare. All of us on the White House staff, who in a chorus
had clung to our mantra "I believe the President," had been made to look
foolish, but no one was made to look more foolish than she. Her reserve
became a measure of her dignity, as it always had been, but now in a very
different sense. How she deported herself mattered more than anything
else in the political equation. She had been the model of the modern professional woman but was obviously not immune to the trouble that af-
flicts marriages of every class. In a way, this blow to her pride made her
in the eyes of many a more accessible and sympathetic figure. As she
steeled herself, she drew warm concern. Her private relationship with
her wayward husband had a magnified effect through her every word and
gesture. She must not display her rage against the prosecutor who had

pried into her life to degrade her and spoil her marriage. To protect her family, she had to protect the presidency. To accomplish both, she had to practice self-control beyond any she had exercised before.

Each member of the White House staff believed that his or her political advice to the President was sound, of course. Some drew upon their religious notions of contrition. Some felt ashamed for themselves. The kind of confession they wanted Clinton to make was also the kind they wanted for themselves to be granted expiation. They were upset by having been exposed as defending a falsehood, yet they were still determined to defend Clinton as president. Others had political reasons for wanting Clinton to make a self-abasing statement. They were in constant touch with the Congress, the ultimate seat of judgment, "the only audience that matters," as many of them—and the Democratic leaders there—wished devoutly for contrition, to remove the stain from them, too.

The congressional Democrats resented having to bear this final indignity, as they saw it, of the many they believed they had suffered from Clinton. Some still blamed him for the loss of their majority in Congress in 1994. Some believed he had not campaigned enough for them to recapture it in 1996. Some opposed every policy he advocated that reformed the party's position and image: NAFTA, welfare reform, the crime bill. Now they wanted him to remove this stain from them as they faced the midterm election, at which they believed they would suffer certain losses. They wanted the whole thing to go away. Clinton could not abase himself enough, even if he threw himself prone on the ground before them or stood in the snow outside their windows for a week barefoot on one leg. Above all, they wanted it to go away because they knew that they would have to defend him.

In the Map Room of the White House, on August 17, Ken Starr appeared for the first time to obtain the testimony of a witness. The grand jury viewed the proceeding through video transmission. Bob Bittman, Jackie Bennett, and Sol Wisenberg, leaders of the Likud faction, were given the job of taking the President's deposition. "Mr. President," began Bittman, "were you physically intimate with Monica Lewinsky?" To this, Clinton responded by reading a prepared text:

> When I was alone with Ms. Lewinsky on certain occasions in early 1996 and once in early 1997, I engaged in conduct that was wrong. These encounters did not consist of sexual intercourse. They did not constitute sexual relations as I understood that term to be defined at my January 17th, 1998, deposition. But they did involve inappropriate intimate

contact. These inappropriate encounters ended, at my insistence, in early 1997. . . . While I will provide the grand jury whatever other information I can, because of privacy considerations affecting my family, myself, and others, and in an effort to preserve the dignity of the office I hold, this is all I will say about the specifics of these particular matters. . . . That, Mr. Bittman, is my statement.

For three and a half hours, Bittman and Wisenberg asked Clinton questions about Lewinsky, including questions about precise forms of sexual contact with her, and then Jackie Bennett asked him questions about Kathleen Willey. Most of these questions were attempted perjury traps. One, about Bob Bennett's claim in a deposition in the Jones case that "there is absolutely no sex of any kind in any manner, shape or form, with President Clinton," drew Clinton's legalistic response: "It depends on what the meaning of the word 'is' is." At one point, Wisenberg bore in about details of "sexual contact": "Including touching her breast, kissing her breast, or touching her genitalia?" Clinton's answer reflected upon the nature of sex and memory: "This is—you're dealing with, in some way, the most mysterious area of human life. I'm doing the best I can to give you honest recollections." In the final minutes, Starr asked questions about executive privilege, as though Clinton's invocation of it constituted an obstruction of justice.

When Clinton finished he was tired, upset, and infuriated. He was handed one draft of a remorseful speech. His lawyers, for their part, argued that he should criticize Starr. Hillary entered the White House solarium where this conference was going on, I learned later, and said, "It's your speech. You should say what you want to say." She knew what he wanted to say, and it was what he did say.

Clinton was acting not only on his sense of the politics of the moment but also on his sense of his marriage. His emotions weren't just about the prosecutor but about his wife. He wanted to win back her respect and he did not want to appear belittled and weak before her. He would have many occasions for expressing his regret and remorse to her. But in defending his privacy now, in public, he would also be defending hers. It was their marriage—together—that had been invaded. He knew how she felt about that, and he wanted to defend her honor. He was acting as a husband who had betrayed his wife and wanted to heal the wound, a man who had been publicly shamed and wanted to protect his family. He was acting as a human being.

Philip Roth wrote in his novel *The Human Stain*:

No, if you haven't lived through 1998, you don't know what sanctimony is. . . . It was the summer in America when the nausea returned . . . when the moral obligation to explain to one's children about adult life was abrogated in favor of maintaining in them every illusion about adult life, when the smallness of people was simply crushing, when some kind of demon had been unleashed in the nation. . . . I myself dreamed of a mammoth banner, draped dadaistically like a Christo wrapping from one end of the White House to the other and bearing the legend A HUMAN BEING LIVES HERE.*

Clinton spent a half hour rewriting his speech himself and went on the air:

Good evening. This afternoon in this room, from this chair, I testified before the Office of Independent Counsel and the grand jury. I answered their questions truthfully, including questions about my private life, questions no American citizen would ever want to answer. Still, I must take complete responsibility for all my actions, both public and private. And that is why I am speaking to you tonight. As you know, in a deposition in January, I was asked questions about my relationship with Monica Lewinsky. While my answers were legally accurate, I did not volunteer information.

Indeed, I did have a relationship with Miss Lewinsky that was not appropriate. In fact, it was wrong. It constituted a critical lapse in judgment and a personal failure on my part for which I am solely and completely responsible. But I told the grand jury today and I say to you now that at no time did I ask anyone to lie, to hide or destroy evidence or to take any other unlawful action. I know that my public comments and my silence about this matter gave a false impression. I misled people, including even my wife. I deeply regret that.

I can only tell you I was motivated by many factors. First, by a desire to protect myself from the embarrassment of my own conduct. I was also very concerned about protecting my family. The fact that these questions were being asked in a politically inspired lawsuit, which has since been dismissed, was a consideration, too. In addition, I had real and serious concerns about an independent counsel investigation that began with private business dealings twenty years ago, dealings, I might add, about which an independent federal agency found no evidence of any wrong-

*Philip Roth, *The Human Stain*, Houghton Mifflin, 2000, pp. 2–3.

doing by me or my wife over two years ago. The independent counsel investigation moved on to my staff and friends, then into my private life. And now the investigation itself is under investigation.

This has gone on too long, cost too much and hurt too many innocent people. Now, this matter is between me, the two people I love most—my wife and our daughter—and our God. I must put it right, and I am prepared to do whatever it takes to do so. Nothing is more important to me personally. But it is private, and I intend to reclaim my family life for my family. It's nobody's business but ours. Even presidents have private lives.

It is time to stop the pursuit of personal destruction and the prying into private lives and get on with our national life. Our country has been distracted by this matter for too long, and I take my responsibility for my part in all of this. That is all I can do. Now it is time—in fact, it is past time—to move on. We have important work to do—real opportunities to seize, real problems to solve, real security matters to face. And so tonight, I ask you to turn away from the spectacle of the past seven months, to repair the fabric of our national discourse, and to return our attention to all the challenges and all the promise of the next American century. Thank you for watching. And good night.

During that day, we had driven from Florence to Rome in order to get our flight back to Washington. I talked repeatedly with Hillary, and Jackie and I stayed up until the middle of the night to watch Clinton give his speech, broadcast on CNN International. About ten minutes after it ended, my hotel phone rang: it was the President, asking me what my reaction was. I told him that it was all right. Hillary asked me what I thought. I told her the same. The President said he was pleased with it. Hillary also approved. That was the most important thing of all. They handed the phone to James Carville and Mark Penn, and I spoke to them, too. I could hear the President and Hillary bantering in the background. Whatever they would have to do between themselves to get over this episode, in the challenge to their marriage and the presidency they were still working as a team. Without that, nothing was possible.

Penn told me that his polling showed that two-thirds of Americans regarded Clinton's speech favorably; they believed that he had apologized and was sincere, and that was sufficient for them. An ABC News poll taken after the speech also revealed that 69 percent wanted Starr to end his investigation immediately—a jump of ten points. The Republicans predictably attacked Clinton. Republican House Whip Tom DeLay, with

Gingrich's permission, urged Clinton to resign. But congressional Democrats were critical, too, claiming he had not been sorry enough, and they resented being put on the spot.

No one knows what might have happened if Clinton had delivered a completely self-abasing speech. If he had apologized abjectly, it is possible that it would have been said that his political capital was gone and that he was too weak to govern. Gingrich and DeLay might have become even more emboldened. No abject contrition, in fact, was going to forestall his impeachment. The Republican leaders wanted him in a position where he could no longer govern. Nothing was going to stop them, including the will of the people.

On August 20, the President addressed the nation again, this time to announce that the United States had launched missile attacks against Osama bin Laden at his sanctuary within Afghanistan and against a factory of weapons of mass destruction in the Sudan. "With compelling evidence that the bin Laden network of terrorist groups was planning to mount further attacks against Americans and other freedom-loving people, I decided America must act." The missiles missed bin Laden by an hour. He had evacuated just before they hit.

By the time I got back to Washington, the President and his family had repaired to Martha's Vineyard, and I found his staff debating the need for him to make further statements of contrition. When Clinton returned, he was initially irritated by this suggestion, since he felt he had already addressed his testimony in his televised speech, but he quickly assented.

Those further apologies continued to help his standing with the public, which needed no more apologies, and to assuage the Democrats, who had no choice but to defend him, but they failed to quell the Republicans, who were now noisily gearing up the chains and pulleys of impeachment in anticipation of Starr's formal report.

On September 7, David Kendall sent Starr a letter concerning the articles and features about his report already saturating the media. He cited Judge John Sirica's decision in transmitting the Watergate special prosecutor's report to the House Judiciary Committee: "It draws no accusatory conclusions. . . . It contains no recommendations, advice or statement that infringe on the prerogatives of other branches of government. . . . It renders no moral or social judgments. The Report is a simple and straightforward compilation of information gathered by the Grand Jury, and no more. . . . The Grand Jury has obviously taken care to assure that its Report contains no objectionable feature, and has throughout acted in the interest of fairness."

Starr, responding the next day, brushed aside Kendall's request to review any report and his citation of the Sirica precedent. In Orwellian fashion, Starr wrote, "The term 'information' is not, as you would construe it, limited to factual evidence." He seemed to equate "information" with his own "judgment."

While his prosecutors were composing the report, they came to him to express their doubts about including salacious sexual material, which they considered irrelevant to the legal case. But Starr insisted that every detail be jammed in. "We need to have an encyclopedia," he said. "I love the narrative!" Lewinsky's lawyers, Cacheris and Stein, had not set parameters on her testimony when they delivered their client to Starr with her proffer, and from the media accounts, they learned that Starr intended to include unedited transcripts of the phone conversations she had had with Linda Tripp, which contained unfiltered sexual talk and denigrating references to the Lewinsky family. On September 9, the lawyers met with Starr to tell him of their objections to the possible inclusion of this material. But he explained it was necessary. "We don't want to leave stuff out because it will look like we are concealing or not giving them all of the facts," he said. Bob Woodward described Starr saying this as he "folded his hands and rubbed them together." Starr added, "I don't think we can remove all of the F-words."* In its detail and tone, Starr was truly the author of the Starr Report.

Almost immediately after his conference with Cacheris and Stein, the previously notified television networks broadcast pictures of two vans loaded with boxes of the report and supporting material being driven slowly to the House of Representatives. Two days later, without any member having read it, the House made the report public, posting its 452 pages instantly on the Internet.

The Starr Report is among the strangest sex books ever written. Its two main characters are an infatuated, needy young woman and a middle-aged man who tries time and again to end the affair but allows his instinct to override his sense. The story is ordinary, squalid, and unhappy. What distinguishes this dreary tale from countless others of its kind is the unusual narrator. He is omniscient, hovering even in the bathroom. He sees everything, recording every sexual gesture bloodlessly.

---

*Woodward, *Shadow*, pp. 453–58.

Every sexual encounter is footnoted. He is cloaked as an antiseptic clinician—pornography in a white laboratory coat. The graphic detail is relentless, the prose as antierotic as possible. The characters are described as complementary in their mutual debasement: the woman is depicted as guilty and innocent, bad and wronged; the man is innocent and guilty, susceptible and wronging. But the narrator's obsession extends beyond his two protagonists. He introduces another character who is always on his mind, but whose absence is his only reference: "Mrs. Clinton was in Africa. . . . Mrs. Clinton was in Ireland." The author's intent to humiliate focuses on her, too. He wishes her to be stained as well. There is no other reason for her inclusion. The inference is that what offends the narrator was not so much the affair as the marriage.

The White House was hushed while staff members read the report on their computer monitors. In the East Room that morning, the President attended a long-scheduled National Prayer Breakfast, telling more than one hundred religious leaders, "I don't think there is a fancy way to say that I have sinned. It is important to me that everybody who has been hurt know that the sorrow I feel is genuine . . . Legal language must not obscure the fact that I have done wrong."

Later that day—September 11—President Clinton addressed the memorial service at the National Cathedral for the twelve Americans killed in the terrorist attacks on the U.S. embassies. (In Kenya, 213 people were killed; in Tanzania, 11 were murdered, and about 5,000 were wounded.) Pledging that he would not "rest as terrorists plot to take innocent lives," he said, "For our larger struggle for hope over hatred and unity over division is a just one. . . . We owe to those who have given their lives in the service of America and its ideal to continue that struggle most of all." In the media, busy with the tumultuous response to the Starr Report's release, the struggle against terrorism was a mere footnote if it was mentioned at all.

The weeks surrounding the release of the Starr Report were like one continuous day for me, for the Republicans were ratcheting up my evil profile. The degeneration of politics into personal demonization reflected the growing frenzy of the effort to overthrow the President. On Sunday, September 6, the unveiling of the Starr Report had been prepared for by two conservative panelists on ABC's *This Week*. George Will stated, "We have the experience recently of a member of the White House staff, Sidney Blumenthal, calling journalists in an attempt to smear Henry Hyde." Bill Kristol jumped in: "It is a fact that Sidney Blumenthal has called members of the press to try to get them to look into congressmen's private lives."

Though I was unsurprised at being used as a scapegoat, I still registered alarm at hearing false allegations about me on national television. The charge was, of course, completely false. It was not, as Kristol blithely said, "a fact," and neither he nor Will would or could offer any facts. In the curious ambit of Washington, these ideologues with their counterfactual slurs were accorded respect, deference, and, most important, time on television. In their punitive ad hominem style, their insults substituted for facts. They indulged in character assassination while parading as the ones exposing it.

A correspondent at ABC News told me that Dorrance Smith, executive producer of *This Week* and communications director in the previous Bush administration, was pushing the line against me hard. My lawyer wrote the ABC News Washington bureau chief a sharp letter:

> Mr. Blumenthal has never—never—attempted to smear Representative Hyde in any way. . . . Neither Mr. Will nor Mr. Kristol presented any facts in support of their false and defamatory allegations, and neither cited any sources for their remarks. Neither Mr. Will, Mr. Kristol, nor anyone else from ABC News spoke with Mr. Blumenthal or anyone at the White House about these accusations before you aired them, or so much as attempted to do so. Your broadcast disregarded the truth. While no one harbors any doubt that both Mr. Will and Mr. Kristol reflect a partisan line, that your show would present their false propaganda as "news" reflects poorly on your standards and practices.

It was apparent from this preemptive strike at ABC that there must be a story floating out there about Hyde. That week a number of journalists had bantered casually about Hyde and sex, as though the subject were a commonplace one. One, Jeffrey Toobin, my former colleague at *The New Yorker*, raised the subject with me. I recalled that my mother, who had been in secretarial pools in Chicago in the 1940s, had told me that she and others avoided Hyde's office because of his reputation, but that was all I knew about the subject.

Henry Hyde was the chairman of the House Judiciary Committee and therefore would preside over an impeachment hearing. The fiction broadcast by Will and Kristol had a patently political intent. Claiming that the White House was smearing him could not have had a more jagged partisan edge. I asked Chuck Ruff his advice, and he suggested that I write a private letter to Hyde. I wrote, "I was appalled to hear George Will on ABC's *This Week* this past Sunday suggest my name in connection with raising personal questions about you. I simply want you to know that I have not and would not do that, and that there is no truth to it." I had the letter hand-delivered to his office by a White House courier. I did not make it public; nor did Hyde.

On the eve of the Starr Report's being thrown onto the Internet, Erskine Bowles summoned me to his office to hear a report from Larry Stein, the White House legislative liaison. Stein said that Gingrich's aide was claiming that I was spreading sexual stories about the Speaker. Bowles asked if that were true, and I replied that it was not. And I resented the question. Gingrich, in fact, would later leave his second wife for a woman with whom he had been having an affair for years and whom he had placed on the House payroll. Many journalists had long heard rumors about this dalliance, and Gail Sheehy, in an article in *Vanity Fair* in 1995, had mentioned the name of his "frequent breakfast companion," Calista Bisek. Clearly, Gingrich was worried about being exposed. His office had been a center for sexual smearing for a long time, since in 1989 it had put out the false rumors that then Speaker Thomas Foley was gay. Perhaps Gingrich made the projective assumption that everyone operated the way he did, but I wasn't engaged in sexual outing. Nor did I know of anyone in the White House doing it. Frankly, given the incendiary political environment, if any of us had chosen to float that rumor it would undoubtedly have been published instantly. Quite on their own, the Republicans had created a political free-fire zone in which their hypocrisy now invited exposure.

Indiana's own Mr. Conservative, the inquisitor of the House, Dan Burton, who had called the President "a scumbag," was the first to have his hypocrisy revealed. His hometown newspaper, *The Indianapolis Star* (owned by the family of Dan Quayle), reported that he had an illegitimate child. Burton defended his private life, even the principle of privacy, while trying to cast aspersions on Clinton's. "I have never perjured myself," he protested. "I have never committed obstruction of justice. I have been as straight as an arrow in my public duty. But this is private."*

Then Idaho's advocate of right-wing militias, Representative Helen Chenoweth, the one who had promoted theories about a United Nations

---

*Edward Walsh, "Burton Fathered Child in Extramarital Affair," *The Washington Post*, September 5, 1998.

invasion with black helicopters, ran a television commercial against her Democratic opponent in the upcoming election: "Bill Clinton's behavior has severely rocked this nation and damaged the office of the president. I believe that personal conduct and integrity does matter." Her hometown newspaper, the *Idaho Statesman*, took that as license to expose her affair with her married former business partner.

Some Republicans nimbly defended this hypocrisy as simply the double standard of traditional values and therefore another mark against Clinton. Bill Kristol was quoted: "I'm not at all convinced it helps Clinton to have the Burton and Chenoweth stories come out. Republicans have old-fashioned extramarital affairs with other adults. Those really are moral lapses that are private and more easily forgiven and very different from taking advantage of a young person who works for you when you're president."*

The week after that ABC broadcast and just as the Starr Report was released, Jackie and I spent days being deposed for my suit against Matt Drudge. In April, federal judge Paul Friedman had decided to remove America Online from the case, even though it had hired Drudge, had paid and promoted him, and had editorial control over his content when the corporation disseminated it over the Internet. "If it were writing on a clean slate, this Court would agree with plaintiffs," the judge wrote. But, he ruled, the Congress had "conferred immunity from tort liability . . . even where the self-policing is unsuccessful or not even attempted." But he kept Drudge as a defendant, writing, "Drudge is not a reporter, a journalist or a newsgatherer. He is, as he himself admits, simply a purveyor of gossip."† We had been disappointed that AOL was no longer in the case, because we wanted to make a larger point, bringing the Internet under the same law that applied to the rest of the press. Now the recent torrent of slander made us only more intent on proving our case.

When I'd first met David Brock in August 1997, he had told me about his ongoing conversations with Drudge about the libel against me. "Drudge said," according to Brock, "that he doesn't care if his reputation is lowered. He said, 'I'll be the brightest star in the sky and Sidney Blumenthal will be nobody.' " And Drudge confided in Brock that he had

---

*Howard Kurtz, "A Chill in the Marble Halls: Others Fair Game for Scandal in Wake of Clinton Affair," *The Washington Post*, September 11, 1998.

†U.S. District Court for the District of Columbia, *Sidney Blumenthal and Jacqueline Jordan. Blumenthal v. Matt Drudge and America Online, Inc*, Civil Action No. 97-1968, April 22, 1998.

been put up to libeling me by several Republican sources. One of them, he said, was Richard Carlson, ambassador to the Seychelles during the first Bush administration and a close associate of Richard Mellon Scaife. Drudge also said he had relied for advice upon Michael and Barbara Ledeen; Michael was a figure involved in the early stages of the Iran-Contra scandal who became a resident scholar at the American Enterprise Institute, a conservative think tank, while his wife worked for the Independent Women's Forum. Drudge suggested that another source was John Fund, an editorial writer for *The Wall Street Journal* who had been a ghostwriter for Rush Limbaugh and was close to Newt Gingrich. Brock told me that Tucker Carlson, Richard Carlson's son, then a writer for *The Weekly Standard*, had informed him that he had written an article in 1997 that would have exposed Fund as Drudge's source but that the editors had spiked it.* After Jennet Conant wrote an article about Drudge published in *Vanity Fair*, I called her. "Fund spread the story," she told me. "He told the world. He told everyone in conservative circles. As soon as your appointment was announced, he started. I couldn't find anyone who didn't hear it from Fund."

In July, the Ledeens' testimony yielded the information that they had arranged through a friend, David Horowitz, for Drudge's defense to be paid for and handled. Both the Ledeens volunteered their "hate" for me because of an article I had written in *The Washington Post* recounting Michael Ledeen's role in the Iran-Contra scandal. Horowitz shared their animosity, in his case because of an article I had reported for the *Post* about a political project of his that became a public embarrassment. Horowitz now headed a conservative group funded by Scaife, and he would serve as a conduit for Scaife's underwriting of Drudge's defense and provision of a lawyer employed by a Scaife-funded front group.

We also sent a subpoena to Fund, but his lawyer, provided by *The Wall Street Journal*, argued that he had not received proper notice. While my lawyer was trying to reschedule Fund's deposition, the *Journal* ran an editorial: "Sidney Strikes Out," claiming that my motive in subpoenaing Fund was "a political jihad on behalf of the President of the United States."† What was truly political had been the organized libel of me on my first day of work in the White House.

A year later, in November 1999, at a restaurant, I was surprised to be

---

*For Brock's account, see Brock, *Blinded by the Right*, pp. 314–15.

†Howard Kurtz, "Blumenthal's Suit Has Become More Than a Drudge Match," *The Washington Post*, August 3, 1998.

stopped by John Fund, who then made what I regarded as a confession. "I'm sorry for the mistake I made about you," he said. "It was a mistake. I don't bear a grudge against you and I hope you don't bear one toward me." I told him, "I'm glad you feel that way." And I walked away.

In my deposition, on September 8 and 9, Drudge's lawyer, Manny Klausner, trying to paint me as a scoundrel, asked if I had planted stories about the personal lives of Henry Hyde, Dan Burton, Helen Chenoweth, and a host of others, including, most perplexingly in that lineup, Mrs. Colin Powell. "How does it feel to read how loathed you are?" he asked.

"I think that some people who feel very, very strongly about President Clinton do feel that way," I replied. "I regard it as a measure of the charged political atmosphere."

Strangely, he asked if I had read in college "the works of Marx and Freud." I admitted that I had, and that I had read other books as well.

"Does it distress you to learn that this rumor about potential wife beating has been in circulation for ten years?" he asked.

"What kind of wife beating?" I answered.

"Potential, possible, alleged."

"Potential?" I said. "Does this mean I am a potential wife beater?"

Klausner used his deposition of Jackie, on September 10, to try to humiliate and belittle her as a price for our pursuing the suit. "Have you changed your diet at all since August of 1997?" he asked.

"I keep trying to," she replied.

"In what respect?"

"I'd like to eat less."

"So that you would photograph better?"

Drudge's lawyer treated Jackie as a nonperson apparently because she was not the intended target of defamation, as the following exchange made clear. In reply to a question, Jackie had described Drudge's accusation: "He's reporting something he didn't check which he just reported recklessly in order to smear my husband and in the end accuse me of being beaten."

"Where did he accuse you of that?"

"If my husband is a wife beater and I'm the wife, I'm the one that got beaten."

"Do you see any reference to you here?"

"Excuse me?"

I had felt compelled to file suit against Drudge to make absolutely clear the falsity of his smear. I had also thought there should be an element of responsibility on the Internet, extending to it the same standards that applied to the rest of the press, but unfortunately the court had not kept AOL in the case. Without any pressure or pain, being financed by Scaife, Drudge was now basking in the negative publicity. For him and his conservative backers, the suit became an instrument for tarnishing me further. But, with the impeachment beginning, I put the suit on a back burner. There would be no more discovery in the case.

III

At the same time that I was being deposed in the Drudge case and during the two weeks before the Starr Report and the days after its immediate release, I was immersed in helping to formulate the President's response to the extraordinary economic crisis then unfolding in Asia. The "Asian contagion" that had begun with efforts in Southeast Asia to repay debt to floundering Japanese banks was spreading. Since July 1997, when Thailand had devalued its currency, other countries had been drawn in, causing the International Monetary Fund to make more than $100 billion in loans. Uncertainty was gripping investors, and the Brazilian and Russian economies appeared wobbly. On August 4, I had written a memo to the President, with copies to Bowles and Gene Sperling, on the danger of "passivity" on the "economic message." If the President acted as though the economy were on "autopilot," then the "Republicans' blockage" of our proposals might be perceived as "perversely" justified: "A new dynamic must be set in motion. The President must make clear that the management of the economy is a day-to-day matter. . . . If the President is not the master economic manager, the risks are manifold: (a) If the economic program that the President has developed is not pursued, the economy might unravel; (b) If the forces of the accelerating global economy are not constantly balanced and stabilized, the economy might slide."

On August 30, I told the President that he should make a major speech to restore confidence in the global economy. Clinton agreed that he should speak, but this was only the beginning of a process to make the speech happen, and someone had to act as a catalyst. The next day I wrote a memo to the President with a copy to Bowles, laying out the idea of his giving a speech on "global economic stabilization," its themes, proposals, venue (the Council on Foreign Relations in New York), and political rationale: "It is better for the President to ride events than to be ridden by them. It is best for him to be steering them where he sees they should be going." A day later the Dow-Jones average dropped 6 percent on fears of the Asian contagion. To set the speech in motion, I gained the approval of the administration's economic policymakers: Secretary of the Treasury Robert Rubin, Council of Economic Advisers chairperson Janet Yellen, and National Economic Council director Gene Sperling, who was in charge of organizing the administration's economic policy. Michael Waldman, the chief speechwriter, and I—with Gene's continual contributions—began to draft the speech.

On September 14, the President delivered his speech, laying out a program for global economic growth, stability, and renewal of the "international financial architecture." "This is the biggest financial challenge facing the world in a half-century," he said. "And the United States has an absolutely inescapable obligation to lead, and to lead in a way that's consistent with our values and our obligation to see that what we're doing helps lift the lives of ordinary people here at home and all around the world." He urged the Republican Congress to stop balking at funding the American contribution to the IMF. But he did more than provide a laundry list of policies, however essential that was to calming the markets, which it did. He made an important statement of social and political policy. Clinton compared the challenge on the global economy to that faced by the New Deal on the U.S. domestic economy:

For half a century now in our national economy, we have learned not to eliminate but to tame and limit the swings of boom and bust. In the twenty-first century, we have to find a way to do that in the global economy as well. . . . What is at stake is more than the spread of free markets and their integration into the global economy. The forces behind the global economy are also those that deepen democratic liberties: the free flow of ideas and information, open borders and easy travel, the rule of law, fair and even-handed enforcement, protection for consumers, a skilled and educated work force.

Each of these things matters not only to the wealth of nations but to the health of freedom. If citizens tire of waiting for democracy and free markets to deliver a better life for them, there is a real risk that democracy and free markets, instead of continuing to thrive together, will begin to shrivel together. This would pose great risks not only for our economic interests but for our security. . . . We now have a chance to create opportunity on a worldwide scale. The difficulties of the moment should not obscure us to the advances of the last several years. We clearly have it within our means, if we do the right things, to lift billions and billions of people around the world into a global middle class and into participation in global democracy and genuine efforts toward peace and reconciliation. That is a possibility, but recent events show it is not a certainty.

At this moment, therefore, the United States is called upon once again to lead—to organize the forces of a committed world; to channel the unruly energies of the global economy into positive avenues; to advance our interests, reinforce our values, enhance our security.

In this room, I think it is not too simple to say we know what to do. The World War II generation did it for us fifty years ago. Now, it is time for us to rise to our responsibility, as America has been called upon to do so often so many times in the past.

But while the President could smooth the roiling waters of the global economy, he could do little back in Washington to subdue the political uproar over his impeachment. The Starr Report had unleashed animosities that hardly anyone anticipated would now rip into the drama.

Over the past seven and a half months, a retiree in Florida, Norman Sommer, had sent out fifty-seven letters and made dozens of phone calls to news organizations prodding them to write a story about his friend Fred Snodgrass. Snodgrass had been a furniture salesman in Chicago whose marriage was broken up in 1967 when his wife, Cherie, had an affair with a forty-one-year-old lawyer and aspiring politician named Henry Hyde. Snodgrass was still bitter, and Sommer was acting as his agent.

On September 16, *Salon.com*, the online magazine, published Snodgrass's account. Cherie, through a daughter, also acknowledged it. Hyde issued a statement assigning it to his "youthful indiscretions." Snodgrass was quoted: "And all I can think of is here is this man, this hypocrite who broke up my family. . . . I hate the man. He destroyed my kids, me. I'm not a vengeful person. And I don't have anything against Cherie anymore. Of course, it takes two to tango and maybe I wasn't the best of husbands. But he got away with it. He doesn't deserve all this ovation, this respect."*

The editor of *Salon*, David Talbot, published an accompanying article

*David Talbot, "This Hypocrite Broke Up My Family," *Salon.com*, September 16, 1998.

explaining why he was publishing the piece. "The White House had nothing whatsoever to do with any aspect of this story," he wrote. "We did not receive it from anyone in the White House or in Clinton's political or legal camps, nor did we communicate with them about it. Norman Sommer, the man who did lead us to the story, categorically denied to us that he had any connection to the Clinton administration." Then he offered as *Salon*'s justification for releasing this information the following argument: "If the public has a right to know, in excruciating detail, about Clinton's sexual life, then surely it has an equal right to know about the private life of the man who called the family 'the surest basis of civil order, the strongest foundation for free enterprise, the safest home of freedom'—and who on Monday indicated that he believes impeachment hearings are warranted."*

When the article was posted on the Internet, I was in my office working on a Third Way conference, "Strengthening Democracy in the Global Economy," that was going to be held in less than a week at the New York University School of Law. The private conversations about progressive politics that Clinton and Blair had had at Chequers and the White House were going public, and for months I had been organizing this conference. I had recruited the Progressive Policy Institute of the Democratic Leadership Council and the World Policy Institute at the New School for Social Research as cosponsors along with NYU. In July, we had had a meeting at the White House with Hillary and leading center-left figures from think tanks, foundations, and journals, trying to work out the common themes we would address in anticipation of the conference. Prominent scholars, United Nations officials, economists, and legal experts were to meet from morning until night, the centerpiece being a discussion among President Clinton, Prime Minister Blair, Prime Minister Prodi, and President Stoyanov of Bulgaria, elaborating on the very themes that the President had discussed in his Council on Foreign Relations speech. As I was making last preparations, Bowles sent a message that he wanted to see me.

Erskine asked me if I was responsible for the *Salon* piece on Hyde. I told him categorically that I was not. John Podesta was in Erskine's office as well, reading through the article. "It says here," he said, " 'The White House had nothing whatsoever to do with any aspect of this story.' "

*David Talbot, "Why We Ran the Henry Hyde Story," *Salon.com*, September 16, 1998.

Blaming me was nothing new, an aspect of the campaign against the President. The lawyers, inside and outside the White House, understood that well but warned that it was a shaky political moment.

The days after the Starr Report's release produced the greatest fear inside the White House since the first week of the scandal. A new NBC News/*Wall Street Journal* poll showed that 60 percent of the American people believed the President had obstructed justice. Some congressional Democrats were unsteady. Senator Joseph Lieberman had given a speech denouncing Clinton's behavior as "immoral" and went up to the edge of calling on him to quit. Most of us on the White House political and legal staffs believed that Starr had written his salacious report to shame Clinton into resigning. No one knew what would come next. Gingrich called Clinton a "misogynist" and was demanding that the networks broadcast his videotaped deposition. The video might be even more damaging than the Starr Report—a coup de grâce. In living color, in everyone's living room, a whole nation might be repelled. The Hyde incident provided the Republican leadership an opening for calculated attack, allowing them to provoke the media into delirium and to push the White House, stoked with concentrated fear, into a defensive crouch.

Mike McCurry, the press secretary, issued a statement: "We were in no way connected to the *Salon* story." That evening, all three networks broadcast bulletins about Henry Hyde, with ABC reporting in an early broadcast that two anonymous sources claimed that I had peddled it to them. In a later version I became an unnamed White House official.

The next day, Bowles sent a letter reassuring Hyde that the White House had had nothing to do with these reports, that it "is informing news organizations that it waives any right to journalistic confidentiality about the sources of such stories," and that "any staff who are found to be engaging in such conduct will be fired." This was a Kafkaesque position, fending off a false charge but attempting to show good faith by expressing willingness to punish the nonexistent offender.

At a press conference, Tom DeLay released a letter calling for an FBI investigation signed by the Republican House Leaders—Speaker Newt Gingrich, Majority Leader Dick Armey, Deputy Whip John Boehner, and himself: "Whether or not that specific story originated with the White House or its allies, clearly there is credible evidence that an organized campaign of slander and intimidation may exist. If these reports are true, the actions of the individuals responsible are pure and simple intimidation—no different than threatening jurors to change their verdicts in organized crime trials." No evidence was offered, no examples cited.

When asked what proof he had that the White House was behind the Hyde story, DeLay blurted out, "No, I don't have any evidence." Then he said darkly, "We have reason to believe that top aides that have access to the Oval Office have been orchestrating a conspiracy to intimidate members of Congress by using their past lives." As he went on, he grew more certain: "A number of published reports have pointed to Mr. Blumenthal as at the heart of the White House strategy. We know why these stories happened. We know others are coming." He finished with a flourish: "If we find out who is responsible, this could be added to the impeachment inquiry."*

Throughout the day, I watched this spectacle unfold and decided I had to speak in my own voice, and within that news cycle. I told Erskine, who thought it was a good idea, and conferred with Ruff, who was supportive. Then I issued a statement: "I was not the source of, or in any way involved with, this story on Henry Hyde. I did not urge or encourage any reporter to investigate the private life of any member of Congress. Any suggestions otherwise are completely false." But my disavowal did not quell the fury. Nor did the accurate report on CBS News that night by Bob Schieffer: "Several Washington reporters told us a Florida man named Norman Sommer" was responsible for the story and that "Sommer says he was operating on his own, not at the request of the White House."†

The following day, September 18, the *New York Post* ran my photo on its front page next to a huge headline: "BILL'S DIRT DEVIL." Above that ran another headline: "GOP Suspects Clinton Henchman Is Top White House Smear-Meister." Inside, there were more headlines—"White House Eyed in GOP Sex Smears" and "Controversial Aide at Center of the Storm"—with the lead story, which read, "Furious Republicans yesterday called on FBI chief Louis Freeh to probe whether the Clinton White House is running a slime machine to fight Sexgate by slandering its enemies." It ended, "Republicans wondered aloud who would be next—perhaps Gingrich?"‡

In *The Washington Post*, Representative Ray LaHood, an Illinois con-

*Donald Lambro and Nancy E. Roman, "Republican Leaders Ask FBI to Look for Source of 'Dirt,' " *The Washington Times*, September 18, 1998.

†Media Research Center, "CyberAlert," September 18, 1998, https://secure. mediaresearch.org/news/cyberalert/1998/cyb19980918.html.

‡Deborah Orin, Brian Blomquist, and Vincent Morris, "White House Eyed in GOP Sex Smears," *New York Post*, September 18, 1998.

gressman close to Hyde, continued the finger-pointing: "I think this is Sidney Blumenthal's MO. Blumenthal is a sneak. He's out to destroy people's careers, and he ought to be fired." Asked for proof, LaHood replied, "Process of elimination." Joe Lockhart, the White House deputy press secretary, suggested that LaHood "should forward to us any credible information he has. If he has no such information, he should keep his thoughts to himself. Otherwise he's engaging in rumor, innuendo, and anonymous gossip."*

The efforts to demonize me got so outlandish that I jokingly greeted my White House colleagues with the Rolling Stones' lyric from "Sympathy for the Devil": "Please allow me to introduce myself . . ." And after a briefing of the President in the Oval Office that I and a number of others attended, Clinton asked me to stay behind. Once we were alone, he said, "Listen, I know all this stuff about you and Hyde is total bullshit. Don't let it bother you." "Thanks," I said. Within the White House, the Kafka-like trial was over.

Once I had been proclaimed the "devil," the television talk shows on Sunday morning, September 20, devoted themselves to probing my satanic works. On ABC's *This Week*, the guest was my attorney, Bill McDaniel. Sam Donaldson began the proceedings by saying that I was "widely suspected of being the person who has disseminated these stories about Hyde and others. . . . Mr. McDaniel," Donaldson demanded, "ABC News, as I said, has reported that we have talked to two individuals who have told us that Mr. Blumenthal discussed the Henry Hyde story with them. Now, are they lying?"

"Do you have their names?" McDaniel asked. "Because if you do I'd like to write them down and talk to them face-to-face."

"We have their names, but we of course promised them confidentiality, as we had to when they spoke to us. But we are putting the faith of—credibility of ABC News behind what we've just said to you."

"Now, I'd like that person to come forward and say, 'I talked to Sidney Blumenthal and he told me these things.' Because it's false."

On NBC's *Meet the Press*, John Podesta was the guest. He made it clear that the White House had "a zero-tolerance policy for dealing in this kind of information about people's private lives. Anybody in the White House who has gotten—done anything in that regard will be fired," he said. "It was not Mr. Blumenthal."

---

*Howard Kurtz, "Hyde Story Stirs Hostilities," *The Washington Post*, September 18, 1998.

Tim Russert, the host, persisted: "The FBI is going to investigate this matter. Will you provide White House phone logs from Mr. Blumenthal to the FBI?"

"Well, I'm not going to predict what the FBI's going to do with regard to this matter, but I think it's—I think it's actually kind of frightening that the House of Representatives and Mr. DeLay specifically would push an FBI investigation, when he stood before the American public and said he has no evidence of a crime. None. Zero."

On CBS's *Face the Nation*, my White House colleague Rahm Emanuel was the guest. "We in Washington have got to stop criminalizing and politicizing people's private lives," he said. "We have a zero-tolerance policy in the White House. If anybody is found to be involved in this, I'd personally kick their butt on the other side of Northwest Gate, and hopefully it'd hit the turnstile on the way out."

Bob Schieffer, the host, spoke as if he had forgotten that he had reported just three days before that I was not involved in the story about Hyde: "But there are journalists out there who say that Sidney Blumenthal, the aide in the White House closest to Mrs. Clinton, has been talking to them about this stuff."

"Sid has denied it, has said he is not involved in this."

Months later, Michael Kramer put the dilemma this way: "It's the hardest question for a press victim who denies an allegation made anonymously: How do you prove a negative?" His article quoted journalists who had tried to talk to me about Hyde before the *Salon* article appeared and who remembered my saying, "I don't want to hear anything about it." George Will did not return Kramer's phone calls. Donaldson refused comment. Cokie Roberts said she was "just there." Kristol bemoaned that it was "unfortunate" that there were no witnesses.* Later, an ABC correspondent with direct knowledge about how the story was developed told me that the accusation about me was broadcast without establishing a factual basis: "It did not have anything to do with you. The disinformation was heartbreaking."

This unpleasant episode about Henry Hyde ratcheted up the tension surrounding all the publicity about the videotape of Clinton's deposition, with the Republican drumbeat for its release getting louder and louder.

*Michael Kramer, "Who's Vicious Now?" *Brill's Content*, December 1998/January 1999.

The House Judiciary Committee announced that it would be made public. The television networks planned to broadcast it uncut, for hours, on Monday, September 21.

Early that morning I went to New York with Hillary Clinton for the planned Third Way conference at NYU. She spent the entire day at the law school, appearing on the first panel, about civil society, and attending the others. Thus she was shielded by work of substance from the downpour of this potentially horrendous day. I had my hands full, too.

Uptown, at the United Nations, the President addressed the United Nations General Assembly that morning on terrorism. When he entered the room, all the world leaders rose to give him a sustained ovation—a telling commentary of their own on his domestic travails. Clinton's speech was specific and prophetic. Terrorism, he said, was not just "an American problem":

> Terrorism has a new face in the 1990s. Today terrorists take advantage of greater openness and the explosion of information and weapons technology. The new technologies of terror and their increasing availability, along with the increasing mobility of terrorists, raise chilling prospects of vulnerability to chemical, biological, and other kinds of attacks, bringing each of us into the category of possible victim. This is a threat to all humankind.
>
> Beyond the physical damage of each attack, there is an even greater residue of psychological damage—hard to measure, but slow to heal. Every bomb, every bomb threat has an insidious effect on free and open institutions. . . .

The President argued for wider democracy, economic programs of reconstruction to end the conditions of "despair and alienation" in which terrorism thrives, and diplomacy to end ethnic strife. He called for greater airport security and international police cooperation to break up terrorist networks. (In the United States, strict airport security measures had been proposed by the presidential commission, chaired by Vice President Gore, set up after the crash of TWA Flight 800 in 1996, but these had mostly been blocked by the airline industry and the Republican Congress.) Finally, Clinton sought to undermine the rationale of the terrorists' distorted view of a holy war:

> Some people believe that terrorism's principal fault line centers on what they see as an inevitable clash of civilizations. It is an issue that deserves a

lot of debate in this great hall. Specifically, many believe there is an inevitable clash between Western civilization and Western values, and Islamic civilizations and values. I believe this view is terribly wrong. False
prophets may use and abuse any religion to justify whatever political objectives they have—even cold-blooded murder.

. . . Let me urge all of us to think in new terms on terrorism, to see it
not as a clash of cultures or political action by other means, or a divine
calling, but a clash between the forces of the past and the forces of the future, between those who tear down and those who build up, between
hope and fear, chaos and community.

Then the President headed downtown to the NYU conference.
Hillary and I waited for him in a room upstairs from the main meeting
hall. He told us about the reception he had gotten, marveling at the ovation he'd been given when he entered the General Assembly. Gene Sperling and I began to brief him for his appearance on the conference panel.
Doug Sosnik, a political aide, mentioned that the television airing of the
deposition did not seem to have provoked a negative reaction. Clinton
nodded and related what a Latin American ambassador had told him at
the UN: "We have coups in our country, too, but they're with guns." We
went on with the briefing.

At the panel with Blair, Prodi, and Stoyanov, the President was relaxed yet concentrated. He was expansive in his remarks, responding to
Blair's call for a "new progressivism." His performance was incisive, his
composure unfailing. Afterward, he spent more than an hour at the reception, talking to participants and guests. The event ended with a call
for another, even broader conference.

Only late that night was I able to view excerpts on television of Clinton's deposition. Two days before, his lawyers had briefed some of us on
the White House political staff about it, and we had learned that contrary
to media stories, he had not lost his temper. The numerous media reports claimed Clinton would appear as an angry man, failing to restrain
his rage, and that the people would be shocked by the sexual imagery.
Given my own experience in the grand jury, I had believed all along that
seeing the President being questioned would elicit support for him. He
would be the only person seen, answering disembodied questions from
the prosecutors. Much of the audience could not help but sympathize
with his predicament.

On the video appeared the familiar Bill Clinton, voluble, captivating,
sometimes wearing his reading glasses, drinking from a can of Diet Coke.

He avoided discussing any salacious detail and defended himself without being overly defensive. He was polite, never argumentative, even when hectored by the droning voices of the unseen men. And he was humane—about his wife, his daughter, and Monica Lewinsky, and in acknowledging his own flaws. He was still Bill Clinton, likable even under these circumstances. And whatever his sins, those circumstances struck most of the public as deeply unfair.

A new poll by the Pew Research Center showed 70 percent wanted Clinton to stay in office and only 26 percent favored removing him.* A CNN/Gallup poll revealed that only a third of the public approved of how the Republicans were handling the controversy.† The darkness of the previous two weeks, after the Starr Report, partially lifted. Hillary went out into the country to campaign for the administration's programs again. Clinton pounded away at the agenda. The Democratic leadership in Congress rallied against impeachment, proposing a censure. The midterm election was six weeks away.

Henry Hyde's immense bulk, his gray hair, florid manner, and soft voice, created the image of an avuncular figure above politics, just the man for the delicate job of chairing the House Judiciary Committee. He seemed to some the beau ideal of bipartisanship who had met his moment. Hyde was in fact a highly conventional product of the Illinois Republican Party, just as much a machine as its Democratic counterpart in Chicago; for decades the Republicans had held control of the state, doling out patronage, favors, and spoils. Hyde had toiled loyally and without much notice in the state legislature for eight years before being promoted to congressman in a safe Republican suburban district. His great crusade was against abortion, and his crowning achievement was the Hyde Amendment, which deprived poor women of federal funding for abortion under Medicaid. He even testified as a character witness in the trial of Joseph Scheidler, an activist who was convicted in 1998 of conspiring to incite violence against abortion clinics. "He has the guts I wish more of us had," Hyde said.‡

*John Harris, "Clinton Team Regains Optimism as Battle Moves to Political Realm," *The Washington Post*, September 25, 1998.

†CNN AllPolitics, "Poll: Release of Clinton's Testimony Creates Backlash Against GOP," September 24, 1998, http://www.cnn.com/ALLPOLITICS/stories/1998/09/24/clinton.poll/.

‡Robert Scheer, "Abortion Fight Drives Hyde's Prosecution," *Los Angeles Times*, December 15, 1998.

The antiabortion movement was in part a reaction to the reordering of family life that had come about with the "women's revolution" beginning in the 1960s. It was an aspect of the conservatives' culture war against this reordering, and the impeachment of Clinton was the climax of this war. Hyde's antiabortion extremism gave him an authentic basis for his participation in it.

Within the Republican Party, now dominated by Southern conservatives, Hyde came to stand for its old Midwestern wing. His rise was that of a small-town man on the make in the city, craving position and success, glad-handing and eager for approval, his hypocrisy of a piece with his ambition. He was a figure out of a Sinclair Lewis novel. With age, an appearance of gravity was ascribed to him, and he was reinvented as a paragon of tradition. His main effectiveness for the Republicans before the impeachment was to project his benign visage in defense of the administration in the Iran-Contra scandal and of Gingrich's program, and to represent the antiabortion cause.

Most of the House Democrats I knew saw Hyde as usually partisan, lazy, and often sarcastic in private. They understood from the start that he would be no barrier to Gingrich and DeLay's hell-bent pressure for impeachment. Hyde was also an unquestioning believer in Kenneth Starr. His rationale for an unlimited impeachment inquiry was that Starr might just have more scandals to divulge. "Based upon what we now know, do we have a duty to look further or to look away?" he said in his opening statement on October 5. Whitewater? Filegate? Campaign finance? Hillary? More women? Who knew?

Hyde brought in as his counsel a crony from Chicago, a former prosecutor and lawyer, David Schippers, who was also an opinionated conservative of the Limbaugh variety despite his being a registered Democrat. He was inexperienced with the protocol of Congress and the byways of Washington. At every turn, he acted as Hyde's goad. On the first day of committee proceedings, Schippers, not understanding his role as a mere staff member, took to lecturing the elected representatives. "Members of the committee," he declaimed in a stentorian tone, "you are not being watched only by the individuals in this room or even by the immense television audience throughout the world. Fifteen generations of Americans, our fellow Americans, many of whom are reposing in military cemeteries throughout the world, are looking down on and judging what you do today."* He could not have been more effective in unifying the Democrats.

*Peter Baker, *The Breach*, Scribner, 2000, p. 122.

With the launch of the House Judiciary Committee impeachment proceedings, Starr opened his unreleased files to congressional staff assistants on a "top secret" basis. Democratic lawyers sifting through the mounds of material discovered an overzealous prosecutor whose dragnet had included Kathleen Willey's dentist and White House window washers. But they also found evidence that would have had an exculpatory effect had Starr made it public: Vernon Jordan had not pressured Revlon to hire Lewinsky, for example. For Republicans, Starr's files were a mesmerizing new "Clinton Chronicles," for they included raw FBI files filled with uncorroborated hearsay, mirroring the uncorroborated hearsay of the Jones case—the same unreliable witnesses, the same stories, only more—a witness who claimed he knew a man who claimed he was Clinton's cocaine dealer, for example. David Schippers was enthralled, and he came away captivated by the conspiracy theory that the President, his lawyers, and the White House staff had intimidated women into silence about his sex life.* The Jones case had not died: it had gone to Starr's heaven, and now it lived on in the overheated imaginations on the House Judiciary Committee.

Backstage negotiations to censure President Clinton rather than impeach him came to naught. Tom DeLay brushed aside anything but impeachment. "We're going to win by losing," Dick Gephardt told an aide. But that Democratic strategy required a presumption that the Republicans would unwaveringly maintain their hard line: it was an assumption that was always borne out. On October 8, the House of Representatives voted on two resolutions on impeachment. The Democratic one, proposed by Representative Richard Boucher of Virginia, required that an impeachment inquiry be limited to the Lewinsky matter and have a time limit of a month. The Republican one, proposed by Henry Hyde, drew no limits on anything, and it passed 258–176, with only 31 Democrats voting in favor. In private, the Democrats regarded their loss as an important victory: the Republicans were making their partisanship an issue.

Meanwhile, the budget deadline had passed, on October 1, an invisible line the crossing of which put a burden on the Republicans. Their inability to settle with Clinton on a federal budget before that date raised the specter once again of a government shutdown. During the next week, the President forced the Republicans into a corner. On October 15, he

*Baker, *The Breach*, pp. 137–39.

won funding for 100,000 new teachers and other educational programs and for additional money for the IMF. Over the previous year, the Republicans had blocked many of his administration's initiatives—the patients' bill of rights, more child care tax credits, an increase in the minimum wage, school construction—but in the decisive budget battle they crumbled. Outfoxed by Clinton even as they were impeaching him, they were flummoxed and fuming.

After announcing his budget victory, the President boarded *Marine One* to fly to the Wye Plantation in Maryland, where he would negotiate the next phase of the efforts to achieve a Middle East peace. For eight days he was isolated there, returning on September 23 with an agreement. Bringing together the intransigent Yasser Arafat and the implacable Benjamin Netanyahu, he sat them down on either side of him on a stage in the East Room to sign the Wye River Accord. The painstaking negotiations were exhausting, and they nearly collapsed twice when Netanyahu threatened to walk out. At the last minute, his demand for the release of Jonathan Pollard, imprisoned for handing over U.S. national security secrets to the Israelis—a demand the President could not grant—nearly blew up the conference. But Clinton managed to win concessions from each side. He got the Israelis to turn over additional sections of the West Bank to Palestinian Authority control. From the Palestinians he wrung an agreement to drop anti-Israel paragraphs from the Palestinian National Charter and, under CIA supervision, to turn over terrorist suspects to Israel. The accord set the stage for the even more difficult negotiations for "permanent status."

In this Israeli-Palestinian work, Clinton regarded himself as a legatee, a political son, of the murdered Yitzhak Rabin, whom he revered above all other leaders, except perhaps Nelson Mandela. Clinton had erected private shrines to Rabin throughout the living quarters of the White House: he kept a plate of dirt from his grave and the yarmulke he had worn at Rabin's funeral, as well as a crystal sculpture of a dove that Hillary had given him to memorialize Rabin, displayed on a mantel. In the Oval Office, a bust of Rabin joined the busts of Kennedy, Roosevelt, Truman, Franklin, and King.

At Wye, the President had invited King Hussein of Jordan to help him persuade the recalcitrant parties. Hussein was dying of cancer, and he came to the meetings between chemotherapy treatments, his hair fallen out, his energy visibly flagging. He was one of the Middle East's ultimate survivors, and he despised Arafat and Netanyahu, about whom he had no illusions, but he harbored to the very end of his life the hope for peace. The White House staff packed the East Room to hear him speak before the signatures were scratched onto paper. King Hussein addressed himself to Clinton:

> Mr. President, I have had the privilege of being a friend of the United States and its presidents since late President Eisenhower. Throughout all the years that have passed, I have kept in touch. But on the subject of peace, the peace we are seeking, I have never—with all due respect and all the affection that I hold for your predecessors—known someone with your dedication, clear-headedness, focus, and determination to help resolve this issue in the best possible way.
>
> Mr. President, permit me to say what I feel—I was mentioning it more than once in the last few days. You have the tolerance and the patience of Job, and you are the subject of our admiration and respect. We hope that you will be with us as we see greater successes and as we help our brethren and our friends move ahead towards a better tomorrow.

That day Representative James Hansen, Republican from Utah, told reporters he was only joking when he had said something that week on a local radio talk show about assassinating President Clinton. "Well," he had said, "over 90 percent are saying impeach. They're saying censure, they're saying all kinds of crazy things. Some are saying assassinate. I'm not saying that."* Newt Gingrich, campaigning for a congressional candidate in Michigan, listened at the rally as a warm-up speaker made wisecracks about "President Gore." And a subcommittee of the House Judiciary Committee announced it would hold a hearing on the history of impeachment once it reconvened after the November election, now only twelve days away.

President Clinton could show the public his good faith in office by pursuing his policy work in their interest, but that only went so far. The case needed to be made that impeaching him was a fundamental assault on the American constitutional system. As the polls proved, most Americans understood this instinctively, but the point was rarely articulated in the daily press or even the opinion journals. With each passing day, Washington was becoming more inward and insular than ever, a closed

---

*Associated Press, "Rep. Hansen Faulted on Assassination Remark," *The Washington Post*, October 24, 1998.

city conducting its business as though the outside world would not and should not intrude.

Then a completely unexpected factor entered. Liberal intellectuals hardly seemed a force to be felt in 1990s politics. If ever a group of individuals appeared to be without an organizing center, it was they. They had no headquarters, no office, not even a bulletin board. Since the Vietnam War, their presence in American politics had been negligible, a reversal of the trend of influence that began with Franklin Roosevelt's brain trust. They had contentiously split with the Johnson administration over the war and gone into hostile opposition under Nixon. During the Reagan years, it was members of the conservative counterestablishment who rode high in the saddle, placing their cadres throughout the administration and expanding their infrastructure of think tanks, publishing outlets, and foundations. That growth continued through the first Bush administration.

When Clinton took office, policy-oriented experts of the center-left gravitated to the new administration. But his early difficulties, especially the defeat of the health care bill and labor's opposition to free trade, destroyed many of their hopes, and some of them were disillusioned. Newt Gingrich's rise began to alarm them, however, and they recognized the political stakes. Clinton's outmaneuvering of Gingrich showed his personal political skills, but some intellectuals on the left saw his virtues as vices, his political finesse as an unprincipled sellout, mistaking tactical necessity for treachery.

Black intellectuals were the great exception, despite the Lani Guinier fiasco. From John Hope Franklin to Henry Louis Gates, Jr., they understood Clinton's political predicaments, the nature of his Southern liberalism, and his commitment to racial equality. In the immediate aftermath of the Starr Report's release, the first political support event for Bill Clinton was held in Oak Bluffs on Martha's Vineyard, a historic community of freed slaves. Skip Gates presided, and Toni Morrison, the Nobel Prize–winning novelist, proclaimed Clinton "the first black president." Black intellectuals, like blacks generally, saw the assault on Clinton as an assault on themselves.

The entire year of 1998 was a political education for liberal intellectuals. No longer could they take for granted that the basic institutions and ideals of the American government, secured since the New Deal era, would survive the attack on Clinton's presidency. Even more, the Constitution itself was endangered. Repelled by Starr and Gingrich, they gradually came to realize what Clinton had been battling all along.*

In September, the distinguished Princeton historian Sean Wilentz, author of a seminal work on Jacksonian politics, *Chants Democratic*, whom I had known from my *New Republic* days, came to Washington as a fellow for a year at the Woodrow Wilson International Center for Scholars. Sean came up with the idea of having American historians make a statement on the impeachment, and he contacted Arthur Schlesinger, Jr., the Pulitzer Prize–winning historian and former aide to President Kennedy. Together they composed a draft they circulated among their colleagues.

On October 28, more than four hundred "Historians in Defense of the Constitution" published their statement in a full-page advertisement in *The New York Times*. In Washington, Wilentz, Schlesinger, and the great Southern historian C. Vann Woodward held a joint press conference about the statement:

> As historians as well as citizens, we deplore the present drive to impeach the President. We believe that this drive, if successful, will have the most serious implications for our constitutional order.
>
> Under our Constitution, impeachment of the President is a grave and momentous step. The Framers explicitly reserved that step for high crimes and misdemeanors in the exercise of executive power. Impeachment for anything else would, according to James Madison, leave the President to serve "during pleasure of the Senate," thereby mangling the system of checks and balances that is our chief safeguard against abuses of public power.
>
> Although we do not condone President Clinton's private behavior or his subsequent attempts to deceive, the current charges against him depart from what the Framers saw as grounds for impeachment. The vote of the House of Representatives to conduct an open-ended inquiry creates a novel, all-purpose search for any offense by which to remove a President from office.
>
> The theory of impeachment underlying these efforts is unprecedented in our history. The new processes are extremely ominous for the future of our political institutions. If carried forward, they will leave the Presidency permanently disfigured and diminished, at the mercy as never before of the caprices of any Congress. The Presidency, historically the

---

*For one account of some episodes of Clinton and the intellectuals, see Barber, *Truth of Power*.

center of leadership during our great national ordeals, will be crippled in meeting the inevitable challenges of the future.

We face a choice between preserving or undermining our Constitution. Do we want to establish a precedent for the future harassment of presidents and to tie up our government with a protracted national agony of search and accusation? Or do we want to protect the Constitution and get back to the public business?

We urge you, whether you are a Republican, a Democrat, or an Independent, to oppose the dangerous new theory of impeachment, and to demand the restoration of the normal operations of our federal government.

Not since Vietnam had the intellectuals intervened in politics with such effect. The ad had a profound and immediate effect on editorialists across the country, especially in the metropolitan press. It provided unapologetic arguments against impeachment that became the heart of President Clinton's case. Republicans had been striding around Washington like triumphant gladiators in an arena, but that turned out not to be the whole picture. The statement also stunned the pundits and social cliques that thought of the capital as their own preserve.

"October surprise," shrieked Walter Berns of the American Enterprise Institute on the *Wall Street Journal* editorial page. William Bennett, the former Reagan and Bush administration official who sat on the board of the Scaife Foundation (approving grants to his own group, Empower America), and the author most recently of *The Children's Book of Virtues* and *The Death of Outrage: Bill Clinton and the Assault on American Ideals*, vented his fury. "Do serious historians really believe such felony charges cannot constitute grounds for an impeachment inquiry?" he asked. "To the extent that the institution of the presidency has been damaged, it has been damaged by Bill Clinton."* He accused the historians of a "sleight of hand" by referring to sex, suggesting that if Clinton were charged with child molestation there would be no difference.†

But the assertion by the true academy, filling the civic assignment scholars must from time to time, revealed the ramshackle and marginal

---

*Quoted by Wendy Koch, "Hyde Joins Dem's Request for More Info from Starr Watergate Panel Chairman: Removal Isn't Warranted," *USA Today*, October 29, 1998.

†John Harris, "400 Historians Denounce Impeachment," *The Washington Post*, October 29, 1998.

nature of the conservative counterestablishment, however well funded by wealthy Republicans. The historians' statement showed that people like Bennett were acting as propagandists lacking a fundamental knowledge of American history. The intellectual emptiness of these incantations against Clinton about the rule of law and higher morality was exposed.

The Washington pundits long hostile to Clinton were also threatened, and their cudgel was taken up by the "dean of the press corps," David Broder. He called the historians' statement "ridiculous," a "broadside," and a "tantrum." Arthur Schlesinger, he wrote, was "like James Carville in a cap and gown." He defended the Republican Congress as though its partisan actions were constitutionally mandated by the framers. "But the House is following the process set forth in the Constitution," he argued. "This tenured trashing of Congress for meeting its responsibility says more about the state of the history profession than about the law of the land." He concluded on a sarcastic note of contempt: "Class dismissed."* But he had no substantive rebuttal, just disdain and anti-intellectual caricatures.

Two days before the midterm election, *The Washington Post* published a long article by Sally Quinn that elaborately declared her well-known sentiment that President Clinton did not belong to the "Washington establishment," that he should "resign" and "spare" Washington "any more humiliation." On the one hand, she wrote, Washington's elite "are not unlike any other small community in the country"—say, Gopher Prairie, Minnesota?—"But this particular community happens to be in the nation's capital. And the people in it are the so-called Beltway Insiders—the high-level members of Congress, policymakers, lawyers, military brass, diplomats and journalists who have a proprietary interest in Washington and identify with it." One of them was Ken Starr. "Starr is a Washington insider, too. . . . Their wives are friendly with one another and their children go to the same schools." But Bill Clinton was decidedly not an "insider." Indeed, "the Washington Establishment is outraged" and "Washington insiders are particularly appalled." Quinn offered a catalog of commentators to make the point. David Broder: "He came in here and he trashed the place, and it's not his place." Tish Baldridge, Jacqueline Kennedy's social secretary and "a frequent visitor since" to the White House: "Now it's gone, now it's sleaze and dirt. We all feel terribly let down. It's very emotional. We want there to be standards. We're used to

*David Broder, "The Historians' Complaint," *The Washington Post*, November 1, 1998.

standards." Muffie Cabot, Nancy Reagan's social secretary: "This is a demoralized little village. . . . Watergate was pretty scary, but it wasn't quite as sordid as this."* What Quinn was describing was not a governing class, but a faux aristocracy. "The lions of yesteryear have become the unicorns of today," as David Cannadine wrote in *The Decline and Fall of the British Aristocracy*.†

Over on Capitol Hill, Speaker Gingrich confided in his aides that he expected the Republicans in the House to gain twenty-two seats in the election. In April, he had said about the scandal, "I will never again, as long as I am Speaker, make a speech without commenting on this topic." But Starr's unpopularity had made Gingrich reticent and he had fallen silent for months. A month before the election, when Republican pollsters noticed that GOP congressional candidates did not have the momentum they ought to have, Gingrich ordered television ads to be made on the scandal to motivate the Republican base. One featured distressed mothers saying to each other, "What did you tell your kids?" The amount spent on these commercials, the National Republican Congressional Commitee's "Operation Breakout," was an extraordinary $37 million. Yet on October 29, an NBC/*Wall Street Journal* poll showed that 68 percent disapproved of Congress's handling of impeachment.

We had been holding political meetings about the midterm election in the White House ever since May. The struggle seemed steeply uphill. Unlike in a presidential election year, the electorate that turned out would skew to older, more rural, and conservative voters. Yet, after the airing of the Starr Report and the broadcast of President Clinton's deposition video, Democratic voters were unusually galvanized. Gingrich's television ads excited even more their outrage at the attempt to remove Clinton. We believed that Gingrich, out of hubris, had made a strategic mistake. Still, every pundit on the television talk shows predicted great Republican gains.

On the evening of November 3, the tallies on the races came in one by one. In the Senate, Lauch Faircloth and Al D'Amato, both of whom had chaired Whitewater investigations, went down to defeat. Hillary Clinton had campaigned hard in New York against D'Amato (and for the winner, Charles Schumer). In the House, losses on the Republican side

---

*Sally Quinn, "Not in Their Backyard: In Washington, That Let Down Feeling," *The Washington Post*, November 2, 1998.

†David Cannadine, *The Decline and Fall of the British Aristocracy*, Papermac, 1996, p. 708.

ticked up, including Michael Pappas of New Jersey, who had sung on the House floor his own composition: "Twinkle, twinkle, Kenneth Starr/Now we know how brave you are"—a performance that his victorious opponent made the centerpiece of a radio advertising campaign. In the end, the Senate balance stayed as it had been, and the Republicans lost five seats in the House.

This was a smashing victory for the Democrats. There had been only one previous midterm election in the century where the party of the incumbent President had gained seats—in 1934, when the country was still in the grip of the Depression and unrelenting in its wrath against Republicans, even after electing Roosevelt two years earlier. (Only once in the nineteenth century had this phenomenon occurred—in 1822, under President Monroe, in the Era of Good Feelings, before the modern party system.) The results gave a sharp, clear statement against impeachment. That was the message—a rebuke to the Washington elites, but most of all to the Republican Congress.

On election night, in his Georgia district, Gingrich had greeted his cheering supporters in a ballroom under a sign announcing, "It's a Brave Newt World." The day after, he blamed the media for the Republican losses. Gingrich, who had sought universal acclamation, had become unloved by his Republican Conference. After Clinton had outplayed him time and time again, the members who had elected him Speaker learned to mistrust him. They had shut down the government twice, but they had not forced Clinton to his knees. They had not passed much of their vaunted program, the Contract with America, either. They had lost on the budget negotiations every year they were in the majority. And they had been unable to dislodge Clinton in the 1996 campaign. They had lost seats in every election since 1994, when they captured the Congress. And most of them were dismayed by Gingrich's support of much of Clinton's internationalist foreign policy. In the next Congress, the Republican's House majority would be a mere five votes, nearly unworkable, and very likely unable to impeach Clinton. The Republican Revolution of 1994 was in tatters.

On November 6, Representative Robert Livingston of Louisiana sent Gingrich a "personal and confidential" letter demanding conditions that would grant him augmented powers in the House leadership, or else he would challenge Gingrich for Speaker. Gingrich dismissed Livingston's conditions as "ridiculous" and didn't bother to call him. Hours later, Livingston, standing in front of the Capitol and before the television cameras, announced his candidacy against Gingrich. Almost in an instant,

Gingrich's support evaporated. Frantically, he called around to his closest supporters, who suddenly distanced themselves. Some even counseled him to quit. Overcome with anger and anxiety, worried that his extramarital affair would be exposed, he decided in a fit of pique to resign, and on a conference call that evening, he told the Republican leadership he was quitting. "I am willing to lead, but I won't allow cannibalism," he said.* (His remark was an eerie echo of that of Speaker Jim Wright, who, in resigning in 1989, under pressure organized by Gingrich, had urged the House to "bring this period of mindless cannibalism to an end.") The world-historical figure, the professor of futurism, who had dreamed of becoming president after forcing out both Clinton and Gore, was at his end. The Republicans' Robespierre made his last appearance before his Committee for the Public Safety, the House Republican Conference, symbolically turning over his gavel to Bob Livingston, and then walked out of the room holding hands with his wife, to return to his Georgia redoubt, where he soon left her for his mistress.

Long before the election, Jackie had planned a fiftieth birthday party for me on November 7. No one could have foretold that this event would become such a celebration. White House staff and administration officials, journalists and lawyers, ambassadors and British government officials, my oldest friends, and family gathered to read tributes, tell stories and jokes, recite poems. The birthday cake was decorated with my nicknames: "Bill's Dirt Devil . . . Hillary's Sock Puppet . . . Grassy Knoll . . . Sid Vicious." John Podesta, now Clinton's chief of staff since Erskine Bowles had left in October, read his entire grand-jury testimony about alien abduction, and then he gave me an inscribed picture from the President. Jackie misread the inscription aloud: "To Sid, who helps make sure I understand what I need." " 'What I *read*,' " shouted Podesta over the laughter. "It says 'what I *read*.' "

Finally, my son Max, then a student at the University of Pennsylvania, read his epic Clintoniad:

> *Goodbye Dr. Jekyll and Henry Hyde*
> *You cast the first stone into a river of lies*
> *A double minded man shoulda never tried*
> *Goodbye Newt you fat fruit*
> *Go back to Georgia and play your skinny skin flute*
> *Goodbye Ken Deathstar*

*Baker, *The Breach*, pp. 146–59.

You can't shine a light when you hyde from your own shadow
Your lizardly molestigation is
Just a crutch for pale political pyromania
Burning America in a cast of stagnation
But that cast cracked when we turned our votes in . . .

The crowd that dispersed happily into that cool November night thought that the threatened impeachment of Bill Clinton was over.

THIRTEEN

Show Trial

I

Inside the White House we thought impeachment was about to end with a whimper. After the midterm election, nothing else seemed to make sense. The matter should devolve into one that could be resolved among reasonable people. It should not be a pitched battle, but a compromise of the sort that was the daily fare of the capital. And we had approached the best connected people in Washington to try to work out with the Republicans the terms of the censure. Big wheels were in motion: Lloyd Cutler, senior partner of Wilmer, Cutler and Pickering, former counsel to both Presidents Carter and Clinton; Vin Weber, former Republican congressman, who was part of Gingrich's inner circle and head of a lobbying firm; Kenneth Duberstein, former chief of staff to President Reagan and chief of the Duberstein Group, a lobbying powerhouse; and Bob Michel, former Republican House leader.

Censure is a statement of reprimand, essentially a disapproving letter, and it has no constitutional significance, as impeachment does. Only one president had previously been censured, Andrew Jackson, in 1834 by a hostile Whig Senate who were enraged that he had vetoed the bill establishing the Bank of the United States. (Three years later a Democratic Senate expunged the record. Had the Whigs dominated the House of Representatives as well in 1834, they might have impeached Jackson on this issue.) Jackson ferociously denounced this motion as an intrusion into executive authority. But President Clinton encouraged negotiations for a censure as the least contentious way to conclude the controversy.

For weeks, even after the House Judiciary Committee had begun impeachment hearings, we continued to believe that there would be a rational solution. As late as Saturday, November 21, 1998, we were still strategizing about censure. We met in John Podesta's corner office in the West Wing to discuss the state of play and to prepare Gregory Craig, the newest member of President Clinton's senior staff, for his appearance the next day on NBC's *Meet the Press*. He had come to the White House the week of the Starr Report as a legal counsel. Greg had been an aide to Senator Edward Kennedy, director of the State Department Policy Planning staff, and a senior partner at Williams and Connolly. He was experienced, savvy, articulate, and—perhaps most important—fresh. His brief for *Meet the Press* was to declare that the White House would consider any "reasonable" offer for censure. Our key word now was "reasonable."

The Washington Post that morning had published an article: "Judiciary GOP Closer to Impeaching." On Sunday, Bob Livingston said that the House should vote on impeachment even if there was no majority for it. By Monday it struck me that we in the White House were in denial. Why should reason prevail? We were operating on a series of false premises: rationality, self-interest, and common sense. Why should an election result unprecedented in American history reverse the dynamics of the House Republicans? Defeat might well intensify their radicalism. I told Hillary that I thought we would never get the votes to stop impeachment. "That never occurred to me," she said. Even Hillary, usually the pessimistic realist, had joined in the Pollyanna-like chorus. But why should we be right on the basis of being "reasonable"? By Thanksgiving, first Podesta and then everyone else concluded that a battle over impeachment was inevitable.

On November 24, ABC's *20/20* broadcast Diane Sawyer's hour-long interview of Ken Starr, who was trying to restore his image and eagerly answered a question about adultery: "The answer to the big question is no. I have not been unfaithful to my spouse. I try to, and I, you know, I'm not trying to pat myself on the back, but I've tried to live by what I believe is my obligation and my responsibility."* Starr was unchangeable in mistaking his own sanctimony for moral bravery.

The Republicans on the House Judiciary Committee inhabited a world of their own and resisted intrusions that might upset it. They had expected they would win the midterm and believed with every fiber of their beings they should have. They knew they had lost the midterm be-

---

*Howard Kurtz, "In TV Interview, Starr Lets the Questions Get Personal," *The Washington Post*, November 25, 1998.

cause of their insistence on trying to impeach a popular president, but they could not reverse themselves. The more the White House tried to move forward from the election result, the more they rebelled against it. The more they thought about it, the more they believed they were right. Their losing, they decided, was another of Clinton's offenses.

"The White House was arrogant," James Rogan, then a key Republican member of the Judiciary Committee, told me later. "The White House was saying, Screw you, you don't have a mandate." The account of how the Republicans were thinking that he related to me while I was writing this book was curious in its contradictions. Rogan explained the Republicans' raised expectations that fall: "Gingrich was telling us in October that we would pick up twenty or thirty seats—plus. We were going to come back with a windfall of seats." Gingrich, I learned, had even called up the President to warn him to resign before a delegation of House Democrats asked him to. "But not only did the Speaker miscalculate," Rogan said, "the way we read the results, Americans took a look at impeachment. There weren't many people on our side disputing that. There was almost no will on our part to pursue a losing strategy any further. We had hung on by our fingernails."

Right after the election, both Gingrich and Livingston talked to Rogan. Neither one thought the impeachment should go any further, he told me. And yet it did. "There was a missed opportunity, a window there," Rogan insisted, but he couldn't spell out exactly what it was. The more the White House spoke of a censure resolution instead, something "reasonable," and the more Democrats criticized the idea of impeachment, the more abused the Republicans on the Judiciary Committee felt. They didn't want to go further, but they went ahead. It wasn't their fault, but the White House's: "The White House was arrogant."

This was the logic of a vanguard consumed with its mission. They felt themselves to be "warriors," as Rogan put it. They had separated themselves from all society except their own, from any notion of political consequences, and from Republicans who didn't share their hard-shell militancy. "It happened because we were the only ones in town," Rogan said about their isolation. The House had adjourned before the election, and with Gingrich's resignation there was no Speaker; Livingston couldn't assume his position until formally elected by the next Congress. In early November, only the members of the House Judiciary Committee were in Washington. "If this had happened in March 1999," Rogan said, "when you had 535 members, there would have been a heightened sense of nervousness. You just had the small band, comfortably elected except for me." (Rogan was politically vulnerable, having squeaked by with 50.8 percent of the vote in his district in suburban Los Angeles.) "And there was nobody there who felt pain."

The "small band" of "warriors" was the tattered remnant of the Republican "revolution." They knew they couldn't sustain an impeachment vote in the next Congress—they would have had to accept defeat and slink away, but rather than acknowledge that, they became warriors imagining victory. Alone in their bunker, they were not about to give up this fantasy, especially for politics as usual, which would reduce them to being mere congressmen among hundreds trudging through the problematical, complex tasks of cutting deals to gain appropriations for local interests and servicing the incessant needs of constituents. The more embattled they became, the greater their faith in the righteousness of their cause and the more grandiose their self-image. They could not imagine how Americans could fail to support their shining example. The scandal became their myth, and the myth became their theater of impeachment.

But the drama needed to be played out before the new Congress convened in January. The process for the impeachment and removal of a president is described in the Constitution. First the House of Representatives must draft the articles of impeachment. If a majority of the House approves any or all of these articles, the president is impeached. A trial in the Senate is prosecuted by so-called House Managers with the Chief Justice of the Supreme Court serving as judge. A two-thirds majority in the Senate is required to remove a president from office.

The House Republicans would establish no standards about what constituted an impeachable offense or how to go about assessing it, but instead replay backward almost the whole reel of Clinton scandals in a surreal kaleidoscope. In the end, a majority was forced to vote not on the actual evidence, but in reaction to these gaudy tales. The chairman of the Judiciary Committee, Henry Hyde, and the designated Speaker of the House, Robert Livingston, deferred to the true power in the House, the Republican whip, Tom DeLay. Through the political machine he had constructed and controlled—the engine of the GOP in the House, linking the party's constituency groups, corporate interests, campaign contributions, and dominance over the committee structure—he whipped the Republicans into line, with threats if he had to. And after the House Managers entered the Senate, they contrived a desperate last gambit— focused on me—to topple the President.

Tom DeLay had always suspected Gingrich of weakness, had always regarded him as a rival. He had opposed him for whip in 1989, and with the Republican capture of the Congress in 1994 and Gingrich's elevation to Speaker, he had clawed his way into the post. After the government shutdowns of 1995 and 1996, when Republican senators had wanted to end the self-defeating conflict with the President, DeLay had said, "Screw the Senate. It's time for all-out war!"* Secretly, he had mobilized opposition to Gingrich, plotting to overthrow and replace him, yet when his internal coup had failed in 1997, his power was so secure that Gingrich dared not punish him. Now, with the equivocal Gingrich gone, Speaker-designate Robert Livingston quaked in DeLay's presence and did what DeLay told him to do.

DeLay lacked Gingrich's patchwork of neuroses, and having seen how Gingrich had become a bogeyman by appearing constantly on television, drawn to the light like a helpless moth, he accepted only occasional guest spots on the talk shows, preferring to operate with the curtains drawn. DeLay's plotting was unrestrained; his machinations on behalf of impeachment were the Founders' nightmare of American politics turned Roman. He held his vanity in check to focus his wrath on the President— a wrath he believed was divinely inspired. In 2002, DeLay preached to the First Baptist Church of Pearland, Texas, that God was using him to promote "a biblical worldview" in politics, and that he had pushed for Clinton's impeachment because the President held "the wrong worldview."†

Just days after the election and within hours of Gingrich's resignation, Henry Hyde held a conference call with the members of the House Judiciary Committee. According to James Rogan, he said: "We've seen the results, but the House passed a resolution. We have an objective. Come back to Washington." Hyde posed his call in terms of grim duty. His heart wasn't in it, in fact, and he was willing to entertain private proposals for a censure motion instead. But he allowed them to fall flat and, pushed by conservative Republicans, fell back on his march, putting one foot ahead of the other and insisting wearily he had no choice. Yet he also saw himself as a statesman, playing a role that would gloriously cap his career.

On November 6, 430 law professors, leading scholars from every region who represented an important consensus, did what the historians had done and issued a public statement about the impeachment. To them,

*David Plotz, "A Bug's Life," *Slate*, December 5, 1998.

†Alan Cooperman, "DeLay Criticized for 'Only Christianity' Remarks," *The Washington Post*, April 20, 2002.

Starr's "allegations . . . do not justify presidential impeachment under the Constitution" and "Members of Congress would violate their constitutional responsibilities if they sought to impeach and remove the President for misconduct, even criminal misconduct, that fell short of the high constitutional standard required for impeachment."

When the Judiciary Committee Republicans convened on November 9, Hyde conveyed the instructions he had received from the Republican leadership: "I have been told in no uncertain terms that we need to finish the inquiry, take it to the floor, and get it voted up or down before the Christmas recess," he said.* The only witness would be Ken Starr, he announced. David Schippers, his old pal from Chicago, the irascible conservative former prosecutor, protested, "We've got more!" He had been combing the detritus of pseudoscandals past. He wanted to stir the members from their doldrums and to the barricades. Rogan urged the others forward, and they marched into a session that they had scheduled before the election on "The Background and History of Impeachment."†

Henry Hyde gaveled this first session of the House Judiciary Committee's impeachment proceedings to order. It was a sprawling committee of thirty-seven members—twenty-one Republicans and sixteen Democrats—spanning the spectrum from the most conservative (Bob Barr of Georgia) to the most liberal (Barney Frank of Massachusetts). A majority of the Republicans, eleven in number, were Southern conservatives, and six were from the party's old Middle Western bastions. There was not a moderate among them.

Defeat had not tempered the Republicans, and in their trench, they fixed bayonets. Charles Canady of Florida began by asserting that the President was "guilty of impeachable offenses," according to "the evidence" assembled by the Independent Counsel. Bob Barr, urging the Democrats to join in impeaching Clinton, cited God's voice urging Abraham to sacrifice Isaac. Bob Goodlatte of Virginia argued that there could be no "fixed standard for impeachment." Lamar Smith of Texas said that if a business executive had done what Clinton had, his "career would be over." Ed Bryant sneered at the idea of censure: "That will come in handy the next time he vetoes the partial birth abortion bill." Asa Hutchinson of Arkansas was the most reasonable, citing a "growing consensus of scholars" who, he claimed, found no basis for censure in the Constitution—an apt point, though he did not cite President Jackson's

*David Schippers, *Sellout*, Regnery, 2001, p. 102.
†Baker, *The Breach*, pp. 160–61.

sulfurous defense of the presidency. Outside the hearing room, before the event began, Hutchinson remarked to a reporter, "I don't see any change in mood."*

The witnesses the Republicans had assembled were mostly minor academic scholars or conservative political figures—such as Jonathan Turley, the environmental law specialist and cable TV commentator, and Charles Cooper, an assistant attorney general during the Reagan administration—who made the tendentious case that whatever the Republicans decided fit the definition of an impeachable offense. On the other side were preeminent scholars, including Cass Sunstein of the University of Chicago Law School, the historian Jack Rakove of Stanford University, Laurence Tribe of the Harvard Law School, Arthur Schlesinger, Jr., of the City University of New York, and Father Robert Drinan, former dean of the Boston College Law School, who had been a member of the House Judiciary Committee that voted for the impeachment of President Nixon. Their account of the constitutional standard was unvarying, and they strongly cautioned the House against overreaching.

Sunstein underlined that "with respect to the President, the principal goal of the impeachment clause is to allow impeachment for a narrow category of large-scale abuses of authority that come from the exercise of *distinctly presidential powers*. Outside of that category of cases, impeachment is generally foreign to our traditions and prohibited by the Constitution." Drinan noted the role of the public, in effect pointing to the recent election: "Impeachment is not a criminal matter or a judicial procedure. It is one that depends in significant ways on the people. It is the people who elected a president who should be consulted before the Congress seeks to impeach him and remove him from office."

Tribe stripped the illusions from the House Republican argument that it had a constitutional "duty" to proceed, once having started: "Some argue that, at least if something that might technically fit the definition of a high crime or misdemeanor is believed to have been committed by the President, the House has a 'duty' under the Constitution to impeach the President and hand him over to the Senate for trial. But there is no more in the Constitution to support that argument than there is to support the argument that, having begun a formal impeachment inquiry, the House must see the matter through. The Constitution, in this matter as in many others, leaves ample room for judgment, even for wisdom, in the

---

*Ruth Marcus, "Panel Signals It Will Pursue Impeachment," *The Washington Post*, November 10, 1998.

deployment of power. What it leaves no room for is the impeachment of a president who has not committed 'Treason, Bribery, or other high Crimes and Misdemeanors.' "

All the scholars were agreed upon the history of impeachment. In the Constitutional Convention of 1787, George Mason argued that impeachment must only be for "great crimes" and "attempts to subvert the constitution." James Madison insisted that a low standard for impeachment would create a weak presidency existing "at the pleasure of the Senate." Alexander Hamilton, in *Federalist Paper* Number 65, wrote that the premise of impeachment must be that it was a political crime, emphatically capitalizing the word "POLITICAL." Immediately, he followed with a warning:

> The subjects of its jurisdiction are those offenses which proceed from the misconduct of public men, or, in other words, from the abuse or violation of some public trust. They are of a nature which may with peculiar propriety be denominated POLITICAL, as they relate chiefly to injuries done immediately to the society itself. The prosecution of them, for this reason, will seldom fail to agitate the passions of the whole community, and to divide it into parties more or less friendly or inimical to the accused. In many cases it will connect itself with the pre-existing factions, and will enlist all their animosities, partialities, influence, and interest on one side or on the other; and in such cases there will always be the greatest danger that the decision will be regulated more by the comparative strength of parties, than by the real demonstrations of innocence or guilt.

The original wording of the Constitution had allowed for impeachment when the president committed "other high crimes and misdemeanors against the state." The Committee on Style took out the words "against the state," but the meaning was intended. Among the framers, there was no division whatsoever: impeachment was the punishment for the most serious political crimes "against the state." The word "other" in the phrase "other high crimes and misdemeanors" was placed there to convey that these crimes must be on the level of "Treason and Bribery." As Arthur Schlesinger, Jr., testified, "The term 'high misdemeanor,' inherited from the British tradition of impeachment, referred to such offenses as treason; it is not to be confused with 'misdemeanor' in its present-day usage as a petty offense."

President Andrew Johnson, who acceded to the office after the assassination of President Lincoln, refused to follow Lincoln's policies of Reconstruction and enforce its early laws in the South. The Congress passed a law, the Tenure of Office Act, barring the President from firing Lincoln's cabinet. Later ruled unconstitutional as a violation of the separation of powers, the law was then still the law, and Johnson willfully trampled on it, firing Secretary of War Edwin Stanton, knowing full well that he was precipitating a battle royal with the Congress. In 1868, he was impeached and the Senate came within one vote of removing him. His partisan impeachment weakened the presidency and helped create a long period of congressional government.

Every one of the articles of impeachment against President Nixon described a crime against the state. One proposed charge, cheating on his income tax, was removed because it concerned a personal issue that had nothing to do with his conduct in public office. From the beginning, Nixon's impeachment was bipartisan, and as it went on it became more bipartisan, until he had few defenders. Before the articles were ever voted on by the full House, Nixon resigned.

The testimony against overreaching and favoring constitutional standards had little effect on the "small band" of "warriors." Now the Republicans hastily hammered together a novel theory of impeachment. First, the president could be impeached not for a high crime against the state, but for anything the House arbitrarily decided was a crime, and the definition of a crime was whatever they felt it was.

Second, the Republicans proposed to convert the impeachment into a grand-jury proceeding, with themselves as prosecutors and the Senate as jury, although the Constitution prescribes that the House must vote on impeachment as a vote to remove the president, not to advance an indictment. But if they were a grand jury, they needed no high standard, needed nothing proved at all, needed only a suspicion. This was the opposite of the framers' design, which set the highest possible bar for removing a president.

Third, the House Judiciary Committee Republicans deferred to the extraconstitutional Office of Independent Counsel in collecting and interpreting evidence for them. In this, Starr had already violated the precedent set by Leon Jaworski, the Watergate special prosecutor, who drew no conclusions whatsoever from the material he collected and composed no articles of impeachment, specifically leaving that action to the House. Making recommendations, Jaworski had stated, would transgress the boundaries of his office and usurp the power of the House. Having aggressively broken these bounds with the composition of the Starr Report, Starr was now invited to usurp the constitutional role of the House

Judiciary Committee. With the connivance of the Republican majority, his standards and practices infected theirs.

The Democrats on the Judiciary Committee were as unified against impeachment as the Republicans were in favor. Four of the Democrats, a quarter of their number, were black; three others were from Massachusetts, and two from New York. (Only one Republican among the twenty-one was a woman—Mary Bono of California, who had replaced her husband, Sonny, when he died.) Three of the Democrats were women, and six were Jewish. They were diverse not only in background but in political complexion, comprising the Southern moderate Rick Boucher of Virginia as well.

In the House hearing room, behind the dais, hangs a portrait of Peter Rodino, the Democratic congressman who presided as chairman of the Judiciary Committee during the impeachment proceedings against Richard Nixon. Rodino had conducted a nine-month investigation into Nixon's crimes by first interviewing all relevant witnesses behind closed doors and without a single leak. (Hillary Rodham was on his staff.) When the committee held public hearings, it called the witnesses whose testimony made a case that could gather bipartisan support. Hyde cited Rodino as a role model, but Rodino himself had declared in October that in his view Clinton had committed no impeachable offenses and that the Starr Report was "tawdry."* His picture loomed as a constantly disapproving visage.

On November 19, Kenneth W. Starr was the witness before the committee—the only witness to be called in the case against the President. The hearing began with rancor, on a sharp motion and points of order, and ended with partisan display. Hyde hammered his gavel. The Democrats asked for two hours for the President's attorney to question Starr, the only witness. William Delahunt of Massachusetts cited a precedent: Nixon's attorney had been granted unlimited time to question all witnesses before Rodino's Watergate committee. Hyde took a vote, and on a straight party-line count, the motion was overruled. Hutchinson remarked about Hyde allowing the vote at all: "His whole sense of fairness overwhelms him."†

For the Republicans, Starr was the guiding light of truth. He had to

*"Ex-Nixon Panel Chief Says Don't Impeach Clinton," Associated Press, October 28, 1998.

†Guy Gugliotta and Julie Eilperin, "Hearing Opens with Party Lines Drawn," *The Washington Post*, November 20, 1998.

be because they had performed no independent fact-finding or checking of their own. "Today the search for truth continues," said Hyde in his opening remarks. Repeatedly, he invoked "the rule of law" and compared the impeachment to the Civil War, raising the image of "a small military cemetery in Pennsylvania" and asking whether the nation "can long endure." His rhetoric until the end followed this pattern of vaporous grandiloquence and patriotic non sequiturs.

John Conyers, Jr., of Michigan, the ranking Democrat on the House Judiciary Committee, spoke next. To him, Starr was the opposite—"a federally paid sex policeman spending millions of dollars to trap an unfaithful spouse"—and Conyers laid out the case against him. Starr's record was sullied with his conflicts of interests, prosecutorial zealotry, illegal leaking, a "salacious" report. The real issue, Conyers concluded, was whether Starr had "created a climate for the purpose of driving a President from office who has twice been elected by the people of this great Nation."

Two days before he testified, with Hyde acting as his conduit, Starr dumped on the media Linda Tripp's taped telephone conversations with Monica Lewinsky, and they were broadcast around the clock. Releasing these tapes was like a rerun of the sensational parts of the Starr Report, but without any claims of fact. The intent could only be to poison the atmosphere against the President. Filled with raw accusations, sexual innuendo, idle gossip, and denigrating references to members of Lewinsky's family, the tapes were also a reminder of Tripp's vicious character and the prosecutor's reliance on her. Tripp's voice was ringing in everyone's ears as Starr assumed his seat under Rodino's portrait.

Starr appeared in his favored role of Olympian jurist. Before the hearing, he had requested to speak from a podium, as if he were presenting a case to the Supreme Court, and to be addressed as "judge." These requests had been denied; even the lower body of the Congress had its protocol and dignity.* Starr began with benign condescension, remarking that he was "proud of the diligence" of the committee. His praise was a form of self-congratulation, since he was, after all, the only witness.

The author of the Starr Report daintily used the words "sex" and "sexual" only four times, while uttering the word "truth" more than sixty times. Starr insisted that his investigation had concerned not a "private matter" but the abuse of power, and he rattled off ten reasons for impeaching President Clinton. They ranged from alleged perjury in his

---

*Jeffrey Rosen, "Starr Crossed," *The New Republic*, December 14, 1998.

Jones deposition and in Starr's grand jury to his misleading the cabinet, his aides, and the public about his relations with Lewinsky and his supposedly improper invocation of executive privilege. On the chief article against the President—perjury—Starr made a constitutional mistake: "Perjury has been the basis for the removal of several judges. As far as we know, no one questioned whether perjury was a high crime or misdemeanor in those cases." But the Founding Fathers in the Constitutional Convention had carefully discussed the distinction, a debate recorded by James Madison, and they had decided that the basis for a president's impeachment should be different from the basis for judges, because if a standard of "misbehavior" were applied to the presidency, according to the founder Rufus King, it would be "destructive of his independence and of the Principles of the Constitution." In fact, the Republicans on the Judiciary Committee during the Nixon impeachment had successfully argued that the president was "unlike a federal judge" and that his removal "should not be too easy of accomplishment."* Starr either had little grasp of constitutional law or was distorting it to make a case.

Starr's list of designated high crimes included one—deceiving the public—that would arguably have required an impeachment trial for every politician seated before him. He tried to maintain his lofty tone, but he could not help descending into peevishness. Among the charges he listed against the President was misleading his aides "about the nature of the relationship—with the knowledge that they could testify to that effect to the grand jury." He argued that this "tactic" was "related" to criticism of his own office, "to declare war" against him in a political effort to "shape public opinion." By listing criticism of himself among the President's offenses, Starr was defensively making a case for his own clean hands and pure heart.

His novel theory linked speaking against him to obstructing justice, the same link he had made when he had subpoenaed me. But when the President had misled me along with everyone else about Lewinsky, he had had no reason to imagine that I would ever be summoned before the Independent Counsel's grand jury. I had never met Lewinsky and knew nothing about her involvement with him. The reason I was subpoenaed, as the subpoena itself made clear, was that Starr wanted to suppress my political work with the press corps and the public. In that, he was starkly

---

*Impeachment of Richard M. Nixon, President of the United States, Report of the Committee on the Judiciary, House of Representatives, August 20, 1974, pp. 362, 379.

political, a motive he wished to cloak before the House committee. "We go to court and not on the talk-show circuit," he said. "We are officers of the court who live in the world of the law."

For more than two hours Starr held forth, concluding with a lengthy summary of his own career, an apologia pro vita sua: "I am not a man of politics, of public relations, or of polls—which I suppose is patently obvious by now. I am not experienced in political campaigns." At last, he quoted Lincoln on "reverence for the law."

Abbe Lowell, the Democratic counsel for the committee, discovered through questioning that Starr's "reverence for the law" allowed for human frailty when it concerned himself. His answers became slippery; he retreated into legalisms; and his memory began to suffer lesions. Lowell began by asking Starr, "Part of being independent, I think you would agree with me, is being free of conflicts of interests that might bias your investigation, correct?"

"Yes," said Starr.

Later he pursued this issue: "You do recall, though, that it was a matter that you admit that on at least six occasions you personally had had conversations with Paula Jones's attorneys over legal issues in the Paula Jones case."

Starr: "I'm not sure. . . . Fault my judgment, if you will, but it just frankly did not occur to me, as I think happens to a lot of us in life, that you just don't view that as relevant information. . . ."

Lowell: "To use your phrase, did it not occur to you that you should tell the Attorney General, who was making a decision about whether you were an independent counsel, that your law firm, Kirkland and Ellis, in addition to being asked to be Paula Jones's attorney, was providing legal advice, free legal advice, to a conservative women's group called the Independent Women's Forum who were thinking about participating in the Paula Jones case itself? Did that not occur to you either?"

Starr: "Well, again, it's not whether it occurs or not. . . . And the fact that I had these discussions had all been, to the best of my knowledge, part of the public domain. That is to say, they were reported. And by virtue of that, I do think it's unfair, I really do, to suggest that someone should, when circumstances were moving so quickly, go do a Nexis search, making sure that everything is in the public domain and the like. . . ."

Lowell: "Mr. Starr, you're suggesting that when you told the Deputy Attorney General that he had to move with haste because this investigation was fast-moving that you had no responsibility to also inform the

Attorney General about these contacts that you and I are talking about, which might make the Attorney General, as you pointed out, have a choice to make between giving the investigation to you or giving it to somebody whose independence, bias, and involvement in the case was not questioned."

Starr became huffy: "Well, I utterly disagree, with all respect, with your premise. . . ." He cited high, nebulous principles: "It has everything to do with what the presidency is, and the nature of our relationship to one another as individuals and whether we are all equal under the law." Flustered, he blurted, "So it did not occur to—" Finally, he admitted, "And these issues did not, in fact, arise." They did not arise because he did not raise them.

In questions from committee members, Representative Zoe Lofgren, Democrat of California, took issue with Starr's veracity: "I note that you, Mr. Starr, are under oath yourself this morning, and on page 36 of your testimony, you swear that you go to court, not on the talk-show circuit. This very morning, you appeared on *Good Morning, America*. Isn't that a false statement under oath? And should you be prosecuted for perjury because of this false statement? . . . I would not urge that. I think that is preposterous. That cannot be what is meant by the Founding Fathers regarding impeachment."

In fact, Starr and his press secretary had appeared thirteen times on talk shows. In response to Lofgren, he was silent.

She then asked him a question about when he first learned of the Lewinsky tapes, and his reply was vacant. "I am not recalling that," he said. When she asked him about the illegal leaks from his office to the press and whether "you release the press from their vow of confidentiality to you and your deputies so this can be fully investigated," he sputtered until Representative James Sensenbrenner, Republican of Wisconsin, acting as chairman in Hyde's momentary absence, rushed to his rescue, interrupting her. An absurd colloquy then ensued.

Sensenbrenner: "Could she please give Judge Starr the courtesy of allowing him to answer the questions."

Lofgren: "I would love to get an answer."

Starr: "I have concluded what I need to say. Thank you."

Sensenbrenner: "The witness has concluded. The gentlewoman's time has expired."

Representative Barney Frank, Democrat of Massachusetts, interjected: "There was only one answer. There were three questions."

Sensenbrenner: "The witness will respond."

Starr: "What was the first question? I am sorry."

This routine went on for a few more minutes, with Starr failing to answer, until Sensenbrenner declared Lofgren's time to be up. A bit later, he opined that he was "getting sick and tired" of Democrats: "They're the ones who are being unfair and partisan."

Barney Frank's acerbic wit was in the service of an acute intelligence. He had noticed that in the course of his testimony, Starr had briefly slid over the fact that he had exonerated the Clintons of all charges in the FBI file and the Travel Office cases. These were mainstays of the conservative scandal legends, and Frank had observed the highly political timing involved.

Frank: "You say in page 9 of the referral that . . . you send us information based on a referral as soon as it becomes clear to you. That is what bothers me about the FBI file and Travel Office issues. You say on page 47 of the testimony, 'Our investigation . . . found no evidence that anyone higher than Mr. Livingston or Mr. Marceca [low-level White House employees who mistakenly received the wrong FBI files] were involved.' When did your investigation determine that?"

Starr: "Well, under 595(c)—"

Frank: "Excuse me. That is a simple factual question, Mr. Starr. When did you determine that . . . nobody higher than Mr. Livingston or Mr. Marceca was involved?"

Starr: "We determined that some months ago."

Frank: "Okay. Well before the election. You also have with regard to the Travel Office a statement that the President is not involved. When did you determine with regard to the Travel Office that the President was not involved? . . . Be factual, Mr. Starr. When?"

Starr: "It is not a date certain. We have no information with respect to—"

Frank: "I will take a date ambiguous. Give me an approximate."

Starr: "First of all, there is an investigation that is continuing, and as of this date of reporting, we do not have any information that the President is involved."

Frank: "Let me just say this, and here's what disturbs me greatly. You say on page 9 that yes, you should send us this information. Before the election, you sent us a lot of information about the President that was to his discredit in some cases, and you found it very derogatory in other cases. You also have been studying for far longer than the Lewinsky case the FBI and the Travel Office. You tell us that months ago you concluded that no—that the President was not involved in the FBI files and you've never had the evidence he was involved in the Travel Office. Yet now, several weeks after the election, is the first time you're saying that. Why did you withhold that before the election when you were sending us a referral with a lot of negative stuff about the President, and only now, despite your saying that the statute suggests you tell us as soon as possible, you give us this exoneration of the President several weeks after the election?"

Starr: "Mr. Frank, what we have tried to do is be responsive to Congress, which has said provide us with information. Is there any other additional information that would be useful?"

Frank: "Why didn't you tell us before the election about this according to your reading of the statute?"

Starr: "Congressman Frank, the reason is because what we provided you in the referral is substantial and credible information of possible potential offenses. The silence with respect to anything else means necessarily that we had not concluded—"

Frank: "In other words, you don't have anything to say unless you have something bad to say."

The Republican members mostly tried to toss Starr questions that elicited answers about his honesty and wonderful credentials, and about Clinton's alleged crimes. Mary Bono said that it was "nice to see" that "behind the spin . . . there is a human." She lobbed a slow pitch in his direction: "Judge Starr, you and your family have been subjected to an enormous amount of personal persecution during your tenure as the independent counsel, particularly over the last year. What motivates you to keep going forward?"

Starr's answer traveled from coast to coast in its bathos, as he wound up confusing himself with George Washington: "Well, I thank you for that question, and I hold no animosity and would love to be back in private life. I received questions today with respect to, well, didn't you accept a deanship at Pepperdine, and look who [Richard Mellon Scaife] made a contribution—so, you're right. I would prefer to be almost your constituent, a little bit farther west—I would like to be—and I'd even looked at a house in Malibu Country Estates; that's where I would like to be. . . . I tried to retire. I think George Washington was very wise in saying eight years is enough. 'I would rather go back.' Of course, he wasn't across the river where the capital was then, but, 'I would rather return to Mount Vernon, thank you very much.' " With that, the committee recessed for dinner.

The next questioner was David Kendall, the President's attorney. "My task," said Kendall, "is to respond to the two hours of uninterrupted testimony from the Independent Counsel, as well as to his four-year, $45 million investigation, which has included at least 28 attorneys, 78 FBI agents, and an undisclosed number of private investigators, an investigation which has generated, by a computer count, 114,532 news stories in print, and 2,513 minutes of network television time, not to mention 24-hour scandal coverage on cable, a 445-page referral, 50,000 pages of documents from secret grand-jury testimony, 4 hours of videotaped testimony, 22 hours of audiotape, some of which was gathered in violation of state law, and the testimony of scores of witnesses, not one of whom has been cross-examined. And I have 30 minutes to do this. It's a daunting exercise, but let me begin with the simple but powerful truth that nothing in this overkill of investigation amounts to a justification for the impeachment of the President of the United States. Mr. Starr, good evening."*

The grand-jury witnesses knew that the Independent Counsel had never been present when they testified. Now he was the only fact witness in the impeachment, though he had never heard one word of testimony except the President's and had never seen a single witness, much less interviewed one. The author of the Starr Report was a hearsay witness. In a court of law, Starr would never have been allowed to take the stand.

When Kendall began, Starr called him "David" and he returned the familiarity by calling Starr "Ken." Within the Washington legal fraternity, they knew each other fairly well. But the clubby salutations were an illusion. David Kendall was in most respects the opposite of Starr. He was a Quaker from Indiana, motivated by a moral sense but discreet and contained. After graduating from Wabash College and studying at Oxford as a Rhodes scholar, he went to Yale Law School, where he was a classmate of the Clintons and a friend of Hillary's. For three years, he worked as a lawyer at the NAACP Legal Defense Fund, and he won the abolition of the death penalty for rape in a case before the Supreme Court. As a senior partner at Williams and Connolly, he represented a number of media companies, including *The Washington Post*, and he also represented the Graham family occasionally.

---

*According to the *Final Report of the Independent Counsel*, "Special Agents, Investigators, Deputies, Agents, and employees were also detailed to the Office of the Independent Counsel from the Federal Bureau of Investigation, the Internal Revenue Service, the United States Customs Service, and the United States Marshals Service. . . . The names of the hundreds of active agents and employees detailed to this office over the years remain unlisted . . . ," p. 6.

Kendall quoted from a press release that Starr had issued on February 6, 1998, justifying his rejection of Monica's Lewinsky's first proffer. We did not know then or at the time of Kendall's interrogation about the profound split within Starr's office over it, but we knew that the second proffer's contents were no different from those of the first, despite Starr's fanfare that his lengthy investigation had wrested it at last from Lewinsky. And we knew that the proffer exonerated the President on the charges of subornation of perjury and obstruction of justice.

Kendall: "I want to direct your attention to your statement, and you are addressing the fact that you have not been able to talk to Ms. Lewinsky yet, and you say in your press release, 'We cannot responsibly determine whether she is telling the truth without speaking directly to her. We have found that there is no substitute for looking a witness in the eye, asking detailed questions, matching the answers against verifiable facts, and, if appropriate, giving a polygraph test.' Did you issue that press release saying that, Mr. Starr?"

Starr: "Yes, I did."

Kendall: "And questions have been addressed to you today about the credibility of various witnesses, including Ms. Lewinsky. It is true, is it not, that you were not present when Ms. Lewinsky testified before the grand jury?"

Starr: "That is true."

Kendall: "And you were not present at her deposition."

Starr: "At her deposition?"

Kendall: "Yes. Were you aware that Ms. Lewinsky was deposed?"

Starr: "I am sorry, in our deposition. I am sorry, I misunderstood you. Yes, I was not present."

Kendall: "You were not present on any occasion when she was interviewed by FBI agents, were you?"

Starr: "That is correct, I was not."

Kendall: "And you have never really exchanged words with Ms. Lewinsky, have you?"

Starr: "That is correct. The answer is yes, I have not had occasion to meet or otherwise to look her in the eye myself."

The same was true for Lewinsky's mother, Marsha Lewis. "Yes, that is true as well. That is true." And Betty Currie. "Yes." And Vernon Jordan. "Well, in connection—I happen to know Mr. Jordan, but yes, in connection with this—" And for 115 individuals before the grand jury. "That is correct." And for the nineteen depositions submitted as part of the Starr Report. "I think you are correct that I was not actually present for any of the depositions themselves, including the Secret Service officers." And for the 134 FBI interviews of witnesses. "That is correct. I would ordinarily not be present for an interview of a witness."

Kendall: ". . . You are not a fact witness, is that correct?"

Starr: "Yes, in terms—well, I can testify to a number of facts in the investigation."

Kendall: "Such as your own autobiography. I am talking about facts of this investigation."

Starr: "Could I answer the question? I believe that there are a number of facts that I can, in fact, testify to, but with respect specifically to this investigation and most particularly with respect to the abuse of power issues. But with respect to other questions, the President's perjury and obstruction of justice and the like, to the extent that one is talking about fact witnesses, you are quite right."

Kendall's questions sought to illustrate Starr's methods—dissembling, vendetta, illegal leaking, coercion, collusion, cover-up, and conducting a sexual investigation of the President for almost a year before Lewinsky came to his attention. Asked if his office had investigated the adoption of an eight-year-old Romanian orphan by Julie Hiatt Steele, the woman who said that Kathleen Willey had asked her to lie and whom Starr had indicted, Starr's answer wandered. He presented himself as ignorant of his own investigation and as a martyr: "Mr. Kendall, my investigators work very hard and diligently to find relevant evidence. I believe that the questions—and I have conducted no specific investigation, and you just spent a good deal of time establishing that I don't go with my FBI agents on every single interview. Indeed, I don't go—may I finish? You asked the question. I don't go with them on interviews. They have a fair amount of discretion as professionals as to what is appropriate to inquire into. But let me simply say this: There is an enormous amount of misinformation and false information that is being bandied about with respect to that particular witness and the circumstances of questioning. . . ."

Asked if, given his stated policy of terminating employees who leaked information to the press, he had fired anyone, Starr answered, "No, because I don't believe anyone has leaked grand-jury information, Mr. Kendall." But this matter was still under investigation by a federal court, which had already found Starr in contempt on the issue. Asked how many prima facie leak violations Judge Johnson had found among the twenty-four charged, Starr answered testily, "I think you know the answer to that."

"I think the answer to my question was all twenty-four," replied

Kendall. "And are you saying that the journalists invented sources like 'prosecutors painted a different picture,' 'sources in Starr's office tell us,' 'sources near Starr,' 'prosecutors suggest'—does the media make up those quotes, Mr. Starr?"

Starr tried to deflect the question without answering: "I am not here to accuse the media of anything."

"Mr. Starr," Kendall continued, "in fact there has been no case remotely similar to this in terms of the massive leaking from the prosecutor's office. I think we know that."

Starr became a self-righteous victim: "I totally disagree with that. That is an accusation, and it is an unfair accusation."

Shortly after that, Kendall's half hour expired. He asked for another hour and Hyde gave him a half hour. Asked if the purpose in detaining Monica Lewinsky at the Ritz-Carlton Hotel on January 16, 1998, was to get her to wear a wire secretly to tape-record the President and Vernon Jordan—"Was it not?"—Starr bristled: "It was not." Kendall confronted him with the FBI report and Lewinsky's testimony stating that it was: " 'And did you tell them you didn't want to do that?' 'Yes.' Was that Ms. Lewinsky's testimony?"

"Yes, that is her testimony," conceded Starr, who had moments before denied it.

Asked about one of the elves, that band of conservative lawyers manipulating the Jones case, namely, his partner at Kirkland and Ellis Richard Porter, involved in dirty tricks ever since the 1992 campaign and a key figure in guiding Linda Tripp to Starr's office, Starr turned blank: "I know Richard. I am not aware of what his role was. I have since read about what his role was, but I did not in any way have any involvement whatsoever or participation in any way with whatever he did, and I have not conducted an investigation."

Kendall read to him that section of the Ethics in Government Act governing the Office of Independent Counsel, stipulating that if anyone associated with his law firm were involved in any aspect of an investigation it would be an illegal conflict of interest; then Kendall read from an FBI report: " 'Goldberg called around to friends she has, including one in Chicago who works at the same firm Ken Starr does. This person recommended Goldberg to call Jackie Bennett at the OIC. Goldberg advised that the OIC knew who this person is, and that this person is very nervous at this time.' Did you ever have any reports from any source that some person at your law firm had expressed nervousness about this contact with Linda Tripp?"

"Well, you just brought this to my attention," said Starr. "But I do not—no, I do not have a recollection of something being brought— you're talking about to my attention? No." The issue of conflict of interest was, he claimed, "very technical" and "very much a judgment."

Asked whether he had investigated "rumors of affairs that the President had while he was Governor of Arkansas," interviewing twelve to fifteen women in early 1997, as *The Washington Post* had reported, Starr answered that "we had reached out and interviewed anyone who might have relevant information." Asked whether he had received authority from the Attorney General to expand his investigation in order to do that, he bumbled, "I guess I wasn't clear."

Kendall continued, racing the clock: "Did you use private investigators to do this investigation into the twelve to fifteen women?"

Startled and alarmed, Starr replied: "I beg your pardon? Private investigators?"

Kendall went on: "Your GAO [Government Administration Office] report, for the last three times, has a line item of approximately—it varies, but it's about half a million dollars for, among other things, private investigators."

Starr angrily threw out the name of the private investigator who had worked under Kendall's aegis: "No, we have never hired Terry Lenzner, David. . . . But what we do do is we do hire retired FBI agents. And those are—I will have to look at—you are talking about an audit report. And if you want to guide me to the audit report, that's fine."

With that, Starr was saved. "The chair has got to intervene," said Hyde. "One must have some compassion for Mr. Starr."

"Thank you, Mr. Chairman," said Starr. ". . . We are almost at my bedtime."

Kendall asked to return the next day to continue and was denied.

David Schippers, the Republican counsel, took over on the mound as batting-practice pitcher. His easy lob about illegal leaks encouraged a more relaxed witness after Kendall's departure, and the more relaxed Starr undermined his own earlier testimony. Now, Starr was not adamantly denying that his office had ever leaked, but saying that his leaks were not illegal: "Well, again, it depends on what one means by 6(e), because there are issues. . . . Within my understanding, and I think that my understanding is correct, no. . . ."

Schippers proceeded to mangle the Constitution, suggesting that the House had no right to call witnesses in the impeachment, only to be corrected gently by Starr: "Well, I am not sure I would necessarily agree with that. . . ." Schippers then set up Vernon Jordan for a smear. Starr ought to have known that his famous report, about which he was testifying as an expert witness, documented that Vernon Jordan's remark about "mission accomplished" referred to a job offer made to Lewinsky, not to an affidavit. Schippers commented, "We don't know which he [Jordan] was referring to [saying 'mission accomplished'], whether it was the job [for Lewinsky] or 'We got the affidavit signed,' do we?"

"No," Starr said, "I don't think we do know that. We just know he said, you know, 'Mission accomplished.' " He was either ignorant of his own work or still intent, despite the truth, on using Jordan to get at the President.

Schippers tossed a few more easy ones: "You are a recognized scholar in constitutional law and in law in general. You have been the solicitor general of the United States; is that correct?" And: "And you have been pilloried and excoriated, charged with unbelievable things of which you are incapable of being guilty?" When Starr finished describing his glorious career, Schippers led the Republicans on the committee in a standing ovation. The Democrats sat silently.

Starr alone, representing all the possible witnesses, had made his case for the impeachment of President Clinton. He defended himself from critics, as though proving his virtue was essential to the work. But on this day that he had labored so hard to reach, when at last he could vindicate himself, he was caught out—having hidden his exonerations of the Clintons for months, having constructed various falsehoods, misleading obfuscations, and defensive rationalizations of his illegalities. Starr was visibly relieved when David Kendall's examination was abruptly cut short, for against a well-informed, experienced adversary, he grew increasingly testy and his answers increasingly uninformative. Yet his performance galvanized the Republicans in their determination to impeach the President, just as it cemented the Democrats in theirs to resist. If Starr's intention was to rally his side, he succeeded. If it was to create bipartisan support for impeachment, it failed. If it was to restore his reputation, it sealed it. In leaving the hearing room, he left the public stage.

The next day there was a footnote to Starr's appearance—Sam Dash, ethics adviser to the Independent Counsel, quit in protest. Dash believed, as he wrote in a letter released on November 20, that Starr had no right to "serve as an aggressive advocate for the proposition that the evidence in your referral demonstrates that the president committed impeachable offenses. In doing this you have violated your obligations under the independent counsel statute and have unlawfully intruded on the power of impeachment which the Constitution gives solely to the House." Dash told me later that he had argued with Starr from the moment Starr had received an invitation to testify: "I said, 'You can't do that; it violates the Constitution and the separation of powers; you don't have authority; you cannot go there and become an active participant.' "

Dash had approved the Starr Report, with its gratuitous sexual material, and Starr's testimony was no different. But Dash suddenly saw a distinction. The independent counsel was lodged in the executive branch, and the Constitution provided for impeachment to be conducted by the Congress, he argued. Of course on those grounds, the Starr Report should not have been a document of advocacy at all. Nonetheless, Dash now took his stand, even if belatedly and futilely. Starr replied, "But the Republican leadership wants me to do it." Dash told Starr he would resign. Starr begged him to withhold his announcement until after Starr had testified, to which Dash agreed "as a courtesy," he explained. In his testimony, Starr cited Dash's "great wisdom," but a day later, Dash's resignation crashed unexpectedly onto Starr's credibility. It made no dent in the Republicans' will.

Starr's appearance had given them heart. President Clinton's response to Hyde's questionnaire gave them an incident: the day after the election, Hyde had submitted eighty-one "admit or deny" interrogatories to the President. For gathering evidence, it was a needless exercise, since the Judiciary Committee already had Clinton's grand-jury testimony. The questions covered the same ground as the grand jury had, but were couched so as to make any answers look dishonest. It was a political instrument crafted in bad faith and could be used only to construct a perjury trap. Another intent, we in the White House believed, was to give Starr a reason to subpoena the President again, this time to answer detailed sex questions. Hyde's first interrogatory was phrased: "Do you admit or deny that you are the chief law enforcement officer of the United States of America?" President Clinton's lawyers labored to ensure that the answers on the questionnaire gave no opening. Some of us on the presidential political staff did our best to polish the answers so that they wouldn't seem rigidly legalistic. But in the end, it was an airless legal document, referring back to his grand-jury testimony at every turn and offering no new facts.

The interrogatories were returned on November 27, a dead news day, the Friday after Thanksgiving. The House Republicans received the answers as confirming their opinion of the President's guilt and took the implacable legal tone as a flagrant act of disrespect. Now, they believed, they held in their hands eighty-one reasons to impeach. "How can we nail this guy?" demanded Representative Lindsey Graham, Republican of South Carolina.* Over that Thanksgiving weekend, it finally became apparent to everyone in the White House that the Republicans really did mean to impeach President Clinton.

The Republicans were already infuriated by Attorney General Reno's decision on November 24 not to appoint an independent counsel to investigate Vice President Gore for perjury. He had been exonerated in the campaign finance probe of 1997, the single largest investigation in U.S. history, and now they were pursuing him again, this time for allegedly lying in his testimony to the FBI. FBI director Louis Freeh had assigned three hundred agents to look into campaign finance charges, and had demanded of Reno that she appoint a special prosecutor. "The Vice President was a very active, sophisticated fund-raiser who knew exactly what he was doing," Freeh wrote. "His own exculpatory statements must not be given undue weight."† (Charles LaBella, head of the Justice Department Task Force on Campaign Finance, an ally of Freeh, had also sent Reno a memo urging Gore's prosecution.) But she had decided, "I find the evidence fails to provide any reasonable support for a conclusion that the Vice President may have lied."

On December 2, another independent counsel investigation came to an end when a jury acquitted former secretary of agriculture Michael Espy of thirty counts of corruption. For four years and at a cost of more than $17 million, Donald Smaltz, a partisan Republican prosecutor, had tried to convict Espy, once the most promising black public official in his native Mississippi. He was charged with accepting gifts and gratuities on the order of football tickets, and Smaltz called seventy witnesses to the stand. When he lost the case, Smaltz remarked, "The actual indictment of a public official may in fact be as great a deterrent as a conviction of that official." Espy's brilliant public career was ruined, yet the prosecutor justified his effort by proclaiming this chilling legal doctrine. Then who would deter the prosecutor?

Hyde, by now, was intoning the phrase "the rule of law" every day, and to demonstrate his seriousness, he gaveled into session a bizarre hearing of the Judiciary Committee on December 1. The witnesses were two women with weird, convoluted stories. Pam Parsons was a former

---

*Baker, *The Breach*, p. 181.

†Cited in editorial, "Would Anything Change?" *The Wall Street Journal*, September 13, 2000.

basketball coach at the University of South Carolina who had recruited players on the basis of their sexual availability. She had been exposed by *Sports Illustrated*, had sued the magazine for defamation when she knew their report was accurate, and had lied during her trial about going to a lesbian bar. "Well, it is really kind of funny," Parsons rambled incoherently. "There is a gay bar called Puss 'N Boots in Salt Lake City, Utah. It wasn't easy to say I'd been there. That occurrence was two years after the things that I was suing *Sports Illustrated* for. It wasn't a pretty picture for me. I thought I had many reasons for why I could say no. But it was an out-and-out lie. I had been there."

The next witness was no less baffling and strange. Barbara Battalino had been a Veterans Administration hospital psychiatrist who had been sued for malpractice by a patient upon whom she had performed oral sex. She won the case but then sued for her legal fees, lied in her deposition, and wound up pleading guilty to perjury. She testified that it was important to "take seriously the rule of law and liberty and justice for all."

Congressman Bill McCollum, Republican of Florida, conducted the questioning. "You were in a position at one time of leadership?" he asked Parsons.

"Absolutely," she replied. "I was also an athletic director."

"There you go," said McCollum. "The President of the United States is the top leader in this country."

Beyond this absurd statement, no explanation was given as to exactly what these irrelevant women's stories about sex, perjury, and false lawsuits had to do with the high crimes and misdemeanors required for the impeachment of a president.

Hyde, perhaps sensing the emptiness of the inquiry, increased the drama by asking the witnesses, "Have you been to Auschwitz? Do you see what happens when the rule of law doesn't prevail?" It was his view, he made clear, that "Lying poisons justice." Yet in the Iran-Contra scandal that had scarred the Reagan administration, Hyde had defended the Republicans accused of perjury by saying it was "too simplistic" to condemn all lying, and had been a chief defender of Oliver North and John Poindexter, Reagan's national security aides who were charged with serious violations of U.S. policy and laws. Hyde had gone so far as to attend the sentencing of North for bribery and perjury, jumping up and shaking North's hand when he was sentenced to six months in jail for lying to the Congress. About Poindexter, who had also lied to the Congress, Hyde declared, "It is an emotional and gut-wrenching experience to go through these hearings and to see good people who have made errors in judgment have to sit here and go through the tortures of the damned."*

But there were other, more expert witnesses that day. Elliot Richardson, who had resigned as President Nixon's attorney general rather than follow his order to fire Archibald Cox, the special prosecutor investigating Watergate, counseled against impeachment: "The initial wrongdoing was not criminal and did not, in contrast to that of Richard Nixon, entail the abuse of power."

Alan Dershowitz of the Harvard University Law School testified: "The false statements of which President Clinton is accused fall at the most marginal end of the least culpable genre of this continuum of offenses and would never even be considered for prosecution in the routine case involving an ordinary defendant." In an exchange with Hyde, Dershowitz called the Republican witnesses "a sham."

A. Leon Higginbotham, Jr., also of the Harvard University Law School, cited Justice Oliver Wendell Holmes, Jr., on degree and proportionality in law: "Perjury has gradations. If the President broke the 55-mile-per-hour speed limit and said under oath he was going 49, that would not be an impeachable high crime. And neither is this. . . . President Clinton's alleged perjury regarding consensual sexual relations clearly falls on the end of the spectrum with my example of perjury regarding a traffic violation. Assuming his statements were false and material, they did not cause anywhere near the gravity of injury required by the Constitution for impeachment."

Congressman Bob Barr, a very right-wing figure from Georgia who had been an advocate of impeachment even before the Lewinsky story had broken, dismissed Higginbotham as not truly American: "I'd be depressed but I realize there are two Americas out there. There's a real America that doesn't buy the professor's talk about gradations. Real Americans know that perjury amounts to impeachment."

Higginbotham, a former federal judge and one of the most distinguished black jurists and legal scholars in American history, gazed at Barr above the reading glasses resting on the bridge of his nose. He raised his finger: "I am in profound dispute when you speak about the real America. The forty-nine percent who voted for the President, were they not real Americans? Those who disagree with you about impeachment, are they

*David Savage, "Hyde View on Lying Is Back Haunting Him," *Los Angeles Times*, December 4, 1998.

not real Americans? Sir, my father was a laborer, my mother a domestic. I came up the hard way. Don't lecture me about the real America."

"Utterly irrelevant," Barr replied.

Dershowitz interjected, "Whenever I hear the word 'real Americans,' that sounds to me like a code word for racism, a code word for bigotry, a code word—"

"That's the silliest thing I ever heard," said Barr.

"We may have a disagreement about the merits of these issues," said Dershowitz, "but I would no more impugn your Americanism than you should impugn mine, sir."

Higginbotham noted that Clinton had brought more diversity to the federal bench: "And I think that there's a real America which President Clinton took in terms of fairness."

Two days later, Dershowitz sent a letter to Hyde detailing Barr's involvement with the Council of Conservative Citizens, a racist group that was a successor organization to the White Citizens' Council: "Congressman Barr, who was fully aware of this organization's racist and anti-Semitic agenda, not only gave the keynote address to the CCC's national board, but even allowed himself to be photographed literally embracing one of their national directors." Barr claimed that the accusations were "unfounded and deplorable," but photographs of his appearance at the CCC meeting were soon published. And articles in *The Washington Post* by Thomas Edsall documented Barr's and Senator Trent Lott's activities with the group. Barr's point that impeachment was about who was a "real American" was not "utterly irrelevant" after all.

Immediately after the December 1 hearing, the Republicans on the committee voted to subpoena Louis Freeh and Charles LaBella, and they got a federal judge to order their memos to Attorney General Reno unsealed. These memos urged investigations of the President and his advisers about alleged violations of campaign finance law, though they did not document any instances of these. The Democrats on the Judiciary Committee angrily objected, and Hyde withdrew the subpoenas within forty-eight hours. Possessing a modicum of political realism, he knew that if he wandered into the quagmire of campaign finance he would never get to impeachment.

His counsel, David Schippers, a true believer in virtually all the so-called Clinton scandals, was enraged. He had begun looking for conspiracies from the moment he was hired. His first foray had been into the Immigration and Naturalization Service on the surmise that immigrants had been allowed to vote illegally in order to throw the 1996 election to Clinton. But it turned out that the Clinton administration was tougher in enforcing the law in this matter than the previous Bush administration had been. Next, Schippers went on wild-goose chases after Hillary's health care task force, the Drug Enforcement Administration, and the Bureau of Prisons.* "If the case were only about Lewinsky," Schippers wrote in his memoir *Sellout*, "the whole Watergate model fell apart. The rest of the story never got out, and unfortunately it still hasn't."†

Schippers trolled through the backwaters of many supposed scandals. He met with Larry Klayman, the head of the Scaife-funded Judicial Watch, a Mad Hatter of the right who dashed around Washington spouting endless conspiracy theories and filing endless nuisance suits against the White House staff (including me), on behalf of clients such as Linda Tripp and Bob Barr. (Klayman also had sued his own mother, claiming she owed him money. Her affidavit accused her son of "verbal abuse.") Klayman urged Schippers to investigate bribery charges involving the late secretary of commerce Ronald Brown, who had died in 1996 in a plane crash in Croatia, and Schippers met with Dolly Kyle Browning, one of Klayman's clients, a high-school classmate of Clinton's who had written a novel suggesting an affair with him. "If true, her testimony fit perfectly into the pattern of obstruction of justice and perjury charges we had already developed,"‡ he wrote. Schippers wanted to call her to testify but Hyde stopped him. Schippers met with Kathleen Willey and her lawyer and planned to call her, too, until Hyde halted that plan.§ Then Schippers wanted to investigate the unproved allegation that the Chinese government had funneled campaign funds to the Clinton-Gore campaign, so he subpoenaed Freeh and LaBella, telling Hyde he wanted to subpoena Reno and the President, too. He hoped the President would call out federal troops to try to stop him. When he met with Reno over LaBella's memo, according to Schippers's own account, he told her, "At least you won't be going to the slammer today."‖

Hyde had picked Schippers as Republican counsel to the Judiciary Committee because he was a hometown buddy, whose "folksy" style, Hyde hoped, would enhance his own dignity. But Chairman Hyde never

*Schippers, *Sellout*, pp. 37–49.
†Ibid., p. 59.
‡Ibid., p. 119.
§Ibid., p. 116.
‖Ibid., p. 136.

did much to handle Schippers in his sensitive post, except occasionally to stop him from running off cliffs. The Democratic staff people were at first surprised that the Republicans would have such a flaky counsel, and it gave them confidence that there was not much to the competition. After a while, however, Schippers induced anxiety because the majority Republicans followed him into dangerous caverns, and regarded him as mascot, cheerleader, and fraternity brother.

During this period, I was working closely with President Clinton's lawyers, doing research, helping to shape the arguments and select the witnesses, as well as working with the White House political team. At the same time, I was helping Jim Steinberg in preparing for the G-7 Economic Summit that would take place the following year in Germany; planning a Third Way conference for 1999 in Florence, Italy; and participating in early meetings about the State of the Union address and the President's forthcoming budget and program. I had receded from public view, and was happy to be assisting in the real work of Clinton's White House.

The Judiciary Committee allowed two days for the President's defense. Four panels of witnesses were presented, the first devoted to testimony on the history and constitutional standards of impeachment. On December 8, Nicholas Katzenbach, President Johnson's attorney general, said, "Finally, I can't see any constitutional basis for impeachment." Sean Wilentz, professor at Princeton University, issued a historian's warning that if the members voted for impeachment they would take the risk of "going down in history with the zealots and the fanatics. If you understand that the charges do not rise to the level of impeachment, or if you are at all unsure, and yet you vote in favor of impeachment anyway for some other reason, history will track you down and condemn you for your cravenness." Republicans bristled at his testimony. How dare he call them "zealots"?

The next panel consisted of three former members of the House Judiciary Committee that voted to impeach Nixon. Elizabeth Holtzman, an author of the Independent Counsel Act, observed, "We never intended to create a Grand Inquisitor for Impeachment." Father Robert Drinan noted that this Judiciary Committee was "entirely different" from the one in operation in 1974 in "thoroughness and fairness," and anticipated, if it impeached Clinton, "an explosion of anger like that that occurred after the Saturday Night Massacre." Wayne Owens pointed out that "by nature personal misconduct" was "therefore not impeachable."

Then two more veterans of the Watergate Committee were sworn in.

Richard Ben-Veniste, its assistant special prosecutor, unfavorably compared Starr's behavior to Leon Jaworski's scrupulous "independence and professionalism"—Starr's continued private practice, the leaks from his office, his usurpation of the prescribed function of Congress in his advocacy of impeachment, and his failure to submit his report to the supervising federal judge for advance review. James Hamilton, assistant chief counsel to the Watergate Committee, underscored that Clinton had committed no "high crime" and, under questioning, stated that Nixon's crimes "are indicative of the type of conduct we should look at."

The next day, five experienced prosecutors appeared, each of them dismissing the notion that Starr's allegations were "of the nature which a responsible federal prosecutor would present to a grand jury for indictment," as Thomas Sullivan, former U.S. attorney for the northern district of Illinois, put it. "This simply is not the stuff of criminal prosecution," said Richard Davis, a former assistant U.S. attorney and leader of the Watergate prosecution task force. Edward S. G. Dennis, Jr., former acting deputy attorney general, stated flatly that "a criminal prosecution [against Clinton] would most likely fail." Ronald Noble, former undersecretary of the treasury for enforcement and deputy attorney general in the criminal division, declared that "a career federal prosecutor, asked to investigate allegations like those in the Clinton-Lewinsky matter, would not pursue federal criminal prosecution." William Weld, who had been a Republican counsel on the Watergate Committee and head of the criminal division of the Justice Department during the Reagan administration, added that it had not been the policy of the Reagan Justice Department "to seek indictments solely on the basis that a prospective defendant had committed adultery or fornication, which are not lawful."

The President's defense concluded with the last Watergate special prosecutor—Charles Ruff, now the White House counsel. Ruff made a factual case, which, he said, "falls under the heading, I suppose, of legalisms." Point by point, by "point of law," Ruff refuted the charges. Addressing the allegation that President Clinton had committed perjury in his deposition in the Paula Jones case, he said, "It is not legalistic to point out that a witness was asked poorly framed or ambiguous questions, and it is not legalistic to argue that a witness's answer was technically true, even if not complete." Jones's counsel had asked his questions "on the basis of a truncated, artificial definition of sexual relations," and Clinton's responses "were misleading but they were not perjurious." On he went, through every incident, holding all the facts up to the light, turning them so that they reflected on Clinton's innocence. When Ruff was finished, the Republicans homed in on the perjury charge, Charles Canady speaking for many of them in waving away "legal arguments that don't really meet the test of common sense and human experience." Their version of the rule of law ruled out actual points of law.

The last House member Hyde called on was Representative Lindsey Graham of South Carolina, who had made himself into a "folksy" character, attracting publicity by remarking that he didn't know if the scandal was Watergate or Peyton Place. He had been elected as a member of the class of 1994, one of Gingrich's shock troops. "I'm one less vote for an agenda that makes you want to throw up," he said then.* He had campaigned as a "Desert Storm veteran," though during the Gulf War he had been a desk-bound lawyer processing papers for the U.S. Air Force in South Carolina. He had been a plotter against Gingrich for his supposed softness on Clinton, and he had supported Barr's impeachment bill of 1997, proposed before the Lewinsky scandal. Some in the press and even in the White House thought of him as independent, while others considered him erratic and opportunistic. He seemed open to overtures from Greg Craig and Abbe Lowell, but then he never did anything but engage them in odd, fruitless conversations. He basked in attention, remarking later, "You like the limelight." He came from western South Carolina, near Spartanburg, far from Charleston, and had never lived in a big city. One reason he offered for favoring impeachment was that Clinton had made late-night telephone calls. "Where I come from, a man who calls someone up at 2:30 in the morning is up to no good," he said. For all the talk of his independence, Graham boasted a 100 percent voting record according to the American Conservative Union.†

Graham began his questioning of Ruff, who had made a point of courtesy, with a show of disrespect: "I can only believe your defense if I check my common sense at the door, and I forget the way the world really works. I'm singularly unimpressed with this defense." But Graham wasn't interested in Ruff's defense or any matter that had been raised before or that the committee by prearrangement had discussed with Ruff. He had his very own fantastic conspiracy theory.

Graham: "But the most disturbing thing about your client to me goes like this. Do you know Sidney Blumenthal?"

---

*Michael Barone and Grant Ujifusa, *The Almanac of American Politics 1996*, Times Books, 1995, p. 1,207.

†Lauren Markoe, "Senate Race Provides Challenge That Graham Relishes," *The State*, October 2, 2002.

Ruff: "I do."

Graham: "Right after January the 18th, your client, for the first time, in my opinion, got wind of the fact that there may have been something known about Miss Lewinsky that his little collusion with her would not protect. They knew something he didn't know. This is a statement he makes to Mr. Blumenthal after Dick Morris—who's a real character, but a pretty smart guy—tells the President that if he'd just come clean, it may save him, because it might have saved Richard Nixon. And here's Blumenthal's discussion, according to Blumenthal's testimony—are they close friends, by the way?"

Ruff: "Who is close friends?"

Graham: "Blumenthal and the President."

Ruff: "I truly do not know the answer to that."

Graham: "Okay. Well, let's—we'll find out about that later."

Graham began to read my grand-jury testimony on my conversation with the President on January 21: "And I said to the President, 'What have you done wrong?' And he said, 'Nothing. I haven't done anything wrong.' I said, 'Well, then, that's one of the stupidest ideas I've ever heard'—the idea being confessing. 'Why would you do that if you've done nothing wrong?' And it was at this point that he gave his account of what happened to me."

Graham turned left and right, speaking to the committee: "Listen, female members of this committee." And he quoted at length: " 'Monica Lewinsky came at me and made a sexual demand on me.' He rebuffed her. He said, 'I've gone down that road before, I've caused pain for a lot of people and I'm not going to do that again. She threatened me.' She said that she would tell people they had an affair and that she was known as 'the stalker' among her peers and that she hated it, and that if she had an affair or said she had an affair then she wouldn't be 'the stalker' anymore. And I repeated to the President that he really needed never to be near people who were troubled like this, that it was just—he needed not to be near troubled people like this. And I said, 'You need to find some sure footing here, some solid ground. . . .' "

Then Graham turned to Ruff: "Do you agree with me that the President of the United States is telling an operative—for lack of a better word—that Monica Lewinsky was a sexual predator coming on to him?"

Ruff replied: "But the one thing I want to be absolutely certain of, because I think your implication is that this was somehow a directive to go out and trash Ms. Lewinsky or otherwise to denigrate her, and if that's true, let me tell you from someone who was involved I think from day one through today in what the White House was doing and not doing, didn't happen; never was thought of."

Graham's time was up, but other Republicans gave up theirs for him to continue. Ruff went on insisting there was no organized or "authorized" effort to smear Monica Lewinsky. "Please! Please let me continue!" shouted Graham. "You're saying there's no organized effort. I have got a mountain of press stories—" And he read bits and pieces of news articles in no particular order, even quoting Congressman Charles Rangel, Democrat from New York, saying that Lewinsky had "emotional problems." "I have tons of press reports linked back to the White House saying this girl is unreliable, that she is basically crazy and weird and I'm telling you, I believe your client left that deposition, planted a story in Blumenthal's mind, and tried to get Betty Currie to believe, 'she wanted to have sex with me and I couldn't do that—' "

Pandemonium broke out. "Mr. Chairman," demanded Conyers. "Mr. Chairman, a point of order!" He kept shouting, "Point of order!"

Chris Cannon, Republican of Utah, jumped into the fray: "—the press operation in the White House turns on this young lady. They were calling her unbelievably vile names, questioning her sanity, and if it had not been for that blue dress, they would have tore her to pieces."

"Congressman, may I now—" Ruff tried to interject.

"Point of order!" Conyers repeated.

Graham suggested that Rangel was "a very innocent victim of the spin machine, like maybe all of us are around here."

At last, Ruff was permitted to reply: "You have no basis for making that allegation, and I will tell you that to the extent I have any personal knowledge, I will represent to you that to the contrary, a very careful and well-considered decision was made to do our damnedest to ensure that in fact no such personal attack was ever made."

Graham's time was up again. Again he was granted more time. "And shortly after those stories were planted, the White House operation went into effect notifying the press that if you ever hear anything about this witness, you need to know she's unreliable, she's a stalker, she's basically not a responsible person. That Bill Clinton did, in fact, like so many women in the past, so many women in the past—that Monica Lewinsky was going to go through hell. And that the only thing that stopped this was it was just maybe one too many women to trash out, or it became the blue dress. You can think what you want to about Linda Tripp, but I can tell you right now, I believe in the bottom of my heart, ladies and gentlemen, that if she didn't have that blue dress proving a relationship, they would have cut her up."

He continued with his soliloquy: "And that is far more like Watergate than Peyton Place. And I'm going to believe that probably till I die. And I don't ask you to accept my rendition of the facts. I do ask every member, especially the female members here—if you've ever done a rape trial, you know what comes women's way sometimes; they wear their skirts too tight and they're flirtatious, and you gotta watch out for these type ladies; they even called her Elvira at one time in one of the press reports—that this is serious. And I do wish the President would reconcile him with the law, Mr. Ruff—himself with the law."

"Point of privilege!" demanded Maxine Waters, Democrat from California. "Yes. I would like to say that every member of this committee should be offended by the spin that was just—the wild spin that was just put on by Mr. Lindsey [she meant Graham] in attempting to somehow send a message to Monica Lewinsky that she's been undermined by the President of the United States, and thus set her up to be angry at the President in case she's called as a witness. We're no fools."

Ruff: "I must say, even out of the greatest respect for members of this committee, that to be greeted at the end of a long day by the next-to-the-last speaker with a litany of charges never heard before, not even, I believe, included in whatever document it was that I was handed a few minutes ago, does not give us any reasonable opportunity for fair response."

Graham promised to document his charges and explained his sudden inspiration: "And in terms of the timing, as I have said, this became clear to me after trying to figure out what he was saying to Betty Currie."

Once again, watching the spectacle on television, I had been startled to hear my name used in a political fantasy. I had to listen to Graham's ramblings closely, following the absurd twists and turns to discover exactly what foul deeds Clinton and I had supposedly committed. I had become somewhat inured to smears, especially after the Hyde incident, and my instinct to quell my anger had become quicker. I could not act on my own to reclaim my reputation—I was never a free man, never a Lone Ranger—and I had to see if my self-defense would mesh with the overall strategy. But when I heard Graham's concocted charges I was outraged, not least by their patent ridiculousness. I was frankly sick of being abused—and especially sick that the false persona who bore my name was again being made to dance to music composed by politicians twisting the Constitution to try to remove President Clinton from office.

Graham's conjecture was not so original as it seemed; as he made emphatically clear, it was consistent with the wildest, most groundless accusations made against Clinton in the Paula Jones case: that he had conducted campaigns of intimidation using the White House to prevent women from testifying about him. Graham's evidence was as nonexistent as the nonevidence the Jones team had mustered. He was trying to turn women against the President and get them to support impeachment, but in his effort to establish *some* example of abuse of power, he got the facts wrong and tied fictions together with speculation.

The Starr Report documented that Lewinsky *had* demanded to have sexual intercourse with Clinton and that he had rebuffed her, though obviously that was hardly the whole story. She *was* called "the stalker" in the White House by a number of people working there at the time, and she called herself by that name—a name she didn't like. But Clinton had not called her that to me: he had told me that *she* said she was called a stalker. Even on the day the scandal broke, *before* I spoke with the President, news articles had appeared describing Lewinsky as a stalker, beginning with Michael Isikoff's story in *Newsweek* about the Talking Points, the document in which Lewinsky called herself one. Hundreds, if not thousands, of articles had used that word about her. I was not the source of any of them, nor was anyone I knew.

I had joined with others in the White House in setting the policy Kendall had described: that we would not put out negative stories about Lewinsky. This was the right thing to do, and we also did not want to antagonize her or turn her into an unfriendly witness. In January she was still negotiating her proffer with the prosecutor. We could not imagine a more counterproductive strategy at the moment when we felt under maximum siege.

I heard, as others in the White House did, too, many unattractive anecdotes told by younger staff people about Monica Lewinsky, but no one peddled them to the media, which would have eagerly published them. Nor did I relate to anyone outside the legal counsel's office, not even my closest associates on the political staff of the White House, information about the secret messages Lewinsky was sending to the White House in June and July. Nor did I or anyone else prompt the press to publish the obvious truth about the tall tales she had told the prosecutor under oath, such as having had lunch with the First Lady.

Everyone I knew inside the White House talked daily about the stories about the scandal, including the ones about Lewinsky. And of course, we talked to our friends outside, to our families, and to journalists, too, who understood what was a new story and what was not, and knew we were not feeding them new ones. If we had been, it would have made a very big story. *The Washington Post* had reported on January 29, "Given the ambiguities surrounding Lewinsky's credibility, the White House has been careful not to attack the 24-year-old woman's character or truthfulness." It cited our policy not to attack her: "In recent days, the president's aides and friends have suggested only that Clinton had become friends with the young woman, in part because they had shared stories of their mutually troubled childhoods. Indeed the negative portrayal of Lewinsky's mind-set and her behavior has emerged in recent days almost entirely from her acquaintances"—in particular a former lover and college professor, Andrew Bleiler, who described her as having stalked him and who said she had told him she wanted to pursue the President sexually.* This last allegation received extensive coverage, as Bleiler quoted her telling him in 1995: "I'm going to the White House to get my presidential knee pads." The *Los Angeles Times* reported in August, under the headline "Ex-Intern Has Not Been and Will Not Be Attacked, Clinton Aides Say," "From the beginning, the White House has been careful about what it has said of Lewinsky. . . . White House officials and Clinton allies have gone out of their way to nurture whatever positive feelings Lewinsky had about the president."†

Indeed, we on the President's staff decided that we would all say that we believed the President's story. Nobody in the press corps made anything of these statements of affirmation; that the President's aides supported him was not deemed newsworthy. We were all pressed for more than the incantation of "I believe the President." But so far as I know, we told roughly the same sort of story.

Benjamin Barber, with whom I occasionally discussed politics and international affairs, and who participated in a number of White House meetings about those subjects, recalled in his memoir, "Sid ruminated, might it not explain the crush of contradictions emerging about Monica Lewinsky, that she was an overwrought young person with a crush on the president, someone whom the staff and the president liked and with whom he had—perhaps foolishly—gotten overinvolved in trying to help

---

*Amy Goldstein and William Claiborne, "Aide's Interest in President Was Known to Friends," *The Washington Post*, January 29, 1998.

†Elizabeth Shogren, "Lewinsky Is Unique Among Women Linked to Clinton; Strategy: Unlike Jones, Flowers and Willey, Ex-Intern Has Not Been and Will Not Be Attacked, Clinton Aides Say. Why? For One, She Poses a Threat," *Los Angeles Times*, August 8, 1998.

her out?" Barber had heard the same account from others: "I was inclined to believe it was an account conceived by good-willed staffers trying to make sense of the contradictory evidence, an account hardly invented by, but conveniently indulged in, by the president." No one ever told him that this was the President's story. In fact, Barber knew differently:

> Don Baer [former communications director], long gone from the White House when this particular hell broke loose (and was he ever glad!), suggested to me not long after my meeting with Blumenthal that the account Sidney had proposed was actually Don's own effort to make sense of what seemed to be happening, and that it had been taken up by the White House staff only after Don had introduced it to them. Neither Sid nor Don ever even hinted that the story was the official Clinton version perpetrated on gullible staffers by a manipulative president. I didn't feel used. . . . Rather, Sid gave the impression of a loyalist searching for an explanation that would allow him to make some sense for himself out of an emerging embarrassment of major proportions, gave the impression that he was trying out this account (perhaps borrowed from Don) not just on me but on himself.*

Don was a friend, but I hadn't gotten it from him. It was a common story, completely lacking in news value, that many of us told during the months before Clinton admitted the truth.

Lindsey Graham had not cited either *The Washington Post* or the *Los Angeles Times* articles or the hundreds of other news items appearing from the very start that had quoted Monica Lewinsky's friends describing her as a stalker. But at Ruff's request, Graham sent his "evidence" to him, and on December 15 Ruff answered Graham in a letter that was never made public:

> As I said then [December 9], the allegation that the White House (and specifically Mr. Blumenthal) mounted a campaign to denigrate Ms. Lewinsky is utterly baseless. I have now had a chance to review the material that you held in your hand as you made your charges, and they serve to fortify my conclusion.
>
> First, as you knew, the news reports on which you relied consisted primarily of a very few stories that were published in the days immedi-

*Barber, *Truth of Power*, pp. 290–91.

ately following disclosure of the Independent Counsel's investigation and were then simply repeated in various forms in various newspapers. More-over, the Associated Press story of January 31, 1998, which appears to have been the basis for many of the other articles and was one of the only ones that purported to quote White House staff at any level (albeit un-named), specifically reported that White House Communications Direc-tor Ann Lewis had disavowed any statements critical of Ms. Lewinsky and made it clear that the White House had no intention of pursuing any such strategy.

Most of the other articles you attached to your letter are, at best, of modest relevance: they include multiple copies of a column by Tony Snow, the man who introduced Linda Tripp to Lucianne Goldberg, mul-tiple columns by Maureen Dowd . . . citing no identified sources except for the quote from Congressman Rangel you read at the hearing; a col-umn by Michael Kelly . . . citing no sources . . . and a Washington Post story reporting Linda Tripp's complaints.

Perhaps most notable is your decision to include with your letter only one page of a lengthy Los Angeles Times article published on Febru-ary 1, 1998. Based on interviews with Ms. Lewinsky's childhood friends, classmates, and neighbors, the article is a compilation of personal infor-mation, much of which is not flattering. To hold out as proof that there was some White House plan to speak ill of Ms. Lewinsky the brief seg-ment describing Ms. Lieberman's concerns is entirely unfair. [Evelyn Lieberman was the deputy chief of staff who fired Lewinsky in 1996 from her White House job in the correspondence department.] Indeed, it is noteworthy that Ms. Lewinsky herself mentioned, in the "talking points" she gave to Ms. Tripp, that she had been transferred from the White House because she had been accused of "stalking" the President.

Further, although basing your charges on a selection of newspaper ar-ticles, you ignore other reports that flatly contradict your thesis. I direct your attention particularly to an August 8, 1998, article in the Los Ange-les Times: "From the beginning, the White House has been careful about what it has said of Lewinsky. . . ."

Lastly, although you did not raise the issue in your letter, you claimed in your speech at the end of the hearing that the plan you accused the White House of engineering would have been carried out if the existence of a stained dress had not been revealed. Apart from the fact that there is no evidence to support your underlying premise, I would point out that, although the existence of such a dress was rumored in the days after Jan-uary 21, by the end of January Ms. Lewinsky's attorney had denied it and the media had reported that the FBI laboratory found no such evidence. Thus, even if there were proof that such a plan had ever been contemplated, it is unclear now, as you contend, it could have been forestalled by the discovery of the dress.

In sum, now that we have examined the evidence you proffered to support your accusation, we once again reject it.

Ruff's reference to "the material that you held in your hand as you made your charges" was an oblique historical reference to Senator Joseph McCarthy, who had flourished papers in his hand as he, too, made unfounded charges. Undoubtedly, Graham missed the allusion, but Ruff deliberately put it there to reflect his own feelings about such smears. Despite Ruff's efforts to put fact to Graham's fiction, these accusations against me remained a core part of the trial against the President until the very end.

While Graham had been holding forth at the December 9 hearing, and without informing Ruff, the Republicans on the Judiciary Committee had submitted their four articles of impeachment for a Committee vote. They charged the President with two counts of perjury—in the Jones deposition and before Starr's grand jury—as well as obstruction of justice and abuse of power.

On December 10, the respective counsels of the House Judiciary Committee presented their summations. Abbe Lowell went first, using audiotapes and videos of Monica Lewinsky, Betty Currie, Vernon Jordan, Linda Tripp, and President Clinton to refute each point of the four articles of impeachment. He began with perjury—"We cannot find . . . what statements the majority contends were lies"—and went on to the tortured definition of "sexual relations" that Clinton believed he was adhering to when he gave his deposition in the Paula Jones case: "How would you have a trial in the Senate to conclude whether the President was right about what he thought the phrase 'sexual relations' meant?" Lowell made it undeniably clear with the tapes of Lewinsky that Clinton had not suborned her perjury. Nor had he done so with Betty Currie; and of course when Clinton had talked to her, she wasn't a potential witness.

Lowell pointed out that finding Monica Lewinsky a job, which the Republicans wanted to believe the President and Vernon Jordan had tried to do in order to alter her deposition in the Paula Jones case, could not have been an obstruction of justice because "the job search began long before Ms. Lewinsky was even a dream to the Paula Jones attorneys." Nor was Clinton guilty of abuse of power—not by "repeating to his staff the same denial . . . that he had already made to the public," nor by invoking executive privilege, nor by asserting attorney-client privilege. "I have heard the majority state that a president should not be above the law. And yet this proposed article would place him below the law." Lowell concluded by citing Alexander Hamilton on impeachment's being determined more "by the comparative strength of the parties than by real demonstrations of innocence and guilt," and he urged the Republican majority, which "has all the votes it needs to do as it pleases," to "avoid the course on which you are now embarked."

David Schippers came next. Even Republicans agreed later that he lost his argument in weeds of details, though he tried to rescue himself with wisecracks: "Life was so much simpler before they found that dress, wasn't it?" The Democratic counsels privately thought his presentation was like a 1940s radio show—"Schippers's 'Green Hornet' bit." With great drama Schippers made an assertion of the discovery of vast new crimes: "We uncovered more incidents involving probable direct and deliberate obstruction of justice, witness tampering, perjury, and abuse of power." He explained that unfortunately, at the request of the Justice Department and the Independent Counsel, he couldn't "compromise pending criminal investigations" by saying what they were. The Democrats could have had no idea that this flamboyant nonsense would decisively affect the committee's final impeachment vote. Schippers's credibility was so low, his skill as an attorney so discounted, that they failed to take seriously anything he said, even when it enraged them.

As soon as he was finished, the debate on impeachment began—in an inflamed and divided committee, exactly as Hamilton had predicted. It opened with a moment of low comedy when the Democrats confused the Republicans by insisting on specificity in the perjury charge. "You're embarrassed to try and unseat a twice-elected president on this degree of trivia and you have therefore used obfuscatory language to suggest a set of offenses that don't have specific support," said Barney Frank. This was indeed true, for the Republicans did not want to turn their articles into a graphic sexual document. But Bill McCollum, whom the Republican staff members nicknamed "Mr. Genitalia" because of his obsessive concentration on where Clinton supposedly touched Lewinsky, eagerly rose to read at length from the grand-jury testimony on "genitalia." This was precisely what the Republicans wished he would not do.

The most significant moments in the debate were the result of Lindsey Graham's unpredictable and changeable behavior. First, he tried to negotiate with the Democrats, proposing that they would drop the articles if Clinton apologized. Actually, another abject apology from President Clinton had already been announced, to be delivered that very afternoon. "You're abandoning ship!" Barr shouted at Graham. But Graham's notion was that Clinton should apologize for committing crimes, and the Democrats rejected it out of hand. When Clinton went before the cameras in the Rose Garden to apologize again but did not confess criminality, Graham was relieved. "He just can't get there, can he?" he said to the Republicans watching on television, seeking to be reembraced after his heresy.*

Then, Graham decided to oppose Article II, concerning perjury in the Jones deposition, explaining that no prosecutor would file such a charge—which of course was true of Article I, on perjury in the grand jury, as well. But if either was weak and had to be defended, it was perjury in the Jones deposition because it revolved around the convoluted definition of "sexual relations." Graham's inexplicable vote somehow made the Republicans feel that there was something wrong with Article II, and the doubt he instilled would greatly benefit the President's case. The final votes in the committee, on December 11 and 12, were 21–16 on Articles I, III, and IV and 20–17 on Article II.

That Sunday, December 13, Republican leaders—Hyde, DeLay, and Armey—appeared on the morning talk shows as a chorus urging the President to quit. Hyde remarked on Clinton's unwaveringly high popularity and had a strange analogy for his own unpopularity: "If Jesus Christ had taken a poll, he would never have preached the gospel."

Now the impeachment moved to the House floor. Within the White House we set up a boiler-room operation of congressional liaisons to target uncommitted moderate Republicans. We worked mainly through surrogates, Republicans who would work with us. Our lists showed that plenty of Republicans might well vote against impeachment. We drew up lists in two categories—those who we believed would vote against and those who were likely to vote against. There were more than enough, some said. I remained extremely skeptical. Soon reports came trickling into the White House about the intense pressure being exerted on all Republicans by Republican whip Tom DeLay. The pest exterminator from Sugar Land, Texas, surrounded by his centurions—

*Baker, *The Breach*, p. 213.

a staff and sixty Republican members designated as whips—was directing what they called "the Campaign." Peter Baker of *The Washington
Post* wrote:

> Besides his public statements advocating impeachment, DeLay had pri-
> vately been coaching Hyde since the election, advising him on media
> relations and assisting with logistics. DeLay had sent copies of Starr's
> November 19 statement before the Judiciary Committee to each member
> of the Republican conference and was organizing committee members to
> do what he could not do himself—whip their fellow congressmen as the
> vote on the floor approached. The committee staff was provided with
> whip cards and taught how to divide up the caucus to focus on key con-
> gressmen who would move whole blocs of members. DeLay's aides were
> also enlisting prominent Republican fund-raisers and party officials to
> help persuade those on the fence.*

On Saturday, December 12, immediately after the Judiciary Committee vote, DeLay and his staff had circulated a letter against bringing up
censure for a floor vote. They told Hyde that the leadership had already
decided, which it hadn't, so Hyde signed. They told Livingston to sign
and he agreed, but he wasn't physically available, so his aide was ordered
to sign for him while one of DeLay's aides hovered over her. Gingrich,
still nominally the Speaker, was in Georgia, and he agreed over the
phone. DeLay's name never appeared on any letter, but through coercion
and will he had snuffed out any alternative to impeachment.†

We heard from Republicans that DeLay's operation was putting pressure on the campaign finance chairmen of certain individual congressmen. In one case, we learned, a congressman's brother had been called
and told to influence his brother, who would otherwise face a right-wing
opponent in the 2000 primary. Representative Amo Houghton, a moderate Republican from New York who opposed impeachment, had already
been declared a betrayer and a conservative primary opponent had announced against him, even though it was two years to the election. This
was an obvious demonstration case to encourage the others. Houghton
was an heir to the Corning Glass fortune and self-financing, but other
Republicans were not in his protected position. Representative Peter
King, a Republican of New York who also opposed impeachment, was
threatened with being stripped of a subcommittee chairmanship. An aide

*Baker, *The Breach*, p. 223.
†Ibid., p. 219.

to DeLay warned him that the Whip would make "the next two years the longest of his life."*

"Coming out of the election, everyone thought impeachment was dead," Congressman King told me later. "I didn't hear anyone discuss impeachment. It was over. Then DeLay assumed control. DeLay used the eighty-one questions; it gave him the peg he needed. In most districts in the country, a majority was against impeachment, maybe a majority of Republicans. But a majority who voted in Republican primaries was for impeachment. When you put individual members under the gun, a lot of them could get killed in a primary. That was the way he did it. I heard of Christian radio stations going after Republicans. Right-wing groups were stirring it up in parts of the country outside of the Northeast. Most of the pressure went through the Christian right network. It happened over a ten-day period. The whole world changed. I remember talking to people like Rick Lazio and Mike Forbes [both Republicans of New York] and they were saying this is nuts. Then suddenly they were holding news conferences saying their consciences were torn."

The stress exerted on Representative Jack Quinn, another Republican from New York, who told King he would vote against impeachment and told us that he would hold out, was tremendous, and he crumpled under it, so beaten by DeLay that he didn't tell us of his decision despite promising he would do so. Tom Campbell, Republican from California—a bellwether of the moderates, a former Stanford Law School professor whom we had counted on—caved, too. At his press conference declaring his intention to vote for impeachment, he was asked about the substance of the articles and responded, "I couldn't say off the top of my head."† Campbell had higher political ambitions to run for the Senate, and so he made his decision. (He lost in 2000.) On December 15, nine previously uncommitted Republican moderates announced for impeachment.

In the Gerald Ford House Office Building, down a corridor guarded by the Capitol Hill police, was a large fluorescent-lit room with a conference table that contained boxes of grand-jury material that Starr had sent over. They were filled with raw FBI reports and independent counsel interviews with hundreds of witnesses, many of them tracking the women in the Paula Jones case. Some of the material was grand-jury testimony that had been the background to the Starr Report, but the vast bulk of it was not. It was the leftovers of dead-end investigations, the accumulated

*See Jane Mayer, "The Exterminator," *The New Yorker*, May 24, 1999.
†Baker, *The Breach*, p. 224.

leavings from failed surmises—boxes and boxes, hundreds of files. In this room, located across the hallway from the Republican counsel's office (the Democratic counsel's staff was scattered throughout the building), Schippers had been delving into unproved conspiracy theories, and he emerged a believer in them all. A few other Republicans on the committee spent time there, though not most, and despite its antiseptic furbishing, the room held a mesmerizing fascination for them. They called it "the secure room" or "the evidence room." They believed it contained the ultimate secrets of the Clinton presidency, the true stories of a supposed predator and his campaigns to intimidate the women he had ravaged, the White House that was like a mafia. Coming from Starr, these boxes bore a magical imprimatur for the Republicans. "That material was important to me," James Rogan told me later, referring to the "stuff," as he put it, unrelated to the Starr Report. "It was the evidence."

But what it was *not* was "the evidence"—it was the opposite of evidence. It was uncorroborated, undocumented, and legally uncertified; it had nothing to do with the articles of impeachment. For Starr to have dumped it on the Congress in September only invited its abuse. ("I also remember being very cautious," said Rogan, a former judge. "I remember thinking I have to base my vote on what's on the public record.")

The Democratic staff were not apprised when the Republicans changed the rules governing who had access to "the secure room," which they did way back in October. The Democrats believed that the rules stood, enabling only Judiciary Committee members to enter. Julian Epstein, chief counsel for the Democrats on the committee, said to me later about the broad access to Starr's boxes, "It was never discussed that the original session rules were vacated. They never told the Democrats that there was a change in the rules. We never got a change from the House parliamentarian. When we found out, it was too late. If we had known, we would have fought it."

On December 16, at a meeting of the House Republican Conference, Representative Stephen Buyer of Indiana insisted that every member should go to "the evidence room" to see the secret material. The impeachment, he said, wasn't just about public evidence. It was just as much about the undisclosed files that held the terrible truth about the beast in the White House—even rape. "If you're undecided on the information that's already out there," he said, "you have an obligation to yourself and your country to get over there and look at that information."*

*Baker, *The Breach*, p. 232.

DeLay's whip operation organized groups of congressmen—sixty-five of them in total, all of whom wound up voting for impeachment—for field trips to "the evidence room." Schippers was their Virgil leading them on a tour of this Inferno, putting on light-and-sound shows "from 8 a.m. until after midnight," he wrote. "We showed videos, played tapes, and provided transcripts, statements, reports, and any other material we had." None of it was evidence in any legal sense. But Schippers believed, as he wrote, that on the basis of these performances about Clinton's "sinister mentality," the Republicans were able to enforce party discipline and "ensure impeachment."*

Neither the House Democrats nor the White House knew about these private screenings. We heard fragments, but not full accounts, and no major newspaper at the time reported what was happening. Afterward we heard from Republicans that the trips to "the evidence room" were used to force them into line behind impeachment. If they did not vote for it after their visits, then the material would be released, and enraged Republican voters would destroy them. At the White House we later came to believe that the obstruction-of-justice article would not have passed without this coercion.

Congressman King told me about his conversation with another Republican leaning against impeachment. "They got me in the evidence room," he said to King. "They were showing me 'evidence' of rape. I don't know if it's true. It can make us look bad if it comes out." "Does it have anything to do with the four articles or was made known in the hearings?" King asked him. "No," he replied, but he voted for impeachment out of fear.

The Republicans focused in the secret vault especially on an affidavit of "Jane Doe No. 5" in the Paula Jones case, a woman named Juanita Broaddrick, a nursing-home operator who claimed that Clinton had lured her to a hotel room and raped her in 1978. The Broaddrick accusation now became the deep, dark secret about Clinton that credulous Republicans and Clinton-haters took as gospel. Now they had penetrated to his heart of darkness. He wasn't just a husband who strayed, but a sexual criminal, nothing less than a rapist. On its own, the Broaddrick affidavit depicted an awful incident. But was it true?

In the fall of 1997, the Paula Jones legal team had heard about Broad-

*Christopher Matthews, "Late Night Session on Jane Doe No. 5 Sealed Impeachment," *Seattle Post-Intelligencer*, February 25, 1999; Schippers, *Sellout*, pp. 254–55.

drick and approached her. She refused to cooperate with them at first. When she was subpoenaed she gave an affidavit saying, "I do not have any information to offer regarding a nonconsensual or unwelcome sexual advance by Mr. Clinton." Later, she filed another affidavit stating that Clinton had raped her. Given her reversal, she had no standing as a reliable witness, but the Jones team could leak her affidavit and deposition simply to hurt Clinton, which they did on March 28, 1998, three days before the Jones case was thrown out; the material swirled about the Internet at various right-wing websites. None of Broaddrick's denials were in "the evidence room."

When I first learned about the Broaddrick affidavit I called David Brock to see if he had ever heard of it. Indeed he had. In 1995, searching for dirt on Clinton, he had been set on Broaddrick's trail by the vindictive Sheffield Nelson, the source of many such stories. Nelson had given him a letter from a Republican activist named Philip Yoakum, who claimed to be Broaddrick's friend and who had conveyed the rape charge. Brock then trotted off to see Yoakum, who told a story about him and Nelson secretly taping Broaddrick recounting her travail. Brock asked for the tape and Yoakum asked for payment—as well as a percentage of Brock's book advance. When Brock refused, Yoakum "said he didn't have the tape after all and suggested the rape story might not be true. For one thing, he said, Sheffield [Nelson] never believed it."

The story became even more weirdly complicated. Caught up in the mystery, Brock asked Sheffield Nelson about the tape. Nelson told him he had given it to a local private investigator, by now an opposition researcher for the Republican Senatorial Campaign Committee in Washington. Brock interviewed this man, one Marty Rile, but his hopes were swiftly dashed when Rile said, "It's not what she says it is." Even at the height of his Clinton-hating writing, Brock backed off this convoluted story as unreliable. None of this information was available to the Republican members.*

And there was more. The editor of the Van Buren, Arkansas, *Press Argus-Courier* told the journalists Joe Conason and Gene Lyons in 1999 that Juanita Broaddrick had asked him in 1990 to send a photographer to her nursing home, the Brownwood Manor, for a special occasion: the appearance there of Governor Clinton. This was hardly the attitude of a rape victim toward her predator. The two sisters who managed Brown-

---

*Brock, *Blinded by the Right*, pp. 252–57.

wood Manor for her, Norma Rogers and Jean Darden, as it happened, did have a problem with Governor Clinton, who in 1980 had commuted the death sentence of their father's killer. They had led an effective political campaign against him in Crawford County, and his visit in 1990 was at least partly to repair political damage. Clinton had spent a decade trying to turn the county's vote around, and by the year of his visit to Brownwood, he had succeeded. Now the two sisters and Broaddrick's husband were the only ones claiming to be witnesses to Broaddrick's rape story, and it was from the sisters that Paula Jones's lawyers learned of it. None of this information, either, was available in "the evidence room."*

On December 12, the day the House Judiciary Committee voted for the articles of impeachment, President Clinton left for Israel. He visited the grave of Yitzhak Rabin, lit a menorah, and delivered a speech at the Knesset, the Israeli parliament, urging the Israeli people to understand the aspirations of the Palestinians:

> Of course, there have been setbacks; more misunderstandings, more disagreements, more provocations, more acts of violence. You feel Palestinians should prove in word and deed that their intentions have actually changed, as you redeploy from land on which tears and blood have been shed, and you are right to feel that.
>
> Palestinians feel you should acknowledge they too have suffered and they, too, have legitimate expectations that should be met and, like Israel, internal political pressure that must be overcome. And they are right, too.
>
> Because of all that has happened and the mountain of memories that has not yet been washed away, the road ahead will be hard. Already, every step forward has been tempered with pain. Each time the forces of reconciliation on each side have reached out, the forces of destruction have lashed out. . . .
>
> If you are to build a future together, hard realities cannot be ignored. Reconciliation after all this trouble is not natural. The differences among you are not trivial. There is a history of heartbreak and loss. But the violent past and the difficult present do not have to be repeated forever. In the historical relationship between Israelis and Palestinians, one thing, and only one thing, is predestined: you are bound to be neighbors. The question is not whether you will live side by side, but how you will live side by side.

*Conason and Lyons, *Hunting of the President*, pp. 60–64.

The next day he landed at the brand-new Gaza International Airport and addressed the Palestinian National Council, the first time an American president had ever done so, urging the Palestinians to recognize the legitimacy and security of Israel. Before he spoke, the PNC had revoked the declaration in its charter calling for the destruction of Israel, and this was the most dramatic step the Palestinians had thus far taken in the peace process.

> Peace must mean many things—legitimate rights for Palestinians, real security for Israel. But it must begin with something even more basic—mutual recognition, seeing people who are different, with whom there have been profound differences, as people. . . . Palestinians must recognize the right of Israel and its people to live safe and secure lives today, tomorrow and forever. Israel must recognize the right of Palestinians to aspire to live free today, tomorrow and forever. . . . The fulfillment of one side's aspirations must not come at the expense of the other. We must believe that everyone can win in the new Middle East. It does not hurt Israelis to hear Palestinians peacefully and pridefully asserting their identity, as we saw today. That is not a bad thing. And it does not hurt Palestinians to acknowledge the profound desire of Israelis to live without fear. It is in this spirit that I ask you to consider where we go from here.
>
> I thank you for your rejection—fully, finally and forever—of the passages in the Palestinian Charter calling for the destruction of Israel. . . . The time has come to sanctify your holy ground with genuine forgiveness and reconciliation. Every influential Palestinian, from teacher to journalist, from politician to community leader, must make this a mission to banish from the minds of children glorifying suicide bombers; to end the practice of speaking peace in one place and preaching hatred in another; to teach school children the value of peace and the waste of war; to break the cycle of violence. Our great American prophet, Martin Luther King, once said, "The old law of an eye for an eye leaves everybody blind."

President Clinton's speeches on successive days in Israel and Gaza marked a high point in his effort to move negotiations to what was called final status resolution—an agreement that would divide the land for peace, guaranteeing Israeli security *and* Palestinian nationhood. Every step forward had been greeted with new assaults by Hamas, the Palestinian terrorist organization, to try to turn the mistrustful partners against each other. And in Israel, West Bank settlers and elements of the Likud remained adamantly opposed, since they regarded the peace process as undermining Israel in its claim to the biblically promised land of Judea and Samaria. Clinton was edging the nations ahead over treacherous ground.

On the morning of December 16, the President did something he never did—he appeared at the senior staff meeting, bleary-eyed and tired. We rose to give him an ovation for his work in the Middle East and to encourage him on the eve of the impeachment debate in the House, which was scheduled to begin the next day. "Don't stop fighting," he said. "The American people are with us. I haven't stopped. Keep up the work."

A few hours later I learned that the United States and Britain were poised to launch a sustained bombing campaign against Iraq beginning at five that afternoon. Six weeks earlier, Saddam Hussein had announced that he would no longer cooperate with the weapons inspectors of the United Nations Special Commission (UNSCOM), who had been ferreting out and destroying his biological, chemical, and potential nuclear weapons of mass destruction. The UN Security Council voted unanimously to condemn his stance and to demand his compliance. At first, he was defiant, but under threat of military force he backed down. President Clinton decided to pursue diplomacy to make him comply before launching an attack, but Saddam's assent was another one of his ruses, and while refusing to cooperate he actually imposed new restrictions on the inspectors. He was trying to manipulate his way out of his self-created crisis, but he had only postponed the reckoning. UNSCOM's report on his failure of compliance now triggered a military response.

I watched the President tell the American people about Operation Desert Fox on a television set in the office of Steve Richetti, deputy chief of staff, down the corridor from the Oval Office, where Clinton was speaking. Minutes before he went on the air, television correspondents reported that Senator Trent Lott, Republican majority leader, was denouncing the attack on Saddam Hussein. "I cannot support this military action in the Persian Gulf at this time," Lott said. "Both the timing and the policy are subject to question." Casting aspersions on the President's motives, Lott suggested that Clinton was authorizing the bombing of Saddam's hidden weapons of mass destruction only to impede the impeachment. Lott's statement marked the first time in American history a congressional leader had ever criticized a president while U.S. forces were about to go into action. Other Republicans soon joined in making the same accusation. Dick Armey said, "After months of lies, the President has given millions of people around the world reason to doubt that he has sent Americans into battle for the right reasons." We learned later that the House Republican Conference had watched the President's speech on Iraq together, jeering and booing.

Preceded by the contentious and contemptuous statement of Lott, the President explained the urgent reasons for Operation Desert Fox:

> Heavy as they are, the costs of action must be weighed against the price of inaction. If Saddam defies the world and we fail to respond, we will face a far greater threat in the future. Saddam will strike again at his neighbors; he will make war on his own people. And mark my words, he will develop weapons of mass destruction. He will deploy them, and he will use them. Because we are acting today, it is less likely that we will face these dangers in the future.

> Let me close by addressing one other issue. Saddam Hussein and the other enemies of peace may have thought that the serious debate currently before the House of Representatives would distract Americans or weaken our resolve to face him down. But once more, the United States has proven that, although we are never eager to use force, when we must act in America's vital interests, we will do so.

As soon as he finished, the President came to Richetti's office. He could not believe that Lott had said what he said—that Clinton had invented reasons to put Americans in harm's way just to try to stop the impeachment. He wished, he said, that Gingrich were back. Gingrich was more responsible, more of an internationalist. Then, almost without a stop, he went on to talk about the points in Abbe Lowell's summation, praising particular ones as especially apt. Reviewing political events was Clinton's style, partly as a way to figure out what worked and what didn't and partly as a way to unwind.

That evening, Secretary of Defense Bill Cohen, Director of the CIA George Tenet, and Chairman of the Joint Chiefs Henry Shelton hastily convened a meeting with congressional leaders to dispel the falsehood that there was any political motive for launching the attack on Saddam Hussein. "Is there any reason why we shouldn't go ahead [with impeachment]?" shouted Tom DeLay.

On December 17, Speaker-designate Livingston announced that the floor debate would begin the next day. "That is wrong!" said Dick Gephardt. "That is wrong!" The bombing of Iraq continued until the middle of the day of the impeachment.

In the afternoon, while a group of us were meeting in John Podesta's office to plan strategy for the impeachment debate, Press Secretary Joe Lockhart (who had replaced McCurry a month earlier) burst in to relate an extraordinary story that he had heard from a Capitol Hill source: Livingston was about to be exposed for having an adulterous affair. Our reaction was astonishment. We didn't know where the story had originated. We didn't know where it would break. But we certainly knew we should maintain silence.

A few hours later, Bob Livingston called a full meeting of the House Republican Conference. As he was speaking, his press secretary whispered in his ear, "The press has got it." For days, he had been agonized by the realization that news of his sexual indiscretions would be published. And now he unfolded a prepared statement to read to the unprepared Republicans: "I have on occasion strayed from my marriage . . . I sought marriage and spiritual counseling . . . a small but painful part of the past . . ." Republicans leaped up shouting, first at Livingston, then at each other. DeLay defended him, arguing that adultery wasn't the same thing as perjury. "My fate is in your hands," Livingston pleaded.

Roll Call, a newspaper about Capitol Hill, instantly posted the story on the Internet, and the network television news shows soon led with it. In the twinkling of a wandering eye, the wrong man's sexual peccadilloes were being exposed. The question of who was going to quit now revolved around the Republican Speaker-designate.

The demiurge behind this chaos was the publisher of an empire of smut whose jewel in the crown was a magazine called *Hustler*—America's leading pornographer, Larry Flynt. "I've been Larry Flynted," Livingston had confessed to DeLay earlier in the day.

Flynt's rags-to-riches story had begun in an Ohio strip club, where he got the vision of creating a raunchier magazine than any other. In 1978, he was shot and left paralyzed in a wheelchair by a white supremacist fanatic (the same one, as it happened, who two years later shot and wounded Vernon Jordan). In 1983, Flynt ran an ad depicting Jerry Falwell, then the most prominent leader of the religious right, having sex with his own mother. Falwell sued and lost in the Supreme Court, which ruled in favor of the right to parody.

On October 4 of the impeachment year, Flynt had taken out a full-page ad in *The Washington Post* offering up to $1 million to anyone with documentary evidence of "an adulterous sexual encounter" with a member of Congress or high-ranking Republican or party official. Ken Starr, through his report, had spread graphic sexual detail across the country, and now the professional got in the ring. If the issue was exposing the private lives of politicians, then no one could do it better than a proud pornographer. Flynt believed in pornography. He wasn't ashamed or embarrassed by it. To him, pornography was his method of reaching what Ken Starr would call "the truth"—in his case, a representation of people's innermost and forbidden desires. By making them public Flynt believed he was striking a blow for honesty, and he made every close-up shot in his magazine hyperrealistic. Starr had presented himself as Sergeant Joe Friday, "Just the facts, ma'am." Flynt was the Joe Friday of the erotic. He got the facts on the ma'am.

The secret lives of Republicans attracted Flynt because of the scent of hypocrisy. The Starr Report was like an engraved invitation to him. "I just wanted to expose hypocrisy," Flynt said in an interview. "If these guys are going after the president, they shouldn't have any skeletons in their closet. This is only the beginning."* He didn't have any information, but he knew that plenty would come his way—and it did. Flynt's faith was vindicated. "I just can't believe that somebody would do that to me," Livingston said. "Welcome to the big leagues. Welcome to the big world. Welcome to the world of Larry Flynt."†

Flynt also showed up the hypocrisy of the press corps. What for them was a matter of smarmy euphemism was for him the headline. When they investigated sex, they pretended they weren't and acted as though they were engaged in a higher form of investigative journalism. Flynt had no use for such artifice. He was happy to be recognized as an "investigative pornographer," as the *Post* called him, the real thing. "I felt I had to employ a very high standard of journalistic proof for this investigation," Flynt said.‡ The politicians were stunned, but the journalists' chagrin at Flynt's role was especially galling. When it came to impertinence, Flynt could not be matched. No one put the self-deluded players of this decadent fin de siècle psychological drama in clearer perspective than the forthright pornographer.

The Republicans filed out of their conference in a state of shock. "It breaks your heart because we're all subject to human frailties," said Representative Asa Hutchinson.§ Their first impulse was to blame the White

---

*Howard Kurtz, "Larry Flynt, Investigative Pornographer," *The Washington Post*, December 19, 1998.

†Martin Kettle, "The Political People Against Larry Flynt," *The Guardian*, December 23, 1998.

‡Kurtz, "Larry Flynt."

§Francis X. Clines and Katherine Q. Seelye, "Speaker-Elect Informs Caucus of Past Affairs," *The New York Times*, December 18, 1998.

House, an accusation given impetus by Cokie Roberts that night on *ABC World News*: "I will tell you that someone close to the White House did tell me a rumor along those lines a couple of weeks ago. And I was shocked to have that person spreading that rumor."

Joe Lockhart immediately responded, "There is no evidence that anyone at the White House had anything to do with this story. It doesn't surprise me the Republicans are doing this. What is surprising is that the media will roll over as easily as they do and assume the burden is on us to prove we had no involvement." He called the president of ABC News, David Westin, suggesting that for ABC to be evenhanded it should report if any Republican had ever speculated at a party about the Lewinsky scandal. Westin said he would get back to Lockhart, but he never did. Cokie Roberts was unabashed. Well, you just *know* Democrats were saying this, she told Lockhart. The next day, on air, she offered greater specificity: she had heard something from someone at a party. Flynt's standards, as he claimed, *were* higher. Through a spokesman, he denied that there was any White House involvement and said his sources included "someone involved in Republican politics." He'd have more to say about "Republican hypocrisy," he added.

On December 18, the debate over impeachment was overshadowed by the crisis over the Speaker-designate, but it began nonetheless—with the reading of the four articles of impeachment by the clerk of the House, Paul Hays (whose wife had been the chief fund-raiser for the Paula Jones legal defense fund). Sitting in the chair, Representative Ray LaHood, Republican of Illinois, announced, "The rules prohibit members from engaging in generally personal, abusive language toward the President and also from engaging in comparisons to personal conduct of sitting members of either House of Congress." Democrats audibly chortled.

Hyde arose to deliver an impassioned oration: "It is not a question of sex. . . . The vote that all of us are asked to cast is, in the final analysis, a vote on the rule of law." He whipped up a mélange of authorities and symbols of patriotism and religious devotion: Ben Franklin, the Ten Commandments, "Mosaic law," "Roman law," the Magna Carta, 1776, Abraham Lincoln, and, in closing, "catch the falling flag."

Gephardt came next: "The politics of smear and slash and burn must end." He was making a gesture to the Republicans over Livingston as well as referring to their treatment of Clinton. But the Republicans refused to allow a vote on censure. "In your effort to uphold the Constitution," railed Gephardt, "you are trampling the Constitution."

One by one the representatives took their turns speaking, for two to four minutes. Off the floor, Congressman Patrick Kennedy confronted Bob Barr, who had quoted his uncle, John F. Kennedy. "Anybody who has been to a racist group has no right invoking my uncle's memory!" Barr called him "some punk."* There was also a brief haunting by a ghost, Newt Gingrich, who wandered into the chamber as the speakers droned on and wandered out minutes later. He said not a word, and then his spectral presence was gone, no longer even sensed.

The day of the impeachment vote arrived on December 19. By Republican lights, it was to be the day of Clinton's disgrace. Since long before he ran for president in 1992 he had been the object of a Republican campaign to remove him from politics. Richard Mellon Scaife had invested millions looking for dirt about him. A flood of books and articles, videotapes, and radio talk shows had spread malicious stories that he had murdered dozens to cover up his crimes. If he was not a murderer, then he must be a rapist. The Republicans had tried to corner him, expose him, and eliminate him for years. Now they believed he was done at last.

Hillary Clinton was calm, composed, and defiant. At 8:30 in the morning she appeared before the House Democratic Caucus. "I love and care deeply about my husband," she said. "We have committed our lives to the values of equality of opportunity and a better life for the children of America." She asked the Democrats to support the Constitution and "the commander-in-chief, the President, the man I love." She received a standing ovation.

The House proceedings opened with the reciting of the Pledge of Allegiance: ". . . with liberty and justice for all." "All! All! All!" chanted the Democrats.

Robert Livingston walked to the podium and addressed his remarks to the President: "Sir, you have done great damage to this nation. . . . I say that you have the power to terminate that damage and heal the wounds that you have created. You, sir, may resign your post." The Democrats, already outraged, shouted: "You resign! You resign!"

Livingston continued reading: "I can only challenge you in such fashion that I am willing to heed my own words. But I cannot do that job or be the kind of leader that I would like to be under current circumstances. So I must set the example that I hope President Clinton will follow. I will not stand for Speaker of the House on January sixth." For a moment, everyone was still. Then the Republican leaders jumped up and quickly

*Baker, *The Breach*, pp. 241–42.

escorted Livingston from the chamber. Some Republicans applauded, others cried. "He understood what this debate was all about," DeLay said on the floor, ". . . about relativism versus absolute truth." Livingston had spent the days of his "intended" speakership, as he called it, in fear and trembling.

In the White House, Livingston's resignation came as a bolt from the blue. But we instantly saw it as part of Tom DeLay's strategy to drum up pressure for Clinton's resignation. The President was in the White House Residence. Lockhart ran over, got his remarks, and immediately briefed the press. We could not allow DeLay's strategy to gain the slightest momentum. Clinton, Lockhart explained, had enjoyed working with Livingston, was dismayed by his resignation, and wished he would reconsider. That response closed off DeLay's effort to use Livingston against the White House.

After Lockhart gave the press the President's comments on Livingston, we held another meeting on the State of the Union address, deciding on various social initiatives to be mentioned in it and communicated to the press beforehand. It was business as usual on the most unusual day.

Back at the House, Gephardt delivered a stem-winder: "We are now rapidly descending into a politics where life imitates farce, fratricide dominates our public debate, and America is held hostage to tactics of fear and smear." The Democrats stomped and cheered and wouldn't stop, as if they could forestall the inevitable. When the roll was called on the first article, the Democrats marched out onto the Capitol steps to protest, returning after fifteen minutes to cast their votes. Article I, perjury in the grand jury, passed 228–206. Five members on each side had voted against their party's majority—mostly Southern conservatives defecting from the Democrats, Northern moderates from the Republicans. Then came Article II, perjury in the Jones deposition. Lindsey Graham's eccentric opposition brought 27 other Republicans along to vote against it, and it failed, 229–205. Then, Article III, obstruction of justice, passed 221–212. And, finally, Article IV, on abuse of power, especially in President Clinton's response to Henry Hyde's eighty-one questions, lost 285–148. The President of the United States was impeached.

Dozens of Democratic representatives boarded buses to take them to the White House, where they congregated in the East Room. A number of us on the staff joked that there was no protocol for an impeachment party. The Christmas decorations were up, and soon the White House would be filled every night with cheery throngs. We all milled around under the portraits of George Washington and Dolley Madison, a room-ful of Democrats, not at all mournful, but political people who knew each other, closing ranks by schmoozing.

When the President came in with Hillary, Gephardt spoke: "We will stay with you and fight with you until this madness is over." Vice President Gore had words for the members who had just rejected impeachment: "History will judge you as heroes." Then Clinton came to the microphone. Subdued but sharp, he drew distinctions between Republicans and Democrats, one party seeking power for its own sake, the other seeking to use government for the common good. "That's what this thing is about. It's about power." He added, "I would give anything if you had not been in the position you were in today, and if I had not acted in such a way as to put you there."

Now everyone marched out to the Rose Garden to speak before the media. Gephardt denounced "a partisan vote that was a disgrace to our country and our Constitution." Gore introduced the President: "What happened as a result does a great disservice to a man I believe will be regarded in the history books as one of our greatest presidents." And Clinton spoke: "We must stop the politics of personal destruction. We must get rid of the poisonous venom of excessive partisanship, obsessive animosity, and uncontrolled anger." He called for "one America," took Hillary's hand, and walked into the White House.

I joined them in the outer Oval Office. Betty Currie was taking phone messages. The President started flipping the pages of a newspaper. Hillary and I gave each other a reassuring hug. Clinton grabbed my arm and asked me to come into the Oval Office. He asked me what I thought. I gave him my views on the Republican strategy, on DeLay and his tactics. The Republicans were ruthless, Clinton agreed. They know what they want: power. They don't have another agenda. Their agenda is a means to an end: power. He was sorry about what everybody had been through because of the scandal. He was apologetic that he had given ammunition to our enemies. He was sorry about Lewinsky and the whole thing, but no apologies would be enough. That's not what they're interested in. They want him out because he's there. They can't accept him as president. They never did and never will. This is about nothing except power. After they won the Congress in 1994 and he didn't roll over and die, they wanted him out even more. The more we do, the more they want him out. Everything that's happened to them—losing the midterm election and losing Livingston—they've brought on themselves because they want to destroy him. They don't care if all of them are exposed as hypocrites. They just don't care. They'd sacrifice every Speaker just to try to get rid of him. Because this is just about power.

II

On the afternoon of the impeachment, while the Democrats rallied at the White House thirteen House Managers trooped across the Capitol building to deliver the articles of impeachment to the Senate. The Republican leaders had handpicked them—and there was not a woman, a minority member, or a Democrat among them, nor any moderate Republicans—to represent the breadth and width of conservatism within the Republican Party. Two (Henry Hyde, Charles Canady) were crusaders in the war against abortion. Another one (George Gekas) was noted for his belief in the death penalty. Still another (Bill McCollum) was a passionate opponent of gun control and a partisan of the NRA. Three (Ed Bryant, Steve Chabot, Lindsey Graham) were "revolutionaries" from the Gingrich "class of 1994." There was a wealthy heir to the Kimberly-Clark fortune who was a leading opponent of the ban on assault weapons (James Sensenbrenner); a prominent opponent of environmental policies and a top recipient of funds from timber political action committees (Stephen Buyer); a proponent of antigay legislation who was also the oil industry's advocate for drilling in national parks (Christopher Cannon); and two extremists on social issues across the board (Asa Hutchinson, Bob Barr). Mostly they were provincial politicians from small-town districts; none besides Rogan and Hyde had experience in a large city. The most metropolitan of the bunch was James Rogan, whose political vulnerability gave him a special status within the militant group.

Two days after he was impeached, Clinton's popularity reached 67 percent in the *Washington Post*/ABC News poll.* The festive Christmas parties at the White House went on as planned. At each one, the President and the First Lady stood for hours, as they did every year, to pose for holiday pictures with guests in the Dish Room—a room located between the Diplomatic Reception Room and a portrait gallery of first ladies that exhibits the representative dishware of the presidents since Washington. At the party held for members of Congress, I observed Re-

---

*Richard Morin, "Public Wants Punishment of President, Not Removal," *The Washington Post*, December 21, 1998.

publicans who had voted for impeachment standing patiently and excitedly in line with their wives to have their photographs taken. Merry Christmas!

Throughout the vacation, while the Congress was adjourned, we worked on the State of the Union address. The day after the impeachment the President had held a meeting in the Cabinet Room to discuss how to frame the Social Security debate. Republicans were already pushing a new exorbitant tax cut that would swallow the surplus. In his 1998 State of the Union address, Clinton had declared, "Save Social Security first." Rather than siphoning the surplus to a regressive tax cut, he wanted to make Social Security solvent for decades to come, and he had held public forums across the country on the subject. Now we debated whether to recommend investing a portion of Social Security in the stock market, then in its most bullish phase. Privatizing Social Security by transforming the system into one of private accounts invested in the stock market was a pet Republican scheme. How could it be countered? "Our mission," Gore said, "must be to defeat individual accounts. They would undermine Social Security." Gene Sperling, director of the National Economic Council, laid out various options. Working with the Treasury Department he had devised an ingenious plan for individual accounts that was the diametric opposite of the Republican one: in addition to Social Security, which would remain sacrosanct, every worker would be vested with a private pension, subsidized by tax credits and matching government funds on a highly progressive basis based on income; this plan obviously especially benefited the working poor. On January 6, at another meeting, the President agreed to this plan, "conceptually," he said. He demanded more work on the specifics.

On January 7, 1999, the trial opened with the entrance onto the Senate floor of the House Managers (having first prayed together). Chief Justice Rehnquist was escorted to the podium by an honor guard of senators. He took an oath and swore in the senators in turn, and the House Managers read aloud the articles of impeachment. Watching the ceremonies on television in my office, I talked on the phone with Arthur Schlesinger, Jr. "The whole thing lacks legitimacy," he said. "Two-thirds of the people are against it. The comparative strength of the parties has driven the whole thing." That evening, Clinton's political staff and key cabinet secretaries met with him for a political strategy session. The President concentrated solely on the issues he would talk about in the State of the Union, conducting a long discussion of Social Security.

During these very difficult months, I saw President Clinton in numerous briefings, speech preparations, and meetings. Almost every day we exchanged newspaper and magazine articles we'd marked up about politics, various policy proposals, the political state of play in important foreign countries, and the impeachment—he did this with a number of us on the senior staff. His comments were practical and precise, though sometimes, when he encountered the bizarre charges made by the Clinton-haters, even he could be astonished. On one article, reporting a particularly fantastic claim, he simply wrote, "Amazing."

Two mutually exclusive theories about him gained currency with the media at this time. Either Bill Clinton was too distracted by his impeachment to focus on governing, or he was able to compartmentalize these subjects and live in eerily separate mental worlds. Both were untrue, and there was no actual evidence to support either. If anything, his formidable powers of concentration were sharper than ever. Above all, he understood that the war against him was really a war against his ability to govern. Clinton knew that his strength depended upon his doing his job for the public, and he neglected no area of policy. But he also devoted his attention to the impeachment and the Senate trial, occasionally expressing anger and wonder but always handling the situation as a political crisis, which it was. He didn't make public remarks about how he felt about Starr or DeLay and kept his views private. Throughout the days of the trial, his focus on his public agenda was unwavering and his discipline unvarying.

Senators, being members of the upper body of the legislative branch, consider themselves far above the rabble of the House of Representatives. While there are 435 members of the House, there are only 100 senators, elected for six-year terms, with only one-third standing in any given election. The Senate is far more intimate, clublike, and devoted to its arcane protocol. A month earlier, on December 8, the full Senate had convened purposefully in the Old Senate Chamber for the first time since 1859. Enveloped by their tradition and setting themselves off from the riffraff banging at the door, they discussed how the trial would proceed. Senator Robert Byrd, Democrat of West Virginia, the second oldest member, who filled his floor speeches with references to Roman history and Shakespeare, denounced the House of Representatives as "the black pit of partisan self-indulgence" trading in "salacious muck which has already soiled the gowns of too many." His sentiment that the senators' togas should remain unsoiled was widely shared. A proposal by Senator Slade Gorton, Republican of Washington state, and Senator Joseph Lieberman, Democrat of Connecticut, well expressed that view.

They suggested that the senators simply hear opening statements and vote. If the articles of impeachment failed to receive a two-thirds vote in favor, there would be no trial. But the House Managers had become folk heroes to the Republican minions in the country, and Senate majority leader Trent Lott could not dismiss them so easily.

Many Republican senators regarded the Republican House members as asylum seekers: if the senators could have deported them without anyone noticing, they would have. Tom DeLay, meanwhile, attempted to intimidate senators into removing the President on the same basis that the House had impeached him: the loose material in "the evidence room." He was unabashed in using this tactic. "The reason the House adopted articles of impeachment was due to the overwhelming evidence against the president," he said. "Before people look to cut a deal with the White House or their surrogates who will seek to influence the process, it is my hope that one would spend plenty of time in the evidence room. If this were to happen, you may realize that sixty-seven votes may appear out of thin air. If you don't, you may wish you had before rushing to judgment."* His remark was a thinly disguised threat: *You may wish you had.*

Half a dozen Republican senators agreed to have the House Managers present "the evidence" to them. But the offer was not made to the Democrats, nor was Chief Justice Rehnquist aware of this egregious irregularity. "We had a nine-page presentation," Rogan told me. "It mutated into a private show for senators. I just wanted them to sit down, shut the door, and listen to the evidence." But more than anything else, these shows frightened the senators about the spectacle that the House Managers might make in the Senate. "The senators wanted us to go away and not be there," said Rogan.

The Managers had a frantic, far-fetched strategy: call live witnesses onto the Senate floor before a national television audience, especially Monica Lewinsky; have this show turn public opinion against the President; force him to defend himself by coming onto the Senate floor; and somehow have the roof collapse on him. "The only threat to the Clinton presidency," Rogan told me, "was if we could try the case in a way that changed public opinion. If public opinion changed, I don't think Clinton could have avoided going to the Senate." The strategy had several flaws, not least that every time Clinton appeared in public his poll ratings improved. Rogan, in the event, was charged with being the President's

---

*Juliet Eilperin, "DeLay Warns Senate on Censure," *The Washington Post*, December 24, 1998.

interrogator: "I'd sit up all night preparing to cross-examine President Clinton. But did I think we were going to get witnesses? No."

Hyde, too, demanded live witnesses from the start, having importuned Senator Lott in a December 30 letter claiming that the House of Representatives had such a "constitutional duty" as "the accusatory body." The Managers drew up a plan for calling sixteen witnesses, including Judge Susan Webber Wright in the Jones case, FBI Director Louis Freeh, Dick Morris, Revlon CEO Ronald Perelman, and Kathleen Willey and her lawyer. ("Lindsey Graham was hot on Willey," said Rogan.) On January 6, 1999, Hyde and Schippers had met with Senator Lott, who refused to commit to their elaborate presentation. When Hyde told him the Managers wanted the loose cannon, Schippers, to address the Senate, Lott said, "We can't do that."*

When they learned on January 7 that they would not get their way, the Managers almost decided to walk out. "I took the position we should not proceed in the trial," Rogan told me. "It's a sham trial. It wouldn't be a trial. They were making it impossible for me to make my case. What I wanted us to do was to announce that we were not able to present on behalf of the House. Without live witnesses, they'd vote overwhelmingly not to convict and we'd look like a bunch of assholes. But most of us felt if we walked out we'd look like crybaby schoolboys. It ended up being just three of us—me, Cannon, and Barr. But I think if we'd done it, they would have had to reverse themselves. I don't think Lott would have withstood the demands of Republicans. Lott's base would have burned him down."

The Senate Democrats, for their part, were hostile to the very idea of witnesses. During the impeachment in the House, the Republicans had claimed they needed none. Why did they need witnesses now? Paul Sarbanes, Democrat of Maryland, reflected Democratic sentiment about the Senate as a forum for sexual storytelling: "They didn't call witnesses in the House because they didn't want to be embarrassed with that kind of testimony. But now they say that we have to call witnesses? That's outrageous."†

On January 8, Republican senators met in Lott's conference room with Hyde, Schippers, and the House Managers. Hyde pressed them to review "the evidence." When Senator Ted Stevens, Republican of Alaska, told them, "We'll look goofy," the Managers exploded in anger. Rogan

*Baker, *The Breach*, p. 275.
†Toobin, *A Vast Conspiracy*, p. 371.

told them they had to do exactly as the House Republicans had in coming to impeachment. "We did—why don't you?" said Rogan. "How else can you reach a rational decision on guilt or innocence?" Hyde kept referring to "the evidence." The senators repeatedly said they would not allow "sex" into the Senate. "Henry," said Stevens, "I don't care if you prove he raped a woman and then stood up and shot her dead—you are not going to get sixty-seven votes." "The system doesn't work," Schippers muttered loudly.*

Three days before the Managers were to begin making the case for the prosecution in the Senate, Larry Flynt appeared on a cable television talk show, *Rivera Live* on CNBC, hosted by Geraldo Rivera, and unveiled new information about Bob Barr. "I'm looking to expose the hypocrites," Flynt announced. Barr's second wife, Gail, had signed an affidavit for Flynt stating that Barr had committed adultery and had refused to answer questions about it in their divorce proceeding. The next day Flynt held a press conference to say that Barr, an antiabortion and "family values" advocate, had insisted that his second wife have an abortion, and that he drove her to the clinic and dropped her off there, without even accompanying her inside.

"I've never perjured myself," Barr shot back, and denounced "the politics of personal destruction," declaring that he would not be "discussing our personal lives in any way, shape or form with the news media."†

On January 14, the first Manager to address the Senate was James Sensenbrenner, who pled for live witnesses as "essential to give heightened credence." Hyde had not winnowed his list of presenters, so all the Managers had the chance to speak, and they argued both a repetitive and a diffuse case. The star was Asa Hutchinson, who appeared to have suddenly exposed the irreducible, unexplainable facts that drew the threads of the conspiracy together. On December 11, 1997, he said, Judge Wright allowed women alleged to have had relationships with Clinton to be subpoenaed in the Jones case, and that very day—that very day— Vernon Jordan had intensified his job hunt on behalf of Lewinsky: "The witness list came in. The judge's order came in. That triggered the President to action. And the President triggered Vernon Jordan into action. That chain reaction here is what moved the job search along." Hutchinson's point was acclaimed by the other Managers.

*Schippers, *Sellout*, pp. 21–23.

†Howard Kurtz, "Rep. Barr's Divorce Answers Draw Flynt Fire," *The Washington Post*, January 12, 1999.

Next came Rogan on perjury, then Barr on witness tampering. In the middle of Barr's argument, Senator Thomas Harkin, Democrat of Iowa, decided to object. The senators had been sitting for an eerily long time for them, unable by the rules of the proceeding to wander to the cloak-room or their offices, or to talk on the phone or to each other, or to hold forth as they wished on the floor, now occupied by denizens of the House. "Mr. Chief Justice, I object," said Harkin, "to the use and continued use of the word 'jurors' when referring to the Senate sitting as triers in the trial of the impeaching of the President of the United States." The House Republicans had argued in their peculiar theory of impeachment that the House was a grand jury and the Senate a jury. Now the Chief Justice ruled: "The Chair is of the view that the objection of the Senator from Iowa is well taken. Therefore, counsel should refrain from referring to the senators as jurors." With that, the House Managers' concept of the whole proceeding was dismissed.

They continued, nonetheless: Buyer on obstruction, Graham on why the President should be treated like a federal judge, Canady on why the President's acts were high crimes, Gekas on the Managers' purity of heart, and, finally, Hyde. Back came the Ten Commandments, Mosaic law, and the Magna Carta. Now came nine battles in American history, beginning with Bunker Hill. There were also brand-new non sequiturs: "The families of executed dissidents know that this is about the rule of law—the great alternative to the lethal abuse of power by the state." *The lethal abuse of power?* Had the President killed someone? Hyde read from a letter by a third-grader who suggested the President be punished by writing a hundred-word essay. Hyde described visiting a military cemetery at Normandy and crying. He described Washington's Vietnam Memorial and touching the names engraved on its stones. He evoked "sacred honor." He ended, "My solitary—solitary—hope is that 100 years from today people will look back at what we have done and say, 'They kept the faith.' "

On January 19, Charles Ruff rolled his wheelchair into the well of the Senate to open the President's defense. His presentation benefited, first, from the fiasco in November over the eighty-one questions Hyde had posed to the President. Clinton's lawyers had answered them with keen lawyerly precision albeit heedless of political pitfalls. Ruff knew better than to do that again. Also, the absence of an article of impeachment based on Clinton's Jones deposition, with its confusing definition of "sexual relations," cleared the way for a different defense than the lawyers had mounted in the House. Now it was possible to make a thoroughly factual rebuttal, point by point.

Ruff first exposed the shabby construction of the Managers' case by observing that despite "numerous efforts" on his part to obtain specific charges from the Republicans on the House Judiciary Committee, he had been informed of them only as he was *finishing* his testimony before the committee. Then he addressed the question of witnesses: "The Managers spent much of their time last week explaining to you why, if only witnesses could be called, you would be able to resolve all the supposed conflicts in the evidence. Tell me, then how is it that the Managers can be so certain of the strength of their case? They didn't hear any of these witnesses. The only witness they called, the Independent Counsel himself, acknowledged that he had not even met any of the witnesses who testified before the grand jury. . . . I suggest that what you have before you is . . . the product of nothing more than a rush to judgment."

The "constitutional deficiency" of the articles of impeachment was apparent in their vagueness, he continued, enabling the Managers to use them as "empty vessels, to be filled with some witches' brew of charges considered, charges considered and abandoned and charges never considered at all." By failing to specify the exact charges against the President, the Managers had violated the Sixth Amendment, denying the accused the right to know the accusation he faced. "This is not some mere technicality; it is the law."

Ruff launched into the central part of his defense with an admonition: "Be wary, be wary of the prosecutor who feels it necessary to deceive the court." He quickly dispensed with Article I, perjury in the grand jury, given that the President had admitted in his testimony to an "inappropriate" relationship with Lewinsky. "Now, to conclude that the President lied to the grand jury about his relationship with Ms. Lewinsky, you must determine—forgive me—that he touched certain parts of her body, but for proof you have only her oath against his oath. Those among you who have been prosecutors or criminal defense lawyers know that perjury prosecutions, as rare as they are, would never be pursued on the evidence available here."

On Article II, obstruction of justice, Ruff cited passages of testimony from Betty Currie and Monica Lewinsky, refuting each charge directly on the facts. On the most ludicrous point of this article, he said: "Article II alleges that the President obstructed justice by denying to his closest aides he had a sexual relationship with Monica Lewinsky. . . . These allegedly impeachable denials took place in the immediate aftermath of the public revelation of the Lewinsky matter, at the very time that the

President was denying that relationship to the entire country on national television . . . It is simply absurd, I suggest to you, to believe that he was somehow attempting corruptly to influence the senior staff when he told them virtually the same thing, at the same time."

Then, Ruff came to the obstruction charge that Hutchinson had carefully supported by establishing a time line for "the magic date of December 11." He displayed on an easel the same time line chart that Hutchinson had used and quoted him at length: "Now, it appears to me that the Manager was suggesting—again, with not a great deal of subtlety—that Vernon Jordan, one of this country's great lawyers and great citizens, was prepared to perjure himself to save the President." Ruff staged an interrogatory session with Jordan, providing the questions and answers:

QUESTION: Mr. Jordan, isn't it a fact that you met with Ms. Lewinsky on December 11 to help get her a job?

ANSWER: Yes.

QUESTION: And isn't it a fact that before and after you met with her, you made calls to potential employers in New York?

ANSWER: Yes.

QUESTION: Isn't it true that the reason for all of this activity on December 11 was that Judge Wright had on that very day issued an order authorizing the Jones lawyers to depose certain women like Miss Lewinsky?

ANSWER: No.

QUESTION: What do you mean "no"? Isn't it true that the judge had issued her order before you met with Ms. Lewinsky and before you made the calls?

ANSWER: I had no knowledge of any such order. The fact that Ms. Lewinsky was a potential witness had nothing to do with my helping her. I had made an appointment to see her three days earlier.

QUESTION: Why? Isn't it a fact that Judge Wright filed her order on December 11, before you met with Ms. Lewinsky?

ANSWER: Well, actually no.

QUESTION: Let me show you the official report of the judge's discussion with the lawyers in the Jones case on that date. You have this before you, as well. The conference call between the judge and the lawyers—which is memorialized in a formal document prepared by her clerk and on file in the case in Arkansas—notes that the conference call began at

5:33 p.m., Central Standard Time. If I have my calculations right, that is 6:33 p.m. in Washington.

"By the way, I was"—this is Mr. Jordan testifying again—"I was actually on a plane for Amsterdam by the time the judge issued her order." So he testified in the grand jury. "I left on United flight 946 at 5:55 from Dulles Airport and landed in Amsterdam the next morning."

So the conference call begins at 6:33 Eastern Standard Time and the court takes up another—a variety of matters. And the judge didn't even tell the lawyers that she was going to issue an order on their motion to compel these various depositions until the very end of the call, around 7:45 Eastern Standard Time, and that the clerk would actually fax them a copy at that point.

And so to return to Mr. Jordan's mythical testimony. To summarize, let me show you something that tells you what the real sequence of events was on December 11. Vernon Jordan makes a possible job call at 9:45, another at 12:49, another at 1:07. He meets with Ms. Lewinsky from 1:15 to 1:45. He gets on his plane at 5:55 in the afternoon, and an hour or so later the lawyers are informed that the judge had issued her order.

In fact—just as a little fillip—the President is out of town and returns to Washington at 1:10 a.m. And actually, Judge Wright's order is filed not on the 11th, but on the 12th.

QUESTION: Oh, I see. Well, never mind. . . .

Ruff's elegant and powerful deconstruction had found every fissure in the Managers' case and broken it apart, leaving it the shambles that it was. Ruff's methodical legal argument also revealed more: he exposed the sloppiness and lack of professionalism of the prosecution case. Hutchinson had been sent out with materials that the majority counsel had put in his hands. The Managers' side was betrayed by sheer carelessness, a profound will to believe their own politically inspired speculations, and an unexamined premise that the country shared their hostile assumptions about Clinton. They had not even mastered their own case. With the factual crushing of the prosecution, the Managers were left to demand live witnesses even more vociferously than before.

"We, the people of the United States, have formed a more perfect Union," Ruff concluded. "We formed it. We nurtured it. We have seen it grow. We have not been perfect. And it is perhaps the most extraordinary thing about our Constitution that it thrives despite our human imperfections. When the American people hear the President talk to Congress tonight, they will know the answer to the question, 'Neighbor, how stands the Union?' It stands strong, vibrant, free."

Back in the White House we had been working full bore on the State of the Union for weeks. When we handed the President the first draft right after New Year's, a very long one that would have taken two hours to deliver, he cracked, "Maybe it will come out of our twenty-four hours," which was the time his defense in the Senate trial had been allowed. We cut, pasted, and prepped. On January 13, Michael Waldman, the chief speechwriter; Bob Shrum, the Democratic consultant; Mark Penn, the pollster and strategist; and I reenacted our feat of the previous year, staying up almost all night to produce a polished version.

Once again, the President rehearsed in the family movie theater. As he spoke he added phrases and subtracted others. During these sessions Clinton lifted up and brought into prominence a major economic policy that was implicit in his program but not yet well known. In generating the surplus, the United States was starting to pay down the federal debt, which had quadrupled since Reagan's tax cuts. Paying down the debt had two effects: it freed funds for social programs, specifically ensuring the long-term solvency of Social Security and Medicare; and it did so while allowing the President to realize fiscal discipline. By pointing out that he was dramatically reducing the debt, Clinton was stealing the thunder of rock-ribbed Republicanism and putting it to Democratic uses.

Another significant policy made it into the speech on the day before its delivery. For months, we had been waiting for the Justice Department to conclude its review of a lawsuit that would be filed against the tobacco companies. At last, it was ready. And Clinton decided that all the funds that would be recovered through the suit would be dedicated to the solvency of Medicare.

The White House had none of the tension it had had a year before, when the Lewinsky story had just broken. On the day that his counsel opened his defense in the first Senate trial of a president in 130 years, President Clinton took his motorcade up Pennsylvania Avenue in a confident mood. His only anxiety before he left for the Capitol was whether Rosa Parks, whose refusal to move to the back of a segregated bus in Birmingham, Alabama, had catalyzed the civil rights movement, would be seated in the First Lady's box.

Once on the podium, the President turned to the new Speaker, Dennis Hastert, Republican of Illinois: "Mr. Speaker, at your swearing in you asked us all to work together in the spirit of civility and bipartisanship. Mr. Speaker, let's do exactly that." Clinton extended his hand to a somewhat stunned Hastert, who shook it in return. With that gesture, the President made the politicians seeking to remove him appear petty and zealous. Then he launched directly into his speech, not a defense at all but his explanation of the progress the United States had made under his presidency.

> . . . America has created the longest peacetime economic expansion in our history—with nearly 18 million new jobs, wages rising at more than twice the rate of inflation, the highest homeownership in history, the smallest welfare rolls in 30 years—and the lowest peacetime unemployment since 1957.
>
> For the first time in three decades, the budget is balanced. From a deficit of $290 billion in 1992, we had a surplus of $70 billion last year and now we are on course for budget surpluses for the next 25 years.
>
> Thanks to the pioneering leadership of all of you, we have the lowest violent crime rate in a quarter century and the cleanest environment in a quarter century.
>
> America is a strong force for peace from Northern Ireland, to Bosnia, to the Middle East.
>
> Thanks to the pioneering leadership of Vice President Gore, we have a government for the information age, once again, a government that is a progressive instrument of the common good, rooted in our oldest values of opportunity, responsibility, and community, devoted to fiscal responsibility, determined to give our people the tools they need to make the most of their own lives in the twenty-first century, a twenty-first century government for twenty-first century America.

As the President rolled out his proposals, cheering Democrats greeted each one with roars of approval.

> Now, last year, we wisely reserved all of the surplus until we knew what it would take to save Social Security. Again, I say, we shouldn't spend any of it, not any of it, until after Social Security is truly saved. First things first. Second, once we have saved Social Security, we must fulfill our obligation to save and improve Medicare.

Hastert was unsure of how to react, and he looked to Tom DeLay for direction. When DeLay applauded, Hastert would applaud, and the Republicans would take his cue.

The speech was tightly packed with policy, paragraph after paragraph: new national school standards; funds to modernize five thousand schools; child care; after-school programs; funds for medical research against diseases; a patients' bill of rights; a new tax credit for family leave from work; a dollar increase in the minimum wage; health insurance for disabled people who can work; a five-year training program for upgrading workers' skills; 100,000 federal vouchers for affordable housing for the poor; funds for community development banks to spur investment in neglected neighborhoods and regions.

With each announcement, the Republicans became grimmer and more disconcerted. The cameras were on them. Were they applauding? Now they were the ones on trial, not Clinton—and Clinton sensed it. "And let's make sure that women and men get equal pay for equal work by strengthening enforcement of the equal pay laws." The Republicans had to clap. "That was encouraging, you know," Clinton said, extending his arms like wings to encompass the whole chamber. "There was more balance on the seesaw. I like that. Let's give 'em a hand! Give 'em—that was great." He was floating like a butterfly, stinging like a bee. The Democrats were gleeful, the Republicans sullen.

The President took special time to address the controversy over trade that had led to the defeat of Fast Track the year before:

> I think trade has divided us and divided Americans outside this chamber for too long. Somehow we have to find a common ground on which business and workers, and environmentalists, and farmers and government can stand together. . . . When you come right down to it, now that the world economy is becoming more and more integrated, we have to do in the world what we spent the better part of this century doing here at home—we have got to put a human face on the global economy.

And he advocated a new round of international negotiations to drop tariffs, strengthen enforcement against dumping of foreign goods in U.S. markets, and promote transparency in international economic institutions and new labor standards:

> Tonight I say we will work with the International Labor Organization on a new initiative to raise labor standards around the world. And this year, we will lead the international community to conclude a treaty to ban abusive child labor everywhere in the world.

Clinton then warned of the threat of terrorism, specifically from Osama bin Laden:

> As we work for peace, we must also meet threats to our nation's security, including increased dangers from outlaw nations and terrorism. We will defend our security wherever we are threatened, as we did this summer when we struck at Osama bin Laden's network of terror. The bombing of our embassies in Kenya and Tanzania reminds us again of the risks faced every day by those who represent America to the world.

And he spoke of Operation Desert Fox, the bombing of Iraq's weapons factories, and of his continuing policy against Saddam Hussein: "For nearly a decade, Iraq has defied its obligations to destroy its weapons of terror and the missiles to deliver them. America will continue to contain Saddam, and we will work for the day when Iraq has a government worthy of its people."

Clinton urged payment of America's United Nations dues, long blocked by Senator Jesse Helms, and asked the Senate to ratify the Comprehensive Nuclear Test Ban Treaty, which the Republicans were determined to kill, as they soon would. He pleaded for an extension of gun control legislation—and for trigger locks that would make it hard for children to use guns. He proposed billion-dollar funds for expanding natural spaces and conservation; he protected more land in the lower forty-eight states than any other president. He urged the expansion of AmeriCorps, the domestic version of the Peace Corps that had been created on his initiative in 1993; it had already given more than 150,000 people the chance to serve local communities while earning money for college or for skills-training programs—more volunteers than in the Peace Corps' first twenty years. And he once again asked the Congress to pass campaign finance reform, which the last Congress had defeated.

Clinton introduced Rosa Parks when he got to the part of his speech calling for new laws against employment discrimination, a Hate Crimes Prevention Act, and new programs to assist immigrants. In a wheelchair, she could not rise to greet the applause, but the woman who in 1955 refused to stand and let a white man take her seat on a segregated bus, and who now in 1998 was seated next to the First Lady, waved.

Back at the White House, a couple hundred staff members and friends of the Clintons watched on large-screen television, and when President Clinton returned from the Capitol he was wildly greeted. Congressmen and senators poured in after him. He spoke animatedly with knots of people eager to press upon him their good wishes, moving around the room to talk politics and policy. The instant poll numbers arrived: more than 80 percent approval! In the Red Room, beneath the bust of Martin Van Buren, the first president to come from New York, Hillary was surrounded by Charles Rangel from Harlem and other New Yorkers who were urging her to run for the U.S. Senate. They covered her with flattery as she laughingly demurred but did not refuse.

The next morning, the defense of the President continued in the Senate. Gregory Craig systematically dissected the perjury charges of Article I. He demonstrated their vagueness, falsity, lack of corroboration, the subparts that had already been dismissed by the Independent Counsel, and the Managers' deliberate confusions of Clinton's depositions in the Jones case and to the grand jury—a "double charging."

> But the most striking thing about Article I is what it does not say. It alleges perjury generally, but it does not allege a single perjurious statement specifically. . . . Imagine a murder indictment without identifying a victim. . . . But this requirement is even more stringent for perjury prosecutions. Descriptions, paraphrases, summaries of testimony that is alleged to be perjurious are not acceptable. . . . The allegations are frequently trivial, almost always technical, often immaterial and always insubstantial.

At its strongest, the charge of perjury depended upon the different accounts Lewinsky and Clinton had given about where he had touched her: "She says one thing, he says another. This is precisely the kind of oath against oath swearing match that is never prosecuted in the real world."

Cheryl Mills, White House deputy legal counsel, followed Craig with a further defense on the obstruction-of-justice charge. Earlier, in his shambling faux-folksy manner, Lindsey Graham had accused the President of violating the civil rights of Paula Jones and other women, a comment that, coming from a reactionary South Carolinian attempting to topple a president beloved by blacks, had a clear, implicit political point. Cheryl, a young black woman herself, was highly conscious of the text of her brief—and its subtext.

> Over the course of the House Managers' presentation last week, I confess I was struck by how often they referred to the significance of the rule of

law. House Manager Sensenbrenner, for example, quoted President Theodore Roosevelt, stating, "No man is above the law and no man is below it."

As a lawyer, as an American, and as an African-American, it is a principle in which I believe to the very core of my being. It is what many have struggled and died for, the right to be equal before the law, without regard to race or gender or ethnicity, disability, privilege, or station in life. The rule of law applies to the weak and the strong, the rich and the poor, the powerful and the powerless. If you love the rule of law, you must love it in all of its applications. You cannot only love it when it provides the verdict you seek, you must love it when the verdict goes against you as well. We cannot uphold the rule of law only when it is consistent with our beliefs, we must uphold it even when it protects behavior that we don't like or is unattractive or is not admirable or that might even be hurtful. And we cannot say we love the rule of law but dismiss arguments that appeal to the rule of law as legalisms or legal hairsplitting.

I say all this because not only the fact, but the law of obstruction of justice protects the President. It does not condemn him.

"Piece by piece," as she put it, she demolished Article II, factually refuting each false implication and distortion about the President's gifts to Lewinsky and his conversations with Betty Currie. She cited both Lewinsky's and Currie's grand-jury testimonies, which exonerated Clinton on every point. What the House Managers had produced was "conjecture about the President's state of mind" that was the opposite of its reality.

Mills was not going to end there. She removed the artifice from the proceedings in her person and by her words, making plain the American dilemma that was at the heart of the trial of Bill Clinton:

Before I close, I do want to take a moment to address a theme that the House Managers sounded throughout their presentation last week: civil rights. They suggested that by not removing the President from office, the entire house of civil rights might well fall.

While acknowledging that the President is a good advocate for civil rights, they suggested that they had grave concerns because of the President's conduct in the Paula Jones case. And some Managers suggested that we all should be concerned should the Senate fail to convict the President, because it will send a message that our civil rights laws and our sexual harassment laws are unimportant.

I can't let their comments go unchallenged. I speak as but one woman, but I know I speak for others as well. I know I speak for the President.

Bill Clinton's grandfather owned a store. His store catered primarily to African Americans. . . . And he taught his grandson that the African Americans who came into his store were good people, and they worked hard, and they deserved a better deal in life. The President has taken his grandfather's teachings to heart and he has worked every day to give all of us a better deal, an equal deal.

I'm not worried about the future of civil rights. I'm not worried because Ms. Jones had her day in court and Judge Wright determined that all of the matters we are discussing here today were not material to her case, and ultimately decided that Ms. Jones, based on the facts and the law in that case, did not have a case against the President.

I'm not worried because we've had imperfect leaders in the past and we'll have imperfect leaders in the future. But their imperfections did not roll back nor did they stop the march for civil rights and equal opportunity for all of our citizens. Thomas Jefferson, Frederick Douglass, Abraham Lincoln, John F. Kennedy, Martin Luther King, Jr.—we revere these men. We should. But they were not perfect men. They made human errors. But they struggled to do humanity good.

I'm not worried about civil rights, because this president's record on civil rights, on women's rights, on all of our rights is unimpeachable.

Ladies and gentlemen of the Senate, you have an enormous decision to make. And in truth, there is little more I can do to lighten that burden, but I can do this. I can assure you that your decision to follow the facts and the law and the Constitution and acquit this president will not shake the foundation of the house of civil rights.

The house of civil rights is strong because its foundation is strong. And with all due respect, the foundation of the house of civil rights was never at the core of the Jones case. It was never at the heart of the Jones case. The foundation of the house of civil rights is in the voices of all the great civil rights leaders and the soul of every person who heard them. . . . The foundation of the house of civil rights is in all of us who gathered up our will, to raise it up and keep on building. . . .

I stand here before you today because President Bill Clinton believed I could stand here for him. Your decision whether to remove President Clinton from office, based on the articles of impeachment, I know will be based on the law and the facts and the Constitution. It would be wrong to convict him on this record. You should acquit him on this record. And you must not let imagined harms to the house of civil rights persuade you otherwise.

The next day, David Kendall set up the charts the Managers had been displaying to show Clinton's alleged crimes and exposed them as "riddled with errors" and based on a "strained theory." Again and again, he quoted Lewinsky's testimony: "No one ever asked me to lie, and I was never promised a job for my silence." Kendall asked: "Is there something difficult to understand here?" Once again, he destroyed Congressman Hutchinson's notion of a conspiracy between the President and Vernon Jordan involving Lewinsky's getting a job: "Quid pro quo, no." Kendall repeated the phrase again and again. He made it clear that the Managers' case not only had no direct evidence but didn't even have circumstantial evidence either. He reduced the impeachment case to dust.

But the defense was not yet finished. The methodical case for President Clinton was concluded with an oratorical tour de force. Dale Bumpers, who had just retired as the senior senator from Arkansas, took the floor. He had known Bill Clinton since the moment the younger man had burst upon the political scene:

> Colleagues, I come here with some sense of reluctance. The President and I have been close friends for twenty-five years. We've fought so many battles back home together in our beloved Arkansas, we tried mightily all of my years as governor and his, and all of my years in the Senate when he was governor, to raise the living standards in the Delta area of Mississippi, Arkansas and Louisiana where poverty is unspeakable, with some measure of success, not nearly enough. We tried to provide health care for the lesser among us, for those who are well-off enough they can't get on welfare, but not making enough to buy health insurance. We have fought, above everything else, to improve the educational standards for a state that for so many years was at the bottom of the list or near the bottom of the list of income, and we have stood side-by-side to save beautiful, pristine areas in our state from environmental degradation. . . .
>
> So if Bill Clinton the man, Bill Clinton the friend were the issue here, I'm quite sure I would not be doing this. But it is the weight of history on all of us, and it is my reverence for that great document, you heard me rail about it for twenty-four years, that we call our Constitution, the most sacred document to me next to the Holy Bible. . . .

"Ah, colleagues, you have such an awesome responsibility," he said, appealing to the senators' sense of their institution and its duties.

He then described a woman who had been pulled into the Independent Counsel's dragnet and had run up hundreds of thousands of dollars in legal bills. The senators were men and women of high honor. Starr's investigation had set before them no crimes, only a squalid tale:

> But after all of those years and $50 million—of Whitewater, Travelgate, Filegate, you name it—nothing, nothing, the President was found guilty of nothing, official or personal.
>
> You're here today because the President suffered a terrible moral lapse, a marital infidelity, not a breach of the public trust, not a crime against society, the two things Hamilton talked about in Federalist Paper number 65—I recommend it to you before you vote—but it was a breach of his marriage vows.
>
> It was a breach of his family trust. It is a sex scandal. H. L. Mencken said one time, "When you hear somebody say, 'This is not about money,' it's about money."

The senators joined in laughter. But this was not Bumpers's punch line; it was his setup. As a friend of the Clinton family, Senator Bumpers for the first time in the trial put the scandal in human terms:

> And when you hear somebody say, "This is not about sex," it's about sex.
>
> You pick your own adjective to describe the President's conduct. Here are some that I would use: indefensible, outrageous, unforgivable, shameless. I promise you the President would not contest any of those or any others.
>
> But there is a human element in this case that has not even been mentioned, and that is the President and Hillary and Chelsea are human beings. This is intended only as a mild criticism of our distinguished friends in the House, but as I listened to the presenters—to the Managers make their opening statements, they were remarkably well prepared, and they spoke eloquently. More eloquent than I really had hoped.
>
> But when I talk about the human element, I talk about what I thought was, on occasion, unnecessarily harsh and pejorative descriptions of the President. I thought that the language should have been tempered somewhat to acknowledge that he is the president. To say constantly that the President lied about this and lied about that, as I say, I thought that was

too much for a family that has already been about as decimated as a family can get.

The relationship between husband and wife, father and child, has been incredibly strained, if not destroyed. There's been nothing but sleepless nights, mental agony, for this family for almost five years, day after day, from accusations of having assassinated, or had Vince Foster assassinated, on down. It has been bizarre.

But I didn't sense any compassion, and perhaps none is deserved.

Bumpers addressed Clinton's motive for his misleading words and conduct:

Why would he do that? Well, he knew this whole affair was about to bring unspeakable embarrassment and humiliation on himself, his wife whom he adored, and a child that he worshipped with every fiber in his body and for whom he would happily have died to spare her this or to ameliorate her shame and her grief.

The House Managers have said shame and embarrassment is no excuse for lying. Well, the question about lying, that's your decision. But I can tell you, you put yourself in his position, and you've already had this big moral lapse, as to what you would do.

We are none of us perfect. Sure, you say, he should have thought of all that beforehand. And indeed he should, just as Adam and Eve should have. Just as you and you and you and you, and millions of other people who have been caught in similar circumstances, should have thought of it before.

Clinton the man had suffered his fall, but the zealous Managers were guilty, Bumpers explained, of another sin: "I'll tell you what it is: It's wanting to win too badly. . . . There's a total lack of proportionality, a total lack of balance in this thing. The charge and the punishment are totally out of sync."

Bumpers recounted the history of the impeachment provision in the Constitution and Hamilton's cautionary words against its abuse by partisans.

Mr. Chairman, we've also learned that the rule of law includes presidential elections. That's a part of the rule of law in this country. . . . It is a solemn event, presidential elections, and it should not—they should not be undone lightly, or just because one side has the clout and the other one doesn't.

With that, Bumpers pivoted to turn on Congressman Hyde's abstract invocation of military battlefields and patriotic symbolism. He did this in order to separate the senators from the House of Representatives, the House Managers from the country, and patriotism from serving as an ideological refuge. He pointed to his colleagues in the chamber: Senator Daniel Inouye—

He left an arm in Italy. . . . I think his relatives were in an internment camp, so ask him what he was fighting for. Or ask Bob Kerrey, certified Medal of Honor winner, what was he fighting for. You'll probably get a quite different answer. Or Senator [John] Chafee, one of the finest men ever to grace this body and certified marine hero of Guadalcanal—ask him. And Senator McCain, a genuine hero—ask him. You don't have to guess. They're with us, and they're living.

And then he closed:

The people have a right, and they are calling on you to rise above politics, rise above partisanship. They're calling on you to do your solemn duty. And I pray you will.

All the senators rose to applaud but one—Senator Inouye, who sat weeping and pounding his arm on his chair.

Senator Robert Byrd, the one figure whom we in the White House feared most as a potential defector, walked over to shake hands with Bumpers. He patted Greg Craig and Cheryl Mills, at the counsels' table, saying, "You did a good job for your client." The next morning, he issued a press release: "Statement by U.S. Senator Robert C. Byrd—A Call for Dismissal of the Charges and End of the Trial." His motion was the signal that the battle had been won. But the trial was far from over.

III

The President was very likely to be acquitted, yet the show trial had to go on. The whole year 1998 had been marked by show trials—trial by

media, trial by grand jury, now the grandest show trial of all. Bob Barr
had insisted there were two Americas, one "real" and one false. Tom De-
Lay had proclaimed that impeachment was "about relativism versus absolute truth." Henry Hyde had summoned every symbol he could in
defense of "honor" and the past. Through Clinton these Republicans believed they could bury the 1960s, politically and culturally. This was the
show trial of their culture war.

The House Managers, having been outlawyered, outmaneuvered, and
outclassed, had become more desperate than ever. Their sense of embat-
tlement, embarrassment, and embitterment intensified, and they fell back
once again on demanding live witnesses. They also had one other far-
fetched hope. Under Tom DeLay's watchful whip, the House Republican
Conference had been marshaled into "the evidence room" and then out
in lockstep to vote for impeachment. If only, the Managers believed, the
horrors in that vault could be sprung on the public, it would recoil from
Clinton. On January 22, the day after Bumpers's speech, Senator Lott,
asked by a reporter what might derail the President's likely acquittal, remarked obliquely, "That depends on what NBC broadcasts on Sunday."
He was referring to an interview that had been conducted by an NBC
correspondent, Lisa Myers, with Juanita Broaddrick, whose story Matt
Drudge was trumpeting.

Matt Drudge had begun the season of the Senate trial for himself by
pushing the old tale that Clinton had had an illegitimate black son by a
prostitute. At a New Year's Eve gathering of conservatives called the
Weekend (formerly called the Dark Ages Weekend, intended as a counter-
point to the Renaissance Weekend retreat that the Clintons often attended), he entertained the crowd with the sensational story, which he
promised would end Clinton's presidency. This racist invention had an ancient provenance in Southern politics, having been rolled out against progressive politicians from time immemorial. In Arkansas, it had been used
against Governor Winthrop Rockefeller, and it came up again during the
1992 Democratic primaries. Now, on January 1, 1999, the *Drudge Report*
blared, "WHITE HOUSE HIT WITH NEW DNA TERROR; TEEN TESTED FOR
CLINTON PATERNITY." A tabloid, the *Star*, was behind this ruckus, he
wrote: "Word of the shocking new DNA showdown spread through the
ranks inside of the White House on Friday, causing near blind chaos!" On
January 3, Rupert Murdoch's *New York Post* headlined on its front page:
"CLINTON PATERNITY BOMBSHELL." On January 4, Fox News carried the
item on its website. On January 5, late-night comedians weighed in. "Only
President Clinton could distract people from a sex scandal with another

sex scandal," Jay Leno, host of NBC's *Tonight Show*, cracked in his opening monologue. On January 6, Drudge claimed he had seen "a shocking new videotaped confession" by the black prostitute. "Media Abuzz with Rumors That Clinton Fathered Boy," headlined *The Washington Times*, citing Drudge and the *Star*. However, on January 9, *Time* magazine reported that the DNA test in fact proved that Clinton was not the boy's father. An unapologetic Drudge set the stage for the next round: "And while the elite media will bark that it was wrong to report the DNA chase that was unfolding behind the scenes—until after it is all over, of course—Drudge Report readers of all stripes have come to expect details on events rocking and shocking those unfortunate souls who rise to power!"*

On January 25, Drudge promoted vague innuendos about Juanita Broaddrick's story: "NBC HOLDING INTERVIEW WITH 'JANE DOE'; WHITE HOUSE PRESSURE HAS NETWORK BRASS ON PAUSE, SAY SOURCES." Three days later, he continued the drumbeat: " 'JANE DOE' INTERVIEW CAUSES DEEP SPLIT INSIDE OF NBC; BROADDRICK FEELS 'BETRAYED' AFTER NETWORK PUTS STORY ON ICE." Don Imus, a radio talk-show host, asked Tim Russert, NBC's Washington bureau chief, about this: "So, are you people at NBC News sitting on this Lisa Myers interview with Juanita Broaddrick?" "This is one of the most amazing stories that I've ever been involved in, because it just hit the Internet, and hit talk radio," said Russert. "The answer is very simple. If we honestly had a buttoned-up bombshell, we would go with it in a flash." Soon lapel buttons appeared as a fashionable accessory among Republicans: FREE LISA MYERS. Senator Charles Grassley, Republican of Iowa, took to wearing one as he sat in judgment on the Senate floor.

The two days of January 23 and 24 had been reserved in the Senate trial schedule for questions from senators. Democratic senators Herb Kohl of Wisconsin and John Edwards of North Carolina asked: "Even if the President engaged in the alleged conduct, can reasonable people disagree with the conclusion that, as a matter of law, he must be convicted and removed from office—yes or no?"

Congressman Lindsey Graham leaped up to answer: "Absolutely!" His response, giving permission for the senators to vote to acquit, threw the House Managers into a state of consternation. Graham rambled on, refusing to allow the others who were trying to shut him up to speak. "In a second," he said to his distraught colleagues.

---

*J. D. Lasica, "A Cybersleaze Timeline: Anatomy of a Smear," *Online Journalism Review*, January 11, 1999, http://ojr.org/ojr/ethics/1017969295.php.

Ruff seized the floor: "Mr. Chief Justice, this is something I won't have an opportunity to say very often, but I believe that Mr. Manager Graham has, in fact, stated for you the essential of the role that this body must play." For the rest of the day, the Managers tried to put the genie back in the bottle by offering different definitions of "reasonable people."

While this lifeless debate plodded on in the Senate, at the federal courthouse in Washington the House Managers were arguing another case. David Schippers, on his own, had asked Starr's office to intervene and somehow force Monica Lewinsky to submit to an interview with the House Managers. By this gambit, they hoped to set in motion a chain reaction that would lead to the calling of live witnesses in the Senate. Starr readily agreed. His function had not ended, after all. By delivering Lewinsky to the House Managers under her immunity agreement, he was giving his last assistance to their cause. Judge Johnson granted Starr's motion, and Lewinsky was ordered to talk.

On January 24, three Managers—Hutchinson, McCollum, and Bryant—trooped to the presidential suite at the Mayflower Hotel, where Lewinsky was staying. "All of a sudden this whole impeachment thing is back on my shoulders," she told the ghostwriter of her memoir, Andrew Morton. "It's not my fault that there's not really a case here."* The Managers tried to ingratiate themselves with her. Seeking common ground, Bryant compared his own recent brush with celebrity with hers. "Having just been through that, I can't imagine going through that the way you have," he said. They left convinced she had warmed to them. But according to Peter Baker of *The Washington Post*, "she and her lawyers were contemptuous."† Many Republican senators, seeing Lewinsky headed toward their sanctum sanctorum, were near panic.

That day, the Senate voted on Byrd's measure: "The Senator from West Virginia, Mr. Byrd, moves that the impeachment proceedings against William Jefferson Clinton, President of the United States, be, and the same are, duly dismissed." All fifty-five Republicans, and one Democrat, the idiosyncratic Russ Feingold of Wisconsin, voted against the motion. However impatient they may have been for the trial to end, they could not offend their base. But the vote demonstrated that there would not be sixty-seven votes to remove President Clinton from office.

On January 25, another motion to dismiss, made by the President's defense, was defeated. In the debate on that motion, Henry Hyde expressed

*Quoted in Baker, *The Breach*, p. 346.
†Ibid., p. 350.

the Managers' hurt feelings: "I sort of feel that we have fallen short in the respect side because of the fact that we represent the House, the other body, kind of blue collar people, and we are trying to survive with our impeachment articles." Hyde's scorn for the Republican senators who were trying to distance themselves from the House Republicans prompted him to question their patriotism. "I'm glad they weren't at Valley Forge or the Alamo," he remarked as he walked into a Managers' meeting.

Ruff, closely reviewing recent statements made by Congressman Hutchinson, realized that Hutchinson could have learned that the Jones lawyers had put Betty Currie on their witness list for subpoena only by improper collusion, since there was still an enforced court-ordered seal on everything to do with the Jones case. Ruff sent a brisk letter to the Chief Justice asking for guidance, but Rehnquist declined to reply. Hutchinson was obviously in contempt of the Arkansas court ruling, but Ruff decided to withhold this information, perhaps for later deployment; he never did use it.

Now, the House Managers again publicly asked for witnesses. In fact, Hyde had already struck a deal with Lott that they would be granted a sop: three witnesses, whose testimony would be taken first in videotaped depositions held off the Senate floor. Whether or not live witnesses would appear before the full Senate was still an open question. On January 26, the motion was debated, though the outcome was a foregone conclusion. David Kendall spoke for the President's defense against the motion:

> First, they filed the charges, which have been spoon fed by Mr. Starr. They don't bother to check these out; they take them at face value, and now they finally want to talk to the witnesses, and they again use Mr. Starr to threaten Ms. Lewinsky with imprisonment unless she cooperates with them. . . .
>
> The House Managers are like the character in *David Copperfield*, Mr. Micawber, who was always hoping that something would turn up. They continue to hope that something will turn up for them. They don't know what it is, but they believe they will know it when they see it and they hope if, for the first time in these proceedings they actually talk to the witnesses on whom they have relied, they will find something to persuade you to overcome the evidence in the record.

Kendall paused and then remarked, "Now, I don't want to be uncharitable to the House Managers—" and before he could complete his sentence the entire Senate spontaneously burst into laughter. The Managers had no case, but they would have witnesses. The witnesses had been announced even before Kendall spoke, and the Senate voted two days later in favor of calling them, on a straight party-line vote: 54–44.

I was watching the Senate trial on television with Steve Richetti in his office when the names of the witnesses were flashed on the screen: Monica Lewinsky, Vernon Jordan, and Sidney Blumenthal. Betty Currie boogied down the hall from the Oval Office with a wide smile on her face. "Free at last! Free at last!" She pointed at me. "Congratulations," I said. "Congratulations," she replied. She gave me a big kiss. On a split screen suddenly appeared pictures of the three witnesses to be called alongside a shot of the Pope, landing that day in St. Louis, Missouri. Hillary, who was on her way to see the Pope, called me to say, "It's an honorable feat [being subpoenaed]. I'm seeing the Pope. He has a different agenda."

I telephoned a Republican friend of mine who was well connected to the House Managers and who, from time to time, discreetly gave me information. He underscored the Managers' strategy: "They want to shove it onto the Senate floor. They think they can do it with you. That's all they've got." The plan was to force Lewinsky into the well of the Senate, using my grand-jury testimony as the foil to upset her, and hoping against hope that then they could get her to cry over her treatment at the hands of the President, which would arouse hatred toward Clinton.

That morning, *The Wall Street Journal* had run a lead editorial headlined "The 'Stalker,' " demanding that I be called as a witness. It laid out what my Republican friend had confirmed:

> For a jobless 25-year-old, Monica Lewinsky sure is terrifying. She's so scary she has managed to unite President Clinton and some Senate Republicans in trying to short-circuit their trial to keep her off the impeachment stage. . . . The value of her testimony has nothing to do with sex. . . . They [House Republicans] want to talk about obstruction of justice, among other things what she thought when she learned that the President she loved had told aide Sidney Blumenthal she was a "stalker" who had "threatened him."
>
> This line, we now know, was vital to the Clinton cover-up. . . . And we know that not long after the President's "stalker" remarks to Mr. Blumenthal on Jan. 21, 1998, media reports began to appear that attacked Ms. Lewinsky. . . . This is ugly stuff, turning consensual sex into a predatory cover-up. Monica is lucky she saved that dress; without Bill Clinton's DNA this would be the White House line today. . . .
>
> All of this is directly relevant to the obstruction case, and is why wit-

nesses including Mr. Blumenthal should be called. Monica's testimony in particular would be an O.J. verdict moment, the one time when just about everyone in America would be watching TV. It is the one event that could change public opinion. Democrats—especially Senate women who make an issue of sex harassment—want these facts swept away before that happens.*

The Managers of course had to have Lewinsky and Jordan as witnesses. Betty Currie would have been the natural third witness, if three were all they were to be allowed. But, Jim Rogan told me later, "The senators told us that it'd look like you're beating up on black people." So they named me as the third and final witness. To the House Managers, I was the devil at Satan's right hand. Just as they believed in their fantasy identity as warriors, they believed in their fantasy of the evil Bill Clinton in his evil White House. They had lost the midterm elections, watched two Speakers resign in ignominy, and listened to an immensely popular president deliver an acclaimed State of the Union address. But they still wanted Americans to believe that Clinton was a merciless godfather who preyed upon women and then ordered his consigliere to do the dirty work of shutting the women up—or else. That had been the theory behind the Jones case, which had failed; behind the theory of Starr's sex hunts disguised as searches for obstructions of justice, which were never found; behind "the evidence room"; and now, transmuted reductio ad absurdum, behind the "stalker" issue.

Starr, who had not recovered from the political effect of my remarks on the courthouse steps excoriating him, a month before the impeachment began had gotten his office to help reconstruct his image by trashing me as a liar. Starr went at me through an "ethics adviser" to his staff, Ronald Rotunda, a conservative law professor at the University of Illinois who had been hired (at $300 an hour) to trump the increasingly unpredictable Sam Dash. Articles suddenly appeared in the right-wing press claiming I had never been questioned in the grand jury about my media contacts—a grotesquely ridiculous claim on its face—and including a distorted reference to the chairwoman of the grand jury who had admonished me about my supposed misrepresentations on the courthouse steps, the statements that in fact my lawyer had made, and made accurately.

A *New York Post* editorial began a smear campaign—"Sidney Blumenthal Exposed": ". . . The White House's premier sleazemeister now

*Editorial, "The 'Stalker,' " *The Wall Street Journal*, January 26, 1999.

stands exposed before the entire nation as an unmitigated liar."* The *Wall Street Journal* editorial page held forth: "Who can forget Mr. Blumenthal's own oratory as he stood outside the courthouse after his grand jury appearance, proclaiming shock at the violations of his First Amendment rights he had allegedly just endured? . . . Mr. Blumenthal's version of events was . . . at odds with the truth."† ABC News broadcast the same story. Finally, Starr's office, in the person of Professor Rotunda, stepped from behind the curtain. "Everybody in this office knew since last February that Sid Blumenthal was lying, but that never leaked," he told the *New York Post*.‡ My lawyer, Bill McDaniel, wrote sharply first to Starr and then to the Justice Department asking for an investigation of this ludicrous remark: "These statements made by Mr. Rotunda, a paid advisor to you [Starr], are false in every particular." With the letters, this round of innuendo stopped.

When Lindsey Graham began his promotion of the "stalker" issue on December 9 in the House Judiciary Committee, Charles Ruff wrote him a sharp letter refuting his false claims, but Graham continued his pitch on every television and radio talk show that would give him airtime. Ruff was disgusted by these antics, and with his permission I told *The State*, a newspaper in Graham's native South Carolina, "I deserve an apology from Lindsey Graham for his dishonorable, false statement, but I don't expect one." He whined about this in a letter to Ruff, which he also released to conservative media, complaining about the "personal attack" on him.§ Ruff replied in a private letter on December 17: "With all due respect, I do not believe that Mr. Blumenthal acted inappropriately. . . . It was not some unattributed remark intended as a 'personal attack.' It was a request for an apology by one who felt that he had been wronged."

One hope the House Republicans continued to have was that an aide would emerge from the White House to squeal against President Clinton or reveal a hitherto unknown detail of his horrible crimes, just as John Dean had turned into a witness against President Nixon. They hoped I would be a kind of Dean analogue. "Without Nixon-style tape

---

*Editorial, "Sidney Blumenthal Exposed," *New York Post*, October, 6, 1998.

†Dorothy Rabinowitz, "True and False," *The Wall Street Journal*, October 30, 1998.

‡Brian Blomquist, "Starr Staffer Blasts Clinton Aides," *New York Post*, November 15, 1998.

§Deroy Murdock, "We Have Ways to Make You Vote," *The Washington Times*, December 17, 1998.

recordings or a John Dean informer," wrote Robert Novak, who was close to Lindsey Graham, "it can only be speculated whether Blumenthal—a former journalist with a penchant for secretly investigating Clinton's adversaries—triggered the Lewinsky smear."* And they also hoped that I would frighten Lewinsky. "Here's what I want to know," said Congressman Graham on ABC's *This Week* on January 24. "When the President told Mr. Blumenthal, you know, she's threatening me . . . I want to ask how she felt about those statements being made about her, how she felt about what was coming out in the press when people thought maybe she's a little unstable, she's a little overweight, she comes from a broken home. I'd like to ask her how she felt about that."

Now, on January 26, having been named as a witness, I read through every published article from January and February 1998 that I could find in the databases on Monica Lewinsky as a "stalker" and prepared a memo for my own and the White House lawyers:

> There is no evidence whatsoever that the White House was directing or involved in any campaign against her. The evidence, however, does prove that the description of her as a "stalker," "a clutch," and "obsessed" was commonly used by the media, her former lover, her friends, and her attorney. This was deliberately overlooked by the Republicans, as they sought to cast a false light on the White House. It is clear that they decided they would not present articles that showed others describing Lewinsky in the terms the Republicans insist came from the White House. They could make their accusation only by distorting the stream of media reportage. Yet they still failed to produce any evidence.

The House Managers were counting on the scary persona of me that they had created. How wicked was I? It was hard to tell. A week earlier, the Reverend Jerry Falwell announced, "Who will the Antichrist be? . . . Of course he'll be Jewish. . . . If he's going to be the counterfeit of Christ, he has to be Jewish. The only thing we know is he must be male and Jewish."†

I fitted their stereotypes. They didn't know me, but from every reasonable surmise, they could observe that I was Eastern educated, a 1960s

---

*Robert Novak, "The Troubled-Girl Defense," *The Washington Post*, December 14, 1998.

†Quoted in Sonja Barisic, "Falwell: Antichrist May Be Alive," Associated Press, January 16, 1999.

graduate, from the liberal media, Jewish, intellectual—and they believed I was guilty of practicing black political arts against them. For all they knew Drudge was right about me—and *The Wall Street Journal*, too. Why shouldn't they believe all those newspaper articles?

Then the subpoena, signed by Chief Justice Rehnquist, arrived:

Greeting:

You and each of you are hereby commanded to appear before the Senate of the United States, on the third day of February, 1999, at 9:00 o'clock a.m., for a deposition to be taken before two Members of the United States Senate appointed pursuant to Senate Resolution 30, One Hundred Sixth Congress, First Session, at Room S-407, The Capitol, in the city of Washington, then and there to testify to your knowledge in the case which is before the Senate in which the House of Representatives have impeached William Jefferson Clinton, President of the United States.

Fail not.

But the next morning when I woke up, far too early, I realized that I had to do more than tell the truth about the media coverage of Monica Lewinsky. I had to shatter the evil stereotype of me. For almost a year I had wondered which of my traits had invited this invective, but now this question didn't interest me anymore. I had more pressing things to attend to.

I knew that perjury traps would be set for me. I knew that I would be asked about my grand-jury testimony. And I knew that if I deviated from it, I would open myself to perjury charges. Jackie and I sat up a whole night at our kitchen table drilling. She read the prosecutors' lines, and if I missed my own lines she would repeat them until I got it exactly right.

I spent every day with my lawyers and with Lanny Breuer, who was now assigned to me full time. Lanny was extremely thoughtful, assiduous, and not given to histrionics. Also—and very important for me—he had considerable courtroom experience. When he was detailed to help me, I felt assured that I could completely count on his quietly masterful competence. For the White House, my appearance was a matter of great anxiety, since I was the only White House aide to be called and I would be the last witness. My grand-jury appearances had prepared me, but this was going to be very different. I had been one of many grand-jury witnesses in closed proceedings, but this testimony would be videotaped to show to the Senate and the entire nation.

In our preparations, Bill and Jo, my lawyers, acted as House Managers along with Lanny. They asked me questions I couldn't have anticipated, trick questions, questions that stumped my memory. What exactly did I remember about certain incidents? Who did what in the White House? Did I know? Did I even recall what I did? For almost a week, I was a virtual prisoner while this work went on. I inhabited a bubble. I shuttled between my office in the White House, where I attended a skeletal schedule of regular political and policy meetings, a conference room at the Williams and Connolly law firm, and McDaniel's office in Baltimore. The practice bouts went around the clock.

In the meantime, the first two witnesses were called, one day after another. Monica Lewinsky was questioned on February 1 in her Mayflower Hotel suite. Henry Hyde had decided that only one House Manager would act as interrogator for each witness, and for Lewinsky, Congressman Bryant, who had tried to curry favor with her in her preinterview, was designated. Lindsey Graham and James Rogan, however, had a scheme to push him aside and replace him with Graham, who would flourish articles describing her as a "stalker," read her my grand-jury testimony, get her upset at Clinton—and then out would flow her answers incriminating the President at last. But Hyde had promised Bryant the job and stuck by the promise. If he started shuffling assignments, he would set the Managers against each other.

"Oh, the Linda Tripp version," said Lewinsky as she was fitted with a microphone.

Monica Lewinsky befuddled these conservative, provincial, middle-aged Republicans. She had confused Starr and most of the men in Starr's office, too. They had not believed her when she said there were no crimes, which was why they had rejected her first proffer. An articulate young woman of her worldly sophistication was beyond their comprehension or ability to acknowledge. For them, there were only two types of women, good and bad. If she had done "bad" things, she must be a victim. She couldn't have willingly, eagerly been a sexual partner or sexual equal. The House Managers presented themselves as her rescuers, her big brothers, saving her from a wolfishness she could not possibly understand. They were unprepared for the actual Monica Lewinsky.

"Do you still have feelings for the President?" asked Bryant.

"I have mixed feelings."

"What, uh—maybe you could tell us a little bit more about what those mixed feelings are."

"I think what you need to know is that my grand-jury testimony is truthful irrespective of whatever those mixed feelings are in my testimony today." Lewinsky wasn't about to yield any ground. She was self-possessed, matter-of-fact, dismissive, and protective of her complex emotions about Clinton. Bryant rehearsed her previous testimony, gaining nothing. In fact, she was less ambiguous in supporting Clinton's version of events than she had been in her grand-jury deposition.

"Did the President ever tell you, caution you, that you had to tell the truth in an affidavit?"

"Not that I recall."

"It would have been against his interest in that lawsuit for you to have told the truth, would it not?"

"I'm not really comfortable—I mean, I can tell you what would have been in my best interest, but I—"

"But you didn't file the affidavit for your best interest, did you?"

"Uh, actually, I did."

Bryant was flummoxed by this answer, which he had not expected. For all intents and purposes, she had destroyed his performance. Almost as if dazed, he wandered into the brambles of the Paula Jones case, setting himself up for Lewinsky subtly to chastise him for his questions and to deliver another unanticipated response that made it clear she did not share the Managers' general view that Clinton was a sexual predator.

"You believe the President's version of the Paula Jones incident?"

"Is that relevant to—"

"I—I just asked you the question."

"I don't believe Paula Jones's version of the story."

"Okay, good. That's a fair answer."

Bryant then tangled himself in a semantic quarrel that was not simply about words. The dispute was really about Lewinsky's notion of her relationship with Clinton. She challenged their presumption of its being somehow dirty. And Bryant had no idea how to defend his lascivious, condemnatory point of view.

"Let me shift gears just a minute and ask you about—and I'm going to be delicate about this because I'm conscious of people here in the room and my—my own personal concerns—but I want to refer you to the first so-called salacious occasion, and I'm not going to get into the details. I'm not—"

"Can—can we—can you call it something else?"

"Okay."

"I mean, this is—this is my relationship—"

"What would you like to call it?"

"It was my first encounter with the President, so I don't really see it as my first salacious—that's not what this was."

"Well, that's kind of been the word that's been picked up all around. So—"

"Right."

"—let's say on this first—"

"Encounter, maybe?"

"Encounter, okay."

Gingerly, Bryant tried to get Lewinsky to describe herself as a sexual victim, a passive partner to the Big Bad Wolf. He stammered, "Okay. Did—did—did you come on to the President, and did he never touch you physically?"

"I guess those are two separate questions, right?" she swatted back.

"Yes, they are."

"Did I come on to him? Maybe on some occasions."

Bryant now sprang the "stalker" line on her. In the House Managers' version, there was a perfidious scheme concocted by the President and his henchman (me) to obstruct justice by tarnishing her reputation. Here was their chance to get Lewinsky to confirm their account.

"Regarding stalking, you never stalked the President; is that correct?"

"I don't believe so."

"Okay. You and the President had an emotional relationship as well as a physical one; is that right?"

"That's how I'd characterize it."

"Okay. He never rebuffed you?"

"I think that gets into some of the intimate details of—no, then, that's not true. There were occasions when he did."

With one more question, Bryant was done.

For the House Managers, Lewinsky had been worse than a hostile witness. She had been in control throughout and had undermined their case in every way. She had refuted their premises of Clinton's criminality almost offhandedly. And she had asserted her sexuality unabashedly and unapologetically. But her self-descriptions floated by them, for they were incapable of seeing her as she was. They continued to project their one-dimensional, dirty-minded fantasy of her.

On February 2, the second witness, Vernon Jordan, took the stand, speaking in the Senate hearing room where I would be questioned, too. His questioner was Asa Hutchinson. They had had to call Jordan—he was essential to their conspiracy theory—but they gained nothing of value in doing so. Jordan's regal bearing, his eminence in the legal profession and in Washington, and his unconcealed contempt for the white, right-wing Republican Southerner who had the audacity to ask him questions dominated the proceedings.

"When you did bill by the hour, what was your billable rate the last time you had to do that?"

"I believe my billable rate at the last time was somewhere between $450 and $500 an hour."

"Now, would you describe—"

"Not bad for a Georgia boy. I'm from Georgia. You've heard of that state, I'm sure."

Congressman Hutchinson, in trying to show that Jordan had acted as Clinton's agent, his exalted valet, provoked another exchange rich in Southern connotation: "And did the President ever give you any other instruction other than to find Ms. Lewinsky a job in New York?"

"I do not view the President as giving me instructions. The President is a friend of mine, and I don't believe friends instruct friends. Our friendship is one of parity and equality."

Hutchinson tried to corner Jordan about the conversation he had had with Lewinsky in which she had discussed notes she'd sent to the President: "And did you make a statement to her, 'Go home and make sure they're not there?' "

"Mr. Hutchinson, I'm a lawyer and I'm a loyal friend, but I'm not a fool, and the notion that I would suggest to anybody that they destroy anything just defies anything that I know about myself. So the notion that I said to her go home and destroy notes is ridiculous."

"Well, I appreciate that reminder of ethical responsibilities. It was—"

"No, it had nothing to do with ethics, as much as it's just good common sense, mother wit. You remember that in the South."

Here was a spectacle out of the New South: a civil rights pioneer, distinguished lawyer, and presidential intimate clashing with a Bob Jones University graduate, Republican-groomed former prosecutor, and redeemer of "traditional values." Hutchinson was blithe and smug in his condescension to a proud and far more accomplished man. Once again, the racial dynamic in the Clinton wars had come to the fore. The burden of Southern history, as C. Vann Woodward called it, remained.

My turn was next. I received notes and calls from my friends. "We are all thinking of you and wishing you well. You'll do great. Just tell it like it is! Yours ever, Tony," wrote Blair. But I knew that in the witness chair, I would be on my own. For the House Republicans, this was their very last chance. They had struck out with Lewinsky and Jordan. (When the videotape of Monica Lewinsky's testimony was played to the Senate on February 6, Senator Fred Thompson, Republican of Tennessee, walked out in disgust in the middle of Bryant's questions, muttering, "I can't take it anymore.") I was what they had left. But the conservative media whipped up more justifications for calling me as a witness. *The Wall Street Journal* said:

> House impeachment managers have been criticized for choosing Sidney Blumenthal as their third witness to depose. . . . The suggestion has been they were afraid Betty Currie would break into tears, and didn't want two black witnesses out of the three. But . . . in the context of the Senate's limit, Mr. Blumenthal was an easy pick; he was a pivotal witness in moving the House itself toward impeachment. . . .
>
> Mr. Blumenthal is the third witness, that is, because he shows the President at his worst—so eager to obstruct justice that he is willing to ruin a young woman who unwisely loved him. . . .
>
> Now, we suppose that in his deposition today Mr. Blumenthal will come up with some cover story to deny that he planted the stalker smear in the media. But everyone, and most of all the press talking to him afterward, should remember his performance when he emerged from the Starr grand jury last February. . . .
>
> Mr. Blumenthal is an apt witness, that is, because he so neatly represents the standards of the Clinton White House.*

On February 3, I awoke in the darkness. I turned on the lights in my kitchen to make coffee and looked out the window to see a horde of paparazzi. My home had become the site of a media encampment. Trucks with satellite dishes filled the street. While the coffee brewed, I took my dog, Wiley, into the backyard, and a dozen paparazzi started jumping the fence. Flashes went off as they snapped pictures. Wiley and I beat a hasty retreat into the house. I called the police, requesting that they ask the reporters to leave my property and stay on the sidewalk. Having cleared the swarm back, the police called me back to say that they'd been told the reporters were only seeking to interview me. I thanked them. In a short while, Jackie and I walked to our car as klieg lights shone on us and photographers shot away.

From the White House we and my lawyers took a car to the Capitol.

---

*Editorial, "Sidney on Point," *The Wall Street Journal*, February 3, 1999.

Lanny Breuer and two other White House counsels, Michelle Peterson and Max Stier, followed. The Capitol police escorted me inside to be met by the Senate sergeant-at-arms, who asked me if I wished to walk past the gathered press corps, an offer I declined. I wanted to do everything I could to minimize the significance of my appearance.

I was taken to the top floor in an elevator, guarded by police. The deposition was conducted in a sealed, windowless room usually used for intelligence briefings and called the "tin can." My lawyers and I were given a small side room, a senatorial hideaway, for private conferences. Two senators, one Democrat and one Republican, had been named as "judges"—Senator John Edwards, Democrat of North Carolina, a former trial lawyer, and Senator Arlen Specter, Republican of Pennsylvania, a former district attorney. James Rogan, who was to interrogate me, was joined at the last minute by Lindsey Graham—a ploy designed, as they later explained to reporters, to ruffle me.*

I conferred with my lawyers, and then we walked into the "tin can." The participants in this exercise were mingling—Specter and Edwards; Senators Christopher Dodd, Democrat of Connecticut, Patrick Leahy, Democrat of Vermont, and Michael DeWine, Republican of Ohio; Asa Hutchinson; Tom Griffith, the Senate legal counsel; Robert Bauer, a lawyer advising the Senate minority leader; and Morgan Frankel, Griffith's deputy. I knew many of these people and began chatting with them. My lawyers wanted me to take my seat and separate myself, but I refused their suggestion. This was not simply a legal proceeding; it was in every respect a political one. I had been demonized, and by quietly talking with the senators and others, I was making a point: I was not as the House Republicans had advertised. I had a pleasant conversation with Specter about his niece, who happened to be a neighbor of my parents in Chicago. With DeWine, I discussed my family's Ohio roots and where they had lived in Columbus and what they did.

Rogan and Graham came in. Rogan headed straight for me and extended his hand. I shook it. "If there's anyone here who wants to be here less than you, it's me," he said. "Oh," I replied. "That's right," he said, "I'm, we're, on the wrong side of history." I made a point of shaking Graham's hand.

Then we assumed our stations. I sat at the center of a semicircular table, flanked by my lawyers. To the left were the judges, Specter and Ed-

*Baker, *The Breach*, p. 377.

wards. At a table across from me to my left sat Rogan and Graham; next to them sat Lanny Breuer and Michelle Peterson. The others constituted the audience, including Jackie.

Specter began by reading the rules, later flagrantly broken:

I note that according to the terms of Section 205, all present must maintain the confidentiality of the proceedings. For Senators and Senate employees, they should be aware that this deposition is a confidential proceeding of the Senate, under Senate Rule 29.5. This deposition may be discussed only with Members of the Senate and staff designated by Members. House Managers and House employees may only discuss this deposition with fellow managers and staff designated by the managers. The President's counsel may only discuss this deposition with the President and counsel and staff representing the President in this matter. The witness, his counsel and his wife may only discuss this deposition with each other.

I stood, raised my right hand, and was sworn in. Rogan's questioning was straightforward, professional, and narrow. His goal was to get me to restate my grand-jury testimony, particularly the part of it that dealt with my conversation with the President on January 21, 1998. Whatever I was saying, I did my best not to reveal my emotions. I kept my hands in front of me on the table, holding a pen, and didn't gesticulate if I could help it. My responses were flat, direct, and unembellished.

"After you were subpoenaed but before you testified before the federal grand jury, did the President ever say that he did not want you to mislead the grand jury with a false statement?"

"No. We didn't have any subsequent conversation about this matter."

"So it would be fair also to say that after you were subpoenaed but before you testified before the federal grand jury, the President never told you that he was not being truthful with you in that January 21st conversation about Monica Lewinsky?"

"He never spoke to me about that at all."

"The President never instructed you before your testimony before the grand jury not to relay his false account of his relationship with Monica Lewinsky?"

"We didn't speak about anything."

Rogan passed the baton to Graham, whose manner and skill could not have been in sharper contrast to his colleague's. He ran his hand through his lanky hair repeatedly, jiggled his leg under the table, and read from an array of disorganized notes, some of which he pulled from his pockets and unfolded.

He began by asking, "Knowing what you know now, do you believe the President lied to you about his relationship with Ms. Lewinsky?"

"I do."

He seemed genuinely surprised. "I appreciate your honesty," he said. But of course, Clinton had lied to the entire nation about Monica Lewinsky at the same time. My admission was unexceptional, I thought, and moreover, the question had no bearing on the articles on perjury or obstruction of justice before the Senate.

Graham then got bogged down in a question concerning executive privilege, leading to objections from my lawyers. Senator Specter's irritation at Graham's ineptitude was obvious, and he began to refer to him as "Congressman Lindsey." Graham abandoned that line of questioning and tried to insert into the proceedings Kathleen Willey and Jane Doe No. 5 (Juanita Broaddrick)—i.e., the horror show of "the evidence room." (In fact, Hutchinson had interviewed Willey as a prospective witness in the impeachment trial and decided that her credibility could be cast into doubt.) This was strenuously opposed by Lanny Breuer, who rightly pointed out that any questions about Willey "have nothing to do with the Articles of Impeachment, nor do they have anything to do with the proffer made by the Managers [in questioning me], and it's beyond the scope of this deposition." The senators called a half-hour recess to confer on this issue, and decided that Graham could ask me about Willey at the end, so that if the White House objection to the question was sustained it could be cut off the tape and never enter the public domain.

When the recess ended, Graham brought up the *Washington Post* article breaking the news of Monica Lewinsky on January 21, 1998. He asked a circuitous, compound question, and I answered, "Well, there are a lot of questions in there." "Okay, yeah, and I'm sorry." He meandered into imprecise formulations, prompting McDaniel to object: "I really object to the question where we mix 'you' and 'we' and the 'White House.' "

"Did you have any discussions with White House press people about the nature of this relationship after this article broke?"

"No."

"Did you have any discussions with White House lawyers after this article broke about the nature of the relationship?"

"No."

"After you had the conversation with the President, sometime the week of the 21st—I believe that's your testimony—shortly after the news story broke, this thirty-minute conversation where he tells you about—" He paused.

"There's not a question," I said.

"Okay. Is that correct? When did you have this conversation with the President? Do you recall?" Rogan had already trod this ground.

"Yes. It was in the early evening of January 21st."

"Early evening of January 21st?" Graham was echoing my answer as a repetitive question.

"Yes."

"The same day the story was reported?"

"Yes."

"Okay. So, from your point of view, this was something that needed to be addressed?"

"Your Honor," objected McDaniel. "Senator, I object to the question about 'this' is something that needs to be addressed. I don't understand what the 'this' is, exactly, that the question refers to. Does it refer to the story? Does it refer to the President's statement to Mr. Blumenthal?"

Senator Specter asked Graham to rephrase his question, and he wound up posing it even more vaguely: "Okay. So it was certainly on people's minds, including the President, is that correct, the essence of this story?"

"I object," said McDaniel, "to the question about whether it's on people's minds. I think he can answer about what he knew or about what he learned from people who spoke to him, but the question goes far beyond that."

"Well, let me ask you this. We know it was on the President's mind."

An exasperated Specter whispered back and forth with Senator Edwards and then ruled in favor of McDaniel: "Perhaps," he said to Graham, "you can avoid it by just pinpointing it just a little more."

"Yes," Graham replied. "We'll try to be laser-like in these questions." He rambled on about strategy meetings in the White House, whether we had been alarmed, whether we thought the scandal was a "bad story," and then he eventually circled back to his conspiracy theory. "So is it your testimony that this accusation comes out on January 21st, and the accusation being that a White House intern has an inappropriate relationship with the President, filed a false affidavit on his behalf, and nobody at this meeting suggested let's find out who Monica Lewinsky is and what's going on here?"

"Well, I wasn't referring to any meeting, but in any of my discussions with members of the White House staff, nobody discussed Monica Lewinsky's personal life or decided that we had to find out who she was."

Graham directed me to a ringed notebook filled with news articles. I had been shown the notebook at the beginning of the session, and I knew it contained the same discursive, opinionated, and hearsay pieces that Graham had given to Chuck Ruff three months earlier and that had elicited Ruff's withering letter. Graham asked me to read an article whose writer, without citing sources, attributed to White House "aides" and "sources" a "behind-the-scenes campaign to portray her as an untrustworthy climber obsessed with the President." He asked, "Do you have any direct knowledge or indirect knowledge that such a campaign by White House aides or junior staff members ever existed?"

"No."

He was working his way to the heart of his theory: "And this is after the President recants his story—recounts his story—to you, where he's visibly upset, feels like he's a victim, that he associates himself with a character who's being lied about, and you at no time suggested to your colleagues that there is something going on here with the President and Ms. Lewinsky you need to know about. Is that your testimony?"

"I never mentioned my conversation. I regarded that conversation as a private conversation in confidence, and I didn't mention it to my colleagues, I didn't mention it to my friends, I didn't mention it to my family, besides my wife."

"Did you mention it to any White House lawyers?"

"I mentioned it many months later to Lanny Breuer in preparation for one of my grand-jury appearances, when I knew I would be questioned about it. And I certainly never mentioned it to any reporter."

"Do you know how, over a period of weeks, stories about Ms. Lewinsky being called a stalker, a fantasizer, obsessed with the President, called the name 'Elvira'—do you have any idea how that got into the press?"

"Which question are you asking me? Which part of that?"

"Okay. Do you have any idea how White House sources are associated with statements such as 'She's known as "Elvira," ' 'She's obsessed with the President,' 'She's known as a flirt,' 'She's the product of a troubled home, divorced parents,' 'She's known as "The Stalker" '? Do you have any idea how that got in the press?"

"I have no idea how anything came to be attributed to a White House source."

Graham reached into his pocket and rummaged for a scrap of paper, finally pulling it out and smoothing it to read its contents. "Do you know a Mr. Terry Lenzner?" Graham's conspiracy theory was now being entwined with Starr's old make-believe obstruction plot, which I had been confronted with in the grand jury. The end of the House Manager's case was looping back to the beginning of Starr's subpoenas.

"I met him once."

"When did you meet him?"

"I met him outside the grand-jury room." Graham asked me if I knew what he did, and I replied that he was a private investigator who worked for clients including the President.

"Okay. Mr. Blumenthal, I appreciate your candor here." Then he asked, "Do you know Mr. Harry Evans?"

Of all the peculiar questions, this was the most unexpected. I was certain Lindsey Graham did not have the slightest idea who the great former editor of London's *Sunday Times* was, not a clue.

"*Harold* Evans?" I asked.

"Yes, sir," Graham replied as though he knew.

"Yes, I do."

"Who is Mr. Harold Evans?"

"Harold Evans is—I don't know his exact title right now. He works for Mort Zuckerman, involving his publications, and he's the husband of my former editor, Tina Brown." Graham's blank reaction suggested that he had no idea who Mort Zuckerman or Tina Brown was.

"Has he ever worked for the New York *Daily News*?" The *Daily News*, which Zuckerman owned, had published critical articles and editorials about Starr and his prosecutors. Breuer objected to this irrelevance, and a baffled Specter asked Graham what he was doing.

"I'm going to ask Mr. Blumenthal if he has ever at any time passed on to Mr. Evans or anyone else raw notes, notes, work products from a Mr. Terry Lenzner about subjects of White House investigations to members of the press, to include Ms. Lewinsky." He was making stabs in the dark, based on already disproved conjecture, and his lunging produced Alice in Wonderland exchanges.

"Relating to Monica Lewinsky?" asked Specter.

"Yes, and anyone else."

"That's a good question," McDaniel opined. "I think we don't have any objection to that question."

"Well, we still have to rule on it," said Specter. "Overruled. The objection is overruled."

"All right. Now I think I know the answer. So let's phrase it very clearly for the record here. You know Mr. Evans; correct?" asked Graham.

"I do."

"Have you at any time received any notes, work product from a Mr. Terry Lenzner about anybody?"

"No."

"Okay. So, therefore, you had nothing to pass on?"

"Right." One conspiracy theory was demolished, having already been shattered a year earlier when I testified before Starr's grand jury. But there were more to come.

"Fair enough. Do you know a Mr. Gene Lyons?" I explained that I did and that Lyons was a columnist for the *Arkansas Democrat-Gazette*. In fact, I had been friendly with him for years. From his vantage point in Arkansas, knowing all the local players and forces, Lyons had early grasped the emptiness of the Whitewater pseudoscandal. When he wasn't writing his column or teaching literature at Hendrix College, this fiercely independent man spent a good deal of time talking about dogs (he raised beagles) and horses (he had two) and his complex ideas about human and animal behavior.

"Are you familiar with his appearance on *Meet the Press*, where he suggests in an article he wrote later that maybe the President is a victim similar to David Letterman in terms of somebody following him around, obsessed with him?"

"Is this one of the exhibits?" I asked.

"Yes, sir."

"I wonder if you could refer me to it."

"Sure," said Graham. He looked at his jumbled notes and paged haplessly through the notebook of articles. "I can't read my writing," he confessed. "Well, while we are looking for the exhibit, let me ask you this. Do you have any independent knowledge of him making such a statement?"

"Well, I'd like to see the exhibit so—"

"Okay." Graham looked put-upon as he continued to riffle through the notebook pages.

"—so I could know exactly what he said."

"Okay."

"If I might, Congressman," McDaniel interjected helpfully, "I don't know whether the one you're thinking of is—I note in Exhibit 20, there are—well, it's not a story by Mr. Lyons—"

Graham flipped to it. "And that's it."

After I read the article, Graham asked if Lyons's speculation about the *Late Show* television host was "very much like the characterization" of Lewinsky in the story President Clinton told me. "Could be," I answered. I knew Graham wanted to ask if I were Lyons's source, but Gene's goofy analogy to David Letterman's stalker was all his own.

"Did you ever at any time talk with Mr. Gene Lyons about Ms. Lewinsky or any other person that was the subject of a relationship with the President?"

"I did talk to Gene Lyons about Monica Lewinsky."

"Could you tell us what you told him?"

"He asked me my views, and I told him, in no uncertain terms, that I wouldn't talk about her personally. I talked about Monica Lewinsky with all sorts of people, my mother, my friends, about what was in the news stories every day, just like everyone else, but when it came to talking about her personally, I drew a line."

"So, when you talk to your mother and your friends and Mr. Lyons about Ms. Lewinsky, are you telling us that you have these conversations, and you know what the President has told you and you're not tempted to tell somebody the President is a victim of this lady, out of his own mouth?"

"Not only am I not tempted, I did not."

My answers made several clear-cut lines of demarcation: I had not mentioned to anyone except my lawyers, my wife, and the White House counsel that the President had told me anything about Lewinsky. I had an obligation to honor the confidentiality of my working relationship with him. However, although I did talk about the published news stories on Lewinsky with many people—from my family to dozens of journalists—I was not a source for anything in them. My guess was that the so-called White House sources consisted of a few of the younger staffers who had known Lewinsky, but I didn't really know that, and I was never asked about it. The whole impeachment and Senate trial came down to a false hypothesis about the gossip trail on Lewinsky, and this had no bearing whatsoever on the articles of impeachment. The concoction was Graham's hobby horse, all that was left in the House Managers' stable.

"You don't know how all this information came out? You have no knowledge of it at all: about her being a stalker, her being obsessed with the President, the President being like David Letterman in relationship to her. You had no knowledge of how that all happened in the press?"

"I have an idea how it started in the press."

"Well, please share that with us," said Graham expectantly.

"I believe it started on January 21st with the publication of an article in *Newsweek* by Michael Isikoff that was posted on the World Wide Web and faxed around to everyone in the news media, in Washington, New York, everywhere, and in the White House. And in that article, Michael Isikoff reported the contents of what became known as the Talking Points. And there was a mystery at the time about who wrote the Talking Points. We know subsequently that Monica Lewinsky wrote the Talking Points. And in that document, the author of the Talking Points advises Linda Tripp that she might refer to someone who was stalking the 'P,' meaning the President, and after that story appeared, I believe there were a flood of stories and discussions about this, starting on *Night-line* that very night and *Nightline* the next night and so on. And that's my understanding from observing the media of how this started."

When I finished there was a moment of silence. Senator John Edwards, former trial lawyer, was grinning from ear to ear. Isikoff, in fact, had put his story of Lewinsky as "stalker" in circulation *before* I met with the President that evening. And undoubtedly he had been handed the Talking Points by the Independent Counsel. Kenneth W. Starr therefore was the ultimate source of the "stalker" story.

"How long have you been involved in the media yourself?"

"Before I joined the White House staff, I was a journalist for twenty-seven years."

"Is it your testimony that the Isikoff article on the 21st explains how White House sources contact reporters in late January and mid-February trying to explain that the President is a victim of a stalker, an obsessed young lady, who is the product of a broken home?" Graham's voice rose in frustration as he developed his new farfetched theory. "Is that your testimony?"

"No."

Breuer objected to the question, Specter and Edwards allowed Graham to ask it again, and Graham got peevish. "Is it your testimony that the White House sources that are being referred to by the press are a result of the 21st of January Isikoff article? That's not what you're saying, is it?"

"No."

McDaniel jumped in. "I don't think that there ought to be argument with Mr. Blumenthal. . . . I also think the questions are remarkably imprecise, in that they do not specify what information it is this questioner is seeking to get Mr. Blumenthal to talk about, and in that regard, I think the questions are both irrelevant and unfair."

Senator Specter chided Graham: "We're still looking for that laser."

Graham retrod the same ground about "White House sources," admitting that he wasn't getting new information. "Strike that," he said about a repetitive question.

Then Rogan, clearly irritated with Graham, announced, "We have no further questions."

The judges, however, granted Graham additional time to ask me questions about Kathleen Willey. Graham wanted to insert Juanita Broaddrick into the proceedings, asking me if the President had ever admitted to a relationship with her, but Specter, prompted by Breuer's objection, ruled that Graham could ask me only about Willey. He wandered into asking me whether White House strategy meetings discussed Willey's "checkered past."

"No, absolutely not."

And then he asked if I knew who within the White House had possession of Willey's letters to the President, which I didn't.

"You have no knowledge whatsoever of how those letters came into the possession of the White House to be released to the press?"

"No, I don't. I don't know—"

"Thank you. I—"

"—who had them—"

"—don't have any—"

"—in the White House."

"—further questions."

With that, the deposition was over. Before I could rise from my seat, Graham leaped up and rushed over to shake my hand. "Listen," he said, leaning in, "when this is over, when you're going to introduce a patients' bill of rights, would you let me be the cosponsor?" I nodded, stunned at his sudden transition from inquisitor to implorer, but said nothing. "Just think about it." He bounded over to shake hands with Jackie. "I'm sorry," he told her. "I just don't know what to say."

Was it all an elaborate prank? Rogan came over to shake hands, too.

"In Breaking No New Ground, Blumenthal Blunts His Sharp Edges," read the headline in *The New York Times*, which quoted Rogan: "I found him to be a gentleman, and I hope he felt the same way about us."* A handwritten note from him was carried to me at the White House by messenger: "I wish my involvement in the trial was as positive for my im-

*Lizette Alvarez, "In Breaking No New Ground, Blumenthal Blunts His Sharp Edges," *The New York Times*, February 4, 1999.

age as yours apparently has become! No ambiguity was meant by my description." Senator Specter wrote in his memoir, "Sidney Blumenthal was not as billed."*

The White House lawyers had been able to add several exculpatory newspaper articles to the official record, which Graham's highly selective anthology of news reports on "White House sources" on Lewinsky had excluded. These other articles were appended to the copy of the transcript of my deposition, which I received on February 4. I was ordered to guard this document closely until the Senate decided to make it public, within a few days. On its cover, it read, "The material contained herein constitutes 'confidential business of the Senate' and is subject to the provisions of Standing Rule XXIX. Unauthorized disclosure of this information may result in expulsion from the Senate, dismissal from Senate employment, and to punishment for contempt."

The morning after my deposition, John Podesta asked me to speak at the White House senior staff meeting. I was lighthearted. The pall, it seemed, was lifting. "It's been a very expensive form of therapy," I said. Everyone laughed.

That afternoon, in the midst of my regular schedule of meetings, to which I was happily returning, I was telephoned by Gene Lyons. He told me that he had received a strange call from Senator Specter, who read him my testimony and asked if it was true. Lyons, unsuspecting that anything was amiss, was nonchalant and told him that what I had said was the truth. "He not only never told me what Clinton said in the Jan. 21, 1998, talk, he never let on that it had taken place at all," Lyons wrote.

> I first learned about it when I read his grand jury testimony. He never provided me hurtful information about Lewinsky or Kathleen Willey, about whom Specter also asked. . . . To the extent that Blumenthal affected my reporting and opinions, it was to temper my inclinations to polemic. . . . As I told Specter, there were scores of newspaper and TV stories describing Lewinsky in most unflattering terms from the scandal's earliest days. "Presidential kneepad" entered the national lexicon on Jan. 25, 1998, courtesy of The Oregonian and CNN. . . . It is preposterous to assert that Blumenthal inserted this concept into the national conversation.†

*Arlen Specter with Charles Robbins, *Passion for Truth*, Morrow, 2000, p. 504.
†Gene Lyons, "Sex Inquiry Spills into the Press," *Arkansas Democrat-Gazette*, February 10, 1999.

Specter, in his memoir, has explained that Congressmen Graham and Rogan came to him with some story about "a guy in London who says that Lyons told him that Blumenthal told him . . ." Henry Hyde wouldn't let the two congressmen call Lyons, but they handed Specter his number, trotted after him to his office, and prompted him while he spoke on the phone. When Lyons answered that what I had said was true, "Congressmen Graham and Rogan looked mystified." A short time later, Graham got his supposed London source on the phone and summoned Specter to talk to him. According to Specter, Michael Mewshaw, a novelist and travel writer, contradicted what Lyons had said: "Mewshaw said he had received a fax [it was not clear from whom] on January 29 telling him that Lyons' source was Sidney Blumenthal." And on this basis, Specter believed, the House Managers might "reopen the Blumenthal hearing" and "affect the trial."*

Lyons telephoned me the next day with interesting news. His friends William Harrison, a novelist, and Roy Reed, a former *New York Times* correspondent, had been called by Asa Hutchinson, who asked them about a party in Fayetteville, Arkansas, where supposedly an unnamed source had claimed Lyons had boasted about receiving information on Lewinsky being a "stalker" from me. "Both men say they told Hutchinson it never happened," wrote Lyons later. "It never did."†

In this whole strange ex parte investigation, Senator Specter was violating the Senate rules on confidentiality he had gravely read at the beginning of my deposition. Purely in theory, he could have been expelled. Also, by questioning Lyons about sealed testimony he was prying into a journalist's sources. And when he didn't get the answers the Managers wanted him to get, Congressman Hutchinson tried to find other contradicting sources among Lyons's friends and thus to impeach his credibility. The plan was to trap me in alleged perjury—an implausible ploy to turn the trial of President Clinton around.

A group of Democratic Senate press secretaries then learned of Specter's egregious breach and wanted to publicize it. I restrained them, arguing that nothing would come of his harebrained investigation, that publicity would only divert attention and might adversely affect the final vote, including Specter's.

Months later, Lyons located Mewshaw, an old graduate school chum. Mewshaw told him he had no idea how the Republicans had heard about

*Specter, *Passion for Truth*, pp. 506–507.
†Lyons, "Sex Inquiry."

him. He thought it might have been through his father-in-law, a wealthy Pittsburgh businessman and acquaintance of Specter. By this time, Specter's book, *Passion for Truth*, had been published. Mewshaw wrote to Lyons, "I'll just say that Sen. Specter is wildly inaccurate on several points. Perhaps I should say he's more economical than passionate about the truth." And Mewshaw confirmed what Lyons already knew: there had been no incriminating fax at all. "In legal terms, I reminded them both [Graham and Specter] that anything I said would be hearsay of hearsay and completely inadmissible. . . . It was possible I pointed out that you had mentioned Blumenthal and that I jumped to conclusions." That is exactly what Lyons supposed had happened.

Specter's probe went up in smoke without ever sending up a signal. The Senate voted to bar live witnesses—the House Managers' last hope—the day after I testified. On Saturday, February 6, the House Managers and the White House defense lawyers made their summations during which they showed on the Senate floor video excerpts from the witnesses' depositions. Pictures of Monica Lewinsky, Vernon Jordan, and me began flashing, as the House Republicans and the White House reiterated their cases. This was Lewinsky's first appearance on television, and the national audience was enormous. She appeared in sixteen excerpts, Jordan in eleven, and I in twelve.

"Well, there's nothing explosive here," said Asa Hutchinson, acting as narrator. The Managers were virtually admitting their defeat. Still, the television show went on, an all-day extravaganza. Watching at home with Jackie, I was uncomfortable seeing the depositions used this way, but I was also relieved. This, I thought, would be the end of it.

Then I got a call from Bill McDaniel. "There's an affidavit from a British journalist claiming you committed perjury," he told me. That seemed incomprehensible. What lunatic twist was this? I couldn't imagine who or what he was talking about. "Who is this person?" I asked. "It's signed by someone named Christopher Hitchens and he cites his associate Carol Blue." "That's his wife," I said. "Christopher Hitchens is my friend. That can't possibly be true." "Well, it is," said McDaniel.

IV

McDaniel read me the affidavit Hitchens had filed with the House Managers:

I am self-employed and contribute articles to Vanity Fair and The Nation.

Sidney Blumenthal and I are social friends and journalistic acquaintances.

On March 17, 1998, Sidney Blumenthal, Carol Blue, and I met for lunch at the Occidental restaurant in Washington, D.C. [Hitchens handwrote the date.]

If called to testify, I would testify on personal knowledge to the following facts.

During lunch on March 17, 1998, in the presence of myself and Carol Blue, Mr. Blumenthal stated that, Monica Lewinsky had been a "stalker" and that the President was "the victim" of a predatory and unstable sexually demanding young woman. Referring to Ms. Lewinsky, Mr. Blumenthal used the word "stalker" several times. Mr. Blumenthal advised us that this version of the facts was not generally understood.

Also during that lunch, Mr. Blumenthal stated that Kathleen Willey's poll numbers were high but would fall and would not look so good in a few days.

I have knowledge that Mr. Blumenthal recounted to other people in the journalistic community the same story about Monica Lewinsky that he told to me and Carol Blue.

I was amazed and bewildered. The document was absurd. By the time Hitchens claimed we had had this lunch, hundreds of articles about Lewinsky as a stalker had been published. I had testified that like everyone else I had talked every day about the Lewinsky stories with my friends. If the point of the affidavit was to prove I had obstructed justice by prodding Hitchens, by then a vehement Clinton-hater, to write a "stalker" story, that was ludicrous. If the point was to charge me with perjury, that, too, was nonsensical, because Hitchens's affidavit didn't contradict my sworn testimony.

Even more perplexing, Hitchens's affidavit was utterly irrelevant to the articles of impeachment and could have no effect on the outcome of the President's trial. While McDaniel was reading it to me on the phone, reporters broke into the television broadcasts of the trial with the startling news that a surprise affidavit had been filed charging me with perjury. As soon as I hung up, my phone started to ring, of course. Some of the reporters who telephoned said Hitchens had instigated their queries.

Lanny Breuer, seated at the defense table on the floor of the Senate, was prepared to debunk Lindsey Graham. He had carefully written out and practiced his presentation, which would have demonstrated that there was no campaign against Monica Lewinsky. He would have cited exculpatory news articles omitted by Graham, explained why such an effort defied common sense, and shown videotape of my testimony that the House Managers had excluded. His statement would have been delivered with fact and logic in a soft-spoken manner, devastating to Graham's contrived smear, and would have cleared me in a dramatic moment on national television.

On the Senate floor, David Kendall rose and spoke: "Now I introduce my colleague, Lanny Breuer—" But Breuer waved at him to stop. Kendall had no idea why. Lanny and Ruff had just learned about Hitchens's affidavit, and they had also learned that if Breuer began his statement, Senator Specter intended to object, wave the affidavit, and call for Hitchens as a witness. (Specter's memoir airbrushes out this ploy.) Lanny had had to calculate quickly. The momentum of the trial was going the President's way. But Lanny's presentation, his chance to vindicate me, would sidetrack it. If he spoke, Specter would seize the spotlight, and whatever Lanny had to say would be wiped away in a sensational television drama. And I would be smeared further; the damage would be compounded. "As much as it breaks my heart, I ought not to speak," he told Ruff, who agreed.

Lanny knew that Hitchens's claim was ridiculous, but he and the other lawyers agreed that it was counterproductive to wind up the President's defense by dealing with it. Lanny telephoned me to explain, and I told him I understood and concurred. I issued a terse statement to the press: "My testimony to the Senate was truthful. If someone is saying it's not, they are mistaken." I was stunned that Hitchens's affidavit was being blown up in a cause célèbre. Ruff believed that the House Managers were playing the Hitchens card vindictively because I had been an effective witness—destroying, as they saw it, their last, best chance. "After your deposition," said Lanny, "they were desperate and so they used Hitchens."

The day after the House Managers released Hitchens's affidavit, they made public a second affidavit, signed by his wife, Carol Blue. Suddenly, the plot became clearer—and more threatening. Blue's affidavit included "facts in addition to those set forth" by Hitchens. Now it was apparent that the goal was to accuse the President of obstructing justice through me—Graham's original obsession—and that I was covering it up with perjury. Hitchens's affidavit hadn't been sufficient, so the one now submitted by his wife added this charge:

> During that lunch, in the presence of myself and Christopher Hitchens, Mr. Blumenthal stated that the President told him that he [the President] was the "victim" of Monica Lewinsky's sexual advances and that she was a "stalker," and was "crazy." Mr. Blumenthal used the word "stalker" several times to describe Ms. Lewinsky. Mr. Blumenthal conveyed his conviction that the President's version of the events were [sic] true.

I chose not to reply to these charges. There were only days to the Senate vote. If I fanned the flames of an absurd side issue, even though it involved my reputation, I might give the House Managers a way to prolong the trial. The multiple untruths would have been impossible to disentangle; the details would be lost in the din. It was better, I decided, to weather the allegations than engage with the person that Hitchens had become. The virulence of his attack would have to be its own answer.

When Hitchens's affidavit was revealed, I couldn't remember the lunch or that it had ever happened. I searched my calendar and found nothing except that on March 17—the day Hitchens cited—I had been in Puerto Rico on official business. Then on February 8, a third affidavit was released by the House Managers. This one had been submitted by Scott Armstrong, a former *Washington Post* reporter and, as it happened, the father of a classmate of my older son. It read:

> On or about March 18, 1998, I was on a panel discussion at the National Press Club with Christopher Hitchens among others concerning national security reporting. Following that panel discussion, I met with Christopher Hitchens and Carol Blue at which time they recounted to me a conversation they had had with Sidney Blumenthal in which Mr. Blumenthal had related to them among other things that Monica Lewinsky was a "stalker."

While I was watching reports of Armstrong's affidavit on television in my White House office, he suddenly telephoned me. "I got a call from Carol Blue over the weekend, on Saturday," he said. "She gave me a long story. Did I remember being with them at the Press Club and that they mentioned a conversation with you. If I were called, would I verify their account? Then I got a call from an investigator from the House Judiciary

Committee, Susan Bogart. She asked if I recalled the conversation. I checked my time manager. On March 18, after a panel, we had a brief discussion. I got another call from Bogart. Would I sign an affidavit? Before I read it, I got a call from ABC News. I was going to be the second person to say that you said Lewinsky was a stalker. Is this Hitchens or the Judiciary Committee who leaked it?" Armstrong seemed equal parts upset and muddled.

I asked if he had spoken with a lawyer. He hadn't. I asked if he wanted to speak to my lawyer. He said he had already signed the affidavit and faxed it back. "I'm not completely sure about my memory," he said.

"Well, Scott, we'll just see what happens. Thanks for calling."

A few hours later, Armstrong started telephoning reporters to protest his own affidavit. "This is ludicrous," Armstrong told *The Washington Post*. "I don't want to become part of any political witch hunt."* "They were using me to set up Blumenthal," he said to *Newsday*. "I said I didn't have any information to relate, except for the date. But Susan Bogart insisted." Before he had signed, his affidavit was leaked. "So I called up Susan Bogart and said: 'If you're going to leak stuff about me, at least leak something that's true.' "†

With Armstrong's and Blue's affidavits, it seemed to me that Hitchens either was panicked or was being prodded by the House Republicans, or likely both. I tried to recall such a lunch. He and I had had many over the years. Then my lawyer received a fax from the manager of the Occidental Grill, who, on his own, had located a receipt signed by Hitchens for lunch on March 19. (The bar bill before I arrived was $18.84.) Now I remembered that lunch. It wasn't March 17, and it was impossible for Armstrong to have heard Hitchens's story on March 18. But I refrained from giving my account, not wanting to feed the frenzy.

To understand what had really happened at our lunch, or even why I had broken bread with such a fervent Clinton-hater, it's necessary to understand the history of our friendship. I first met Christopher Hitchens at a think-tank seminar, but didn't really get to know him until Jackie and I moved to Washington in 1985. At the very first dinner party we attended, a week after coming from Boston, at the home of Peter Pringle, a British journalist, and his wife, Eleanor Randolph, then my colleague at

---

*Lloyd Grove, "The Lunch That Sticks in Capital's Craw," *The Washington Post*, February 9, 1999.

†Michael Dorman, "More Controversy over Blumenthal," *Newsday*, February 17, 1999.

The Washington Post, we encountered Hitchens. He rose at the table to toast our hosts, reciting several bawdy English limericks, and then launching into a gleeful and scurrilous story about a high Reagan administration official, "Reagan's whip master," who he claimed was a secret lesbian. It was impressive how anyone could be so lubricated and articulate. When Hitchens concluded, to laughter and downed glasses of wine, another guest, who had seemed asleep, suddenly came to life and stood up. Henry Fairlie was a once-prominent British journalist who was now writing at *The New Republic*, where I had met him. He was the epitome of a certain Washington archetype—the Oxbridge-educated, facile, politically nonconformist, dissolute British journalist. (Contrasted against this was the other type of British journalist in Washington—the suave establishment denizen of C. P. Snow's "corridors of power"—Henry Brandon, for example, whose wife, Muffy, had been Nancy Reagan's social secretary.) Now Fairlie delivered a masterful performance, full of irony and erudition, topped with more limericks than Hitchens had memorized. In the English way, he was putting the upstart in his place.

Early on, Jackie and I gave Hitchens's son boxes of toys that our boys had outgrown. We invited him to celebrate American holidays like the Fourth of July and Thanksgiving with us. Sometime in the late 1980s, he announced dramatically that we were related. He claimed to have learned from his dying grandmother that he was Jewish and that his family name was really "Blumenthal." He took to calling me "cousin" as a greeting. I took his self-dramatizations with a grain of salt, but when he decided that he was part of our family, we invited him to our Passover seder. His separation from his eight-months-pregnant wife, Eleni, whom we all adored, did not lead to any break or censure. We were supportive of Eleni, but we remained friends with Christopher, tolerant of his "bad boy" persona. We understood that other people's marriages were mysterious. We befriended his new girlfriend and soon-to-be wife, Carol Blue. And I made friends with Hitchens's friends the novelists Martin Amis and Salman Rushdie.

After I left *Vanity Fair* to join *The New Yorker* and Hitchens was hired by *Vanity Fair*, his perpetual money problems seemed to be alleviated. At last, he had his own Condé Nast expense account. Jackie gave him the idea of holding a *Vanity Fair* party after the White House Correspondents Dinner, the first of these now annual events being held in his apartment. He was delighted when I helped him compile guest lists, especially of Clinton administration figures he didn't know.

In the early Democratic campaign in 1992, Hitchens had favored

Jerry Brown's quixotic effort, seeing in him some leftist crusader. He muttered after Clinton's election about how it was bad for the left; he'd rather have Bush: the worse, the better. None of this eccentricity bothered us. Who would take Christopher Hitchens seriously on American politics? He knew little about America's history, traditions, or Constitution. I told him fairly frequently when he was holding forth that he should go cover an extended political campaign in the Midwest. That never quieted him; he continued to cite Noam Chomsky on the perfidy of U.S. imperialism.

Though he paid scant attention to actual American politics, he caught the drift of things and applied his sensibility with the intent to shock, bedazzle, and entertain. He did not concern himself with domestic policy issues, not health care, education, or the economy. That would have been too prosaic for him, requiring precise knowledge about institutions with which he couldn't be bothered. While freed from commitment to practical political outcomes, he could purport to be more committed than any American precisely because of his roots in a European radical tradition. London was a good place to be from.

As a political writer, Christopher was a literary critic. As a literary critic, his specialty was not irony so much as mockery—that very English form of implicit superiority and disdain, difficult for Americans to master. As a political reporter, he was, in a word, unreliable. "Why would you ever be fair?" Hitchens once said about his own method of debating. I never took him seriously as a reporter of fact, and I didn't know anyone in Washington who did.

By the mid-1990s, I began to wonder if he was morphing into someone I didn't quite recognize. When our mutual friend Martin Walker of *The Guardian*, an English paper, was leaving Washington for a new assignment, Hitchens (who had been best man at his wedding) hosted the going-away party, but just as it began he rushed off to appear on television shows on the deaths of Mother Teresa and Princess Diana, two public figures he had already vilified in print, in order to besmirch their legacies. If nothing else, this abandonment was no way to treat his friend Walker. Soon he was spending months on end in California, living at his in-laws'. When he came back to town, he would call ahead to set up a lunch, where he would press me for news on what he'd missed in Washington.

By the time I was working in the White House, Hitchens and I had been having conversations and lunches and dinners and drinks and bar mitzvahs and book parties and holidays together for a dozen years, and he had become vociferous in his invective against President Clinton. This had no effect on our relationship. I paid no attention. Hitchens continued to make a great show of being a devoted friend to his "cousin," greeting me with an embrace and even a kiss. No matter what the political difference, a friend was a friend. He made professions of friendship at every turn. He might leave a wife, but not a friend. He had friends for life.

When Starr issued his subpoena to me, Hitchens proclaimed about us in *The Nation*: "Together we have soldiered against the neoconservative ratbags. Our life à deux has been, and remains, an open book. Do your worst. Nothing will prevent me from gnawing a future bone at his table or, I trust, him from gnawing in return."*

For the entire period from January to mid-March 1998, when the Monica Lewinsky scandal was raging, Hitchens was in California. Upon his return, he called, as usual, and asked me to meet him at the Occidental Grill, a restaurant near the White House. Hitchens and Carol were at the bar when I arrived, and he was drinking a Johnnie Walker Black Label. "Cousin," he said. His embrace and kiss followed. Carol kissed me, too. We ordered our food—and California cabernet—and they demanded that I tell everything. They could barely contain themselves. They had been cooped up in faraway California. What had really happened? What was it like now in Washington?

I gave what I thought was an entertaining retelling of the story to date: how the scandal had broken, the media frenzy, the old boyfriend of Monica's holding a news conference right before the State of the Union address, how he had called her a stalker, the whole antic cast of characters—Lucianne Goldberg (who had been sued by Kitty Kelley, did they know that?), Linda Tripp, Ken Starr—and the complete story of my appearance at the grand jury, what it was like inside the room, the ridiculous questioning. As we ate and drank, they laughed and laughed. Tell us more, what happened then? Each incident seemed more absurd to them than the next. Hitchens roared, Carol giggled. Along the way, they asked if I believed Clinton. Hitchens made some mocking derogatory comments. I said I did; they said they didn't. When the espressos were served, I handed Christopher a large envelope with copies of articles. The packet was one I was giving to a number of journalists—I still have the original file—and it consisted of articles on what I now told Hitchens about: the Arkansas Project, Richard Mellon Scaife, how Whitewater was bogus—

*Christopher Hitchens, "Conspiracies with Sidney," *The Nation*, March 30, 1998.

they had heard the Whitewater part from me before. Nothing about Lewinsky. Hitchens wasn't very interested, but I said he should read the articles. When Christopher paid the bill on his *Vanity Fair* expense account, I rose to go back to work. They asked if I could stay longer, but I did have to go. Hugs and kisses again. See you soon.

In late May, Christopher and Carol invited Jackie and me to dinner at their Washington apartment, where he regaled his guests with stories of Monica Lewinsky. She had posed for a photo spread for *Vanity Fair* and he had written the short text to accompany it. He described the unreleased pictures for us. She had posed on the beach with pink fans. The retouching, he said, was extensive. "She's a rhino! A tank!" He roared and Carol giggled. On and on he went with ridicule of Lewinsky.

By the fall, Hitchens was contending in print that the U.S. attempt to kill Osama bin Laden with a missile attack on his training camp in Afghanistan and the bombing of a suspected al-Qaeda factory in Sudan were "cynical" political ploys to distract from the scandal.* To him, these events were a real-life version of the movie *Wag the Dog*, in which a president and a public-relations man fabricate a war to sustain the politician's popularity. A staff member on the National Security Council, who had worked for both Republican and Democratic administrations, was enraged. He wrote a memo carefully refuting Hitchens's polemics and circulated it to others at the NSC and to me. Didn't Hitchens know that the joint chiefs approved of these actions? That the CIA had signed off on them? One question after another demonstrated ignorance and irresponsibility. But, I explained, "It's just Christopher Hitchens." "Ignore him," said another NSC staff member. The author of the memo conceded grudgingly that it was best to let the issue fade. But he worried whether leaving the falsity of the article unchallenged was the right thing to do: Wouldn't some people take the story at face value?†

On October 9, Hitchens invited us to a book party for Gore Vidal and to dinner at a restaurant afterward. Steve Wasserman, editor of the *Los Angeles Times Book Review*, came with us. Hitchens spoke to Vidal with slightly mocking deference as "maître," or "master," while Vidal, over

---

*Christopher Hitchens, "It's Not the Sin. It's the Cynicism," *Vanity Fair*, December 1998.

†A factual refutation of Hitchens's charges appears in Daniel Benjamin and Steven Simon, *The Age of Sacred Terror*, Random House, 2002, pp. 360–63. Benjamin was director for counterterrorism and Simon senior director for counterterrorism at the NSC.

dinner, whipped into a jeremiad against the right wing and Ken Starr. Whenever Hitchens piped up with an effort to trounce Clinton, "maître" rebuffed him, declaring Starr "a traitor." He was clearly upset that Vidal had sided against him.

A month later, at my fiftieth birthday party, Christopher and Carol mingled with the other guests, wandering often out to the porch, enclosed and heated for the occasion, where the bar was stationed and smoking was permitted. After the toasts, Hitchens seemed glum, and he explained to my friend Christina Ritch that he had been promised he could deliver one. Her impression was that he had a toast prepared and was let down because he hadn't been called on. Jackie remembered later that he had asked her if there would be toasts and that she had said there would be; he must have assumed he would be asked to give one.

Just before Thanksgiving, Jackie and I attended a black-tie dinner at the Swedish Embassy in honor of the American Nobel Prize winners, and Christopher and Carol were at our table. Hitchens started up with a stream of his usual denunciations of Clinton. By now, with impeachment at full throttle, he was calling the President "a rapist and war criminal." One of our tablemates, a human-rights advocate from Stockholm, Monica Nagler-Wittgenstein (the niece, by the way, of Ludwig Wittgenstein), was shocked. "He is a friend of yours?" she asked me. I explained that though we disagreed we remained friends. "That's right," said Hitchens. "We still love each other."

On February 3, I found a phone message from Carol Blue upon my return home after testifying in the impeachment trial. She was in California, expressed support and "love," and said that when she and Christopher were back in town we'd all have dinner.

The next day, after work, I went to a book party for a friend, David Fromkin, whose *The Way of the World* had just been published. That morning *The New York Times* had printed its article with Rogan's comment about my being "a gentleman," and people congratulated me for having survived the ordeal unscathed. To my surprise, Hitchens was there, looking the worse for wear, sporting a beard. I approached him, but he was strangely cold. I mentioned that Carol had called. He murmured something inaudible. I observed that his beard had a white stripe in it. "Skunk," he said. The next day he signed his affidavit.

That very evening Jackie and I had dinner with Andrew and Leslie Cockburn, who were among Christopher's closest friends. None of us yet knew about his affidavit. But the conversation naturally turned to him, and the Cockburns were worried. Andrew remarked on how Hitchens's

Clinton-hating seemed part of a general rightward drift. They had been with him on election night, when Hitchens had muttered imprecations at the reports of Republicans suffering defeats. "He's turned into Paul Johnson," said Andrew, referring to the former left-wing editor of the *New Statesman* who transmuted into a conservative, a figure whose sex life Hitchens had taken special pleasure in ridiculing in print. "He's more like Peter Hitchens," I replied. "That's it," said Andrew.

Peter, Christopher's younger brother, was in many respects his perfect mirror opposite. Or was he? A former student Trotskyist like his brother, he was now a thorough reactionary who believed that the Tories had sold out to modernity and that Tony Blair was destroying Britain root and branch. (His book on Blair was entitled *The Abolition of Britain*.) Like Christopher, he was a columnist who expressed extreme opinions with vehement invective. The next day, February 6, the House Republicans released Christopher's affidavit.

On February 7, the day after the videotaped testimonies of Lewinsky, Jordan, and me had been broadcast, Hitchens was the first guest on NBC's *Meet the Press*. He was unkempt, grizzled, and bleary-eyed. Tim Russert, the host, played a tape of my testimony. "As far as I saw from your tape," said Hitchens, "Sidney has not lied to Congress. I mean, what he said was he had no idea how that got into print. That's notionally possibly true." Having already filed a legal document, he now claimed he wouldn't testify. "I won't testify if it's just against him."

McDaniel faxed a statement from me to *Meet the Press*, which Russert read on the air: "I was never a source for any story about Monica Lewinsky's personal life. I did not reveal what the President told me to any reporter. As I testified to the Senate, I talked every day about the stories appearing in the news about Monica Lewinsky to my friends and family, as everyone else was doing. Though I do not recall the luncheon with my 'then' friend of fifteen years, the notion that I was trying to plant a story with this rabid anti-Clinton friend is absurd."

Hitchens replied to this fax with a self-contradicting remark: "Well, the last bit is true. If he thought—I can't believe he would have ever thought I would pass it on." So what I had said was now "notionally possibly true" and "true."

"With us now," intoned Russert, "House Republican Managers Ed Bryant and Asa Hutchinson. Mr. Hutchinson, let me turn to you first. You've just heard Mr. Hitchens; you've read his affidavit. What fate awaits Sidney Blumenthal?"

"Well," said Hutchinson, "I think it's a very serious matter. The Senate should deal with this, should investigate it, determine whether there was any perjury committed before the United States Senate. It also points up how difficult it is to get to the truth in this case and how much of an obstacle it is for the House Managers to make the case, to get to the bottom of it."

By now, the controversy was a heated subject at the top of the news. *The Washington Post* reported, "The House impeachment managers are in full cry over Blumenthal and the Washington media-political complex . . . is obsessed with the affair."* Both the *Post* and *The New York Times* published several articles apiece about it.

The *Drudge Report* screamed, "HITCHENS TURNS IN BLUMENTHAL, SAYS WHITE HOUSE AIDE DID SMEAR LEWINSKY." Soon Alexander Cockburn called him "Hitch the Snitch."† Michael Kelly, in a column in the *Post*, weighed in on Hitchens's side: "There you had it, a presidential aide caught out, a major Republican claim proved."‡ In another *Washington Post* column, Robert Novak wrote, "Beyond legalistic accusations of perjury and obstruction of justice, Blumenthal has unwittingly exposed institutional White House corruption that most closely resembles the conduct of Richard M. Nixon."§ The *National Review* featured an illustration of me with a manacle around my neck, wearing prison stripes, being led away on a chain.‖

Hitchens now began a series of performances on TV shows and in newspapers and magazines. Immediately after the House Managers released his wife's affidavit, he was asked on CNN if he could confirm her more detailed and damning version. "Would I swear he said this is what the President wants you to know? No, I would swear he did not say that."

Hitchens's accounts—of what had happened between us, of what he had heard and what his wife had heard, of how he had come to the attention of the House Republicans and how they had learned of his story, and of his own motives—changed almost daily and gained gaudier embellish-

---

*Grove, "The Lunch That Sticks in Capital's Craw."

†Alexander Cockburn, "He Planted a Big Fat Judas Kiss," *Los Angeles Times*, February 11, 1999; Alexander Cockburn, "Hitch the Snitch," *CounterPunch*, February 10, 1999.

‡Michael Kelly, "Aides and Abettors," *The Washington Post*, February 10, 1999.

§Robert D. Novak, "Blame It on Sidney," *The Washington Post*, February 11, 1999.

‖Mark Steyn, "Sid 'n' Hitch," *National Review*, March 8, 1999.

ment over time. His stories expanded, contracted, and contradicted each other. The effect was Rashomon-like in its altered perspectives.

At first Hitchens claimed he had been called out of the blue by the Republicans on the House Judiciary Committee and had no idea why. "So when . . . I was asked a question by someone who already knew the answer, I wondered for a while who had preempted me," he wrote in a column in a London newspaper. And he told *The New York Times* that he was working in ignorance of my testimony when he was sought out by House Republican investigators.

> In retrospect, Christopher Hitchens said yesterday, the only thing he really regrets about signing an affidavit that could land his longtime friend Sidney Blumenthal in criminal trouble is that he did not break the news himself to Mr. Blumenthal, the Presidential adviser. . . . "I kept thinking, 'Can I phone them? If I get the answering machine, I can't leave it on an answering machine message. If I faxed them . . .' " At the time of the call from House members, Mr. Hitchens said, he did not know Mr. Blumenthal had just testified to the Senate that he was not the source of negative stories to reporters about Ms. Lewinsky.*

(He did not tell the *Times* reporter that the night before he filed his affidavit he had strangely told me he was a "skunk.")

Then he offered another version. In this one, Hitchens was searching for my Starr grand-jury testimony in order to write his own exposé of me. (The testimony was in fact readily available on numerous websites, including those of major newspapers and television networks.) "In the course of getting hold of the transcripts and so forth, I had a number of conversations with staffers at various House committees. One of them evidently called the House Judiciary Committee, which contacted me on Friday, February 5, while this column was being written."†

Soon he added new elements, including the portentous anecdote that "he [Blumenthal] left me two folders of pro-Clinton clips and documents, which I wish I'd kept, and went off back to the White House." And Hitchens also offered new information as to why he had been contacted: "When Susan Bogart, senior investigative counsel of the House Judiciary Committee, contacted me in the closing days of the trial, she

---

*Randy Kennedy, "Writer Who Turned Lunch into an Affidavit," *The New York Times*, February 10, 1999.

†Christopher Hitchens, "What Really Happened," *The Nation*, March 1, 1999.

asked a question to which she already knew the answer. I had put a version of the lunch with Sidney in print, in the London *Independent* of September 13, 1998." (In that article, he had written obliquely, "I've forgiven a good friend of mine, who sincerely lied for Clinton before a grand jury, for looking me in the eye last March and telling me that Monica was a 'stalker.' ") Hitchens also justified his affidavit as a brave effort to right the scales of justice and to override the established procedures of the Senate trial: "I thought it was a disgrace to have a mock trial, invisibly sponsored by the stock market and opinion polls, at which the defendant didn't appear and at which all efforts to mention Kathleen Willey and Juanita Broaddrick were quashed."*

Yet Hitchens claimed he was still my friend. He insisted publicly he meant no harm to me—only to the President: "I made it plain to the House counsel and lawyers that I regarded myself as witnessing only for their Senate trial, and only against the President . . . I would not testify in any separate or subsequent case against Blumenthal." Hitchens had a picture in his mind of how the drama would play out. I was "another Clinton human sacrifice," he continued, and he would be the hero, acknowledged in the end as the true friend:

> The Senate lets Bill Clinton walk. Judge Starr decides to proceed against Sidney, who by his excess of loyalty has become one of Clinton's victims. And I withdraw my affidavit (as I then would) and am cited for contempt.
>
> The U.S. Senate then finds out, having "put everything behind us and moved on," that everything we could even suspect in the Kathleen Willey case turns out to be true. A perfect victory for justice.
>
> So, for the moment, I am putting myself under the protection of America's love of the ironic. And, when this is over (and if it matters) I look forward to seeing Sidney again, and to having no differences with him except about politics.†

Hitchens's plot thickened when his anti-Clinton polemic, entitled *No One Left to Lie To: The Values of the Worst Family*, appeared. In it he deepened his suspicions and added unnamed coconspirators: "I believe that

---

*Christopher Hitchens, "I'll Never Eat Lunch in This Town Again," *Vanity Fair*, May 1999; Christopher Hitchens, "It's a Scandal, but Nothing like the One About to Break," *The Independent*, September 13, 1998.

†Christopher Hitchens, "Another Clinton Human Sacrifice?" *The Washington Post*, February 9, 1999.

clippings [about Lewinsky as 'stalker'] were in a folder of material that he brought along to give me, and which I no longer possess. I also believe that at least two other senior White House aides were involved in spreading the smear against a defenseless and vulnerable young woman."* These he did not name.

Three years later, Hitchens was no longer presenting himself as my rescuer or friend. He told an English reporter:

> "He looked as if he'd suddenly gone to work for John Gotti. He was shifty, he was looking around the room, he was uninterruptible and paranoid and he said, 'We're going to take care of these bitches' [Lewinsky and Kathleen Willey]. He was talking out of the side of his mouth—like a real thug—and it was very horrible and ugly and scary. Carol and I didn't know where to look, and she was obviously very upset and horrified. So I said, 'Look, Sidney, are you sure this is the kind of work you want to be doing? Is this what you signed up with the White House to be doing? I mean, hunting down these women?' No, I don't remember what he replied to that."

He had only been seeking to find a way to confront me, he explained:

> "But my regret is that I didn't have a crisis with him before I did." A case in point was the night of Blumenthal's birthday party, the November before Clinton's impeachment crisis, when he and Carol umm-ed and ah-ed about whether it was hypocritical to attend. In the event they did, and Hitchens spent a miserable evening on the deck in the freezing cold, refusing to go inside. "A pathetic compromise," as he says. The house was full of Clinton people who were clearly surprised to see one of the President's most persistent critics among their number. "And I thought, 'Oh well, the unspoken question I can see in your eyes is a very fair one, and I've only just begun to really face it myself.' "†

But the "freezing cold" deck was nicely heated; the bartender hadn't needed to wear a jacket.

In the days right after Hitchens emerged with his affidavit, two other witnesses stepped forward to cast some perspective on the issue of calling

---

*Christopher Hitchens, *No One Left to Lie To: The Values of the Worst Family*, Verso, 1999, pp. 145–46.

†Ginny Dougary, "Friendship and Betrayal," *The Times* (London), July 17, 2002.

Monica Lewinsky a stalker. One was Michael Isikoff, appearing on National Public Radio. On the air, Monica Lewinsky's tape of her conversation with Linda Tripp on December 22, 1997, was played for him, in which she said, "I think people call me that stalker. I think that's what they say. Oh, my God. That gets me so mad. I hate that." Isikoff commented,

> Well, actually, it goes back a little further than that. It goes back to the time in April of 1996 when Monica Lewinsky is evicted from her position in the White House. . . . It is true that people called her the stalker. . . . At the time that the President was meeting with Blumenthal, which was the evening of January 21st, we were publishing in *Newsweek* our first story about this diary of a scandal, which included reporting for the first time about the so-called Talking Points that Lewinsky had handed Tripp. And those Talking Points did include a sentence in which Monica Lewinsky is referred to as a stalker.

Of course Lewinsky, as she testified, was the author of the Talking Points.

The other witness was Linda Tripp, on NBC's *Today Show*. "Monica," she said, "was named a stalker far before Sidney Blumenthal saw fit to share it with his peers. This is not news. Monica was called a stalker when she was forced to leave the White House."

On February 8, Henry Hyde tried to reopen the Senate trial on the basis of Hitchens's affidavit. He sent a letter to Republican majority leader Trent Lott and Democratic minority leader Tom Daschle, pleading to "admit new evidence and to authorize and issue subpoenas" for Hitchens, his wife, and Scott Armstrong. Hyde described Hitchens as having "credible evidence" that "the President may have engaged in an intimidation campaign against potential adverse witnesses in a civil rights action brought against him and in a criminal investigation of his misconduct." This gambit was the very, very last one.

Lindsey Graham, on CNBC that day, remarked on Hitchens's affidavit: "I think this scenario will bring us votes we didn't have, that it went from being about concealing an affair, to turning on people and obstructing justice." " 'I will never again laugh at a Southern accent or confuse it with right-wing drivel,' " Hitchens told *The Washington Times* about Graham and Hutchinson.*

---

*Ralph Z. Hallow, "Hitchens Charges White House Plot," *The Washington Times*, February 13, 1999.

My lawyer prepared a ten-page brief he had written on his own initiative, categorically refuting every allegation and falsehood made as a result of Hitchens's affidavit. In it, he noted that the Nexis database contained 439 stories about Lewinsky as stalker published between the day the scandal broke and the day of my lunch with Hitchens. The White House exhibits, the exculpatory articles that the House Managers had excluded in their batch of articles on the subject, were appended. McDaniel urged me to let him send the document to Lott and Daschle and to release it to the press. I consulted with Chuck Ruff, but in the end this was my decision, and I decided that no matter how much I wanted to defend myself, the best decision was not to respond to Hitchens.

Within the Senate, Lott attempted to gain unanimous consent to subpoena Hitchens and the others, but Daschle, under the rules of the trial, vetoed. There would be no more witnesses. Still, Republicans demanded a Justice Department investigation to determine if I had committed perjury, and David Kendall explained to me that any member of the House could refer it to the Justice Department, which would then be obligated to investigate. Of course, he said, they would conclude not to prosecute, but that could take months. Even though the trial would be over, my ordeal would be on-going. There were still several days to go before the Senate vote. John Podesta asked me if I was holding up, and I said I was steady. Within the White House, my colleagues went out of their way to be supportive through small gestures.

I deliberately kept silent about Hitchens, and as the story faded his tone toward me changed from that of concerned friend to hostile foe, attracting new attention. When *The Washington Post* reported in January 2001 that I would be writing this book, he was quoted: "As everyone now knows—too late—the Clinton presidency was a racket and a shakedown operation. I don't begrudge Sidney his small share of it. It's the price of his soul."* In March 2002, the *Post* quoted him again, apropos of nothing: "It's right that we should be enemies." The paper noted, "Blumenthal declined to comment."†

From the moment I learned about Hitchens's affidavit, I wanted to know what really had happened and why he had done what he had. Initially I hoped that his stumbling explanations somehow meant that he had regrets. I wanted to attribute his overheated, overwrought self-

---

*Lloyd Grove, "Reliable Source: Blumenthal Cashes In, Hitchens Lashes Out," *The Washington Post*, January 30, 2001.

†Lloyd Grove, "Reliable Source," *The Washington Post*, March 6, 2002.

justifications to an inner recognition of what he had done. However, as I was trying to clarify the events while writing this book, a very different sequence emerged. Unraveling Hitchens's actions required finding those with whom he had collaborated, and the tale of the innocent truth-seeker faded in these new shafts of light.

A year after the trial, a Republican staff member on the House Judiciary Committee told me that far from being a reluctant witness, Hitchens had "eagerly volunteered," that initially his wife was upset and the Republicans feared she would "squelch it." Knowing this led me to ask James Rogan about Hitchens. "Hitchens may well have called Lindsey, who was a habitué of the talk shows back then," Rogan said. "That may also be why Lindsey wanted in on the questioning with you."

This suggestion—that Hitchens had been in touch with Congressman Graham *before* the Senate trial—prompted me to contact an old conservative source of mine whom I had known when I was a reporter on *The Washington Post*. I recalled that during the impeachment Jude Wanniski had been a cheerleader for Lindsey Graham.

Wanniski had been an editorial writer for *The Wall Street Journal* in the late 1970s, who helped promote supply-side economics. (He gave the "Laffer Curve" its name—the theory President Reagan adopted from the work of his then adviser, Art Laffer, that tax cuts would increase government revenues.) The voluble, opinionated Wanniski attached himself to politicians and pundits whom he badgered into becoming mouthpieces for his pet ideas. For many years, he was close to Jack Kemp. As a private financial analyst, Wanniski published a newsletter in which he pushed his causes. He called Black Muslim leader Louis Farrakhan "one of the nicest men I've ever met," crusaded against military action against Saddam Hussein and Slobodan Milosevic, and called for Clinton's impeachment because the United States had bombed Iraq. Wanniski also promoted Matt Drudge as his "Man of the Year."* During the impeachment and trial, Wanniski wrote memo after memo addressed to Lindsey Graham and devoted to "The Importance of Sidney Blumenthal," which he posted on his website and circulated to political acquaintances; they eventually found their way to me. Wanniski, in fact, had incessantly left me phone messages, which I thought prudent not to return.

Now I contacted Wanniski on the off chance that he might know something. He told me he had telephoned Lindsey Graham right after Graham had questioned Ruff about the "stalker" story on December 9,

*Jude Wanniski, "Hurray for Matt Drudge!!!," *Polyconomics.com*, October 7, 1998.

and from then on had been in regular touch with him. Having become a fan of Hitchens's anti-Clinton screeds, Wanniski also conversed with him fairly often "in this period," he said. His obsession was the "stalker" story—"I was drawing Graham's statements to everyone's attention"—which he said he raised with Hitchens.

This prompted Hitchens to tell Wanniski a version of the lunch with me, and Wanniski said he instantly called Graham. "I told him about Hitchens's story as soon as I heard it," Wanniski e-mailed me. I asked Wanniski, "When did Hitchens tell you his story? Was it before the Senate trial?" "Yes," he replied. "Did Hitchens know of your role with Graham and that you had told Graham his story?" "Yes." Wanniski explained, "Hitchens told me you had mentioned the 'stalker' story at that meal with his wife, not that you were complicit in its fiction, but that if you were bringing it up with him, you were surely bringing it up with others, which is what the Pres. would have expected from you, as a defender. That really sums up what was in my mind."

I asked Rogan how Hitchens had come to the House Managers. Had they stumbled across his story through the grapevine or an obscure newspaper clipping, as he had claimed? Rogan said he would ask David Schippers for me. Schippers, through Rogan, replied, "Hitchens called us and said what you testified to was untrue. He [Schippers] says that's how the Hitchens thing popped up." *Hitchens called them.*

I discovered another peculiar incident, related to me by Steve Wasserman, which shed light on Armstrong's affidavit. Wasserman told me that Carol Blue had telephoned him the very day she filed her own affidavit, sounding panicked and pleading that she and Christopher needed him to help them. Could Steve corroborate her memory of a conversation she had with him, telling him about Blumenthal's "stalker" story at the time? Wasserman remembered no such conversation, then or later. She asked again. Again he insisted that he recollected no such thing.

For reasons unknown to me, Hitchens, having already imagined I was doing the bidding of an evil manipulator, was posing as the saint for whom nothing, not even friendship, would stand in the way of virtuous revelation. It was a familiar story. Both Linda Tripp and Christopher Hitchens had seen fit to relate patently private conversations to prosecutors, knowing the material might be used in criminal proceedings. But unlike Linda Tripp, who had betrayed actual confidences, Hitchens had purveyed what he claimed were confidences and were not.

Lifestyle and "contrarian" politics explained little about Hitchens's motives. My mistake had been to think that he was a harmless entertainer. The surprise was that he was capable of doing harm without conscience or regret. That remains the mystery.

V

On February 7, President Clinton flew to Jordan to attend the funeral of King Hussein. The next day, he and other world leaders marched down the streets of Amman behind the casket and met with the new king, Hussein's son, Abdullah, to convey his sympathy. It was also important to discuss the place of Jordan in continuing its support for the peace negotiations between Israel and the Palestinian Authority.

Meanwhile, the Senate trial ground on. On February 6, while the House Republicans were brandishing the Hitchens affidavit to fan their final media firestorm, the President's defense attorneys shredded the House Managers' case. Nicole Seligman, of Williams and Connolly, the lawyer who had been present during Lewinsky's deposition, took the floor after the Managers had shown their video excerpts. She explained the reason she had asked Lewinsky no questions: "Why? Because there was no need. Her testimony exonerated the President." She explained that now the Senate would see a longer segment of the video, "unvarnished, not in snippets, because the snippets you have seen are terribly misleading." The Managers, she said, had "distorted, they have omitted, and they have created a profoundly erroneous impression."

For an uninterrupted twenty minutes, Lewinsky on tape was shown giving answers that the Managers had not presented, making her interlocutor, Ed Bryant, appear flustered and foolish. A few senators could not help laughing out loud at Bryant's ineptitude as the tape rolled on and on. Seligman then showed another excerpt, in which Lewinsky corroborated the President's statements to the grand jury: "Again, the Managers did not play these excerpts for you either. They don't want you to know Ms. Lewinsky's recollection, which is that the cover stories and the affidavit were not connected in that telephone call. And that's the call that's at the heart of that first obstruction charge."

On and on the tape of Lewinsky went, her words refuting each of their articles of impeachment. "Through this proceeding," said Seligman,

the Managers have consistently told you how credible a witness Ms Lewinsky is and they have invoked her immunity agreement as the reason that she must be honest. And today they again credit her testimony, but carefully, only in snippets, only when it suits their purposes. The responses Ms Lewinsky provided about the cover stories that were mentioned on Thursday by Mr. Manager Bryant are not new; they are the same responses Ms Lewinsky gave to the Independent Counsel. The truth is that she didn't tell the story that the Managers wanted to hear. So, remember those stubborn facts.

Lewinsky's testimony, Seligman pointed out, was exactly as it had been before the grand jury on the so-called cover story, exonerating Clinton.

Perhaps most notably, her testimony also provides corroboration for the President's testimony that he told her she had to turn over to the Jones lawyers what gifts she had. That's new evidence. But it undermines the Managers' case; it doesn't help it. In one of the most extraordinary points in the deposition—and we'll get to this in a moment—we learned that the Office of Independent Counsel failed to disclose to the House, to the Senate, to the President, Ms Lewinsky's exculpatory statement on this point. Since the OIC evidently had chosen not to share the information with us, with the House or with this body, we owe the Managers a small debt of gratitude for allowing us to learn of it here.

Monica Lewinsky had been the trump card the House Managers had wanted to play against the President. But her testimony at every crucial juncture upheld his, and her self-possession had unnerved the Managers. Even more, she had provided additional testimony sufficient to impeach the Independent Counsel for suppressing evidence. The Managers' dream of forcing Lewinsky as a live witness on the Senate floor had been a misbegotten chimera. If she had been put into that uncomfortable position, she would undoubtedly have continued to prove them false.

After Seligman had demolished their case yet again, the Managers retreated sullenly to the Marble Room off the Senate floor, where they deliberated. Senator Rick Santorum, Republican of Pennsylvania, one of their conservative supporters, wandered by to buck them up. "You're doing great!" he said. "So make a motion to let us call more witnesses," answered Rogan. But Santorum couldn't do that; the Republican Senate leaders had already ruled against it. "Then get the fuck out of here!"

shouted one Manager. The others joined in the jeering, shouting obscenities at Santorum as he ran out the door.*

On February 8, Henry Hyde spoke for the last time, presenting himself as a humble and already defeated petitioner: "We are blessedly coming to the end of this melancholy procedure, but before we gather up our papers and return to the obscurity from whence we came, permit, please, a few final remarks." Some senators burst uncontrollably into laughter. Now, "in speaking to my managers," he recited Shakespeare's *Henry V*'s St. Crispin's Day speech; quoted King Edward VII's remark made famous in Terence Rattigan's play *The Winslow Boy*: "Let right be done" ("I saw the movie; I saw the play; and I have the book," said Hyde); cited Horace Mann and Charles de Gaulle; and cited Edward Gibbon on a corrupt emperor, Septimius Severus, described in *The Decline and Fall of the Roman Empire*. "I guess those who believe history repeats itself are really onto something," said Hyde.

Hyde had always invoked "the rule of law" as his underlying motive. But now a more forthright phrase replaced that high-flown one: "I wonder if, after this culture war is over, this one we are engaged in, an America will survive that is worth fighting for to defend." With this admission, Hyde acknowledged the raw political struggle to overturn the forces in American life they believed President Clinton represented. This is what the House Republicans had been engaged in all along.

Charles Ruff, the last speaker for the defense, rolled his wheelchair one more time into the well of the Senate. Once again, he refuted the prosecution case, point by point. "Nice try—no facts," he said. And he set into a larger perspective the impeachment and trial that were about to come to a conclusion:

> Now, you have heard the Managers' vision—or at least some part of it— of the process we have been engaged in and the lessons we have learned and what it will look like at the end of our journey. . . . I believe their vision could be too dark, a vision too little attuned to the needs of the people, too little sensitive to the needs of our democracy. I believe it to be a vision more focused on retribution, more designed to achieve partisan ends, more uncaring about the future we face together.
>
> Our vision, I think, is quite different, but it is not naive. We know the pain the President has caused our society and his family and his friends.

---

*Toobin, *A Vast Conspiracy*, p. 388.

But we know, too, how much the President has done for this country. And more importantly, we know that our primary obligation, the duty we all have, is to preserve that which the founders gave us, and we can best fulfill that duty by carefully traveling the path that they laid out for us.

The trial was almost done, and it was obvious that President Clinton was about to win the Senate vote. For two more days, the senators orated. Senator Specter bizarrely announced that his vote would be a "Scottish" verdict—"not proved." But the parliamentarian advised that any vote that was not "guilty" would be ruled "innocent." By the afternoon of February 11, the senators were submitting written statements rather than making floor speeches. They were impatient for the trial to end.

Within the White House, we enforced a rigidly impassive tone. The White House, we said, would be a "gloat-free zone." The weather had turned unusually balmy, reaching near seventy degrees, and at the end of the day I walked across Pennsylvania Avenue from the White House to a park bench in Lafayette Park, where I joined Philip Bobbitt, a counterterrorism expert and University of Texas Law School professor on the NSC, and Princeton historian Sean Wilentz to discuss the ideas in what would become Bobbitt's seminal book on the nature of the modern state and warfare, *The Shield of Achilles*. Phil broke out cigars, and for a moment the tension seemed to be going up in a puff. But with a jangle my beeper went off: "Urgent. See Joe Lockhart." I wondered what unforeseen last-minute crisis this might be. I trotted back into the White House to Joe's office. "Thank God you got that message quickly," he said. At the morning press briefing he had been asked about gloating aides, and he had replied sarcastically, "They're in Lafayette Park smoking cigars." He had just learned that a Fox News camera crew was on its way to film me. At least, from this one potential scandal I had been spared.

On February 12, Lincoln's birthday, the Senate voted. A small group of us sat in John Podesta's office to watch the proceedings on television. On Article I, perjury, the President was acquitted, 55–45. On Article II, obstruction of justice, the President was acquitted, 50–50. Thus the President was acquitted on all charges.

"Mr. Chief Justice," said Senator Lott, "I ask unanimous consent that the February 5, 1999, affidavit of Mr. Christopher Hitchens and the February 7, 1999, affidavit of Ms. Carol Blue, and the affidavit of Mr. R. Scott Armstrong be admitted into evidence in this proceeding, the full written transcripts of the depositions taken pursuant to S. Res. 30 be included in the public record of the trial at this point. This matter has been cleared on both sides of the aisle."

My colleagues, sitting around, jocularly pointed their fingers at me. "Without objection, it is so ordered," said Chief Justice Rehnquist. That was the last matter of business, and the court of impeachment of the President adjourned sine die. An honor guard of senators escorted the Chief Justice from the chamber.

Podesta called the President, who was in the Residence, and he emerged in the Rose Garden to make one final statement: "This can be and this must be a time of reconciliation and renewal for America." "In your heart, sir," asked a reporter, "can you forgive and forget?" "I believe," said Clinton, "any person who asks for forgiveness has to be prepared to give it."

At the next weekly political strategy meeting in the Yellow Oval, the President joked, "They've spent so much energy trashing me I'm surprised anyone is willing to be in a room with me." Michael Waldman observed that for the first time the cable channels had new scandals on. "They're just reloading, boys," Clinton warned. At the meeting's end, he announced, "I've got to go to the dentist. Anyone want to go for me?"

As we walked out of the room, Clinton put his arm around me and made a remark that echoed what I had told him the day the scandal broke, in our Oval Office conversation. "You know," he said with a grin, "you shouldn't be hanging around crazy people." I laughed and said, "You know, that's good advice."

A month later, on March 18, I was a guest of CBS News at the Radio and Television Correspondents dinner at the Hilton Hotel. At the CBS reception held beforehand, I ambled up to Bob Bennett and Lindsey Graham to join their banter. A semblance of Washington etiquette, where partisan disagreements give way to bonhomie, was beginning to emerge. "I can't get rid of *your* friend," said Graham. "Hitchens is *your* friend. I can't get him off the phone." Hitchens wouldn't stop calling Graham, he said, and kept pestering him with new schemes on how to attack the President. "He *really* doesn't like the President. If you have any ideas on how I can get rid of him, let me know."

On my way to the CBS table, I ran into Jim Rogan. "I hope you don't think badly about me," he said. "You were a perfect witness—totally professional, honest. If I were presenting a case, you're exactly the kind of witness I'd want."

A year later, on March 27, 2000, I appeared at a charity event for the Arena Stage's educational programs by joining a cast of political and media figures in a makeshift comedy called *Washington Confidential*. I kicked in a chorus line with Senator Fred Thompson, Congressman Dick Gephardt, Jacob Stein (Lewinsky's attorney), Cokie Roberts, and Securities and Exchange Commission chairman Arthur Levitt. Backstage, I ran into Representative Mary Bono, Republican from California, who had been on the House Judiciary Committee. As we waited for our cue to go on, she said, "Impeachment was tough on everyone." "Yes," I agreed. She continued her patter. "Lindsey Graham sure had a good time making fun of your name," she said. "Oh," I replied. "That's right, he did." She chuckled. She was just trying to be friendly.

The amateur theatrics about to occur onstage were all in good fun. But the "fun" Mary referred to was a different kind of fun. It wasn't the first time that that sort of "fun" for the purpose of ridicule and denigration had surfaced—Bob Barr's "real Americans" had been another example. Mary Bono's cheerful mindlessness didn't make her account of it any less disturbing.

VI

Six months after the Senate trial concluded, on August 24, 1999, I was summoned back by the Office of Independent Counsel. There was no publicity or saturation media coverage. Instead of being issued a subpoena, I was asked for an interview, to which I could bring my lawyers. I didn't know the subjects that would be raised, but an incident had occurred a few months before that would be relevant. It concerned the only act of violence surrounding the entire Starr investigation—a truly serious crime.

In late 1998, Kathleen Willey had told the OIC prosecutors a story that on January 8 of that year, two days before she was to give her deposition in the Jones case, her cat had mysteriously disappeared and her car tires had been studded with nails. She claimed that someone she called "the jogger" had run by her on the street and said, "You aren't getting the message, are you?" Conservative media widely reported this story, suggesting it as another example of the intimidation campaigns run by the President. No evidence of any kind to support that suggestion ever emerged.

In the early spring of 1999, I had dinner with one of my oldest friends, Derek Shearer, whom I had known since we worked together as journalists on *Boston After Dark* in 1970. Derek had just finished serving as the U.S. ambassador to Finland. I was also friendly with the rest of his family. His father was Lloyd Shearer, a famous Hollywood reporter; his sister, Brooke, was married to Deputy Secretary of State Strobe Talbott; and his brother, Cody, ran an international student program. Cody had been a journalist for decades, and both Brooke and Cody had once worked as researchers for Terry Lenzner, the private investigator. Cody was also at the dinner that evening at Derek's, and he told me that the Independent Counsel had subpoenaed him and questioned him about being "the jogger." He had been outraged. He had nothing to do with any of this. Also, he had been in California for weeks during the time Willey claimed the incident had taken place and could prove it. His seatmate on the airplane trip back from Los Angeles to Washington had happened to be former secretary of state Warren Christopher.

On May 11, Chris Matthews interviewed Kathleen Willey on his CNBC cable TV talk show, *Hardball*. Matthews had been a speechwriter for President Carter and a press secretary for the Democratic Speaker of the House Thomas P. "Tip" O'Neill before becoming a talk-show host. He had lobbied the White House to replace DeeDee Meyers as press secretary, but the job had gone to Michael McCurry. Even before the impeachment Matthews had turned into a detractor of Clinton. He freely told perplexed friends that as a consequence, his ratings had improved.

Before Willey appeared on his show, she had told Matthews about "the jogger," and he was determined to name him once she was on the air.

"Who was that guy?" he asked. "I'm going to ask you again, because I think you know who it was."

"I do know," said Willey. "I think I know."

"Is it someone in the President's family, friends? Is it somebody related to Strobe Talbott? Is it a Shearer?"

"I can't say . . . I've been asked not to dis—"

"You've been asked not to admit that?"

"Yes, by the Office of Independent Counsel, because they are investigating this."

Matthews was persistent: "Let's go back to the jogger, one of the most colorful and frightening aspects of this story."

Willey said Jackie Judd of ABC News had shown her a picture of someone and she had identified it "positively." Exactly how the ABC correspondent had this picture, why she had failed to report it, and why she was acting as an arm of the prosecutor was left unexplained.

Matthews blurted, "So it's Cody Shearer."

"I can't tell you," Willey replied.

That night, Drudge posted Matthews's revelation, and the next day Rush Limbaugh regaled his listeners: "She says Ken Starr asked her not to reveal the identity of the man who she says threatened her two days before her testimony in the Paula Jones case. Here's who it is. It's Cody Shearer, S-H-E-A-R-E-R . . ."

That day, a man with a history of mental illness living in suburban Maryland heard of the Matthews allegations. He drove to Shearer's home in Washington with a gun. Shearer was not there, but several of the international students in his program were. The man broke into the garage, slashed tires, waved his gun, and threatened the students before speeding away. They jotted down his license-plate number and he was soon apprehended. His name was Hank Buchanan, and he was the disturbed brother of Patrick Buchanan, the conservative pundit and presidential candidate. After he was arrested, the family checked him into a mental hospital and the charges were dropped.

Death threats flooded in to Shearer, who demanded that Matthews apologize to him on the air. The regretful talk-show host broadcast a retraction: "I now regret having spoken—having spoken about him—not [having] spoken beforehand with him before I mentioned his name on the air. I should have never brought his name up till we had vetted it."*

Now I was in a suburban Virginia office complex to be interviewed by prosecutors from the office of Independent Counsel. There were four of them in the shabby windowless room with cracked plaster. The rough transcript that follows is based on my lawyers' notes:

You came on to the President's staff around the time that Kathleen Willey's story surfaced in *Newsweek*. When you were hired did you have any discussions about Willey?

No. I hadn't heard of her before that article was published.

The prosecutors asked with whom inside the White House I had discussed the release of Willey's fawning notes written to Clinton after she had claimed he sexually mauled her. I said I had known about the notes perhaps a day before they were released, but that I was out of the country, in Puerto Rico, when the decision was made to give them to the press. The prosecutors asked who outside the White House I had discussed the notes with, and I named a reporter at *The New York Times*.

---

*Joe Conason, "Hardball Strikes Out," *Salon.com*, May 18, 1999; Jake Tapper, "Buchanan's Brother Threatens Clinton Associate," *Salon.com*, May 20, 1999.

Do you have any information about the jogging incident regarding Willey?

No.

Then the prosecutors asked about Christopher Hitchens. One of them pulled out photocopies of pages from *No One Left to Lie To: The Values of the Worst Family*. The prosecutor read a passage quoting me as saying about Willey, "Her poll numbers look good now, but you watch. They'll be down by the end of the week." I replied that I had no recollection of saying that or anything like it.

A prosecutor asked if I had had a face-to-face meeting with Hitchens. I said that the date he gave for it was inaccurate.

But you did have a lunch with him, didn't you?

Yes, I said.

What do you remember about it?

The first thing, I said, was that he was drinking Johnnie Walker Black when I arrived.

Could it have been Jim Beam? asked a prosecutor.

Jack Daniels? said another.

Those are bourbons, said the first. How about Johnnie Walker Red? They were all now having a laughing fit. J&B? said one. Dewar's, shouted another.

For five minutes, the prosecutors went back and forth among themselves, uncontrollably laughing about Hitchens's drink of choice, while I sat, waiting for the next question.

Finally, I was asked what I thought about what Hitchens had said about our conversation.

I said I had never regarded him as a reporter of fact or someone who got his facts straight.

All right, a prosecutor said, waving away the topic. This prosecutor had done his due diligence on Hitchens.

Do you know Cody Shearer?

I've known him for about thirty years.

Did you ever have a conversation with him about Kathleen Willey?

Yes, recently, at his brother's house. Cody said he didn't know why you had contacted him, that he was in California during the so-called jogging incident, had the documents to prove it, and wanted to know why he was being harassed.

Harassed?

Yes, he wanted to know why you were harassing him.

What do you mean by harassed?

He feels he is being treated unfairly. He says he was not involved in any way.

Did you have other conversations with Shearer about Willey?

Yes, I said, and I told them about Willey's appearance on Matthews's show and Hank Buchanan's gun brandishing. Willey had told Matthews Shearer's name off-camera and before she went on the air. What happened afterward was a serious crime—someone with a gun had come looking for him. There had been death threats. Shearer was understandably upset.

Are you blaming us? Are you saying that we're responsible?

My lawyer objected. Mr. Blumenthal, he said, is here as a fact witness, not to be asked his opinions.

For a desultory five minutes more, the prosecutors asked questions they had already asked. And thus my appearances before the Office of Independent Counsel came to an end.

On April 14, 1999, a farewell party for Gregory Craig was held in the Yellow Oval in the White House. His work completed, Greg was returning to private practice. The members of the legal and political teams that had fought throughout the impeachment and trial gathered to cheer him on and thank him. We delivered encomiums to Greg as a way of paying tribute to the whole experience. Cheryl Mills read a hilarious satire, heavy on the first-person pronoun, of George Stephanopoulos's just published memoir. Drinks had already been poured, a cake was about to be cut. Chuck Ruff delivered the closing statement, doling out praise and humor, as he had before the House of Representatives and the Senate. While he was discussing the trial and just as he uttered by chance the word "guilty," the President walked into the room.

"Innocent," said Clinton.

FOURTEEN

The Twenty-first Century

I

On the day after the Senate trial ended, February 13, 1999, President Clinton delivered his weekly Saturday radio address, on the subject of Kosovo. (The practice of giving these talks was begun by President Reagan, out of admiration for FDR's "fireside chats," and Clinton used them to good effect.) His attention on this particular Saturday to an obscure corner of Europe, a rebellious province of Serbia, seemed almost like a return to tranquillity after the tumult of the impeachment drama.

But the latest turn in the Balkan wars that had plagued the West for a decade was about to confront Clinton with the gravest foreign policy crisis of his presidency and the first war fought by NATO forces in its fifty-year history. This crisis threatened to discredit the leadership of every government in Western Europe, set Russia against the United States, and undermine Clinton just as he was freed from the constitutional crisis at home. The Kosovo war would require all of the President's deft political skills to sustain a strained international coalition. His entire foreign policy rested on his ability to carry out a campaign that faced intense opposition from both right and left, from his familiar enemies in the Republican Congress and a rising chorus of discontent about his strategy and motives. The war was his ultimate international juggling act.

Throughout 1998, Clinton had conceived and executed against Slobodan Milosevic a sequenced strategy of diplomacy, sanctions, and force. As the Serbian dictator's ethnic cleansing rolled through Kosovo, Clinton closely monitored the growing crisis, and on September 23, the United States had won approval of a UN Security Council resolution con-

demning Milosevic's campaign in Kosovo, demanding that he enter negotiations to end it, and authorizing the use of force should he fail to
do so.

Now, in February 1999, the President dispatched Secretary of State
Albright to conduct negotiations between the Serbs and the Kosovars. In
the fourteenth-century chateau of Rambouillet, outside Paris, Albright
tried to get the hostile parties to reach an agreement. In his radio address
on February 13, Clinton recalled recent events: "Bosnia taught us a lesson: in this volatile region, violence we fail to oppose leads to even
greater violence we will have to oppose later at greater cost. We must
heed that lesson in Kosovo."

Like Joseph Stalin, Slobodan Milosevic was a mediocrity and an apparatchik with the soul of a mass murderer: the man without qualities as
tyrant. Like Stalin, he manipulated nationalism to promote his atavistic
power. He was ruthless in his corruption, which was a family enterprise,
in his brutality, and in pitting his enemies against each other. In 1989,
Milosevic had invested himself with the founding myth of Serbia. At the
Field of the Blackbirds, he had addressed a million people drawn to celebrate the six hundredth anniversary of the Ottoman Empire's victory
over the Serbs in the Battle of Kosovo. On that sacred ground, Prince
Lazar had been slain by the Turks, vanquished only to rise again spir-
itually in the Serbs' continuing holy warfare. Kosovo was the Serb
Jerusalem, site of Serbian martyred nationalism, holy crossroads of the
battle between Christianity and Islam. "Again we are in battles and quar-
rels," Milosevic told the roaring crowd. In the whirlwind he summoned,
he was going to forge a greater Serbia, a new empire crushing the other
parts of Yugoslavia. His image was as victim and avenger at once. Then,
a decade later and on the eve of the bloody war over Kosovo, Milosevic
defiantly boasted, "I am ready to walk on corpses and the West is not.
This is why I shall win."

His war was not a war of Christian crusaders against Islamic hordes,
nor was it a set battle with an opposing army in an open field. Ethnic
cleansing, a term first used by the Serbs, was a unique form of total war
against an entire population—a new kind of genocide, a war fought
against a people because of who they were. The war in Bosnia had shown
that the Serbs' ethnic cleansing differed from the systematic thoroughness of the Holocaust and, despite its murderous rampages, from what
had gone on in Rwanda. Its savagery was a policy endorsed by the state
and carried out by the army. Its methods included forced expulsions; the
looting and burning of cities and towns; the separation of men from their

families and their detention; summary executions, including targeted ones of professionals, intellectuals, and civic leaders; state-sanctioned rape; destruction of hospitals and clinics; and the eradication of forms of identity—passports, property registries, legal papers, even license plates.

In 1998, in Kosovo, Milosevic promulgated a virtual law of apartheid against the overwhelmingly Albanian population, denying them employment, health care, and rights. His plan was to drive them from their land and occupy it solely with Serbs. The Kosovar leader, Ibrahim Rugova, was a gentle, hapless father figure preaching nonviolence and easily ignored. In this vacuum, a rebel band calling itself the Kosovo Liberation Army began harassing the Serbs. In January, in the town of Racak, the Serb army staged a massacre, an echo of Srebrnica that precipitated U.S. involvement in trying to work out a peace agreement. While the negotiations proceeded, Milosevic massed forty thousand troops, three hundred tanks, and one thousand pieces of artillery at the Kosovo border. His ethnic cleansing had already created 250,000 refugees.

The Clinton of 1999 was a more toughened, more experienced, and shrewder president than the Clinton who had taken office in 1993. He had entered the office naïvely believing that the world could be held at bay, or that he could subcontract international affairs to his foreign policy team while he himself dealt with domestic policy. Now he knew that he could not repeat that mistake and that his own persistent leadership was needed. He had learned the harsh lesson of Bosnia: diplomacy without the threat and use of force would not work in the Balkans.

In the earlier phase of dealing with the crisis in the Balkans, Clinton had been captivated by the idea that eternal, unyielding ethnic antagonisms, about which the West could do very little, had driven the conflicts there. He had gleaned this notion especially from Robert Kaplan's profoundly pessimistic and elegiac book *Balkan Ghosts*. But in his instinctive search for practical answers, Clinton's political sense reasserted itself, and he eventually grasped that it was politics above all that was behind the Balkan conflagration. Clinton peered into Milosevic's heart and saw a politician—an evil one, but a politician nonetheless. For Clinton, on the Balkans, this was the beginning of wisdom and recovery. Passivity and fatalism in foreign policy were self-defeating. As Richard Holbrooke wrote:

Had the United States not intervened, the war would have continued for years and ended disastrously. . . . By the spring of 1995 it had become commonplace to say that Washington's relations with our European allies were worse than at any time since the 1956 Suez crisis. But this comparison was misleading; because Suez came at the height of the Cold War, the strain then was containable. Bosnia, however, had defined the first phase of the post-Cold War relationship between Europe and the United States, and seriously damaged the Atlantic relationship. In particular, the strains endangered NATO itself just as Washington sought to enlarge it. . . . Dayton changed this almost overnight. Criticism of President Clinton as a weak leader ended abruptly, especially in Europe and among Muslim nations. Washington was now praised for its firm leadership—or even chided by some Europeans for *too much* leadership.*

Clinton had also learned a lesson in Rwanda during the Hutu massacre of Tutsis in 1994. The massacre occurred right after the Somalia fiasco, and intervention was not considered by any Western power, nor was there domestic pressure to intervene—not from editorial writers of major newspapers, not from groups like Trans-Africa, not from Capitol Hill. Within the National Security Council, the capable Richard Clarke (soon to become the head of counterterrorism) directed a task force that suggested creating a protected zone to which refugees could flee, but the United Nations had rejected this option. "Would I have done the same thing again?" Clarke replied when asked about the U.S. record. "Absolutely. What we offered was a peacekeeping force that would have been effective. What [the UN] offered was exactly what we said it would be— a force that would take months to get there. If the UN had adopted the U.S. proposal, we might have saved some lives. . . . The U.S. record, as compared to everyone else's record, is not something we should run away from. . . . I don't think we should be embarrassed. I think everyone else should be embarrassed by what they did or did not do."†

When he went to Africa in March 1998, President Clinton offered a formal apology for Western inaction, and he soon proposed U.S. funding and support for an Africa Crisis Response Initiative. "The international community must bear its share of responsibility for this tragedy," he said in Kigali, Rwanda's capital.

Genocide can occur anywhere. It is not an African phenomenon. We must have global vigilance. And never again must we be shy in the face of

---

*Richard Holbrooke, *To End a War*, Random House, 1999, pp. 360–61.
†Samantha Power, "Bystanders to Genocide," *The Atlantic Monthly*, September 2001.

the evidence. It may seem strange to you here, especially the many of you who lost members of your family, but all over the world there were people like me sitting in offices, day after day after day, who *did not fully appreciate* the depth and the speed with which you were being engulfed by this *unimaginable* terror.

Clinton realized that in both Bosnia and Rwanda, the United States, with its preponderance of power, had made a statement to the rest of the world by its inaction. Being the indispensable nation put added burdens on the United States to assume a greater, more varied responsibility for international stability. Clinton had never been hesitant about the use of force, but by his second term he felt thoroughly comfortable using it, having ordered the U.S. military into action many times. In 1996, when China fired missiles over Taiwan in gestures of intimidation, the commander in chief had sent a naval carrier group swiftly to the Taiwan Straits, and China backed down. But the eventual success in Bosnia, more than anything else, had established a precedent.

President Clinton was carving a path between the left, which advocated an international system upholding the rule of law but was leery of the use of force, and the right, which believed that U.S. strength should compel the rest of the world to line up behind it. The weakness of the first was matched by the arrogance of the second. Both corroded the international alliances needed for collective security and action in the long run.

Kosovo was the central challenge remaining to full European integration after the fall of the Soviet Union. If the crisis there were allowed to fester and ethnic cleansing allowed to succeed, Europe would be inundated with refugees. The human tragedy would be appalling. This might well demoralize the center-left political parties, but right-wing ones would seize on the developments to gain influence, exploiting fears about increased immigration and asylum seeking. NATO would seem a feckless, purposeless organization: if it could not be mobilized to ward off this new threat in Europe, what use was it? The incentive for former Warsaw Pact countries to join it would be drastically reduced. NATO expansion would become an empty exercise. Moreover, the absence of U.S. power would trigger traditional rivalries among the European countries and hamper Britain's influence, given its link to the United States. Reform in Russia would be slowed down or be derailed, as conservative political forces there would be galvanized by Serbian defiance of the West. And without the Balkan puzzle solved, Turkey and Greece might also be propelled into renewed conflict.

In the United States itself, if Clinton's new internationalism seemed merely the impotent gesture of a Democratic president, foreign policy would be viewed as the projection of narrow national interest rather than as the means to create an expansive community of nations, as Clinton believed it was. Isolationism, unilateralism, and protectionism would gain ground. New global initiatives for international labor standards, environmental protection, and women's rights—putting "a human face on the global economy," as Clinton described the Third Way between command economies and laissez-faire policies—would be radically set back.

Creating an internationalist foreign policy had been a beleaguered mission of the progressive presidents throughout the twentieth century. Franklin Roosevelt helped to form the United Nations, remembering his experience in the administration of Woodrow Wilson, who had failed to win a Republican-dominated Senate's approval of U.S. participation in the League of Nations after the First World War. Wilson's presidency had crashed with his political and physical collapse, as he exhausted himself in a whistle-stop nationwide campaign for his League. Roosevelt had maneuvered against the isolationists in 1940 to gain Lend Lease aid for a Britain facing Nazi Germany alone, and he barely won approval from the Congress. And Harry Truman won Senate approval of the Marshall Plan aid program for Europe and of NATO, and promulgated the Truman Doctrine, in the face of bitter Republican isolationist opposition—and against often hostile public opinion. Yet from 1940 on, this liberal internationalism was sustained against the totalitarian threats, first from National Socialist Germany and then from the Soviet Union.

With the ending of the Cold War, President George H. W. Bush had little conception of what policy would be best to follow, apart from supporting the unification of Germany. His invocation of a "new world order" after the successful prosecution of the Gulf War in 1991 remained a phrase in search of a definition. He was a self-proclaimed realist who could not describe the world he was in or what he thought it would become. His indifference to the Bosnian crisis and his abandoning of the imperative learned from two world wars that the United States must enforce Europe's peace and stability laid a decade-long crisis in his successor's lap.

President Clinton had to build upon the institutional framework left by the Cold War and weakened by Bush's nonpolicies, and he had to direct it to new purposes. After the Bosnian war, he recognized that he had to persuade the NATO allies to join in action in Kosovo from the very beginning. In Bosnia, Bush had left the allies to pursue their own self-serving interests; the British and French played treacherous games with Milosevic and then connived to confound the Americans. And just as Clinton had learned lessons from this disaster, different leaders in Britain, France, and Germany had also learned from the failures of their predecessors. Clinton was no longer dealing with British and French governments undermining his intentions. On the contrary, he was enthusiastically supported. He had also strongly advocated the expansion of NATO, so that it now included Poland, the Czech Republic, and Hungary, bordering on the Balkans. Kosovo would test this expanded Western alliance.

Clinton was no longer the junior figure among the Western powers that he had been when he became president. Now he was a senior statesman, the one longest in office and the most experienced, and the political role model for a new generation of center-left leaders. The natural alignment of the United States and Britain was cemented in shared objectives as never before—closer than Franklin Roosevelt and Winston Churchill had been (Churchill rightly suspected that FDR sought the dissolution of the British Empire), or John F. Kennedy and Harold Macmillan (who fought over defense policy), or Ronald Reagan and Margaret Thatcher (who fretted over Reagan's remoteness and limited intellectual capacity). Already, the Clinton-Blair relationship had been tested during the bombing of Iraq. Across Europe, leaders of entrenched social democratic parties looked to Clinton as a political trailblazer—reforming his party, the welfare state, and global economics all at the same time. He was the most sophisticated, knowledgeable, innovative—and European—American president in their lifetimes.

Kosovo was a crisis for them all. If they succeeded in Kosovo, they would gain a strengthened platform for the Third Way and for their new ideas about globalization and interdependence. Clinton himself well understood the stakes.

Clinton's foreign policy team in his second term was better suited to his ambitions and sensibility than the one in his first term. Secretary of State Warren Christopher had been emotionally reserved and stoic, a classic deputy who had risen to his position on experience and the appearance of gravity, but without a vision. He had sided with Clinton during his difficult primary contests in the 1992 campaign, and his support of the embattled candidate was much appreciated. But he did not have a clear idea of the damage that would be done to the President and U.S. policy by deferring to the Europeans over Bosnia. Christopher listened closely to Clinton's anxieties about Bosnia during his first two years in of-

fice and did not present another view. He had a lawyerly notion of his office, as if the job of secretary of state were faithfully to represent the
client. The national security adviser, Anthony Lake, a former foreign
service officer and a professor at Amherst College, had argued for lifting
the embargo on Bosnia and bombing the Serbs, but he undercut Ambassador Albright when she challenged Colin Powell over the use of force.
Despite their long careers and involvement with politicians, neither
Christopher nor Lake was intrinsically political. They favored international law and higher abstractions in foreign policy. Clinton chafed at
this stance and wished for a sharper, more political performance.

In the second term, a more experienced and confident Clinton got
the team that expressed his now more coherent and activist tone, that was
congruent with his personality and perspectives. At its center was Samuel
"Sandy" Berger, his national security adviser, who had been Lake's
deputy. Like Clinton, Berger was a small-town boy, from upstate New
York, whose father had died when he was young. He was a meritocrat of
ambition and achievement (Cornell, Harvard Law), having done it all on
his own—the dominant pattern of the Clinton administration. His
lengthy, varied political résumé included working for the liberal Republican mayor John Lindsay of New York City and an upstate New York
Democratic congressman, Joseph Resnick, and writing speeches for Secretary of State Edmund Muskie during the Carter administration. He
had helped provide political intelligence to Pamela Harriman, the influential widow of Averell Harriman, and her network of Democrats for the
Eighties, bringing onto her board the young governor of Arkansas and
giving Clinton his first regular Washington institutional connection.

Henry Kissinger had unsympathetically remarked about Berger, "You
can't expect a trade lawyer to be a global strategist."* But in an era of
global economics, being a trade lawyer certainly wasn't a disadvantage.
Berger was politically canny, knew Clinton well, had earned his implicit
trust, and had had extensive foreign policy experience. His deputy, James
Steinberg, former director of policy planning at the State Department,
was another formidable expert. Berger was a liberal internationalist dedicated to pragmatic methods. He was adamantly opposed to doctrines of
any kind and knocked down any effort to invent a Clinton doctrine
around this or that idea. As the head of the National Security Council,
Berger was a superb manager, eliciting all the staff's concerns, and orga-

---

*Halberstam, *War in a Time of Peace: Bush, Clinton, and the Generals*, Scribner,
2001, p. 408.

nizing the flow of policy through the interagency process and then the Principals Committee meetings in the Situation Room, so that everyone was on the same page. He was down to earth, funny, and smart. He never operated behind people's backs, as Kissinger had, and he had no ulterior motives or agendas apart from the President's, but he also did not hesitate to offer his unvarnished views. As a former speechwriter he understood the importance of the written and spoken word, and he involved himself in the preparation of every one of the President's foreign policy speeches. Like Clinton, he wanted to transform the foreign policy image of the Democratic Party. Unlike the anguished Lake, the Vietnam syndrome did not haunt him. In that, he was of a similar mind with Albright.

On the Kosovo crisis, Secretary of State Madeleine Albright remained as insistent on confronting Milosevic as she had been for years. In a meeting at the White House in late 1998, she was unyielding on this point. Assistant Secretary of State James P. Rubin remembered, "Midway through her argument, one of her colleagues cut her off and exploded in frustration. 'What is it with you people at the State Department, always wanting to threaten force and bombing? It's not always the solution. What is it with you?' But Albright held her ground. 'I remember five years ago when I was U.N. ambassador, Tony Lake cut me off time and time again and he wouldn't let us really discuss this issue. Well, now I am Secretary of State and we are going to have this discussion.' "*

At the Rambouillet conference, the Kosovo Liberation Army accepted the proposed terms of an agreement that gave Kosovo considerable autonomy but stopped short of independence. The Serbs, however, walked out. Holbrooke was sent to Belgrade for a last time to speak face-to-face with Milosevic, who had refused to come to Rambouillet and who now rejected his last-minute plea. On March 24, the bombing of Serb positions in Kosovo started, and Clinton addressed the nation. Thus began NATO's first war, the first war ever fought to reverse an act of genocide.

From its inception, Russian president Boris Yeltsin was adamant in his censure of NATO, and his anger ushered in "the most severe, dangerous and consequential crisis in U.S.-Russian relations of the post–cold war period," as Deputy Secretary of State Strobe Talbott, who had principal responsibility for U.S.-Russian affairs, wrote. The Clinton-Yeltsin relationship had been warm and productive thus far, though the hoped-for

*James P. Rubin, "A Very Personal War," *The Financial Times*, September 30, 2000.

fostering of reform in Russia had not been wholly successful. Nonetheless, the continued tie between the leaders had bolstered the cause of
democracy, defused potential crises, and brought Russia ever closer to
the West. But Yeltsin was furious at Clinton about Kosovo and, as early
as October 1998, had declared in a telephone call that the use of force
against Milosevic was "forbidden" and then had hung up. The night the
bombing started he slammed the phone down again on Clinton. But
Clinton's personal link—and Talbott's diplomacy—later proved decisive.*

Clinton and Talbott had been roommates at Oxford as Rhodes scholars, where Talbott had translated the manuscript of Soviet leader Nikita
Khrushchev's memoir while Clinton made him tea. Members of the vibrant Russian emigré group that clustered at Oxford came and went, including members of the Pasternak family, and Clinton, partly inspired
by Talbott, went to Russia and Eastern Europe then. When he was
elected U.S. president, he asked Talbott, by then a columnist for *Time*
and the author of numerous books on U.S.-Soviet arms control, to become his Russia hand; in 1994 Talbott became deputy secretary of state.
Soon, Clinton would ask him to take charge at a critical diplomatic
moment.

Milosevic took the bombing as a signal to accelerate his ethnic cleansing. His army swept into Kosovo and drove nearly one million Kosovars
from their homes. The world's media broadcast pictures of the effects of
NATO's bombing but not of Milosevic's atrocities. Serb tank battalions
were not credentialing CNN correspondents to ride with them. Public
support in most of Europe was fragile and shaky. An aide to Chancellor
Gerhardt Schroeder, Bodo Hombach, came to my office in the White
House. His briefing on German public opinion was not encouraging. In
western Germany support was at 60 percent, but in eastern Germany
only about one-third. A majority of Greens, the Social Democrats' coalition partner and the party of Foreign Minister Joschka Fischer, were opposed to the use of force in the Balkans; only 28 percent of all Germans
believed that Milosevic would be forced to admit defeat. In Italy, public
opinion was even shakier, and in Greece, an overwhelming majority were
opposed. "We need to win quickly," Hombach told me.

Only when television pictures showed trains bearing the Kosovars
fleeing from their countryside, images reminiscent of trains bearing Jews
being shipped to concentration camps by the Nazis, was the European
public horrified. Suddenly, scenes from recent films about the Holocaust

*Strobe Talbott, *The Russia Hand*, Random House, 2002, p. 297.

like Steven Spielberg's *Schindler's List* and Roberto Benigni's *Life Is Beautiful* appeared re-created in modern Europe.

On March 30, after a political strategy meeting in the Yellow Oval, the President took me aside to discuss the war. His popularity, after less than a week of bombing, was beginning to slip. "I feel quite comfortable, even if it takes weeks and weeks," he said. "Building up popularity is for this. If the popularity isn't for this, what's it for?" At a meeting of his national security advisers about this time, he said, "I know you're taking criticism, that the critics are calling it 'Madeleine's war.' Well, it's my war and we're going to see it through to the end."

Clinton gave me his assessments of the alliance. Great Britain was firm and would be staunch to the end. (Blair had declared that the Kosovo war was a humanitarian war "in defense of our values, rather than our interests.") Clinton said he'd told Blair that the bombing had to be kept up: there could be no pause, not even for Easter. Blair had to help Clinton to keep the alliance together and avoid being "nickel and dimed." Blair took on the task of asking Javier Solana, then defense chief of NATO, to approve broader bombing targets, which he did. Prime Minister Massimo D'Alema of Italy had asked for a bombing halt, but Clinton talked him out of it, helping him with his political efforts to win public support for the bombing campaign as it widened. Schroeder, who also faced a difficult domestic political situation, was supportive. Milosevic had tried, with Russian help, to wrangle a cease-fire, but Schroeder had conferred with Clinton and then told Russian prime minister Primakov that any such deal would be rejected. The Germans were checking the Russians.

The bombing did not stop Milosevic. After a week, the political stresses on the NATO coalition grew exponentially, and within the U.S. administration debate continued on the proper strategy for conducting the war. In his speech on March 25, Clinton had said, "I do not intend to put our troops into Kosovo to fight a ground war," a line that National Security Council speechwriters, with Berger's approval, had inserted and that Clinton did not question at the time. He thought the bombing might force Milosevic to concede within days. Clinton's reasoning was to do everything he could to maintain national and international unity; otherwise, he felt he would be playing into Milosevic's hands. He didn't want to set off a debate about ground troops with the Congress. Equally important, he didn't want to spark a debate among the allies. Even if ground troops had been planned at the beginning, it would have taken two to three months to deploy them, and Milosevic would have rolled through

Kosovo in any case. As a practical matter, in the short run, it didn't make a difference. But that early calculation could not last over time.

Clinton made it plain that he was willing to persevere regardless of the political pressures on him. But his stalwart attitude did not diffuse these pressures. He came to regret the line about ground troops and in private railed about its having limited his options. Once he had said it, though, he had put down a marker, and it became a source of rising frustration. In April, Berger went on television to say that all options were open.

General Wesley Clark, the Supreme Allied Commander in Europe (SACEUR), was caught in the crosswind between "political aims and military means," as he later wrote.* The Pentagon as a whole resisted a ground war that might well produce many casualties and that had no clear exit strategy, one of the stipulations of the Powell doctrine, the military codification of the Vietnam syndrome. Nightmarish visions of Somalia danced in the generals' heads. When it began to seem that the war would be prolonged, Clark pressed for NATO to be given additional means, and he requested the deployment of the deadly Apache helicopters. But the Pentagon opposed this suggestion, seeing it as a cloaked effort to commit American troops to a ground war. Its planners told the White House that the Apaches would suffer perhaps a 50 percent loss ratio, an utterly contrived figure intended to destroy the option, as Clark saw it. General Hugh Shelton, chairman of the Joint Chiefs of Staff, eventually agreed to the deployment of a symbolic force of Apaches in Albania, but these were ultimately withdrawn and never committed to combat.

Clark himself was a controversial commander. His assets were regarded within the Pentagon as his liabilities: He was decisive, highly intelligent, a West Point graduate, a Rhodes scholar, but not one of the boys. He had climbed too far, too fast; was perceived as being political (though he was not especially close to Clinton, despite coming from Arkansas and having been a Rhodes scholar); and was suspected of operating out of channels (with the British). He was a general under suspicion. Clark wrote about the situation he and the President faced:

> While the air campaign was simple enough in concept, its execution was repeatedly constrained and distorted by political forces such as hope that just a few strikes would compel Milosevic's surrender, thirst for a bomb-

*Wesley K. Clark, *Waging Modern War*, Public Affairs, 2001, p. 244.

ing pause, fear of civilian casualties, exaggerated fear of the Serbs' military capabilities, and the American military's reluctance to risk the Apache helicopters. The air campaign began with enough forces to punish the Serbs, but it lacked the mass and capabilities needed to halt the ethnic cleansing. . . . Throughout the campaign, and especially as it contemplated ground intervention, the Pentagon was distracted by its preference for focusing on Northeast Asia and the Persian Gulf, despite the fact that the only real conflict was in Europe. Other nations, such as France, also kept a wary eye on balancing their operations in various areas.*

Clinton was on the phone every day with his counterparts, and he and Blair worked as a tag team, dividing up the allies to speak to them. "We need to ramp up operations," he told Blair on April 1. That same day, he told Schroeder, "Milosevic needs to understand that we are prepared to escalate this campaign for the next couple of weeks. We have no timetable or deadlines." Schroeder agreed. But Clinton found it difficult to convince President Jacques Chirac to agree to a targeting strategy that included Milosevic's military and communications infrastructure within Serbia proper. So far the bombing had been restricted to targets in Kosovo. Wary of the United States as the "hyperpower," France was hesitant to expand the war. Clinton went on trying to cajole Chirac, but he also used others to get Chirac's agreement for the new targets. When President José Maria Aznar of Spain visited the White House in mid-April, Clinton talked of his problems with Chirac, and Aznar took on the task of persuading Chirac, which he did. After a civilian convoy was mistakenly hit by NATO bombs on April 16, Clinton swayed Chirac not to walk out on a NATO leaders' meeting, arguing that his abrupt departure would be interpreted as a sign of open disunity. "We must be upbeat, resolute, and not defensive about our mistakes," Clinton pleaded with him.

The humanitarian crisis within Kosovo, meanwhile, was becoming a greater and greater nightmare. Refugees were flowing by the hundreds of thousands into camps in Macedonia and Albania. On April 2, the President met in the Cabinet Room with representatives of voluntary relief organizations coping with the food, housing, and medical needs of the Kosovars. Unlike some critics, they did not blame the displacement of the Kosovars on the U.S.-led military action against the Serbs. But they were being overwhelmed. After the meeting, the President and I discussed the danger of disorganization and how it might adversely affect

*Clark, *Waging Modern War*, p. 424.

both the conditions of the Kosovars and public opinion about the war. That week, he appointed Brian Atwood, administrator of the U.S. Agency for International Development, as the overall chief of the relief effort in Kosovo.

On April 12, the seventh lecture of the White House Millennium Program was held in the East Room. The speaker was Elie Wiesel, winner of the Nobel Peace Prize and witness to the Holocaust, and his subject was "The Perils of Indifference." "What is indifference?" he asked. "Etymologically, the word means 'no difference.' A strange and unnatural state in which the lines blur between light and darkness, dusk and dawn, crime and punishment, cruelty and compassion, good and evil." He described the universe of the Holocaust: "In the place that I come from, society was composed of three simple categories: the killers, the victims, and the bystanders." He asked why the railroads to the concentration camps had not been bombed in 1944 and why the *St. Louis*, a ship loaded with Jewish refugees, had been turned away from American shores. Now, in Kosovo, "crimes against humanity" were being confronted. "But this time, the world was not silent. This time, we do respond. This time, we intervene."

The President, responding with impromptu remarks to Wiesel, said:

The history of our country for quite a long while had been dominated by a principle of nonintervention in the affairs of other nations. Indeed, for most of our history we have worn that principle as a badge of honor, for our founders knew intervention as a fundamentally destructive force. George Washington warned us against those "entangling alliances."

The twentieth century, with its two world wars, the Cold War, Korea, Vietnam, Desert Storm, Panama, Lebanon, Grenada, Somalia, Haiti, Bosnia, Kosovo—it changed all that; for good or ill, it changed all that. Our steadily increasing involvement in the rest of the world, not for territorial gain, but for peace and freedom and security, is a fact of recent history. . . .

The central irony of our time, it seems to me, is this: most of us have this vision of a twenty-first-century world with the triumph of peace and prosperity and personal freedom; with the respect for the integrity of ethnic, racial, and religious minorities; within a framework of shared values, shared power, shared plenty; making common cause against disease and environmental degradation across national lines, against terror, organized crime, weapons of mass destruction. This vision, ironically, is threatened by the oldest demon of human society—our vulnerability to hatred of the other.

In the face of that, we cannot be indifferent, at home or abroad. That is why we are in Kosovo.

But the war went on without conclusion, and from the right and left came harsh criticism. "A colossal failure," railed George Will on ABC's *This Week*. Some argued that ground troops should have been put into the field at once, that NATO's failure to do so showed cowardice, perhaps even a special generational cowardice, a desire to achieve results without sacrifice but with politically clean hands. The liberal writer Mark Danner suggested, "Perhaps one day there will be a method to calculate how many Kosovars had to be displaced, how many had to die, for the West to prosecute its 'perfect' war."*

The President was planning the fiftieth anniversary summit meeting of NATO to be held later in the month in Washington. "Blair and Schroeder and I could ride into the sunset, but we've got to do this with NATO intact, having done this as an alliance," he said to me on April 7. "Either it comes out right or we get cremated." But even weeks later the war was still not going well; progress seemed stalled. Criticism was growing and Clinton's popularity continued to drop. He seemed strategically boxed in by his early statement against ground troops, for which Blair was now agitating. Within the administration, Albright supported Blair's position. General Clark, too, favored the use of ground troops, but the Pentagon was blocking him.

The night before the NATO summit, on April 23, Blair and Clinton met at the White House. Blair argued in favor of a ground force short of an invasion force that could be deployed in what the military called a "semipermissive environment," that is, in areas where they would not be required to seize territory from an entrenched enemy. Clinton was insistent that the issue of ground troops not be raised in the context of the summit meeting for fear that it would blow up the entire event. None of the other allies were as aggressive as Blair, and if the United States joined the British position, the alliance might fall apart. Blair agreed not to bring the matter up and Clinton agreed that Clark should draw up contingency plans. This was not a commitment to ground troops; it was a

---

*Mark Danner, "Kosovo: The Meaning of Victory," *The New York Review of Books*, July 15, 1999.

decision to have the option on paper. They pledged to each other that the war must be won on NATO's terms: the strategy was open-ended. Clinton was determined that the allies must plan a more intense bombing campaign in Serbia itself, targeting Milosevic's military, his communications, his bridges, and even his and his cronies' homes, and must leave the summit reaffirming the war's aims. In this, he succeeded.

Right after the summit meeting ended, Clinton, Blair, Schroeder, D'Alema, and Prime Minister Wim Kok of the Netherlands appeared on April 25 at a joint discussion on Third Way center-left perspectives which I organized under the auspices of the Democratic Leadership Council. There these men all demonstrated the connection they believed tied the war to the fate of their politics.

"What gives rise to this kind of politics, when the old order is destroyed or when the realities of daily life or popular dreams can no longer be accommodated by a given set of political arrangements through a political debate?" asked Clinton. Gesturing to the others onstage with him, he went on, "What is giving rise to all these people's [winning] elections? Why is this happening everywhere? It's not some blind coincidence. I believe it is because the social arrangements which were developed within countries and the international arrangements among them, which grew up from the Great Depression through the Second World War, and then the Cold War, are no longer adequate to meet the challenges of the day." The right, he explained, had been "beating us in elections" by campaigning against government itself. "So they had quite a run in the 1980s. And then it became readily apparent that that didn't really solve any problems." For the center-left now, Clinton posed several questions:

> The great question that any political party that purports to represent ordinary citizens must answer is, how do you make the most of the economic possibilities of the global information economy and still preserve the social contract? What can governments do to help make sure that every responsible citizen has a chance to succeed in the global economy? And how can we discharge our responsibilities, as the leaders of wealthy countries, to put a human face on the global economy so that in other countries, as well, no one who's willing to work is left behind?

Blair responded that the internationalism of the center-left was essential to this political equation: "This applies internationally as well as nationally. And, therefore, when we say what is happening in Kosovo is utterly unacceptable and we are not going to tolerate it. . . . [This] is every bit as much about our values as it is about strategic interest."

D'Alema, a former communist, now leader of the Italian left coalition, reflected on the demise of the old left and the rise of a new one, still working to gain a footing. "The Third Way," he said, "is the effort to find a meeting point between the positive aspects of these two major experiences. Is it possible to have a dynamic economics and a society based on solidarity? I think it is. But . . . there is no prescription that you can write down for this. It is an attempt, an effort that is pursued day after day. . . . The need for a Third Way is the result of a crisis of ideologies, not of the victory of ideologies."

When a newspaper article about the forum was published under the headline "NATO's 'Third Way' Leadership Faces Foreign Policy Test," Clinton marked it up and gave it to me. He had underlined key portions: ". . . the third way leaders . . . have shown the left can once again start a war, if need be; they have yet to prove it can do what it takes to win one. . . . With an eye on the 1995 NATO bombing campaign that had helped push Milosevic to the bargaining table in Bosnia, today's crop of NATO leaders rejected the imprisoning assumption that the only choice in Kosovo was all or nothing; in that sense, Clinton's generation arguably has been less bound by the Vietnam precedent than Bush's."* And indeed, President Clinton was exploring every possible diplomatic and military option available to the Western powers.

On April 28, the House of Representatives voted a resolution on the air war in the Balkans. Speaker Dennis Hastert had assured the White House that he could secure a majority in favor, but the true power within the Republican Party unmasked Hastert once again as a figurehead. Republican whip Tom DeLay ensured that there would be no positive vote for President Clinton. The final vote in the House was a carefully stage-managed tie, 213–213. "Shame! Shame!" chanted the Democrats in unison. But DeLay gloated. He saw Kosovo as "act two of impeachment," according to representative Peter King. DeLay believed, as he told Republicans, "When the sun rises following the election of 2000, I think we will control both ends of Pennsylvania Avenue because of it."† "I don't

---

*Ronald Brownstein, "NATO's 'Third Way' Leadership Faces Foreign Policy Test," *Los Angeles Times*, April 26, 1999.

†Jane Mayer, "The Exterminator," *The New Yorker*, May 24, 1999.

respect the President, but I don't agree with the President either," he explained on NBC's *Meet the Press* on May 16.

In early May, the bombing ramped up with devastating effect, the raids now penetrating into Belgrade. Serb surface-to-air missile batteries and radar sites, armored units, governmental buildings, and safe houses for Milosevic's mafia were systematically taken out. Serb soldiers started to desert. A mutiny was reported. Then, on May 7, a precisely targeted missile hit the new Chinese embassy in Belgrade, killing two people. The truth, not publicly acknowledged, was that the CIA had been operating with an old map drawn before the construction of the new building, and had assumed the strike was against a Serb target. No one in the CIA or in any of the armed forces thought to seek information from any American who had recently been in Belgrade. The Chinese persisted in believing that the hit had been deliberate. It was a public relations disaster. Clinton called Blair and vented his frustration: "If we had one TV picture of the fifteen [Kosovar] men being roped together and burned alive [by the Serbs], they would be demanding that we bomb the hell out of them. People would be wondering why we haven't leveled the place."

Clinton used a press appearance with King Abdullah of Jordan to shift his position on ground troops while making it appear that his policy had never been set in concrete at all: "I don't think that we or our allies should take any options off the table, and that has been my position from the beginning." The Pentagon almost instantly issued a statement saying that the use of ground troops was not an option, but the President was, in fact, moving toward authorizing precisely that.

After the bombing of the Chinese embassy, already precarious public support for the war plummeted by 25 percent in Germany. Three weeks earlier, on April 13, the Green Party had nearly come apart at the seams at its annual conference. The "realos," or realists, and the "fundis," or fundamentalists of the ecological and pacifist persuasion, could not agree on whether the party should back the German government and NATO. When Foreign Minister Fischer entered the conference hall, he was physically assaulted, pelted with objects and drenched in red paint to symbolize blood, and his eardrum was broken. He threw his prepared speech at the crowd and told the delegates that if they did not vote in favor of the war they might as well elect Milosevic as their party leader. With that bravura performance, the Greens elected to support NATO, and the German coalition held. But Blair's push for ground troops prompted Schroeder to declare that such an option was "unthinkable" and called it, on May 20, "British war theory."

On May 24, Joschka Fischer came to Washington to confer about the war, and that night at a dinner held in his honor at the German embassy, I was seated next to him. We had an intense conversation about the German position, particularly on ground troops. We were two members of the generation of '68, easily recognizable to each other politically, trying to find common ground. Fischer, the son of a Hungarian immigrant butcher and a German mother, had been a scruffy oppositional militant in Frankfurt; was a former roommate of Daniel Cohn-Bendit, "Danny the Red," with whom he had organized a group called Revolutioner Kampf, or Revolutionary Struggle; and had been arrested in street demonstrations. By the 1990s his left-wing associates were accusing him of being a changeling, trading in his black leather motorcycle jacket for an establishment Armani suit in an act of surpassing opportunism. But in the German Foreign Office he was respected as capable, strong, and very well prepared for his work. His odyssey and political predicament paralleled in an especially dramatic way that of American and British activists who had undertaken their own journeys from the 1960s to the center-left of the 1990s. The charge against Fischer that he was a hollow opportunist was a kind of German echo of the "character issue" that conservatives raised about Clinton. Fischer, of course, had been a true radical, which Clinton never was, but the accusation was similar: Fischer's idealism and his character must be false because he had power, because he had fought for it, and because he used it.

Fischer was morally and politically serious as he worked through the German question of "the ghosts of the past," as he put it to me, the ghost of war and the ghost of the Holocaust. Fischer's generation had been imbued with the idea that "no more war" and "no more Auschwitz" were complementary. But the Kosovo war confronted Germans with a choice: to be pacifist meant to accept genocide. And now the choice was becoming even more difficult. What would it mean for NATO to let Milosevic win? Shouldn't all the options be pursued to end the greater evil? Couldn't Germany support a "coalition of the willing" that would deploy troops, if by a given time the air war had not turned in NATO's favor? Germany would not have to join that coalition, but couldn't it support it? At the end of the conversation, Fischer said he was coming to the conclusion that he could agree to such a formulation, and he soon held a press conference announcing it.

On May 27, the President sent Secretary of Defense William Cohen to a secret meeting of NATO defense ministers in Brussels to assess the ground troops option. The ministers agreed that since it would take perhaps three to four months to assemble a force, the decision would have to be made soon.

On May 30, the President went to a Democratic Leadership Council retreat that I had organized at White Oaks in northern Florida. White Oaks is a large, lush preserve, containing a private zoo of animals threatened with extinction and Mikhail Baryshnikov's dance studio, owned by the Howard Gilman Foundation. At this weekend event, key Democratic officials and supporters were joined by my counterparts from Britain, David Miliband, director of policy, and Peter Mandelson, a member of Parliament and among Blair's closest advisers. During the day we held seminars on politics during which both Hillary and the President made presentations. That night, before dinner, Mandelson talked with Clinton, conveying Blair's belief that unless NATO ground troops were used against him, Milosevic would continue to hold out. Clinton replied that although committing to ground troops might be further than Congress and public opinion wanted to go, he would support it if that would be what it took to make Milosevic come to his senses.

The President and I then spoke alone. He had heard the opinions of his national security advisers on ground forces, and they properly had not made political arguments, but I believed Clinton now should hear the political reasons for the policy, too, put in the light of history. I told him that he should reflect on the previous Democratic presidents of the twentieth century, one after another ending their terms ruined by foreign policy crises. Leaving aside FDR and JFK, who had died in office, consider that Woodrow Wilson could not win passage of the League of Nations. Harry Truman could not run for reelection in the midst of the Korean War. Lyndon Johnson was destroyed in his handling of the Vietnam War. Jimmy Carter was voted out of office in great part because he was seen as ineffectual during the Soviet invasion of Afghanistan and when the Iranians took the American hostages. Winning the Kosovo war was imperative, I told the President. If it required ground troops, he must not rule out that possibility. He could not allow the war to drag on or lose control of it. Clinton nodded in agreement. He did not really need reinforcement of his will to persevere, and he had made it plain that he would endure whatever political pain was necessary until victory. But historical reminders of Democratic tragedies could not but underline the urgency of the decision.

When he returned to the White House, planning for NATO ground troops in Kosovo moved to a practical level. Sandy Berger submitted a new options memo on June 2, saying that ground troops were necessary if negotiations with Milosevic should fail. The scenario that would then go into effect was called Plan B-minus, and it would comprise 175,000 troops, including 100,000 Americans and 50,000 British, who would invade in early September. That very day, *The New York Times* reported that the President had scheduled a meeting with the Joint Chiefs at the White House for the next day, "when they are to discuss options for using ground troops if NATO decides to invade Kosovo, NATO and Administration officials said today."*

The meeting took place on June 3 as scheduled. As usual, Clinton withheld his own opinions as he went around the Cabinet Room asking each of the generals to speak. Then others presented their views. Secretary Cohen was the most reluctant to support ground troops and Gore the most aggressive. Clinton was prepared to move forward, but just after the meeting ended, he received word from Strobe Talbott that Milosevic had capitulated. The diplomacy that had been quietly pursued for weeks had suddenly achieved success.

The diplomatic effort began on the last day of the NATO summit meeting, April 25, when Clinton and Yeltsin had a ninety-minute telephone conversation. In the face of allied unity, Yeltsin had decided to cut himself loose from the Serbs, whose cause was alienating Russia from its larger interests with the West. Clinton told Yeltsin, "I don't think the refugees will go home [to Kosovo] unless there is a NATO and an American presence." Yeltsin wondered if a bombing halt would do the trick, but Clinton told him that while that might be "helpful," all of Milosevic's troops had to be withdrawn, and this was a condition backed by all nineteen members of NATO. "I am bound by the decision the group has taken, and I think it is a good decision." He added, "I do not believe there can be a settlement without Russia's leadership and involvement."

Now Yeltsin could see a way out for himself. He appointed Viktor Chernomyrdin, the former prime minister and a close ally, as his special envoy to the Serbs. "I don't care what you have to do, just end it. It's ruining everything," Yeltsin said to him.† After initial conversations with Vice President Gore, with whom Chernomyrdin had conducted productive joint U.S.-Russian communications on various issues for years, Strobe Talbott was sent as the U.S. negotiator. And—an American suggestion—a neutral party was brought in to buttress Chernomyrdin,

*Jane Perlez, "Clinton and the Joint Chiefs to Discuss Ground Invasion," *The New York Times*, June 2, 1999.

†Halberstam, *War in a Time of Peace*, p. 476.

Finnish president Martti Ahtisaari. The three became an effective team, working together for weeks to bring Milosevic to his senses. On June 3, at Milosevic's palace in Belgrade, when Ahtisaari spelled out for him the havoc that would be wrought on him if he persisted, Milosevic turned to his fellow Slav, looking for support, but Chernomyrdin was a blank wall. He told him to sign the Russian draft of an agreement that called for "all Serb forces out." Milosevic crumbled.

Within hours of receiving the news, Clinton held a long-scheduled cabinet meeting. "The agreement may be great, but we don't know that yet," he told his cabinet. Albright spoke next: "Yes, there are a lot of moving parts." "We got into Kosovo immediately compared to Bosnia," the President reflected. "This is not just about beating Milosevic, but [about] reversing ethnic cleansing. That's the ultimate test." Cohen offered congratulations: "There are two successes here: the success of the air campaign and the diplomatic success." But Berger the pragmatist jumped in: "Put your pride in a lockbox. There's still no better than a 50–50 chance. Less is more here."

Clinton emphasized the politics of the allied coalition as essential to victory: "NATO never had to wage a war for fifty years. This is the first operation this alliance has had to engage in for fifty years. The best thing Bush did in Desert Storm was to get Arab countries to go along. Bosnia took four years. Running a campaign by committee is a challenge. There was second-guessing from the moment it began. But our crowd maintained a positive frame of mind. I will go to my grave grateful we hung together."

The President then discussed the war's tactics, first referring to the air campaign and then to ground troops: "There was a gross underestimation of the damage we have done [in the air campaign] to the Serb army—and we kept all options open." Seamlessly, without a stop, he linked this foreign crisis to his domestic politics: "We haven't allowed the White House to become paralyzed. Under the most adverse circumstances, we have got a lot done." Some Democrats believed that if he flatly rejected dealing with the Republican Congress it would "rebound to the Democrats' credit," he noted. But "those Democrats who believe that are wrong," and he had managed to "get the Republican Congress to get a good deal of what we want." Not only did he have faith in his political ability, but he also argued that producing results was essential for the Democrats: "If you're progressive, you always have to legitimize the government enterprise. We need to do those things that we can do. We won't get everything we want, but we need to push for them. Stay up-beat. We'll get good results. There's always going to be an adverse environment. We have to have a multi-front war here we're waging for the American people." And he launched into a discussion of his latest education bill.

The debate over the means of victory in Kosovo began immediately. The noted British military historian John Keegan wrote, "There are certain dates in the history of warfare that mark real turning points. . . . Now there is a new turning point to fix on the calendar: June 3, 1999, when the capitulation of President Milosevic proved that a war can be won by airpower alone."* But at Downing Street, the view was that President Clinton's willingness to put the ground troops option forward was in the end decisive, that it had given a final impetus to the Russians to seek an agreement and had created a doomsday scenario for Milosevic.

On June 22, President Clinton visited the Stenkovic refugee camp in Macedonia, just across the mountainous border from Kosovo. About half its inhabitants had already left to go home, but about twenty thousand people remained in the sea of tents and mud. Upon our arrival, children surrounded us, many of them speaking English and asking to meet with the President. Clinton spent more than an hour sitting with groups of families, listening to their harrowing stories. Then he climbed atop a wooden crate to address the thousands assembled before him: "We're proud of what we did because we think it's what America stands for, that no one ever, ever should be punished and discriminated against or killed or uprooted because of their religion or their ethnic heritage." They chanted "Clinton!" and "U.S.A!" It wasn't long before all the people at Stenkovic were returned to their villages and the camp disappeared.

At the Pentagon, a graceless note was struck in July, however, when General Clark was summarily retired early as SACEUR. This was a personal slap at him for having insisted on ground troops against the Pentagon's recommendation and for his sharpness in pursuing that strategy. And the White House had been snookered without realizing it when it had earlier agreed to what Berger and others thought was a routine replacement process at SACEUR. But if it was held against Clark that he

*John Keegan, "Yes, We Won This War: Let's Be Proud of It," *The Daily Telegraph*, June 24, 1999.

was a political general, it was a mistaken impression. Clark had in fact put his strategic concerns above politics and above his career.

Clark was called at night and informed of the Pentagon's decision without being given any recourse. He instantly received a call from a *Washington Post* reporter, who had been tipped off by the Secretary of Defense's office, to confirm the story. When the President learned what had happened, he was furious—"I'd like to kill somebody," he told me— but there was nothing to be done. Clark's enforced early retirement from the European post was a fait accompli. Secretary Cohen and General Shelton had considered Clark insubordinate. Clinton awarded Clark the Presidential Medal of Freedom, and the British gave him an honorary knighthood. But the Pentagon's treatment of Clark left a sour taste amid the triumph.

The Kosovo war was the last war fought on European soil in the "century of total war." Conflict ended in the Balkans except for spasms in Macedonia. Both the European Union and NATO continued to expand without disruption. On October 5, 2000, the last revolution toppling a remnant regime from the communist era took place in Yugoslavia: a beleaguered Milosevic announced an election and then tried to void its results when he lost it; instead of succeeding in imposing his rule, however, he provoked his overthrow. He was arrested and placed on trial for crimes against humanity at The Hague before the United Nations War Crimes Tribunal.

In 1999, two weeks after Milosevic's defeat in the war in Kosovo, President Clinton traveled to Cologne, Germany, for the G-7 Economic Summit. On his way, he stopped, on June 16, at the International Labor Organization offices in Geneva, to declare that the U.S. government would ban the purchase of any products made by child laborers and would join initiatives to raise global labor standards around the world. Clinton also made the case for more international trade, arguing that increased standards and trade must go hand in hand: "Globalization is not a proposal or a policy choice, it is a fact. But how we respond to it will make all the difference. We cannot dam up the tides of economic change any more than King Canute could still the waters. Nor can we tell our people to sink or swim on their own. We must find a third way—a new and democratic way—to maximize market potential and social justice, competition and community."

Clinton acknowledged the skepticism about the benefits of globalization and stated that policies of social investment must accompany the inevitable spread of trade:

Unfortunately, working people the world over do not believe this. Even in the United States, with the lowest unemployment rate in a generation, . . . working people strongly resist new market-opening measures. There are many reasons. In advanced countries the benefits of open trade outweigh the burdens. But they are widely spread, while the dislocations of open trade are painfully concentrated. . . . If we allow the ups and downs of financial crises to divert us from investing in our people, it is not only those citizens or nations that will suffer—the entire world will suffer from their lost potential.

The G-7 summit at Cologne had loomed as a potential danger point if by then the Kosovo war was not concluded. On President Clinton's national security staff and among the allies much anxiety was fixed on that meeting. But Cologne was suffused with the glow of the allied victory and the success of Clinton's leadership. Now the President led the other six nations in approving an initiative that slashed the debt of heavily indebted poor countries by 70 percent—a reduction stipulating that the funds would go instead to social expenditures in education, children's health care, and AIDS prevention. Clinton also led in creating with the Europeans a stabilization pact for the Balkans, a diplomatic instrument for establishing the mechanisms and financing for reconstruction. He polished an agreement on international financial stabilization. And he met for the last time with Yeltsin, an exhausted volcano, who agreed to the last touches on the peace agreement with Serbia.

After the Kosovo war, other world leaders regarded Clinton with a deference that extended beyond his role as the chief of state of the number-one power. They considered him a first among equals because of who and what he was, not only because of the country he represented. They knew that he understood in depth their own countries' economics and history and politics like no other U.S. president before him. Because of their implicit trust in him, U.S. prestige reached a zenith it had not enjoyed since perhaps the presidency of John F. Kennedy, when the Western leadership had not been so close. "Because of his empathy and understanding, the world felt included and not resentful of America," a British cabinet minister told me.

Politically like-minded leaders discussed with Clinton their conundrums, and he often had answers he could frame in their own terms. He had bonded initially with Chancellor Schroeder during a conversation about the German economy in which Clinton had offered policy solutions involving the intricacies of apprenticeship and worker-retraining programs peculiar to Germany. I once sat with the President and Tony Blair as, in about fifteen minutes, the two men easily thrashed out a prickly trade problem involving bananas and cashmere. Then Clinton, mentioning a book he had just read, *King Leopold's Ghost*, by Adam Hochschild, about the devastation wrought in the Belgian Congo by colonialism, engaged Blair for an hour in an intense discussion about what they could do to advance African issues in international forums.

For Africans there was never before an American president like Clinton—given his commitment to Africa's progress in economic development, the conquest of AIDS, and the advancement of human rights. On his trip to Ghana, more than one million people greeted him, the largest outpouring he had ever seen. The same was true in India, where, as BBC World Service reported, "Clinton mania" broke out during his March 2000 visit. In Hyderabad, India's high-technology center, he said, "Millions of Indians are connected to the Internet, but millions more aren't connected to fresh water. India accounts for 30 percent of the world's software engineers, but 25 percent of the world's malnourished." He announced billions of dollars' worth of new investment, while also discussing the need for India to support efforts to control global warming. Latin American leaders viewed him as a guarantor of democracy, stability, and development, and conferred with him on everything from trade issues to drugs. He worked tirelessly to make North and South Korean reconciliation possible, and his negotiating skills brought the hermit kingdom of the north to the edge of dismantling its nuclear missile program. Throughout Asia, he was seen as the president whose alert and swift actions had headed off an economic disaster and helped to stabilize financial markets. In China, on his visit there in 1998, he spoke forthrightly in response to complex questions students asked him at Beijing University about the practical meaning of democracy: his theme was that "true freedom means more than economic freedom." In private talks with President Jiang Zemin, Clinton pointedly raised specific human-rights violations in China's record, and a number of political prisoners were released thereafter. A year before, at a joint White House press conference, Clinton had flatly proclaimed that on human rights China was "on the wrong side of history." Yet in 2000 the President also won approval from the Congress for normal trading status for China (risking splitting the Democratic Party again), because he believed that China must be as fully integrated as possible into the world trading system before its power inevitably expanded. In November 2000, Clinton visited

Vietnam to promote democracy, commerce, and reconciliation. America, he said, could now see Vietnam as "a country, not a war."

Nearly a year to the day after Milosevic's capitulation in the Kosovo war, Clinton became the first American president ever to be awarded the Charlemagne Prize, the greatest European honor bestowed on figures who have advanced European unity and progress. The prize, granted since 1950 by the German city of Aachen (once the French city of Aix-la-Chapelle), had been given to Winston Churchill, Konrad Adenauer, Václav Havel, King Juan Carlos, and Tony Blair. Two Americans had previously been recipients: Secretary of State George C. Marshall, who had engineered the reconstruction of postwar Europe, and the German-born Henry Kissinger. The prize was conferred in a formal ceremony in the ancient cathedral where rest the remains of Charlemagne, the eighth-century ruler who created the Holy Roman Empire. Then, in the sun-drenched cathedral square, the President spoke. His vision of Europe in the twenty-first century embraced both Russia and the Balkans: "No doors can be sealed shut to Russia, not NATO's, not the European Union's. . . . Our goal should be to debalkanize the Balkans." But he also addressed the issue that the tragic twentieth century had forced time and again: America's influence in Europe. "The simple fact is that since Europe is an idea as much as a place, America is also a part of Europe, bound by ties of family, history, and values," he said. "Europe and America should draw strength from our transatlantic alliance. Europe should not be threatened by it and America must not listen to those who say we should go it alone."

Clinton's vision of international relations in the twenty-first century was not a rhetorical trope. He did not peer through a hazy lens into a nebulous future. Rather, he saw sharply defined problems requiring constant engagement to achieve practical solutions. He assumed nothing, not least eternal American preeminence, nor did he believe that the world was there for the taking or the ordering. Globalization, he thought, gave rise both to the dire threat of terrorism, which exploited the world's new openness and technologies, and to the progressive possibility of fostering worldwide economic opportunity through social justice. In his intensive battle with terrorism, a mostly secret war that was largely screened from the public, the President contended with the new forces of fear. And in his organization of the center-left leaders who gathered strength and numbers after the Kosovo war, he encouraged the new forces of hope.

II

On June 21, 1995, Clinton had signed Presidential Decision Directive-39, the first U.S. policy document of its kind. Never before had terrorism, or "asymmetric warfare," in the language of the directive, received such urgent government attention in the United States. As a result of the directive, the "consequence management" of federal agencies was reorganized in the event of terrorist attack. For the first time, agencies were subjected to a common budget review on counterterrorism. At the National Security Council, Richard A. Clarke was appointed chairman of the Coordinating Subgroup (CSG), in charge of centralizing control within the White House of the interagency groups. Clarke was a Foreign Service officer, an intelligence specialist, with a thorough grasp of the byzantine national security bureaucracies, tough-minded and more than persistent. Another document, PDD-62, designated him the first person to hold the position of coordinator of counterterrorism.

Since the bombing of the World Trade Center in New York in 1993, the President had proposed antiterrorism measures, only some of which had been approved by the Congress. And although after the bombing of the Murrah Federal Building in Oklahoma City in 1995 many of his proposals were enacted, the Republican-dominated Congress, supported by some civil libertarians, still refused to agree to roving wiretaps (on any phone used by a suspect) and identifying markers on explosives.

In August 1996, Clinton had delivered a major address on terrorism, which he called "the enemy of our generation," and he signed a bill that levied sanctions against firms that did business in the energy sector with Iran or Libya. By then, Clarke was issuing warnings about Osama bin Laden, then operating out of Sudan, a center for worldwide terrorism; but bin Laden was, thanks to U.S. pressure, soon to be expelled and would move to Afghanistan as it fell under the control of the Taliban. At Clinton's instigation, federal programs virtually unknown before—to protect the nation's "critical infrastructure" and to curb weapons of mass destruction—received $3.6 billion over the next four years, and traditional counterterrorism funding was increased by 43 percent. Clinton insisted on spending whatever Clarke and the other intelligence agencies believed was necessary.*

During this time Clinton became virtually obsessed with the dangers of bioterrorism, especially after a conversation he had with Dr. J. Craig

---

*Benjamin and Simon, *Age of Sacred Terror*, pp. 247–48.

Venter, head of the Institute for Genomic Research, and after reading Richard Preston's frightening novel *The Cobra Event*. He held a secret roundtable on bioterrorism at the White House in April 1998 with intelligence experts and a group of scientists including Venter. Immediately after, he ordered the federal stockpiling of antidotes and vaccines.

For more than a year, Sandy Berger, working with Clarke, had been sending urgent alerts to U.S. forces abroad to guard military facilities, including ships in port. In the summer of 1998, at Blair House, across the street from the White House, Berger and Clarke led a secret "tabletop" full-dress rehearsal for cabinet secretaries, deputies, and intelligence agencies of the different possible scenarios of terrorist attacks that could occur with nuclear, chemical, or biological weapons. The participants were shocked by their own poor preparation for these possibilities. The CIA, in the meantime, was mobilized on this front and dramatically increased the number of those listed as "wanted" for terrorism, getting them moved from their refuges to third countries where they could be put on trial—a process called "rendition."

Then came August 7, 1998, and al-Qaeda's bombings of the U.S. embassies in East Africa. Clinton signed one secret presidential "finding" after another, authorizing a lethal campaign against bin Laden. The first approved covert action against bin Laden's network; then he signed three classified "memoranda of notification" that "authorized killing instead of capturing bin Laden, then added several of al-Qaeda's senior lieutenants, and finally approved the shooting down of private civilian aircraft on which they flew," as *The Washington Post* later reported.*

The Principals Committee, consisting of the highest officials with national security responsibilities, voted (with the exception of Attorney General Reno) to approve the President's plan for missile strikes against bin Laden and an al-Qaeda factory of weapons of mass destruction in retaliation for the African embassy bombings. Though the Tomahawks on August 20 just missed bin Laden, his camp in Afghanistan and the Sudanese factory at al-Shifa were destroyed.

Before the embassies were bombed, the CIA had determined that al-Qaeda was trying to build weapons of mass destruction. Daniel Benjamin and Steven Simon, former director and senior director of counterterrorism at the NSC, who worked closely with Clarke, wrote in their authoritative account:

*Barton Gellman, "Broad Effort Launched After '98 Attacks," *The Washington Post*, December 19, 2001.

What made this news riveting was evidence that the group might already be preparing an attack with the chemical agent VX, an extraordinarily lethal substance that could be used to kill hundreds of people, or more. Proof came in the form of a clump of dirt—a soil sample collected near the al-Shifa chemical plant in Khartoum. It contained the chemical O-ethyl methylphosphonothioic acid, or EMPTA, which is produced near the completion of the process to synthesize VX. The Central Intelligence Agency concluded that there was no other reason, including accident, for this precursor to be present in the quantity demonstrated in the soil sample, except in connection with the production of this chemical weapon.*

The U.S. strikes in East Africa, especially the one at al-Shifa, coming as they did within a week of Clinton's deposition by Ken Starr's investigators, were described by the President's foes as a "wag the dog" strategy, as if Clinton were following the script of the recent movie of that name. NBC News and other networks broadcast clips from the movie repeatedly. Among those casting doubt on the U.S. attacks on al-Qaeda were the Republican Senators Arlen Specter and Dan Coats. At the time, the CIA's protection of its sources and methods precluded it from releasing certain information it had that bin Laden was an owner of the Military Industrial Corporation, which controlled the al-Shifa factory, and that its manager lived in bin Laden's villa in Khartoum. The "wag the dog" scenario became a staple of Clinton's critics and the subject of hundreds of articles and editorials in serious publications, not to mention grist for late-night television comedians and radio talk-show hosts.

The circularity of the cynical controversy over al-Shifa had an effect. "The dismissal of the al-Shifa attack as a scandalous blunder had serious consequences, including the failure of the public to comprehend the nature of the al-Qaeda threat," Benjamin and Simon wrote. "In 1999 and 2000, there was no glimmer of support in the U.S. public or the Congress for decisive measures in Afghanistan—no one was even thinking about it." These authors observed matter-of-factly, "Throughout this period and the remainder of the Clinton presidency . . . no member of Congress ever called the national security adviser to discuss the rising problem of al-Qaeda."†

Yet President Clinton spoke continuously about terrorism in major

---

*Benjamin and Simon, *Age of Sacred Terror*, p. 259.
†Ibid., pp. 358, 380, 359.

speeches during his last years in office—at the United Nations in 1998, for example, and in many others. Within the NSC, "threats meetings" were held three times a week to assess potential conspiracies. Intelligence showed no links of consequence between al-Qaeda and the governments of either Iran or Iraq. "The NSC analysts found it difficult to accept that al-Qaeda acted alone, but no other conclusion was warranted," wrote Benjamin and Simon.* In late August 1998, an al-Qaeda plot to bomb the U.S. embassy in Albania was thwarted. Throughout late 1998 and early 1999, more than a dozen embassies were shut down as a result of threat assessments. The administration secured $1.5 billion from the Congress for security upgrade at embassies. And in many unheralded cases, one terrorist cell after another was rolled up: "But the takedowns could never be discussed in any detail."†

Clinton wanted the assets of bin Laden and al-Qaeda frozen, which would allow the CIA and Treasury to track al-Qaeda's finances, but unfortunately, Secretary Rubin was opposed to covert actions that would block bin Laden's bank accounts because, he thought, such a move would violate the international financial system's integrity. In March 2000, the President proposed new laws to ban American residents and firms from doing business with banks in countries that were havens for al-Qaeda money laundering. The bill passed in the House, but the Senate killed it at the behest of Banking Committee chairman Phil Gramm, Republican of Texas, who argued that it was "totalitarian." Thus the Senate declined to attack the financial roots of al-Qaeda. Clinton continued to try to hamper al-Qaeda's money network, reaching an agreement through the Organization for Economic Cooperation and Development for twenty industrial nations to close tax havens for al-Qaeda, but he had to leave completion of this task to the new Bush administration. *Time* reported on how the Bush administration soon undermined the agreement:

Officials from the banking-industry-friendly Center for Freedom and Prosperity sat down with top Bush economic advisers Larry Lindsey and R. Glenn Hubbard and urged them to keep the U.S. out of the coalition and firmly support the status quo in many tax havens. The group's pitch: Americans should be free to seek out lower tax rates anywhere in the world; competition from tax havens helps keep tax rates in the U.S. down. The conservative Heritage Foundation met with Treasury Secre-

*Benjamin and Simon, *Age of Sacred Terror*, p. 264.
†Ibid., pp. 267–68.

tary Paul O'Neill and presented a similar argument. And the C.F.P. helped Don Nickles of Oklahoma, the No. 2 Republican in the Senate, draft a letter to O'Neill applying still more pressure.

By June [2001], the lobbyists got what they wanted. O'Neill told the Organization for Economic Cooperation and Development (OECD), which was leading the campaign against tax havens, that the U.S. was out. And without the world's financial superpower, the biggest effort in years to rid the world's financial system of dirty money was short-circuited.*

The Clinton administration also entered into negotiations to get the Taliban to hand over bin Laden to a third country to face justice. The Taliban were totally uncooperative and protective of their ward; bin Laden was showering money on their regime and on their leader, Mullah Omar. Pakistan, the nation most closely supportive of the Taliban, was also unhelpful. In a meeting with Pakistani prime minister Nawaz Sharif in December 1998, Clinton upbraided him for not arranging to hand over bin Laden and for escalating war threats against India. Sharif backed down on the Indian front but did nothing about bin Laden. He had little control over his army, which in October 1999 overthrew him; its chief of staff, Pervez Musharraf, was installed in his place. On July 4, 1999, Clinton froze assets of the Taliban regime, and in March 2000 in Pakistan, he pressed Musharraf to use his influence on the Taliban to apprehend bin Laden. "I will do as much as I can," Musharraf said—and did nothing.†

In another aspect of the war on terror, Clinton ordered Los Angeles class attack submarines stationed off the Pakistani coast. They were kept there for almost two years after the events in East Africa. Three times missiles were "spun" in preparation to launch against bin Laden, but each time he moved before action could be undertaken. And Clinton demanded of General Shelton that other military plans be readied against al-Qaeda. "Clinton wanted to hear about 'boots on the ground,' plans that put U.S. soldiers in Afghanistan to get the Saudi terrorist. A request for options was made to the Pentagon," wrote Benjamin and Simon. Shelton explained the impracticability of deploying troops there by presenting an overwhelming plan that could not be executed: "One participant remembered the presentation as the Pentagon's 'usual two-division, $2 billion option.' . . . Sandy Berger felt he was having déjà vu, reliving

---

*Adam Cohen, "Banking on Secrecy," *Time*, October 22, 2001.
†Benjamin and Simon, *Age of Sacred Terror*, pp. 317–18.

the discussions from 1993–1995 about intervening in Bosnia, which the military opposed."*

Still frustrated, President Clinton tried to get the Pentagon to think about a Special Forces operation. In late 1999, he suggested to Shelton, "You know, it would scare the shit out of al-Qaeda if suddenly a bunch of black ninjas rappelled out of helicopters into the middle of their camp. It would get us enormous deterrence and show those guys we're not afraid." But Shelton "blanched." The generals subsequently argued to the NSC that a small operation was too risky: "The White House had little recourse; it would not work to order the military to undertake a mission it believed to be suicidal."†

The Federal Bureau of Investigation was the most dysfunctional agency of the government and the one most resistant to cooperation with the National Security Council on al-Qaeda. Its director, Louis Freeh, had for years treated the White House as his enemy. When scandals about FBI mismanagement and misconduct appeared about to swamp him in 1995–96, he had become an ally of the Republicans in Congress in their endless investigations of the Clintons, and serious congressional oversight of the bureau stopped; so did any meaningful internal reform. As the Justice Department inspector general would report in 2002, it was an agency rife with favoritism, where senior officials accused of misconduct were given promotions and cash bonuses while under investigation. Freeh was eventually charged by the Inspector General with "poor judgment" for his part in sending the message that the bureau would "overlook serious allegations of misconduct and even reward the subject of the allegation with a major promotion."‡ Throughout, Freeh's encouragement of institutional squalor was masked by his self-righteousness.

Freeh's hostility to the White House dictated his lack of cooperation with the war against bin Laden. He had been deeply involved in the investigation into the Khobar Towers bombing in Saudi Arabia in 1995, an investigation thwarted by the Saudi refusal to share information or grant access to suspects. The American government suspected that Iranian intelligence agents had been behind the attack, but there was no way to gain evidence that would lead to any convictions. With the emergence in 1997 of the reformist Iranian president Mohammad Khatami, who was

*Benjamin and Simon, *Age of Sacred Terror*, pp. 294–95.

†Ibid., pp. 318–19.

‡Dan Eggen, "FBI Plays Favorites in Discipline, Report Says," *The Washington Post*, November 16, 2002.

challenging Iran's conservative forces, President Clinton believed that diplomacy with Khatami might be "the best bet for reducing tensions between the countries and ultimately securing convictions in the case."

But Freeh, although he had no experience in international affairs and no mandate to develop it, did not agree. "His mistrust of the White House grew so strong that it seems to have blinded him and made him susceptible to manipulation," wrote Benjamin and Simon. Prince Bandar bin Sultan, Saudi Arabia's ambassador in Washington, whispered in Freeh's ear that the administration "showed no interest in the [Khobar] case and only wanted out of the box it was in with Iran." Freeh concluded wrongly that President Clinton was sacrificing the Khobar investigation and became "a man nursing a secret grudge."* He never voiced his qualms or disagreements with any member of the National Security Council. Instead, wrapped in his illusions, he developed his animosities. "Berger, Freeh later thought, was not a national-security adviser; he was a public-relations hack, interested in how something would play in the press," as Elsa Walsh wrote.† And Freeh decided, without telling anyone at the Justice Department, the NSC, or the State Department, to withhold until President Clinton left office any FBI information about the Khobar case that might lead to indictments, presuming that the President, because of his negotiations with Khatami, would not permit the indictment of Iranian officials. When indictments were finally handed down on June 22, 2001, the objects of attention were thirteen Saudis, an unnamed Lebanese, and no Iranians. "Freeh, in his hatred of Clinton, had lost touch either with the standards of evidence required in federal courts, or with the foreign-policy dimension of the case, or both," wrote Benjamin and Simon.‡

The FBI refused to share information with the NSC counterterrorism operation.

Every day a hundred or more reports from the CIA, DIA [Defense Intelligence Agency], the National Security Agency, and the State Department would be waiting in their computer queues when they [NSC staff] got to work. There was never anything from the FBI. The Bureau, despite its wealth of information, contributed nothing to the White House's understanding of al-Qaeda. Freeh, whose interest in Khobar was

*Benjamin and Simon, *Age of Sacred Terror*, p. 301.
†Elsa Walsh, "Louis Freeh's Last Case," *The New Yorker*, May 14, 2001.
‡Benjamin and Simon, *Age of Sacred Terror*, p. 332.

renowned inside the government, showed little interest in the growing phenomenon of Sunni terrorism and played no notable role in U.S. strategizing against al-Qaeda.*

Yet John O'Neill, head of the FBI's terrorism office, cared deeply about the issue. However, he was turned down for the job of FBI assistant director for national security, and he moved to the FBI's New York office, where he told everyone he knew working in counterterrorism that the bureau had almost no understanding of al-Qaeda. Finally he quit and took a new job as chief of security at the World Trade Center, where he died on September 11, 2001.

President Clinton garnered every penny he could from the Congress for the FBI's counterterrorism work. He was told and believed that it was being put to productive uses. But as Benjamin and Simon wrote:

> After September 11, the FBI acknowledged to senior administration officials that despite hundreds of millions of dollars of budget increases over several years, it had no more agents working on counterterrorism cases than it had in 1996. Although the Clinton administration, using information supplied by the Bureau to OMB [Office of Management and Budget], declared on numerous occasions that the number of agents working in counterterrorism had more than doubled, the Bureau had actually assigned most of these new personnel to the National Infrastructure Protection Center, the FBI's cybersecurity unit.†

Freeh and his deputies seemed to have a visceral antagonism against Clinton. In evaluating a routine White House request to brief Secretary of State Madeleine Albright for an upcoming trip to China, Assistant Director Robert "Bear" Bryant "adamantly opposed sharing information that could be relayed to the President. 'Why should we brief him?' he asked [Freeh]. 'He's a crook. He's no better than a bank robber. Would we tell a bank robber about our investigation?' "‡ Freeh agreed and the information was withheld.

The China-bashing pseudoscandals—having nothing whatsoever to do with Ken Starr's investigations—swept across the last two years of the Clinton administration as unnamed "federal" sources stoked the flames.

*Benjamin and Simon, *Age of Sacred Terror*, p. 304.
†Ibid., pp. 348–49.
‡Walsh, "Louis Freeh's Last Case."

On April 4, 1998, Jeff Gerth of *The New York Times*, who had been responsible for the first Whitewater story in 1992, had a new scoop. Citing unnamed sources close to a "federal inquiry," he reported that an investigation into whether "two American companies illegally gave China space expertise that significantly advanced Beijing's ballistic missile program" had been "dealt a serious blow two months ago when President Clinton quietly approved the export to China of similar technology by one of the companies under investigation." The President must by law grant a waiver for every U.S. commercial satellite that is launched by the Chinese government. Loral Space and Communications was the company in question. Bernard Schwartz, its CEO, was a large contributor to the Democratic Party, and the suggestion was that Clinton was doing a favor for a backer. At last, here was the smoking gun—or Chinese rocket.*
William Safire soon held forth in his column on "the sellout of American security," and Gerth was awarded the Pulitzer Prize for his "articles that disclosed the corporate sales of American technology to China, with U.S. government approval despite national security risks."†

It did not become clear until May 23, 2000—a year after Gerth won his Pulitzer—that a Justice Department internal investigation of this transaction had exonerated both Bernard Schwartz and President Clinton of any wrongdoing shortly after Gerth's first article was published in 1998. According to the federal prosecutors in an internal document, there was "not a scintilla of evidence—or information—that the president was corruptly influenced by Bernard Schwartz." As a *Los Angeles Times* article reported, other Justice Department documents showed that Charles LaBella, chief of the task force, "regarded the Loral executive as a victim of Justice Department overreaching. . . . And in an addendum to his original report, LaBella flatly advised that the Schwartz case 'was a matter which likely did not merit any investigation.' 'Poor Bernie [Schwartz] got a bad deal,' one former task force investigator said in an interview. 'There never was a whiff of a scent of a case against him.' "‡

Notwithstanding this Justice Department exoneration of Schwartz and Clinton, which occurred in 1998, on March 6, 1999, another scoop claimed that "China Stole Nuclear Secrets for Bombs, U.S. Aides Say."

---

*Jeff Gerth with Raymond Bonner, "Companies Are Investigated for Aid to China on Rockets," *The New York Times*, April 4, 1998.

†Benjamin and Simon, *Age of Sacred Terror*, pp. 378–80.

‡William C. Rempel and Alan C. Miller, "Internal Justice Memo Excuses Loral from Funds Probe," *Los Angeles Times*, May 23, 2000.

Gerth and James Risen reported that Chinese spying had been significantly advanced by the espionage committed at a Los Alamos National Laboratory. Two days later, a Chinese-American scientist working at Los Alamos, Wen Ho Lee, was fired. The FBI conducted three investigations of his having downloaded classified files onto his personal computer. Agents showed him one of Gerth's articles and asked him if he knew "who the Rosenbergs are," then explained that they had been executed for being spies. Committees in the House and the Senate held twenty-five hearings. Republicans demanded the resignations of Attorney General Reno and National Security Adviser Berger. Lee was indicted for fifty-nine felonies unconnected to espionage and jailed in solitary confinement for nine months. Prosecutors later conceded that they had no evidence that he had given secrets to another country or had contributed to building the nuclear weapon described in Gerth's original article. Finally, they dropped the case against him in exchange for his pleading guilty to one count of mishandling classified material. Federal judge James Parker (a Reagan appointee) declared that the government's case "embarrassed our entire nation and each of us who is a citizen of it."*

After the impeachment crisis was over and President Clinton had been acquitted, the China-related pseudoscandals continued to create a din of suspicion about his administration. The FBI, the Republican Congress, and a scandal-obsessed press played complementary, self-interested parts in filling the public space with these false distractions while al-Qaeda plotted. If they had paid as much attention to the real terrorist threat as to the fictional dramas they fostered, perhaps the public, which President Clinton was trying to inform, would have been better alerted. Public opinion polls showed that huge majorities of the American people regarded terrorism as a significant danger, so they were not sidetracked; nor was the President, who warned constantly about the threat and tried to thwart it. However, an incompetent FBI director, a partisan Republican Congress, and a press corps grasping for the glittery prizes to be had from scandal diverted themselves with—and diverted attention to—fantasy China-bashing scandals about the Clinton White House. The behavior of the FBI director, and the support of those who encouraged him, bore on the Bureau's practical failures, including its suppression of vital information, to prevent the al-Qaeda attack on September 11, 2001.

On December 31, 1999, the White House Millennium Program

*Benjamin and Simon, *Age of Sacred Terror*, pp. 378–79; Robert Scheer, "The Persecution of Wen Ho Lee, Redux," *Los Angeles Times*, August 7, 2001.

staged a spectacular celebration to mark the coming of the new millennium. At the Lincoln Memorial, we heard John Glenn and John McCain
talk, the sonorous voices of Jessye Norman and Renée Fleming singing,
Muhammad Ali and Will Smith, the poets Robert Pinsky and Rita Dove;
we watched troupes of tap dancers, heard the U.S. Army Band and various choruses, viewed an impressionistic film directed by Steven Spielberg
with music by John Williams—and listened to President Clinton; and the
event was topped by brilliant fireworks illuminating the skies over Independence Mall. Then we hopped onto buses that took us to the White
House, where the Marine Band played swing upstairs and the Rose Garden was transformed into an enclosed disco.

Al-Qaeda had plotted terrorist attacks that night for Washington and
at the Los Angeles International Airport. Simultaneous attacks were also
planned against the Amman Radisson Hotel in Jordan, holy sites in Israel, and the USS *The Sullivans*, docked in port in Yemen. But all these
plots were thwarted. Sandy Berger, at the White House party, made his
last phone call to CIA director George Tenet at three in the morning.

Five months later, on May 17, 2000, at the Coast Guard Academy, the
President gave another speech about terrorism. And for the first time, he
revealed the existence of the millennium plots and how they had been organized by bin Laden's terror network. He began with these words: "And
I want to tell you a story that, unfortunately, will not be the last example
you will have to face."

III

Sir Harold Acton, British poet, historian, and aesthete, who had pledged
war on "philistines," bequeathed his estate on a hilltop overlooking Florence to New York University, which took possession of it after Acton's
death in 1994. The Villa La Pietra is a sixty-room, fifteenth-century
mansion containing priceless artworks and surrounded by acres of mani-
cured Tuscan gardens filled with statuary. Through the pines, more than
a mile in the distance, can be seen Brunelleschi's magnificent dome on
Florence's Duomo. At La Pietra on November 20, 1999, a dinner was
held to open a summit meeting of the Third Way movement—Progressive Governance in the Twenty-first Century.

Around the tables sat European Commission president Romano
Prodi, European Union foreign minister Javier Solana, Director-General
of the International Labor Organization Juan Somavia, Prime Minister

Tony Blair, Prime Minister Massimo D'Alema, Chancellor Gerhard Schroeder, Prime Minister Lionel Jospin, and President Fernando Henrique Cardoso of Brazil. As Clinton's point man on the Third Way, I also played impresario and had invited the actor Roberto Benigni, star of *A Beautiful Life*, who threw himself at our entourage with hugs when we entered ("Podesta!" he shouted. "We were in the war together!") before taking a seat between Hillary Clinton and Cherie Blair; and the tenor Andreas Bocelli, who concluded the evening with arias. Under the auspices of New York University and the European University Institute in Florence, prominent intellectuals from the United States and Europe joined the party. At Chequers the year before, Clinton had envisioned the Third Way as a "floating opera," without a central directorate, but growing in political strength. Now the opera had a new act.

The United States had entered the 1990s under the shadow of decline. After the Cold War, both Americans and foreigners believed that without an ability to compel alliances against the Soviet Union, America's power would inevitably wane. Now, after the settlement of the European war in the Balkans, and with unsurpassed prosperity in America under the aegis of a Democratic president, U.S. power and prestige were greater than before. There was no power anywhere in the world that could challenge the United States. But Clinton pointedly rejected a unilateral declaration of American hegemony as being either rational or realistic. He did not dismiss the Europeans' preference for multilateralism as just an attempt by a declining continent to undercut U.S. power. He did not see the United States and Europe as divergent in interests and values. He rejected "the arrogance of power," as Senator Fulbright had called it, and embraced a strategy that he believed in the long term would best enhance the U.S. position in the world.

The President could grasp this opening partly because he understood the history of the European left. The center-left parties had belonged nominally to the Socialist International, a largely impotent and inconsequential organization. Before 1914, social democrats in a world of expanding colonialism, great power rivalries, and mass industrialism had envisioned the democratic replacement of capitalism with a completely new economic, political, and social order. They had mass followings but no national power; none of these parties held responsible positions in ruling governments. What there was of communism resided among the Russian exiles in the cafés of Zurich. Now, almost a century later, a communist empire had risen and fallen; a capitalist system that the socialists thought irredeemable had been reformed; colonialism had crumbled;

previously disenfranchised groups had gained representation; and social democrats themselves had become part of the regular alternation of power. The anticommunist socialist parties had to deal with entirely new political configurations, and they all confronted new questions: how to reform the welfare states, modernize economies, and deal with popular resentment of immigrants and minorities.

Existing economic and political institutions faced unfamiliar problems arising from the new global economy, and neither conservatism nor social democracy had ready answers. President Clinton argued that globalization must be accepted and its excesses regulated. Domestic policies—education, environment, health care, child care, family leave, welfare—must be attended to, and the more they could be adapted and synchronized around the world, the more advancement was possible.

The old nineteeth-century balance-of-power game was an anachronism, and so was the bipolar Cold War. Yet Clinton favored the expansion of NATO and the growth of the European Union, building up the unity and strength of Europe, because he believed that U.S. power would not thrive in isolation or by fiat. Strategic objectives could be reached more easily through international cooperation, which must be a principal goal itself.

Moreover, democracy and free markets were still fragile in many parts of the world. The "democratic revolution," as Clinton called it, was hardly a given, and the automatic operation of markets could certainly not maintain it. The President understood that these fragile gains would be threatened unless living standards were raised. Fundamental policy choices had still to be made in Latin America, Africa, and Asia—and in the former Soviet Union—that might adversely affect U.S. security. Terrorism was only one part of the dark side of globalization.

President Clinton had a political conception of progress—not as occurring on its own, a fairy tale of laissez-faire, but as something that occurred when concerted political forces acted through governments to shape economy and society. The Third Way movement was a politically advanced aspect of his new internationalism, a belief in the necessity of a new social contract for the new global economy—and for an informal network working constantly toward its framing. It could not be created within one country alone or by the domination of one country.

Through organizing the Third Way summits, Clinton's administration had encouraged the sharing of what we called "best practices" of social policy with other governments. The most intensive cooperation existed with the British; traffic about domestic issues between British ministries and American departments became a regular part of the relationship. But discussions also began with the other Europeans—and they responded in kind. Constant exchanges are obviously integral to a healthy foreign policy, but this was a new dimension in international affairs. It was also natural that the political actors would hold many conversations about politics—opening informal but regular channels on political strategy.

After the La Pietra dinner, Clinton spoke. He raised questions about science and progress, about the aging of societies in the West, about the reform of government. At each point, he tried to draw closer the connections between the United States and Europe, even where the two might be thought to diverge. Whenever in the past the United States had surged forward economically, Europeans had grown anxious about their own pace of innovation—"the American challenge," as the French thinker Jean-Jacques Servan-Schreiber called it in 1967. Though the American Century was over and a new century was starting, with the United States more powerful than it had ever been, Clinton wanted to find ways for Americans and Europeans to benefit mutually from their social and economic experiences. And he was drawing into the Western orbit the important emerging other countries—hence the significant presence of Cardoso of Brazil, every bit an intellectual and political equal, though coping with harsher inequalities than those faced by his European counterparts.

Clinton was at the height of his international influence, but his tone was not lordly. It was reasoned, open, and liberal—an American tone:

> In the United States, we have proceeded for the last seven years under a rubric of opportunity for all, responsibility from all, and a community of all Americans. We have also recognized something that I think is implicit in the whole concept of the European Union, which is that it is no longer possible, easily, to divide domestic from global political concerns. There is no longer a clear dividing line between foreign and domestic policy.

Rather than indulge in triumphalism or hold up the American example as an unblemished model to follow, Clinton did not hesitate to acknowledge American problems at home in order to make his points:

> In America, we have the lowest unemployment rate in thirty years, 4.1 percent. On the Pine Ridge Indian Reservation in South Dakota, the home of the Lakota Sioux, the unemployment rate is 73 percent. And in

many of our inner cities, in many of our rural areas, this recovery simply has not reached because of the lack of educational level of the people or because of the digital divide or because of the absence of a conducive investment environment.

But every advanced society that seeks social justice and equal opportunity cannot simply rest on economic success in the absence of giving all people the chance to succeed. . . . There has, by and large, in all of our societies with heavy reliance on the market been an increase in income inequality. I'm happy to say it is moderating in the United States. In countries that have chosen to make sure that did not happen, very often there have been quite high levels of unemployment, which people also find unacceptable—and which is another form of social inequality.

Among the radical changes occurring throughout the West that Clinton discussed was the change in family life, which was assuming new forms, especially with women in the workforce, and he praised European social policies that recognized this:

I think virtually every European country has done a better job than the United States in providing adequate family leave policies, adequate child care policies, adequate supports. But let me just put it in this way. If most parents are going to work, either because they have to or they want to, then every society must strive for the proper balance, because if you have to choose between succeeding at home and succeeding at work, then you are defeated before you begin.

Discussing potential developments in technology and science, Clinton insisted on setting forth the largest, most difficult issues of inequality, because they were related to global governance. One problem is that putting new policies into place takes time. Sacrifices are required until the results kick in. And appeals to patience don't always work. Clinton noted that the Democrats had lost control of the Congress. He urged the other leaders to understand the widespread disquiet about the global economy:

Ordinary people all over the world are not so sure about the globalization of the economy. They're not so sure they're going to benefit from trade. They want to see if there can be a human face on the global economy, if we can raise labor standards for ordinary people, if we can continue to improve the quality of life, including the quality of the environment. And if we believe—we, who say we believe in social justice and the market economy, really want to push it—we have to prove that the globalization of the economy can really work for real people. And it's a huge challenge.

. . . About half the world still lives on less than two dollars a day, so for most of [these people], most of this discussion tonight is entirely academic, which is why debt relief is so important. . . . While we talk about having smaller, more entrepreneurial government, the truth is that a lot of poor countries . . . don't have any government at all with any real, fundamental capacity to do the things that have to be done. Even in a lot of more developed countries, they have found themselves blindsided by the financial crisis that struck in 1997.

So we have to acknowledge while we, who say we are developing a Third Way—and in our case, we've been able to do it with the smallest federal government in thirty-seven years—we have to acknowledge the fact that some countries need more government. They need capacity. They need the ability to battle disease and run financial systems and solve problems, and that it is fanciful to talk about a lot of this until you can basically deal with malaria, deal with AIDS.

Once again, as he did in every important speech on international affairs, President Clinton underlined the urgency of the new threat from terrorism. He was not making a utopian plea for abstract ideals but spelling out the conditions of the modern age, good and ill, that political and governmental leaders must contend with:

I believe that the biggest problems to our security in the twenty-first century and to this whole modern form of governance will probably come not from rogue states or from people with competing views of the world in governments, but from the enemies of the nation-state, from terrorists and drug runners and organized criminals who, I predict, will increasingly work together and increasingly use the same things that are fueling our prosperity: open borders, the Internet, the miniaturization of all sophisticated technology, which will manifest itself in smaller and more powerful and more dangerous weapons. And we have to find ways to cooperate to deal with the enemies of the nation-state if we expect progressive governments to succeed.

Clinton alluded to the Florentine setting and mentioned the Renaissance. He suggested the possibility of a new renaissance in the twenty-first century, even though modernity was plagued by hatreds and fears:

The supreme irony of this time is that we are sitting around talking about finding out the secrets of the black holes in the universe, unlocking the mysteries of the human gene, having unprecedented growth, and dealing with what I consider to be very high-class problems—finding the right balance between unemployment and social justice, dealing with the aging of society—isn't it interesting to you that in this most modern of ages, the biggest problem of human societies is the most primitive of all social difficulties: the fear of people who are different from us. That, after all, is what is at the root of what Prime Minister Blair has struggled with in Northern Ireland, at the root of all the problems in the Balkans, at the root of the tribal wars in Africa, at the root of the still unresolved, though hopefully progressing problems in the Middle East.

Now, this is in an age where 800,000 people were slaughtered by machetes in ninety days in Rwanda a few years ago, when a quarter of a million Bosnians lost their lives and 2.5 million more were made refugees.

So that's the last point I would like to make. We need a little humility here. . . . If I had to leave tonight and never have another thing to say about public life, I would say, if we could find a way to enshrine a reverence for our common humanity, the rest would work out just fine.

The next day at the Palazzo Vecchio, the center of Florentine government in the Renaissance, the participants grouped on a stage in the Hall of the Five Hundred, the cavernous hall lined with gigantic epic paintings from the school of Vasari where the elected leaders of the Florentine Republic once deliberated. (On an upper floor in the palazzo, a room is devoted to the public servant who once occupied it, Niccolò Machiavelli, before his arrest and banishment.) A debate was held on "Equality and Opportunity," in which various intellectuals—Norman Dorsen, director of the Global Law School Program at New York University; Anthony Giddens, director of the London School of Economics; and Yves Meny, president of the European University Institute—presented their perspectives. (President Clinton responded to Meny's apt citation of Machiavelli: "He quoted that wonderful section from Machiavelli, where he says something to the effect that there is nothing so difficult in all of human affairs than to change the established order of things. The next part . . . is also very important, where Machiavelli goes on to say . . . that is so because the people who will lose are absolutely sure of the consequences and will go to any lengths to avoid them.")

The complexity of modernizing the center-left was apparent in the maneuverings in and around the conference. For the host Italians, the ramshackle center-left coalition in power was in constant danger of shifting and the government in danger of falling. That was how Prodi's prime ministership had ended; D'Alema was engaged in a shaky balancing act. In June 1999, the Blair and Schroeder governments had issued a joint paper, "Europe: The Third Way, *Die Neue Mitte*," which advocated fiscal discipline, targeted tax cuts, and acceptance of the market economy. Germany's traditionalist Social Democrats had denounced the document and attributed to it the Social Democratic losses in the European parliamentary elections. The tactically adroit Schroeder was facing large strategic problems, particularly structural ones in the German economy, which needed welfare reforms and greater labor market flexibility.

Prime Minister Jospin used the conference to separate himself from what he saw as a creeping "Anglo-Saxon" hegemony. By criticizing and distancing himself from the Third Way he hoped to hold his own Socialist Party together, yet at the same time he was advocating the privatization of state-owned companies in France. He assumed that his political prospects would brighten so long as he did not openly create a new French synthesis but instead adhered to the well-known golden rhetoric of Jean Jaurès and Léon Blum. His presence at the Third Way meetings resulted in tensions because he was suspicious of Clinton's and Blair's intentions and clung to old socialist ways of speaking. Clinton wanted a broad, inclusive "floating opera," with as many participants as possible. But Jospin did not want too many leaders of parties belonging to the Socialist International to become part of the Third Way, because he saw it as a cooptation that would diminish the virtually irrelevant organization, in which he believed he exercised influence. He did not understand the historically unique opportunity that the others grasped about Clinton. (When he ran for the French presidency in 2002, this refusal to make choices for the future and his unyielding nostalgia led to his crushing defeat. A book about him entitled *Ni, Ni*, "Neither, Nor," became a French best-seller.) His political geometry—"yes to the market economy, no to the market society"—could not square his circle. About it, Tony Blinken, head of the European section on the National Security Council, and I joked: It works in practice, but will it work in theory?

Another Third Way meeting was held on June 1, 2000, in Berlin, at Charlottenburg, the palace of the Hohenzollerns. This time thirteen leaders sat around the dinner table (Clinton had gotten his way, and Jospin was trumped), including the new members: Prime Minister Wim Kok of the Netherlands, Prime Minister Goran Persson of Sweden, President Fernando de la Rua of Argentina, Prime Minister Jean Chrétien of Canada, Prime Minister Costas Simitis of Greece, Prime Minister Helen Clark of New Zealand, Prime Minister Antonio Guterres of Portugal, President Ricardo Lagos of Chile, and President Thabo Mbeki of South Africa. Prime Minister Giuliano Amato replaced D'Alema, who had slipped from power.

Before the conference, my counterparts from the various governments and I had worked on a joint communiqué stating the democratic principles of the Third Way and advocating a comprehensive global program embracing education, health care, the alleviation of poverty, a more equal distribution of digital technology, market stability, environmental protection, trade, reformed government services, equal rights—"a new international social compact." All the participants signed it.

A session on June 2 was closed to the public so the leaders could be free to have an open, spirited discussion. Schroeder was chairman. Clinton was eager that the process continue, that it move beyond where it had gone so far. He wanted the communiqué to be a first step toward enacting specific policies in a unified way. He talked about the issues raised by poverty in the developing world, and by global warming. He believed the Third Way network could be used to advance a progressive agenda in other international forums such as the G-8. Schroeder heartily agreed. Cardoso argued for a "Berlin consensus" as opposed to "the Washington consensus," by which latter term he meant the draconian policies imposed around the world by the International Monetary Fund and the World Bank. He also warned about an overemphasis on "civil society." It was "a vague entity," he said. "I don't want to belittle civil society. But we are transferring tools to it that belong to government."

All the leaders chimed in—Guterres on debt relief, Lagos and Simitis on capital flows, Persson on human rights, Kok on education, Amato on democracy and cultural diversity. Chrétien discussed health care in Canada. Then for some reason he veered into talking about Viagra, explaining that it was not covered—and ought to be—by his country's national health insurance. At this Jospin suddenly piped up: "Viagra," he pronounced, "is not successful in France. French men do not need it!" After the laughter died down, Clinton leaned forward and remarked, "That's cultural imperialism if ever I heard it."

President Clinton returned the discussion to the future of Third Way politics:

Why are we here? We have an enormous potential to solve problems. In the 1980s, with the single exception of Wim Kok, right-wingers were running the world. The Cold War ended, the global economy arose. There was a general consensus that the economy could run off half-cocked without a role for government in the greater relations among nations. People like us began to get elected. We began to realize some common ground across the divides we represent. So we started these meetings. I thought we could help each other do well. More of us could be elected and the world could take another direction. This is both political and substantive. It's one and the same. Now, to start with we have to issue the communiqué. But that's just a starting point. We can then build up our network and begin to work on specific issues.

Once again, there was a murmur of agreement.

Clinton's program was concrete, his politics pragmatic, but his tone was taking on a valedictory edge. He became more insistent and urgent; time was running out for him. One more Third Way meeting was planned for New York at the millennium session of the United Nations General Assembly in September. The unstated yet keenly felt assumption among the leaders was that the new internationalism required at its center a certain kind of American president. Whether the global momentum Clinton was trying to marshal would continue depended upon the outcome of the 2000 U.S. elections. That had already been clear at the Florence conference. I missed the lunch of the leaders because in a small room, in an upper turret of the Palazzo Vecchio, Hillary and I and a couple of other White House aides were intently planning strategy for her Senate campaign.

FIFTEEN

A New York State of Mind

The first thought of Hillary Clinton running for the United States Senate flickered in 1996 at the Democratic National Convention in Chicago, her hometown, when she gave such a successful speech. Some prominent Democrats thought she had the makings of a Senate candidate—for Illinois, if and when a seat opened up. But then Democrats held both of them, so it was an indefinite scenario for an imagined campaign.

In 1998, Hillary barnstormed across the country in the midterm elections campaign. In New York, she plunged for the first time into its politics on behalf of Congressman Charles Schumer, helping him raise money for his senatorial race and speaking across the state on his behalf. Schumer was a very capable representative from Brooklyn, a Harvard Law School graduate, keenly attuned to his constituents, who also had made a national reputation for himself as an advocate of gun control, and he had battled against President Clinton's impeachment as a member of the House Judiciary Committee. Hillary's presence beside him raised his profile and stature and helped broaden the statewide appeal of this outer-borough candidate. He needed all the support he could get because his opponent was a fierce combatant who had grabbed and kept the Senate seat by doing whatever it took to demolish anyone who ventured to run against him.

Senator Alfonse D'Amato was the product of Long Island's Republican Party fiefdom, rooted in a population in middle-class flight from the city. The Nassau County Republican Party in which D'Amato had risen from Island Park executive to Hempstead town supervisor to the U.S. Senate was as finely honed a machine as Tammany Hall in Boss Tweed's heyday. It controlled more than thirty thousand county jobs dispensed through patronage, whose holders were obligated to kick back 1 percent of their salaries to the political organization. In 1980, D'Amato had run as an upstart conservative against the venerable liberal Republican Senator Jacob Javits. His television commercial blared, "And now, at age seventy-six, and in failing health, he wants six more years."

D'Amato's style was vulgar, self-dealing, and brutal, and he formed an odd couple with the exalted senior senator from New York, the Democrat Daniel Patrick Moynihan. After coasting to an easy win in 1986, D'Amato had faced a tough race in 1992 against State Attorney General Robert Abrams. D'Amato's ad: "Bob Abrams. Hopelessly liberal." D'Amato won by two points. Two years later, he handpicked George Pataki, an obscure upstate state senator and former mayor of Peekskill, as the Republican candidate to run for governor against the Democratic incumbent, Mario Cuomo, progressive bearer of "the New York idea." "I'm going to take out Cuomo," D'Amato boasted to a group of Republican senators. On election night, when Rupert Murdoch, publisher of the *New York Post*, called to congratulate the winner, the man he telephoned was D'Amato, who passed his cellular phone to Pataki. "It's Rupert," D'Amato told him.

In 1994, as the Senate turned Republican, D'Amato was in line to become the chairman of the Banking Committee, the overseer of Wall Street. Having eliminated his rivals in the state with Borgia-like cunning, he had power in New York unequaled since the titanic Nelson Rockefeller had ruled as governor. In Washington, as D'Amato began lengthy televised hearings on Whitewater, Senate majority leader Bob Dole gave him a bottle of perfume labeled "White Water" for him to sprinkle over his malodorous work. And in 1996, when Dole ran for president against Clinton, he named D'Amato as his national campaign chairman and publicly dubbed him "King Alfonse." The 1998 campaign against Chuck Schumer was D'Amato's fourth, and he was confident of victory.

Hillary took to the stump against her tormentor. D'Amato's popularity in New York had in fact never recovered from its fall as a result of his endless Whitewater investigation; President Clinton was far more popular than D'Amato in the state, and Clinton's wife had come to thrash him. She compared D'Amato to Senator Jesse Helms, the Dixiecrat Republican from North Carolina, calling D'Amato a tool of the National Rifle Association, and condemning his legislative votes against the interests of women.

Schumer proved to be a quick counterpuncher, knocking away D'Amato's slurs. This had never happened to D'Amato before. Schumer demonstrated how a Democrat who was not the nonpareil Moynihan could run a national race in New York. Local politics has terrific gravitational pull in any state, especially in New York, but he kept himself above the fray of ethnic politics and avoided making promises to beseeching interest groups, with their inevitable effect of reducing a candidate to fractions.

Schumer's victory taught his helper several lessons: Hillary learned that she had been an effective campaigner; she had settled a score; and even during the impeachment of her husband she had beaten back the attacks. And she had done it all in New York. Schumer's success offered an incentive: a New York race could be won.

In the week after the election, Senator Moynihan announced that he would retire from the Senate at the end of his term in 2001. His desire not to run again in 2000 was no surprise. Now something more rare than a full eclipse of the sun came into view: there had not been an open Senate seat in New York since 1958. In September, Hillary had taken a congressional delegation to the Dominican Republic to survey the damage wrought by Hurricane Mitch, and Representative Charles Rangel from Harlem, on the mission, had slyly told her in his inimitably raspy voice that he knew who could win the Moynihan seat. She asked just who that might be and he said, "You." The week after Moynihan made his announcement, Bob Herbert's column in *The New York Times* was headlined, "Run, Hillary, Run!" The idea was widespread as the impeachment hearings began in the House of Representatives.

From the day after the 1998 election, Hillary had contemplated the pros and cons of running for the Senate. Most of her staff were against it. They were frankly tired, and they didn't look forward to the prospect of a withering campaign, enduring again the slings and arrows. I suggested to her that when the President left the White House she would be a world-renowned personage, able to call attention to a myriad of worthy causes, but that it was always better to hold elective political office if one wanted to work toward large public policy goals. Still, the risks were enormous. If she lost, she would be permanently tarnished. Nonetheless, I said it was a risk she should take if she wanted to play a major part in future political debates and accomplish her aims. Hillary went back and forth, though she was inclined from the beginning to run. There was no rational way to make such a decision. No poll, no single piece of advice could balance the imponderables. It was entirely a shot in the dark. Less than a week after the Senate impeachment trial of her husband had ended with his acquittal, she agonized but at the same time was progressing toward a decision. "It's not a lock and I'm throwing myself to the wolves and fate," she said.

On February 18, Senator Moynihan came to the White House with elaborate maps and charts of the voting patterns of every county in New York. He showed her how hard it was for a Democrat to win, especially upstate. He was not trying to discourage her, but acting as the professor to a promising pupil. She absorbed the material as someone determined to get an A. In the beginning, she even memorized the names of the counties and the state bird (bluebird).

At the end of the month, Hillary's instinct was to run. Accumulated goodwill surrounded her as a result of her dignified reserve while maintaining support for her husband. But she did not care to stand on a pedestal. "What do you save an aura for?" she said. In late March, Tom Freedman, the White House aide who had once been Schumer's chief of staff, and I met with her to discuss political strategy. Performing his due diligence, Tom laid out the hardships of a campaign and the alternatives that would be open to her. But she waved off this talk. "You're not a leader if you haven't been elected," she said. "You have to test your ideas in a public forum." Her tone was not ambivalent, though she still expressed private doubts for months, "still very torn," she said. "To throw myself into the maelstrom, it's pretty daunting." She knew she had "incredible built-in obstacles. The incredibly organized opposition that hates Bill and me is difficult to combat. The carpetbagger business is serious. The only thing to deal with it is time." Then she joked, "One reason I might run is to stop raising money for other people."

Her plausibility as a candidate in New York was partly a function of the vacuum in the New York Democratic Party, the oldest part of the oldest political party on earth. Founded by Aaron Burr, the rogue among the Founding Fathers, and allied with Thomas Jefferson to forge the Democratic Party; reorganized by Martin Van Buren, the Red Fox of Kinderhook, to create the dynamic northern component of Jacksonian democracy—the party of Grover Cleveland, Alfred Smith, Franklin D. Roosevelt, Robert Wagner, Herbert Lehman, and Robert F. Kennedy had no figure of standing to turn to to run for the Senate. The most obvious and available was Nita Lowey, a congresswoman from suburban Westchester, a person of many fine qualities, but not well known in the state as a whole. Moynihan's stature had established an invisible benchmark and the expectation that his replacement should be a considerable personage. The only one like that waiting in the wings was Hillary.

Her New York roots were nonexistent. Robert F. Kennedy at least had had some: he had grown up partly in Bronxville, after all. The absence of any true New York background—no sense of place or memories of Walt Whitman's densely packed *Manahatta* or the Empire State that stretched beyond it—was her liability and her credit. She was an outlander, and that would inevitably raise the question of how much she knew or cared about New Yorkers. But, like Bobby Kennedy, she was a larger-than-life character who fit New Yorkers' idea of their own significance—a president's wife, close enough to being a president's brother. Being a Clinton mattered in a state where the President was extremely well regarded. Parachuting in from above, she had an asset that no one else in New York politics possessed: she was unmarked by its nasty internecine struggles. Almost everyone else was cut and wounded. Hillary was not of any faction, was not beholden to any interests, had not crossed any other politician. She belonged to nobody but herself and therefore could be claimed by everybody. She was not compromised by difficulties in the Democrats' New York history and thus could win.

There was also the matter of her ambition. Who was she to descend from the heavens onto the sidewalks of New York? Her claim appeared to some New Yorkers as sheer ambition, mere presumption. But if there was one place in the country where the ambition of people who come from other places to "make it" was unabashedly celebrated, it was New York City. She was, like millions of others, drawn to the greatest city of all. (She discovered that her Rodham ancestor from England had landed on Ellis Island.) Her running there could not but flatter New Yorkers' self-conception. Hillary had spent eight years in Washington. She was shaking those "little town blues." Now it was time for Broadway.

But first there was the tryout. On July 7, 1999, Hillary strolled with Daniel Patrick Moynihan down the long unpaved driveway of his farm in Pindars Corner, a pretty location in the very center of the state, north of the Catskill Mountains. They arrived at a bank of microphones set up by a throng of reporters, and there he bestowed his blessing on her and she announced that she would go on a "listening tour" of New York state voters before throwing her hat into the ring. For the next four months, she traveled around New York, mostly upstate, to discuss issues with groups of about 150 local people in each town she visited.

As she went from place to place, from Oneonta to Syracuse, from Cooperstown to Jamestown, the traveling media thinned out. The locales were not glamorous enough for them. She continued the discussions with New Yorkers long after the camera crews packed up. She mastered her briefing books on the Northeast Dairy Compact, on hospital reimbursement formulas, and on cancer rates on Long Island. And she discovered that upstate New York was not foreign to her at all: its conditions and people were like those of the Middle West and Arkansas. Hillary had an instinctively greater grasp of the state than most other New York politicians, who tended, like most politicians, to be parochial. She actually listened to people, and she learned about more than their local problems. She found that upstate voters felt neglected and ignored by the Republicans, for whom the region was supposedly a base. Republican support there was softer than expected. The closer she got to the ground, the more attuned she became to its politics. And her constant presence sent a signal that as a senator she would be there for these voters. She convinced people in these long "listening" sessions that she was different from her stereotype: not haughty, cold, and aloof, but approachable. In small, struggling upstate towns, the non–New Yorker gained something of a New York identity. She felt at home, felt comfortable, and the people liked her. So she became a kind of upstate personality. The more time Hillary spent there, the more she escaped the censorious ambit of the Washington and New York City press corps, and upstate coverage of her work differed radically from theirs. "When Hillary hit an upstate city, not only was her mere presence news, but the papers would actually lead with what she said in her speech," wrote Michael Tomasky, chronicler of her campaign for *New York* magazine.*

Still, every trap was baited for her. Throughout 1999, she walked straight into some of them. Almost all these rites of passage had to do with the snares of local politics. The first mistake was minor but telling, and it riveted attention on her status as an interloper. On June 10, the President received the World Champion New York Yankees at the White House, and both he and Hillary were presented with Yankee caps. She put hers on and it became an early symbol of her lack of authenticity. The truth was that she had been a Yankee fan growing up in Chicago—she had rooted for both the hometown Cubs (a National League team) and the Yankees (her American League club)—but that didn't matter. She was showing a tin ear for New York politics. She hadn't yet grasped that New Yorkers are at once sophisticated and parochial, that aspiring to be a New Yorker was acceptable, but pretending to be one too soon excited local prejudices and latent hostilities.

In August, the President announced that he was granting clemency to sixteen Puerto Rican nationalists, members of a group that had commit-

*Michael Tomasky, *Hillary's Turn*, Free Press, 2001, p. 120.

ted acts of violence, though these particular people had not. His act was the result of painstaking work by the White House counsel Charles Ruff, and Hillary had had nothing to do with it. But, instantly, she and the President were accused of abusing presidential powers on behalf of her political ambition. A week after the President's statement, she declared her disagreement with it, which only made her seem more opportunistic and drew the fire of Puerto Rican leaders, who claimed they hadn't been consulted about the decision to begin with.

These were teacup wars compared to the explosion that occurred following Hillary Clinton's trip to Israel. On November 11, she appeared at a day-care center in Ramallah with Yasser Arafat's wife, Suha, who gave a speech denouncing what she called the "daily and intensive use of poison gas" by the Israeli Defense Forces against the Palestinians, and claiming that Israel was poisoning the water supply in Palestinian areas. Hillary listened politely to the speech, given in Arabic, and, following protocol, kissed Mrs. Arafat on both cheeks when she finished. The cameras snapped.

The next day, the *New York Post* ran a screaming headline—"Shame on Hillary"—and a subheadline referring to Suha Arafat's "blood libel." Hillary said that she had not been given a translation of Mrs. Arafat's remarks until later, but, once again, the facts didn't matter. A Democratic candidate requires about two-thirds of New York City's Jewish vote to win in New York state, and she had aroused the furies in what should have been one of her most secure bases. The kiss seemed to be an error of biblical scope. Hillary was trapped in the contradiction between her two roles: if she was only the first lady, she could brush off the incident; but she was a candidate for office in New York who had not yet established her credentials with Jewish voters. Among Jews, the range of opinion is vast—from those who backed President Clinton's peace initiatives to those adamantly opposed to them. Hillary as first lady was advancing her husband's foreign policy, having been asked by the State Department to be at the event with Mrs. Arafat to help enhance negotiations that were fluid and vital. But she hadn't staked her own ground yet as a candidate. When she was on the platform in Ramallah, she was engaged in more than international relations; but she might as well have been in Brooklyn.

Hillary did not end the year without making another mistake. On December 8, at an Irish breakfast, where leaders of the Irish community in New York lauded her contributions to peace in Northern Ireland, a reporter asked a trick question that seemed on the surface to be a simple one. Would she march in the St. Patrick's Day parade? "I sure hope to," she replied. For almost a decade, the official parade, conducted by the Ancient Order of Hibernians, had been a matter of great controversy because it had refused to allow the Irish Lesbian and Gay Organization to join the march. Every year, the event had been marked by noisy demonstrations and arrests. Hillary's innocent eagerness led her to become caught between two contentious constituencies. Once again, there was a flurry of negative stories, fanned by partisans on all sides. Eventually, she marched in both parades, to everyone's satisfaction.

But Hillary's errors were creating the picture of a naïve and potentially disastrous candidate. When the Clintons had come to Washington they had misplayed much in their first two years. In the first year of Hillary's campaigning, it looked as though she might be repeating these missteps in New York. With the advent of 2000, she trailed her prospective opponent, Mayor Rudolph Giuliani, by nine points, 49–40, and her favorable ratings had fallen below 50 percent. But soon she gained her bearings. The hallmark of her campaign was her ability to learn and recover. Her listening tour had been the opposite of her closed, controlling formulation of the health care plan in 1993. Most important, her travels had shown her how the issues she had advocated in the White House related specifically to New York and, at the same time, showed New Yorkers that her White House experience was directly relevant.

Hillary's stumbles were also useful in teaching her the natural political landscape of New York. New York City was the cultural mecca of the country and the capital of the global economy, but it was also proudly provincial. Each balkanized element in New York City and state presented its own test to any politician seeking its approval. The reactions to anyone who made mistakes, as she learned, were unsparing, harsh, and insistent. She would be thrown to the wolves, and whether she survived would depend upon her own skills. The sharp elbows and jostling she encountered were educating her as an adoptive New Yorker. She learned even more when, in September, President Clinton and she purchased a five-bedroom house in Chappaqua, Westchester County.

On January 12, 2000, she was a guest on the David Letterman *Late Show*—her biggest and least protected appearance in public so far. Letterman joked with her that since she had moved into her new house in Chappaqua, "every idiot in the area is going to drive by honking." "Was that you?" she replied spontaneously. She had used the quick-witted

comic as a straight man, but she was doing more than firing off a one-
liner. She was becoming more comfortable being herself in public, and
she was getting into a New York state of mind.

When Hillary entered the arena her persona shadowed her. All her
failures and successes were held against her. The residue of pseudoscandals still hung in the air like soot. For a decade, she had been depicted as
a power-mad Lady Macbeth. Because she was actually running for office,
the old innuendos might factor into her fate rather than fade from memory. Some professional women of her own age were suspicious of her
motives, and for them she was a subject of endless speculation: Did she
feel entitled? Was she an enabler? Was she coldly calculating? Focus
groups conducted by her campaign in the summer of 2000 showed that
suburban women were reluctant to support her, being especially critical
precisely because she was an ambitious woman. I watched tapes of these
sessions, and the talk was negative, circular, and almost entirely conjectural. "Indeed intelligence and strength, usually not seen as pejoratives,
became, as these women saw them in Hillary, negative qualities," wrote
Tomasky.* Hillary said she was their "Rorschach test."

She was running not just against a political opponent but also against
a negative image of her that a string of right-wing women tried to vivify
in a series of pathographies. There was *The Hillary Trap: Looking for Power
in All the Wrong Places* by Laura Ingraham, according to whom Hillary
had made a "devil's bargain," was in a "sham marriage," was "a dupe . . .
or a Machiavellian who craves power so much she'll do anything to keep
it," was "an old-fashioned doormat," was "clinging to her abuser," and
was personally responsible for "schools that don't teach" and "a permissive sexual culture."† There was *The Case Against Hillary Clinton* by
Peggy Noonan: "Lying, of course, is not the Clintons' only distinguishing characteristic. They are marked, too, by an absence of grace, a lack of
personal humility that is actually jarring, perhaps because it threatens to
lower both standards and expectations for our leaders." Noonan urged
that her book "be read aloud in bed" by married couples.‡ There was
Hell to Pay: The Unfolding Story of Hillary Rodham Clinton by Barbara
Olson: "I have come to know Hillary as she is. . . . A woman who has
persuaded herself and many others that she is 'spiritual,' but who has

---

*Tomasky, *Hillary's Turn*, p. 192.
†Quoted in Mary McGrory, "Hillary Wars," *The Washington Monthly*, June 2000.
‡Quoted in Sean Elder, "Looney Noonan," *Salon.com*, March 24, 2000.

gone to the brink of criminality to amass wealth and power."* Finally, there was Gail Sheehy's *Hillary's Choice*, a volume of almost unremitting psychobabble.

In April, the conservative American Enterprise Institute cosponsored a conference with the (Scaife-funded) Center for the Study of Popular Culture devoted entirely to the obsessive subject of Hillary Clinton. Christopher Hitchens held forth: "I attended Oxford with Bill Clinton (at one point sharing a girlfriend in common—she later became a radical lesbian), so I have a deep-rooted understanding of both the President and the President's wife, Hillary Rodham Clinton." Joyce Milton, author of *The First Partner*, yet another pathography, remarked, "I don't see the many social engineering plans in Hillary's background as left-wing so much as I see them as a kind of corporate fascism." John Fund of the *Wall Street Journal* editorial board called her a "celebrity candidate," predicted that President Clinton would launch "an October surprise or two in this campaign" to rescue her candidacy, and warned that as a senator "she'd find things to bomb all around the world." Lynne Cheney, the wife of Dick Cheney and a scholar at AEI, said, "What really drives me crazy is when Hillary acts like the happy wife. Walking hand in hand off the helicopter together at critical moments. It is just so distressing to me."†

The intense reactions she provoked were given daily shape and focus by the *New York Post*. "Shortly after the Listening Tour started," wrote Tomasky, "the paper asked its readers to name the most notable and most evil people of the century that was drawing to a close. On the Most-Evil list, Hillary came in seventh and Bill fourth, right behind Hitler, Stalin, and Saddam Hussein. They were write-in votes [from] readers who took their cues from the newspaper to which they mailed their ballots."‡

New York City has a twenty-four-hour, seven-day media cycle, with its competitive tabloids tearing at every subject they can get their hands on and local TV news shows gleefully amplifying the sounds and sights of the carnage. Very early, Hillary tried to arrange a meeting with Rupert Murdoch, but he refused to see her. From the *Post* there would be only antipathy. In February, for example, when Hillary was treated to breakfast at a diner in the upstate town of Albion and she and her aides forgot to leave a tip, it became a running story in the *Post* for days, broadcast by

*Barbara Olson, *Hell to Pay*, Regnery, 1999, p. 2.
†See *The American Enterprise*, July/August 2000, Vol. 11.
‡Tomasky, *Hillary's Turn*, pp. 62–63.

Fox News, and churned by local television news and radio talk shows. Nothing was too trivial to blow out of proportion to attempt to magnify the negative image. "She's Nothing But an Empty Carpetbag," ran a typical *New York Post* news headline.

One of Hillary's chief antagonists at the *New York Post* was its new weekly columnist, none other than Dick Morris, who was also now a commentator on Fox News. The triple drumbeat of Morris's one-man campaign at the *New York Post* against Hillary's candidacy was that she wouldn't run, she wasn't a real New Yorker, and she couldn't win. "The Clintons Are Freaking Out"; "Hillary on the Ropes?"; "Hillary's Ahead, But Losing"; "Is Hillary Going to Bail Out?"; "No Good News for Hillary."

Hillary was not alone in coping with all this mayhem. She had assembled a campaign staff highly experienced in the byways and folkways of New York. Principal among them was Harold M. Ickes, who had been deputy chief of staff in the White House during Clinton's first term and had been immersed in New York politics seemingly from birth, being intimately connected to Democratic, union, and black political leaders. (His father, Harold L. Ickes, FDR's interior secretary, had urged Eleanor Roosevelt to run for the U.S. Senate from New York in 1946 after her husband's death, but she declined.) On February 12, 1999, the day the impeachment trial ended, Harold came to the White House to confer with Hillary about the Senate race. He was initially skeptical, but willing to do whatever he could. As her pollster, Hillary drew in Mark Penn, who had worked in New York campaigns ever since Ed Koch's mayoral races. Mandy Grunwald produced the television commercials, and as the daughter of Henry Grunwald, former managing editor of *Time*, her contacts were also invaluable. Mandy had worked on Moynihan's Senate campaigns and now served as a bridge to the Senator. Howard Wolfson, Hillary's press secretary, was recruited from Representative Lowey's staff; he knew the nuances and habits of the bumptious media and never lost his composure. Hillary's choice of her seasoned team was itself a message that she knew what she was doing.

She had another adviser: the President. He had been enthusiastic about her running. On February 4, 2000, he joined a small group of us to help prepare the candidate for her formal announcement speech, to be delivered on February 6. We rehearsed in the White House movie theater, just as we did for the President's State of the Union addresses. But it was Hillary, not Bill, at the podium, and he sat with the rest of us, offering pointers and word changes. Clinton had a hard time staying seated.

He'd leap up excitedly, advising, "You need to say *why* you're running here and now."

"Because I'm a masochist," Hillary said. We all burst out laughing.

He began rearranging the sequence at the beginning of the speech. "She'll announce. They'll cheer and dance around. That's fine. Why is she doing it? Why not Illinois, Arkansas, Alaska? Why not rake in some dough? Why ask to be trashed right now? What I wish you could do, Hillary, is a sentence here: The overwhelming reason is that I don't want to give up my life in public service." That was, after all, her motive.

"I'm just a little policy wonk," she joked. "I just want to make life better for little children." Then she sighed, "I have to memorize too much."

Clinton was dancing in front of her: "You have to be totally, totally comfortable. It's something that I had to learn when I got here. You have to listen to your heart and head and get rid of the awkwardness. If you do this, you give the election back to them. So you're not arrogant, you're not entitled. You want people to see you with new eyes. You have to look like you're not reading the script. Give it to them. Act like one of them has been asking you." He hugged her and she laughed. Then he told a story about his race for the Congress from Arkansas in 1974, when he had a television ad featuring a dog that barked at his opponent's falsehoods about him.

"I want one of those dogs," said Hillary.

Clinton had always been a good and generous political adviser. He wished he could run again himself, but having Hillary do it was the next best thing. (In April, he said, "I'm not running for anything. And most days I'm okay about it.") His judgments of her race were remarkably disinterested. "Trashing me is fine if it helps Hillary," he told me about the endless articles about their marriage. He just wanted her to win.

And Hillary wanted his advice. She was proud of him and his presidency, and she knew that most people in New York were, too. She considered him the best political mind she knew, and she discussed her speeches and strategies with him several times a day. Hillary was after all the one person who had paid the closest attention to Bill Clinton as a political figure over the years. Even Democrats who admired him often caricatured how he did things. Their most frequent error was failing to grasp the difficulty of the policy positions he took and how he nonetheless integrated them into his politics. His smoothness made it look too easy.

Hillary also observed the physical and emotional differences between herself and her husband, especially since she had become a candidate. "It helps to be a big man," she said. "I'm at a subway station. People are kissing me, enveloping me. They throw themselves at me. I'm going through an emotional wringer. The amount of emotion is overwhelming. It's all projected. Bill is supernatural. Bill can work a crowd. He can stretch his arm out three or four people deep. He can do it so fast. People can feel touched." Hillary was intent on standing on her own, and for her that meant not separating herself from her husband and his administration. That was her decision alone; she was willing to absorb whatever criticism and speculation attached to her as a result, and he proved as an adviser, touchstone, and symbol to be one of her most valuable resources.

On February 6, on the stage in the gymnasium at the State University of New York at Purchase, Senator Moynihan introduced his choice to be his successor. "Eleanor Roosevelt would love you," he said.

"I am honored today to announce my candidacy to the United States Senate from New York," Hillary told the crowd. "I may be new to the neighborhood, but I'm not new to your concerns." And: "I know it's not going to be an easy campaign, but hey, this is New York."

From the start, one of the chief reasons that Hillary's intentions were taken seriously was her willingness to run against the formidable Mayor Giuliani. Rudolph Giuliani had been elected and reelected as the savior of New York City. Under his mayoralty, it had become prosperous for many people and was virtually free of crime. The causes of the city's revival extended beyond his ministrations: national policies advocated by President Clinton had had similar effects in cities across the nation; the collapse of the crime rate was the same in New York as in other large metropolitan areas; some of the policies credited to Giuliani had been initiated before he assumed office. Nonetheless, he had cleaned up the streets, advocated community policing and other "quality-of-life" programs, and driven the pornography shops from Times Square. To many New Yorkers he represented a civic ideal of stern fairness.

Giuliani was a representative of the upwardly mobile, ethnic, and outer-borough New Yorker. The grandson of Italian immigrants, he had graduated from Manhattan College and the New York University Law School and become U.S. attorney for the Southern District of New York in the classic mold of crime busters going back to District Attorney Thomas E. Dewey. He was a Catholic, a Yankees fan, and a subscriber to the Metropolitan Opera. DiMaggio and Verdi were his household gods.

The eventual collapse of "the social democratic city" of Fiorello LaGuardia, the mayor of the 1930s who had led the city's own version of the New Deal, made Giuliani's eventual rise possible. "New York, for all of its many social democratic institutions, had kept costs and hence taxes in check," wrote the sociologist Fred Siegel. But after the militant 1960s, with threats of riots and waves of strikes, New York "lost 35 percent of its manufacturing and 16 percent of its overall jobs, roughly 700,000 in all. . . . The 1970s meant the end of New York's white working class, as more than a million fled the city during that decade."*

In 1989, David Dinkins became the first black mayor by defeating Giuliani by two points. The city had grown weary of racial conflict and the tart tongue of Mayor Edward Koch. Dinkins, who promised to weave the city's ethnic groups into a "gorgeous mosaic," had a mandate to govern as a racial healer, but his mismanagement of the city's budget was a sign of indecisiveness. His refusal to enforce a court order against a black boycott of a small, Korean-owned grocery store, a boycott conducted by a notorious demagogue, turned most people against him. He appeared weak in the face of the self-promoting identity politics that had torn the city apart and that he had been elected to resolve. Dinkins could not disentangle himself from the "race men" like Al Sharpton, and Giuliani's uncompromising severity seemed an appropriate remedy. In 1993, he beat Dinkins by three points. New York was still a Democratic city—but the Republican Giuliani received 57 percent of the vote in his reelection in 1997 and widespread respect for him was shown in the endorsement from *The New York Times*.

Still, Giuliani began to curdle as he prepared to run for the U.S. Senate. The harsh side of him became harsher. His temperament became an issue: autocratic, contemptuous, suspicious, insulting, and bitter. Those who questioned him he regularly called "jerks." He was, in fact, a man of many vendettas. He had many powerful enemies within his own party. As U.S. attorney he had investigated Senator D'Amato, and D'Amato had sworn revenge. When Pataki ran for governor, Giuliani endorsed Mario Cuomo, and when Pataki won his calls to the victor were disregarded for three weeks. In 1999, one of Pataki's major backers privately approached Hillary's campaign to communicate that, even if Pataki felt compelled formally to endorse Giuliani, he would do whatever he could to help Hillary.

In December, Hillary criticized the way Giuliani was handling the growing number of homeless people. He had imposed new rules that permitted officials to put children in foster care if parents lost their spots in the homeless shelters. "Breaking up families that are homeless is

*Fred Siegel, "The Social Democratic City," *The Public Interest*, Spring 2000.

wrong," Hillary said to a gathering of black ministers. It was a counterintuitive stroke. Giuliani, after all, had gained his support by being tough on those who had not met the stringent rules he set. She was still commonly thought of as another soft liberal, a perfect foil for him. But she hit him hard on a specific issue that turned his toughness into a political vulnerability. His response was to say dismissively that she wasn't from New York. He played into her hands by illustrating his harshness.

Giuliani began his campaign by trying to solidify his Republican base on the right. In September, he denounced an exhibition at the Brooklyn Museum of Art, "Sensation," containing a painting of the Virgin Mary by a black British artist of Nigerian origin who had used elephant dung in its composition. "Sick stuff," said Giuliani, and he tried to cut off the museum's public funding. A federal court ruled against him. In January, Giuliani laced into Hillary for "old-fashioned, classical left-wing thinking." He used extensive direct-mail appeals to raise money from Clinton-haters around the country. The letters called her "the darling of the left-wing elite." His aides estimated that about 40 percent of the $11.5 million he raised in 1999 came from these mailings and that most of the donors were from outside New York. The invective prompted President Clinton to step forward to defend his wife, charging Giuliani with ginning up the "right-wing venom machine" against her. "The only way they can win is to convince people that we're space aliens," Clinton said.

On February 25, 2000, a jury handed down a verdict acquitting four police officers of second-degree murder in the case of Amadou Diallo, a West African street vendor whom police said they had mistaken for a serial rapist they were seeking on the night of February 4, 1999. They had said they believed he was reaching for a gun when they shot at him forty-one times. The unarmed Diallo was, in fact, reaching for his wallet to show them his identification. The case was so heated that the trial had to be moved from the Bronx to Albany. The day after the acquittal, thousands of blacks marched in peaceful protest in New York.

Diallo's fate was linked in many minds with that of Abner Louima, a black man of Haitian origin who, in 1997, had been held down in the bathroom of a police station by one cop while another shoved his baton up his rectum, almost killing him. Louima claimed that one of the policemen shouted, "It's Giuliani time, not Dinkins time." (In June 1999, one policeman pled guilty to assault and in September 2002 another pled guilty to perjury in this highly dramatic case.) Popular alienation from Giuliani, who made no gesture of conciliation with the city's blacks during the Louima business, grew after the Diallo verdict.

Hillary was out of the city when the verdict was handed down. Some of her campaign aides wanted her to rush back immediately, but she made a judicious decision to act calmly and at a bit of a remove. Rather than making a hurried political statement, she spoke on March 5 at Riverside Church, near Columbia University. She said that minorities "do believe if Amadou had been a white man in an all-white neighborhood, he would still be alive." She criticized Giuliani by clear inference, saying "the leadership of this city refuses to reach out." Then she methodically proposed a program for police reform, including increased pay for officers, more minority recruitment, and community involvement. "I reject the false choice between effective policing and mutual respect," she said. She was poised, constructive, and sympathetic. She had risen above the rancorous politics while Giuliani further submerged himself in them.

On March 16, in the early morning, two undercover narcotics policemen approached a young black man, Patrick Dorismond, asking him to sell them marijuana. Dorismond was angry at the request for drugs, said he didn't have any, and pushed one of them away from him. One of the cops shot him dead. News articles about this occurrence highlighted Dorismond's past arrests, information that was drawn from juvenile court records supposedly sealed but released to the press by Giuliani's administration. (In truth, Dorismond was literally a church altar boy and his arrests had been for disorderly conduct misdemeanors.) On March 19, Giuliani went on Fox News to attack Dorismond for "arrests and convictions" and to insist that the public had a "right to know" about his "pattern of behavior." Condemnation of the mayor was universal.

On April 7, the *Times* published a poll showing Hillary beating Giuliani 49–41. His support among black voters was measured at zero. An emphatically local figure, he was even losing in the city he loved. He had little grasp of national issues, even as they related to New York, and he had put out not a single position paper. Hillary had him on the defensive on a host of issues, beginning with the homeless, and he didn't know what to do on the minimum wage, Republican tax cuts, or the Nuclear Test Ban Treaty that had been rejected by the Republican Senate. He was completely out of his depth on foreign policy; his idea of international relations was to attempt to enforce parking regulations on UN diplomats. He could not control his anger and frustration at his political plight. Asked at a press conference about Hillary's proposal on the federal debt, he shouted at reporters: "Oh, come on! Mrs. Clinton, Mrs. Clinton. You guys are unbelievable. You're like knee jerk, knee jerk, knee jerk. Thank you. Why don't you just join the Democratic National Committee."*

For all his sharp edges, Giuliani was also showing an uncharacteristic ambivalence. Instead of attending a sold-out Republican Women for Giuliani luncheon in Rochester, he went to a Yankees game. Some close observers wondered if he really wanted to run. Soon it became obvious that his uncertainty had more profound sources than politics.

On April 20, Donna Hanover Giuliani, a former television correspondent and actress, and the mayor's second wife, announced that she would appear in *The Vagina Monologues*, a feminist play about sexuality. She seemed to be trying to embarrass her husband. In interviews, she admonished reporters not to call her "Mrs. Giuliani," but just "Donna Hanover." Since 1995, the couple had rarely been seen together, in either public or private. A week later, on April 27, Giuliani held a press conference at which he announced he had prostate cancer, the disease that had killed his father. Asked about his political plans, he said, "I don't think it's fair to answer questions about the Senate race right now."

On May 2, the New York *Daily News* published an item saying that Rudy had been spotted out with "a friend" for dinner—his mistress, Judith Nathan. "She's a good friend, a very good friend," the mayor said at a press conference. Then on May 10, he held another press conference to declare that he and his wife led "independent and separate lives" and were separating. But this was something he had failed to tell his wife. Two hours later, she held her own press conference, letting the people of New York know that this was how the mayor had conveyed the news of their separation to her, and letting it be known that she knew he had had an affair with "one staff member," an open secret to the City Hall press corps. Two nights later he walked Judith Nathan home from dinner before the press corps and kissed her. Hanover retreated to her parents' home in Los Angeles. On May 19, Giuliani dropped out of the Senate race to undergo cancer treatment and sort out his private life. Hillary wished him well. "Now I know why he likes opera," she said to me.

Conservatives now praised the Republican mayor for the manner in which he had conducted his illicit affair, for being "unscripted," "nothing if not forthcoming," and "ragged and human."† The *National Review* called him "a real class act" with "respect for [his] constituents to be

*Tomasky, *Hillary's Turn*, p. 152.

†Peggy Noonan, "Exit Stage Right, Rudy," *The Wall Street Journal*, May 12, 2000.

forthright and honest." It added, "Everyone has known that Rudy and Donna have been past-tense for years. It is and has been no secret."*

Giuliani was overcome by his tribulations. But he was already losing to Hillary before his marriage unraveled and his cancer became public. Since he had launched his campaign he had become increasingly abrasive, strident, and self-defeating. He had gone from eight points ahead to eight points behind—a sixteen-point movement downward—at a cost of about $25 million. He had developed no idea of how to run against Hillary, trying to pigeonhole her as "left-wing" but unable to engage her policies. By contrast, Hillary appeared increasingly knowledgeable, hardworking, and compassionate about New York issues. (It was not until September 11, 2001, that Giuliani's finest qualities were called upon and displayed.) She had defeated him. Now she had to face a new candidate, to run a second campaign.

Enter Congressman Rick Lazio, forty-two years old, nicely married with two little girls, smooth, suburban, smiling, from Long Island. He appeared to be the anti-Rudy, his opposite in every respect. Lazio had wanted to run from the start, but his political sponsor, Governor Pataki, had held him back while Pataki endorsed but tried to undermine Giuliani. Now the field was clear. Lazio's leading trait was his uncomplicated ambition. He was prepared to say or do anything to get the job. In the House he claimed to be a moderate, followed the conservative Republican line to get ahead, and never took a risk. "There seemed to be nothing that he was finally and fundamentally and unalterably for, beyond the idea of Rick Lazio becoming a senator."†

On July 14, Matt Drudge posted "news" on his Internet website based on yet another pathography, entitled *The State of a Union*, whose author, Jerry Oppenheimer, was a former *National Enquirer* tabloid reporter. The book was serialized by the *New York Post* and published by HarperCollins (also owned by Murdoch). Oppenheimer claimed that in 1974, during Clinton's losing congressional race in Arkansas, Hillary had called one of his campaign aides a "fucking Jew bastard." For anyone who knew Hillary Clinton in the slightest, this charge was patently ridiculous. (The long-ago aide from Arkansas whom she had once criticized, Paul Fray, happened to be a Baptist, whose paternal great-grandmother was Jewish, a fact unknown to Hillary.) "Fucking Jew bastard here," I said when I

---

*Quoted in Joe Conason, "Righteous Hypocrites Excuse Rudy's Behavior," *The New York Observer*, May 22, 2000.

†Tomasky, *Hillary's Turn*, p. 186.

reached Hillary on the telephone. "Glad *you* said it," she replied. She issued a statement calling the smear an "outrageous lie." The President, exercised about the fracas, called the political editor and the publisher of the *Daily News* to try to get a different story into the news cycle: "My wife has never, ever uttered an ethnic or racial slur against anybody, ever." She fell nine points behind Lazio. But within two weeks the incident had nearly faded.

"HILLARY'S GAY AFFAIRS: The Shocking Truth" read the headline on the *National Enquirer*. It quoted Oppenheimer's book:

> One particularly peculiar tale circulated among Washington cognoscenti around the time of Clinton's impeachment trial—that a well-known Washington veterinarian, visiting the White House to treat Socks the cat, had opened the wrong door and discovered Hillary locked in a passionate embrace with another woman. The oddest thing about this tale was who was telling it: It had been passed on by a stalwart Clinton loyalist, a man who had repeatedly demonstrated his willingness to fall on his sword in defense of the president.

As I read the lurid tale while standing in the supermarket line it dawned on me that I was the one the tabloid was claiming was the source of the story. I recognized that anecdote—it had been lifted and distorted from my satirical play *This Town*. *The Washington Post* investigated, and Oppenheimer insisted to the newspaper, "I didn't make a mistake. It's a very bizarre story for Blumenthal to have put into his little playlet. Maybe he missed his calling. Maybe he should be working for the *National Enquirer*." The *Post* quoted me: "Life imitates satire."*

While Hillary tirelessly traveled around New York state discussing concrete programs every day, Lazio set out a customary line of attack against her. He claimed the election was about her "character" and "integrity"—and, in one fractured phrase, about "whether or not the rule of law applies to all or just a privileged few." He declared that stopping Hillary was his "patriotic duty." The slogan on his ads hammered, "You just can't trust her."†

On September 6, at the millennium session of the United Nations General Assembly, attended by almost every world leader, Cuba's Fidel

---

*Lloyd Grove, "Reliable Source: Next: The Lesbian Affairs of Buddy the Dog," *The Washington Post*, July 26, 2000.

†Tomasky, *Hillary's Turn*, pp. 216–18.

Castro managed to station himself in front of President Clinton after lunch and shake his hand. Lazio seized upon the incident. "I think we send the wrong message when we embrace, whether it's Mrs. Arafat or Fidel Castro," he said. A week later the White House released to the press a photograph of a glowing Lazio shaking hands with Yasser Arafat at a White House reception in 1998. Lazio protested that shaking hands with Arafat was "absolutely nothing like what Mrs. Clinton had done. . . . It wasn't a kiss, it wasn't a hug, it wasn't a call for a Palestinian state."

But his gambit had backfired. He looked utterly tactical, inventing controversies rather than discussing issues. Lazio was a perfect Republican candidate of his kind: clean-cut, youthful, conservative without passionate belief, glib, willing to be a transmission belt for his handlers' talking points. But the shallowness that had allowed his ambition to skim the surface this far and this fast was betraying him. He could not stop himself from attacking Hillary. By following instructions to go negative, busy at his task like a managerial trainee, he let his transparent opportunism become his message, in the absence of a positive one. Hillary's television ads, meanwhile, called attention to his position as deputy whip to Speaker Newt Gingrich and to his right-wing votes (for cutting Medicare by $270 million, for shutting down the federal government, for abolishing the Department of Education). The slogan on her ads: "The more you know, the more you wonder."

On September 13, the candidates met in a debate moderated by the host of NBC's *Meet the Press*, Tim Russert. Lazio's momentum carried him into the ring, jabbing at Hillary about "character and trust." Then the moderator decided to take control of the debate himself. "The issue of trust and character has been raised repeatedly in this campaign," said Russert. "Mrs. Clinton, I want to start with you. In January of '98, you went on the *Today Show* and talked about what had occurred at the White House. I want to play that for you and our viewers and our voters and give you a chance to respond." So Russert played a tape from January 27, 1998, in which Hillary said that she believed her husband when he told he hadn't had an "adulterous liaison," as her interviewer put it.

"Regrettably, it was proven true. Do you regret misleading the American people?" asked Russert. He had gone to the heart of the issue that made women most uncertain about Hillary, and he had posed his question so that it underlined the attacks on her. She paused before answering: "Well, you know, Tim, that was a very painful time for me, for my family, and for our country. It is something that I regret deeply that anyone had to go through. And I've tried to be as forthcoming as I could, given the circumstances that I faced. Obviously, I didn't mislead anyone. I didn't know the truth. And there's a great deal of pain associated with that, and my husband has certainly acknowledged that and made it clear that he did mislead the country, as well as his family."

When asked by Russert to respond to these comments, Lazio charged ahead: "I think that, frankly, what's so troubling here with respect to what my opponent just said, is somehow that it only matters what you say when you get caught. And character and trust is about, well, more than that. And blaming others every time you have responsibility? Unfortunately, that's become a pattern, I think, for my opponent."

Lazio moved on without stopping to another tack. Earlier, he had raised the issue of "soft money" used on behalf of candidates by independent groups because she had more of it, although he had exceeded her in raising "hard money," contributions that could only be spent directly by the candidates' campaigns. He whipped out a piece of paper from his suit jacket, held out a pen in his other hand, and marched over to her. "Right here, here it is," he said. "Let's sign it. It's the New York Freedom from Soft Money Pact. I signed it. We can both sit down together. We can all get all the media in here. We will make sure it's an ironclad deal. And I am happy to abide by anything that we all agree on, but let's get it done now. Let's not give any more wiggle room."

"Mrs. Clinton, do you want to respond?" asked Russert.

"Well, yes, I certainly do. You know, I . . . I admire that. That was a wonderful performance and—"

"Then why don't you sign it?" demanded Lazio, who was back at his own podium.

"And you did it very well."

"I'm not asking do you admire it, I'm asking you to sign it."

"Well, I would be happy to when you give me the signed letters—"

"Well, it's right here. It's right here."

"When you give me the signed—"

"Sign it right now." He was pounding his podium.

"Well, we'll shake on this, Rick."

"No, I want your signature, because I think that everybody wants to see you signing something that you said you were for. I am for it, I haven't done it. You have been violating it. Why don't you stand up and do something important for America? While America is looking at New York, why don't you show some leadership, because it goes to trust and character?"

"And this new radio ad from the Republican party using soft money is not part of your campaign?"

"What are we talking about here? Let's put things in perspective."

"We are out of time," interjected Russert. "We have to—"

"Six million dollars, seven million dollars, eight million dollars that you have been spending," shouted Lazio.

"We have to allow time for closing statements," said Russert.

Hillary began speaking: "I will use the thirty years of my experience to go to work for the people of New York. But, look, I know that there may be some who think that the most important issue is who has lived here the longest. That's the test. And if that's the test, I can't pass that test. But if you want someone who will get up every day and be on your side and fight for better schools, health care, and jobs, I can pass that test, and I would be honored to serve as a senator on behalf of the people of New York."

"Now," said Lazio, "you have got to decide in this campaign how you define character and trust. My opponent has talked and talked, but she has done nothing for New York. I've delivered for New York. And as that old Yankee manager Casey Stengel used to say, 'You can check it out.' "

Before the debate many women had been unsure about Hillary. But after it they made up their minds. In June, she had led Lazio by five points and then the race had been frozen until the debate. A week afterward, she was ahead of him by ten points, 51–41. Her boost had come from the very women who had been holding themselves back. According to a poll conducted by *The New York Times* and CBS News, Lazio's lead of 43–36 among suburban women in June had become a Clinton lead of 54–38.* Russert's embarrassing question, Lazio's invasion, and Hillary's composure were decisive. Actually seeing her fend off overbearing men made these women identify with her.

On September 22, Hillary announced that she would renounce Democratic Party soft money and urged Lazio to impose a similar ban on the Republican Party. Lazio agreed, but his desperation soon got the better of him.

On October 12, al-Qaeda terrorists attacked the USS *Cole* in port in Yemen, killing seventeen sailors. Shortly afterward, New York voters received telephone calls telling them that Hillary had accepted money from

---

*Adam Nagourney with Marjorie Connelly, "In Poll, Mrs. Clinton Makes Gains Among Women from the Suburbs," *The New York Times*, September 21, 2000.

an Arab organization that "openly brags about its support for a Mideast terrorism group, the same kind of terrorism that killed our sailors on the USS *Cole*." The calls urged voters to "tell her to stop supporting terrorism and give the money back." The group in question was the American Muslim Alliance, which had also endorsed George W. Bush for president. The Republican National Committee was paying for these calls with soft money. "This hits a new low," said Hillary, who returned the contribution. Governor Pataki, appearing on a local talk show, denounced the RNC calls. With that, he cornered the Republican candidate. Lazio was at a dead end.

On the day of the election, November 7, Hillary won by 55 to 43 percent, topping her opponent by more than 800,000 votes of the 6 million plus cast—a landslide. She carried three-quarters of the vote in New York City and half of the vote upstate, winning ten upstate counties. She had been deeply engaged in politics as Bill Clinton's wife, but on her own she had mastered every aspect of campaigning from shaking hands at the state fair to debating. She had, in effect, defeated two Republicans, who had collectively outspent her by about $60 million to $35 million, and she had run the closest thing to a nonstop presidential race that a senatorial candidate could approximate.

"They did their worst," I told her, "but you came from the toughest neighborhood in New York."

"Where's that?" Hillary asked.

"Chicago," I said.

In the bedroom of her suite in the Grand Hyatt Hotel in New York City, she was wearing a terrycloth bathrobe and getting her hair done when the news was broadcast that she had won. She simply smiled. One part of the Clinton succession was secured. In a corner her aides tinkered with her victory speech. Out in the main room, the President had positioned a television set in the middle of the space, and he stood with his face just inches away from the screen, talking to it, urging that the election be called for Vice President Gore. Earlier in the evening, cheers had gone up when Florida had been given to Gore, but then the state had been shifted into the undecided column. The polls were still open in the Western states, and Clinton got himself onto a Nevada radio talk show to exhort voters there to turn out for Gore. He was talking on the phone, to aides in the room, and to the television set at the same time. Then Hillary appeared, all ready to go. It was time for a break from the nail-biting presidential contest, to go downstairs to the ballroom for Hillary's speech.

Standing on the stage, flanked by her husband and her daughter and Senator Moynihan, she declared victory: "Sixty-two counties, sixteen months, three debates, two opponents, and six black pantsuits later, because of you, here we are." She had become the United States Senator from New York.

Back up in the suite, the watch went on. Hillary went to sleep. The President stayed up. Bush was announced as the winner; then the election was declared too close to call. Hillary woke up and wandered in. "What's happening?" she asked.

SIXTEEN

The Stolen Succession

I

Ebenezer Baptist Church, built in 1922 on Auburn Avenue in Atlanta—"Sweet Auburn," the historic heart of the black community in Georgia's largest city—had had the King family in its pulpit for forty years, ever since Martin Luther King, Sr., "Daddy" King, had come there in 1927 as the assistant pastor. Three years later he took over as pastor, and thirty years after that he made his son co-pastor. From this pulpit, two months before his assassination, Martin Luther King, Jr., preached a sermon envisioning his own death and funeral: "Yes, if you want to say that I was a drum major, say that I was a drum major for justice. (*Amen.*) Say that I was a drum major for peace. (*Yes.*) I was a drum major for righteousness. And all of the other shallow things will not matter. (*Yes.*) I won't have any money to leave behind. I won't have the fine and luxurious things of life to leave behind. But I just want to leave a committed life behind. (*Amen.*) And that's all I want to say."

On January 17, 2000, Vice President Al Gore climbed to the same pulpit at the Ebenezer Baptist Church to speak in commemoration of Martin Luther King, Jr. He had launched his presidential campaign seven months earlier, and his appearance at this event was reported as ceremonial and minor, but for Gore it was an intensely personal moment, expressing what he cared about most deeply as his father's son and a son of the South.

Albert Gore, Sr., congressman and senator from Tennessee, while he was never one of the Senate's great powers or a clubman in the sanctum sanctorum of Southern barons like Richard Russell or Harry Byrd or

Lyndon Johnson, had been an important liberal voice in the Senate of the 1950s and 1960s. He had refused to sign the notorious Southern Manifesto of 1956 signed by all other Southern senators except him and Lyndon Johnson, a document that denounced the Supreme Court decision in favor of integration in *Brown v. Board of Education*. When Strom Thurmond approached him about it on the Senate floor, Gore had bellowed, "Hell, no!" But in 1964, up for reelection, he was stricken with a crisis of courage and voted against the Civil Rights Act. His son, Al, then sixteen, strenuously argued with him, and so did his elder child, Al's sister, Nancy, whose friends included journalists covering the civil rights battles. Senator Gore later said that vote was the worst mistake in his life, and from then on he became, as his son proudly said, "a crusader" for civil rights.

Al's childhood was split between the small town of Carthage, Tennessee, and Washington, between the rural and the metropolitan, between the farm and an apartment in the Fairfax Hotel, between his parents' roots and their aspirations. His mother, Pauline, who had a firm view on civil rights, enrolled him in St. Albans because it was one of the few integrated private schools in the capital; in Tennessee, she made sure her children had black playmates and required them to read Harper Lee's *To Kill a Mockingbird*. Pauline was the tenth female graduate of the Vanderbilt Law School, and in the 1930s she worked answering correspondence for Eleanor Roosevelt, whom she saw as a model. She constantly prodded her husband to take liberal policy positions, as Eleanor had encouraged Franklin. Al recalled, in his eulogy for his father, an incident in the year when his father refused to sign the Southern Manifesto:

When I was eight years old, we lived in a little house on Fisher Avenue, halfway up a hill. At the top of the hill was a big old mansion. One day, as the property was changing hands, the neighbors were invited to an open house. My father said: "Come, son, I want to show you something." So we walked up the hill and through the front door. But instead of stopping in the parlor, or the ornate dining room, or the grand staircase with all the other guests, my father took me down to the basement and pointed to the dark, dank stone walls—and the cold metal rings lined up in a row. Slave rings.

Long after he left the classroom, my father was a teacher. And I thank God that he taught me to love justice. Not everyone was eager to learn. One unreconstructed constituent once said, in reference to African-

Americans—though that was not the term he used—"I don't want to eat with them, I don't want to live with them, I don't want my kids to go to school with them." To which my father replied gently: "Do you want to go to heaven with them?"

Senator Gore vainly tried to become the Democratic vice-presidential nominee in 1956 and again in 1960, and he bequeathed his ultimate ambition to his son. Al was his father's and mother's arrow to the sun. Observing Al plow a field behind a team of mules, as he had taught him, Senator Gore said to his wife, "I think a boy, to achieve anything he wants to achieve, which would include being president of the United States, ought to be able to run a hillside plow."

When Senator Gore came out in opposition to the Vietnam War, Nixon's White House directed a flood of illegal money into a campaign to unseat him in 1970 through an enterprise called Operation Townhouse. This was part of Nixon's "Southern strategy"—turning Dixiecrats into Republicans—and a test of the dirty tricks that would lead to Watergate. (Operation Townhouse was also siphoning large sums of cash to the losing Senate campaign of George H. W. Bush in Texas.) Senator Gore's television ads featured pictures of him with his son; when he conceded defeat, his speech was widely interpreted as a prophecy: "The causes for which we fought are not dead. The truth shall rise again!" In his eulogy, Al said, "The night he lost—in 1970—he made me prouder still. He said: 'Defeat may serve as well as victory to shake the soul and let the glory out.' And then he turned the old Southern segregationist slogan on its head, and declared: 'The truth shall rise again.' I heard that."

On December 19, 1997, as part of the national dialogue about race issues that he conducted throughout his presidency, Clinton had invited a group of conservatives to the White House for a private meeting. They came determined to voice adamant opposition to affirmative action. The President wanted to listen to them, in the hope that he might find some way to persuade them to tone down their harsh rhetoric. Gore found their views offensive and did not hesitate to say so. They took the usual anti-affirmative-action line that class and cultural issues mattered more than the race factor. "It is naïve in the extreme to assert that there is no persistent vulnerability to prejudice rooted in human nature," Gore told them. Bigotry can lead "to an unleashing of evil. I think that evil lies coiled in the human soul. . . . To deny that there is this factor called race that is persistent is, I think, just wrong."

Though he knew it would receive only cursory attention, Gore prepared his speech at the Ebenezer Baptist Church with as much care as he had devoted to the speech announcing his presidential candidacy. He asked me to help him and I participated with his staff in the lengthy process; he held a long meeting with civil rights leaders in the Roosevelt Room and had several discussions in his West Wing office about everything from specific policies to the theological basis of civil rights.

At meetings like these, I realized that the closer you got to Gore the more complex and interior he became. Systematic, deliberate, and logical, he devoted enormous effort to his work, but sometimes he would make a wholly abstract remark that seemed like a flying fragment of a larger pattern of thought he was not sharing. Gore combined command of detail with a reach for the holistic. In public he cloaked his sharp sense of humor, which could be biting, wry, and intellectual in private. He had a sophisticated understanding of the world around him, but he would sometimes appear impenetrable and inaccessible. Both when he waded enthusiastically into crowds and when he held himself back slightly, he revealed a hint of discomfort. Clinton, in contrast, had a preternatural quality of being present, totally accessible, and completely focused on the person in front of him, and this manner distracted nearly everyone from noticing his self-consciousness. In truth, Gore was more like most people, while Clinton, drawing the multitudes closer and closer, was nonpareil. The more Gore tried, the more labored he sometimes appeared, though he could often be completely natural, neither stentorian nor stilted—as I saw him when he gracefully talked about his own commitment to civil rights at a book party at his house for his friend Congressman John Lewis, who had been bloodied with Dr. King on the Pettus Bridge at Selma. Gore was funny, warm, and utterly convincing. That was in him, too.

After his Harvard years, during which he had opposed the war in Vietnam, Gore had enlisted in the army and served there; when he returned, he had attended divinity school at Vanderbilt, where he was influenced by the thought of Reinhold Niebuhr, the realist liberal theologian who also influenced Martin Luther King, Jr. In *The Children of Light and the Children of Darkness*, published in 1944, Niebuhr had written that the children of light must temper their "foolish" idealism with an astute pessimism in order to counter the malice and cynicism of the children of darkness. Gore's lecture to the conservatives about the "vulnerability" of "human nature" to "evil" had shown his understanding of Niebuhr's view.

Ascending to King's pulpit, Gore explained perhaps more clearly and passionately than in any other speech he gave during the campaign the essence of his thinking and the sweep of his strategy. He listed the accomplishments of the Clinton administration, but offered them as just a start:

> We have come many miles toward justice, but have not yet fulfilled the dream. . . . African-American unemployment has fallen to the lowest level in history. African-American poverty has fallen to the lowest level in history. And African-American child poverty has fallen to the lowest level in history. In [the last] two years, African-American home-ownership has risen to an all-time high. And in those two years, we have continued to surpass every past mark for appointment of African-Americans to Cabinet seats, judgeships, and other high-ranking posts. If Dr. King were with us now, I believe he would celebrate our gains, because they nourish our dreams, and then he would summon us on.

Gore's agenda was not just an unfinished legislative program but a moral cause. He believed that the conservatives' insistence that it was needless was mistaken about the realities of the enduring American dilemma and also morally flawed:

> I hear some in America arguing that our nation's historic struggle for justice and equality is over—that we have already reached the Promised Land—that we now have a color-blind society.
>
> They're confusing the wilderness with Canaan. Like thirsty men too long in the desert, they see fountains in the sand. They gaze at the shimmering mirage of a city on a hill. But their eyes are playing tricks on them. Our journey is not over. The city we seek still lies ahead—beyond the horizon of justice.
>
> This is what Dr. King would have called moral blindness. It is a condition that affects the heart as well as the eyes. Those who suffer from it have the capacity to look and not see. They look at African-American poverty, and diminished opportunity, and increased infant mortality, and unequal law enforcement, and they don't really see a cause for affirmative action. . . . Yes, they have eyes, but they do not see. They do not see that we must live together and advance together. . . .
>
> "We shall overcome" has got to be more than a line we sing; it must be a fight to make things right—so all God's children can hear the freedom bell ring. And then "the crooked places shall be made straight, and the rough places plain: And the glory of the Lord shall be revealed."

Al Gore had command of an almost infinite array of intricate details and technicalities of science and social policy. He had mastered difficult fields, one after another, and arrived at innovative solutions to persistent problems. When he told an aide he wanted to write a book called "Salt," the aide thought he was referring to the Strategic Arms Limitation Talks, but Gore explained it would be about how salt affects human life.* A genuine expert on nuclear strategy, he had done much to restore the Democratic Party's reputation for realism in the post-Vietnam period. His book *Earth in the Balance*, published in 1992, was only partially about how greenhouse gases create global warming. It was a spiritual affirmation of his belief that humanity could become whole by shaping and protecting the environment and establishing "the link between our intellect and the physical world."† He and his wife, Tipper, had also been holding annual conferences on family and children's policy for more than a decade.

It was no surprise, then, that within the Clinton administration's councils, Gore had had important and far-ranging influence. He had worked for the unpopular budget of 1993 that virtually eliminated the deficit (casting the deciding vote in the Senate to break the tie), for military action in Bosnia, NAFTA, welfare reform, and affirmative action. He, together with former Prime Minister Viktor Chernomyrdin, spearheaded a joint commission on U.S.-Russian relations. He was in charge of the National Performance Review for "reinventing government," which by 2000 had reduced the number of federal employees to the lowest level since the Kennedy administration and had wiped thousands of outdated rules off the books. He helped initiate the low-cost "E-rate" for schools to be wired to the Internet, resulting in more than 95 percent of them being hooked up. On all these issues and more, he had been prescient, effective, and principled.

Gore had trained to run for the presidency. He had suffered ambivalence about that ambition when he returned from Vietnam but had long since overcome that feeling. He had campaigned in 1988 when he was only forty. He might have run in 1992 if not for his son's life-threatening accident: when he accepted Clinton's offer to be his running mate, he told his aides he wanted to be president. And for eight years, he had been grooming himself for the inevitable 2000 campaign.

---

*Maraniss and Nakashima, *Prince of Tennessee*, p. 241.

†Cited in Louis Menand, *American Studies*, Farrar, Straus and Giroux, 2002, p. 256.

His mastery of many issues notwithstanding, what Gore believed was his paramount distinction was his character—serious, hardworking, honorable, dutiful, sincere, dignified, and trustworthy. He took brave stands. He had been a reformer in many fields. He had a practical vision of the future and a deeply rooted sense of social justice, and he was a person of integrity.

But now it was his turn to be the target. By late 1996 he had developed new vulnerabilities because he was the imminent threat to future Republican control of the White House. In the final week of the 1996 election, as Bob Dole was about to be overwhelmingly defeated, a number of Republican senators had called for an independent counsel to be appointed to investigate the financing of the Clinton-Gore campaign. The Republican campaign against Gore had been at full throttle ever since. In 1997 and 1998, the Republicans adroitly created a swirling storm around his character. Their drive for power, having created the impeachment crisis, moved directly into the presidential campaign of 2000.

The Republican political operation targeted Gore's greatest strengths and virtues and systematically turned them upside down. He was called a liar, an exaggerator. The media, in large part, accepted this portrait of an untrustworthy, sleazy, and phony man and transmitted the false stories originating in the Republican camp.

The doubts raised about his character in the campaign finance controversy profoundly bothered Gore. He felt defensive and tainted. During the 1996 campaign, he had proved himself once again, as he had his whole life, as loyal and diligent, an achiever, accomplishing the objective—this one to raise money for the Democratic cause—and he had done it even more assiduously than Clinton. Once Gore cleared one list of prospective donors, he'd get another, and another. But when his image was besmirched, his sense of himself as a reformer was assaulted. His father had been elected to the Congress by defeating the corrupt political machine of Edward H. "Boss" Crump of Memphis, and as a journalist at the *Nashville Tennessean*, Al had done reporting that had led to indictments. Early in his own career in the House, he had introduced bills on campaign finance reform, which he saw as part of his overall approach to good government. When he himself was stigmatized as a symbol of a rotten system, he was naturally enough disconcerted and sought to distance himself from the damage.

The negative Republican campaign against Al Gore, once begun, never ended, and it became the salient factor in the public perception of the Vice President. The doubts this campaign raised among many voters who were otherwise politically in concert with Gore were decisive. According to a study based on the 2000 National Election Survey conducted by the Center for Political Studies at the University of Michigan, more than 3.5 million liberals voted against him, despite their natural inclinations to favor him, because of reservations they had come to have about his personal traits: he received only 57 percent of the vote of sympathetic liberals.* The Republican campaign against him—mendacious, false, and distorting—had been wildly successful.

In 1969, Harvard senior Al Gore had written his honors thesis on "The Impact of Television on the Conduct of the Presidency 1947–1969." "A key factor in this trend is the increasing importance of the president's personality," he wrote. "Because of this, it is possible to speculate that a 'role requirement' of the president in the future might become 'visual communication,' just as an effective speechmaking technique has been a role requirement in the past." Gore's paper recounted how John F. Kennedy had bested Richard Nixon in the visual medium and how the cameras "seemed to intimidate" Lyndon Johnson "from being himself."† Now the media had changed again, with the emergence of the Republican permanent negative campaign, which had radically altered the structure of American politics.

The main effect of the Republican campaign was disorientation in the Gore camp. Gore did not fully grasp until later just how the Republicans had created what he would call in 2002 "a fifth column" within journalism, and how they had distorted the political atmosphere. The Republicans inflated every minor error he made on the stump into a revelation of supposedly fraudulent character. They twisted truths he uttered to make the same point. He found himself in a ceaseless battle with phantoms of himself.

The more he was attacked, the more Gore stubbornly tried to go ahead with his own message, disregarding the campaign against him. But this strategy exacerbated the problem. Republicans depicted every effort he made to present his authentic self as inauthentic, and they denigrated as another "reinvention" every attempt he made to overcome the con-

*David Gopoian, "Making Sense of the 2000 Presidential Election: Lessons for 2004," unpublished paper, February 24, 2002.

†Deb Riechmann, "Gore's College Thesis: Personality Is a 'Role Requirement' for Presidents," Associated Press, June 26, 1999; David Grann, "Al Gore's Campaign Against Himself, the Hard Way," *The New Republic*, November 20, 2000.

trived figure of himself. Gore's efforts to rise above their low tactics and the shabby reporting made him appear out of touch and aloof. He tried to sidestep them with self-deprecating humor and, finally, by abjectly apologizing for trivialities—both of which were incitements to further trouble.

He had ideas about why this or that reporter or broadcaster might be hostile to him, but he was shocked by the media's general enmity. His efforts to reaffirm his own real self confirmed for the press that he was vulnerable, clumsy, and self-righteous.

On October 27, 1999, Al Gore and his principal Democratic primary opponent, former senator Bill Bradley of New Jersey, held their first debate at Dartmouth College in New Hampshire. "The 300 media types watching in the press room at Dartmouth were, to use the appropriate technical term, totally grossed out," *Time* reported. "Whenever Gore came on too strong, the room erupted in a collective jeer, like a gang of fifteen-year-old Heathers cutting down some hapless nerd." (*Heathers* is a 1988 movie about cliquish, nasty high-school girls.)*

Margaret Carlson, a *Time* columnist, explained on the Don Imus radio show, "It's really easy, and it's fun, to disprove Gore. As sport, and as our enterprise, Gore coming up with another whopper is greatly entertaining to us."

"Somewhere along the line," said Mark Halperin, the ABC News political director, "the dominant political reporters for most dominant news organizations decided they didn't like him, and they thought the story line on any given day was about his being a phony or a liar or a waffler. Within the subculture of political reporting, there was almost peer pressure not to say something neutral, let alone nice, about his ideas, his political skills, his motivations."†

From the beginning of the campaign, the innuendo against Gore was relentless. In May 1997, *The Weekly Standard* had published an article consisting of what was already then conventional invective, labeling Gore "shiftier and more disingenuous than just about anybody currently in national office." In it, the conservative writer Tucker Carlson offered a sen-

---

*Eric Pooley, "Please Don't Leave Me, Don't You Go," *Time*, November 8, 1999.
†Howard Kurtz, "By Stepping Aside, Gore Stands Out," *The Washington Post*, December 23, 2002. The most comprehensive coverage of the media treatment of Al Gore can be found at www.dailyhowler.com, a website written by Bob Somerby. See also Paul Waldman, "Gored by the Media Bull," *The American Prospect*, January 13, 2003.

sational new charge. "The day [his sister] died must have been a very busy one for Al Gore, for at some point during the same day, July 11, 1984, he also found time to give a speech before the Kiwanis Club in Knoxville, across the state from his sister's deathbed. He also squeezed in an interview with a wire-service reporter. Whether he managed to do these things before or after his sister's last words to him isn't clear, since Gore didn't mention her in the UPI interview he gave." Nancy Gore Hunger, who died of lung cancer at the age of forty-six, was Al's only sibling—ten years older than he, the family rebel, a natural politician, the center of the liberal crowd at Vanderbilt, the first volunteer at the Peace Corps in Washington—and she had watched over Al, guided him, and prodded him. While Al was campaigning for his first term in the Congress, Nancy had been in and out of the hospital for months, and he would drive across the state from wherever he was to be with her. When her husband reached him on the telephone to tell him she was nearly at the end, he was, indeed, at a political event, and he quickly sped to her bedside to be with her when she died. In his speech at the 1996 convention, Gore described this sequence of events and used her death as a summons to "take on the tobacco companies." But *The Weekly Standard*'s story fit the carefully constructed image of him as someone who would even misrepresent his last moment with his dying sister for political gain.

"I can hardly remember a time when it wasn't on our radar screen that Al Gore had a propensity to both exaggerate and fabricate," Clifford May, spokesman for the Republican National Committee, told *The New York Times*. In December 1997, the RNC announced it was launching a contest for a Gore slogan. "The R.N.C. wants your best 'Love Means . . .' slogan for Al and Tipper Gore," said its press release. The party suggested its own entry: "Love means never having to tell the truth."*

This mockery referred to an item in *Time* about Gore and his wife being the models for the couple in the popular novel and 1970 film *Love Story*, by Erich Segal. The story originated in a conversation Gore had had about the movies with several reporters, in which he told them that the *Nashville Tennessean* had quoted Segal, who had been at Harvard in 1968 and befriended him, as saying that he and Tipper were his models for the young lovers, Oliver Barrett IV and Jenny Cavilleri. *Time* left out

*Alison Mitchell, "The 2000 Campaign: The Credibility Issue: A Sustained G.O.P. Push to Mock Gore's Image," *The New York Times*, October 14, 2000.

Gore's mention that it was the *Tennessean*, not he, that had made this point. Segal himself, when asked, explained that the figure of Oliver was indeed loosely based on both Gore and his roommate, Tommy Lee Jones. But this supportive clarification never caught up with the myth, and the notion that Gore had self-aggrandizingly lied about *Love Story* was regularly cemented into reports on his "credibility."* Gore's response was to have his press secretary apologize if there had been a "miscommunication." Gore thought it reasonable to assume that such a frivolous incident would simply evaporate into the ether.

Another example of the same dynamic began on March 9, 1999, when Gore was asked about his legislative record in an interview on CNN and remarked, "During my service in the United States Congress, I took the initiative in creating the Internet." He was, in fact, the legislative father of what was early called "the information superhighway," having sponsored the Supercomputer Network Study Act in 1986 and the High-Performance Computing Act in 1991. Vinton Cerf, the scientist who is most credited as the "father of the Internet," said, "The Internet would not be where it is in the United States without the strong support given to it and related research areas" by Gore.†

Two days later, a conservative writer, in an article in *Wired* entitled "No Credit Where It's Due," cited as an authority on the Internet a spokesman for the Gingrich-sponsored Peace and Freedom Foundation, who said, "Gore played no positive role in the decisions that led to the creation of the Internet as it now exists."‡ For days thereafter, the RNC sent out press releases ridiculing Gore for having claimed to have invented the Internet.§ Soon, this claim was repeated as factual in many news reports. Republican leaders joined in the merriment. Senator Trent Lott said, "During my service in the United States Congress, I took the initiative in creating the paper clip." House Majority Leader Dick Armey cracked, "If the Vice President created the Internet, then I created the interstate highway system." "We all just leapt on it. We would just kind of compile stuff and send it out to talk radio and to members," said Armey's

---

*Sean Wilentz, "Will Pseudo-Scandals Decide the Election?" *The American Prospect*, September 24–October 2, 2000; Eric Boehlert, "The Press v. Al Gore," *Rolling Stone*, December 6–13, 2001.

†Wilentz, "Will Pseudo-Scandals Decide the Election?"

‡Declan McCullagh, "No Credit Where It's Due," *Wired*, March 11, 1999.

§Cited in Wilentz, "Will Pseudo-Scandals Decide the Election?"

press secretary.* Armey's office (where Justice Clarence Thomas's wife worked as a researcher on the Democratic opposition) became a clearinghouse for negative material against Gore. For more than a week, Gore did not dignify this activity with a response, but finally, on March 20, he joked to the Democratic National Committee, "I was pretty tired when I made that comment because I had been up very late the night before inventing the camcorder." Trying to make light of the incident without correcting the record allowed the falsehood to stand, however.

On March 16, in an interview with the *Des Moines Register*, Gore observed that his father had assigned him farm chores when he was a boy.† Though plenty of press reports had already verified the truth of this statement, the RNC leaped on it as yet another instance of dissembling. RNC chairman Jim Nicholson sent out a press release: "Mr. Vice President, with all due respect, you're shoveling a lot more of it right now than you ever did back then."

Conservative columnists and publications beat the drum. Michael Kelly dubbed Gore "Farmer Al": "The Gore farmhouse occupied six big rooms on the top floor of the Fairfax, and Al was proud of that; there weren't many farm families in Washington whose penthouses boasted views of sunrise and sunset."‡ "Internet Al, Down on the Farm" went the version in *The Weekly Standard*. The *Washington Post* reporter assigned to Gore's campaign wrote, "Critics say the latest Gore gaffe fit a pattern of personal puffery. Remember, they noted, in 1997 when Gore suggested he and wife Tipper were the models for Erich Segal's teary Love Story? And last week, Gore was lampooned for his gauzy recollections of days on the family's Tennessee farm where he chopped wood, slopped hogs and took 'up hay all day long in the hot sun.' "§

On July 22, 1999, Gore wanted to draw attention to environmental issues, and campaigning in New England, he paddled down the Connecticut River in New Hampshire. The next day, *The Washington Times* reported that four billion gallons of water had been released to lift Gore's canoe for a photo opportunity, and that the cost to the utility was $7 mil-

---

*Mitchell, "The 2000 Campaign."

†David Yepsen, "Gore Makes His Candidacy Official," *The Des Moines Register*, March 16, 1999.

‡Michael Kelly, "Farmer Al," *The Washington Post*, March 24, 1999.

§Ceci Connolly, "Gore Exhorts Core Democrats to 'Stand with Me,' " *The Washington Post*, March 21, 1999.

lion, implying that this expense would be passed on to consumers.* Those figures, though no source was attached to them in the paper, came from the RNC, as *The Washington Post* later noted.

Newsweek called it the "photo op from hell."† For weeks, *The Washington Times* and the RNC kept pumping the story, and it continued to flow through the media. The New Hampshire State Republican Party filed a complaint against Gore with the Federal Election Commission, creating another round of reporting.

In Rutland, Vermont, however, the local *Herald* reported that the $7 million number was bogus and that the utility and its consumers had lost nothing: "The GOP's claim that the water was wasted may be based on some slippery calculations. An official from the utility that released the water said Friday that the company didn't waste the water. It generated power—and made money—during the dam release."‡ The amount of water released was only a quarter of the volume that was now widely believed to have been used, and it would have been released that day in any case. "I felt like we'd fallen through the looking glass," said Sharon Francis, executive director of the Connecticut River Joint Commissions; she later described the media coverage, "spun to sound like something corrupt," as "fictional" and "nasty."§

On November 30, Gore appeared before a group of students at a Concord, New Hampshire, high school, where his theme was to encourage them to participate in public life. He told them that it was a letter he'd gotten from a student that had alerted him in 1978 to dangers of toxic waste in Toone, Tennessee, about how he then learned, as he explored the problem, about Love Canal, New York, and in the end launched congressional hearings. "Had the first hearing on that issue, and Toone, Tennessee—that was the one you didn't hear of, but that was the one that started it all." The next day, Ceci Connolly in *The Washington Post* misquoted him as saying, "I was the one that started it all," a

---

*Bill Sammon and Laura R. Vanderkam, "New Hampshire Opts to Float Gore's Boat; 4 Billion Gallons Released for Photo Outing," *The Washington Times*, July 23, 1999.

†See also Dan Balz, "Gore, Bradley and the Soft-Money Shootout: Four Billion Gallons for a Photo Op," *The Washington Post*, July 25, 1999; Howard Fineman, "A War Over Who Controls the Left," *Newsweek*, August 9, 1999.

‡John Dillon, "GOP Goofs in Attack on Gore Dam Opening," *The Sunday Rutland Herald* (Vermont), July 25, 1999.

§Boehlert, "The Press v. Al Gore."

statement, she wrote, that was "reminiscent of earlier attempts to embellish his role in major events."* *The New York Times* also published the misquotation.† The RNC issued a press release: "Al Gore is simply unbelievable—in the most literal sense of that term." A day later, in an article headlined "First 'Love Story,' Now Love Canal," Connolly added, "Add Love Canal to the list of verbal missteps by Vice President Gore. The man who mistakenly claimed to have inspired the movie Love Story and to have invented the Internet says he didn't quite mean to say he discovered a toxic waste site when he said at a high school forum Tuesday in New Hampshire: 'I found a little place in upstate New York called Love Canal.'" She noted that Gore had told an Associated Press reporter, "If anybody got the misimpression that I claimed to do what citizens in Love Canal did, I apologize."‡ His apology only gave further license to radio and television talk shows whipping up a frenzy.

Chris Matthews, host of CNBC's *Hardball*, asked his guest, Lois Gibbs, the Love Canal resident who was responsible for arousing interest in the town's crisis, "I mean, isn't this getting ridiculous? . . . Isn't it getting to be delusionary?" But Gibbs credited Gore as the congressman who first cared about the plight of her town: "I actually think he's done a great job. I mean, he really did work, when nobody else was working, on trying to define what the hazards were in this country and how to clean it up and helping with the Superfund and other legislation." Her rebuttal made no difference. The next night, Matthews held forth again: "Now you've seen Al Gore in action. . . . What is it, the Zelig guy who keeps saying, I was the main character in Love Story. I invented the Internet. I invented Love Canal."

That Sunday, December 5, both the *Post* and the *Times* published corrections to their misquotations, but on the ABC News program *This Week*, George Stephanopoulos, now a regular member of its panel, remarked, "Gore, again, revealed his Pinocchio problem."§ And instead of

---

*Ceci Connolly, "Gore Paints Himself as No Beltway Baby; On Stump in New Hampshire, Vice President Highlights Days as 'Home Builder,' Soldier," *The Washington Post*, December 1, 1999.

†Katharine Q. Seelye, "Gore Borrows Clinton's Shadow Back to Share a Bow," *The New York Times*, December 1, 1999.

‡Ceci Connolly, "First 'Love Story,' Now Love Canal," *The Washington Post*, December 1, 1999.

§Quoted in Robert Parry, "Al Gore v. the Media," *Consortium News*, February 1, 2000, http://www.consortiumnews.com/2000/020100a.html.

assigning reporters to examine Gore's actual record, newspapers favored analyzing his "credibility." "Gore Record Scrutinized for Veracity" ran a headline in *The Boston Globe*.*

As these trivial attacks mounted, President Clinton made plain the high stakes in carrying on the policies of the Clinton-Gore administration. Clinton used the 2000 State of the Union address to explain the historical moment. From this bully pulpit, he was intent on setting the theme of continuity and change for the years to come. The record, he demonstrated, had established the success of his approach:

> We begin the new century with over 20 million new jobs; the fastest economic growth in more than thirty years; the lowest unemployment rates in thirty years; the lowest poverty rates in twenty years; the lowest African-American and Hispanic unemployment rates on record; the first back-to-back budget surpluses in forty-two years. And next month, America will achieve the longest period of economic growth in our entire history.
>
> We have built a new economy. And our economic revolution has been matched by a revival of the American spirit: crime down by 20 percent, to its lowest level in twenty-five years; teen births down seven years in a row; adoptions up by 30 percent; welfare rolls cut in half to their lowest levels in thirty years.

None of the achievements of his administration were passive accomplishments, happening by accident. They required planning, struggle, and will. And in setting out an agenda for the future, Clinton was making the case for further progress:

> In 1992, we had a road map; today, we have results. More important, America again has the confidence to dream big dreams. But we must not let our renewed confidence grow into complacency. We will be judged by the dreams and deeds we pass on to our children. And on that score, we will be held to a high standard, indeed, because our chance to do good is so great.

The program he had proposed in January 2000 would pay off the national debt within thirteen years. He called for doubling federal invest-

*Walter V. Robinson and Ann Scales, "Gore Record Scrutinized for Veracity," *The Boston Globe*, January 28, 2000.

ment in troubled schools, $1 billion for the Head Start preschool program, and a $30 billion tax credit so that families could deduct $10,000 in college tuition a year. He demanded another increase in the minimum wage. He urged that the Congress make a simple health insurance improvement: include the low-income parents of children already receiving insurance under the federal plan he had enacted in 1997—an expansion that would cover one-quarter of the still uninsured. He proposed a fully funded prescription drug plan for senior citizens and a tripling of the tax credit for long-term care to $3,000. He wanted investment in Medicare to make it solvent until 2055. He advanced a child care plan to cover four hundred thousand low-income children. The House of Representatives had rejected his proposals for gun safety, and after the Columbine High School massacre in Colorado, when two gun-toting students had killed twelve of their schoolmates in April 1999, he had resubmitted it. He proposed new initiatives to fight infectious diseases. He called for federal investment to support clean energy technology. He demanded that the Congress pass the Hate Crimes Prevention Act and the Employment Non-Discrimination Act—and proposed "the largest-ever investment to enforce America's civil rights laws":

> One of America's leading scientists said something we should all remember. He said all human beings genetically are 99.9 percent the same. So modern science affirms what ancient faith has always taught: the most important fact of life is our common humanity. Therefore, we should do more than tolerate diversity—we must honor it and celebrate it. . . .
>
> After 224 years, the American Revolution continues. We remain a new nation. And as long as our dreams outweigh our memories, America will be forever young. That is our destiny. And this is our moment.

II

After the crisis over President Clinton's impeachment ended, Gore had assumed that the force of his own decency would wipe the slate clean, that with a political situation restored to normal he would prevail, that he could be his own man. But he was perplexed by the problem of defining his vice presidency and his relationship with the President. The day after the State of the Union address in January 2000, Clinton's popularity rose while Gore's fell by four points. His physical presence, standing behind the President on the Senate podium, had reminded people that he was the number two, and they did not necessarily credit him with any of the administration's successes. This would have been a problem under any circumstances, but the impeachment complicated it. Bill Clinton had brought Al Gore to the highest reaches of the national government and gave him prominence he had not had before, but being number two, which had never been his intention, was both a gift and a burden, and Clinton's reliance on Gore's counsel heightened the paradox.

Gore worried that voters concerned above all about personal moral qualities might not choose him because of his association with Clinton. On June 16, 1999, the day that Gore announced his bid for the presidency, he was interviewed on the ABC News program *20/20*, where he sharply criticized Clinton for his conduct with Monica Lewinsky. "What he did was inexcusable," said Gore. "And particularly as a father I felt that it was terribly wrong, obviously." He was concerned when Clinton's personal favorability ratings hovered in the high forties, believing that popular disapproval of Clinton's behavior would rub off on him. And he believed in a theory much discussed in the press called "Clinton fatigue," according to which, voters were exhausted by the struggles surrounding the President, wanted no more to do with him, and were ready to reject him and anyone associated with him.

But the "Clinton fatigue" theory was derived from poll numbers about personal, not job performance, assessments. Throughout his presidency, there had been a significant gap between the two with Bill Clinton. But only when the job approval numbers fell, as they did in 1994, was there a negative political outcome. In the 1992 and 1996 elections, Clinton had won, and in 1998 he had helped Democrats to win. Now his job performance numbers were higher and more sustained than ever. In fact, he was the most popular second-term president since Franklin D. Roosevelt. (Every president since FDR had experienced a decline in their job approval ratings in their second terms, even Eisenhower.)

Clinton was also more popular than Ronald Reagan had been. At his high point, in May 1986, Reagan had reached 68 percent. But in November of that year, with the exposure of the Iran-Contra scandal, his job approval rating fell below 50 percent, and he did not recover until June 1988, when he signed the arms-control agreement with Gorbachev and declared the Cold War over; even then he did not recover his former standing. Only after the election of George H. W. Bush did Reagan's numbers rise as high as 63 percent, which left him with the aura of a president who had always been popular. As for Clinton, after his reelection in 1996 his popularity ranged in the mid-fifties for a few months, then rose to the sixties, spiked at 69 percent during his impeachment, fell to 56 percent during the Kosovo war, and then climbed in 2000 to the mid-sixties.*

Clinton's job approval ratings had been predictive of election outcomes before. Given the administration's record of peace and prosperity, which Gore could claim as indicative of his own future intentions, the polls in 2000 showed public opinion should favor him. To be sure, Gore would have to step out of Clinton's shadow. But that was an inevitability for which the stage of the Democratic convention was made.

Gore could not separate from Clinton either as a matter of record or in the mind of partisan Republicans. The Vice President was self-evidently part of a team. To imagine him as having been a valuable vice president to an ineffective president was illogical, and in any case Clinton had been a successful president with a strong record of achievement. Moreover, no one confused Gore with Clinton. Voters watched Gore to see how he treated the man who had made him vice president, as an indication of how he might deal with them. What kind of friend was Gore? What kind of leader? Sometimes he expressed "disappointment," sometimes he condemned Clinton, sometimes he fervently defended the administration's successes, sometimes he spoke as though he had only just now suddenly appeared on the scene.

Gore's uncertain handling of his own relation to the Clinton administration turned into an issue itself and reinforced the qualms that were induced by the Republicans' negative campaign against him. With his remarks about Clinton on the day of his announcement, he created an ongoing issue about his relationship with Clinton, his autonomy, and his identity, and he gave the press a basis for incessant chatter and psychobabble. He had not brought himself into sharper focus, and instead of resolving people's questions, he had turned his own predicament into a Shakespearean subplot.

In October 1999, Gore fired his pollster Mark Penn, who also was President Clinton's pollster, after the two had an argument about "Clinton fatigue," a notion Penn did not support. Gore's new pollsters emphasized the marginally depressing effect that Clinton was having on his chances. He moved his campaign headquarters to Nashville and announced he had not consulted Clinton about this move. Gore told his advisers that he had helped to get Clinton elected twice, but was now bequeathed the weight of Clinton's impeachment. For his part, Clinton was

*See Sean Wilentz, "Yawn," *The New Republic*, February 28, 2000.

willing to do whatever helped Gore, including staying in the background if that was requested. The President offered his political advice but delivered it circuitously through his aides to former secretary of commerce William Daley, now Gore's campaign chairman.

On Labor Day, former senator Bill Bradley had tied the Vice President in a *Boston Globe* poll in New Hampshire. Bradley—who had been an All-American basketball player at Princeton, the gentleman scholar-athlete of his generation, a Rhodes scholar at Oxford (just before Clinton arrived), a player for the New York Knicks who had helped the team win National Basketball Association championships, and then eventually was elected to the Senate from New Jersey—had been touted from his earliest days as a potential presidential candidate. In 1992, the logical year for him, President Bush seemed unassailable after the Gulf War, and he demurred. Two years later, he retired from the Senate. Now "Dollar Bill" was making his run. Surrounded by the NBA stars of his heyday, he held a fund-raiser that filled Madison Square Garden, hearing the roar of the crowd there once again.

Bradley was disdainful of Gore, and his staff called the Vice President "a joke." Presenting himself as a candidate of "big ideas," Bradley proposed a large health insurance program as the centerpiece of his campaign as a programmatic contrast to the diminished Gore. But after stumbling for months, Gore righted himself. Overnight, he began hewing to the record of the Clinton-Gore administration, countered criticism quickly and efficiently, and campaigned strictly on the issues. He criticized Bradley's health insurance plan for including a proposal to eliminate Medicaid and elements of Medicare without having worked out what would replace them, and for having been put together without heed to the costs; he warned that it would consume the surplus and eat into other social programs. In a series of debates, Gore was aggressive and even harsh in his criticism of Bradley, and under pressure, Bradley admitted he hadn't calculated the costs of his health care proposal. His policy position and poll numbers crumbled.

Bradley's response to falling behind was to attack Gore in a way that reinforced the negative image the Republicans had already painted. Bradley became the clean one, Gore the dirty one. He accused Gore of a "pattern of misrepresentation." "Why should we believe that you will tell the truth as president if you don't tell the truth as a candidate?" he asked in one debate. His campaign distributed a flyer in New Hampshire: "The symptoms: uncontrollable lying. The medication: truth serum. The patient: Vice President Al Gore." But Gore won in New Hampshire on

February 1, 2000, and it was finished for Bradley.* Gore's strategy had worked, but at a price. What had played well with the voters played terribly with the press. The press did not like it that he had won the nomination against the beautiful loser Bradley.

Unlike Gore, Governor George W. Bush of Texas suffered defeats in the primary campaign. The son of the former president—endorsed by virtually the entire Republican Party establishment, and endowed with a bulging war chest of money—found himself flailing in New Hampshire, where Senator John McCain trounced him 49–31 percent.

George W. Bush's advantages had been carefully arranged for him his whole life. Having been rejected by the St. John's Preparatory School, he attended the Phillips Academy at Andover, where his father had gone. His distinction there was as chief cheerleader. He was accepted at Yale University not for his grades but as a legacy—his father and grandfather were alumni—and he was tapped for the secretive club Skull and Bones, to which both father and grandfather had belonged, and became president of his fraternity, Delta Kappa Epsilon, known for its parties. When he graduated in 1968, during the Vietnam War, one of his father's friends called the Speaker of the Texas House of Representatives, and young George suddenly gained a slot as a pilot with the Texas Air National Guard, jumping long waiting lists. For about a year of his service he was unaccountably absent without leave. After being rejected by the University of Texas Law School, he was accepted by the Harvard Business School. Then several of his father's friends invested in an oil venture for him, which failed. His next venture failed, too. But the Harken Energy Corporation, owned by some of his father's friends, acquired his losing holdings, and ultimately he escaped with a large profit while ordinary investors saw their shares plunge. Many of the internal financial machinations at Harken during his years as a director remained unexplained and mysterious. A group of businessmen, including his father's campaign manager, next invited him to join in purchasing a Texas baseball franchise. According to his contract, his 2 percent share would become 11 percent if the team became profitable, which of course it did: $650,000 soon became $15.4 million.†

Bush had run unsuccessfully for Congress in 1978, defeated by a far-

*Eric Pooley with Karen Tumulty and Tamala M. Edwards, "How Al Came Back to Life," *Time*, March 13, 2000; Mitchell, "The 2000 Campaign."

†Molly Ivins and Lou Dubose, *Shrub: The Short but Happy Political Life of George W. Bush*, Random House, 2000, p. 42.

right-wing opponent. During his father's campaigns for the vice presidency and presidency, he was a hanger-on and picked up valuable political lessons from Lee Atwater, the cutthroat negative campaign specialist whom Bush's father assigned to him as his minder. In the 1994 midterm election, the year of the Republican sweep, Bush was elected governor of Texas, and in office he served those business interests that aided him, awarding them extensive state contracts, appointments, and favorable legislative policy.

After his reelection to the governorship in 1998, his clever political handler Karl Rove at once began to organize his presidential campaign, devising a public relations strategy to position him and his party as moderate and unthreatening, avoiding the harsh image of Newt Gingrich while continuing the policies of the Gingrich "revolution." Rove presented Bush as the proponent of "compassionate conservatism." This slogan was styled to give an impression that it referred to new forms of assistance for the poor, minorities, and the needy, but its actual substance involved the creation of government patronage for the religious right and breaching the wall of separation between church and state. Bush and Rove did everything they could to disguise their policy agenda in order to win over suburban moderates with soothing rhetoric.

As he began to campaign, Bush declared that his personal behavior before he had been forty years old should be forgiven and forgotten, whatever it might have been. By his own admission, he had spent much of that time on drunken sprees. Though his father had had a career as United Nations ambassador, the U.S. plenipotentiary to China, and CIA director, the son had scant interest in or knowledge of international affairs—and he had hardly traveled outside the country. His fractured syntax and constant misstatements created the misimpression, especially among the media, that he was intellectually hapless. But the truth was that he was politically cunning, determined, and ruthless—with a messianic streak about his destiny gained from his born-again religious conversion, which had led him away from alcoholism. However, his ingrained sense that he was born to rule came more from his privileged class and family background than from his relationship with the deity.

John McCain, Bush's most serious opponent, was anathema to the Republican Party leadership. His style was open and outspoken, and in the Senate, he had cosponsored with Democrats legislation for campaign finance reform, for a patients' bill of rights, and against the tobacco companies. He drew a majority of independents' votes in state primaries that allowed them to participate, like New Hampshire's. McCain had been a war hero, a prisoner in Vietnam for five years, and he saw his battle against Bush as a war against the Republican establishment.

In South Carolina, Bush took his stand. He curried favor with the religious right at Bob Jones University, a fundamentalist school that banned interracial dating, and he refused to endorse the Republican governor's opposition to flying the Confederate battle flag above the statehouse. A Texas financier named Sam Wyly, one of Bush's biggest backers and a member of his inner circle of fund-raisers, "Team 100," created a front group called Republicans for Clean Air that spent $2.5 million in radio and television ads attacking McCain and distorting his record. A long-time Republican activist named Richard Hines, who was one of the leaders of the movement in favor of the Confederate flag, created a political action committee called Keep It Flying that sent out 250,000 letters to South Carolina voters attacking McCain on the flag issue and praising Bush. Thousands of voters got phone calls and e-mails telling them McCain had an "illegitimate" or "black" child. (He and his wife had adopted an East Asian girl.) McCain, who had announced he wasn't engaging in negative campaigning, seemed surprised by the onslaught. Bush won the crucial primary by eleven points, 53–42 percent. Then, in Michigan, Pat Robertson of the Christian Coalition sponsored automated telephone calls attacking McCain for favoring abortion, which was not true. Yet McCain stunned Bush in Michigan—51–43 percent. In New York, Republicans for Clean Air was back with new ads, trashing McCain for opposing breast cancer research, even though his sister was battling the disease—another untruth. "They know no depths, do they? They know no depths," McCain said. Eventually, Bush crushed McCain's challenge to his candidacy.

Bush's sharp shift to the right in the South Carolina primary and his reliance on the resources of wealthy supporters had tarnished his original image as a "compassionate conservative." Nonetheless, he sought to restore it as if nothing had occurred. He called himself "a uniter, not a divider" and brought back the theme of "compassionate conservatism." And he borrowed a page from McCain's book about openness with the press. For Bush, it was only a question of appearances. He "not only slaps reporters' backs but also rubs the tops of their heads and, in a few instances, pinches their cheeks. It is the tactile equivalent of the nicknames he doles out to many of them and belongs to a teasing style of interpersonal relationship that undoubtedly harks back to his fraternity days," as

Frank Bruni wrote in *The New York Times*.* At the same time, Bush's advisers gave the press no quarter on serious articles or research and made it difficult to get to the bottom of his murky history.

Gore used the late spring and early summer months to prepare for the Democratic convention, to begin the process of selecting his running mate, and to prepare for the fall campaign. For the most part he allowed Bush breathing space and time to reinvent himself. Bush's strategy could not be based on the issues because very large majorities favored Gore on them. Nor could he permit the campaign to turn on experience and competence, which were Gore's strong suits. He had to win over swing voters on the pivotal perception that they simply liked him better than Gore. So the Republicans set out to ensure that Bush's opponent was disliked and distrusted. "The seething research room at RNC headquarters" was beefed up, according to *Time*, to "ply a rough trade . . . to change Al Gore's image from that of wooden Boy Scout into untrustworthy liar." A large sign hung over the main operations center: "On my command—unleash hell on Al."†

In July 2000, the Project for Excellence in Journalism and the Committee of Concerned Journalists issued an unusual study of the "character issue" as it had been reported thus far by the media. This extensive survey of articles and bulletins published and broadcast between February and June 2000 showed that the press had carried an overwhelmingly high proportion of positive stories about Bush and negative ones about Gore:

> In general, the press has been far more likely to convey that Bush is a different kind of Republican—a "compassionate conservative," a reformer, bipartisan—than to discuss Al Gore's experience, knowledge or readiness for the office. . . . Fully 40% of the assertions about Bush were that he was a different kind of politician, one of Bush's key campaign themes. Yet the public associates these bipartisan qualities more with the vice president than with the Texas governor. In contrast, only 14% of the time did the press assert the message that Gore has wanted to convey, about his experience and competence. Despite that, the public has this impression of Gore anyway. The media have not particularly pushed the idea that

*Frank Bruni, "For a Suddenly Accessible Bush, Everything Is on the Record," *The New York Times*, April 14, 2000.

†Martin Lewis, "This May Be a Pre-Mortem of the 2000 Campaign," *Time*, November 3, 2000.

Bush has gotten where he is largely on family connections. Nonetheless, this is one of the most dominant impressions the public has about the likely GOP nominee.*

The study also concluded that "reporting on Bush during the preconvention era involved surprisingly little digging into his record and background." Only 15 percent of the coverage of him mentioned his father or his brother Jeb, governor of Florida, or his grandfather, senator from Connecticut. A host of unanswered questions about his own past—his having been absent without leave from the Texas Air National Guard for a year, his business dealings in Harken Energy, his policies and associations in Texas—remained largely unexamined. The press corps that inflated pseudostories about Gore largely failed to investigate Bush's political, financial, and military history in any serious way.

The study found that 80 percent of the coverage of Gore concerned the manufactured issues either of his lack of truthfulness (34 percent) or of his being tainted with scandal (46 percent). Only 2 percent of the Gore-as-liar stories bothered to include an opposing point of view. Also, "fully 17% of the statements about Gore's ties to scandal came from just one prime-time talk program, Hardball with Chris Matthews on CNBC." Meanwhile, more than half of all Americans, 51 percent, told the Pew Research Center for People and the Press that Gore's experience would make them more likely to vote for him.

The Republican National Convention, which opened on July 29 in Philadelphia, was chaired by Senator Trent Lott, and it began with the theme of "Leave No Child Behind." Colin Powell and Condoleezza Rice were featured as speakers, and scores of minority singers and dancers performed on the platform. (There were only eighty-five black delegates, however, 4 percent of the total, the same percentage as in 1992 and 2 percent less than in 1912. By contrast, 872 delegates at the Democratic convention were black, 20 percent of the total, including the convention cochairman and the platform committee chairman. In his keynote address, Powell said, "Some in our party miss no opportunity to roundly and loudly condemn affirmative action that helped a few thousand black kids get an education, but you hardly hear a whimper when it's affirma-

*Project for Excellence in Journalism and the Committee of Concerned Journalists, "A Question of Character: How the Media Have Handled the Issue and How the Public Has Reacted," July 27, 2000, http://www.journalism.org/resources/research/reports/campaign2000/character/default.asp.

tive action for lobbyists who load our federal tax code with preferences for special interests." Asked about Powell's statement, Bush said, "I don't know what specific policies he had in mind."*) Dick Cheney, who had been the head of Bush's selection committee for the vice presidency and decided in the end to put himself forward, with the approval of George H. W. Bush, was nominated as vice president.

Richard Cheney was a central figure at the top of the Republican hierarchy with a lifetime of experience on Capitol Hill, in the White House, and in the oil industry. He had served as the deputy to Donald Rumsfeld when he was counselor to President Nixon and chief of staff to President Ford, then succeeded Rumsfeld in the latter position. After Ford lost the 1976 presidential election, Cheney ran for the Congress from Wyoming. Cheney rose to become the House minority whip; he was bureaucratically skillful and ideologically conservative. His phlegmatic, inexpressive manner masked his sharp, hard views. President George H. W. Bush appointed him secretary of defense. Cheney's wife, Lynne, a conservative scholar at the American Enterprise Institute who saw herself as a Valkyrie in the culture war against liberalism, was appointed chairman of the National Endowment for the Humanities. When Clinton defeated Bush, Cheney became chief executive officer of the Halliburton Company, an oil services firm based in Texas. To George W. Bush, the older Cheney was his father's loyal friend, a Republican leader and mentor, and an oilman.

Bush's acceptance speech was a paean to "compassionate conservatism." "Mr. Chairman . . . Instead of seizing this moment, the Clinton-Gore administration has squandered it." The evidence of misdeeds was, he said, the feeble and prostrate condition of the American armed forces: "We have seen a steady erosion of American power and an unsteady exercise of American influence. Our military is low on parts, pay, and morale. If called on by the commander-in-chief today, two entire divisions of the army would have to report, 'Not ready for duty, sir.' " (The army issued an official statement the next day that Bush's statement was untrue.) Bush went on, "America has a strong economy and a surplus. We have the public resources and the public will, even the bipartisan opportunities to strengthen Social Security and repair Medicare. But this administration, during eight years of increasing need, did nothing." How the largest surplus in American history had been created under Clinton,

---

*Arianna Huffington, "A Tale of Two Parties—and 1000 Parties," August 3, 2000, http://www.ariannaonline.com/columns/files/080300.html.

when he had inherited the largest deficit from Bush's father, was left unexplained.

Bush proposed privatizing Social Security and using the surplus for tax cuts. He told of a visit he had made to a juvenile prison in Texas, where he met a teenaged inmate who asked, "What do you think of me?" Bush interpreted his question as meaning, "Frankly, do you, a white man in a suit, really care about what happens to me?" Bush answered that he believed in "compassionate conservatism." He said he would "change the tone in Washington" and added, "I do not reinvent myself at every turn." He warned the Republicans, "Their war room is up and running, but we are ready. Their attacks will be relentless, but they will be answered. We are facing something familiar, but they're facing something new. We are now the party of ideas and innovation, the party of idealism and inclusion, the party of a simple and powerful hope."* At the end of his speech, Bush's lead over Gore, according to the Gallup poll, was 54–37 percent.

The week after the Republican convention, Gore chose as his running mate Senator Joseph Lieberman of Connecticut. Lieberman was the first Jewish candidate on a national ticket. The son of a liquor store owner in New Haven, he had studied at Yale, where he'd been the editor of the Yale *Daily News* and had gone to Mississippi as a Freedom Rider for civil rights. As attorney general of Connecticut he had been a consumer advocate, and as a senator he had supported Clinton's New Democratic initiatives on trade, welfare reform, and other issues. Lieberman had a streak of moral censoriousness, which was more a political asset than not, but he was also engaging and charming. Gore's unpredictable selection attracted renewed interest in his campaign.

President Clinton set the themes on the opening night of the Democratic convention. He had been worried that America's thriving economy was fostering complacency. The boom was now the longest in American history, and people's memories were dimming of the recession of 1990–91 and of the struggle he had waged, at considerable political price, for a new economic policy. Instead, amid ever-increasing affluence, people had begun to imagine that the economy would continue to expand ef-

---

*In his acceptance speech, Bush said that his "compassionate conservatism" would be substantiated in the presidency by three signature pieces of legislation: tax credits for the "low income" for health care insurance, providing rental housing for the "low income," and "the next phase of welfare reform" by providing funding for "homeless shelters and hospices, food pantry and crisis pregnancy centers." None of these measures has been enacted during his presidency to date.

fortlessly. Many voters didn't believe it mattered who was president. President Clinton's mastery of economic policy, steering the country through domestic political turmoil and unsteady Asian financial markets, ironically reinforced the voters' sense that the economy was taking care of itself. Even the deflation of the dot-com bubble was not causing widespread anxiety. His constant ministrations with such beneficent results had encouraged a smug, self-satisfied sentiment that was helping to buoy Bush and was undermining Gore.

So the President made clear that "America's success was not a matter of chance, it was a matter of choice. And today America faces another choice. It's every bit as momentous as the one we faced eight years ago, for what a nation does with its good fortune is just as stern a test of its character, values, and judgment as how it deals with adversity."

Clinton feared that the political effect of complacency would be to enhance Bush's prospects. He stressed that the prosperity that his policies had made possible could not be taken for granted. As he had in the State of the Union address, he laid out the achievements of his administration in precise numbers: he wanted to show there were real, demonstrable consequences to the choice of occupant in the White House. Having established the record, he set the Vice President within its context not only as his partner but as the right person to carry on the work. Gore's virtues as a public and private person were exactly counter to what the Republican campaign against him asserted.

Clinton's peroration was a cautionary message about the cycles of American history. The President underlined his central warning about blind contentment, argued against Americans' ahistorical tendency, and recalled the tragedies of the 1960s so that the continuity of progress might not be broken again:

Now, I want the young people especially to listen to this. I remember this well. I graduated from high school in 1964. Our country was still very sad because of President Kennedy's death, but full of hope under the leadership of President Johnson. And I assumed then, like most Americans, that our economy was absolutely on automatic; that nothing could derail it. I also believed then that our civil rights problems would all be solved in Congress and the courts. And in 1964, when we were enjoying the longest economic expansion in history, we never dreamed that Vietnam would so divide and wound America.

So we took it for granted.

And then, before we knew it, there were riots in the streets, even here. The leaders that I adored as a young man, Martin Luther King and Robert Kennedy, were killed. Lyndon Johnson—a president from my part of the country I admired so much for all he did for civil rights, for the elderly and the poor—said he would not run again because our nation was so divided.

And then we had an election in 1968 that took America on a far different and more divisive course. And you know, within months, after that election, the last longest economic expansion in history was itself history.

Why am I telling you this tonight? Not to take you down, but to keep you looking up. I have waited, not as president, but as your fellow citizen, for over thirty years to see my country once again in the position to build the future of our dreams for our children.

Three nights later, it was Al Gore's turn to mount the stage, taking his place at last as the presidential candidate of his party. He began by embracing President Clinton. And then he, too, set out the theme of continuity and change: "This election is not an award for past performance. I'm not asking you to vote for me on the basis of the economy we have. Tonight I ask for your support on the basis of the better, fairer, more prosperous America we can build together." Having put down this marker, he could present himself not just as a carrier of past successes but as an independent figure: "We're entering a new time. We're electing a new president. And I stand here tonight as my own man." Gore talked about education, health care, the environment, and civil rights as issues that Democrats cared about and Republicans preserved for special interests. "And that's the difference in this election. They're for the powerful. We're for the people."

Gore talked about issues that did not yet have electoral resonance, but he showed his broad internationalism and stressed the problems he believed were important to address. "We must confront the new challenges of terrorism, new kinds of weapons of mass destruction, global environmental problems, and new diseases that know no national boundaries and can threaten national security." He was also responding to a virtually unreported section of the Republican platform that had explicitly criticized him. The Republicans had written, "Reacting belatedly to inevitable crises, the administration constantly enlarges the reach of its rhetoric—most recently in Vice President Gore's 'new security agenda' that adds disease, climate, and all the world's ethnic or religious conflicts to an undiminished set of existing American responsibilities. If there is some limit to candidate Gore's new agenda for America as global social worker, he has yet to define it."

At the end, Gore spoke about himself, his strengths and flaws, his substance and image, and how the superficial perception of style should be assessed:

Yes, we're all imperfect, but as Americans we share in the privilege and challenge of building a more perfect union. I know my own imperfections. For example, I know that sometimes people say I'm too serious, that I talk too much substance and policy. Maybe I've done that tonight. But the presidency is more than a popularity contest, it's a day-by-day fight for people. Sometimes you have to choose to do what's difficult or unpopular. Sometimes you have to be willing to spend your popularity in order to pick the hard right over the easy wrong. There are big choices ahead, and our whole future is at stake. And I do have strong beliefs about it. If you entrust me with the presidency, I know I won't always be the most exciting politician. But I pledge to you tonight, I will work for you every day, and I will never let you down.

Immediately after this speech, a *Newsweek* poll showed Gore leading Bush, 52–44 percent. He had not only erased a fifteen-point deficit but had vaulted ahead by eight points. But the next Gallup poll, taken a week later, showed Gore and Bush in a dead heat.

At the very beginning of the general campaign, in early September, Bush took some missteps. During the negotiations between the two parties over televised debates featuring the two candidates, he appeared fearful of them because he had demanded short ones and asked for Larry King, renowned for his genial questions, as the moderator. A second blunder occurred when a Republican National Committee television ad attacking "The Gore Prescription Plan" was shown to have subliminally flashed on the screen for a fraction of a second the word "rats" before dissolving into the words "bureaucrats decide." There was a great outcry, and Bush had to withdraw the commercial. "We don't need to play cute politics," he said. "We're going to win this election based upon issues."

One of the issues he was referring to was another Gore imbroglio. On September 18, *The Boston Globe* reported that Gore had misspoken in Florida about prescription drugs:

Vice President Al Gore, reaching for a personal example to illustrate the breathtaking costs of some prescription drugs, told seniors in Florida last month that his mother-in-law pays nearly three times as much for the same arthritis medicine used for his ailing dog, Shiloh. But Gore, the master of many policy details, mangled the facts, and late last week his aides could not say with certainty that Shiloh or Margaret Ann Aitcheson actually takes the brand-name drug, Lodine, that Gore said they do. Even if they take the drug, Gore's assertion that his black Labrador retriever's monthly bill is $37.80 and Aitcheson's is $108 is wrong. The Gore campaign admitted that it lifted those costs not from his family's bills, but from a House Democratic study.*

For the next two days, though a spokesman admitted to one reporter that the Bush campaign had no transcript of Gore's remarks—and indeed none was ever directly reported or found—it sent out six press releases about Gore's "misleading" remarks. Hyping the story, both Bush and Cheney jumped into the fray. Karen Hughes, Bush's press secretary, told the press corps, "I hope you all will ask him today about the *Boston Globe* story." "America better beware of a candidate who is willing to stretch reality in order to win points," Bush said. "I have always been concerned about Vice President Gore's willingness to exaggerate in order to become elected." "It looks like another Al Gore invention," said Cheney. "It strikes me that this was the kind of statement we have heard in the past from Al Gore and frankly, I would expect better from the vice president."† On September 19, a *Washington Times* headline blared, "Aides Concede Gore Made Up Medicine Story." That was completely untrue.‡

In fact, all Gore's aides had said was that they didn't know if his mother-in-law paid for her medicine herself or whether it was covered by her insurance.

Gore's mother-in-law and the dog both did take the drug, and the costs cited in the House Democratic study were accurate ones. Gore's campaign people calculated that his mother-in-law's drug, under her health plan, cost 2.315 times more, not three times more, per capsule

*Walter V. Robinson, "Gore Misstates Facts in Drug-Cost Pitch," *The Boston Globe*, September 18, 2000.

†Jake Tapper, "A Campaign's Dog Days," *Salon.com*, September 21, 2000.

‡Dave Boyer and Sean Scully, "Aides Concede Gore Made Up Medicine Story," *The Washington Times*, September 19, 2000.

than the dog's; but the wholesale price, as the study had indicated, was three times higher for humans than for pets. This information took a few days to unearth, of course.

The facts did not stop the usual machinery from rolling ahead. On September 21, *The Washington Post* published an op-ed article by William Kristol elevating the Gore-as-liar storyline into Gore-as-barbarian:

> From the Bible and Aristotle on, the family has been understood to be crucial to tempering our self-love. It has also been understood to be a barrier—the barrier—to the totalizing of politics. Al Gore is not a totalitarian. But his willingness to use his family members for political purposes reveals a self-regard and self-absorption, a ruthlessness and lack of restraint, that have taken him into new territory, well beyond George W. Bush, beyond even his master, Bill Clinton.*

The next day, Peggy Noonan advanced a less intellectually challenging theme in *The Wall Street Journal*, contrasting Bush as "dumb-good" versus Gore as "evil-smart": "I suspect people are starting no longer to be amused but actually concerned by Mr. Gore's tendency to lie in speeches and interviews. In the past five days he unspooled a heartfelt story of how his mother-in-law and dog both take the same arthritis medicine, but the pooch's meds are cheaper and this is a scandal. It certainly might be if it were true, but apparently not a word of it is."† But not a word of her piece was true.

Stretching out this story, the Bush campaign set the stage for the debates, a three-act play featuring the elements of distortion, disorientation, and ambiguity. In the beginning, Gore triumphed, unleashing furies that made him lose his bearings, only to recover his senses enough to steady himself, but at the price of creating confusion among voters about his character.

For the first debate, Gore gave one of his classic performances of a kind that had dominated Dan Quayle, Ross Perot, and Jack Kemp. He was in command of his facts and in control of the issues, he conveyed earnestness about public policy and respect toward his opponent, and he never criticized him personally. He had statistics to support every pro-

---

*William Kristol, "Gore's Family Values," *The Washington Post*, September 21, 2000.

†Peggy Noonan, "Dumb-Good vs. Evil-Smart," *The Wall Street Journal*, September 22, 2000.

gram he proposed; he poked holes in Bush's tax-cut plans by showing easily that they would benefit primarily the wealthiest 1 percent of Americans, drain money from Medicare and Social Security, and deplete the surplus; he stressed his own government experience; and he showed his knowledge of the complexities of foreign policy while refuting Bush's claim that the armed forces had become weak. He also made a point of saying when he agreed with Bush and explicitly declared he would not attack his character. He pressed his arguments strongly, used a plausible explanatory tone, and avoided sarcasm.

Bush began by attacking Gore for using "phony numbers," which he also called "fuzzy math" and "Washington fuzzy math." The surplus didn't belong to the government, he said, but to the people, and he would "share it" through a tax cut. He emphasized, "I'm not of Washington. I'm from Texas." He charged that Gore wanted to expand federal bureaucracies like "Lyndon Baines Johnson." His sarcasm expanded as the minutes ticked by. After Gore pointed out the wealthiest 1 percent would benefit most from Bush's proposed tax cut, the moderator, Jim Lehrer of the Public Broadcasting System, called for the "next question," and Bush interjected, "I hope it's about wealthy people." When Gore warned that under Bush's prescription drug plan for senior citizens, 95 percent of them would receive no benefit for four or five years, Bush replied, "I guess my answer to that is, the man's running on Mediscare." When Gore said that an elderly couple earning $25,000 a year would be ineligible under Bush's proposal, Bush shot back, "Look, this is the man who's got great numbers. He talks about numbers. I'm beginning to think, not only did he invent the Internet, but he invented the calculator."

The debate turned to foreign affairs, and to the recent crisis provoked by Milosevic's refusal to accept the results of the Yugoslav election on September 24, when his opponent trounced him by eight points. Bush advised, "This'll be an interesting moment for the Russians to step up and lead." Gore suggested otherwise: "In this particular situation, no . . . I think the governor's instinct is not necessarily bad, because we have worked with the Russians in a constructive way, in Kosovo, for example, to end the conflict there. But I think we need to be very careful in the present situation before we invite the Russians to play the lead role in mediating." Gore played the gentle diplomat in puncturing Bush's naïve posturing.

Asked to illustrate his ability to stand up under crisis, Gore spoke of the long and difficult diplomacy with the Russians that had successfully brought an end to the Kosovo war. Bush said, "Well, I've been standing up to big Hollywood, big trial lawyers—what was the question? It was about emergencies, wasn't it?" He had dealt with fires and floods as governor. Gore was very polite: "I want to compliment the governor on his response to those fires and floods in Texas. I accompanied [Federal Emergency and Management Director] James Lee Witt down to Texas when those fires broke out."

When he was asked to speak about his opponent's character, Bush answered, "I don't know the man well, but I've been disappointed about how his administration has conducted the fund-raising affairs. You know, going to a Buddhist temple and then claiming it wasn't a fund-raiser is just not my view of responsibility." Gore refused to take this bait: "Well, I think we ought to attack our country's problems, not attack each other. I want to spend my time making this country even better than it is, not trying to make you out to be a bad person. You may want to focus on scandals; I want to focus on results." But when he said that he would support campaign finance reform as the first measure of his administration, Bush replied, "You know, this man has no credibility on the issue." Again, Gore kept his temper: "Look, Governor Bush, you have attacked my character and credibility and I am not going to respond in kind. I think we ought to focus on the problems and not attack each other."

One postdebate analysis rated the credibility of the various claims that Bush and Gore had made. Gore's account of what the effects of Bush's tax cut would be, it reported, was "in the ballpark." In contrast, "Bush insisted he devotes one-half of projected federal budget surpluses over the next decade to Social Security, one-quarter to important priorities, and one-quarter to give back to the people in tax cuts. But he comes up with those figures by ignoring the interest costs that accrue from opting for tax cuts or new spending instead of paying off the national debt." Though Bush repeatedly attacked Gore for "fuzzy math," Gore's budget numbers were "more accurate."And while Bush claimed his prescription drug plan would cover all poor senior citizens, "it would not reach elderly people earning more than $14,600 and it would not provide any relief until a retiree had spent $6,000 out of pocket."

Gore's criticism of Bush for failing to explain how he would finance his privatization scheme for Social Security was well-founded, the analysis said: "As Gore said, Bush has not adequately explained how he would finance his plan, especially when he also proposes a large tax cut." And Bush "misspoke when he said, 'I want to get a better rate of return for your own money than the paltry 2 percent that the current Social Security trust gets today.' The trust fund is invested in special Treasury bills, which earn at least 4 percent."* Yet the discrepancies in Bush's figures were not a tack that most reporters would take.

All the television networks conducted polls immediately after the debate, and they all showed Gore as the winner, the CBS News poll by fourteen points. But there were two more debates ahead. So the first barrage against Gore began that very evening. The Republican attack line that Gore was disrespectful, overly aggressive, and arrogant was quickly established. On Fox News, Morton Kondracke insisted that Bush "did not make any mistakes," and Fred Barnes (editor of *The Weekly Standard*) criticized Gore's "sighing and mugging." On MSNBC, Peggy Noonan echoed, "He sighed, he rolled his eyes, he almost put his hands in his mouth and made funny faces. He was quite sneering toward Bush. I don't know how the American people will accept that." On ABC News *Nightline*, the guest was Dick Cheney: "I noticed the way he, he kept sighing into the microphone when Governor Bush was talking. It was weird. I don't know whether it was a deliberate tactic of some kind to disconcert the governor. It didn't work, clearly."†

By the following morning, Gore's sighing had become a staple. Tim Russert, on Don Imus's radio talk show, added his view: "Yeah, I was in the hall. I'm familiar with the Al Gore sighing. He did eighteen in the December debate with Bill Bradley. We were tightly sitting next to each other on the set and every time Bradley would try to give an answer, 'Hhhhhh.' It's unbelievable."‡ Cokie Roberts was quoted the morning after in *The Washington Post*: "I do think women were turned off by Gore's demeanor." She cited "sighing."§

While the debate was being conducted, the RNC was already creating new stories in the Gore-as-liar saga, its opposition research unit churning out material to an eagerly awaiting press. This whirl was captured by a British Broadcasting Corporation documentary, "Digging the Dirt" (never aired in the United States); the film showed the RNC unit deputy director, Tim Griffin, exclaiming about Gore's reference to hav-

---

*Glenn Kessler and Ceci Connolly, "Dueling Data Reflect Divides," *The Washington Post*, October 4, 2000.

†Bob Somerby, "Where Does Spin Come From?" *The Daily Howler*, June 2, 2001, http://www.dailyhowler.com/ho60201_1.shtml.

‡Bob Somerby, "Seven? Add Eleven," *The Daily Howler*, October 5, 2000, http://www.dailyhowler.com/h100500_2.shtml. Somerby reported that the Bradley campaign had counted seven Gore sighs, not eighteen, as Russert stated.

§Howard Kurtz, "Instant, Ephemeral Analysis: Debating the Debates," *The Washington Post*, October 5, 2000.

ing gone to Texas with Witt, "Get one of these AP reporters or somebody on it for the next few days and then we get a lie out of it . . . and
roll a few days with a new lie!" *Time* reported on what the BBC had
shown:

> We see RNC glee as the Associated Press accepts their oppo research on
> a Gore misstatement during the first presidential debate. During their
> months of filming BBC producers also observed producers for NBC's
> Tim Russert, among others, calling to enquire if the team had any new
> material. This was apparently normal practice. "It's an amazing thing,"
> says RNC researcher Griffin in the film, "when you have top-line
> producers and reporters calling you and saying 'We trust you . . . We
> need your stuff.' . . . We think of ourselves as the creators of the ammu-
> nition in a war," he said. "Research digs up the ammunition. We make
> the bullets."*

The television morning shows seemed obliged to follow the Republican leads. On ABC's *Good Morning America*, Gore was asked about Witt.
He explained that he had made eighteen trips to disaster sites with Witt
but had misspoken about the Texas fire one, when he had met with the
FEMA regional director. On NBC's *Today Show*, he was asked about sighing: "Well, I guess sometimes the mike picks up your reaction to the
other person. I'll try to be more careful on that." The day unfolded with
still more Republican attacks on Gore's character. Bush thought Gore's
"pattern of exaggerations says something about leadership." Cheney reinforced the line. Gore's mistake should "begin to raise doubts about
whether or not he would deal straight with the American people," he
said, and compared him to "somebody" who "embellishes their résumé
in a job interview." Karen Hughes told the press, "This is another disturbing pattern, when under pressure the Vice President simply makes
things up."

Gore's response to the furor was to try to dismiss it as unworthy:
"Even though Governor Bush and I have a lot of differences, mostly, I
think it's better to spend time attacking America's problems than attacking people personally."† But the clamor over his credibility had become
the lead story in the campaign. *Time* later reported, "The post-debate

---

*Lewis, "This May Be a Pre-Mortem."

†Ceci Connolly and Terry M. Neal, "Nominees Carry Debate Themes Back on
Road," *The Washington Post*, October 5, 2000.

spin cycle becomes about Gore's perceived chronic character flaw. And so it has gone every week since the debates. The image is enshrined."*

The night of the first debate Gore's team had been exultant, giving each other high fives. Their candidate, they were certain, had aced the match. Within days, they were panicked. The attack on Gore and his apologies swamped them. His advisers began to doubt their own judgment. In the preparation session for the next debate they told Gore he must be less aggressive, less policy-oriented, less detailed—more likable. Some of them even wanted him to apologize for any misstatements at the previous debate. President Clinton, for his part, thought Gore had done well but had missed a couple of opportunities where he could have cornered Bush on specific policies and cited the administration's accomplishments on health care. His comments were transmitted to Gore through intermediaries.

Gore set out in the second debate to do battle with the stereotype that the Republican negative campaign had projected in the media. "Broadly speaking," *The Washington Post* reported, "Gore comes here for Wednesday night's 90-minute debate at Wake Forest University needing to present a calmer, more human side that shows he can relate to the average American, the analysts said. No loud sighs, no interrupting, fewer statistics and more anecdotes."†

In the first part of the debate, Gore seemed deflated, even passive, engaged in an apparent tense, internal struggle of self-restraint. The subject was his strong point, foreign policy, but at nearly every turn he graciously conceded ground to Bush. Gore's early remarks were a series of concurrences: "I agree with that. I agree with that. . . . I haven't heard a big difference, right—in the last few exchanges. . . . Well, I don't disagree with that." When the moderator, Jim Lehrer of PBS, listed examples of U.S. military interventions, from the one in Lebanon in 1983 to the Gulf War in 1991 to Kosovo in 1999, Gore gave terse monosyllabic answers, saying yes he supported all of them, except no for Lebanon. (In 1983, President Reagan had sent marines to act as peacekeepers in the Lebanese civil war but soon supported the Christian government challenged by Muslim factions supported by Syria. The USS *New Jersey*, stationed off the coast, had bombarded the Muslim positions, and then on October 23, a terrorist car bomber attacked the marines' compound in Beirut, killing 241

*Lewis, "This May Be a Pre-Mortem."
†Terry M. Neal and Ceci Connolly, "Debate Challenges Are Same as Before," *The Washington Post*, October 11, 2000.

American soldiers. The U.S. force was quickly evacuated, and the incident was universally considered disastrous.) When Bush said he had approved of the Lebanon intervention, it was clear he was clueless. But instead of making note of this, Gore sat mute.

Then Bush attempted to smear Gore, falsely suggesting that former Russian prime minister Chernomyrdin had personally pocketed International Monetary Fund loans. Chernomyrdin was Gore's diplomatic counterpart on the commission that for years had worked productively on many bilateral U.S.-Russian problems, yet Bush was insinuating that Gore had simply been engaged with a thief. "We went into Russia, we said, 'Here's some IMF money,' and it ended up in Viktor Chernomyrdin's pocket and others," Bush said. (This charge was later dismissed by the International Monetary Fund, which stated that its auditors had discovered no such funds diverted.) Bush had defamed a prominent foreign leader and tarred Gore with guilt by association. When Bush finished, Lehrer suggested, "Let's move on." Instead of rebutting Bush, Gore simply said, "Far be it from me to suggest otherwise."

In talking about the Balkans, Bush said, "I think it ought to be one of our priorities to work with our European friends to convince them to put troops on the ground." But European troops already comprised the majority of peacekeeping forces there, which he apparently didn't know. Gore did not call attention to this error.

Bush summed up what he claimed his foreign policy would be by making a crude isolationist argument that echoed the conservative Republican past: "I'm not so sure the role of the United States is to go around the world and say, 'This is the way it's got to be. We can help.' And maybe it's just our difference in government, the way we view government. I mean, I want to empower people, I don't—you know, I want to help people help themselves, not have government tell people what to do." Gore took issue with Bush on this way of talking about what he considered the American responsibility for nation building, but he did not challenge the isolationist tack.

Toward the middle part of the debate, Gore slowly came to life, notably after Bush claimed that as governor he had favored hate crimes legislation in the wake of the racist murder of a black man, James Byrd, in Texas, and that he had worked to extend health insurance for Texas children. In fact, Bush had opposed a new hate crimes bill and had arranged for the Texas Senate Republicans to kill the measure before it might reach his desk, and while he bragged that in Texas he was signing up children for the Children's Health Insurance Program (CHIP) as "fast as any other state," he had in fact tried to limit access to the program.*

When Gore pointed out his record, Bush responded quickly, "If he's trying to allege that I'm a hard-hearted person and I don't care about children, he's absolutely wrong." "But it's not a statement about his heart," Gore replied. "I don't claim to know his heart. I think he's a good person. I make no allegations about that. I believe him when he says that—that he has a good heart. I know enough about your story to admire a lot of the things that you have done as a person. But I think it's about his priorities."

"Last question for you, Governor," said Lehrer. The final segment of the debate, it turned out, would be devoted solely to the charges Republicans had made about flaws in Gore's character. Lehrer, a person of impeccable fairness, felt required to bring this up: "This flows somewhat out of the Boston debate. You, your running mate, your campaign officials have charged that Vice President Gore exaggerates, embellishes, and stretches the facts, et cetera. Are you—do you believe these are serious issues—this is a serious issue that the voters should use in deciding which one of you two men to vote for on November 7?"

"Well," replied Bush, "we all make mistakes. I've been known to mangle a syllable or two myself, you know. But . . . I think credibility's important. It's going to be important—for the president to be credible with Congress, important for the president to be credible with foreign nations. And, yes, I think it's something that people need to consider."

Gore took this as a cue for an apology: "I got some of the details wrong last week in some of the examples that I used, Jim. And I'm sorry about that. And I'm going to try to do better. One of the reasons I regret is that it—getting a detail wrong interfered several times with a point that I was trying to make. . . . I can't promise that I will never get another detail wrong. I can promise you that I will try not to anymore. But I will promise you this, with all the confidence in—in my heart and in the world, that I will do my best, if I'm elected president, I'll work my heart out, to get the big things right for the American people."

"Does that resolve the issue, Governor?" asked Lehrer.

"That's going to be up to the people, isn't it?"

"Does it resolve it for you?"

*Glenn Kessler and Steve Mufson, "For Both Debaters, a Few Missteps," *The Washington Post*, October 12, 2000.

"It depends on what he says in the future in the campaign."

"But, I mean, your folks are saying some awful things."

"I hope they're not awful things."

"Well, I mean . . ."

". . . his own words."

"No, no, what I mean is, you calling him a serial exaggerator."

"I don't believe I've used those words."

"No, but your campaign has."

"Maybe they have."

And then it was time for closing statements. So the entire debate had ended on the issue of Gore's credibility. Gore had been apologetic, Bush belligerent; Gore had been cast as the offender, Bush as the the authority on his offense.

On the eve of the next debate, *The Washington Post* published a poll showing Bush leading Gore 48–44 percent and Gore's political position hanging on his credibility. "There has been a clear shift in the balance of the race since the debates began on Oct. 3 in Boston," the paper reported. "Last month, more than six in 10 voters said Gore was honest and trustworthy. Today, fewer than half shared that view."[*]

In the third debate, on October 17, Gore time and time again hammered away at the obvious truth that he and Bush had a "huge difference of opinion" on issue after issue. Now he was fighting. "If you want someone who will . . . end up supporting legislation that is supported by the big drug companies, this is your man," he said, pointing at Bush. "I want to fight for you." When Bush claimed that Gore's budget would be the largest ever, he shot back, "Absolutely not, absolutely not. I'm so glad that I have a chance to knock that down." Bush seemed pushed back on his heels. "Well, he's wrong," he complained. "Just add up all the numbers; it's three times bigger than what President Clinton proposed." Gore came right back at him: "That's in an ad . . . that was knocked down by the journalists who analyzed the ad and said it was misleading." "My turn?" said Bush. "Forget the journalists."

On civil rights, Gore brushed Bush's rhetoric aside: "I don't know what affirmative access means; I do know what affirmative action means. I know the governor's against it and I know that I'm for it. I know what a hate crime statute pending at the national level is all about, in the aftermath of James Byrd's death. I'm for that proposed law; the Governor is

---

[*]Dan Balz and Richard Morin, "Bush Has Slim Lead on Eve of 3rd Debate," *The Washington Post*, October 17, 2000.

against it." Bush was on the defensive. His responses became petulant, and when Gore spoke he vamped for the camera, smirking and "several times could be heard laughing or snorting in what appeared to be an effort to deflate his opponent."*

In conclusion, Gore addressed the matter of his own credibility: "I'd like to tell you something about me. I keep my word. I have kept the faith." And now he raised the record of the Clinton-Gore administration like a banner: "We've made some progress during the last eight years. We have seen the strongest economy in the history of the United States, lower crime rates for eight years in a row, highest private home ownership ever. But I'll make you one promise here: You ain't seen nothing yet. And I will keep that promise." All the polls taken immediately afterward showed the public judging Gore the winner, in the ABC News poll by fourteen points. He pulled even with Bush.† There were only twenty days to the election.

Still, the mocking of Gore in the media did not stop, and now he was ridiculed for his precision. On television and radio talk shows, he was criticized for having stated during the third debate the exact name of the bipartisan patients' bill of rights legislation that he favored: the Dingell-Norwood bill. As George Stephanopoulos tried to explain the substance of that bill, on ABC News *This Week*, Cokie Roberts (herself the daughter of the late House Democratic majority leader, Hale Boggs) interrupted him: "Actually, I don't think that is the important point there." "Why not?" asked Stephanopoulos. "Because," she said, "that's not what comes across when you're watching the debate. What comes across when you're watching the debate is this guy from Washington doing Washington-speak."‡

Gore had respect for traditional opinion leaders in Washington's press corps, and he believed throughout the campaign that he could convince them of his integrity. After all, they knew him and had known him, in some cases, since he was a boy. (He had gone to St. Albans with Donald Graham, the publisher of *The Washington Post*.) And he refused to play the game of the politician as star, even proclaiming himself "unexciting." In that game, the press knew its place as star makers reflecting the ambi-

---

*Dan Balz and Mike Allen, "Bush and Gore Clash Sharply on Health, Education," *The Washington Post*, October 18, 2000.

†Richard Morin and Claudia Deane, "Instant Polls: Debates Leave Race at a Draw," *The Washington Post*, October 18, 2000.

‡Jonathan Cohn, "Yuck, Yuck," *The New Republic*, November 6, 2000.

ent light of the stars. However, Bush had one impalpable advantage over Gore: belief in his star power, rooted in his sense of class and family superiority. For the star-reflecting press, Bush's arrogance presented itself as ease. His condescension to the press, giving reporters nicknames and joshing with them, acting the sportive Tory with his gamekeepers, made them feel as though they had an intimate tie, but actually he was putting them in their place, fostering a reflexive deference toward him. The more they put out their story line of Bush as nonintellectual, the more he outplayed them, happily dispensing nicknames like treats around his campaign plane. Mostly, the press that was disrespectful toward Gore was submissive toward Bush. By trashing the one, they proved their independence; by going soft on the other, they demonstrated their fairness.*

The press corps had tilted against Gore, but ultimately the reporters did not make the decisions about which aspects of the campaign or the candidates to cover, how to present them, or what their content would be. Their editors made those decisions—and the editors and publishers were strongly in favor of Bush. Newspapers (that is, their publishers) endorsed Bush over Gore by a two-to-one margin; editors voted for him in the same proportions, according to one survey. Publishers voted for Bush by a whopping three-to-one margin.†

In the final weeks of the campaign, President Clinton was frustrated, for Gore was not asking him to campaign, and he felt he could help. Gore took the advice that in the battleground states Clinton's presence would hurt among the swing voters. Gore's strategists were particularly focused on conservative-leaning working-class white middle-aged men in Pennsylvania and Michigan—and on Florida. (They virtually ignored New Hampshire, which Gore did not visit, and victory there, it turned

---

*"Neutrality has gone by the wayside in coverage of Campaign 2000," reported a study of the last two months of the campaign. "Less than a third of all stories were neutral in tone. . . . Vice President Al Gore has gotten the worst of it. . . . In contrast, George W. Bush was twice as likely as Gore to get coverage that was positive in tone . . . 24% of Bush stories were positive, nearly double the 13% for Gore. In contrast, the coverage of Gore was more negative. A full 56% of the Gore stories had a negative tone, compared to 49% for Bush. The remaining stories were neutral. . . . Fewer than one-in-ten of these stories considered policy differences between the two candidates." Committee of Concerned Journalists, "The Last Lap: How the Press Covered the Final Stages of the Presidential Campaign," 2000, http://www.journalism.org/resources/research/reports/campaign2000/lastlap/default.asp.

†Greg Mitchell, "Newspaper Editors and Publishers Predict Bush Victory: Bush Also Wins Newspaper Endorsement Race," *Editor and Publisher*, November 2, 2000.

out, would have put him over the top.) Gore concentrated many resources belatedly on his home state of Tennessee, which had gone out of
his reach. He allowed Clinton to campaign once in Arkansas, in the end,
a state which by that time was also gone. Reporters sniffed out Gore's
concern with Clinton's potential negatives, and it, too, became a negative
for Gore.

Gore's main theme throughout the campaign until the third debate
had been "the people versus the interests." This stirred some of the
Democratic base, but it failed to express the real quality of reinvented
liberalism that he had helped so much to consolidate during the Clinton
administration. After the last debate, however, even as he kept Clinton in
a box, he sprinted to the finish line with plenty of talk about the administration's record.

There was one more factor: Ralph Nader's Green Party candidacy.
Nader had been there all along. His was a strangely colorless voice that
expressed remnants of the American left, and none of its storied socialist
past. There were no red banners, hymns, manifestos, poetry, or hairsplitting arguments in the Nader campaign. In fact, he had started politically
on the far right, writing for *The American Mercury*, but with his crusades
for consumer safety and fairness he had famously become a model of the
useful citizen. By 2000, that Ralph Nader, who had been focused on constructive and specific battles, was gone. Now he was whipping up a thin
populist gruel around the fringes of college towns. In his candidacy he
offered no ideas about the federal budget and no foreign policy. In public
policy, his program, such as it was, was more congruent with Patrick
Buchanan's than anyone else's in politics: protectionism, anticorporatism,
anti-Israel, proimpeachment.

Nader had had an open door at the Clinton White House he chose
not to enter. A number of his former aides (Nader's Raiders) worked in
the administration and still held him in high esteem, but he remained a
stranger. In December 1999, I ran into him at a friend's Christmas party
and asked him what he was up to. He told me he was involved with a
team of army doctors at the Walter Reed Institute of Health doing research on tropical diseases. I told him the administration had been working on a new policy on diseases, which the President would unveil in his
State of the Union address in January, and I invited him to bring the
army doctors to a meeting at the White House with Chris Jennings,
Clinton's health care expert.

In that State of the Union address, Clinton was the first president to
propose an initiative to do something about global diseases (an approach

condemned in the Republican Party platform). Clinton said, "Last year in Africa, ten times as many people died from AIDS as were killed in wars—ten times. The budget I give you invests $150 million more in the fight against this and other infectious killers. And today, I propose a tax credit to speed the development of vaccines for diseases like malaria, TB, and AIDS. I ask the private sector and our partners around the world to join us in embracing this cause."

Then, on March 3, President Clinton held a conference on the Millennium Vaccine Initiative (the chief Walter Reed scientist was a participant), at which he announced that four drug companies had agreed to donate tens of millions of doses of vaccines for use in developing countries, that the World Bank and other international financial institutions had decided to devote variously $400 million to $900 million in low-interest loans for public health, that the Gates Foundation was giving $750 million for the purchase and distribution of vaccines, and that he would ask the Congress for significant increases in research funding, and ask other advanced industrial nations at the next G-7 summit to join in this effort.

One of my jobs at the time, which I had undertaken at the President's request, was to serve as editor of a collection of articles solicited from scientists, economists, historians, and other thinkers addressed to what they thought were the problems of the future, and I asked Nader to write for it. His memo, focusing exclusively on tropical diseases, was included in the long *Visions of the Future* I gave to the President, the Vice President, and the senior staff.* By that time, Nader had begun his campaign.

By October 2000, Nader was deliberately acting as spoiler for one of the most progressive candidates ever to run for president. "If it were a choice between a provocateur and an anesthetizer, I'd rather have a provocateur. It would mobilize us," he told a college crowd in the last

---

*Nader's account in his campaign memoir of his interaction with the Clinton White House is disingenuous: "In discussing foreign policy initiatives on the campaign trail, I would repeatedly stress the need for the United States to launch a major program against these scourges, coming toward the United States with drug-resistant strains, which take millions of lives a year, mostly in the Third World. The Pentagon's tiny enclave at the Walter Reed Institute of Health is one of the best-kept secrets in Washington. The press had never heard of it, nor had anybody in Congress, nor had Bill Clinton's White House aides. The latter, led by Sidney Blumenthal, did meet at the White House earlier with the same army and navy scientists and me to discuss what more could be done." Ralph Nader, *Crashing the Party*, St. Martin's Press, 2002, p. 108.

week of the campaign. His intention was to help Bush, the "provocateur." Nader's strategy was: the worse, the better. A group of Nader's Raiders pleaded with him on the eve of the election not to campaign in swing states, but he disdained them and made a point of doing precisely that. Members of his family and closest friends begged him to stop, but he dismissed them, too.*

At the end of October, the Republican Leadership Council, a GOP "soft money" front group, spent $100,000 in television attack ads against Gore that featured a clip of Nader; these were broadcast in states where votes for Nader might tip the state for Bush: "Al Gore is suffering from election year delusion if he thinks his record on the environment is anything to be proud of," Nader was seen saying. "Eight years of principles betrayed and promises broken." Nader refused to ask that the commercials be taken off the air. A spokesman for the RLC remarked on Nader's previous complaint that he had no money for advertising: "We'll put an end to that."†

"Do you really want a Pat Buchanan answer—about what I will do when I am president?" Nader asked a reporter. "The truth is you can't lose. . . . You cost the Democrats a few states. They'll never be the same again."‡

If his remarks were taken in good faith, Nader was trading on a hoary left-wing (and far-right-wing) myth: that the major parties and candidates were essentially the same and that a third-party effort, by galvanizing alienated and discontented voters, could pave the way for the destruction and replacement of one of those parties. It was either an ignorant or a cynical misreading of American history. (Abraham Lincoln's Republican Party, the only party in American history that ever replaced another one, arose only after both the Whigs and the Democrats had already split over slavery and the Whigs had disintegrated. As late as 1854, Lincoln was still a Whig.) By campaign's end, Nader's work had become completely destructive, and it was directed at only one party and one candidate. The narrowness of his appeal, the vainglory of his cause, and his distance from the historic tradition of the left was glaringly

*Jacob Weisberg, "Ralph the Leninist," *Slate*, October 31, 2000, http://slate.msn.com/id/1006380.

†Laura Meckler, "GOP Group to Air Pro-Nader TV Ads," Associated Press, October 27, 2000.

‡John B. Judis, "Ralph Nader Betrays Himself: Seeing Green," *The New Republic*, May 29, 2000.

apparent in the utter absence of support for his candidacy among black voters.

In the last week of the campaign, despite Nader's determined effort to undermine him, Gore was closing in on Bush's lead, and so the Bush campaign's final move was to broadcast a negative television ad: "Remember when Al Gore said his mother-in-law's prescription cost more than his dog's? His own aides said the story was made up. Now Al Gore is bending the truth again. The press calls Gore's Social Security attacks 'nonsense.' "

On the day before the election, Bush's chief political strategist, Karl Rove, told the press that he believed Bush would win the popular vote by six points and a landslide of 350 votes in the Electoral College. Rove's obvious motive in making this bold prediction was to foster the notion of Bush's inevitable victory. This bravado notwithstanding, the Bush campaign was anxious that their candidate would find himself in the awkward position of winning the popular vote but losing the Electoral College and therefore the presidency. Contingency plans were being drawn up for just this event. "The one thing we don't do is roll over. We fight," a Bush aide told the New York *Daily News* a week before the election. The newspaper reported:

> The core of the emerging Bush strategy assumes a popular uprising, stoked by the Bushies themselves, of course. In league with the campaign—which is preparing talking points about the Electoral College's essential unfairness—a massive talk-radio operation would be encouraged. "We'd have ads, too," says a Bush aide, "and I think you can count on the media to fuel the thing big-time. Even papers that supported Gore might turn against him because the will of the people will have been thwarted."[*]

Another journalist got the same story: "The Bush camp, sources said, would likely challenge the legitimacy of a Gore win, casting it as an affront to the people's will and branding the Electoral College as an antiquated relic."[†]

On election night, immediately after the polls closed, the television

[*]Michael Kramer, "Bush Set to Fight an Electoral College Loss," New York *Daily News*, November 1, 2000.

[†]Andrew Miga, "Electoral, Popular Vote Split Could Get Ugly," *The Boston Herald*, November 3, 2000.

networks gave Florida to Gore at 8:05 p.m., and the country knew that this almost certainly assured his victory. At 9:55 p.m., however, they retracted this prediction and declared the Florida vote too close to call. By then it was clear that whoever won Florida would certainly win the presidency. At 2:16 a.m., Fox News announced that Florida was in the column for Bush and he was the victor. The person who made this decision to call it for Bush was the director of the Fox News "decision desk," John Ellis, George W. Bush's first cousin, who had been in constant telephone contact all that day and night with both Governors Bush: George, and John Ellis "Jeb" Bush, the candidate's brother, of Florida.

With the Fox News announcement, pressure instantly fell on the other networks to follow suit. What happened next remains a mystery. At NBC News, the flamboyant and willful Jack Welch, chief executive officer of General Electric, which owns the network, was in the control booth reviewing voting results, and witnesses claim he demanded that the network declare Bush the winner, which it did minutes after Fox did so. Despite efforts by Representative Henry Waxman, Democrat of California, to obtain a videotape of Welch's demands, NBC has refused to release it. (Perhaps some future historian will secure this document, if it still exists.)

Gore immediately telephoned Governor Bush to congratulate him, and then he drove to the War Memorial in Nashville to make a concession speech to his followers. As he prepared to walk onstage, frantic aides gave him the news that Florida had once again been judged too close to call. It was not clear that Bush had won after all. So Gore called Bush back and withdrew the concession he had made earlier. About to deliver his victory speech, an incredulous Bush protested, "Let me make sure I understand. You're calling me back to retract your concession?" "You don't have to get snippy about this," Gore replied. Bush told Gore that his brother, the governor of Florida, had assured him he had won. "Let me explain something," said Gore, "your younger brother is not the ultimate authority on this."

By the next morning it was clear that Gore had won the overall popular vote, but it took weeks to determine his margin—539,947 votes, considerably more than the 118,574 edge that John F. Kennedy had over Richard Nixon in 1960. But Bush had won many small states, and he had 21 votes more than Gore's total in the Electoral College, 267–246. Florida's 25 electoral votes would therefore decide the election.

Just as Ralph Nader hoped, he had damaged the Democratic Party candidate. In Florida, Nader captured 96,837 votes, 2 percent of the total. Without Nader's candidacy most of these would have gone to Gore and given him the election. In New Hampshire, where Bush beat Gore by 1 percent, about 6,000 votes, Nader got 22,156 votes, 4 percent; most of these, also, would have been Gore's and handed him victory.*

The Republican campaign against Gore's character had succeeded at least enough to enable Bush to push the election into overtime. In the end, association with Clinton affected Gore less than the "net loss from perceptions of Gore's leadership skills and Gore's personal traits," which together amounted to a loss of 5.6 percentage points. Those and other findings, based on figures taken in the University of Michigan 2000 National Election Survey, were reached by David Gopoian, senior survey research associate at Consumers Union and former professor of political science at Kent State University, in his exhaustive study of the election.†

The ruthless Republican campaign against Gore's credibility, the media's complicity in it, and Gore's disoriented response, with his hesitant, apologetic performance in the second debate, landed him in Florida.

Yet Gore had won the votes of a majority of the American people.

---

*On June 12, 2001, Nader attended the Wednesday Group, a weekly strategy meeting of right-wing constituency groups organized by the Republican lobbyist Grover Norquist, adviser to Tom DeLay. Among those included were the Christian Coalition, National Rifle Association, Eagle Forum, Free Congress Foundation, and Republican National Committee. They cheered Nader for his help in the 2000 election. "Nader responded by pointing to his favorite political cartoon, in which a George W. Bush figure, upon hearing that 'A Vote for Nader Is a Vote for Bush,' announces his intention to 'Vote for Nader.' " Marc J. Ambinder, "The Strangest Bedfellows: Conservative Strategy Meeting Gets a Dose of Naderite Populism," *ABC News.com*, June 12, 2000, http://abcnews.go.com/sections/politics/DailyNews/Nader_020612.html.

†Among white Southerners, Gopoian wrote, these poor perceptions of Gore's image cost him 20.2 percent, while hostile views of Clinton cost him 2.3 percent. Clinton was a particular drag among white Northern religious voters, but Gore's leadership and personal image hurt him more decisively among secular voters in both the North and the South. Those who agreed with him on the issues supported him by only 57 percent. Among blacks, "Clinton's effect did more to secure nearly monolithic support for Gore than any other single factor. The net gain for Gore was approximately 34 percentage points." Gopoian concluded, "The most realistic scenarios indicate that Gore would have picked up between 1.3 to 2.0 percentage points more than he actually did if he had been a better liked and more trusted candidate." Gopoian, "Making Sense of the 2000 Presidential Election."

Would he win the presidency? For thirty-five days the struggle over Florida—and democracy in America—would be waged.

III

President Clinton was often intensely frustrated during his last year in office. He had attained full mastery of the powers of the presidency and could see clearly what needed to be done. He was fifty-four years old, younger than many presidents when they first assumed office, and he didn't want to leave the job. "I wish I were running this year," he told me in the Oval Office on August 2. "I'd run their ass down." He especially didn't care for the thought that the Republicans might return to the White House. "The whole Bush crowd is spoiled and angry they don't have West Wing offices," he had said to me in February during the Republican primaries. He thought John McCain made a terrible mistake by failing to make an issue of Bush's "Texas money"—not only the "soft money" that paid for the negative ads against him but the whole structure of special interests that Bush had built through his use of the state government. And in the general election, the President was worried that the distinctions between the two candidates might not be drawn sharply enough: "If we go into the election and the people don't know what the differences are, we'll lose. We have to get our people out of their lethargy and get them rooted in what is going on."

Clinton had been sidelined by the Gore campaign, but on the eve of the Republican National Convention he could not restrain himself. On July 27, he publicly described George W. Bush's message as being "I've been governor of Texas, my daddy was president, I own a baseball team, they like me down there." This single sentence, defining Bush as the child of privilege he was, provoked a furious and sputtering response from former president George Bush, who appeared on the NBC *Today Show* on the morning of the first day of the Republican convention. "If this continues, then I'll tell the nation what I think of [Clinton] as a human being and as a person," said the elder Bush. But this defensive outburst by the riled-up father had unwittingly diminished the son. Clinton could not have been more pleased by this stumbling display, for it only called attention to his point. "All I did was say 'Daddy,'" he said playfully to me. "It's another word for father. He uses 'father.' I just said, 'Daddy.'" He laughed: "As a rule, I like white people."

As he prepared for his speech at the Democratic National Convention, Clinton repeated time and again, "Clarity of choice is the key to the outcome of this election. I really believe this." Right after the Democratic convention, on August 16, the Gore campaign stage-managed a passing of the torch at a rally in Monroe, Michigan, the first and last campaign appearance of Gore and Clinton together. "He is the right person to be the first president of the twenty-first century," the President said. And Gore replied, "The question in this election is whether we erode that foundation [laid in the Clinton years] or build on it." Clinton shook Gore's hand and left him alone on the stage. Hillary returned to New York to her own campaign.

On September 6, at the last of the Third Way conferences, held during the millennium session of the United Nations General Assembly, thirteen national leaders gathered for dinner at the Waldorf-Astoria Hotel—the same group as had been at the Berlin conference minus Prime Minister Jospin and plus Prime Minister Blair. Anxious about the forthcoming U.S. election, the departure of Clinton, and its effect on global politics, they asked the President to give them an analysis of the American campaign thus far. He explained how Bush was using the rhetoric of "compassionate conservatism" to blur the distinctions between him and Gore and to cloud the actual Democratic program. "Bush gave a speech that could have sounded like us," he said. "It was a rhetorical triumph, but had no specifics. The Republicans are running ads saying they're for what we're for even though they're not." Legislation passed while he was president had removed the contentious issues of welfare and crime, staples of conservatism in the past, from political debate, and Gore's positive platform was "very specific." But "what's working for us, a sense of well-being, forward motion," could also "work against us, by creating a sense of complacency." There was another danger: "Nader could imperil Gore's election if he gets enough of the vote." He emphasized, "Our whole message has to be clarity of choice, clarity of choice."

Tony Blair didn't think the basic debate was so different from elsewhere: "The progressive parties win when people understand they need a government on their side. In Europe we call it solidarity. The right in Europe now will move to race and identity—issues where they can appeal to a set of prejudices that are not upfront but lie underneath."

"Fear of the future is the basis of the right-wing parties," said Prime Minister Persson of Sweden.

"I see weakness in our position in Europe," said Prime Minister

Guterres of Portugal. "We face a dangerous combination of social populism with demagogy."

Several leaders shook their heads over the prospect of a Bush presidency. "It would be a terrible blow," said one. "Gore's victory is essential," said another.

President de la Rua of Argentina asked Clinton what in his judgment would be the future of U.S.–Latin American relations, and Clinton said he foresaw no large differences between Gore's and Bush's basic policies. Continuity would prevail. Unfortunately, Clinton's optimism was misplaced; when Argentina's dire economic crisis virtually exploded in November 2002, after the nation defaulted on a World Bank loan, President George W. Bush chose a policy of studied indifference to it—the opposite of what Clinton's policy had been toward Mexico during its economic turmoil in 1995. (As the Argentine economy collapsed and its middle class was reduced to penury, Clinton was upset. "Oh, I cry for Argentina," he said.) The meeting ended on an unresolved note, with Clinton talking of the "next generation of reforms" and the need for "mechanisms to help each other." It sounded like an unfinished symphony.

At the end of January 2000, Bob Squier, a pioneer political consultant who had worked on both Clinton presidential campaigns and had been especially close to Gore, died at the age of sixty-five. I had known him since Gary Hart's presidential campaign of 1984. Squier was unusual among politicos for his literary and epicurean interests. He had made PBS documentaries about Hemingway, Faulkner, and Fitzgerald, and he had operated a wine press at his Virginia country home. After his funeral at the National Cathedral, where the President delivered a eulogy, a friend of Bob's told me that Bob had learned about his colon cancer too late for it to be cured. I decided I would schedule a colonoscopy.

In late July, the procedure revealed that I had colon cancer. It had been caught at an early stage, though, and at a subsequent physical exam, my physician told me my condition was generally superb: I had only the one problem of cancer. Feeling as fit as I did, I would not have gotten the colonoscopy if I had not been spurred to do so by Bob's death. Like Bob's, the cancer might have been discovered too late. I felt indebted to him and wished I weren't.

Of course, I also felt what other cancer patients experience—the anxieties, the fear, and the sense of the body's betrayal. But I was extremely lucky, not least because I had my work, which did more than keep me busy and preoccupied. And at the White House I was fortunate to be able to have a practical effect on how U.S. medicine went about treating colon cancer. When I learned that I had cancer, I studied the public policy about it. In a memo to the President, I wrote, "Currently, only about a third of colon cancers are diagnosed in the early stage, before the cancer has begun to spread. Less than 25 percent of Americans over 50 years of age are currently being screened. Colon cancer mortality could be cut in half within two years." And I detailed the programs that could accomplish this goal.

I was operated on on September 14 at the Johns Hopkins Hospital in Baltimore. One-third of my colon was removed. Three days after my operation, my surgeon told me that the cancer had not spread and that I would not require chemotherapy or radiation. I was cured. Before going into the hospital, an event for which I had responsibility had been put on the President's schedule, and it was to take place three weeks later. I was determined to be back on my feet by then, and, a bit wobbly, I was.

On October 5, President Clinton addressed a conference of historians on "The Progressive Tradition" at Princeton University:

> I believe the time in which we live bears the most resemblance to the progressive era. . . . You can see it in the fight we had with the Republican Congress that led to the shutdown of the government. You can see it in our efforts to build one America across all the lines that divide us. You can see it in our struggle to end genocide and ethnic cleansing in the Balkans. . . . The central lesson of the progressive tradition is that you either have to shape change consistent with your values, or you will be shaped by it in ways that make it more difficult for you to live by your values. To retreat from responsibility is to invite instability. . . . In this time, we can have a progressive era that outlasts the one you came here to study, if we are faithful to its values; if we understand we have to change even more rapidly, and perhaps even more profoundly than they did.

The next day, the President devoted his weekly Saturday radio address to the subject of colon cancer: "Good morning. Every year, more than 56,000 Americans die from colorectal cancer, and another 130,000 are diagnosed with the disease. These are people we know and love: our families, our friends, our neighbors. . . . Today I am announcing several new actions in the war against cancer." One was that the National Cancer Institute would invest $30 million over the following five years in improving screening techniques. Another was that every Medicare recipient would receive an annual reminder to get a screening, and the President asked the Congress to expand Medicare coverage to cover these screening tests for people of average risk and without symptoms. And he repeated his demand that the Congress pass a patients' bill of rights that would ensure that "cancer patients—and all patients—have access to the specialty care they need." Though the Republican Congress refused again to do so, President Clinton succeeded in his final budget negotiations to secure Medicare coverage for colon cancer screening—a major gain in public health care.

On October 12, a small boat rammed the USS *Cole*, anchored in the harbor of Aden, killing seventeen sailors and tearing a gash in its side. The counterterrorism experts on the National Security Council believed that al-Qaeda was almost certainly responsible for this attack, but it took weeks to assemble the proof. In 1997, the NSC had sent the Pentagon a memo warning about terrorist dangers to American ships in foreign ports. "The Navy disregarded these admonitions and the known threat conditions in Yemen, which was second only to Afghanistan on the list of states infested with terrorists," wrote Daniel Benjamin and Steven Simon. "The Navy possessed virtually the entire body of intelligence on al-Qaeda and disregarded it so thoroughly that an institution built on the concept of the personal responsibility of the commander decided that no individual should be punished for the security lapses. . . . A more telling display of the persistent disbelief concerning the threat from al-Qaeda would be hard to imagine."*

President Clinton and Vice President Gore carefully avoided using the bombing of the *Cole* as a pretext to attack Bush's unsure command of foreign policy during the campaign, however. The war on terrorism was politically out of bounds, they believed; it would have been contrary to national security interests to turn it into a political debating point.

The very next day, Dick Cheney suggested that the Clinton-Gore administration was to blame. "It's relatively easy to sit back and say look, the Cold War is over with, nothing to worry about, why should we spend any time concerned about the U.S. military today," he railed at an American Legion hall in Ohio. "And then something happens such as happened this morning and we lose sailors." For a week, Cheney kept on making political hay of the attack on the *Cole*. On October 16, he even lambasted the Democrats for urging bipartisanship: "Our opponents in this campaign, Al Gore and Joe Lieberman, have sometimes argued when I raise issues about the status of the U.S. military today, we shouldn't talk

*Benjamin and Simon, *Age of Sacred Terror*, pp. 323–24.

about it. Shouldn't bring it up. Somehow it's unpatriotic to have this conversation. I think they're dead wrong. I can't think of a more important time to have this conversation than when we are making this decision."

Meanwhile, in New York, the Republican National Committee launched a telephone campaign against Hillary Clinton's Senate candidacy, accusing her of "supporting terrorism . . . the same kind of terrorism that killed our sailors on the USS *Cole*" because she had accepted campaign contributions from a Muslim group—a group, incidentally, that had also endorsed Bush.

On October 18, President Clinton led the memorial service for the fallen sailors at the Norfolk, Virginia, naval base. After slowly reading the names of the dead, he said, "To those who attacked them, we say, you will not find a safe harbor. We will find you—and justice will prevail."

With the race neck and neck, Gore was asked on October 20 about whether he was receiving campaign help from the President. "This is a campaign that I am running on my own," he said. A week later, though, Clinton invited 150 black leaders to the East Room in the White House to give them a pep talk about the importance of the choice in the election, and he recorded seventy different phone messages to be used on the day of the election to get out the black vote. On October 29, he sang with two different black church choirs and preached sermons. At the Alfred Street Baptist Church, in Alexandria, Virginia, he implored:

> Make sure nobody takes a pass on November seventh. When I hear people say this is not really a very significant election it makes me want to go head first into an empty swimming pool. We really do have a big, clear, unambiguous stark choice here. We don't have to get mad, but we need to be smart. There are differences in education policy, in health care policy, in environmental policy, in crime policy, and on foreign policy, just a ton of things. You need to show on Election Day. We still have bridges to cross. The question is, are we going to be walking in the right direction. Are we all going to walk across, or just a few of us?

President Clinton made a last swing out to California, dropped into Kentucky, and finally landed in New York, where he went to campaign for Hillary and to receive the election returns. He stayed up all night.

On the day after the election, Clinton was even more galvanized. From the start, he saw the postelection contest in Florida as a quintessential political struggle between the Republican and Democratic Parties. In public, during the thirty-five-day battle, he maintained a serene demeanor, making no partisan remarks, reassuring the public that the ship of state was not foundering and that he was at the helm. Behind the scenes, he dispensed strategic and tactical advice to the Gore effort in Florida through his aides, including me. He had ideas about what Gore should do day by day, and just as in the campaign, these ideas were filtered and mostly ignored. Clinton couldn't speak out and he couldn't speak to Gore. So he could make no difference in this decisive battle.

IV

The earliest records of slavery in the New World are to be found in St. Augustine, Florida, one of the oldest cities in North America, settled by the Spanish—documents "dating more than fifty years before 1619, the commonly accepted beginning of African slavery in the future United States," according to Taylor Branch.* By the nineteenth century, northern Florida was part and parcel of the plantation economy based on cotton and slaves. In 1861, Florida seceded and joined the Confederacy. After the Civil War, under Reconstruction, the state was occupied by federal troops and allowed to rejoin the Union in 1868 when its legislature agreed to enfranchise black voters under the Fourteenth Amendment and adopted a new state constitution incorporating their civil rights.

The morning after the presidential election of 1876, it appeared that the Democratic candidate, Samuel Tilden, governor of New York, had defeated the Republican, Rutherford Hayes, governor of Ohio. "Tilden Elected" was the headline in the *New York Tribune*. He had won the popular vote cleanly, by 4,284,020 (or 51 percent) to Hayes's 4,036,572 (48 percent). But in the Electoral College, Tilden's 184 electoral votes were just one short of a majority. Though the initial outcome indicated that Tilden had captured Florida and Louisiana and South Carolina, the remaining states still occupied by U.S. troops, the results there were in doubt. Beginning on the day after the election, the Republican Party launched a political effort to move those states' electors into the Hayes column. The battle turned on Florida. "Flagrantly partisan and arbitrary decisions of the Florida [election] board converted an apparent Tilden majority into Hayes votes," the historian C. Vann Woodward explains.†

---

*Taylor Branch, *Pillar of Fire: America in the King Years 1963–65*, Simon and Schuster, 1998, p. 34.

†C. Vann Woodward, *Reunion and Reaction*, Doubleday Anchor, 1956, p. 19.

On February 9, 1877, the National Electoral Commission, created to adjudicate the election, decided, on a straight party-line vote, eight to seven, to award Florida to Hayes. The Democrats filibustered in the House of Representatives to try to thwart a final count. On February 26, five Southern Democrats and five Ohio Republicans acting on Hayes's behalf held a secret meeting at the Wormley House Hotel in Washington, where they thrashed out a deal to end the filibuster and make the Republican president. In return, federal troops were withdrawn, Reconstruction was finished, and the last three Southern states were placed under the political control of the "Redeemers." In 1887, segregation was officially enshrined in Florida through a series of "Jim Crow" laws. In the 1890s, poll taxes, literacy tests, and other impediments were imposed on black voters to make certain of their disenfranchisement. For decades, the civil rights of blacks were suppressed in Florida as throughout the South.

Harry T. Moore was a black schoolteacher who in 1934 organized the Brevard County chapter of the National Association for the Advancement of Colored People. (Brevard County is on the Atlantic coast, mid-state.) Three years later, he filed the first lawsuit in the Deep South against the Board of Public Instruction for equal salaries for black and white teachers—a suit that was ruled against the next year by the Florida Supreme Court. Moore also started a campaign against lynching—between 1921 and 1946, sixty-one blacks were lynched in Florida, the most in any Southern state—writing letters to the governor and launching his own investigations. In 1944, Moore founded the Progressive Voters' League and registered 116,000 black voters as Democrats— about a third of all black voters in Florida at the time. He was fired from his position as the principal of an all-black school and became the first full-time executive secretary of the Florida NAACP; in 1947 he launched a campaign against the "lily-white primary bill" that excluded black voters.

During the 1930s, the Ku Klux Klan had had an estimated thirty thousand members in Florida, the largest Klan in the South, and a decade later, it was still virulent there. On election night in 1948, the Klan staged large marches through several black areas in support of Strom Thurmond's Dixiecrat candidacy for president. In the election of 1950, Moore's League backed a candidate in a write-in campaign who unseated a segregationist as chairman of the Brevard County Commission in what was called a "miracle." By now, Moore was notorious as "the most dangerous man in Florida." On Christmas Day 1951, his house was bombed, and he and his wife were killed while they slept—the twelfth Klan bombing against black leaders that year in the state, known nationally as the "Florida Terror." Harry T. Moore was the first martyr of the modern civil rights movement. Seven Klansmen were indicted for perjury in Moore's murder, but the charges were dismissed. Northern Florida, especially in Duval County, around the cities of Jacksonville and St. Augustine, remained Klan strongholds.*

In 1962, Vice President Lyndon Johnson went to St. Augustine for its four-hundredth-anniversary celebration. The threat of black protest led him to declare that the events he participated in would be integrated, but the courthouse still prominently displayed a sign over a side entrance that read "Colored"; the library was all white; there was one black poll worker for elections. Through the summer of 1963, dozens of demonstrators were arrested in sit-ins and marches against segregation in St. Augustine. The September night of the funeral of the four black girls who were killed when the Ku Klux Klan bombed a black church in Birmingham, Alabama, the Klan burned crosses and beat civil rights workers in Florida—and the black *victims* were jailed. Vigilantes firebombed cars and homes. In May 1964, more marches were met with arrests and unleashed police dogs. Martial law was declared. On June 1, Martin Luther King, Jr., came to protest alongside "the heroes of St. Augustine." Waders into segregated beaches were beaten and arrested. On June 5, King was shot at in an attempted assassination. On June 11, he was arrested trying to integrate a motel. "The racists in St. Augustine were worse than those in Birmingham," King said.† This struggle in Florida was the dramatic background of the battle going on in the U.S. Senate for the Civil Rights Bill.

The 2000 election in Florida was as much about race and rights as the election of 1876 had been. Its circumstances were the latest symptoms of more than a century's struggle for civil and political rights in the South, where Florida had so often been a major battleground. Those who were disenfranchised in 2000 were the children of those whose voting rights had been secured by the civil rights movement of the 1960s and the descendants of those who had been disenfranchised under Jim Crow. Their votes were the decisive ones that were not counted. The battle over who

---

*See Ben Green, *Before His Time: The Untold Story of Harry T. Moore, America's First Civil Rights Martyr*, Free Press, 1999.

†See Branch, *Pillar of Fire*; Jeffrey Toobin, *Too Close to Call*, Random House, 2001, p. 172.

won the presidential election in 2000 in Florida was, among other things, the latest episode in the struggle for voting rights for blacks in the South.

The political warfare in Florida after the election became an extension of the election campaign, but the situation was unprecedented and the rules were unwritten. It pitted the Republican Party's political machine in Florida, where Jeb Bush was governor, against Gore's and the Democrats' makeshift recount effort. It was already known that the Bush camp would not tolerate a result in which Bush won the popular vote but lost in the Electoral College. Now, having lost the national popular vote and appearing to be in danger of losing Florida's, the Republicans refused to accept that the contested votes should be counted, and they resisted by any means necessary.

On the day after the election, the Associated Press reported that the count in Florida showed Bush leading by 327 votes out of nearly 6 million cast. Under state law, the closeness of the result automatically triggered a recount. And it was already apparent that serious problems had been caused by the chaotic design of the ballots and by malfunctioning voting machines. Counties around the state reported that the design of voting cards and machines often clogged the ballots, producing what became famously known as hanging chads, or incompletely punched-through ballots, though in most cases the intent of the voter was obvious. The Gore camp asked local canvassing boards in four counties for a hand recount.

In heavily Democratic Palm Beach County, on election day, hundreds of voters complained about the "butterfly ballot," which put far-right-wing third-party candidate Pat Buchanan's name above Gore's but on the other side of the ballot, with confusing arrows pointing to a series of holes. It was easy to think one was voting for Gore and actually cast a ballot for Buchanan. Bush, since his name came first on the ballot, suffered from no such confusion. According to the *Palm Beach Post*, Gore had a net loss of 6,607 votes on ballots that were inadvertently double-punched, and he lost an additional 3,000 when those who intended to vote for him mistakenly punched the hole for Buchanan. Many of these voters were elderly Jews for whom the anti-Israel Buchanan was anathema, and Buchanan himself acknowledged that he doubted he had earned these votes.

Gore wanted to win as the one rigorously upholding standards of decency, and he put limits on what he would do, lest the conflict rage out of control; he was not demagogic. Gore held back any public demonstrations, because he did not think the matter should be settled in the streets, and after civil rights leader Jesse Jackson led one, Gore asked him not to organize any more. But Gore was up against a Republican juggernaut that simply wanted to win. Bush did not have any of Gore's compunctions. For him, it was no holds barred, all hands on deck.

Bush delegated his overall legal and political strategy to James Baker, the most commanding and experienced political figure in the Republican Party. His presence in Tallahassee was a clear sign of the Republicans' will to gain power, completely without hesitation or worries about democratic niceties. As he had always been in the past, Baker was cold, efficient, and riveted on securing power. He came from one of the oldest and wealthiest families in Texas, scion of Baker and Botts, the powerhouse Houston law firm, and he had been an indispensable friend to George H. W. Bush throughout his political career. He had also served as President Reagan's first chief of staff, his secretary of the treasury, and as Bush's secretary of state. In the meantime, the candidate himself remained at his Texas ranch, going through the motions of forming a government as though the contest were a fait accompli. "The vote in Florida was counted," Baker said endlessly. "The vote in Florida has been recounted." He repeated these phrases while using every means the Republican team could devise to prevent the votes from being counted.

In Florida, the state government, under Governor Jeb Bush's control, moved quickly to deter Gore. Secretary of State Katherine Harris, whose office was in charge of elections, eagerly put herself at the governor's service. Harris, the granddaughter of one of Florida's early tycoons, had been cochair of George W. Bush's state campaign, an honorific position requiring her to do little more than lend her name to a letterhead. This typified her approach, as airy as it was grandiose. Jeb Bush inserted a trusted Republican operative and lobbyist, his first campaign manager, Mac Stipanovich, into her office. "You have to bring this election in for a landing," he ordered.*

Thus the skirmishing started. On November 9, two days after the election, Harris announced that absentee ballots had to be counted by November 14. When the Palm Beach canvassing board decided it would begin a recount on November 15, she declared that she would accept no results after November 14. A Broward County circuit judge ruled that that county's board didn't have to abide by her deadline. Volusia County completed a recount, netting 98 more votes for Gore. On November 15, Harris said that she would certify the election results on November 18.

*Cited in Toobin, *Too Close to Call*, p. 69.

That day, the Florida Supreme Court, whose judges had all been appointed by Democratic governors, denied her request that it halt the recounts. Gore, who had assembled a team of lawyers, offered to stop his legal efforts if Bush would either agree to a statewide recount or accept the results in Broward, Miami-Dade, and Palm Beach Counties, in addition to the overseas absentee ballots. Bush refused. "Everyone in Florida has had his or her vote counted once. Those votes have been recounted," he said. "The votes of Florida have been counted. They have been recounted." On November 16, the Florida Supreme Court ruled that the recounts could proceed.

The Republicans opened two new fronts. William Kristol called the former executive producer of ABC News *This Week*, Dorrance Smith, who was now in charge of public relations for Bush in Florida, and suggested to him that the overseas absentee ballots could be ginned up into a question of Gore denying members of the armed forces their votes. The Republican Party had run an operation to get its registered members living abroad to file absentee ballots. Not all of these had been mailed before the deadline, as the postmarks indicated. Members of the armed forces typically vote by absentee ballot, and most of them from Florida were Republican. By conflating these with all other absentee voters and making it sound as if all of them were military voters, Kristol tried to make it look unpatriotic if unlawful ballots filed after the deadline were disqualified.

By the next day, November 18, the whole Republican communications team was putting out this theme and trotting out retired General Norman Schwarzkopf to condemn the idea that "men and women . . . serving abroad and facing danger . . . are denied the right to vote." On November 19, Senator Lieberman was asked by Tim Russert on NBC News *Meet the Press* whether Gore was eliminating military ballots by means of "technicalities." Lieberman instantly declared that the Gore camp would never do that and would "give the benefit of the doubt to ballots coming in from military personnel generally." With that, the rules governing all those overseas ballots apparently went out the window.

Of the 4,256 ballots cast by Floridians living overseas, half had been received after November 9, many without postmarks as required. On November 24, the canvassing board of Duval County, composed of four white Republicans, admitted 68 additional overseas ballots for Bush in addition to the 550 it had already accepted. Boards dominated by Republicans across the state followed suit. In the end, 680 questionable overseas ballots were included, according to *The New York Times*, providing just enough for Bush's margin of victory. Thus, not wanting to be branded unpatriotic in excluding military ballots, the Gore camp permitted what became known as the "Thanksgiving stuffing."*

On November 18, Harris had certified the election for Bush, yet three days later the Florida Supreme Court ruled that her action was "arbitrary . . . contrary to law . . . contrary to the plain meaning of the statute," that the unfinished recounts in Broward, Miami-Dade, and Palm Beach were legal, and that the deadline would be extended for five more days. Baker said, "It is simply not fair . . . to change the rules, either in the middle of the game, or after the game has been played." Then he added, "One should not be surprised if the Florida legislature seeks to affirm the original rules." On the same day, Jeb Bush declared that he would sign a bill authorizing the Republican-controlled legislature to send a new slate of electors to the Electoral College to challenge the ones committed to Gore if the recounts went Gore's way. The Republican State House Speaker, Tom Feeney, also suggested the reinstatement of "literacy tests," a legal method used to disenfranchise blacks in the days of Jim Crow. "Voter confusion is not a reason for whining or crying or having a revote," he said. "It may be a reason to require literacy tests."†

The Republicans had two more responses to the Florida Supreme Court decision. First, Baker filed suit with the U.S. Supreme Court seeking to overturn its ruling. And second, on November 22, when the Miami-Dade canvassing board had begun its recount at the Clark Government Center, a crowd of about fifty Republicans rushed the door of the room where the board was working. "Several people were trampled, punched or kicked," according to *The New York Times*, the state Democratic Party chairman was surrounded and kept from returning to the room, and David Leahy, the election supervisor, was hit. Rather than continue, the Miami-Dade board, physically intimidated, declared that it could not count ballots at all. The palpable intimidation "weighed heavy on our minds," Leahy told *The New York Times*.‡

The mob was organized from two sites. From a large recreational vehicle serving as his command central, Roger Stone, a long-time Republican political consultant and lobbyist who had been recruited by James

*Toobin, *Too Close to Call*, pp. 173–74.

†Cynthia Tucker, "Jesse Revisits Roots in Blacks' Voting Rights Battle," *Palm Beach Post*, December 18, 2000.

‡Dexter Filkins and Dana Canedy, "Protest Influenced Miami-Dade's Decision to Stop Recount," *The New York Times*, November 24, 2000.

Baker to come to Florida, sent word to the local Cuban radio station, Radio Mambi, to call for demonstrators to converge on the Government Center. Another band of protestors was already assembled there, consisting of dozens of Republican congressional staffers from Washington—including staff members for Senator Trent Lott and five staffers for House whip Tom DeLay—who had been given plane tickets and expense money to make the trip to Florida. Representative John Sweeney, Republican of New York, led the crowd in chanting, "Shut it down!" Paul Gigot of the *Wall Street Journal* editorial page was there, too. "If it's possible to have a bourgeois riot, it happened here Wednesday. And it could end up saving the presidency for George W. Bush," he wrote.*

The next night, November 23, the Bush campaign operation paid for a Thanksgiving party with free food and drink for the "bourgeois" rioters at the Hyatt Hotel in Fort Lauderdale. The Las Vegas lounge singer Wayne Newton was brought in to serenade them with his rendition of "Danke Schoen." Bush and Cheney thanked the revelers in a phone call broadcast to the party, "which included joking references by both running mates to the incident in Miami."†

In Miami-Dade, more than 10,000 ballots went unrecounted. On November 25, Broward County completed its tally, which netted Gore 567 more votes. Hundreds of Republican-organized pickets massed outside the courthouse to protest the Broward counting. The following day Harris denied a request from Palm Beach County for more time to count its hard-to-discern, chad-ridden ballots, so, its task unfinished, the board simply shut down and submitted no vote totals. That night, George W. Bush went on national television to declare himself the winner. The *Palm Beach Post*, later reviewing the undervotes in Palm Beach County—that is, votes that had initially been registered with no presidential vote but contained indications of voters' intent—discovered Gore would have netted 784 votes there, more than enough to overcome Bush's final margin of 537.

The battle went on. On November 27, Gore filed suit in Leon County demanding recounts and counts in three counties. On November 30, a special committee of the Florida legislature called for a special session to name its own electors, a move openly encouraged by Jeb Bush.

*Paul Gigot, "Miami Heat," *The Wall Street Journal*, November 24, 2000.
†Nicholas Kulish, Jim Vandehei, and Evan Perez, "The Day After: Partying Hardy with the GOP," *The Wall Street Journal*, November 27, 2000.

On December 4, Leon County Circuit Court Judge N. Sanders Sauls, a hidebound conservative, ruled against Gore and in favor of upholding Harris's certification and stopping the recounts. Gore appealed this ruling to the Florida Supreme Court. And the same day, the U.S. Supreme Court, ruling on a Bush appeal, nullified the Florida Supreme Court's decision to extend the deadline for counting, saying that it had failed to defer to the legislature's standard.

On December 8, the Florida Supreme Court overturned Sauls's decision and ordered a manual recount of undervotes in any county where it had not taken place and the inclusion in the final tally of all hitherto uncounted ballots. "In tabulating what constitutes a legal vote," it ruled, "the standard to be used is the one provided by the legislature, 'a vote shall be counted where there is a clear indication of the intent of the voter.'" Furthermore, the court added 215 votes from Palm Beach's previously excluded recount, along with 168 more from the partial and halted count in Miami-Dade, reducing Bush's lead from 537 votes to 154. To stop this court-ordered count, Bush appealed to the U.S. Supreme Court.

By now, news reports had appeared about particular problems affecting districts that were predominantly black. For the 2000 election the NAACP had organized an extensive voter participation program—a legacy going back to Harry T. Moore—which had increased black turnout by 893,000 voters, 65 percent more than in 1996; blacks were becoming 15 percent of the total Florida electorate, a growth of 50 percent. At least part of the cause of their mobilization was as a response to Governor Jeb Bush's abolition of affirmative action in the state's colleges and universities. Many knew that the University of Florida had not been fully desegregated until the late 1960s, after a movement of marches and sit-ins. Black Floridians voted for Gore over George Bush by a margin of nine-to-one.*

The first sign of special trouble came with news articles that reported on Florida's so-called scrub list, which the Secretary of State's office used to purge convicted felons from the voting rolls. Overwhelmingly, those removed were black. Florida was the only state to contract the work of scrubbing the voter lists to a private company, which happened to be

*Thomas B. Edsall, "Bush Lost 9 to 1 Among Blacks: Poll Findings and Fla. Fight Present Challenge to GOP Nominee," *The Washington Post*, December 12, 2000.

owned by major Republican fund-raisers. More than 8,000 of those scrubbed turned out to be not felons but people guilty merely of misdemeanors, and there were also many mistaken names.*

Starting on Election Day, complaints from the rejected had been pouring into the offices of black representatives. A pattern emerged. In heavily Democratic Hillsborough County, which includes the city of Tampa, the election board conducted an investigation. "Of the 3,258 names on the original ("scrub") list . . . the county concluded that more than 15 percent were in error," wrote Gregory Palast, the journalist who first uncovered all this. "If that ratio held statewide, no fewer than 7,000 voters were incorrectly targeted for removal from voting rosters."† Across the state, an unknown number of registered black voters had been rebuffed at the polls because they were listed as scrubbed felons.

Three weeks after the election, Gore strongly insisted that the recounts were essential because it could be seen that the voting technologies used in different districts had had a disproportionate effect on ballots, and this negatively affected black voters. *The New York Times* corroborated the point, reporting that as a result Gore had lost 7,000 votes:

*The U.S. Civil Rights Commission later reported:
During the briefing on June 20, 2002, many panelists spoke of the need to restore former felons' voting rights. Howard Simon of the ACLU, for example, focused his opening statement on this issue and stated that he considered it "the overriding civil rights problem in the state of Florida." A report issued in June 2001 by the Florida Parole Commission and the Executive Clemency Board noted that there are 418,000 Floridians who have permanently lost the right to vote. . . . Mr. Simon noted that at the close of the last decade in Florida there were 139,000 former felons and that 107,000 of them were black men. He added that the 107,000 constituted 9 percent of Florida's voting-age African-American population and 15 percent of Florida's voting-age African-American male population. [State] Senator [Kendrick B.] Meek maintained that the vast majority of these convicted felons are first-time offenders who pled guilty and were sentenced to probation and never incarcerated. Despite the relatively minor nature of most offenders' crimes, Senator Meek noted that Florida has the largest backlog in the nation of individuals who have filled out the necessary paperwork to have their rights restored. Approximately 50,000 individuals in Florida have been on the waiting list for restoration of rights for two to three years.

†Gregory Palast, "Florida's Flawed 'Voter-cleansing' Program," *Salon.com*, December 4, 2000, http://archive.salon.com/politics/feature/2000/12/04/voter_ file/ index.html.

When Florida's votes were counted on Election Day, Gov. George W. Bush of Texas had a tiny but possibly decisive edge: the majority of the state's black voters, Vice President Al Gore's most reliable voters, stalwart supporters, cast their ballots on punch cards that are more prone to voter error and miscounts. Across the state, nearly 4 percent of the type of punch-card ballots most widely used in Florida were thrown out because the machines read them as blank or invalid. By contrast, the more modern, optical scanning systems rejected far fewer votes—only about 1.4 percent of those cast. A New York Times analysis shows that 64 percent of the state's black voters live in counties that used the punch cards while 56 percent of whites did so. While black voters made up 16 percent of the vote on Election Day, that small difference, the analysis suggests, could have had a decisive effect on an election decided by only a few hundred votes out of nearly six million. . . .

The impact of these differences on the outcome will never be known but their potential magnitude is evident in Miami-Dade County, where predominantly black precincts saw their votes thrown out at twice the rate as Hispanic precincts and nearly four times the rate of white precincts. In all, 1 out of 11 ballots in predominantly black precincts were rejected, a total of 9,904.

Had all people cast ballots that could be counted along the same lines as their neighbors, Mr. Gore would have gained nearly 7,000 votes.*

The Washington Post confirmed this conclusion in its own report on the undervotes in Miami-Dade: "According to the Post analysis, in Miami-Dade County precincts where fewer than 30 percent of the voters are black, about 3 percent of ballots did not register a vote for president. In precincts where more than 70 percent of the voters are African American, it was nearly 10 percent. . . . The more black and Democratic a precinct, the more likely it was to suffer high rates of invalidated votes."†

But the most glaring problems had occurred in Duval County, including Jacksonville, the historic center of turmoil during the 1960s. It still had a white majority and Republicans in charge of the election board. In Duval, 27,000 punch-card presidential ballots were voided; in just four predominantly black districts in Jacksonville, 11,300 of the 59,650 ballots

*Josh Barbanel and Ford Fessenden, "Racial Pattern in Demographics of Error-Prone Ballots," *The New York Times*, November 29, 2000.

†John Mintz and Dan Keating, "Fla. Ballot Spoilage Likelier For Blacks: Voting Machines, Confusion Cited," *The Washington Post*, December 3, 2000.

had been tossed out. The ballot in Duval, as confusing as the "butterfly" ballot in Palm Beach, cost Gore even more votes. The names of presidential candidates were spread across two pages, and on the sample ballot printed and distributed by the Republican-controlled board, the instructions read, "Vote all pages." As a result, many blacks voted for Gore on one page and, thinking they were doing the right thing, pressed a mark for a minor party candidate on the next. "Altogether," reported *The New York Times*, "21,942 ballots were rejected because the voter punched the hole beside the name of more than one candidate, and another 4,927 were invalidated because the voter punched no hole next to a presidential candidate, said the Duval County supervisor of elections."*

On December 9, the court-ordered statewide recount of about 45,000 undervotes began. But that afternoon, the U.S. Supreme Court, in a 5–4 decision, accepted Bush's request for a stay on the Florida Supreme Court's order to recount. The counting stopped, never to start again. In a dissent, Associate Justice John Paul Stevens wrote:

> Counting every legally cast vote cannot constitute irreparable harm. On the other hand, there is a danger that a stay may cause irreparable harm to the respondents—and, more importantly, the public at large—because of the risk that "the entry of the stay would be tantamount to a decision on the merits in favor of the applicants." National Socialist Party of America v. Skokie, 434 U.S. 1327, 1328 (1977)
>
> Preventing the recount from being completed will inevitably cast a cloud on the legitimacy of the election. It is certainly not clear that the Florida decision violated federal law. . . . As a more fundamental matter, the Florida court's ruling reflects the basic principle, inherent in our Constitution and our democracy, that every legal vote should be counted.

Stevens's dissent prompted Associate Justice Antonin Scalia to take the unusual step of countering with a concurring opinion on the stay:

> The counting of votes that are of questionable legality does, in my view, threaten irreparable harm to petitioner [George W. Bush] and to the country, by casting a cloud upon what he claims to be the legitimacy of his election. Count first and rule upon legality afterwards, is not a recipe for producing election results that have the public acceptance that demo-

---

*Raymond Bonner and Josh Barbanel, "Democrats Rue Ballot Foul-Up in a 2nd County," *The New York Times*, November 17, 2000.

cratic stability requires. . . . It suffices to say that the issuance of the stay
suggests that a majority of the Court, while not deciding the issues presented, believe that the petitioner has a substantial probability of success.

These sentences exposed the flagrantly political and authoritarian thinking behind the Court's halting of the vote count. Above all, Scalia was
anxious about Bush's "legitimacy" and how public opinion would perceive it. He presumed both that the uncounted votes were of "questionable legality" and that they would be cast for Gore. His use of the phrase
"democratic stability" was telling: democracy was less his concern than
his notion of stability, which he believed was up to the Court to ensure
by imposing itself as the final arbiter of the election. He made it plain
that the result was foreordained.

On December 11, the Supreme Court heard arguments. David Boies,
the prominent litigator who had been the chief presenter of the Gore
case in Florida but had never appeared before the Supreme Court, was
chosen to make the case there rather than Laurence Tribe, the Harvard
constitutional law professor who was experienced as a Supreme Court
advocate and had been prepared to present the argument. For Bush,
Theodore Olson, who had argued many cases before the Court, was
given the responsibility for this one. Olson claimed that counting all the
hitherto uncounted votes violated the Equal Protection Clause of the
Fourteenth Amendment because they would be tallied by different standards in different counties. (Tribe had written in his brief that "it is the
exclusion of these ballots, not their inclusion, that would raise questions
of unequal treatment."*) Associate Justice Ruth Bader Ginsberg provided
a cogent reply to Olson: "How can you have one standard when there are
so many varieties of ballots?" Associate Justice David Souter asked Boies
what standard he would recommend to the Florida courts, and Boies
froze. There the arguments ended. In Florida, the state legislature prepared to vote the next day on a resolution that would authorize it to appoint a new slate of electors.

At 10 p.m. on December 12 the Supreme Court issued its decision. In
a 5–4 vote, with William Rehnquist, Antonin Scalia, Clarence Thomas,
Sandra Day O'Connor, and Anthony Kennedy in the majority, it reversed the state court's ruling on a recount on the grounds of the "absence of specific standards to ensure its equal application," asserting that
the "desire for speed is not a general excuse for ignoring equal protection

*Toobin, *Too Close to Call*, p. 260.

guarantees." The votes had to have been tabulated at the latest by that very day, December 12, it claimed, a date that any new remedy of the Florida Supreme Court could not meet, so it ordered the halt of vote counting. "Because it is evident that any recount seeking to meet the December 12 date will be unconstitutional for the reasons we have discussed, *we reverse the judgment of the Supreme Court of Florida* ordering a recount to proceed."

Reasoning and motive aside, the Florida court had not, in fact, set December 12 as the deadline. It had set no deadline whatsoever. It had simply said "forthwith." Nor did federal law stipulate this so-called safe-harbor date. Indeed, in 1960, Hawaii, after a court-ordered recount, did not declare John F. Kennedy the winner of the state's election until December 28. Associate Justice Stephen Breyer had suggested a "safe harbor" date of December 18, but the majority wrote that this date "contemplates action in violation of the Florida election code," although there was no deadline in the code. "There was no December 12 deadline," observed Jed Rubenfeld, professor of constitutional law at Yale University. "The majority made it up. On this pretense, the presidential election was determined."*

There was a fillip to the decision: it would be "limited to the present circumstances." That is, it would have no further standing; it could serve as precedent and authority for no other decision. With *Bush v. Gore*, the entire edifice of legal philosophy that the conservatives on the Court had argued for over the years was contradicted. "The Supreme Court of the United States does not sit to announce 'unique' dispositions," Scalia had written in a 1996 case, *United States v. Virginia*, and his writings elaborated his fervent belief in the principles of precedent, tradition, and adherence to the textual Constitution. Associate Justice Clarence Thomas, who always echoed Scalia, had written, the "Equal Protection Clause shields only against purposeful discrimination: A disparate impact, even upon members of a racial minority, the classification of which we have been most suspect, does not violate equal protection."† Associate Justice Anthony Kennedy was also renowned for his belief in precedent. Associate Justice Sandra Day O'Connor, having been a state senator and judge, had gone out of her way in the past to defer to state legislatures and

---

*Jed Rubenfeld, "Not as Bad as Plessy, Worse," in Bruce Ackerman, ed., *Bush v. Gore*, Yale University Press, 2002, p. 26.

†Cited in Alan Dershowitz, *Supreme Injustice: How the High Court Hijacked Election 2000*, Oxford University Press, 2001, p. 147.

courts, and she consistently ruled against intrusion of the Supreme Court into political matters.

Chief Justice Rehnquist, as a champion of "state sovereignty" and the Tenth Amendment, always favored states' rights, and he chastised other justices for having "produced a syndrome wherein this Court seems to regard the Equal Protection Clause as a cat-o'-nine tails to be kept in the judicial closet as a threat to legislatures which may, in the view of the judiciary, get out of hand and pass 'arbitrary,' 'illogical,' or 'unreasonable' laws."* But then, Rehnquist was also ruthlessly results-oriented. "Don't bother so much with the reasoning," he once remarked to another justice.†

The arbitrary nature of the Supreme Court's ruling and its sharp contradiction to the usual conservative position of the five justices naturally aroused questions about their political motives. Was the majority's decision intended to ensure that conservatives would be sustained and increased on the Court by appointments of a Republican president? Did the decision involve ambitions to be Chief Justice? Both Scalia and Kennedy were widely reported to harbor just such a desire. And Scalia, for his part, had gone out of his way to bully colleagues in their deliberations on *Bush v. Gore*. When he read a draft of Justice Ginsberg's opinion, which included references to press reports about equal protection violations against black voters by local and state officials, he accused her of "Al Sharpton tactics," comparing her to the notorious black demagogue from New York, and she removed the discussion of race from her opinion.‡

Chief Justice Rehnquist, who was reported to wish to retire, was on the Supreme Court in the first place as a consequence of Nixon's "Southern strategy" to incorporate conservative Southern voters into a new Republican coalition. Nixon had nominated two extraordinary mediocrities with segregationist pasts, Clement Haynesworth and G. Harrold Carswell, both rejected by the Senate, before he named Rehnquist, of whom he had no knowledge and whom he called "Renchberg," but his aide John Ehrlichman informed him that the unknown from Arizona was "to the right of Pat Buchanan."§ As a law clerk to Justice Robert Jackson in 1952, Rehnquist had written a memo in favor of

*Cited in Dershowitz, *Supreme Injustice*, p. 144.

†Ibid., p. 142.

‡Toobin, *Too Close to Call*, p. 267.

§See John Dean, *The Rehnquist Choice: The Untold Story of the Nixon Appointment That Redefined the Supreme Court*, Free Press, 2001.

upholding segregation: "I think *Plessy v. Ferguson* was right and should be reaffirmed." In the early 1960s, he had personally harassed minority voters in Arizona as part of a local Republican Party "ballot security" campaign. He had also owned a home with a restrictive covenant forbidding its sale to "any member of the Hebrew race."* In the Senate hearings on his nomination, Rehnquist denied that his memo for Justice Jackson reflected his own views and claimed it was written to Jackson's specifications, but other former law clerks said this was a lie that smeared Jackson. Rehnquist's use of the Equal Protection Clause in *Bush v. Gore* was another case of not bothering much with the reasoning.

Justice O'Connor, who had been the Republican state senate floor leader in Arizona, was also said to be contemplating retirement. Various reporters told of her private remarks before the decision. One wrote:

> The day of the Supreme Court's first opinion on the election (December 4), O'Connor and her husband had attended a party for about thirty people at the home of a wealthy couple, Lee and Julie Folger. When the subject of the election controversy came up, Justice O'Connor was livid. "You just don't know what those Gore people have been doing," she said. "They went into a nursing home and registered people that they shouldn't have. It was outrageous." It was unclear where the justice had picked up this unproved accusation, which had circulated only in the more eccentric right-wing outlets, but O'Connor recounted the story with fervor. Similarly, on election night Justice O'Connor and her husband had attended a party at the home of Mary Ann Stoessel, the widow of a prominent diplomat. When the states looked like they were not falling in place for Gore, Justice O'Connor said, "This is terrible," and she hastened away from the television, which was located in a basement den. Her husband, John, explained her reaction to the partygoers, saying, "She's very disappointed because she was hoping to retire"—that is, with a Republican president to appoint her successor.†

In his dissent in *Bush v. Gore*, Justice Stevens wrote, "Although we may never know with complete certainty the identity of the winner of this year's presidential election, the identity of the loser is perfectly clear. It is the nation's confidence in the judge as an impartial guardian of the

---

*Dershowitz, *Supreme Injustice*, p. 243.

†Toobin, *Too Close to Call*, pp. 248–49. See also Evan Thomas and Michael Isikoff, "The Truth Behind the Pillars," *Newsweek*, December 25, 2000.

rule of law." The next day, Al Gore conceded to George Bush and called for national unity. The public response to Bush's having been made president by judicial fiat was muted.

Many months later, in April and in November 2001, media organizations released various reports of the way ballots in Florida might have been counted. In six out of nine possible different scenarios, Gore would have won. And what would have happened if the Supreme Court had refused to take *Bush v. Gore* and returned it to Florida's Supreme Court? No one can say for certain, but it is certain that the case would, in turn, have been remanded to Leon County Circuit Court Judge Terry Lewis, and Lewis would very likely have ordered the counting of overvotes— those marked for more than one candidate but where the intent was clear—as well as undervotes. "I'd be open to that," he told *The Orlando Sentinel* a year after the election.* In another interview he said, "I would have addressed that issue. . . . Logically, everything the Florida Supreme Court said was, 'You have to look at the clear intent of the voter.' Logically, if you can look at a ballot and see, this is a vote for Bush or this is a vote for Gore, then you would have to count it. . . . Logically, why wouldn't you count it?"† In one media scenario in which the overvotes were counted, Gore would have won by 171 votes.

The five Supreme Court justices who determined the outcome of *Bush v. Gore* did not specify who or what was being denied equal protection that required their intervention. Ultimately, who was being denied his or her rights? This issue at the heart of the matter continued to be investigated and adjudicated over the course of the following year.

On June 8, 2001, the U.S. Civil Rights Commission, after extensive hearings, approved a report on "Election Practices in Florida During the 2000 Campaign." (Two Republican members of the eight-member commission dissented.) The report stated:

> The Commission's findings make one thing clear: widespread voter disenfranchisement—not the dead-heat contest—was the extraordinary feature in the Florida election. . . . The disenfranchisement of Florida's voters fell most harshly on the shoulders of black voters. The magnitude of the impact can be seen from any of several perspectives:

*David Damron and Roger Roy, "Both Teams Misjudged Strategy to Win Recount," *The Orlando Sentinel*, November 12, 2001.
†Michael Isikoff, "The Final Word?" *Newsweek*, November 19, 2001.

- Statewide, based upon county-level statistical estimates, black voters were nearly 10 times more likely than non-black voters to have their ballots rejected.
- Estimates indicate that approximately 14.4 percent of Florida's black voters cast ballots that were rejected. This compares with approximately 1.6 percent of non-black Florida voters who did not have their presidential votes counted.
- Statistical analysis shows that the disparity in ballot spoilage rates—i.e., ballots cast but not counted—between black and non-black voters is not the result of education or literacy differences.

. . . After carefully and fully examining all the evidence, the Commission found a strong basis for concluding that violations of Section 2 of the Voting Rights Act (VRA) occurred in Florida. . . . The state's highest officials responsible for ensuring efficiency, uniformity, and fairness in the election failed to fulfill their responsibilities and were subsequently unwilling to take responsibility.

After the U.S. Supreme Court ruling, the NAACP and other civil rights groups sued the state of Florida and seven counties in it for violating voting rights. On September 3, 2002, a settlement was negotiated in which the state acknowledged the grievances and agreed to far-reaching reform of election practices. No one knows exactly how many black voters were improperly scrubbed from the rolls or how many ballots marked with clear intent were not counted. But certainly there were more than enough of those ballots to have elected Gore if they had been. Yet the Supreme Court, citing the Fourteenth Amendment, a constitutional guarantee obtained after the Civil War and granting blacks the full rights of citizenship, had denied those Americans their franchise.

The election of 2000 was the last battle of the Clinton wars. These wars were waged between a Democratic Party revived under the leadership of Bill Clinton, who had reordered the progressive tradition and the office of the presidency to meet the demands of postindustrial and post–Cold War America, and the Republican Party and the conservative movement, which had attempted to frustrate and ultimately overthrow Clinton's effort to reinvent liberalism and to deploy a renewed government. The wars had begun in Clinton's 1990 campaign for the governorship of Arkansas, when Republican Party chairman Lee Atwater had sought to derail him. They had heightened in the 1992 campaign. And on the day of Clinton's inauguration in 1993, the wars had entered a new phase, as the Republicans contested his legitimacy. In 1994, when the Republicans, led by Newt Gingrich, succeeded in gaining control of the Congress, the Speaker of the House proclaimed himself virtual head of state. But President Clinton's adroit handling of the Republicans discredited them with the public and paved the way for his reelection in 1996. The Republican campaigns against Clinton inexorably continued, now commanded by Kenneth W. Starr. After years of failing to discover wrongdoing on the part of the President and the First Lady, Starr colluded with the lawyers for the politically driven and bogus Paula Jones case to force a constitutional crisis. The House of Representatives, whipped up by the de facto Republican leader, Tom DeLay, impeached the President on spurious partisan grounds. The Senate acquitted him.

Despite the relentless Republican war against him and the media hysteria, President Clinton forged the most progressive record of achievement in two generations, since John F. Kennedy and Lyndon Johnson. Here was a platform on which his vice president, Al Gore, could run for president and, from time to time, did. And even though Gore became distracted by the sustained attacks on his character, he won the election—not only the national popular vote but also, apparently, the vote in Florida, which was never fully counted. This Florida outcome, which should have elected Gore president, was stopped by the Republican Party operation and, finally, by the intervention of the conservatives on the U.S. Supreme Court. Bush became president with the only vote that counted: 5–4. He was installed, not elected.

The outcome of the 2000 election turned on many factors. But above all, it was the latest, most spectacular, and most consequential case of the systematic abridgment of black voting rights since the era of Jim Crow. Inevitably, historians will be left to question the legitimacy of Bush's ascension to the presidency.

In 1824, John Quincy Adams had come in second to Andrew Jackson in the popular vote in a four-man race in which no candidate had an Electoral College majority. As prescribed by the Constitution, the House of Representatives decided the outcome. Jackson protested because the fourth-place finisher, Henry Clay, had thrown his support to Adams, but the law was followed to the letter. In 1876, the Republicans manipulated the contested states and cut a deal with Southern Democrats, ending Reconstruction behind closed doors to put Rutherford B. Hayes in the presidency. In 1888, Benjamin Harrison lost the popular vote narrowly to President Grover Cleveland but won the Electoral College vote, and there was no controversial aftermath to his election.

In 2000, the procedure that was followed departed from that stipulated in the Constitution. The aftermath was as fraught with political exploitation as that of 1876, and each involved chicanery in Florida and the suppression of civil rights. In 2000 the U.S. Supreme Court imposed itself to determine the result, casting a shadow on its majority's impartiality. In the case of the 2000 election, two branches of the federal government, as well as the state government in Florida, were directly besmirched. Historians may disagree over whether Hayes or Bush had less legitimacy, but none may study the election of 2000 and fail to raise the question.

SEVENTEEN

The Sands of Time

I

On the day the U.S. Supreme Court handed down its decision in *Bush v. Gore*, President Clinton flew to London for his last foreign visit, and I went as part of the traveling staff. On December 14, we stood on the soggy grass of Hyde Park, whipped by a cold wind, waiting to strap ourselves into the military helicopters that would fly us to Coventry, discussing the stolen election, feeling bereft.

At the University of Warwick, the President delivered a lengthy farewell address on the "global social contract." He spoke positively of all the initiatives that he and Blair had worked on together: "More open markets, public investments by wealthy nations in education, health care and the environment in developing countries, and improved governance in those countries themselves." But he warned again of the dangers lurking in the possibilities of globalization: "This open society becomes more vulnerable to cross-national, multinational, organized forces of destruction: terrorists; weapons of mass destruction; the marriage of technology in these weapons, small-scale chemical and biological and maybe even nuclear weapons; narco traffickers and organized criminals, and increasingly, all these people sort of working together in lines that are quite blurred."

In discussing the false, antiquated belief that economic growth requires pollution and will inevitably release the greenhouse gases that produce global warming, the President made a general comment about the oppressive weight of obsolete thinking: "As Victor Hugo said, 'There's nothing more powerful than an idea whose time has come.' The reverse is also true: there's no bigger curse than a big idea that hangs on after its time has gone. And so, I hope all of you will think about that." Clinton had opened a vista of things to come, and his commentary on Hugo was a warning about the oppressive weight of the ossified past on the future.

Several of us, in a final display of esprit de corps, dashed from the hall through the rain to the buses that would take us to the airport. "It's time for us to go!" we shouted. Soaked, as the motorcade pulled away, I looked out the window to see Tony Blair standing there waving. He pointed at me and I pointed back and waved. He shrugged. Now he was left to deal with a very different president.

On *Air Force One*, on the long, last ride home, the President, Hillary, Mark Penn, and I reviewed the painful twists and turns in the presidential campaign and the postelection struggle in Florida. While we talked about what might have been done differently, Clinton played cards with Chelsea. He ran through every scenario, every standard for counting Florida's votes. Then, as we were still talking and with much more to say, the plane landed.

At the Christmas party that week at the Vice President's residence at the Naval Observatory, the Christmas tree was brightly decorated and a choir singing carols greeted the guests just as if it were a normal festive holiday celebration. But for everyone there, Gore's most fervent supporters, the election result was still unsettling and the mood was strained. Across Massachusetts Avenue, a few pro-Gore stragglers from the campaign stood on the street corner holding hand-lettered signs declaring him the true president. The band inside the tent played cheery melodies and the tables were spread with goodies. After the speeches, Gore told me he still couldn't really believe what had happened.

On December 21, he met with President Clinton in the Oval Office, where the two of them thrashed out their feelings. Gore explained where he thought Clinton had been a liability, and the President, in turn, laid out his ideas on how things might have gone differently in the campaign. Gore told me the next day that the meeting had ended with them "patching everything up." We discussed presidential elections where the winner of the popular vote did not become president, and he said he intended to run again. I replied that he could become the first person since the passage of the Twenty-second Amendment to be elected three times, and he laughed.

After the election and the Supreme Court decision, the atmosphere at the White House was of a strange transition. Hillary said that she felt "schizophrenic," neither here nor there. She was still the First Lady and she was also the senator-elect from New York. She was moving out and moving in. On January 3, 2001, she took the oath of office in the well of the Senate, with Vice President Gore swearing her in. The President stood next to her, wearing a button reading, "Hillary." When she walked down the corridors to a party of her supporters being given at the Russell Senate Building, reporters shouted to get her attention: "Mrs. Clinton! Mrs. Clinton!" Then they changed: "Senator Clinton! Senator Clinton!"

On January 6, the President and the First Lady gave a party under a white tent pitched on the South Lawn for everyone who had worked in the White House with them over the eight years. The Clintons rode the short distance from the White House down to the tent in the bus they had driven in the 1992 campaign. Inside the tent, amid the crowd, I encountered Bill Daley, who had been Gore's campaign chairman. We talked about Florida. He said that before the deadlock there, he had observed that if Jeb were his brother, there'd be no way he'd lose the state. "It was predictable," he said resignedly.

At that very moment, Gore as vice president was presiding over the formal count of the Electoral College vote before the joint session of Congress that declared George W. Bush the next president. As he went through the ritual, the entire congressional Black Caucus, joined by Democratic representatives from Florida, stood to protest. They tried to lodge a formal objection to the proceedings, but since not a single senator would sign their petition, it could only be a symbolic gesture. "We keep hearing, 'Get over this.' We will never get over this," said Representative Corrine Brown, who represented the voters of Jacksonville, Florida, tens of thousands of whose ballots had been discarded and not recounted. "The Supreme Court selected George W. Bush as president—he was not elected." Black representatives raised objection after objection. When Representative Jesse Jackson, Jr., of Illinois broke in, Gore replied, "The chair thanks the gentleman from Illinois, but, hey." Representative Alcee Hastings of Florida shouted, "We did all we could." "The chair thanks the gentleman from Florida," said Gore.

In the tent on the South Lawn, the lights dimmed and a valedictory video documentary was projected highlighting the achievements of Clinton's presidency. Then Gore arrived from his sad duty at the Senate. Hillary spoke, saying that he was the winner of the election. Defiant cheers underscored her comments. The President said that the rule of law had been twisted. And Gore as vice president, he went on, had been there every day in every way and had been a part of all the important accomplishments. He had no idea how he would have responded to the

Supreme Court decision or what he would have said about it, the President said, but no one could have done better than Gore in the gracious concession speech he had given. Betty Currie and Nancy Hernreich, the President's personal secretaries, mounted the stage together and announced a surprise: the curtain came up unveiling Fleetwood Mac. The band launched full-blast into "Don't Stop Thinking About Tomorrow," the 1992 Clinton campaign's theme song.

Before the election had turned into a deadlock, almost everyone in the White House believed that Gore would win. The continuity was assumed; Clinton's achievements were to be the foundation for the next four years. Now we were left to applaud with restrained bitterness Gore's dignity in the face of humiliation. Our cheering rose in crescendos to affirm the work that we had all contributed and that was at an end. We could only celebrate the past because the future was lost.

II

"Sometimes time is your friend," President Clinton observed, citing the case of Northern Ireland. "Sometimes time is your enemy," and he pointed to the Middle East. And about the peace negotiations there, he said in early 2000, "Sometimes I wish I were a psychologist. It's just not rational. It's just not rational."

The diplomatic efforts that the President had shepherded ever since taking office reached a critical point in 2000, when it was time to achieve a final-status agreement between the Palestinians and the Israelis. The foundation of the diplomacy was the Oslo Accords, secretly negotiated with Norwegian guidance and eventually signed in a ceremony on the South Lawn of the White House on September 13, 1993, when the President had coaxed Yitzhak Rabin and Yasser Arafat to shake hands. Those accords specified the ultimate goals of Israeli security and Palestinian self-rule.

Prime Minister Rabin, the skeptical and tough former general who had been Israeli Defense Force chief of staff during the Six Days War, had come to believe that only a "hard peace" could guarantee Israel's future safety. When on November 5, 1995, a right-wing Jewish religious zealot assassinated him, Clinton's resolve to achieve an Israeli-Palestinian peace only deepened. He pressed forward with Shimon Peres, the new prime minister, as Palestinian groups began suicide bombings in Israel.

In the Israeli election in May 1996, Benjamin "Bibi" Netanyahu of the right-wing Likud Party, who had campaigned against Oslo, won victory, but as prime minister he grudgingly became a participant in the ongoing negotiations. His reluctance, however, stretched out to years the progress that should have been compressed into months. In 1998, Clinton invited Netanyahu and Arafat to an isolated lodge in Wye, Maryland, and personally took charge of the diplomacy. Netanyahu openly disparaged Arafat, and Foreign Minister Ariel Sharon refused to address him in anything but the third person, but Clinton indignantly insisted that they maintain a respectful tone, which Rabin and Peres had managed. "That's ridiculous," he told Netanyahu about his behavior in front of all those at Wye. With his partly calculated rebuke, the President shook up the negotiations, and the participants moved toward an agreement on new timetables for final-status talks.

On May 17, 1999, after Ehud Barak, a former general and leader of the Labor Party, was elected prime minister, in his first telephone call with President Clinton he expressed his ambition to finish what Rabin had started. He saw himself as completing a mission that had begun with David Ben-Gurion, Israel's first prime minister: to create peace between Israel and its neighbors.

Contrary to advice from the Clinton national security team, Barak decided to negotiate first with the Syrians rather than the Palestinians. He held a summit of misunderstanding with the Syrian foreign minister on January 9, 2000, in Shepherdstown, West Virginia—misunderstanding because he came with no intention of withdrawing to the Syrian-Israeli border of *before* the Six Day War of 1967, while the Syrians mistakenly believed he would. President Clinton later met with Syria's leader, Hafez al-Assad, but he could not restore those wrecked negotiations. Assad died in May 2000, and the Syrian track closed for good.

On May 15, Israel's Independence Day, the West Bank erupted in violence and two Palestinians died. Barak's political stability, as well as Arafat's, was threatened. When Barak's negotiating plans were leaked to the Israeli press, he was convinced that the source was his foreign minister, David Levy, a member of the Likud Party. He asked for another summit meeting, a "pressure cooker," he called it, where all the delegates were contained in a protected environment and the necessary diplomatic give-and-take could occur without any danger of leaks or press coverage. President Clinton agreed, convening a summit on July 11 at Camp David to achieve a final-status accord.

Once there, Barak unveiled his proposals for a divided Jerusalem—a breathtaking reversal of previously untouchable policy on the holy city that was the Israeli capital. Clinton had not been told beforehand of this plan, which came as a surprise both to him and to the Palestinians. But without advance warning, there was little the President could do to work with the other Arab nations to help ensure that Arafat would ultimately accept this daring proposal, and the pressure that might have been applied on him to accept was therefore absent.

On the eleventh day at Camp David, the President was scheduled to go to Okinawa for the G-8 economic summit, but both Israelis and Palestinians pleaded for the talks to continue. Clinton flew to Asia, put in a perfunctory appearance at the G-8 meeting, and returned. Back in his Aspen Lodge at Camp David, he brought the chief negotiators together again to pore over a map of Jerusalem; then he charged them to make a list of the sixty-four civil functions of the jurisdiction and how they would be apportioned between the Israelis and the Palestinians. Sovereignty was an abstraction; Clinton asked them to deal with the concrete realities. He wanted to know who was going to pick up the garbage. The negotiators made a list with sixty-one of the sixty-four civil tasks assigned. In practical terms, the division of Jerusalem was workable.

At Camp David, Barak was taking a more radical position than any Israeli leader had ever done before him: he was willing to consider a Palestinian state with four cantons and with Palestinian control over parts of Jerusalem. The more he gave, the greater the political stress at home, for he had promised that he would submit any settlement to the Israeli people in a referendum for approval. To encourage and support the concessions, President Clinton pledged that he would go to Israel to campaign for the referendum. And to Arafat, he promised that he would personally travel around the world to raise tens of billions of dollars for Palestine's economic development. These numbers were not chimerical; there was no doubt that in the event of a final accord, Clinton could indeed secure such sums for investment from the United States, Europe, the Arab states, and Japan.

But as Barak conceded more and more, Arafat became more and more passive. He made no counterproposal. Other members of the Palestinian delegation told President Clinton that they wanted to accept the deal, but on July 25 Arafat rejected it, insisting on the right of return of all Palestinian refugees to their original homes in Israel. This old Palestinian dogma was central to the argument against Israel as an illegitimate usurper nation, and he knew that it would be rejected.

Immediately, a new wave of Palestinian violence broke over the West

Bank. Arafat made no effort to tamp it down. He must have believed that it worked to his advantage, but it soon spun out of control. On September 29, Ariel Sharon, now the leader of Likud, bulled his way with party followers to the al-Aqsa mosque, the most holy Muslim shrine in Jerusalem, setting off a riot. With that provocation the so-called al-Aqsa intifada began against Israel.

On December 18, Israeli and Palestinian negotiators reconvened in Washington for a last effort to secure a peace agreement. By now, the toll from the intifada stood at 330 people, 224 of whom were Palestinians. President Clinton brought both sides to the Cabinet Room in the White House and formally read to them terms that had been worked out for a final settlement. The main elements were: The Palestinians would gain control of 95 percent of the West Bank and all of the Gaza Strip, whose size would be increased by one-third, and a safe land link between the two would be established; the Arab sections of East Jerusalem would become the capital of the new Palestinian state; Palestinians would have authority over Muslim holy places in Jerusalem; Israel would withdraw from sixty-three settlements on the West Bank; and Palestinian refugees would have the right to resettle in the new state and receive compensation from a $30-billion reparation fund. (This amount did not include the tens of billions Clinton had promised he would raise for economic development.)

"The only answer I want is 'Yes' or 'No,' " said the President. "Will you accept these parameters for final negotiation?"

Once again, the Palestinian diplomats urgently told Clinton they wanted to accept the plan, but Arafat would not let them. So the delegations left Washington. On January 2, 2001, Arafat rejected the formula and reasserted the right of return to a Palestine embracing all of Israel. Thus, President Clinton's effort at forging peace in the Middle East came to its conclusion.

The European Union convened another Palestinian-Israeli meeting in Taba, Egypt, where Barak made additional marginal concessions, but that negotiation ended with only a vague joint statement released after Clinton left office. It was an event after the fact, as it were. Then the intifada whipped into a storm of carnage. On February 6, with Barak's hopes and credibility in tatters, Sharon was elected prime minister.

Over five years, Yasser Arafat signed four agreements with the Israeli governments. Despite the often self-defeating frustrations he fostered, he had in fact kept his part of these bargains. But in the end, he saw himself as the chief of an insurgent movement and by nature was a temporizer, not a leader—always seeking a better deal, willing to sacrifice the whole for living to play another day, as he had always done. Rather than seeing ahead, he was looking over his shoulder at his more militant rivals, who he knew were capable of assassinating him. He had survived in a world of conflict without end. Without conflict what would become of him? Arafat could not reconcile himself to a Palestinian state with normal politics. Almost two years after the negotiations had ended with his refusal to make a counterproposal at Camp David and his unwillingness in principle to approve the President's terms in Washington, amid spiraling suicide bombings and retaliations, Arafat said he would have accepted the terms at Taba. But Taba existed in a vacuum, without President Clinton to move it forward and with Arafat already having wrecked the peace negotiations. Abba Eban, Israeli foreign minister from 1966 to 1974, was referring to Arafat when he had remarked that the Palestinian leadership never missed an opportunity to miss an opportunity.

On January 17, Arafat had his last telephone conversation with President Clinton. He thanked him for all he had done and told him he was "a great man."

"The hell I am," said Clinton. "I'm a colossal failure, and you made me one."

The Israelis and Palestinians would have to find another time to make peace—and another American president committed to it.

III

The coming of the end spurred the President to issue a raft of executive orders. On January 6, 2000, the President issued an executive order stipulating new protections for almost sixty million acres of federal forests covering thirty-eight states, the biggest land conservation act in decades. Since the previous June, when he had announced four new national monuments in Utah and Arizona, he had steadily used his powers to protect the environment. Now he issued new executive orders to protect migratory birds, the Hawaiian Islands coral reef ecosystem, and wilderness trails. He had placed under federal protection more land in the contiguous forty-eight states than any previous president.

On January 15, he sent a statement to the new 107th Congress on "The Unfinished Work on Building One America." It concisely formulated much of the work that still remained to be done: "Raise the minimum wage, provide more child care assistance, and health care coverage to the working poor by covering those whose children are already covered under the Children's Health Insurance Program (CHIP). We should also expand the Family and Medical Leave Act, so more parents can succeed at home and at work. We should make sure women receive equal pay for equal work." And there was more: construction of new schools to reduce class size; more after-school programs; more health care for Native Americans; more investment in training, education, and English training programs for immigrants. More, more, more.

And there should be new legislation: bans on racial profiling; the End Discrimination in Employment Act. More, more, more . . .

Lastly:

> If ever there was a doubt about the importance of exercising the most fundamental right of citizenship, it was clearly answered by the first presidential election of the 21st century. No American will ever again be able to seriously say, "My vote doesn't count." That election also revealed serious flaws in the mechanics of voting, and brought up disturbing allegations of voter intimidation that we thought were relics of the past. . . .
> Recommendation: Appoint a non-partisan Presidential Commission on election reform to ensure a fair, inclusive and uniform system of voting standards, prevent voter suppression and intimidation and increase voter participation. Declare election day a national holiday. Give ex-offenders who have repaid their debt to society the chance to earn back the right to vote.

Inevitably, there were final legal matters that had to be decided. President Clinton worked with the White House legal counsel and the Justice Department on pardons, for he believed he had not issued enough pardons during his presidency, which reflected poorly on the quality of his mercy. (He had granted only 250, far fewer than the presidents he most admired and a small number even compared to Richard Nixon's 926.) The pardon power is granted by the Constitution solely to the president, so it is removed from congressional politics or prosecutorial reach. Alexander Hamilton, in *Federalist Paper* Number 74, wrote, "Humanity and good policy conspire to dictate, that the benign prerogative of pardoning should be as little as possible fettered or embarrassed." George Washington issued the first pardon, to a convicted rumrunner. Abraham Lincoln issued many to deserters in the Civil War. Roosevelt gave out 3,687 pardons, Woodrow Wilson 2,480, and Harry Truman 2,044. Jimmy Carter pardoned thousands of Vietnam War draft evaders who had fled the country, as well as Peter Yarrow of the folk group Peter, Paul, and Mary for taking "immoral liberties" with a fourteen-year-old girl. George H. W. Bush pardoned Armand Hammer, the oilman who had made illegal contributions to Richard Nixon's 1972 campaign; a Pakistani heroin smuggler; the Reagan administration officials like Oliver North and John Poindexter, who had been convicted in the Iran-Contra scandal; and Orlando Bosch, an anti-Castro terrorist jailed for illegal entry into the United States, whom the Justice Department wanted to deport because of his advocacy of violence* Nixon had given a pardon to convicted Teamsters president Jimmy Hoffa. In the end, Clinton granted a total of only 395 pardons during his presidency.

The petitioners all had lawyers, relatives, and clergymen pressing their cases. Former President Carter wrote a letter on behalf of Patty Hearst, the kidnapped heiress turned bank robber, and she was granted one of the 140 presidential pardons and 36 commutations that President Clinton issued on his last day in office. Lady Bird Johnson and Walter Cronkite pleaded for a Texas banker who had been convicted of receiving bribes. The singer Don Henley asked for a pardon for a convicted illegal gambler. I passed on a letter from Arthur Schlesinger, Jr., urging a pardon for Samuel Loring Morrison, a former naval intelligence officer guilty of espionage for leaking classified satellite photos to a magazine. One of those seeking a pardon was a commodities broker named Marc Rich, who lived in Switzerland as a fugitive, who had fled the country under indictment for tax fraud and trading with the enemy (in his case, dealing in oil with Iran). Rich had hired Jack Quinn, who had been the White House legal counsel earlier in the administration. Quinn made the case that no one had ever been charged criminally for what Rich was alleged to have done, and he submitted briefs written on his client's behalf by Rich's previous attorneys—Leonard Garment, former White House counsel to President Nixon, and I. Lewis "Scooter" Libby, who had already been named as Vice President-elect Cheney's chief of staff; the briefs argued that Rich was innocent of tax violations and had been wrongly charged. Rich, like every petitioner, mounted a campaign for his pardon, though in his case he had more resources. King Juan Carlos of Spain wrote a personal letter. Rich's former wife, Denise, who was a large contributor to the Clintons' campaigns, also pled for her ex-husband. Many prominent Jewish leaders asked for his pardon. But the most influ-

*On Bush's pardons, see Joe Conason, "The Bush Pardons," *Salon.com*, February 27, 2001, http://archive.salon.com/news/col/cona/2001/02/27/pardons /print.html.

ential one to weigh in was Prime Minister Ehud Barak of Israel, who asked the President for a pardon for Rich in three separate telephone conversations.

At this particular juncture, the Middle East peace negotiations were failing after the collapse of negotiations at Camp David, and Barak was facing a difficult election campaign. Rich's "philanthropic contributions," which Barak referred to in his first conversation with the President on December 11, included millions of dollars in support of projects in Palestinian areas undertaken at the behest of the Israeli government. In short, Rich was a financier of the peace process. On January 8, 2000, Barak said, "I believe it [the pardon] could be important not just financially, but he helped Mossad [the Israeli intelligence agency] in more than one case." (Among those who wrote letters to Clinton asking for Rich's pardon was the former head of Mossad.)

"It's a bizarre case, and I am working on it," replied Clinton.

"Okay, I really appreciate it," Barak said. On January 19, Barak called again. "The question is not whether he should get it or not," the President explained, "but whether he should get it without coming back here. That's the dilemma I'm working through." Clinton resolved the tangle because he eventually agreed that the charges against Rich should have been considered as civil, not criminal, ones; he pardoned him on the criminal charges but specifically stipulated that Rich had to waive the statute of limitations on all as yet unspecified civil charges (the tax-evasion ones), which would allow for further prosecution of them by the government even after the pardon.

A concatenation of pseudoscandals, a last burst of media frenzy, would continue for weeks after President Clinton left the White House. The new president's press secretary, Ari Fleischer, pumped up these controversies in order to tarnish the departing Democrat and burnish the image of the Republican, who still bore the scars of Florida. Bush's White House press office put out to pliant reporters false stories that the Clinton staff had trashed *Air Force One* and the White House itself—later disproved by a Government Accounting Office investigation. Other reports had it that the Clintons had accepted $190,000 in gifts in their final days to avoid Hillary's new Senate gift requirements, whereas in fact these presents from friends had accumulated over eight years and were roughly the same amount as the preceding Bushes had accepted. The Rich pardon, which was involved with the foreign policy of the Middle East as well as being a matter of complicated law, was turned into a pseudoscandal suggesting that Clinton had been bribed. But, in August 2001, when Congressman Dan Burton in his investigation was handed the transcripts made by the National Security Council of Prime Minister Barak's conversations with President Clinton, his accusatory tone was thoroughly dampened and his little-noticed final report, issued in March 2002, alleged no wrongdoing.*

During his last weeks in office, the president also held small meetings to discuss his future work. A long postpresidency loomed. He had ambitious plans for his presidential library in Little Rock. He was about to establish a graduate school in public service at the University of Arkansas. And he wanted to continue his political efforts for progressive governance.

I had my own lingering legal problem to resolve: Jackie's and my suit against Drudge for his defamation back in 1997. Jackie and I believed that we would certainly win it, but we came to see it as detritus from the past. The case had been on the back burner for years, and it seemed now mainly to serve the purposes of the attention-seeking Drudge. When the judge ruled in November 2000 that we could not depose him directly but had to conduct more than a dozen other depositions before we could put Drudge under oath, that requirement put a heavy financial burden on us. By the end of 2000, we had no savings and were paying college tuition for our younger son. Drudge evidently had access to an endless amount of money to finance his defense, provided through conservative front groups by Richard Mellon Scaife.† Most important, the suit gave Drudge the oxygen of publicity he thrived on. It was time to cut that supply off.

Throughout the spring of 2001 we sought, through the magistrate appointed by the judge to settle the matter, to obtain a simple apology from Drudge. The magistrate composed one. But Drudge refused to sign it, and we decided eventually that we could not convince him to act decently. He even threatened us with a lawsuit of his own to recover his lawyer's expenses for making a trip to Washington. We paid $2,500 for his nuisance value, to prevent him from creating a false controversy by

*See Eric Boehlert, "The Clintons' Gift Rap," *Salon.com*, January 30, 2001, http://archive.salon.com/politics/feature/2001/01/30/clinton/index.html; Kerry Lauerman and Alicia Montgomery, "The White House Vandal Scandal That Wasn't: How the Incoming Bush Team Nudge-Nudged a Credulous Press Corps into Swallowing a Trashy Clinton Story," *Salon.com*, May 23, 2001, http://archive.salon.com/politics/feature/2001/05/23/vandals/index.html.

†Scaife was the principal funder of the right-wing groups that ran Drudge's defense—the Center for the Study of Popular Culture, and the Individual Rights Foundation.

filing a suit, and we dropped our own suit in May. He was furious when we terminated the case, running screeds on his website excoriating the press for ignoring him: "Big Media Silent." We felt a sense of relief. Filing the suit when we did had been right, and dropping it when we did was also right.

I had incurred about $300,000 in legal expenses as a result of Starr's grand-jury subpoenas, the Senate impeachment trial, the Drudge case, and the nuisance suits filed by the Scaife-funded right-wing Judicial Watch. Dozens of other people in the White House were also burdened with very large legal bills. One survey, conducted in July 1998, which was before the impeachment reached a head, estimated that legal costs to the White House staff from Starr's investigation had amounted to $8 million.* Very few of us had independent means to pay off the bills ourselves, but once we were out of the White House, the President helped us to raise funds to take care of the debts.

On January 18, the President delivered a succinct farewell address. He had already given a number of lengthy issue-oriented speeches to sum up his presidency. Ever since George Washington, presidential farewell addresses have contained portentous warnings to the nation. Washington's cautioned against making permanent alliances with any great power, and Eisenhower's alerted the country to the danger of "the military-industrial complex." Clinton couched his warnings as affirmative admonitions. For the last time as president, he stated his credo: "Opportunity for all. Responsibility from all. A community of all Americans." He urged continuation of the economic policies he had put in place that insisted on fiscal responsibility in order to create prosperity and "invest in our future." Second, he advised that the United States continue a foreign policy of internationalism, not unilateralism. He warned against "terrorism," adding, "Global poverty is a powder keg that could be ignited by our indifference. . . . America cannot and must not disentangle itself from the world. If we want the world to embody our shared values, then we must assume a shared responsibility." Then he linked the imperative of American action in the world to American unity at home: "We must remember that America cannot lead in the world unless here at home we weave the threads of our coat of many colors into the fabric of one America. As we become ever more diverse, we must work harder to unite around our common values and our common humanity."

*Robert Dreyfuss, "Collateral Damage: The Personal Costs of Starr's Investigation," *The Nation*, July 27, 1998.

The final draft of this brief speech was composed in the Cabinet Room. Clinton wrote and rewrote, reading aloud his changes in the text as he worked. One of the speechwriters typed them into a computer as he went along. When Clinton finished, only fifteen minutes before airtime, an aide took the disk and sprinted away to get the words onto the teleprompter set up in the Oval Office. "It's just like the beginning," Clinton laughed.

For a couple of weeks, like everyone else, I had been sorting through my files and packing them. Grandstands for reviewing the inaugural parade were being built on Pennsylvania Avenue in front of the White House. Bush officials started wandering through. I pointed Condoleezza Rice to Sandy Berger's office. Karen Hughes, Bush's communications director, popped into my office, saying, "I really want to pick your brain." In almost every corner of every office of the West Wing, piles of paper to be discarded mounted up.

On January 19, the last full day of the Clinton White House, Jackie and I loaded up our car with my belongings, and we went into the Oval Office for a last time. The President was there, sorting through his things, CDs in one hand and a golf club in the other. Moving men were packing his books and memorabilia. It was disconcerting to see the stage set of Clinton's Oval Office being struck.

Clinton told me about the consent order he had just worked out with Robert Ray, Ken Starr's replacement as independent counsel, which tied up loose ends from myriad legal matters. Ray had told David Kendall that there was no basis in Clinton's grand-jury testimony, the heart of the articles of impeachment, for prosecution by his office. In fact, there would be no prosecution of him on any matter whatsoever. Clinton had committed no crimes. However, he had to acknowledge, as part of the agreement with Ray, that in his deposition in the Jones case, though he had tried to speak lawfully, "certain of my responses to questions about Ms. Lewinsky were false." He also accepted a five-year suspension of his law license in Arkansas and a $25,000 fine in exchange for dismissal of a pending disbarment suit, initiated by the Southeastern Legal Foundation, a Scaife-funded right-wing group. (Starr helped the group raise funds by giving a speech for it in 2000.) Ray privately thought the fine was excessive and offered to intervene on Clinton's behalf, but his gesture was declined. The President, Bruce Lindsey, and I then dropped our case against Starr's leaks; Judge Johnson's ruling that he and his prosecutors were in prima facie violation was left standing.

In May, Ray filed his final report, and it found no illegalities on the part of the Clintons. Much of it was filled with defensive rationalizations of the OIC's conduct, like its illegal leaks. The only actual news in it concerned Kathleen Willey: given "the differences between her deposition and grand jury statements, as well as her acknowledgements of false statements to the Office of the Independent Counsel," she had no credibility as a witness in her claims about Clinton, it said.* Once he had filed the report, Ray sounded out Republican fund-raisers and activists about running for the U.S. Senate from New Jersey but discovered little interest. The Independent Counsel Act had been allowed to expire without being renewed on June 30, 1999. No one in either party proposed to extend it. Thus Starr's legacy included the abolition of the very office he had held.

"Let me ask you something," said Clinton in the Oval Office. He asked me what I thought about granting pardons to Susan McDougal and Henry Cisneros, which he worried might become politically controversial acts. Other people, he told me, had expressed opposition to his giving pardons to these two figures. I said that I thought he must grant them. McDougal had been a heroine in standing up to Starr's bullying, and Cisneros had been targeted and abused for absurdly minor offenses. That was my last conversation with Bill Clinton as president. The next day, in reading the list of names of those who were receiving pardons, I was pleased to see McDougal and Cisneros among them.

After I spoke with the President, Jackie and I went back to my office, the old barbershop, and loaded up one more box of keepsakes, including a Lucite paperweight that Chief of Staff John Podesta had given to members of Clinton's senior staff. It depicted a roller coaster encircling the White House and was inscribed, "I SURVIVED THE CLINTON WHITE HOUSE 1993–2001." The paper signs we had recently hung on the doorknobs to our offices in the West Wing swayed slightly as we walked down the corridor. On the signs were the words Clinton had uttered during the New Hampshire primary in 1992, when it had appeared that his political career was over: "Until the last dog dies."

---

*Robert Ray, Independent Counsel, *Final Report*, p. 93.

EIGHTEEN

The American Conflict

For the generation between John Kennedy and Bill Clinton, the reputation of the American presidency had been in decline. One after another, presidents were overwhelmed by events, contributing to the widespread belief that government itself was hapless in solving the problems faced by the people. The idea that "the only national voice," as Woodrow Wilson said, was "the vital place of action in the system" became discredited. Since Franklin D. Roosevelt, the presidency had been at the center of America's political life, not only as the most personal office in the American constitutional system but because FDR had used it to direct the government into action during the Depression and in World War II. But Lyndon Johnson was overcome by the war in Vietnam and racial strife at home—and decided he would not run again. Richard Nixon had to resign because of the criminal abuses known as Watergate. Gerald Ford, his vice president and successor, stumbled in trying to control the inflation of the mid-1970s and failed to win election in his own right. Jimmy Carter succumbed amid economic turmoil and because of the Iran hostage crisis. "The Presidency appeared in rout," wrote Arthur Schlesinger, Jr.* Ronald Reagan imitated Roosevelt's bonhomie and deployed his gestures of confidence—but he did so to stymie government's capacity to act, and once he had induced insolvency with a major tax cut and created a federal deficit larger than that created by all previous presidents combined, he did little: he held a record for enacting fewer bills than any president since Dwight Eisenhower. His illusion of mastery hid

*Arthur M. Schlesinger, Jr., *The Cycles of American History*, Houghton Mifflin, 1986, p. 283.

a reality of passivity. His aim was to paralyze government, not animate it. George H. W. Bush, his vice president, inherited the consequences, and his own inability to deal with deficits and recession rekindled despair about the presidency and compounded the voters' alienation from government.

From the start, Bill Clinton envisioned his task as overcoming an era of disillusionment and antigovernment sentiment, renewing a progressive political tradition that had been stalled since the 1960s. "We pledge an end to the era of deadlock and drift," he declared in his first inaugural address. Yet his first two years in office appeared to reconfirm the worst fears that the presidency was an impossible position. The collapse of his health care initiative, the centerpiece of his program, dramatized his apparent failure to make the government work again. But Clinton's intelligence and adroitness restored his political position after the Republican victories of 1994 and the government shutdowns of 1995–96 assured his reelection and reinvigorated the presidency as an office of action.

Clinton's policies helped the nation to achieve the greatest prosperity in its history, the greatest reduction in poverty and increase in family income and wages since Johnson's Great Society, the greatest conservation of natural resources and public lands since Theodore Roosevelt, the greatest decline in crime in more than a generation, the greatest extension of loans, grants, and tax credits for higher education since FDR's GI Bill, the greatest public health insurance coverage of children, and the greatest budget surplus ever, earmarked for paying off the national debt and guaranteeing Social Security and Medicare. He appointed the most diverse cabinet and administration in our history, helped to define a new national identity for a multicultural, multiracial "One America," defended women's rights, and fought for the extension of civil rights to all. Clinton's new internationalist foreign policy, making the United States the "indispensable nation," judiciously used diplomacy and force to help ensure peace for twenty-first-century Europe, create the conditions for a settlement of the strife in Northern Ireland, define the terms of an ultimate peace in the Middle East, and reestablish collective security for a new age of globalization and interdependence. By 2000, the prestige of the United States everywhere in the world had never been higher.

The Clinton wars over the progressive presidency and its uses of government had a partisan cast, but they were not about one side versus another as in some sporting match. They focused on Clinton the man because he personified his office, but at issue was how the executive branch would use the instruments of government. Would they be

wielded on behalf of the interests of the great majority of citizens, allowing the Constitution to be a living document for advancing the people's
rights and social equality and the nation's needs—"the organic law," as
Lincoln called it—and the United States to be a vital nation advancing
public purposes? Or would the executive branch define the nation as a
shell, a confederation of states, clearing the way for private special interests, and asserting the armed forces as the only expression of national
power?

Since the 1930s, the Republican Party, which, then and now, regarded
itself as the rightful party of power and the true keeper of Americanism,
has responded to the rise of the modern Democratic Party on a rising
curve of incredulous hostility. Republicans attacked Franklin Roosevelt
for destroying free enterprise and promoting war, and conservatives on
the U.S. Supreme Court ruled much of the early New Deal legislation
unconstitutional. FDR won congressional approval of Lend Lease aid to
Britain, then standing alone against Nazi Germany, by only a narrow
margin against Republican isolationists in the Congress, who later accused Harry Truman and his secretary of state, Dean Acheson, of being
communist appeasers. Republican Party leaders used Senator Joseph
McCarthy's vicious smearing of Democrats as communist sympathizers
as a helpful tool until he exceeded bounds by wildly turning on President
Eisenhower. They hounded John F. Kennedy as soft on communism,
and, because of his support of racial integration, Southern reactionaries
launched an impeachment movement against him, his brother Attorney
General Robert F. Kennedy, and Chief Justice Earl Warren—impeachment being their favorite tactic, as nullification and secession had been in
the nineteenth century. They condemned Lyndon Johnson as a crypto-
totalitarian for his Great Society program and as a Southern race traitor
for his Civil Rights Act. They tarred Jimmy Carter for sponsoring the
Panama Canal Treaty, which they thought undermined U.S. sovereignty.

Over the course of these decades, the Republican Party went from
being dominated by a coalition of leaders from the Midwest and the
Northeast to a party increasingly controlled by the South and the South-
west. After Senator Barry Goldwater of Arizona seized its presidential
nomination in 1964, it shifted steadily to the right. Under Nixon, the
party absorbed the old Dixiecrats through his so-called Southern strategy. In 1980, Ronald Reagan began his campaign by extolling states'
rights at Philadelphia, Mississippi, where the Klan had murdered three
civil rights workers in 1964 (a presidential campaign event organized by
Congressman Trent Lott), and in office he fought for the exemption of

segregated institutions from civil rights laws. George H. W. Bush, whose father had been a moderate Republican senator from Connecticut, had transplanted himself to Texas and in his unsuccessful run for the Senate declared his opposition to the Civil Rights Act of 1964. When he was chosen as Reagan's vice president, he altered what remained of his lingering heritage to make his politics congruent with Reagan's. His appointment of Clarence Thomas to the Supreme Court, claiming he was the most qualified choice, was the apotheosis of Bush's tortured politics. By 1992 the Republican center of gravity had moved to the South and radically to the right.

In their efforts to overthrow President Clinton, the Republicans escalated a politics of crisis into almost continual warfare. Some of their hostility came from their desire to avenge the disgraces of past Republican scandals. Apart from the $70 million spent by Ken Starr, other independent counsel investigations against members of the Clinton administration totaled $40 million. But in the end, not a single top official of the Clinton administration was convicted for any crime involving public conduct in office. In a prosecution costing $21 million conducted by a Republican independent counsel, Secretary of Agriculture Michael Espy was acquitted, but his chief of staff was convicted of lying under oath. And in a prosecution costing $10 million conducted by another Republican independent counsel, Secretary of Housing and Urban Development Henry Cisneros pled guilty to a misdemeanor, giving false information to the FBI about the size of payments he had made to a former mistress. By contrast, twenty-seven officials of the Nixon administration were convicted in Watergate, and thirty-two members of the Reagan administration were convicted of crimes committed in the Iran-Contra and other scandals (seven of whom President George H. W. Bush pardoned, and two of whom were subsequently appointed to national security positions by George W. Bush). But their larger goal, which had been set long before Watergate or Iran-Contra, was to use the presidency to cripple the federal power that might inhibit the excesses of private interests and entrenched local elites.

In his final weeks in office President Clinton thought about giving a long speech on federalism. He understood, and opposed, the conservative Supreme Court opinions fostered by Chief Justice William Rehnquist that promoted the old and only true American conservative tradition of John C. Calhoun, using states' rights arguments to strike down federally determined policies, including those that protected rights that benefit the majority. A speech on this subject by Clinton would have laid down a significant marker, especially after the Court had handed the presidency to a Republican candidate in a 5–4 decision that President Clinton privately said was more poorly reasoned than the *Dred Scott* decision. Unfortunately, this speech was not given because of time and opportunity; the number of farewell speeches on international and domestic issues was limited.

Chief Justice Rehnquist had been the longest serving and among the most effective proponents of conservatism. Under his leadership, the Supreme Court struck down law after law enacted by the Congress, citing a radical interpretation of the Eleventh Amendment to assert state immunity from national legisation. In doing so, Rehnquist and the conservative court were constantly brushing aside the Fourteenth Amendment's guarantee of "equal protection of the laws," ratified after the Civil War to override claims of states rights by virtue of national citizenship. Just as Rehnquist adopted an expansive view of the Eleventh Amendment, he enforced the narrowest of the Fourteenth. As a result, individual rights were being increasingly curbed. In 1994, the Rehnquist court struck down the Violence Against Women Act on this basis. In 1999, the court issued the first in a series of decisions limiting the Americans with Disabilities Act; and in a case argued in 2000 and decided in 2001, the court found the Age Discrimination in Employment Act inapplicable to state employers. While the conservatives made high-flown abstract statements about original intent and state sovereignty, they were wielding the law as a political instrument.*

The so-called original jurisprudence notion in which Rehnquist believes, that the United States is merely a compact of the states, that state

*In 2002, a book by Ken Starr celebrating Rehnquist and the conservative majority—and its decision in the 2000 election—attacked "liberals," "cultural elites," the "gay rights agenda," and the "*New York Times* editorial board." Starr hailed the conservative majority on the Court as the "Five Friends of Federalism" against the "Four Foes," whom he denigrated as "forlorn liberals," and praised the Rehnquist Court record for its "moderation and stability." He extolled Rehnquist for being "gutsy . . . willing to stand up—all by himself," and Clarence Thomas for being an "original" thinker. He called *Roe v. Wade*, the decision that defended state laws legalizing abortion as constitutional, "unacceptable" and claimed that in decisions which weakened the wall of separation between church and state the Rehnquist court was upholding the "principle of equality." Kenneth W. Starr, *First Among Equals: The Supreme Court in American Life*, Warner, 2002. In 2002, Starr also campaigned in a Republican primary on behalf of Representative Bob Barr of Georgia, one of the House Managers in the impeachment; Barr lost to another conservative Republican.

sovereignty nullifies national authority, that local control is more representative and expresses a superior "majority," harks back past John
C. Calhoun, ideological forerunner of the Confederacy, to the anti-
Federalists who campaigned against the Constitution in the early years of
the Republic. Calhoun's arguments were taken to their logical conclusion
by the Confederacy. They were reformulated by reactionaries in the
Congress and on the Supreme Court as Social Darwinist imperatives
mobilized against the New Deal. They were adapted by the Dixiecrats'
resistance to civil rights in the 1950s and 1960s, and, in our time, recast
by Rehnquist and Reagan and George W. Bush. The tradition runs from
the framing of the Constitution, through the Civil War and the industrial
revolution, and to the present. If they could, the conservatives would return most federal functions to the states to restore the status quo before
the New Deal. This tradition runs to the anti-Federalists, not to Madison. Calhoun, not Jackson. Buchanan, not Lincoln. Taft, not TR.
Hoover, not FDR. Thurmond and Goldwater, not Kennedy and Johnson. Bush, not Clinton. And the American conflict endures.

Clinton faced conditions that were, among progressive presidents,
most analogous to those faced by Theodore Roosevelt. Neither of them
confronted a single overwhelming crisis; instead they perceived the necessity to frame new national policies in order to deal with great transformations in the economy and society and in America's place in the
world. Just as TR sought to enact new programs that would regulate and
stabilize the new powers of industrialism, Clinton proposed appropriate
policies for the postindustrial global economy. Both faced new waves of
immigration, new questions about race, and recalcitrant, conservative
Congresses. Both redefined American strength internationally, TR projecting an emerging power in the community of nations, Clinton standing at the head of the world's indisputably paramount power. Both were
peacemakers: TR won the Nobel Peace Prize for mediating the treaty
concluding the Russo-Japanese War; Clinton effectively resolved the
conflict in Northern Ireland and worked hard to try to resolve the crises
in the Middle East and Korea. And both left unfulfilled agendas.

Had the proposals Clinton made for new legislation been enacted, the
United States would now have universal health insurance, affordable
prescription drugs for senior citizens, universal day care, more schools,
higher teacher salaries and higher educational standards, more gun
safety, greater voting rights, new civil rights laws against discrimination,
and an even higher minimum wage. Had his foreign policy been fully enacted, the United States would have affirmed the Kyoto treaty to address

the dangers of global warming; more programs for education, disease control, and economic development for Africa; and more trade with Latin America. Had his administration had another year, he would have reached a final agreement with North Korea preventing it from developing nuclear weapons, and perhaps even an altered outcome to the final-status negotiations between Israel and the Palestinians. Certainly he would not have abandoned either of those negotiations, as his successor did.

It was not the distraction of his impeachment that somehow prevented these programs from being enacted. The public's approval of Clinton remained high throughout that ordeal, and he achieved as much as he could have by outmaneuvering the Republican Congress. If Gore had become president, undoubtedly progress would have been made on all these fronts. There would not have been an exploding federal deficit, because his administration would not have proposed a regressive tax cut. Gore would certainly have kept the pressure on the tobacco, health insurance, gun, and pharmaceutical interests. And on civil rights, he would have been a drum major for justice. But, like the ambitious plans of Theodore Roosevelt and Woodrow Wilson, the Clinton promise, at the end of his term, was unfinished. Clinton understood that the social gains the country had made during his presidency were fragile and incomplete. He knew the forces that opposed them remained powerful.

Just as the presidents of the late twentieth century operated in the shadow of FDR, those of the first part of the twenty-first century will stand in the shadow of Clinton. As the first president of his generation, the first after the Cold War, the first of the global economy, he will be the reference point for the progressive presidency for the next generation.

Theodore Roosevelt, in his early fifties, enraged at the conservative dominance of his successor's administration, formed his own party, and the Progressives, with their advanced social platform, finished second in the election of 1912. Former president Clinton will be able to elaborate his ideas long into the future and help the opposition to the conservative forces whose grip on the Republican Party is now even greater than when TR split with it. And Hillary Clinton will carry the tradition forward as a vital voice in the U.S. Senate.

In the short run the Clinton presidency will be viewed through the prism of the presidency of George W. Bush, just as Bush himself must operate in the shadow of the Clinton years. Clinton's political and policy successes made it possible and essential for Bush to campaign as a "different kind of Republican," a "compassionate conservative," and a "reformer with results," to claim that government was not the enemy. No Republican could hope to win on an unabashed conservative platform that expressed hostility to the government—not after the fall of Gingrich and not given the unpopularity of Clinton's impeachment. Especially after Bush's primary victory in South Carolina, where he had spoken at Bob Jones University, a citadel of segregation, he needed to use his "compassionate" rhetoric again, which is why he softened his edges to make it seem as if he had few differences with Gore on the issues.

Once in office, Bush acted as though he had won a mandate in a landslide. He rammed through the Republican-controlled Congress a mammoth regressive tax cut intended to paralyze the capacities of government by inducing insolvency: fiscal policy used to attain political ends. At the same time, he launched a deregulation of industries, a loosening of environmental laws, and a general strategy of meshing his policies to follow the trade association lobbies. "There is no precedent in any modern White House for what is going on in this one: a complete lack of a policy apparatus," said John DiIulio, a University of Pennsylvania professor who worked for a year as Bush's deputy domestic policy adviser and quit. "What you've got is everything—and I mean everything—being run by the political arm. It's the reign of the Mayberry Machiavellis."[*] But the bullying behavior of the White House toward moderate Republican Senator James Jeffords of Vermont prompted him to leave the party, causing the Senate to come under the Democrats' control, and a Democratic Senate then blocked much of Bush's radical program.

Though George W. Bush appointed a number of his father's former retainers to high-ranking positions within his administration, his ascendancy was not a restoration of the earlier Bush years. His father had been a weak, divided political character, of Connecticut provenance and yet unconvincing as an authentic Texas Republican. But the son was the first of his kind in the office, a Southern Republican—the first in the White House—even more radically conservative than Reagan. And Southern Republicans dominated not only the executive branch but the Congress as well.

By September 10, 2001, Bush seemed destined to be one of the most insignificant of American presidents. His popularity was lower than that of any recent president at that early point in his administration. He had lost his party's control of the Senate through arrogance. His policy agenda, beyond administrative deregulation, was virtually nonexistent.

*Ron Suskind, "Why Are These Men Laughing?" *Esquire*, January 2003.

The exposure of the corporate scandals at Enron in 2001 directly affected him, as the Houston-based Enron had been the biggest financial supporter of his political career—and one of the biggest beneficiaries—from its beginning. It appeared that he would join the three previous presidents—John Quincy Adams, Rutherford B. Hayes, and Benjamin Harrison—who had lost the popular vote, whose legitimacy was questioned, and who served only one term.

Bush's approach in most situations seemed a reactive combination of calculations to avoid his father's mistakes and to reject Clinton's policies. This was especially clear in international affairs: in his first nine months he reversed Clinton's policy toward China, proclaiming it no longer a "strategic partner" but a "strategic competitor"; in the Middle East, by withdrawing U.S. involvement from the negotiations between Israel and the Palestinians; toward Korea, by abandoning the negotiated accord that had frozen the North's nuclear program and by humiliating President Kim of South Korea, who was promoting North-South reconciliation, during his March 2001 visit to the White House, contributing to a wave of anti-Americanism in a country that was among the staunchest American allies; by withdrawing U.S. support from the Kyoto treaty on global warming; and by forsaking Clinton's efforts to address the dangers of international terrorism.

During the transition between administrations, National Security Adviser Sandy Berger arranged several extensive briefings on this last subject for Bush's incoming national security adviser, Condoleezza Rice, and others on the Bush team, including Vice President Cheney. One briefing lasted a half day. Berger told them that Osama bin Laden was "an existential threat" and told them he wanted "to underscore how important this issue is." In another briefing, Richard Clarke, head of counterterrorism in the NSC, the single most knowledgeable expert in the government, gave them a complete tutorial on the subject. In yet another briefing, CIA officials were brought in to go over all the intelligence available on terrorism.

Don Kerrick, a three-star general and outgoing deputy national security adviser, overlapped for four months with the new Bush people. He submitted a memo for the new National Security Council warning of the danger of terrorism. "We are going to be struck again," he wrote. But as Kerrick explained to me, he received no answer to his memo. "They didn't respond," he said. "They never responded. It was not high on their priority list. I was never invited to one meeting. They never asked me to do anything. They were not focusing. They didn't see terrorism as the big megaissue that the Clinton administration saw it as. They were concentrated on what they thought were higher priorities than terrorism." The Principals meeting of national security officials took up terrorism only once, after constant pressure from Clarke, on September 4, 2001, and at that meeting they discussed using unmanned Predator drone spy aircraft, but no decision was made. "Unfortunately," said Kerrick, "September 11 gave them something to focus on."

After September 11 and the terrorist attacks on the World Trade Center and the Pentagon, Bush gained the legitimacy he had hitherto lacked. Now he used the presidency to reorder the government according to conservative imperatives as he could not have done before.

In the midterm election of 2002, Bush campaigned for Republicans on the theme of national security, as Karl Rove had said he would at a January meeting of the Republican National Committee. "We can go to the country on this issue because they trust the Republican Party to do a better job of protecting and strengthening America's military might and thereby protecting America," said Rove. In the election, the Republicans recaptured the Senate by the one seat they had lost in 2001 with Jeffords's defection.

With Republicans in control of all branches of government, Bush proposed another large regressive tax cut. Projected estimates of the federal deficit were doubled to a figure exceeding Reagan's. The indices from the Clinton era were reversed under Bush: poverty was on the increase, family income and wages fell, and more than two million jobs were lost in two years. The administration announced plans to weaken the Clean Water and Clean Air Acts. Bush began appointing conservative judges in the mold of Rehnquist and Scalia to the federal bench. He also announced his opposition to affirmative action for black Americans by joining a lawsuit arguing the case before the Supreme Court. (His solicitor general was Ted Olson.) He and Cheney fought in the courts against the release of documents identifying the members of his Energy Task Force, which had included the chief executive of Enron. John Dean, President Nixon's counsel, who was a witness in the Watergate scandal, wrote, "Cheney apparently wants to turn the clock back to the days of the Nixon administration, before Watergate, when Nixon sought to make Congress merely another administrative arm of the presidency."* The imperial presidency was making its return. Using national security

*John Dean, "How the War on Terrorism Is Shrinking Congressional Powers," *Findlaw.com*, October 11, 2002, http://writ.news.findlaw.com/dean/20021011.html.

as a pretext for keeping information secret, the administration in effect was creating an Official Secrets Act. (In 2000, Clinton had vetoed an Intelligence Authorization Act, which provided criminal penalties for leaking classified information—what would have been the beginning of an Official Secrets Act.)

Whether Bush would be judged as a character in a triumphant bildungsroman, as his admirers saw him, a hero who had wasted his privileged youth in drunken frivolity but had come to his senses to become a leader through the test of war, or as a figure in a revenge tragedy obsessed by the ghosts of his predecessor father and the president who deposed his father would depend on unforeseen turns. But there could be no doubt that his presidential decisions were fostering greater problems of inequality—economic, social, and racial—that would create demands for remedy. Bush's efforts to repeal the progressive policies of the twentieth century were bound to provoke a new politics of crisis. The Clinton wars were over, but there would be intense conflicts to come.

Presidential hostility to making positive use of governmental power has always intensified pressures that then erupt in strife and conflict. The complicity of Presidents Franklin Pierce and James Buchanan in the crisis of the Union; the deference to privilege of the Gilded Age presidents; the indifference to economic inequality by the Republican presidents in the 1920s; President Eisenhower's constrained, narrowly legalistic approach to the impending civil rights revolution; Reagan's animosity to the federal government itself; George W. Bush's arrogant dissolution of federal responsibilities on behalf of private interests, including friends and family, in a concerted effort to overturn not only the Clinton era social advances, but the Great Society and New Deal—all were presidents' attempts to avoid the use of national power while enormous forces were forging new realities. They have left the inexorable task of confronting and mastering these realities to the progressive presidents, who saw the White House as the place to "think anew, and act anew," as Lincoln said.

"The president is relevant," Clinton had had to say, defensively, in April 1995, at his lowest ebb. But the next day came the bombing of the federal building in Oklahoma City and then the recovery of his positive political powers. History never ceases to surprise, making what seems solid and inexorable crumble under the weight of new circumstances.

The issue is, finally, the problem of democracy. Old orders always seek to preserve the status quo, and they have succeeded in doing so, sometimes behind the cloak of national security and during emergencies, but not forever. From Jefferson to Jackson, from Lincoln to Theodore

Roosevelt, from Franklin D. Roosevelt to John F. Kennedy, from Kennedy to Bill Clinton, the progressive presidents have met the challenges of new eras by widening the scope of democracy. Their opponents have charged, against them all, that their actions were scandalous and their innovations illegitimate. But the people have made their own judgments. As Abraham Lincoln's great admirer, the poet Walt Whitman, wrote:

> *Why what have you thought of yourself?*
> *Is it you then that thought yourself less?*
> *Is it you that thought the President greater than you?*
> *Or the rich better off than you? Or the educated wiser than you?*

> *You may read in many languages, yet read nothing about it,*
> *You may read the President's message and read nothing about it there,*
> *Nothing in the reports from the State department or Treasury*
>   *department, or in the daily papers or weekly papers,*
> *Or in the census or revenue returns, prices current, or any accounts of*
>   *stock.*

> *The sum of all known reverence I add up in you whoever you are,*
> *The President is there in the White House for you, it is not you who are*
>   *here for him,*
> *The Secretaries act in their bureaus for you, not you here for them,*
> *The Congress convenes every Twelfth-month for you,*
> *Laws, courts, the forming of States, the charters of cities, the going and*
>   *coming of commerce and mails, are all for you.*

ACKNOWLEDGMENTS

Everything that the Clinton administration achieved was a collective effort on the part of the extraordinary individuals who worked in it. For me to thank those who helped me while I was there would require publishing most of the internal White House telephone book. During the writing of this book, literally dozens of former colleagues assisted me with their recollections and perspectives. Without their contributions, this book would not have been possible. My assistants at the White House—Kevin Moran, Jonathan Smith, McKenzie Davis, Shawn Johnson, and Todd Cohen—weathered every storm with aplomb. I thank especially John Podesta for his encouragement throughout. I am deeply grateful to my former colleagues, who remain committed to the great work we started. Most of all, I thank Bill Clinton and Hillary Rodham Clinton for granting me the opportunity and honor to serve with them.

I am thankful to Ben Gerson, my friend from our first days of college, for running my legal defense fund. I appreciate the stalwart support I received during these recent years from many people, including James Carville, John Emerson, Mark Penn, Tony Podesta, Bob Shrum, and Mark Weiner. I acknowledge my attorneys, William Alden McDaniel, Jr., and Jo Bennett, whose efforts and counsel helped rescue me from endless perils. Lanny Breuer and Cheryl Mills of the White House counsel's office and David Kendall, the President's attorney, also gave me much needed advice and support at critical times.

My former assistants at *The New Yorker*, Danielle Mattoon and Nina Planck, did significant research early on that I drew upon. James Chace and Sean Wilentz read portions of the manuscript and provided invaluable comments. I had numerous helpful conversations with friends who should know how grateful I am for their friendship and ideas. I am particularly indebted to the insights of Menno Meyjes, with whom I discussed many of the book's difficulties. The only brief vacation I took was thanks to the kindness of Mary Steenburgen, whose cottage on Martha's Vineyard was a lovely place for writing.

Elisabeth Sifton, my editor at Farrar, Straus and Giroux, was a marvel of wisdom, clarity, and understanding. Her assistant, Danny Mulligan, was indispensable in making the publishing process run more smoothly, as was Debra Helfand, managing editor. Sloan Harris, my literary agent, provided just the right advice and backing at every turn.

Two people who personified the highest standards of their professions during the crises described in this book and who were good friends to me died suddenly and prematurely. Charles Ruff, the White House legal counsel, lived the principles of the law. Lars-Erik Nelson, columnist for the New York *Daily News*, breathed the ideals of journalism. They were both scrupulous in their fairness, imbued with a sense of justice, and fearless.

During the writing of this book, my younger brother, Edward, died tragically on May 4, 2002. He was a blithe spirit with big shoulders about to enter the best years of his life. On January 20, 2003, my father, Hymen, died. He was the strongest man I ever knew, not only in his physical strength but also in his strength of character. I cannot say how much I miss them.

I am fortunate to have the love and support of my mother, Claire, and my sister, Marcia. Dennis Fields, Marcia's husband, has been especially supportive and generous.

This book is dedicated to my wife, Jackie, just as my first book was. She was by my side through everything chronicled here and more, and her love and intelligence have been essential to everything I've done, including this book. And I'm proud of our sons, Max and Paul, who became young men during this period and learned important lessons about family, friendship, and politics.

As I think of it, my own public service did not end when President Clinton left the White House, but has been extended through the writing of this book.

INDEX